The Very Witching
Time of Night

AH-49d

The Very Witching Time of Night

Dark Alleys of Classic Horror Cinema

GREGORY WILLIAM MANK

McFarland & Company, Inc., Publishers

Jefferson, North Carolina

ALSO BY GREGORY WILLIAM MANK
AND FROM McFARLAND

*Bela Lugosi and Boris Karloff: The Expanded Story of a Haunting
Collaboration, with a Complete Filmography of Their Films Together*
(2009; main title first edition, *Karloff and Lugosi*)

Women in Horror Films, 1930s (1999; paperback 2005)

Women in Horror Films, 1940s (1999; paperback 2005)

*Hollywood Cauldron: Thirteen Horror Films from
the Genre's Golden Age* (1994; paperback 2001)

Frontispiece: Ariel Heath, RKO starlet of the early 1940s,
welcomes you to *The Very Witching Time of Night.*

LIBRARY OF CONGRESS CATALOGUING-IN-PUBLICATION DATA

Mank, Gregory W.
The very witching time of night : dark alleys of classic horror cinema /
Gregory William Mank.
p.   cm.
Includes bibliographical references and index.

ISBN 978-0-7864-4955-2 (softcover : acid free paper) ∞
ISBN 978-1-4766-1543-1 (ebook)

1. Horror films—Production and direction—United States.
2. Motion pictures—United States—History—20th century.
3. Chandler, Helen, 1906–1965.   4. Laemmle, Carl, 1867–1939.
I. Title.
PN1995.9.H6M3155 2014   791.43'6164—dc23   2014012459

BRITISH LIBRARY CATALOGUING DATA ARE AVAILABLE

On the cover: Poster art for the 1942 film *Cat People*
(RKO Radio Pictures/Photofest)

Printed in the United States of America

*McFarland & Company, Inc., Publishers
Box 611, Jefferson, North Carolina 28640
www.mcfarlandpub.com*

For my beautiful Barbara.
We thought this would be an easy one, didn't we?

Tis now the very witching time of night,
When churchyards yawn, and Hell itself breathes out
Contagion to this world. Now could I drink hot blood
And do such bitter business as the day
Would quake to look on.
—**Hamlet**, Act III, sc. ii

Table of Contents

Introduction

Most of my books on film history have had a definite dramatic focus. The first, *It's Alive! The Classic Cinema Saga of Frankenstein,* way back in 1981, presented the backstage story of Universal's eight classic Frankenstein films—the talent, the studio politics, the phenomenon. The most recent, *Lugosi and Karloff: The Expanded Story of a Haunting Collaboration,* published by McFarland in 2009, focused on the eight films the two horror superstars made together, the Hollywood in which they worked, and the rivalry and sadness that plagued their personal relationship.

While working on these books and the others, I frequently found fascinating "tangential" material—often striking, sometimes bizarre—that cried out for its own focus and attention. It was colorful, wide-ranging "stuff"—dynamic theater and cinema history—and I became determined that one day, all this material would receive its own worthy and well-deserved book.

Hence, *The Very Witching Time of Night.* The chapters are as follows:

1. **"A Very Lonely Soul": A Tribute to *Dracula*'s Helen Chandler.** The story of the tragic actress whose real life became a pitiful saga more gruesome than her one classic horror film, *Dracula,* as intimately told by her best friend and sister-in-law, Geraldine. Accompanying the story are wonderful (and at times heartrending) family photographs provided by Helen's great-nephew, Kevin Chandler.

2. **Mad Jack Unleashed: *Svengali* and *The Mad Genius*.** John Barrymore, hailed by Warner Bros. as "The World's Greatest Living Actor," gave back-to-back 1931 film performances so brilliantly grotesque that his adoring public rejected both him *and* the films. The account includes the memories of Marian Marsh, leading lady in both movies, and revealing production information from the Warner Archives.

3. **Paramount Horrors: *Murders in the Zoo*.** When it came to spicing horror with sex—and vice versa—no studio did it better than Paramount. The chapter analyzes Paramount's kinky house style and focuses on the deliriously erotic, exotic *Murders in the Zoo*—including coverage of Lionel Atwill's daringly depraved star portrayal and the film's wild climactic animal free-for-all debacle that ended with the real-life mercy killing of a puma.

4. **The Mystery of Lionel Atwill: An Interview with the Son of the Late, Great Horror Star.** After Lionel's death in 1946, what happened to the Atwill family—his 29-year-old widow and his six-month-old baby son? For the first time, Lionel Anthony Atwill gives the answers and also provides a delightfully macabre account of rescuing his father's ashes from "Vaultage" in a Hollywood mortuary where they sat for over 57 years. Atwill also provides some great family photographs.

5. **James Whale, Colin Clive, Lionel Atwill and the Riding Whip: The Real-Life Horror Story of the Censorship of Universal's *One More River*.** Between *The Invisible*

1

Man and *Bride of Frankenstein,* James Whale directed this 1934 super sex-melodrama, starring Colin Clive as a sadist and featuring Lionel Atwill as his lawyer. Whale's defiant insistence on shooting the film his own way and his battles with Joseph Breen and the newly empowered Production Code made this a real-life horror for the director, censor, and studio. The story contains extensive documentation from the Censorship Files of the Academy's Margaret Herrick Library.

6. **"Baby-Scarer!" Boris Karloff at Warner Bros., 1935–1939.** In 1935, Karloff signed a non-exclusive contract at Warners—before he or the studio fully recognized the severity of the anti-horror factions converging upon Hollywood. The chapter reveals how, over the course of five films, Karloff went from a "Triumphant Warner Bros. Star" to a corporate liability the studio was desperate to dump. Contracts and correspondence from the Warner Archives tell the tale.

7. **Libel and Old Lace.** The fully-researched story of the greatest horror comedy hit in theater and (arguably) film history. It includes rich material from the Warner Archives on the production of the film, as well as a full explanation as to why Karloff, who starred in the Broadway play, didn't make the movie—and examines how close he came to a libel suit against Warners that would have rocked Hollywood and horror history.

8. **Production Diaries:** *Cat People* **and** *The Curse of the Cat People.* A day-by-day account of the shooting of both of Val Lewton's feline masterworks, reporting specific behind-the-scenes events and crises as detailed in the RKO Archives. Here are all the production nuts and bolts for both films, including a meticulous analysis of Lewton's revised ending for *Curse* and the toll suffered by this hypersensitive producer.

9. *Frankenstein Meets the Wolf Man* **Revisited.** It's the most fascinating and obsessive of Universal's Monster sagas, and this retrospect in honor of its 70th anniversary presents new discoveries and insights about Bela Lugosi's forlorn Frankenstein Monster and that film's remarkably troubled production history.

10. **Horror Propaganda:** *Hitler's Madman.* In 1942, Hitler's barbaric revenge for the assassination of Gestapo monster Reinhard Heydrich shocked the world. A group of émigré Jews in Hollywood vowed to commemorate the atrocity by undertaking something virtually unheard of in U.S. film industry—an independent production. This chapter tells the fascinating saga of this doomed but passionate film, its many production challenges, its sale to MGM, the Metro retakes, the censorship battle that almost saw the film scrapped, and its nightmarish content that made it far more disturbing than any actual horror film of the era.

11. **John Carradine and His "Traveling Circus."** In 1943, John Carradine decided to make his dream come true by forming his own Shakespearean stage company. To help finance the troupe, he made several infamous horror movies. Audiences soon forgot the short-lived stage triumph but always remembered the horror movies, and the enterprise eventually cost Carradine his wife, home, yacht, and screen reputation. A tragedy almost classical in its consequences, this compelling story receives full coverage, including rare material from the archives of the Pasadena Playhouse, where Carradine opened his company.

12. *Shock! Theatre,* **the "Half-Witch and Half-Fairy" and Dr. Lucifer.** This tribute to the *Shock!* TV sensation of 1957, as Universal released its monsters to TV, covers two aspects of that phenomenon. One is the court battle waged by Mae Clarke against a TV horror hostess who had claimed to be Ms. Clarke while hosting a showing of *Frankenstein*. Included are papers from Mae Clarke's own personal files and a full description of the show, as provided by the surviving script. The other is an interview with the late Richard Dix and the late

Nancy Lee Dix, "Dr. Lucifer" and "Mrs. Lucifer" of Baltimore's *Shock! Theatre,* remembering the madness that went into the show every Saturday night.

13. **Junior Laemmle, Horror's "Crown Prince" Producer.** At age 22, he personally produced *Dracula,* won a Best Picture Oscar for *All Quiet on the Western Front,* and began the Universal horror genre—yet little is known about the man who retired from films forever before he was 30. The late Evelyn Moriarty, Junior's lady friend for almost forty years, cleared up a few mysteries in this 1993 interview about the man who remains one of Hollywood's great enigmas.

As always, there are many people to thank for often above-and-beyond-the-call-of-duty assistance. For granting interviews:

Lionel Anthony Atwill: My wife Barbara and I visited Tony at his home in Vermont, where his father's portrait painting dramatically dominated the dining room. We made a valued friend.

Patricia Morison: The leading lady of *Hitler's Madman* vividly remembers the shooting of that melodrama—even if she prefers to sing (as she did at my request) "So in Love," which she introduced in 1948 in Broadway's *Kiss Me Kate.* Morison is a gallant survivor of Hollywood's Golden Age and a class-act lady.

Also thanks to those who gave interviews and are now gone: DeWitt Bodeen, Ann Carter, Geraldine Chandler, Nancy Lee Dix, Richard Dix, Dean Goodman, Ruth Lewton, Marian Marsh, Evelyn Moriarty, Jane Randolph, Elizabeth Russell, Simone Simon, Curt Siodmak, and Robert Wise.

For archival assistance:

Jonathon Auxier and Sandra Lee Joy, of USC's Warner Bros. Archive, who provided fascinating behind-the-scenes information on the Warners films covered in this book.

Ellen Bailey, genial and indefatigable curator of the Pasadena Playhouse Archives, and its awesome collection of Los Angeles theater history.

Ned Comstock, curator of the USC Motion Picture and Television Library, whose knowledge and generosity did so much to make this book (and many of my books) possible.

Julie Graham of the UCLA Special Collections, who gave me access to the University's RKO Collection, making it possible to trace the day-to-day shooting of *Cat People* and *The Curse of the Cat People.*

Kristine Krueger of the Academy's Margaret Herrick Library, whose expertise and patience made many studio documents available.

The Manuscript Division of the Library of Congress, Washington, D.C.

Thanks to G.D. Hamann whose Filming Today Press produces excellent books filled with information from Los Angeles newspapers, many of which are now defunct. Hamann's books on Lionel Atwill, John Barrymore, John Carradine, Boris Karloff, Carl Laemmle, Jr., and Bela Lugosi were of great help.

Thanks also to (in alphabetical order): John Antosiewicz, who owns one of the finest archives of Universal stills in the world; Kevin Chandler, who made it possible to interview his grandmother Geraldine about her friendship with Helen Chandler, and who provided the wonderful family photos; Arianne Ulmer Cipes, for talking with me about her father Edgar G. Ulmer and *Hitler's Madman*; Jim and Marian Clatterbaugh, who published several of the chapters of this book in earlier incarnations in their magazine *Monsters from the Vault*;

Kerry Gammill, whose remarkable computer talent restored a number of illustrations that appear in this book; Roger Hurlburt, who's always generous with his awesome autograph collection; Neil Lipes, who kindly shared his Junior Laemmle data; John McElwee, whose Greenbriar Picture Show is a wonderful necessity for all film fans; Doug Norwine, former entertainment-memorabilia director at Heritage Galleries and collector *par excellence*, and his wife Kelley; and Gary and Sue Svehla, who published earlier versions of the Richard Dix and Evelyn Moriarty interviews in their magazine *Midnight Marquee*.

Also: Ron Adams (*Monster Bash*), Buddy Barnett (Cinema Collectors), the late Richard Bojarski, Ronald V. Borst of Hollywood Movie Posters, Bob Burns, David Colton and the Classic Horror Film Board, Kirk Crivello, Sonia Darrin, Bruce Forsberg, Scott Gallinghouse, Martin Grams, Jr., Charles Heard, Mark Martucci, Richard and Julie May, Patrick McCray, Constantine Nasr, Bill Nelson, Fred Olen Ray, Alan K. Rode, David Schaaf, David J. Skal, Sally Stark, Dr. Karl Thiede, Laura Wagner, and Buddy Weiss and the staff of Photofest.

A special thanks to Frank Dello Stritto (Cult Movies Press) and to Eileen Wolfberg, who generously offered their expert services as proofreaders. Frank, Eileen, and Eileen's husband Tom Jackson all did much to help the cause and to keep morale high as this book went into its final stages.

There are many more to thank, such as the man who caught me one sunny morning photographing the exterior of the house where Helen Chandler had lived in 1930; he was living in the house that day in 2010, and I appreciate his not calling the police. But special mention must be made of esteemed colleagues Gary Don Rhodes and Tom Weaver, whose names are surely familiar to readers of this book, and who made many dynamic suggestions and contributions.

So, now falls *The Very Witching Time of Night*. As with all the books I've written, it's been an adventure—and I've loved sharing it, as I do all things, with my wife Barbara.

1

"A Very Lonely Soul"
A Tribute to *Dracula*'s Helen Chandler

It is Walpurgis Night—the night of evil—Nosferatu!
—***Dracula***, Universal, 1931

Walpurgis Night ... April 30. "The Night of Evil."

It's an internationally notorious night of unholy revels, precisely six months away from the other pagan sun feast of Halloween. In Germany, some still believe that witches celebrate Walpurgis Night on Brocken Mountain, the highest peak in the Harz range. In Sweden, the faithful traditionally scare away wicked spirits by lighting giant bonfires.

The namesake is St. Walpurga, whose canonization was May 1, circa 870; the satanic rites take place on the eve of her holy day. Historical and pop culture references abound. The "Night on Bald Mountain" climax of Disney's *Fantasia* (1940) takes place on Walpurgis Night. Hitler and Goebbels committed suicide on Walpurgis Night, 1945.

The opening scene of 1931's *Dracula* takes place at sunset on Walpurgis Night. The coach rolls along Universal's back lot Transylvania, delivering Dwight Frye's Renfield for his fateful midnight in Borgo Pass. The sun is setting, the coach rattling, and a fearful passenger is praying:

On this night ... the doors, they are barred, and to the Virgin, we pray.

* * *

Venice, California, 1965.

The lady who lives in the apartment at 15 Paloma Avenue has a scarred face; she was ravaged in a fire years before. She has no resources for cosmetic repair. Once upon a time, the lady had been a beautiful movie star—and her most famous film was *Dracula*. Those neighbors who see her on late night TV in that 1931 milestone probably think her as bizarre as Bela Lugosi's vampire—blonde, cat-eyed, looking like a Jazz Baby angel. Even at the time of *Dracula*'s release, the woman's performance had seemed to be in Never-Never Land–style. *Time* magazine had sniped: "Silliest sound: Helen Chandler's feeble soprano chirrup uttered repeatedly as an indication of superhuman fear."[1]

Many neighbors who watch her walking up to the Santa Monica Pier with a fishing pole to catch her dinner have no idea she had been a top star of Roaring '20s Broadway: a pitiful "flapper" Ophelia in a 1925 modern-dress *Hamlet*; a rapturous Marguerite in the Theatre Guild's 1928 *Faust*. When Charles Lindbergh triumphantly returned from his 1927 trans–Atlantic flight, Helen was his New York City escort.[2] After she arrived in Hollywood,

Iconic horror: Universal's *Dracula* (1931), starring Bela Lugosi and Helen Chandler (John Antosiewicz Collection).

Darryl F. Zanuck, seeing her sensitive performance in the 1930 film *Outward Bound,* wrote to Jack L. Warner:

> By all means take up the [option] on Helen Chandler as this girl is positively the most sensational and talented actress I have ever seen on the screen—she is a young Lillian Gish.[3]

The press had rhapsodized that she "had stars where her eyes should have been" but long before 1965 alcohol had become her own vampire. She has a history of addiction and devastating breakdowns as long ago as *Dracula;* she spent much of the late 1950s in an asylum

A Helen Chandler signed MGM portrait from 1931—the year the world saw her in *Dracula* (courtesy Roger Hurlburt).

in the California desert, committed by her own brother; she survives now by the charity of the Motion Picture Relief Fund. She's had three failed marriages and is the victim of a fanatical stage mother who, after the disfigurement, abandoned her own desperate adult daughter. She seems old, yet she really isn't—records claim she's 56 or 59, and maybe even she isn't sure which is right anymore.

Helen Chandler's own life has become a horror movie more frightening than *Dracula*—in which her demon lover had vowed:

There are far worse things awaiting man ... than Death....

When Death finally comes, it must be a mercy. It is also an irony. Helen Chandler dies on April 30, 1965—the date of Walpurgis Night.

*   *   *

Geraldine, who was affectionately known as "Gerry," Chandler was the friend Helen Chandler needed and loved throughout her life's many cruel perils. She was her sister-in-law, more of a kid sister than an in-law, and she shared many happy times with Helen, remaining devoted, 40 years after Helen's death, to her memory.

Geraldine died in January of 2007. Kevin Chandler had kindly arranged my interview with his grandmother in May of 2003.

Interview

Helen was the sister of my husband Lee. She was a sweet, winsome, loving girl—a little lost child, really, a delicate thing, who never received the love she deserved. Gentle, kind, good. She lived with us off and on for many years, in Hollywood and in our house out in the San Fernando Valley. We had so much fun together! I loved her dearly.

Let's begin with a funny story you have about yourself and Helen.

One time, after Helen's career was over, I think in the mid– or late 1940s, we went into Hollywood together to buy a car. Lee had to use our car to get to work, and I was stuck in our house, the last on Vine Street up in the hills. I didn't have any money, but Helen said, "I have $150," so we took a taxi down Vine Street to where the used car dealers were. Neither one of us knew anything about cars and Helen didn't drive— she'd actually ask the salesman questions like, "Does this car have an engine?"

So, we ended up buying a Flying Cloud Rio coupe, elegant in its day, but *ancient*—and with bud vases on both sides! We'd ride around, each dressed in denim jeans, white shirts and tennis shoes, and white gloves—"The gloves will make them *respect* us," Helen would say. We'd pull up to the Ambassador

The eyes are unmistakable (courtesy Kevin Chandler).

Hotel in my Flying Cloud Rio, hand the keys to the attendant, and he *hated* getting into that car! As we'd go grandly into the hotel for lunch, the attendant would drive the Rio out of sight in the back—because not only was it ancient, but Helen had put *roses* in each of the bud vases!

When did you first meet Helen?

I believe it was June of 1930. Helen was working in Hollywood and sent for her mother and brother Lee to come from New York City and stay in Los Angeles for the summer. She put them up at the Inglaterra Apartments that my mother was managing. Lee and I were married in April of 1931—we were both 17 years old! So that's how I met Helen. I loved her like a sister—we had lots of fun.

If you met her in the summer of 1930, you'd have known her when she was filming* Dracula *... shot in the fall of '30 at Universal City.

Yes! In fact Helen took me on the set.

What were your impressions of Bela Lugosi?

He was very distant. He didn't want to meet somebody's kid sister—I guess he had more important things to do.

Helen, adorned in flapper finery, shows her favored profile in this still from *The Sky Hawk* (Fox, **1929**) with John Garrick.

What did Helen say about him?

She talked about his wife, who came on the set and was *not* a particularly nice person.

According to the records, Lugosi wasn't married at the time. Maybe a lover?

Yes, or maybe it was an ex-wife, or a lady *claiming* to be his wife. But apparently she thought she was *extremely* important, and tried to boss people around. The people on the set didn't like her. Helen said she was a pain in the neck!

As far as Helen was concerned, *Dracula* was just another movie, just another job. But one night, Helen and I were discussing *Dracula*, and—she was kind of mischievous—she *glazed* her eyes, made her hands like *claws*, lifted up her arms as if she were about to *bite* me on the neck—and *really* scared me!

What other movie stories did she share with you?

There was the movie *A House Divided* (1931), that Helen did with Walter Huston and Douglass Montgomery. There was a storm scene, Helen was in water in a tank up at Universal, and she couldn't swim a bit—she almost drowned! She was in the water—she was *terrified* of water—and she was flailing her arms around, and everyone thought it was acting, but it wasn't—she was trying to keep alive! She was actually *drowning!* And finally some young kid working there jumped in and got hold of her, or she would have drowned. She simply could not swim at all....

Helen's home when she was starring in *Dracula,* high above the Hollywood Bowl, as it appeared in 2010 (photograph by the author).

Helen's so elegant in **Dracula**—*it's hard to imagine her splashing for life in a water tank, or dressed casually in your Flying Rio coupe!*

Helen had beautiful dresses, designed by Natacha Rambova, Valentino's ex-wife. Even the seams of the dresses were hand-sewn—really beautiful, sophisticated New York dresses. Helen and I were just about the same size, so she'd give her dresses to me (I didn't have anywhere to wear them to, I was just a kid out here in the Valley!). I had a sister who was my size too, and Helen sent me so many that I'd pick out one or two for dress-up, and I'd give the rest of them to Mary Jane. And she'd pass them on down to nieces, so the clothes traveled all over the Valley.

Meanwhile, I'd give some of *my* clothes to Helen—old, light blue denim jeans, white shirts and old tennis shoes! She always hated high heels—I think her ankles were a little weak—and she would find ways that she could get just little Cuban heels for dress-up. She wouldn't put high heels on unless she had to be in a picture or something, because she really couldn't balance very well on them. Helen always brought the white gloves, and we'd drive around in my beat-up old Rio. Oh, Helen loved it! She had more fun with me than she'd ever had in her life.

At one time, I can remember I asked Helen, "How much do you make?" and she said, "Twelve-fifty." And I said, "Twelve dollars and fifty cents?" and she said, "No, twelve hundred and fifty dollars!" You know, in the middle of the Depression, that was like a fortune!

She was such a wonderful actress ... was she dramatic in real-life?

Oh, yes! She'd prance around our living room—"emoting!" She'd ham it up around the house, and Lee would get so mad he'd be ready to *brain* her! You know, she'd walk up and down the living room, waving her arms and being very dramatic, and he'd say, "Oh, *sit down,* Helen!" But I loved her. She was a very lonely soul, I think.

You say her brother—your husband—had been a child actor with Helen?

Yes. And her mother ... well, she'd treated Lee and Helen when they were children like they were little trained animals. She required them to do certain things and they better damn well do them. But Lee rebelled. Both Helen and her mother always said Lee had been a better actor than Helen, but he said the only reason he was good was that he really couldn't see beyond the footlights and he didn't realize there was an audience watching him. One day, in a play he was in, somebody asked him, "Why are you scratching there?" and he said, "Because nobody else knows where it itches." Well, the audience burst into laughter, he suddenly realized all those people were watching him—and he walked off the stage. He took off his cap, put it on Ann Roth's head (they grew up together—she was the sister of Lillian Roth)[4] and he told his mother, "I'm never going on the stage again." And he never did. But Helen continued to try and please her mother.

Even long after I was married, if anything went wrong, I would just go home and get on my mother's lap. And I knew I could sit on my mother's lap and she would hug me and hold me. But Helen was never able to do that with her mother. Her mother was distant—she had a gentle way of speaking, but an iron fist.

Helen apparently lived with you between her marriages. In 1930 she'd married Cyril Hume, the writer-playwright, who scripted MGM's 1931 hit **Trader Horn** *and 1932's* **Tarzan the Ape Man;** *he also scripted 1956's* **Forbidden Planet.**[5] *Some have claimed he was partially responsible for her problems.*

In *Christopher Strong* (RKO, 1933), Helen, leading lady of *Dracula,* plays the daughter of Colin Clive, star of *Frankenstein.* **Both were tragic alcoholics. Clive died in 1937, 28 years before Helen passed away.**

Oh, Cy was a wonderful man ... he really was. He loved Helen, adored her. He was a brilliant man—a very fine writer. He wasn't a good-looking man—wore glasses on the end of his nose—and he had a daughter, Barbara, by a previous marriage, and she lived with them quite a bit.

Helen, left, with her first husband, writer Cyril Hume, who scripted such films as *Trader Horn* (1931) and *Forbidden Planet* (1956). They wed in 1930. The other woman is Helen's lifelong friend, Lillian Roth (courtesy Kevin Chandler).

But when he and Helen were separating and Helen was back east and drinking, it was the middle of the Depression and Lee and I got into financial difficulty. Lee was so young that most people wouldn't even hire him, and we just had a terrible time. I worked in the dime store on Saturdays and stuff, but we could hardly make ends meet. I turned to Cy many times, and he never failed me. Years later, when Lee and I were on our feet—of course, we were still kids, and weren't very sophisticated—we wanted to thank Cy because he'd saved our lives so many times. Well, we went out and bought a painting—and it probably was one hell of a painting!—but we thought it was pretty, and we gave it to Cy. I think he was very touched that we would try and buy something nice for him after all the times that he'd gotten us out of the hole.

He was a wonderful man, he really was. He finally married again to a really nice woman and he had more children, and he lived a nice, quiet life.

Husband #2 was actor Bramwell Fletcher, whom Helen married in 1935.[6] He'd played in the films Svengali *[1931] and* The Mummy *[1932], and did lots of stage work with Helen.*

Bram was a pain in the fanny. I think he married Helen because he thought it was going to improve his career. As far as pictures were concerned, he was basically a nobody, and Helen was pretty famous. I remember her saying to me about Bram, "You know, he's very

A signed photograph of Helen and Bramwell Fletcher, whom she wed in 1935, in the play *Ruy Blas* (1938). Fletcher starred as "Little Billee" in *Svengali* (1931) and played Norton, the archaeologist who goes mad, in *The Mummy* (1932) (courtesy Kevin Chandler).

pretty!" He was good-looking, almost movie star good-looking, and I think that's what Helen fell for. But they hadn't been married very long at all when—I don't know how it came up—Helen had to get something from Mary Astor's house that she had left there. We drove out there, honked the horn for Mary to come to the window so Helen could tell her what she wanted, and Bram came to the window with Mary—the second story bedroom window. And Helen was absolutely stunned. Of course, you know Mary Astor really had quite a reputation with men. I guess she couldn't stand the idea of Helen having somebody she hadn't had, because she really was a beautiful woman. But I know how crushed Helen was. I'll never forget ... she just sat there, she couldn't even say anything when they both came to the bedroom window.

Helen and Bram later divorced and he latched on to and married Diana Barrymore, and they were *very* unhappy together! I understand she was very volatile, and she really put him through the hoop.

Did you know her last husband, Walter Piascik? There seems to be little information on him and I can't find a record of when they married.

Yes, I knew Walter. I think he met Helen in a bar. He was a merchant seaman—just a nice, easy-going, very handsome, great big *dumb* man! He was like 6'2" or something, and built to go with it—and I think that attracted Helen. But they had nothing in common. I don't think Walter even said three words in a conversation. I guess he was okay in bed, or something. But it was her first husband, Cy, who loved her very much. It's that she just couldn't be a normal person. And you know, that wrecks marriages.

So over the years, between the marriages, Helen lived with you?

Yes. I worked part of the time—I tried to get a steady job, but sometimes I'd just be relief at the dime store or something like that. I remember coming home so many times, and Helen and my son would be waiting on the front porch, on the steps, with the dog and cat, waiting for me to come home. My son, little Lee, adored her—she'd talk to him like little boy to little boy.

Sometimes Helen made me very nervous too, because she didn't know the first thing about cooking a dinner, or anything like that. So when I was trying to cook, she'd stand right behind me at the stove, looking over my shoulder, saying, "Why are you doing that?" and "What is this?" and "What's that?" And it drove me crazy! I couldn't move my elbows, I couldn't back up, I couldn't do anything because she just crowded me. But she really was trying to learn, so ... one time, she tried to make dinner—and she *fried* the *baloney*. It was *terrible!* And Lee, my husband, said, "Don't let her in the kitchen *any more!*" She kept standing over him, saying, "Don't you like it, don't you like it?"—and he *didn't* like it! She didn't know how to do stuff like that—she'd never, even as a child, been around a kitchen. It was her first taste of domesticity [*laughing*]—and her idea of preparing dinner was to fry the baloney!

Helen would be so lonesome all day. There she'd be, sitting on the front porch with little Lee, waiting for me to come home. Helen would try to monopolize my time, and Lee, my husband of course wanted to monopolize my time. So there was always tension in the house, and I was glad when we finally got Helen an apartment, to be on her own.

You've mentioned alcohol a few times, and it's been well-documented that Helen had a drinking problem.

Yes, she was an alcoholic. I'd told her she couldn't drink, because I didn't want our little son to see it. Lee wouldn't have her in the house if she were drunk. We had just a little two-bedroom house, and little Lee slept out in the dinette while Helen used his bedroom. Well, it wasn't until after she'd moved and I went in to fix up the bedroom for little Lee to move back in again, that I looked in the closet. And on every hook in that closet, there were these great big shopping bags ... full of empty bottles.

See, Helen would stay sober all day. Lee and I would both be tired, go to bed around ten—and then she'd drink all night. She'd get in bed, take a book with her, and smoke and read and drink. She was a solitary drinker. When we'd get up in the morning, she wouldn't be up, and when we got home, she'd be cold sober. And she lived that way for quite a while.

Her last theater credit was in 1941. The fire that almost killed her—and that was blamed on her drinking and smoking in bed—took place in a Hollywood apartment house in 1950, reportedly after Walter had shipped out.

Yes, that's how she got burned.

The fire must have been awful.

[*Emotional*] It was just terrible. I'll never forget going down to the hospital in Hollywood and seeing Helen all in bandages there. You know, it just was such a terrible shock.

Helen, after her stardom years, with her nephew Leland (courtesy Kevin Chandler).

And then to see the scars on her face afterwards. It burned around her face, around her breast and arm and face—she was *very* burned. And her hair was burned, and ... oh God.

Did she have plastic surgery later to correct the scars?

No, no. And that was the beginning of the end ... it really was. Helen lived with us for a long time. And she would forget, you know, that she was so scarred. After dinner, my sisters would come over—Helen *loved* to ham it up in front of them—and she would get up and prance around, talking about some play or something that she had been in long ago, and she'd forget that she was so burned. And ... she'd *pose*. It would just break my heart. Most of the time, she was aware of it. But she got caught up in the story of some play or something like that, she'd forget she was burned, and she would get up and in her mind she was not burned.

She was a very lovable person, and she tried so hard to please people....

Did her mother ever come to help her in the later years?

I can't even remember what happened to the mother—she just disappeared from view. I think she went to live with some friend, an old studio friend or person she knew from the stage with whom she'd been friends for a long time. We just never heard from her again. She divorced herself from her children—didn't want anything to do with them. So the mother malfunctioned herself, and it was her fault, really, that Helen had malfunctioned. The only reason Lee didn't is because he broke away from her very young. But that was the mother's idea of punishing the kids—don't let them know where you are, and don't speak to them....

Helen, in the 1950s, spent time in a California state institution. Your husband Lee, Helen's brother, committed her?

Yes. She went into an asylum. It was heart-wrenching.

Did you see her there?

No. We moved, and that might have been while we were in San Francisco. I do remember, in Helen's later years, that she left the asylum, and the Motion Picture Relief Fund took care of her.

I tell you, I used to worry about her so. She lived for a while someplace out on Ventura Boulevard in Encino, like a movie people's boarding house. It was a big, old-fashioned two-story ranch house, which had been part of a ranch before Ventura Boulevard had built up—I guess it was owned by the Motion Picture Association. Other actors lived there. She had a room there, and there were people who dug the same things she did, and there was some sort of housekeeper who served meals and stuff. I'd go out there every day, because I couldn't stand worrying about her so much. I wanted to know she was all right. So she lived out there until very close to the end. It would just break my heart to see her. She'd had to be a little performing animal for her mother, and now....

Helen was living in an apartment in Venice, California, at the time of her death in 1965. The Chapel of the Pines hosted the funeral. Were you there?

No, I think I was in a sanitarium then, with tuberculosis. And Lee and I were getting divorced at that time. But I think I heard it was a beautiful funeral, with the old-time theater and film people.

1825 Whitley in Hollywood. Helen was catastrophically burned here in November 1950 (photograph by the author).

She'd been a great actress ... but what a terrible price to pay.

Oh yes ... she was a *wonderful* actress! I remember seeing her in a play in Hollywood, *Tonight at 8:30,* in the late 1930s. I watched it from the wings ... I think there were eight one-act plays, and this one one-act play was about a married woman who took a train into London or wherever it was, every day at the same time, and a man took the train at the same time, and they kept seeing each other and they finally fell in love. He would tell her he loved her, but she was married and he was married. And Helen walked to the front of the stage, looked out at the audience and did a long monologue about how she loved him, how there wasn't any future in it, how they were going to stop seeing each other, and she was going to have to take another train because she couldn't bear to see him every day. And I tell you, she

A family gathering, May 18, 1960: left to right, Helen, her uncle John, her brother Lee, and Lee's wife Geraldine. Note that Helen's left side, scarred by the fire, is turned away from the camera (courtesy Kevin Chandler).

made me cry every time! She'd stand out there and look out into space and I'd be standing there weeping, and I'd turn around and the people who were watching with me, you know, backstage, they were all weepy. She was a damned good actress, she really was, and she could make her voice sound so wistful and she would be so serious. She'd just be looking into space and kind of talking out loud about how she felt, and ... oh God! It was the most moving performance I ever saw!

It's very good to know she had such a loving friend.

Well, I loved her, and she loved me.... I know she did. I had a lot of fun with her, I can tell you that. We were good companions, the two of us—we found a lot to laugh about. She was one of the most lovable people I've ever known, warm and loving and sweet, and I just loved her to death. I was the one and only person that she could confide in.

When she would get very blue and very down, I'd say, "Come on, let's go do this" or "Let's go do that," and I'd try and snap her out of it. It was a really tragic life that she had, but Helen didn't have a mean bone in her body. She was a very nice person, a very good person, and I miss her terribly ... I really do. The poor little thing....

*   *   *

Helen Chandler Facts

• *Saturday, February 1, 1908*: Helen Chandler is born in New York City. According to Kevin Chandler, Helen's great-nephew, the previously published birth date of 1906 and birthplace of South Carolina are incorrect.

• *Monday, November 5, 1917*: Helen, guided by a very ambitious stage mother, makes her New York stage debut at the Plymouth Theatre in the play *Barbara*. Over two dozen Broadway productions follow for Helen until 1938.

• *Saturday, March 6, 1920*: Helen is a "victim" of John Barrymore as Shakespeare's *King Richard III* opens at Broadway's Plymouth Theatre. She plays one of the little princes whom Richard orders murdered in the Tower of London.

• *Thursday, February 17, 1921*: Helen is a victim of Lionel Barrymore as Shakespeare's *Macbeth* opens at Broadway's Apollo Theatre. She plays Macduff's son, slain by Macbeth's minions.

• *Monday, November 9, 1925*: Basil Sydney's modern-dress *Hamlet* opens at New York's Booth Theatre, with Helen as Ophelia, played in flapper fashion. The producer is Horace Liveright, who two years later produces Broadway's *Dracula*.

• *Thursday, December 9, 1926*: Helen opens at Broadway's Selwyn Theatre in *The Constant Nymph*, which features Claude Rains and stars Rains' then-wife, Beatrix Thomson.

• *Sunday, January 23, 1927*: Fox Studios releases *The Music Master*, Helen's film debut. It was shot at Fox's 56th Street Studios in New York City. She will stay at Fox for several more films.

• *Tuesday, February 7, 1928*: Helen opens in the horror play *The Silent House* at Broadway's Morosco Theatre. She plays the heroine, T'Mala. Tod Browning reportedly sees Helen in *The Silent House* and will remember her two years later when he's casting *Dracula*.

• *Monday, October 8, 1928*: Helen opens as Marguerite in *Faust* at Broadway's Guild Theatre. Dudley Digges plays Mephistopheles and Douglass Montgomery plays Valentine.

• *Monday, February 3, 1930*: Helen marries Cyril Hume, British novelist-playwright then working at MGM, where he'd write such screenplays as *Trader Horn*.

Helen in a picture she signed to her father (courtesy Kevin Chandler).

• *Wednesday, September 17, 1930*: Helen, who'd played in several more films by now—*The Joy Girl* (Fox, 1927), *Mother's Boy* (Pathé, 1929), *Salute* (Fox, 1929), *The Sky Hawk* (Fox, 1929), and *Rough Romance* (Fox, 1930)—stars in Warner Bros.' *Outward Bound*, the metaphysical love saga by Sutton Vance, which opens this date at the Hollywood Theatre in New York. Warners has placed Helen on contract.

• *Also on September 17, 1930*: Darryl F. Zanuck directs the Warner Bros. studio legal office to draw up a contract with Universal to "loan them the services of Helen Chandler" for

Helen on Broadway as T'mala in the melodrama *The Silent House* (1928). Tod Browning reputedly saw the play and remembered Helen when casting the film *Dracula* two years later. The actor menacing her is unidentified (courtesy Kevin Chandler).

Dracula with a four-week guarantee. Universal will pay Warners $750 per week for Helen's services, of which she'll receive the full $750. (Lugosi reportedly is paid $500 per week.) Although various references will claim David Manners receives $2,000 per week for *Dracula,* Warner Bros. correspondence of October 14, 1930 (written two weeks after *Dracula* begins shooting), arranges for Manners to go on loan-out to Universal for *Dracula,* with Warners paying Universal $500 per week for Manners' services—Manners himself receiving $300 per week. One can assume Helen is the highest paid performer in *Dracula.*

- *Friday, November 14, 1930*: Reportedly less than 12 hours after completing her role in *Dracula,* Helen has her appendix removed at Hollywood Hospital.
- *Friday, December 5, 1930*: Warner Bros.' *Mothers Cry* plays New York's Winter Garden Theatre, co-starring Dorothy Peterson, who'd played the female lead in Broadway's *Dracula,* and Helen, who'd just completed the film *Dracula.* Also in *Mothers Cry* is *Dracula's* David Manners. Peterson plays Helen's long-suffering mother, and Helen has a dramatic work-out in the melodrama as she falls from grace with a roué and ends up murdered by her own

Behind the scenes of *Dracula*: Helen (in her lounging robe and with cigarette), Lugosi (with cigar), and director Tod Browning (in beret).

brother. (Note: Boris Karloff, credited with appearing as a murder victim in *Mothers Cry,* isn't in evidence in the 2012 DVD released by Warner Bros. Archives.)

• *Thursday, February 12, 1931*: Universal's *Dracula* premieres at the Roxy Theatre in New York City. It's the baptism of Hollywood Horror for the sound era.

• *Wednesday, August 19, 1931*: Warner Bros.' *The Last Flight* opens at New York's Strand Theatre, featuring one of Helen's best starring performances: she plays Nikki, a wealthy, hard-drinking eccentric who joins up with four "Lost Generation" fighter pilots after World War I. Her leading men are Richard Barthelmess, Johnny Mack Brown, Elliott Nugent and, in his third film with Helen, David Manners. He acted with many of the most famous actresses of Golden Age Hollywood—Katharine Hepburn, Claudette Colbert, Barbara Stanwyck, Carole Lombard, Loretta Young, and many more—but will always say that Helen Chandler was his favorite of them all.

• *Friday, September 18, 1931*: Universal completes *A House Divided,* co-starring Helen and Walter Huston and directed by William Wyler. James Whale is directing *Frankenstein* at the same time and Helen has likely crossed paths with Colin Clive's Frankenstein and Boris Karloff's Monster on the San Fernando Valley lot.

• *1931*: Helen appears as "Miss Information" in a *Voice of Hollywood* short subject from Louis Lewyn Productions. The character of "Miss Information" is recurrent; Helen's *Dracula* co-star Frances Dade played the part in another *Voice of Hollywood* short in 1931.

• *Wednesday, December 9, 1931*: Helen returns to Broadway's Bijou Theatre for *Springtime*

A striking close-up of Helen (left) as Mina in *Dracula,* with Frances Dade as the doomed Lucy (John Antosiewicz Collection).

for Henry, a hit farce co-starring Leslie Banks (Count Zaroff in 1932's *The Most Dangerous Game*), Frieda Inescort (the "female Van Helsing" who defeats Lugosi's bloodsucker in 1944's *The Return of the Vampire*) and Nigel Bruce (Dr. Watson in the Fox and Universal's Sherlock Holmes films).

• *Thursday, March 9, 1933:* RKO's *Christopher Strong,* directed by Dorothy Arzner, opens at New York's Radio City Music Hall, starring Katharine Hepburn and Colin Clive. Helen plays Clive's daughter (although she's only nine years younger). Geraldine Chandler remembered that Helen's "fun and free-spirited" performance was very much like Helen's own personality. Meanwhile, Helen is working on Poverty Row—e.g., Mayfair's 1933 *Alimony Madness.*

• *1933:* Helen, who always dreamed of playing Alice in Wonderland, tests for the role in Paramount's all-star movie version. She loses to Charlotte Henry, who would also play Bo-Peep in *Babes in Toyland* (1934).

• *Late 1933:* Rumor claims that John Barrymore will revive *Hamlet* at the Hollywood Bowl, and Helen will play Ophelia. Possibly due to the personal troubles of both stars, the production never opens. Barrymore and Helen do co-star in *Long Lost Father* (RKO, 1934), directed by Ernest B. Schoedsack of *King Kong* fame.

• *1934:* Helen and Cyril Hume divorce.

• *Thursday, Valentine's Day, 1935:* Helen marries Bramwell Fletcher at the Riverside Church in New York. They'd already starred together in Broadway's *These Two* in 1934; they would act together in such New York plays as *Lady Precious Stream* (1936), with Helen in the title role and both stars in Asian makeup.

• *1935:* Three British films starring Helen are released, including *It's a Bet,* co-scripted by legendary horror-fantasy writer Curt Siodmak and featuring a pre–Hollywood George Zucco.

• *1936:* Helen proves what a great stage comedienne she is in the screwball comedy *Boy Meets Girl,* playing dumb-blonde Susie. She essays the role in London in 1936 (with husband Bramwell Fletcher) and at Hollywood's El Capitan Theatre in 1937.

• *Wednesday, December 9, 1936:* Helen opens on Broadway in the play *The Holmeses of Baker Street* as "Shirley Holmes"—Sherlock's crack-shot daughter!

• *Monday, April 19, 1937:* Helen co-stars with Joe E. Brown on Cecil B. DeMille's *Lux Radio Theatre* broadcast "Alibi Ike."

• *Tuesday, February 15, 1938:* Grand National releases *Mr. Boggs Steps Out.* It plays mainly double features and is Helen's last film.

• *Thursday, December 22, 1938:* Helen stars in a hit Broadway revival of *Outward Bound,* reprising her role from the 1930 film. Bramwell Fletcher stars, Vincent Price is in the cast, and Otto Preminger directs. It will be Helen's last Broadway show. She and Fletcher will divorce shortly afterwards.

• *Summer, 1940:* Helen enters La Crescenta Sanitarium in Los Angeles after suffering a nervous breakdown. Her father tells the press the suspect story that Helen suffers from a rare malady and has spent her fortune searching the world for a remedy.

• *Thursday, April 24, 1941:* *The Hollywood Reporter* writes that Lillian Gish is definitely out of the cast of *Ladies in Retirement* at Columbia, and that Helen Chandler (whom Darryl Zanuck had described eleven years before as "a young Lillian Gish") is the top candidate to replace her. The *Reporter* notes that Helen had arrived in Hollywood by plane from New York the previous night and will film tests that morning. However, Ida Lupino, Elsa

Lanchester and Edith Barrett will win the three female leading roles in *Ladies in Retirement*.

• *July 3, 1941*: Helen co-stars with Joe E. Brown in a revival of *The Show Off* at the Alcazar Theatre in San Francisco. "Helen Chandler does a neat job as Amy," critiques *Variety*. It's the end of her career.

• *Thursday, November 9, 1950*: BADLY BURNED AS FIRE ENGULFS BED, reports *The Los Angeles Daily News*. A picture shows Helen, half-mummified in bandages, tended to by a nurse at Hollywood Receiving Hospital. The manager of the apartment house at 1825 North Whitley in Hollywood had broken into the apartment at the smell of smoke and had found Helen "clad only in a bed jacket" and "severely burned on the side of the face, head, neck, abdomen and leg." Investigators find liquor and sleeping pills in the apartment. Her third husband, Walter Piascik, a Merchant Mariner, had shipped out shortly before the fire. He will be a "sometimes" husband—Helen's death certificate will note that she was divorced.

• *Some time presumably in the mid–1950s*: Helen's brother Lee Chandler has Helen committed. (In the October 1990 issue of *Films in Review* magazine, Randolph Man wrote a letter to the editor regarding *The Thistleball*, the unpublished memoir of Bramwell Fletcher, who had died two years previously. Man wrote that the last Fletcher had heard of Helen "was from an acquaintance who had received a letter in the mid–1950s from an insane asylum in the desert southeast of Los Angeles signed by her. When he went there, he was told by the head nurse that, yes, they did have a patient who *claimed* to be Helen Chandler. Of course, it turned out to be her.")

• *Tuesday, November 3, 1959*: *The Hollywood Reporter* writes that Chandler is making "her first visit outside the walls of DeWitt State Hospital in five years." She pays a call on childhood friend Lillian Roth in Palm Springs.

• *Friday, April 30, 1965*: Helen, who had been living, apparently alone, at 15 Paloma Avenue in Venice, California, dies at Los Angeles County Hospital, having been admitted days before suffering from shock and massive bleeding from an ulcer. According to her death certificate, she was 56 years old. According to her birth certificate, she was 57.

• *Monday, May 3, 1965*: Funeral services take place for Helen Chandler at the Pierce Brothers Hollywood Mortuary. She's cremated at the Chapel of the Pines, where her ashes are in Vaultage, along with such Hollywood figures as Edmund Gwenn, Thomas Mitchell, and H.B. Warner. Lionel Atwill's ashes were also in Vaultage at Chapel of the Pines until his son removed them in 2003.

*   *   *

Quotes from and About Helen Chandler

"Her father, Leland Chandler, raced and bred fine horses. As a little girl, Helen loved to go to the races all through the south with him. 'But it wasn't the horses that interested me particularly,' she says. 'It was the crowd, the clamor and the excitement. I adored watching the people. They were so gay, so taken out of themselves. It had the feeling of theater, good theater. Of course, I didn't realize it, but this is probably when I first wanted to be an actress....'"

"'The technique [between stage and screen acting] is so different that when people ask me which I like best I am completely stopped. I enjoy both, but it's like trying to decide whether you prefer beefsteak or ocean liners. I enjoy each of them in their respective place.'"—*New Movie* magazine, January 1932

"Helen Chandler is not much over five feet tall. She couldn't possibly weigh an ounce over a hundred pounds. Her eyes are blue and childlike and her pixie face is framed with a halo of wavy yellow hair. She's just the most delicate, demure little person imaginable."—*Silver Screen* magazine, January 1932

"'In *Dracula*, I played one of those bewildered little girls who go around pale, hollow-eyed and anguished, wondering about things ... I was. Wondering when I could get to a hospital and part with a rampant appendix without holding up the picture....

"'It would be an awful fate, for instance, to go around being a pale little girl in a trance with her arms outstretched as in *Dracula*, all the rest of my screen career.'"
—*New Movie* magazine, January 1932

"She is interested in swimming and riding as sports and does a great deal of reading. Her pets consist of a small garden toad and a small, white cat with blue eyes."
—Studio biography, early 1930s

"The Cyril Humes live in a picturesque home high up in the Hollywood Hills. Each evening Helen curls up in a window seat to watch the lights come on in the city below. A lover both of the mountains and the sea, she has found an admirable compromise by living there in the winter and at the beach in the summer....

"Motion picture actress, dignified wife, and little girl dreaming in the sand, Helen Chandler seems without a care in the world."—*Silver Screen* magazine, January 1932

[Helen Chandler and Bramwell Fletcher] had planned to marry in the spring, but when Fletcher's play *Within the Gates* was forcibly withdrawn from tour by Boston censors, the couple hastened the nuptials."—Associated Press, February 14, 1935

"[Apartment house manager Sam] Cox told police he first was aroused at 4 a.m. by another tenant, who reported he smelled smoke in the corridor, but after investigating the manager returned to bed. It was not until three hours later that he, too, detected the odor of smoke and removed the lock to gain entry to the woman's apartment."
—*Los Angeles Daily News*, November 9, 1950

"Helen Chandler, 56, former film and stage actress, was reported in improved condition Tuesday in General Hospital."—Unidentified clipping, April 21, 1965

"Services will be held at 3 p.m. today at Pierce Brothers, Hollywood, for Helen Chandler ... who died Friday after a long illness."—*The Hollywood Reporter*, May 3, 1965

Mad Jack Unleashed
Svengali and *The Mad Genius*

> *When he looked at women*
> *With his terrible eyes*
> *They forgot their*
> *Pride and senses*
> **Mr. John BARRYMORE**
> **SVENGALI**
> —Warner Bros. publicity for ***Svengali,*** 1931

> *At Last! The Great*
> ***John***
> ***BARRYMORE***
> *At His Zenith!*
> —Warner Bros. publicity for ***The Mad Genius,*** 1931

Monday, January 12, 1931

Bella Vista is an estate, a virtual castle with its tower and pools, almost fairy tale in its baroque extravagance and nestled on a mountain in Beverly Hills. The entranceway gate bears a coat of arms, personally designed by Bella Vista's master, John Barrymore, and revealing his repellent self-image: a serpent wearing a crown.

As the master arises, he probably doesn't wash—he rarely does. More likely he climbs his tower and looks at the view of the starlit pre-dawn Pacific. Maybe, as is his custom, he visits his glass-domed aviary of over 2,000 birds and the lair of Maloney, Barrymore's king vulture from South Africa.[1] He often feeds Maloney in the garden—dangling worms from his own mouth for Maloney to fly down, snare, and enjoy. Only one problem: The liquor frequently on the master's breath intoxicates Maloney. One of the strangest spectacles in Hollywood, as described by the master's servants, is the sight of a drunken vulture flying crookedly over Bella Vista.

Barrymore might behold his many treasures, such as the black copper armor he wore as *Richard III,* or his dinosaur egg. He might say good morning to the angelically blonde Dolores, his former leading lady and third wife, whom he affectionately calls "Jiggie Wink." Although a stained glass window at Bella Vista presents the couple almost as archangels, she's been a torment to him, as have most of the ladies in his life, all the way back to the stepmother who seduced him when he was ten. Rumors of Dolores' promiscuity so agonize him that he's actually placed bars on the windows. He also despises artist James Montgomery Flagg for tattling that "Jiggie Wink," during her days and nights as a model, once posed for

Portrait: John Barrymore in *Svengali*.

Flagg in lingerie that wasn't entirely clean.[2] Long after John's death, Dolores will live on an avocado ranch, oblivious to the fact that many of her ex-husband's prized ancient religious icons—that she'd snared when they divorced—were now forsaken in her flooded cellar, floating or submerged.

He might or might not visit his nine-month-old baby daughter "Dede"; he'd desperately wanted a son (having had a daughter Diana, with former wife Michael Strange), and had jocularly described "Dede" to the press as looking "a little like Lon Chaney." He dresses habitually in his battered Homburg hat, rakishly cocked over one eye, and a long, dirty sashed overcoat; studio makeup men will tend to his celebrated "Great Profile," which he favors in his films. When he looks full-face into a camera, the effect is startling, mainly due to his eyes—like the eyes one sees in paintings of the saints, and photographs of serial killers.

At 48, he's still a very striking man, and currently "on the wagon," more or less. A chronic alcoholic since age 14, he's never fully abstinent, and there are the Prohibition nights and mornings when, with no liquor available, he drinks Dolores' perfume.

His driver takes him toward Hollywood, for which he has coined many irreverent nicknames—including "Hollywoodus-in-Latrina" and "The Flatulent Cave of the Winds." The actor who'd played Hamlet as (in his own words) "a ranting, pious pervert" and had reveled on screen as Dr. Jekyll and Mr. Hyde and Captain Ahab, is happy to be playing yet another epic tormented soul as he arrives at Warner Bros.–First National Studio, under the mountains in Burbank. This new vehicle provides Barrymore virtually all he could desire—a makeup à la Lucifer, Expressionistic sets, and a juicy death scene. It will also feature a dash of opera, burlesque-style humor, a glimpse of the derriere of the leading lady's double, a suicide, a black cat, a bevy of starlets as Morocco dancing girls, dazzling special effects, and even a dash of foot fetishism.

All in all, it promises to be a John Barrymore feast day.

And on this morning, the actor will begin playing the virtuoso role which many believe to be his greatest all-time screen performance ... Svengali.

*   *   *

Bella Vista: Barrymore's estate, high in Beverly Hills.

Evil Magician of Evil Love!
—Warner Bros. publicity, *Svengali*

When movie audiences had last seen John Barrymore, he had been riding the great white whale.

Moby Dick, 1930. "Mad Jack" Barrymore, of course, was Captain Ahab, complete with peg leg, and the climax saw him atop Moby Dick, vengefully stabbing his harpoon over and over into the infamous monster of the deep. Although portraying Ahab, Barrymore actually evokes Mr. Hyde, whom he had played so chillingly in 1920—his face viciously contorted, his smile wildly demonic, cackling, screaming, the whole effect all the more grotesque as he leers through the prop whale blood that splatters his face, playing the scene as a bestial rape.

The "whale," meanwhile, doesn't seem so much a whale as it does a giant, glistening, sea-going penis, one of incredible size and conceit, hell-bent on winning a Special Oscar as Most Enormous Phallic Symbol of 1930. Manned by a stalwart crew of four, the whale puppet is especially a hoot whenever it opens its Howdy Doody-esque mouth, one of the hapless men inside dropping its plank lower jaw with "teeth" attached to it. The comical monstrosity seems hardly a worthy match for the legendary John Barrymore, be he drunk or sober.

On *Moby Dick,* he was usually drunk.

Barrymore had first played Ahab in Warners' *The Sea Beast* (1926), the silent version of Herman Melville's classic. In *The Sea Beast,* the star looked like a wild-eyed, peg-legged archangel. In *Moby Dick,* he looks at times, despite his "Great Profile," like a Midnight Mission derelict—and in fact was suffering from all-too-obvious alcohol bloat.

Warners proclaimed Barrymore "The World's Greatest Living Actor," and his films made the studio teeming profits: *The Sea Beast,* $100,500[3]; *Don Juan* (1926, the first film with synchronized music and sound), $523,000; *General Crack* (1929, Barrymore's first "talkie"), $89,000. *The Show of Shows* (1929), Warners' all-star vaudeville-style extravaganza, saw Barrymore guest star as Shakespeare's Richard III, chillingly cackling atop a pile of battlefield corpses:

"My devil had long been caged, he came out roaring": John Barrymore in *Dr. Jekyll and Mr. Hyde* (1920).

> Why, love foreswore me in my mother's womb...
> She did corrupt frail nature with some bribe
> To shrink mine arm up like a wither'd shrub;
> To make an envious mountain on my back,
> Where sits deformity, to mock my body...

Barrymore was the class act attraction of *The Show of Shows*—which earned a profit of $251,000.

For 1930 moviegoers, beholding Barrymore on the screen is akin to 21st century audiences watching a rock star—a crazy, unbridled talent, shooting off sparks of what Greta Garbo later hailed as the man's "divine madness." However, Barrymore's previous Warner vehicle, *The Man from Blankley's*, had perilously bombed, with a loss of $253,000. *Moby Dick*, released September 13, 1930, was also a failure, Warners recording its loss at $106,000.

Warner Bros. is worried. Is Barrymore losing his looks, magic, sobriety and box office potency? His most recent contract with the studio, dated July 7, 1928,[4] was one of the most generous in Hollywood existence, packed with lavish assurances:

> Producer agrees to submit to Artist each literary work for his approval....
> Producer agrees to pay Artist for each photoplay, the sum of $150,000, and 10 percent of gross receipts of each picture....
> Producer to supply at own expense and cost all costumes, wigs, and other wearing apparel and wardrobe for representation by Artist....
> Artist shall be sole star and principal actor in each photoplay and no director, author, artist or person other than Artist shall be starred or co-starred or featured therein, without written consent of Barrymore, and Artist shall be announced as such sole star in all press bulletins, advertising and all publicity matter of every name, nature and character issued by Producer....

Warner Bros., deeply in the red, can't risk paying such a fortune to a star in a self-destructive eclipse. Barrymore needs a role to vindicate his fame, salary and legend. He believes he knows precisely what it should be.

* * *

> "Ach, Drilby [*sic*] ... how beautiful you are! It drives me mad! I adore you.... And, ach! What a beautiful skeleton you will make! And very soon, too, because you do not smile on your madly loving Svengali. You burn his letters without reading them! You shall have a nice little mahogany glass case all to yourself in the museum of the Ecole de Medecine and Svengali shall come in his new fur-lined coat, smoking his big cigar of the Havana ... and look through the holes of your eyes into your stupid empty skull, and up the nostrils of your high, bony sounding-board of a nose ... and into the roof of your big mouth, with your thirty-two big English teeth, and between your big ribs into your big chest, where the big leather lungs used to be.... And then he will look all down your bones to your poor crumbling feet and say, 'Ach! What a fool she was not to answer Svengali's letters!'"
> —Svengali, talking to Trilby in George Du Maurier's 1894 novel *Trilby*

Du Maurier named his sensationally popular novel *Trilby* after its doomed heroine. However, it was the villain, Svengali, who fascinated the public—a vile Jewish hypnotist and pianist who fatally mesmerizes milkmaid-artists' model Trilby (or "Drilby," as he pronounces it) into becoming a magnificent singer. Du Maurier captured it all in his lush literary style, often rhapsodizing in French, sometimes lapsing into anti–Semitism (or so his critics say), and now and then devoting ecstatic prose to Trilby's feet. Despite a blind left eye, the former *Punch* illustrator personally provided the novel's charming sketches, one presenting Svengali's bearded face leering atop a spider's body—exultant in his web. "An Incubus," read the caption.

The Victorian women swooned. Here was a lascivious villain who offered a slick variation of the Faust concept: He provided Trilby glorious fame, claiming her body and soul, but as he had hypnotized her into his bed, she couldn't face damnation—or could she? After Svengali's demise, she faces a sad, lingering death, her final words "... *Svengali ... Svengali ... Svengali!*" The romantic lead, Little Billee, wastes away shortly after Trilby's death.

Svengali, if only as a ghost, conquered all.

The success of *Trilby* amazed Du Maurier (father of the celebrated British actor Gerald Du Maurier and grandfather of the five boys who inspired J.M. Barrie's *Peter Pan*), and eventually overwhelmed him. He died at the age of 62 on October 8, 1896, only two years after the book's publication and 23 days before the Halloween 1896 announcement that the city of Macon in Pasco County, Florida, had changed its name to Trilby. *Trilby* would also be a major influence on Gaston Leroux's 1910 novel *The Phantom of the Opera,* as Erik works his spell upon opera singer Christine.

Trilby became a great stage vehicle for powerhouse actors. In England, Sir Herbert Beerbohm Tree triumphed as Svengali; in the U.S., Wilton Lackaye first played Svengali in New York in 1895 at age 33, and followed with three revivals over the next 26 years. In silent days there had been at least six film versions, dating all the way back to a 1908 *Trilby* from Denmark. Tree starred in a 1914 British film version, Lackaye in a 1915 American version.[5] *Trilby* (1923) had starred Andrée Lafayette as Trilby and Arthur Edmund Carew[6] as Svengali. *The New York Times* review (July 23, 1923) noted:

> [W]himsical and charming as Mlle. Lafayette is, it is Arthur Edmund Carew's revelation of Svengali that dominates the production.... He has the long fingers, the sharp, aquiline nose, the hollow, cadaverous cheeks, the black, matted beard and unkempt hair of the Svengali of the book. His dark eyes are scintillating and gruesome....

John Barrymore is determined to revive himself, personally and professionally. He's very familiar with Du Maurier; on April 17, 1917, he'd opened on Broadway in the title role of *Peter Ibbetson,* based on Du Maurier's 1891 novel. His older brother Lionel had co-starred as the evil Col. Ibbetson and the show's big thrill was John climactically (and viciously) beating Lionel to death with a cane. It had been a terrific success for both Barrymores, although John had lamented that his role was basically "a marshmallow in a blond wig."

Barrymore sees Svengali as a role that can mix his love of the macabre with racy humor and ultimate tragedy. He'll follow in the tradition of Sir Herbert Tree and Wilton Lackaye. It could be his ultimate screen triumph.

Warner Bros., however, must secure the rights.

September 1930: Barrymore sets sail on his yacht *Infanta,* with Dolores and baby Dede, to Cape San Lucas, not to return until December. On November 7, Louella Parsons reports that there's a 50–50 chance that Barrymore will remake *Dr. Jekyll and Mr. Hyde* upon his return to Warners. She adds that the star is "definitely set" there for *The Maltese Falcon,* in which Barrymore might have enjoyed a decided change of pace as a very offbeat Sam Spade. On November 20, however, Parsons announces what she calls "the most surprising news of the year": that Warners finally has the rights to *Trilby,* and that "Jack Barrymore, no less, is to play the weird role of Svengali...."

At sea, Barrymore suffers a gastric hemorrhage. Very ill from loss of blood, nevertheless he cables his ideas on *Trilby* to Warner Bros.—insisting Svengali "must be funny and get lots of laughs":

> Although a sinister figure, he is a wise, dirty, glutinous Polish Jew, with no conscience and a supreme contempt for all those nice, clean, straight-thinking Christians. He has an enormous sense of humor. The funnier he is, in the proper way, the better the picture will be, and the greater contrast to all the sinister part, hypnotism, et cetera, in the last part of the picture....
> The female lead must have exactly the correct quality. Otherwise the entire play goes for nothing. The man's is the better acting part, but if the girl is not perfectly right, everything he does is bound to be unbelievable and a little ridiculous....[7]

Warner Bros. believes it has found the "perfectly right" Trilby. She's Evelyn Laye, a wistfully beautiful, 30-year-old British actress known to her cronies as "Boo."[8] Samuel Goldwyn had starred Evelyn Laye in his film *One Heavenly Night,* set for release in January 1931. On November 24, 1930, Warners, eager to sign Evelyn, writes to Sam Goldwyn at the Sherry-Netherlands Hotel in New York City:

> Dear Sam:
>
> In continuation of our several talks we had reference Evelyn Laye to appear in our picture *Trilby* with John Barrymore, we would appreciate your continuing negotiations in our behalf for Miss Laye's services in this particular picture and authorize you by this letter to conclude the arrangement along the terms and conditions we discussed verbally. It is understood we must have Miss Laye at our studio in California no later than January 15th, 1931, or prefer January 1st or even December 29th would be agreeable to us.[9]

In reference to the credit given Miss Laye on film and advertising matter, the billing can read as follows:

JOHN BARRYMORE

in

TRILBY

with

EVELYN LAYE

Warners offers Evelyn Laye billing at 75 percent the size of Barrymore's, as well as $35,000 for ten weeks—remarkable money for an actress the U.S. public had yet to see in a movie. The studio even authorizes Goldwyn to go as high as $50,000, so sold are they on Laye's perfect fit for Trilby. However, the deal collapses. Stories conflict: One says the actress prefers to return to England for a vacation,[10] while a more sinister story claims Laye's exhausted from overwork and confined to a sanitarium. At any rate, Miss Laye will enjoy a very distinguished career, marry Frank Lawton (whom horror fans will remember as the romantic lead in the Karloff and Lugosi *The Invisible Ray* and Tod Browning's *The Devil-Doll,* both in 1936), and die in 1996 at the age of 95.

Trilby has no Trilby.

Dolores Costello would seem perfect for Trilby, but is devoting herself to motherhood—and Barrymore seems intent on keeping "Jiggie Wink" captive in Bella Vista. Meanwhile, on July 24, 1930, Warner Bros. had signed a starlet named Violet Krauth to a contract. Her professional name at the time was Marilyn Morgan; she's blonde, pretty and 17 years old. Marilyn had played a bit in Howard Hughes' *Hell's Angels,* acting a twinkle-eyed mini-vamp who got men to enlist in the Great War by offering them a kiss (a scene directed by *Hell's Angels* "ghost director" James Whale). On October 20, 1930, Marilyn, using the new stage name Marian Marsh, had opened at Los Angeles' Belasco Theatre in *Young Sinners,* a comedy about "rampant youth."[11]

Marian has a curious mix of child-like beauty and an almost teasing sensuality. Jack Warner sees *Young Sinners* and demands, "Who is that girl?" Marian will always remember the "embarrassing situation" of telling Warner she was under contract to his studio. Warners tests the virtual novice for Trilby.

She has lots of competition. *The Baltimore Sun* will wax poetically about Warners' Trilby quest:

> Sixty young women of various degree of charm and talents—tall ones, short ones, blondes and brunettes, baby-like beauties and tall, lissome ladies of dignity—all took the screen test for the occasion. In time sixty samples of comeliness and histrionism were assembled and put together as if the whole constituted a single picture.[12]

Barrymore, still ailing with what the press ominously calls "jungle fever," watches the big parade of Trilbys on a movie projection set in his bedroom. He too likes Marian's test and Jack L. Warner and Darryl Zanuck decide to take her to meet the Great Profile. For the sake of protocol, and considering Barrymore's reputation—especially while in the throes of "jungle fever"—they also take Marian's mother. The limousine heads up Tower Road, and Marian sees Bella Vista. Her mother waits downstairs as Warner and Zanuck take Marian up to the Barrymore boudoir. The actress recalled over 60 years later:

> John Barrymore was in this great big enormous bed in this great big enormous room. As I walked in, he was propped up in bed, lots of pillows around him; he sat up rather straighter....
> "Has anyone ever remarked," asked Barrymore, "that you resemble my wife Dolores?"
> "Yes," I said.
> "Who?" asked Barrymore.
> And I said, "The butcher on Vine Street, who gives me liver for my cat!" Well, Barrymore just laughed his head off![13]

"He looked like a king lying there," the young actress will tell *Motion Picture* magazine. Warner gambles that the 17-year-old will hold her own with the superstar. She can't sing, but Warners can easily recruit a trained singer to dub her.[14]

Wednesday, December 17: Louella Parsons reports in the *Los Angeles Examiner* that, "unless something entirely unexpected happens," Dolores Costello, despite plans to return to the screen, will not play Trilby, rumors to the contrary.

Barrymore gives his blessing: Marian Marsh wins the role of Trilby a few days before Christmas 1930. Warners allows her to announce her good fortune at a Yuletide party at Pickfair after the 11 p.m. late edition newspapers carry the news. She'll also work for far less compensation than Evelyn Laye.

Tuesday, December 23: Jack L. Warner writes to Marian:

> The term of your contract is accordingly extended for an additional period of six (6) months from and after the expiration of the present term of said contract, upon the same terms and conditions as herein set forth, and upon the same rate of compensation, to-wit, the sum of One Hundred Twenty-five Dollars ($125) per week.[15]

Although the salary is a pittance of the fortune that Barrymore is earning, Warner will augment the pay with a blockbuster publicity campaign for Marian.

However, Warners titles the film not *Trilby,* but ... *Svengali.*

* * *

Final choice as Trilby: Marian Marsh.

Svengali—The Shoot[16]

WEEK ONE

Love-Slave of the Man She Hated!
—Warner Bros. publicity for *Svengali*

Monday, January 12, 1931: *Svengali* begins shooting on Stage 8 at Warners' First National lot in Burbank. The sets: Svengali's Upper Hall and Apartment.

Directing *Svengali* is Archie Mayo, a plump, 39-year-old Warners workhorse whose recent credits include James Cagney's *The Doorway to Hell* and Barbara Stanwyck's *Illicit*. Mayo has a ribald sense of humor and the habit of greeting co-workers with a hand buzzer. With the men, he usually buzzes their hands. The ladies usually feel the buzzer's full impact in other areas.

"Script Unfinished" reads the first day's Daily Production and Progress Report. J. Grubb Alexander, who'd scripted Universal's *The Man Who Laughs* (1928) as well as Barrymore's *General Crack* and *Moby Dick,* is providing the scenario pieces at a time; by Wednesday, it's still only about 65 percent finished.

Barrymore is on time for the 8:30 call, having arrived at dawn for his two-hour Svengali makeup, as applied by Johnny Wallace. The star revels in his wicked look, a frightening facsimile from the du Maurier sketches; it's as if Lucifer himself is alive and frightfully well in Burbank. Margot Peters will write in her excellent book *The House of Barrymore*:

> The alcohol bloat so evident in *Moby Dick* disappeared with weeks of abstinence and a bland diet.... he was lean and controlled.... As the dirty, sly, magnetic Svengali, Jack transformed himself into the personification of seductive guile—Lucifer as serpent. He allows enough male sexuality to burn through a repellant exterior to attract. The nose is the key. His own long, quivering nose was phallic; Svengali's nose is an exaggeration of that symbol, rapacious and sensual.... He is like a tomcat watching a mouse hole....

Barrymore is 5'8", so he wears boots with four-inch heels to provide a more looming look for Svengali. Instantly he's the talk of the studio and one wonders if he had a personal inspiration: With his beak of a nose and vulturous aura, the star evokes not only Satan, and Faust's Mephistopheles, but Barrymore's king vulture, Maloney.

Also on call today: Luis Alberni as Svengali's faithful familiar, Gecko. The Barcelona-born Alberni becomes a Barrymore hanger-on and drinking crony and signs on for *Svengali* at $500 per week. Joining Barrymore and Alberni are Adrienne D'Ambricourt as Mme. Vinard, Svengali's battle axe landlady, and Lionel Belmore (soon to play the Burgomaster in *Frankenstein*) as a lawyer—Svengali running afoul of both of them. A cat is also on call, reportedly named "Leo," as is a musician to serenade the first day's shoot.

Barney "Chick" McGill, Archie Mayo's cameraman on *The Doorway to Hell*, is the cinematographer and Anton Grot is the set designer, creating a marvelously Expressionistic Latin Quarter of Paris. Both McGill and Grot will receive well-deserved Academy nominations for *Svengali*.

Mayo shoots over three minutes of what the Daily Production and Progress Report will list as "OK'd Takes" and Day One wraps up at 5:45 p.m.

Tuesday, January 13, and *Wednesday, January 14*: The same players work on the same sets. "Leo" the cat is back, too, and works the whole week. The day runs long Wednesday; with no supper break, Mayo ends at 8:40 p.m.

Thursday, January 15, and *Friday, January 16*: A new player joins the show: Carmel Myers, as Svengali's ill-fated lover-voice pupil, Honori. A great silent screen vamp, best-remembered as the wild-eyed, platinum blonde temptress Iras in MGM's 1925 *Ben-Hur*, Myers had also seduced Barrymore in *Beau Brummel* (1924). Reportedly she had left Los Angeles by train, heading for New York to sign a contract for a vaudeville tour when she received a wire inviting her to return to Hollywood for *Svengali*. The telegram expressed that the role of Honori was "a short one but important to the picture and would give her an opportunity to sing." Ms. Myers claimed it took her "five split seconds" to decide to abandon the tour.[17]

Svengali meets Honori, who's his married lover as well as his adoring pupil. He is posing as the brilliant maestro, holding a quill and fluttering his eyelids:

> *Svengali*: Now ... what did we do last?
> *Honori* (sighing): Don't you remember?
> *Svengali*: I was speaking about *music!*

Miss Myers tugs at her corset as she sings "Tally Ho," Barrymore sitting at the piano, making faces at her caterwauling with the timing of a master vaudevillian. He suggests they "rest" from the lesson and Honori has news:

> *Honori*: I've left my husband.
> *Svengali*: And how much has *he* left *you?*

The "brute" has left her nothing—she's come to Svengali "just as I am." Suddenly the comedy vanishes and the scene becomes very dark. Svengali rises and turns his evil eye on her; the audience doesn't see his face, only Honori's horrified reaction. "Take your eyes off me, Svengali!" She wails into the streets. Come the next scene, as Svengali feeds his black cat, Gecko brings the news that Honori has drowned herself in the river.

"She was very, very sweet," eulogizes Svengali. "Oh, but a bad businesswoman!"

The black-humored episode perfectly sets up *Svengali*. Asked almost half a century later who her favorite person was to work with, Ms. Myers replied, "Barrymore. Because if you were good when you started, you would be great when you finished, because he was an inspiration."[18]

Saturday, January 17: A long day and night: Mayo works the *Svengali* company from 10:00 a.m. Saturday until 2:30 a.m. Sunday. Barrymore, Adrienne D'Ambricourt and Lionel Belmore have worked every day this week; alas, the latter two will see all their footage cut from *Svengali*'s release version.

Week one has rolled along smoothly, Barrymore creating a foul, brilliant, insolvent, womanizing, incorrigible yet charismatic Svengali. Mayo has given the film pace, and the first week's work seems a crazy brew of melodrama and burlesque. Word already runs through Hollywood that the star is giving his most brilliant screen performance.

* * *

WEEK TWO

The Loveliest Feet in Paris Yet They Followed the Evilest Man in the World
—Warner Bros. publicity for **Svengali**

Monday, January 19: Marian Marsh reports to the *Svengali* Apartment set at 8:30 a.m. for her first day, wearing her blonde Trilby wig. She and Barrymore are the only players on call—the World's Greatest Living Actor and a 17-year-old novice. She's nervous. He's patient.

> Mr. Barrymore (as I always called him) worried so about me, which was very pleasant. Whenever we rehearsed, he would say, "Are you comfortable? Don't worry about anything—just be natural."
> ... He was so helpful, and we were so comfortable together—many people remarked on that.

Archie Mayo is helpful too, but progress is slow, complicated by the fact that the underage

Marian must have her teacher on the set. There's no supper break and Mayo works Barrymore and Marsh until 11:45 that night—a nearly 15-hour day.

Tuesday, January 20: Barrymore and Marsh are back at 10:00 a.m., the late start due to the very late night previously. Luis Alberni is on call, and starting today are Donald Crisp and Lumsden Hare as, respectively, the Laird and Taffy, artist cronies of Little Billee.[19] Crisp's film career goes back to 1908; he'll win a Best Supporting Actor Oscar for *How Green Was My Valley* (1941); his last film was *Spencer's Mountain* (1963); he dies in 1974 at age 91. Hare's film career goes back to 1916; he'll later appear in such films as *The Lodger* (1944) and *The Picture of Dorian Gray* (1945); his final credit will be the 1961 *Thriller* TV episode "Hay-Fork and Bill-Hook"; he dies in 1964 at age 89.

Once again, the company skips dinner, working until 7:30 p.m. The day has its problems; the camera staff lists notes such as "Mask wiggled," "Cue mix up," and "Action changed after first six takes."

Wednesday, January 21: Barrymore, Alberni, Crisp and Hare work on the Interior Studio Apartment set; Marian Marsh, likely exhausted after the past two days, gets a day off. The scene includes the badinage as Svengali visits Taffy and the Laird to find Taffy taking a bath. "These Englanders get dirty very quickly," Svengali tells Gecko. Meanwhile, the "Englanders" demand to know when "the Polish scavenger" last took a bath.

"Ha! Not since I tripped and fell in the sewer!" cackles Barrymore.

Thursday, January 22: The same players work on the Interior apartment set, and Marian Marsh joins them, as does one pianist. They also work on the Int. Curtained Enclosure, where the Laird is in the bathtub. They end up tossing Svengali in the tub. "God scrap England," prays a soapy Svengali.

Meanwhile, Darryl Zanuck is very carefully watching the rushes. On the 22nd, he sends this memo to cameraman Barney McGill:

> I think you can photograph Miss Marsh better than you did the first day. While she looked good, I think there is still room for improvement. I think you can always photograph her a little softer than you did, because she must look beautiful at all times. Please look after this personally.[20]

Friday, January 23: It is the first day's shooting for Tom Douglas as Little Billee.[21] Douglas is a Kentucky-born 36-year-old "juvenile," whose Broadway credits include *Seven* (1929), in which he played a doomed World War I pilot and was directed by Lionel Atwill. (Originally set for the Little Billee role was David Manners, who had recently returned to Warners after a loan-out to Universal to play John Harker in *Dracula*.) Warners fires Douglas from *Svengali* after only one day's work.

Saturday, January 24: *Svengali* already has a new Little Billee. He's Bramwell Fletcher, 26-year-old British actor, almost as blond and angelic-looking as Marian Marsh. Fletcher, who signs on for *Svengali* at $450 per week, will soon play Norton, the archaeologist who goes stark raving mad ("He went for a little walk...!") at the sight of Karloff as Imhotep in *The Mummy* (Universal, 1932). In 1935, Fletcher will marry *Dracula*'s leading lady Helen Chandler; in 1942, he'll wed Barrymore's daughter, Diana.

The very sight of Barrymore terrifies Fletcher. Barrymore, realizing it, amuses himself by glaring at the young actor whenever he plays a scene. Mayo works the company until 12:15 a.m. Sunday.

Barrymore and Marsh have a strange chemistry. Appropriately, it's almost as if the actor has hypnotized the actress.

* * *

WEEK THREE

Where Did Hate End! Where did Love Begin?
—Warner Bros. publicity, Svengali

Monday, January 26, and Tuesday, January 27: Barrymore has off Monday, as Marsh, Fletcher, Crisp and Hare work until 9:05 p.m. Barrymore's back Tuesday, working with Marsh, Fletcher, Crisp, Hare, and Alberni until 8:45 p.m. Neither 12-hour day has a supper break.

Wednesday, January 28, through Saturday, January 31: Barrymore is ill, missing these four shooting days. As such he's not present to enjoy a *Svengali* "Event": Trilby's nude scene, shot Friday on the Carrel's Studio Set. Bramwell Fletcher and 28 extras are there to behold the peep show: Trilby posing *au naturel* when the innocent Little Billee happens to see her. She smiles at him, he looks shocked, she looks ashamed, hops off the stage, and runs for cover.

Marsh reports to Stage 8, wearing her Trilby wig, a body stocking and a smile. As she's underage, "an older girl," as Marian remembers, is also on the set, in Trilby wig and what Marian describes as "a nude leotard." So it's actually the double's derriere we see as Trilby jumps off the stage, runs from the room, and basically moons the audience. Mayo wraps up the day at 9:50 p.m. and Warners does its best to quash the gossip that in *Svengali*, Marian Marsh not only wears a wig and has a "singer double," but also has a "derriere double."

Svengali is halfway through its shoot and despite Barrymore's incapacitation this week, is basically on schedule. Trilby's "nude" scene gives the film a special splash of sensation.

In fact, it's all the film needed to launch rumors more sinister than the film itself.

* * *

Idol of Paris—
Venus of Montmartre—
Selling Her Soul to a Sinister Satan of Hypnotic Evil
—Warner Bros. publicity, Svengali

Svengali fascinates the Warner Bros. factory. John Barrymore and Marian Marsh both look as if they leapt out of a first edition of *Trilby,* with its engraved cover of a golden heart with angel wings, trapped in a horrific spider's web.

"Mad Jack" parades about the First National lot in Svengali cloak and high-crowned hat, his beard pointed and scraggly, cackling at his own perfidy and the response his image inspires, looking every bit the Antichrist. Marian Marsh, a pictorially perfect Trilby in her blonde wig and dark eye makeup, evokes a racy archangel, smiling and laughing, thrilled by her overnight stardom, and, according to the *L.A. Times,* "creating a furor on the Warner Brothers lot."[22]

Motion Picture magazine offers Marian's exultations about Barrymore:

> She says that playing Trilby to his Svengali had made her believe in fairy stories. It was a fairy story. One of those incredible happenings that infrequently occur in Grimm's Fairy Tales—and in Hollywood. Quite as much a fairy tale, says Marian, as the transformation of Cinderella or the legend of Snow White.[23]

John Barrymore and *Svengali*'s director, Archie Mayo. Note Barrymore's cigarette (courtesy John Antosiewicz).

She tells *Motion Picture* she believed none of "the weirdish [*sic*] tales about John Barrymore" ... that he was always on time, "chummy and friendly" with the cast ... and that "he *adored* his macabre makeup ... playing with it as a child plays with a putty mask. He'd sit between scenes, day in and day out, fooling with his beard, adjusting his built-out nose, admiring different effects in the mirror. He hated to remove it."

Thus, in an imagery that's both fairy tale storybook and Dante's *Inferno,* John Barrymore and Marian Marsh starkly stand out on a topical, rip-roaring movie lot that offers slick gangsters and sexy molls, jazz singers and leggy show girls. And perhaps inevitably, the dark rumors spread.[24]

After all, he's been so helpful to her.... She so resembles Dolores Costello.... You know his reputation.... She must idolize him....

The gossip sinuously circulates: *Svengali* is truly a sex melodrama: The Antichrist is despoiling the archangel.

The Great Profile and 17-year-old Marian are lovers—or so the Hollywood grapevine vows. The sordid slander goes that Barrymore, madly jealous of Dolores, has sexually recruited a dead ringer, an underage understudy for his wife in the hothouse climate of Warner Bros. The imagery of the satanic Svengali and cherubic Trilby, *in flagrante* in Barrymore's studio bungalow as night falls over the mountains of Burbank, is irresistibly gothic and the rumors persist ... so rich and ripe that Gene Fowler will feel compelled to deny them in his 1944 Barrymore biography *Good Night, Sweet Prince.*

Marian Marsh will refute them too:

> These were happy days for Jack Barrymore. He was on his best behavior, I might add; he was happily married, and he wasn't drinking. Dolores would visit the set, with their little daughter, "Dede," who was just learning to speak then. The little girl didn't like that beard! When Barrymore would want to kiss her, she didn't like that very much—the beard tickled her!

Warner Bros. front office powers intervene. They speak solemnly to both stars. If rumors escape First National of a sex affair between Barrymore and Marsh, *Svengali* sinks, and Marian's career dies on the vine. Nightmares of Lucifer and this little cherub celebrating carnal rites would be horrendous, a sordid anathema to the movie-going public.

"*Nail her nude double, the gal in the body stocking, who* isn't *underage,*" one imagines Jack L. Warner telling Barrymore. "*Put the wig on her and you'll never know the difference.*"

Whatever the truth, the gossip casts a real-life shadow on *Svengali* that never fully diminishes. An aura of sinister sensuality perfumes the film and somehow becomes a part of its ambiguity.

Svengali—cursed by the rumor mill—is becoming a real-life horror.

* * *

Week Four

His Evil Eyes Followed Her—His Power Coiled About Her—Strangled Her
—Warner Bros. publicity, **Svengali**

Monday, February 2, through *Wednesday, February 4*: Barrymore is back. Marsh, Fletcher, Crisp, Hare, and Alberni quickly make up for the time the star has missed.

Thursday and *Friday, February 5* and *6*: Paul Porcasi, a former concert soloist and New York City vocal teacher, joins the show as the concert manager. So does Ferike Boros as Marta, Trilby's servant. Rain has come mid-week and an exterior street shot is cancelled.

Saturday, February 7: Mayo shoots scenes on the Exterior Latin quarter on the back lot and the interior Montmartre studio. There are 62 extras. Meanwhile, production runs smoothly due to a coterie of devoted Barrymore crew members who have worked on his Warners films: Gordon Hollingshead (assistant director), Herbert "Limey" Plews (property man), "Smoke" Kring (wardrobe expert), Johnny Wallace (makeup artist), John Ellis (portrait photographer), Fred Applegate (script clerk), and Dave Forrest (sound engineer). As Warner publicity will report:

> For these men Barrymore ... stands eternally willing to go to bat. He has known them long enough to trust their judgment and their actions and he shows his favoritism for them in many ways.

Important studio officials Barrymore is not above snubbing or openly insulting if a disagreement arises. He enjoys a fight of that kind. But to those who are in no position to answer back he manifests a consideration, a friendly understanding that makes him the most popular star in the business with his particular crew.[25]

* * *

WEEK FIVE

Master of Her Mind but Not of Her Heart!
—Warner Bros. publicity, *Svengali*

Monday, February 9: Barrymore and Marsh have the day off, but Fletcher, Crisp and Hare join 111 extras on Stage 8's Interior Lobby and Foyer of Paris Theatre set.

Tuesday, February 10: Barrymore and Marsh return. Svengali and Trilby have spruced up by this time in the film; his hair is dressed back, and Marsh wears her own hair as Trilby-as-star. Bramwell Fletcher is sporting a mustache as the older and sadder Little Billee. Mayo shoots scenes on the Paris Theatre Stage Door set on First National's back lot.

Wednesday and *Thursday, February 11* and *12*: Mayo copes with clouds, rain, extras and five carriages on the back lot.

Friday, February 13: Only Barrymore and Marsh are on call. The scene: Svengali, frustrated by Trilby's lack of affection for him, hypnotizes her into lust as she lies in bed in their Paris hotel boudoir. The scene, perhaps the sexiest in the show, has the risk factor of shocking audience members *and* of causing derisive laughter that could capsize the whole film.

Barrymore naturally comes through; Marsh is the surprise on this Friday the 13th. "I *do* love you!" she gasps, her eyes wild, and she kisses him passionately.

"Ah, you are beautiful, my manufactured love," says Svengali, freeing Trilby from her hot pants trance. "But it is only Svengali talking to himself again."

It takes until 9:00 p.m. to get the scene, but Archie Mayo—"a rough kind of fellow," remembered Marian Marsh, "loud, boisterous, and anything he thought, he said!"—is delighted. "How did you know how to do that like that, and do it so well?" he teases Marian. Darryl Zanuck sees the rushes the following week and sends a February 20, 1931, memo to editor William Holmes: "Be sure to use the new take on the big Barrymore love scene with Marian Marsh on the bed. I think this is the best of all we have printed. It came in last night's rushes."

Saturday, February 14: A sunny Valentine's Day, and the Svengali Company pays a visit to Universal City. Warner Bros. has rented Universal's Phantom Stage, erected for Lon Chaney's *The Phantom of the Opera* (1925), to serve as the Paris Theatre. Barrymore, Marsh, Fletcher, Crisp, Hare, Alberni, Porcasi and 135 extras are there. Marsh, made up and costumed to appear her most archangelic, lip-synchs to a playback of "Lucia" recorded by Ellen Coutta, a coloratura soprano and pupil of maestro Leon Cepparo of Hollywood. Warners tries to keep Marian's dubbed singing a secret, but the *L.A. Times* will later divulge the truth—complete with a picture of Ms. Coutta—in its "Music and Musicians" section of June 14, 1931.

The Universal lot is in high spirits: *Dracula*, starring Bela Lugosi, opened the preceding Thursday in New York City, and is doing spectacular business.

The company gets box lunches but no supper. The scene of Trilby's triumph plays very dramatically, hitting the desired musical climax; in a nice touch, Barrymore's Svengali, overwhelmed by Trilby's performance, jubilantly knocks over his conductor's podium. Mayo finishes at 6:50 p.m. Zanuck, a hard man to please, hails the sequence in a February 17, 1931, memo as "marvelous."

*   *   *

Sunday, February 15: Barrymore celebrates his 49th birthday. Warner Bros. has a week of shooting left to complete *Svengali.* And on this date, *The New York Times* makes an announcement: *The Genius,* originally slated for Warners' Edward G. Robinson, will now go to John Barrymore. No reason is given for the switch, but surely Warners, delighted by *Svengali,* and convinced that Barrymore is giving his masterpiece screen portrayal, wants a follow-up similar in style and scope. Barrymore himself had discussed filming *Hamlet* for Warner Bros., but *The Genius* impresses the studio as the perfect vehicle to follow *Svengali*—fresh enough to avoid seeming a carbon copy, and melodramatic enough to allow the star to explode in his frenetic fashion.

The Genius lacks *Svengali*'s literary and dramatic pedigree. It's based on a Broadway-bound play by Martin Brown entitled *The Idol,* which had starred William Farnum and had ignobly died before reaching New York in the summer of 1929.[26] The basic difference from *Svengali* is its modern 1931 setting—and a sex change. Rather than Svengali hypnotizing a

Marian Marsh, Bramwell Fletcher and John Barrymore (right) in *Svengali.* **In 1942, a few months after Barrymore's death, Fletcher would marry Barrymore's daughter Diana.**

young milkmaid into becoming a great diva, Tsarakov—a genius with a club foot—transforms a young male waif, Fedor, into the ballet star he himself might have been if not for his deformity.

With *Svengali* still in the works, Warner Bros. blueprints *The Genius* to co-star Barrymore and Marian Marsh, who they see as giving a breakout star performance. Production will begin as soon as possible.

* * *

WEEK SIX

His Eyes Darted Baleful Fire—He Was Her Master—She His Slave—
With All Paris At Her Feet She Groveled Before Svengali
—Warner Bros. publicity, **Svengali**

Monday, February 16: A big day at First National: the studio's own theater set represents the Interior of the Naples Theatre, with 125 extras and 25 musicians. Principals Barrymore, Marsh, Fletcher, Alberni and Porcasi are on call. The studio provides lunch and supper and Mayo ends at 8:45 p.m.

Tuesday, February 17: Only Barrymore and Marsh work. For reasons not noted, the call is 1:00 p.m. The scene: the final exchange—almost a farewell—between Svengali and Trilby, before she takes the stage at a dive of a Cairo nightclub to offer her final, fatal concert. Barrymore's eyes brim with tears as he says:

> Listen, my dear. Tonight, I want you to watch me very closely. Do not take your eyes off mine, even for an instant. And remember ... there is nothing in your mind, nothing in your heart, nothing in your soul, but Svengali ... Svengali ... Svengali....

He exits, looking back at her with a heartbreaking smile. The company fervently applauds. Mayo wraps it up at 10:35 p.m.

Wednesday, February 18, Thursday, February 19, and *Friday, February 20:* Barrymore, Marsh, Fletcher and Alberni report to Stage 8 for *Svengali's* finale, taking place on the wonderfully smoky and sinister Sphinx Café set. There are 57 extras Wednesday and Thursday and 35 on Friday; among them are Mlle. Doro and Her Six Morocco Dancing Girls, who top the Cairo bill over Trilby and Svengali. Mlle. Doro and her troupe wiggle and undulate with abandon.

The 20th is Bramwell Fletcher's 27th birthday. Mayo had tried to lessen Fletcher's fear of Barrymore by taking the young actor up to the star and making him touch him. "See?" says Mayo. "He doesn't even bite!" Yet Fletcher's awe remains. Darryl Zanuck will send editor William Holmes a February 23 memo about the rushes of their final meeting, when Svengali tells Billee that this is Trilby's final concert and drinks to her "freedom":

> Use the first part of the scene in the take in which Bramwell Fletcher blew up in the middle of the scene where they had to stop—then
>> Use for the last part of the scene, the take that picked up the action from where Fletcher forgot his lines, as this is by far the best take.

Svengali's climax is magnificent. Gecko signals with his violin bow for the attention of the filthy patrons. Svengali bows to the non-applauding audience—with a special bow to Little Billee. The concert begins, Svengali conducting Trilby as she sings "Ben Bolt" (again,

Ellen Coutta provides the singing). Svengali suffers a heart attack, Trilby goes woefully off-key, and she too collapses.

The nightclub is in an uproar. Little Billee runs to the stage and scoops up Trilby in his arms. "Trilby, it's Billee. I'm right here with you! Speak to me, darling!"

Svengali, with his dying strength, prays, "Oh, God! Grant me in death, what you denied me in life—the woman I love...."

Trilby awakens. She looks at Billee, then at her loving, dying maestro.

"Svengali," she sighs lovingly—and dies.

Barrymore's joy, as Svengali greets his own death, grateful and with a little song, is unforgettable. He dies in the arms of the loyal Gecko. The final shot is poetic and phallic: Svengali's baton stick slips from his hand and falls to the floor.

Saturday, February 21: It's the last day of shooting. Barrymore, Marsh and Alberni are the only players on call. Mayo shoots the scene of Svengali and Trilby (the latter presumably naked, likely back in her body stocking and wrapped in a dark blanket) in a coach, and various inserts.

Also filmed this final day is what's listed in the daily report as a "Jackman shot." Fred Jackman is *Svengali's* special effects director, and his *tour de force* in the film is Svengali's telepathic summons of Trilby. It's a still-dazzling wonder of 1931 cinematography. A steeple clock strikes midnight. Svengali stands in his garret, his hollow eyes (Barrymore used primitive contact lenses) staring out the window, sending a hypnotic seduction over the Latin Quarter rooftops. The camera sweeps out of the garret, taking the audience on a witch's broomstick wild ride, complete with sounds of wind, over the arched, twisted houses, through Trilby's balcony and into her bed. In their book *Human Monsters*, Michael H. Price and George E. Turner note that Hans Koenekamp was the actual engineer of this episode. In 1989, Koenekamp (who died in 1992 at age 100) told them how it was done:

> The sets of the two apartments were built full scale at the opposite ends of the huge Stage 5. The city of rooftops was a large scale miniature which ran the length of the stage. The camera pulled back from Svengali's eyes, traveled over the miniature rooftops and into Trilby's bedroom.

Barrymore saluted the cinematography wizardry, as noted in *Hollywood* magazine (July 1931):

> If an actor can keep up with the mechanical and technical end of this business, he needn't worry. On the *Svengali* set they have cameras that do everything but read the paper. They turn somersaults, shoot up in the air, flatten down to the floor, slide or gallop, chase me or let me chase them.[27]

It's all over at 5:50 p.m. "Close Production" reads the Daily Production and Progress Report. Barrymore takes off on a nine-day cruise on the *Infanta* down the west coast of Mexico. When he returns to Long Beach on March 3, he tells reporters he likes *Svengali* "better than any other thing he ever did."[28] Archie Mayo has taken a vacation to Del Monte up the coast. Darryl Zanuck prepares *Svengali* for preview. Among his cutting notes (dated March 7, 1931):

> Cut out Barrymore's milk routine with the butler.... Cut out the line of Barrymore, when he refers to Trilby's voice as that of a wounded gorilla.... Try and get a better shot of Billee running on the stage—he looks very awkward.

Two days later, Monday, March 9, 1931—only 16 days after *Svengali* wrapped up—Warners begins shooting *The Mad Genius*.

John Barrymore and Marian Marsh in *Svengali*.

* * *

Once ... ONLY ONCE in the Life of Every Star Comes a Picture So Great—It Remains His Outstanding Screen Triumph.... No Matter How Many Great Successes Precede or Follow. For twenty years **John BARRYMORE** has been waiting for the story that would give full expression to his genius ... to make his supreme contribution to posterity. It has come at last with

The MAD GENIUS
—Warner Bros. publicity, 1931

Warner Bros.' plan for *The Mad Genius*: Set John Barrymore, Hollywood's most Byronic actor, on the loose, complete with a club foot, a wild and wicked finale, and a magnificently over-the-top death scene. Warners also expects it to be a cash-in on what the studio anticipates as the smash hit of *Svengali*.

Warners blueprints the new *uber*-melodrama as a virtual *Svengali* alumnae reunion:

• Marian Marsh is cast as Nana, the ballet dancer who runs afoul of Tsarakov as she falls in love with Fedor. Having had a voice double and nude double in *Svengali,* she'll have a dance double in *The Mad Genius.*

• Luis Alberni wins the showy role of Serge Bankieff, a dope-addicted ballet master.

• Carmel Myers plays Sonya Preskoya, a jealous ex-mistress of Tsarakov. The vampy actress' role is small, but it allows her to snuggle with the star and appear in a negligee.

• J. Grubb Alexander scripts with Harvey Thew.

- Barney McGill is cameraman.
- Anton Grot creates new evocative sets.

There are several major new additions. One is Donald Cook, memorable as James Cagney's brother in Warners' *The Public Enemy* (1931), cast here as the adult Fedor and abetted by a dance double. Then there's Adolph Bolm, famed Russian ballet director, who had danced in the 1922 experimental film *Danse Macabre*. Bolm will stage "The Spirit of the Factory" in tune to Mossolov's "In a Soviet Iron Foundry," the musical highlight of the film.

But the major new face—and a rather glowering one it is—is the director. Rather than *Svengali*'s chubby, practical joke-playing Archie Mayo, the man in charge is Warners' formidable Hungarian wolfhound, Michael Curtiz—fated to direct *Doctor X* (1932) and *Mystery of the Wax Museum* (1933), win an Oscar for *Casablanca* (1943), and become a legend for his directorial virtuosity and mangling of the English language.

"The next time I send a no-good son of a bitch to do something, I go myself!" Curtiz once ranted.

*   *   *

He Creates the Frankenstein
That Destroys Him!
—publicity for **The Mad Genius**

The company call on Monday, March 9, is for 8:30 a.m. for what Warners still calls *The Genius*. The set is the Marionette Tent on Stage 7 at the original Warner Studio on Sunset Boulevard.

On time are Charles Butterworth (as Karimsky, Tsarakov's comic hanger-on), E. Percival Wetzel's puppet troupe, and Barrymore. The star sports a wispy mustache and the club foot boot Warners has prepared for him. Director Curtiz and set designer Grot splendidly create a forlorn atmosphere as the two carnival puppeteers perform in an empty tent on a rainy night, the music wheezing on a gramophone, the pitiful troupe somewhere in the wilds of Russia.

The pre–Code badinage is quickly in evidence. "Careful!" says Barrymore as he and Butterworth pull the strings of the dancing "female" marionettes. "They are virgins!" A moment later, Butterworth mentions he took some pills for a malady, but they haven't helped.

"Perhaps you didn't put them in the right place," says Barrymore. "Use your imagination!"

Curtiz, of course, is a notorious taskmaster. The company takes a one-hour lunch at 12:50, and then works until 8:10 p.m. The next day, Barrymore and Butterworth work all day with the marionettes on Stage 7; come evening, Curtiz takes five horses and ten extras to the Russian village set on First National's back lot. There the special effects crew whips up a storm, and Curtiz films moody shots of the wagons mournfully riding through the rain. He finally calls it quits at 1:30 a.m.

The opening sequence continues shooting the next two days, Curtiz again soaking extras and horses as he returns to the rainy village back lot set on Thursday night, shooting until 11:30. During these days, two players join *The Genius*, each so anonymous at the time in the eyes of Warner Bros. that the daily shooting reports don't provide their names—simply listing both as "extras." One is 13-year-old Frankie Darro, who plays the young Fedor and later stars in such films as *The Mayor of Hell* and *Wild Boys of the Road* (both 1933). He

John Barrymore, as Tsarakov, dominates this unusual composite picture for *The Mad Genius* which includes, among other images, director Michael Curtiz, Marian Marsh, and Barrymore's club foot shoe (Photofest).

sneaks into the tent, impoverished and barefoot, fascinated to see the puppets dancing. Pursued by his father, Fedor runs, leaps, and bounds so impressively (like a "mountain goat!" marvels Tsarakov) that the puppeteer hides him and kidnaps him—intent on transforming the prodigy into a great dancer.

John Gloske, author of the book *Tough Kid—The Life and Films of Frankie Darro,* befriended the late-in-life Darro when the destitute, near-forgotten actor, over 40 years after *The Mad Genius,* lived in a decaying apartment in Hollywood:

> Frankie told me that, for those leaps, the crew hooked him into a harness with wires, and raised and lowered him on a boom—and he loved that! He was only 13 at the time of *The Mad Genius,* but knew it was special to be in a film with John Barrymore. By the way, Barrymore signed a beautiful 11x14" portrait for Frankie. Although he'd sold much of his memorabilia, Frankie had saved some signed photos—John Barrymore among them. There they were, in a box in his really run-down Hollywood apartment. At one point he told me to take them, but I figured he might sell them, as he sure could have used the money, so I turned them down. After Frankie died—on Christmas of 1976—the box disappeared!

Incidentally, Frankie Darro was less sure-footed 25 years later while playing Robby the Robot in MGM's *Forbidden Planet.* After a multi-martini lunch, Frankie almost took a nosedive, coming "this close" to falling flat on his face in the expensive Robby suit—and MGM fired him.

As for the menacing Russian father, the "extra" whipping little Frankie is ... Boris Karloff, five months away from winning the Monster role in *Frankenstein.*

"I break every bone in your body, you dev-il!" growls Karloff in his *faux* Russian accent.

In January, Karloff had triumphed in Columbia's *The Criminal Code,* reprising his West Coast stage role as the murderous Galloway; still, he clearly wasn't about to let any job slip away, even this virtual bit. In late 1935, when Karloff came back to Warners in glory to star in *The Walking Dead,* his director was Michael Curtiz—who then told Karloff why he'd hired the Englishman for *The Mad Genius*: "The reason I called you in," Karloff recalled Curtiz saying, "was because I thought you actually were Russian. Your name is Karloff—it certainly sounds Russian. When you came in, you seemed so anxious to get the job that I decided to let you have it!"[29]

Dancing puppets, a fabricated back lot night storm, and a future Frankenstein Monster stalking about with a basso Russian accent and a whip ... things are coming together nicely. Yet dominating all, of course, is Barrymore. Come Thursday, March 12, on a wagon set on First National's Stage 8, Barney McGill's camera looks right into those saint-serial killer eyes as Barrymore chillingly delivers a Tsarakov soliloquy, truly propelling *The Mad Genius* into darkness and tragedy:

> Have you ever heard of the Golem, made of mud and given a human soul? Or Frankenstein, the monster created by man? Or the Homunculus, the pale being, the product of science? These are all dreams, brought to life by mortals. I will create my own being. That boy—that boy will be my counterpart! He shall be what I should have been. I will mold him—I will pour into him my genius, my soul. In him, all my dreams, all my ambitions, will be fulfilled. I will make him the greatest dancer of all time!

*   *   *

> *BARRYMORE—a tradition to the show world!*
>   *A career studded with unforgettable achievements! But all his superb successes have been but stepping stones ... prologues to the greatest, most amazing characterization the stage or screen has ever known!*—Warner Bros. publicity for ***The Mad Genius***

March 13—a Friday the 13th.

The Mad Genius, its story now set 15 years after its rainy night opening, has moved into a giant theater set at the Vitagraph Studios, the third studio lot owned by Warner Bros. and located at 4151 Prospect Street in East Hollywood. Marian Marsh starts work today, resplendent in a ballerina costume, white tights and black shoes that charmingly show off her shapely legs. Somber-looking Donald Cook begins work as Fedor, vampy Carmel Myers flashes her eyes as Sonya and Luis Alberni, with the look of an enraged poodle left in the rain all night, relishes his first day as Serge, the drug-addicted ballet master. Michael Curtiz is in his glory: This weekend he has Adolph Bolm, 44 dancers and a full orchestra at his disposal, as well as, of course, John Barrymore.

Barrymore as Tsarakov and Donald Cook as Fedor, the Trilby counterpart in *The Mad Genius*.

"Mad Jack" sits in a theater box between scenes, dressed in black top hat and magnificent flowing, fur-collared coat, now sporting a mustache and Van Dyke beard. He smokes a cigarette as he curses, violently smacking his club foot shoe with his walking stick. In his black mood and profane squawks, Barrymore once again evokes his king vulture, Maloney.

Why the star's high dudgeon? There are several reasons. For one thing, he's damned uncomfortable—the club foot shoe hurts like hell. "He walked around on that club foot," remembered Marian Marsh, "and he used to get mad at it once in a while, because it hurt his back; it was awful to walk with it."

Then there's Curtiz. Before shooting began, Barrymore was already aware of his director's notoriety. Curtiz had directed *Noah's Ark* (1928) starring Dolores Costello Barrymore—"Jiggie Wink" herself. Cameraman Hal Mohr had quit the picture because he felt the studio's plan to film the flood was doomed to kill extras. Allegedly, he was right. The legend goes that three extras drowned, one had to have a leg amputated, and about a dozen more suffered serious bone-breaking injuries. (John Wayne, laboring in those days as an extra, reportedly survived unscathed.) As for Dolores ... she, having suffered on *Noah's Ark* under Curtiz's martinet direction, had come down with pneumonia.

Also, there are the hours Curtiz demands. On Friday, the director works *The Mad Genius* company until 8:40 p.m. The Saturday morning call is 8:30 and all the principals report again to Vitagraph, along with the dozens of dancers and extras. The lights on the cavernous theater set are merciless and, late that afternoon, the heat sets off the sprinkler system—soaking the company. Will this Act of God accident cancel shooting and give everyone Saturday night off? No such luck. Curtiz dries off, rallies his forces, works until 6:55 p.m., gives the company an hour off for dinner, then continues shooting—until 11:40 p.m.

The clash is quickly clear: a star practically decadent in his extravagances, and a director sometimes sadistic in his work ethic.

The company wraps up its work on the Vitagraph theater set Monday night, March 16, finishing at 9:20 p.m. Barrymore, for all his loathing of his club foot shoe and Curtiz, is giving a solid, colorful performance—related to Svengali perhaps, but still very much his own *dramatis persona*. A running gag has developed (the script is now complete) as Barrymore greets various wide-eyed ballerinas, such as Olga, played by Mae Madison:

Tsarakov: Do you want to be a ballet dancer?
Olga: Yes!
Tsarakov: Do you want to be a *great* ballet dancer?
Olga: Yes!
Tsarakov (lecherously): Come to my office—three o'clock!

* * *

He Pours His Genius Into Another Man's Veins—
But His Creation Becomes an Avenging God!
—Warner Bros. publicity, **The Mad Genius**

Shooting proceeds. Curtiz is determined to be as flamboyantly volatile as Barrymore. At one point, even little Marian Marsh takes the director to task.

"You're very temperamental!" says Marian.

"Well," replies Curtiz, "I should have been an actor!"

Nevertheless, Marian respects Curtiz's "marvelous flair.... He made things *go*." Many vignettes, as played by the star and staged by the director, are wonderfully striking. The episode where Barrymore threatens to burn Alberni's dope, the fire glowing on Barrymore's face, masterfully presents the star as a handsome, aglow-in-the-dark Lucifer. The humor works too. One of the best bits comes when Tsarakov, about to welcome a female to his parlor, takes an atomizer from his desk and luxuriantly perfumes his mouth.

And the big payoff scene, where Fedor climactically tries to walk out on Tsarakov, is unforgettable. Barrymore stops him, places his hands on his neck, and magnificently builds:

> Now listen to me. For 15 years I've devoted my entire life to you. I've poured my soul, my brain into you. I've sacrificed everything in the world—everything, do you hear?—for your career. I've lied—I've cheated—I've crushed—I've even crushed myself, so that you should appear greater than I. I thought I'd given you strength enough to rise above everything. You haven't risen, you've *fallen*. You're not strong, you're *weak*. But all of me is in you still, all that strength I poured into that weak soul, so you can't fail me now. If you fail me now, I'll kill you. I'll *kill* you!

Helping production roll along, as they had on *Svengali,* are assistant director Gordon Hollingshead and the loyal Barrymore crew. Yet all the while, star and director clash. The hot-headed Curtiz, who hates even breaking for lunch, surely has no sympathy for a man who feeds worms from his mouth to his pet vulture. In a sense, the tension is prophetic of Curtiz's battles with Errol Flynn (later a Barrymore crony and idolater) over the course of their eleven films together. Curtiz would be provoked by (and would sometimes be sadistically responsive to) Flynn's "wicked, wicked ways."

Hostility keeps rising. Barrymore and Curtiz both bristle. During the three weeks of shooting to date, Barrymore has had only one day off. The story goes that Barrymore and a lady friend passed a dance marathon about this time, and the lady expressed sympathy for the dancers on their feet for those many hours.

"Ah," said Barrymore. "I see you've never worked for Michael Curtiz."

The director, anxious to wash his hands of Barrymore and the whole damned movie, makes a decision, with the front office's blessing: He will *not* film the big ballet showpiece, "The Spirit of the Factory," despite the weeks of rehearsal devoted to it by Adolph Bolm.[30] And he vows to slip into high gear and wrap up *The Mad Genius* as quickly as possible, no matter how late the hours ... and no matter how his star curses and rants ... and no matter how humanly or inhumanly.

* * *

Climaxing Triumph of His Stage and Screen Career!
—Warner Bros. publicity, **The Mad Genius**

Monday, March 30: The Theater set on Stage 2, Vitagraph Studios.

The climax that Barrymore and Curtiz are to shoot is as gothic a finale as any melodrama of Hollywood's Golden Age. A lavish, rather sinister ballet is being performed in the theater, before a grotesque centerpiece of a giant Idol head with illuminated eyes—a morbid masterpiece created by Anton Grot. Tsarakov discovers that Serge has overdosed and, rabidly, amok backstage, has decided to destroy the giant head with an axe.

"Look at it!" rants Alberni's Serge to Barrymore's Tsarakov. "It is cardboard! It is plaster! It is *dead!* It should be *alive!* It should be squirming with blood oozing from its veins! It should be a human being! You—*you* are the Idol—if you have any blood!"

Tsarakov confronts Serge, who attacks him, the two men falling off the set, the ballet master madly hacking the maestro to death, the backstage murder shown in shadows. Come the ballet's climax, a scrim curtain rises to reveal the Idol—and Barrymore's Mad Genius—covered in blood and hanging from the monster's face. He falls and tumbles (and tumbles, and tumbles) down the set stairs, all the way to the foot of the stage. A bit actress named Alice Doll, famed for her scream, sounds the first shriek, and soon the whole crowd is scream-

Barrymore, axed to death by a dope fiend and dangling from the stage scenery of "The Idol," in the deliriously baroque climax of *The Mad Genius* (Photofest).

Barrymore's corpse rolls downstage, horrifying all beholders (Photofest).

ing, the exit music blaring, the ballerinas escaping the stage, the audience fleeing the theater. Curtiz delights in the quick shots of aghast female faces staring morbidly at the corpse, other women falling in the aisles, the director delivering all the delirious mayhem of the wild, riotous climax. Indeed, when *The Mad Genius* opens at Warner's Western Theatre in Hollywood, the *Hollywood Citizen News* review will report that the movie house audience, almost violently bewitched by the baroque melodramatics, became nearly as hysterical as the audience in the film!

Curtiz manages to shoot this episode in a whirlwind three days and nights:

Monday, March 30: Barrymore, Marsh, Butterworth, Alberni ... only Cook is off. There are 36 dancers. Curtiz shoots until 10:35 p.m.

Tuesday, March 31: Marsh, Cook and Alberni gather at Vitagraph with 37 dancers—Barrymore has the day off. Shooting starts at 10:00 a.m. and finishes at 10:30 p.m.

Wednesday, April 1: The call is at 9:00 a.m., complete with Barrymore, Marsh, the principals, 37 dancers, and 106 extras. Curtiz revels this April Fool's Day and night, shooting 14 scenes, including 20 "wild shots," finally wrapping at 2:40 a.m.

The film ends with the lovers reuniting. Onstage, a sheet covers Tsarakov's corpse as two policemen take the report. The only mourners are Butterworth's Karimsky and—so it seems—the Idol, its monstrous glowing eyes hungrily staring down at the cadaver. Curtiz frames the final shot so that all we see of Tsarakov's covered corpse is the protruding club foot.

* * *

Michael Curtiz has completed *The Mad Genius* in only 21 days—a remarkable *nine days* ahead of schedule and 15 days less than Archie Mayo took to film *Svengali*. Part of this is possible due to scrapping the ballet, but even with that excision, the pace and results are astounding. The exhausted company leaves Vitagraph under a nearly full moon, and "Mad Jack" Barrymore drives home to Bella Vista, "Jiggie-Wink," Dede, his dinosaur egg, Maloney, and his aviary.

Warner Bros., meanwhile, prepares to preview *Svengali*.

* * *

Together
Greatest Star of Today—
Greatest Star of Tomorrow!
—Warner Bros. publicity, **Svengali**

Warner Bros. mounts a gala promotion campaign for *Svengali*. The pressbook presents all variety of exploitation gimmickry, to cash in on everything from Barrymore's eyes to Marian Marsh's feet:

• "Ballyhoo Herald Stunt": Find a man with "large black eyes" ("Plenty of youths of Continental type can be had for the purpose"), dress him up in a "wide-brimmed and rather battered black hat, and a long black coat," have him wear a "black half-mask which allows the eyes to appear prominently," and send this "Svengali" into the streets to "arrest passers-by with a fiery glare" and hand them a herald for *Svengali*.

• "Most Perfect Feet" Contest: With Marian Marsh publicized as having "The Most Perfect Feet in Hollywood," Warners encourages theaters to have their own contests to find "the prettiest foot in your town." Prizes presented on the stage could be "most exquisite shoes or slippers."

The pressbook is also very specific regarding size of billing: John Barrymore's name in 100 percent size; the title and Marian Marsh's name in 75 percent size. It's the same billing Warners had originally offered to Evelyn Laye.

Friday, May 1: *Svengali* premieres in New York City, where Warners reopens its Hollywood Theatre for the auspicious event. *Film Daily* in Hollywood proclaims the news on page one:

> It is a creeping, intense, human and at times believable *Svengali* that moves into Warner Bros.' Hollywood Theatre on Broadway today…. It is strictly a star production, with the brilliant John Barrymore in the title role…. The production is elaborate, the cast splendid, and the background well in keeping with the feline atmosphere of the story. We believe the tale will still hold a kick for the younger generation, same as it did 30 years ago. John Barrymore, artist *de luxe*, adds another undying screen portrait to the gallery of screen immortals.

However, *Film Daily* feels compelled to add a note of caution: "*Svengali* may be slightly too highbrow to knock 'em over at the box office, but it is a welcome exception to the current film menu and is artistically swanky enough to hold its own in any sort of cinema company."

New York Times film critic Mordaunt Hall is rapturous about Barrymore's Svengali, writing that his performance "surpasses anything he has done for the screen, including the motion pictures of Stevenson's *Dr. Jekyll and Mr. Hyde* and Clyde Fitch's *Beau Brummel*."

Hall also praises the Jackman-Koenekamp special effects flight over the rooftops, "undoubtedly one of the most striking and interesting camera feats ever accomplished in a film."

Variety, however, has definite reservations. Always suspicious of anything "artistically swanky," safeguarding Depression theater owners who cater to Middle America patrons, and ever with an eye on box office, "the show business Bible" condemns *Svengali* for not delivering (in the reviewer's opinion) the female star it had so effusively promised:

> In performance John Barrymore takes care of everything. So much so that they won't go away remembering much of anybody or anything else.... Barrymore's hypnotic powers are interesting until getting a look at Miss Marsh under an unbecoming wig. After which a lot of people will figure it's a waste of expert concentration....

It's a decidedly lowbrow review. Unaware that a double performed Trilby's nude scene, *Variety* hails the vignette as Marsh's finest moment, writing that it "infers that Tril [*sic*] was the Miss France of her day and Svengali isn't the chump that wig makes him out to be." The critic also writes that Marsh "flashes nothing unusual histrionically" and lets the cat out of the bag that her singing was dubbed. Additionally, the romantic but unhappy finale appalls the reviewer ("both principal characters die at the finish")—1931 audiences crave Happy Endings.

"Its b.o. prospects," reports *Variety* of *Svengali*, "are only fair."

The forecast unfortunately, is accurate. In its first three days on Broadway, *Svengali* takes in $17,384[31]—decent money, but hardly sensational. On May 9, Norbert Lusk in New York sends this report to the *Los Angeles Times*, published in the next day's edition:

> In the estimation of the critics, John Barrymore exceeds his past efforts in *Svengali* and offers a character study worthy of a place with his stage portraits ... but in spite of highly favorable notices it is not attracting business commensurate with its merit. This is difficult to explain, except by remarking the mediocre audiences generally encountered on Broadway nowadays.

In its first full week at the Hollywood, *Svengali* earns $30,002; the following week, it takes in $25,441.[32] Meanwhile Warners' *The Public Enemy*, starring James Cagney and playing at Warners' Strand Theatre on Broadway, earns $63,776 its first week, $35,284 its second week, and $28,701 in its third week. At one point, the Warners Hollywood Theatre actually runs an ad that gives the dominant space to *Svengali*'s accompanying short subject *How I Play Golf* with Bobby Jones.

Friday, May 22: *Svengali* has a gala Los Angeles opening at both the Warners Hollywood Theatre and the Warners Downtown Theatre, following Warners' James Cagney hit *The Public Enemy*. Marian Marsh attends the Hollywood premiere and *Los Angeles Times* critic Edwin Schallert reports:

> A classic is revived, and John Barrymore rises to a portrayal marked by its excellent irony and sinister interest.... Smoother, quieter, with a diminishing of the forced and somewhat self-conscious style he has often evidenced, his work in this particular production entitles him to the finer wreathes of approval ... Marian Marsh ... is not the Trilby of tradition ... but there is an uncanny and pervasive sweetness to her personality....

Although the crowds are large on the opening day and night, *Svengali* tanks. It runs only a week at the Warners Hollywood and Downtown Theatres; at the latter, it takes in only $12,000,[33] where the high had been $30,000 for *Office Wife* (1930), a 59-minute Warner sex saga starring Dorothy Mackaill, Lewis Stone, Joan Blondell, and Blanche Friderici as a cigar-smoking lesbian. Warners yanks *Svengali* from both theaters to make way for *Party Husband*, which also stars Dorothy Mackaill and *The Mad Genius'* Donald Cook.

Svengali poster.

To the shock of the brothers Warner, *Svengali,* that had cost $499,000 to produce, tallies a worldwide rental of only $498,000.[34] Compare this to *Dracula,* which by the summer of 1932 had a worldwide rental of $1,200,000.

Come final tabulations—with Barrymore receiving $150,000 and ten percent of the gross—*Svengali* will lose $225,000.

Why the bomb? Was Barrymore's flamboyance losing its appeal? Was Marian Marsh truly a disappointment? Did the tragic ending cause bad word of mouth? Whatever the problem(s), Warner Bros. now had a basic *Svengali* facsimile on its hands—*The Mad Genius,* starring John Barrymore and Marian Marsh and with an investment of $441,000.

Meanwhile, come the summer of 1931, Barrymore, who has departed Warner Bros., cruises the *Infanta* to Alaska, where he picks up a new curio for Bella Vista: a towering 25-foot-high totem pole, supposedly bearing the remains of several Alaskan Indians. A settler warns him that it might offend the gods to take the sacred relic, and Barrymore admits fearing the deities "might take a notion into their whimsical noggins to wreak vengeance on the thief." Nevertheless, the totem pole will loom over his estate for years. Brother Lionel, genuinely believing the totem pole to be cursed, would blame it for his younger brother's spectacular downfall.

*   *   *

All humanity hails it as immortal!
—Warner Bros. publicity for **The Mad Genius**

Friday, October 23: *The Mad Genius* premieres, as had *Svengali,* at Broadway's Hollywood Theatre. Richard Watts, Jr., of the *New York Herald Tribune* delivers the review Warners desperately hopes for:

> Mr. Barrymore, having had his fun with peg legs, hypnotic eyes, grotesque skulls and all the other impediments of perverse physical fortune, offers us the drama of the clubfoot in his new film ... called, with considerable accuracy, *The Mad Genius....* Certainly it is a real Barrymore show, which, naturally, is more concerned with providing a field day for an actor than in exploring the potentialities of drama. Thanks to the star, however, it is a grand show....
>
> ... As drama, it is pretty trashy stuff.... About it, however, there clings an inescapable air of perverse fascination, maniac melodrama, sadistic excitement and, above all, the field day of the picturesque actor who must strut and fret all over the screen before he can be really happy. In addition, the film is handsomely and lavishly staged. The result is, I think, good, if quite decadent entertainment....

Watts signs off praising "the mad melodramatics of the leading actor, who is, after all, the greatest of the Barrymores."

Mordaunt Hall of the *New York Times* also praises the star's "sterling acting and Michael Curtiz's gifted and imaginative direction," but notes that Barrymore's "masterful conception of Tsarakov" outshines the efforts of the other actors. He especially targets Marian Marsh, writing, "[S]he is out of her element ... particularly when she is called upon to appear in scenes with Mr. Barrymore. The contrast of the amateur and the artist is most pronounced."

Tuesday, November 10: The Fourth Academy Award ceremony takes place at the Biltmore Hotel in Los Angeles. There'd been chatter during *Svengali*'s shoot that John Barrymore would win the prize for his brilliant performance. He wasn't even nominated. His brother Lionel is the winner that night for MGM's mega-hit *A Free Soul,* playing a drunken lawyer who drops dead defending his daughter (Norma Shearer) for killing her gangster lover (Clark

Gable). In *The House of Barrymore,* Margot Peters wrote that it was "typical of the Academy to reward big and fundamentally sentimental pieces of acting. In *Svengali,* John Barrymore was always subtly ironic. Who was he mocking—himself, the role, the cast, Hollywood? Oscars didn't go to mockers."

Svengali does rate two Academy nominations: Barney McGill for Cinematography (he loses to Floyd Crosby for Paramount's *Tabu*) and Anton Grot for Interior Decoration (he loses to Max Ree for RKO's *Cimarron*).

Thursday, November 19: The Mad Genius has its Hollywood premiere at Warner Bros.' Western Theatre. The next day, *Frankenstein* opens in several key cities and the world begins a strange love affair with Boris Karloff's Monster. As *Frankenstein* becomes a sensation, *The Mad Genius* crashes and burns. Worldwide rental: $400,000 (compared to *Frankenstein's* $1,400,000). Loss: $241,000.

Who to blame? "Amateur" Marian Marsh? "Mediocre" audiences? Barrymore's Alaskan totem pole? At any rate, the failure of *The Mad Genius* marks John Barrymore's departure from Warner Bros.—his last two films there losing the studio nearly a half million dollars in a year that the company ended up $8,000,000 in the red.

As for the prime movers of *Svengali* and *The Mad Genius*:

Archie Mayo later directs such Warner Bros. films as *The Mayor of Hell* (1933), *Bordertown* (1935) and *The Petrified Forest* (1936). He leaves the studio in the late 1930s, works for Goldwyn and 20th Century–Fox, reportedly becomes tyrannical on his sets, and retires in 1946. Mayo dies in Guadalajara, Mexico, on December 4, 1968, age 77.

Michael Curtiz receives five Academy nominations, winning, as noted, for *Casablanca* and carving himself a place in Hollywood history as Warner Bros.' top dog director. He dies April 10, 1962, age 75. The sadistic legends abound.

J. Grubb Alexander, who scripted both *Svengali* and *The Mad Genius,* dies of pneumonia on January 11, 1932, at the age of only 44.

Barney "Chick" McGill will be cameraman on such Warner films as *20,000 Years in Sing Sing* (1933), leaving in the mid–1930s to join Fox, where he primarily works with the "B" unit. He dies precisely ten years after Alexander, on January 11, 1942, age 51.

Anton Grot works with Michael Curtiz on *Doctor X* (1932) and *Mystery of the Wax Museum* (1933), designs sets for many Warners productions, receives four more Academy nominations and wins a special Oscar in 1941 for creating Warners' "water ripple and wave illusion machine." He dies March 21, 1974, at age 90.

John Barrymore's despised club foot shoe from *The Mad Genius* makes a comeback of sorts in Warners' *Green Light* (1937)—worn by Sir Cedric Hardwicke.

Barrymore's cursed totem pole will become the property of Vincent Price, shortly before Warner Bros. releases Price's 3-D hit *House of Wax* (1953). Price was an avid collector of Indian art.

As for John Barrymore himself ... he enjoys triumphs at MGM in *Grand Hotel* (1932), *Rasputin and the Empress* (1932), and *Dinner at Eight* (1933), at RKO in *A Bill of Divorcement* (1932) and at Columbia in *Twentieth Century* (1934). Then comes the fall. The self-destructive pet devil dominates, cackles, and roars, and the end mercifully will come May 29, 1942.

Finally, there's Marian Marsh. She gives a powerhouse portrayal in Warners' 1931 super-hit *Five Star Final,* starring Edward G. Robinson and featuring Boris Karloff, but her promised super-stardom never will come. Warners dumps her in 1932 and she quickly topples into Poverty Row—a sad, ignominious surprise for Warner Bros.' "Greatest Star of Tomor-

In 1942, shortly before his death, a clearly declining John Barrymore strikes what seems to be a Svengali-like pose for his daughter Diana. Note his Richard III armor in the background (courtesy John Antosiewicz).

row." In 1933, she reports her total income as $5,750, a fair Depression salary, but a pittance for a Hollywood star.[35] Among her deductions are $997.06 in depreciation of clothes and $410.55 in makeup, wig, and beauty parlor expenses.

Marian works in Europe and enjoys something of a comeback at Columbia, where she appears as Boris Karloff's unhappy bride-to-be in *The Black Room* (1935), charmingly holding her own amidst Karloff's virtuoso portrayal(s) of medieval twin brothers and Roy William Neill's superb, storybook-style direction. She prefers *Crime and Punishment* (1935), co-starring Peter Lorre; director Josef von Sternberg lights her with the reverence he'd provided Marlene Dietrich, but the film is a misfire. Come the early 1940s, she retires from the screen.

She lives her later years in Palm Desert, the widow of Clifford Henderson, aviation pioneer (and Palm Desert's founder). Marian Marsh dies on November 9, 2006, at age 93. Her daughter consigns her memorabilia to Heritage Auctions. Among the items: her scripts for *Svengali* and *The Mad Genius,* her first edition of *Trilby,* two paintings of her from *Svengali* that had hung in her home, and her Trilby wig.

* * *

Despite *Svengali's* financial failure, Warner Bros. considers a remake. On October 20, 1944, Herbert Dalmas sends a three-page inter-office communication to Jerry Wald:

> In transferring *Trilby* to the screen, the most important thing to keep in mind it seems to me, is that it is one of the great love stories of literature. It is NOT the story of Svengali.
> Treated as a love story, it achieves a stature equal to and possibly greater than *La Dame Aux Camelias*; treated as a vehicle for the actor who is going to play the part of Svengali, it becomes a run-of-the-mill horror job....

Dalmas goes on at length, arguing his "conviction that *Trilby* is spoiled as soon as Svengali steps to the front of the stage ... he must remain definitely a secondary character...." The

Marian Marsh kept her Trilby wig the rest of her life, 75 years after *Svengali*. Following her death in 2006, the wig (upper left) went up for auction, along with other hairpieces she wore in films, offered by Heritage Galleries of Dallas, Texas, in October 2007 (courtesy Heritage Galleries).

writer sees Svengali as basically Trilby's cause of death, the same way tuberculosis is Marguerite's cause of death in *Camille,* and the remake would focus on Trilby and Little Billee. "The audience should be knee-deep in tears at the end," writes Herbert Dalmas. The new Warner Bros. *Trilby* never comes to pass.

There would be a British *Svengali* (1955), starring Hildegarde Neff as Trilby and Donald Wolfit as Svengali. (Wolfit replaced Robert Newton, who defected from the filming in a blaze of alcohol and personal woes, and can still be glimpsed in long shots.) Noel Langley directs. A 1983 made-for-TV *Svengali* will transform the Latin Quarter hypnotist into a washed-up musical star (Peter O'Toole) and Trilby into a rock singer (Jodie Foster). Anthony Harvey (who had directed O'Toole in *The Lion in Winter*) directs.

In 1991, there is a stage musical *Svengali,* with book and lyrics by Gregory Boyd and music by Frank Wildhorn, composer of the musicals *Jekyll and Hyde, The Scarlet Pimpernel* and *The Civil War.* The show tries out in Houston and Sarasota, with Chuck Wagner (who played the title roles in Wildhorn's *Jekyll and Hyde*) as Svengali and Linda Eder (who'd played Lucy, the prostitute in *Jekyll and Hyde* and later married and divorced Wildhorn) as Trilby.

* * *

On April 10, 1959, almost 17 years after Barrymore's death, United Artists Associated purchased in Probation Court the star's financial interest in *Moby Dick, Svengali,* and *The Mad Genius.* John Drew Barrymore, his son by Dolores Costello, had originally filed objections, but then withdrawn them. Over eight months later, on December 22, 1959, *Variety* reported that Superior Judge Burdette J. Daniels had approved the final accounting of Barrymore's estate the previous day:

> Assets were listed as $10,812 from sale of late actor's interests in three pix, including *Moby Dick, Mad Genius* and *Svengali,* but since Barrymore owed $40,274 in back federal income taxes when he died, balance in estate went toward satisfying this debt.
>
> As a result, actor's three heirs, Diana Barrymore, John Drew Barrymore, and Mrs. John P. Bedell, will receive nothing from the estate.[36]

* * *

Thank God I'm drunk. I'll never remember it!
—John Drew Barrymore, after exhuming and looking at his father's corpse in 1980

Strangely and sadly, yet another macabre role awaits John Barrymore that will exceed his *Dr. Jekyll and Mr. Hyde, Svengali* and *The Mad Genius* ... the role of exhumed cadaver.

In his will, Barrymore specified, "I desire that my body shall be cremated and placed in the family vault at Philadelphia, Pennsylvania." But Lionel, acting as an executor and with his Catholic sensibilities, had vetoed cremation and opted for burial in the Main Mausoleum at Calvary Cemetery in Los Angeles. In 1954, Lionel died and was buried in the crypt above John.

Enter John Drew Barrymore (1932–2004), the son that Barrymore had always wanted but had never really known. Wild-eyed, bearded, looking every bit a Hollywood warlock, John Drew Barrymore, aka "Johnny" Barrymore (and whom we'll refer to as John II), had long ago seen his own career explode in a cloud of alcoholism, spousal abuse, and drug busts.

John Blyth Barrymore, son of John II and actress Cara Williams, has posted an amazing "true story" on the Barrymore family website titled "Invasion of the Body Snatchers." John III wrote that he and his father began enjoying "a greatly improved standard of living" as they "pirated" Barrymore treasures from Dolores' estate after her death in 1979. Eventually, John II decided to grant his father's wish, and bury him in Philadelphia.

"Jake," said John II to John III, "we've got to get my daddy up."

The caper began. John II got John III and his lawyer, Bruce Pedy, to join the crusade. The exhumation demanded dispensation from the Catholic Church (which now allowed cremation) and from the Health Department, as well as signatures from all living heirs. The lawyer handled the church document, and John III admitted to forging the family signatures in lieu of dealing "with my insane Barrymore relatives."

So John II, John III, Bruce Pedy and (as John III wrote) "a one-eyed Carpathian pirate named John Desko" all came to call at Calvary Cemetery, where John II's mother Dolores was now buried outside in Section D, with her parents. At the mausoleum, John II and company waited while Calvary's gravediggers had their lunch. They all ascended to the Main Mausoleum's second floor, opened the crypt, and removed the marble plaque upon which Lionel had personally carved "Good Night, Sweet Prince." (The marble plaque with its quote still remains at Calvary.) The smell from the opened grave was overpowering. The stinking solid bronze casket, despite its glass lining, had presumably cracked and the corpse was still decomposing after 38 years. The leakage had sealed the casket to the marble slab and the gravediggers couldn't budge it.

"Out of the way!" shouted a very drunk John II.

It had always been a Barrymore custom to give a red apple on an opening night. This was, after all, as John III noted, "an opening," and John II had brought apples, which he now handed to the gravediggers. Then he personally grabbed the coffin, placed his feet against the wall of the tomb and "yanked." The coffin surrendered. The gang hefted it onto a hand truck and wheeled it out to a waiting brown Ford van.

"The body fluids were leaking out all the way," wrote John III.

John II and his mourners made a beeline to Odd Fellows Cemetery, locale of the closest crematory. Before the immolation, John II decided to take a look at the father of whom he had so little memory. The Odd Fellows pleaded with him not to do so, but John II gave them apples, remained insistent, and they finally obliged. (John III passed up the viewing—"the smell had been more than enough for me." He went outside.) John Drew looked at the corpse, then left the crematory pale and crying. Bruce Pedy also saw the cadaver, Bruce and John III remembered Pedy's nightmarish description:

> Apparently all the bouncing around we had subjected it to had sort of busted the jaw apart from what was left of the head. They were convinced it was John Barrymore by the very high quality dental work, and because although most of the flesh had decomposed, an incredibly long nose cartilage remained....

It seemed that even in so horrific a state, John Barrymore was still the Great Profile.

John III picked up the cremated remains the next day. John II sold more Barrymorebilia and headed to Philadelphia with the book-shaped urn, eventually finding his way to Mt. Vernon Cemetery. There, as historian Scott Wilson learned from a cemetery official, John Drew Barrymore manically dug his father's grave himself, at his own insistence and by hand.

Mt. Vernon Cemetery itself has decayed so dangerously that authorities have padlocked the gate. Philadelphia historian David Schaaf describes Mt. Vernon as "the most hellish cemetery I've ever seen, overgrown, unsafe.... The fear is that homeless people have broken into the tombs and live there." John Barrymore's ashes now abide in this notorious cemetery, haunted by bums and addicts, his fans unlikely to gain admittance to pay tribute.

"Alas Poor Yorick," reads the inscription on John Barrymore's small marker.

Svengali

Studio, Warner Brothers-First National. Producer, Jack L. Warner. Executive Producer, Darryl F. Zanuck. Director, Archie Mayo. Screenplay, J. Grubb Alexander (from George Du Maurier's 1894 novel *Trilby*). Cinematographer, Barney McGill. Set Designer, Anton Grot. Editor, William Holmes. Wardrobe, Earl Luick. Technical Effects, Fred Jackman and Hans Koenekamp. Vitaphone Orchestra conductor, David Mendoza. Mr. Barrymore's Makeup, Johnny Wallace. Assistant Director, Gordon Hollingshead. Property Man, Herbert "Limey" Plews. Portrait Photographer, John Ellis. Sound Engineer, Dave Forrest. Script Clerk, Fred Applegate. Wardrobe Expert, "Smoke" Kring. Running Time: 81 minutes.

Filmed 12 January to 21 February 1931, at Warner Bros.' First National Studios and Universal Studios. New York City Opening: Warners Hollywood Theatre, 1 May 1931. Los Angeles Opening: Warners Hollywood and Downtown Theatres, 22 May 1931.

The Cast: John Barrymore (Svengali); Marian Marsh (Trilby); Bramwell Fletcher (Little Billee); Donald Crisp (The Laird); Carmel Myers (Madame Honori); Luis Alberni (Gecko); Lumsden Hare (Taffy); Paul Porcasi (Bonnelli); Ferike Boros (Marta); Yola D'Avril (Maid); Julia Griffith (Concertgoer); Henry Otto (Man with Opera Glasses); Eleinor Vanderveer (Concertgoer); In deleted footage: Adrienne D'Ambricourt (Madame Vinard), Rose Dion (Trilby's Mother), Lionel Belmore (Lawyer).

The Mad Genius

Studio, Warner Brothers–First National. Producer, Jack L. Warner. Executive Producer, Darryl F. Zanuck. Director, Michael Curtiz. Screenplay, J. Grubb Alexander and Harvey Thew (adapted from Martin Brown's play *The Idol*). Cinematographer, Barney McGill. Set Designer, Anton Grot. Editor, Ralph Dawson. Wardrobe, Earl Luick. Choreographer, Adolph Bolm. Vitaphone Orchestra conductor, David Mendoza. Mr. Barrymore's Makeup, Johnny Wallace. Assistant Director, Gordon Hollingshead. Property Man, Herbert "Limey" Plews. Portrait Photographer, John Ellis. Sound Engineer, Dave Forrest. Script Clerk, Fred Applegate. Wardrobe Expert, "Smoke" Kring. Running Time: 81 minutes.

Filmed 9 March to 1 April 1931. Warner Bros.-First National Studios. New York opening: Warners Hollywood Theatre, 23 October 1931. Los Angeles opening: Warners Western Theatre, 19 November 1931.

The Cast: John Barrymore (Vladimir Ivan Tsarakov); Marian Marsh (Nana Carlova); Charles Butterworth (Karimsky); Donald Cook (Fedor Ivanoff); Luis Alberni (Sergei Bankieff); Carmel Myers (Sonya Preskoya); Andre Luguet (Count Robert Renaud); Frankie Darro (Fedor as a Boy); Mae Madison (Olga Chekova); Boris Karloff (Fedor's Father); Lee Moran (Montmarte Cabaret Director); Alice Doll (Screaming Woman); Charles A. Bachman, Charles Brimley (Poster Hangers); Walter Miller (Opera Spectator); Charles Williams (Stagehand); Harry Wilson (Curtain Man).

3

Paramount Horrors
Murders in the Zoo

To Lily, The "Snake Man" has his eye on you!! Sincerely, Lionel Atwill
—Autograph to Lily Dirigo, Lionel Atwill's toupee dresser
on ***Murders in the Zoo**, 1933*[1]

Eliminate shot of man with mouth stitched together.... Eliminate shot of alligator chewing up woman's body.... Eliminate scene where husband has hand over wife's breast and dialogue thereto:—"What makes me love you so?"... Eliminate shot of man being choked to death with snake wrapped around his body.
—Kansas Censorship Report on ***Murders in the Zoo**, March 31, 1933*[2]

*Lionel Atwill, in his relatively short film career,
has become the most bloodthirsty villain of them all.*
—Donald Kirkley, *Baltimore Sun*, reviewing ***Murders in the Zoo**, May 6, 1933*

*You don't think I sat there all evening with an eight-foot mamba
in my pocket, do you? Why, it would be an injustice to my tailor!*
—Lionel Atwill, ***Murders in the Zoo***

* * *

It's one of the wildest and wooliest pre–Code horror movies of them all ... *Murders in the Zoo*.

The star was a lascivious Lionel Atwill, remembered in *Parade* magazine in 1989 as a real-life "notorious Hollywood sex fiend," here enjoying a sex fiend frolic as, in a passionate clinch with Kathleen ("The Panther Woman") Burke, he comes very close to grabbing her breast.

The studio was Paramount, where Miriam Hopkins had stripped down to her garter in *Dr. Jekyll and Mr. Hyde* (1931), a gorilla had attacked a naked platinum blonde martyr in DeMille's *The Sign of the Cross* (1932), and Charles Laughton had created the aforementioned "Panther Woman," whom he hoped to mate with a human male in *Island of Lost Souls* (1932).

The film opens with Atwill suavely *sewing* a man's lips together for having kissed his wife, and then gets nastier. Rapacious alligators devour Burke. A giant python strangles Atwill. Comic relief Charlie Ruggles actually gets away with defying a carved-in-stone censor no-no—the dreaded "bathroom humor."

Nevertheless, the most shocking feature of *Murders in the Zoo* is its climactic animal blood-fest—a free-for-all battle of lions, pumas and panthers, all unleashed by Paramount à la the Roman Coliseum and primed to tear each other to shreds. Indeed, the studio actually invited the press and its own contract stars to the filming of this barbaric spectacle to behold what became actual carnage, requiring the mercy killing of a puma. It survives in the film as one of the most excessive, irresponsible, and truly horrifying episodes Hollywood ever offered.

Atwill's slinky audacity, Paramount's shameful exploitation of the animals, and the film's big parade of bestial horrors, madly mixed with comedy, all spark a film rich in exotica and erotica—one that, by at least one report, spawned genuine hysteria in its audience as its climax filled the screen. It still fascinates today ... and at times repels. Appropriately, of all the horror films produced in this legendary early '30s era, *Murders in the Zoo* and its formidable star most powerfully conjure the fascination one feels watching snakes in a reptile house—and the sensation that there might be a hole in one of the cages.

* * *

"The best show in town!"
—Paramount's corporate motto, 1933

Devil and the Deep, a Paramount picture, 1932. Charles Laughton, as a madly jealous submarine commander, crashes his sub, with his wife Tallulah Bankhead and her lover (and his officer) Gary Cooper on board, into a ship. Come the finale, after Laughton drowns while laughing insanely and Cooper is convicted for adultery in a naval court martial, we see Tallulah, slinking forlornly through the rainy streets, without husband or lover.

So she enters a shop and buys a pool stick.

A few moments later, she and Cooper reconcile and jump into a cab. As if there was ever any doubt about why Tallulah purchased a pool stick, the fade-out shot shows her tossing it out of the cab and into the street. After all, what lady needs a pool stick when she has Gary Cooper?

The pre–Code era was a notorious time, especially for Paramount Studios, its famous gate looming at 5451 Marathon Street, Hollywood. Paramount was the most intoxicatingly sensual of the studios—the lair of Marlene Dietrich, the domain of Cecil B. DeMille, the salon of Ernst Lubitsch. As Paramount blueprinted *Murders in the Zoo,* it was preparing to release Mae West's *She Done Him Wrong.* The studio's horror films purveyed its hot house style, perfumed with kinky sexuality, while the sex sagas in turn often had their own degree of horror.

Three examples. Of course, there's *Dr. Jekyll and Mr. Hyde,* which opened Christmas Eve of 1931 in Los Angeles. As brilliantly directed by Rouben Mamoulian, Fredric March's Hyde is a mugging, prancing ape in top hat and cape, bestially eyeballing Miriam Hopkins as Ivy, Jekyll's prostitute fantasy girl. His sadism feeds her masochism. In a scene in a pub, the two stars spar so spiritedly that they regularly spray flit at each other (at one point, March, coping with his Hyde false teeth, actually sprays her). The savagery with which Hyde finally kills Ivy, clearly fueled by his sexual passion, still shocks today, as does March's sly delivery of the chilling, double-meaning line: "Isn't Hyde a lover after your own heart?"

Then there's DeMille's *The Sign of the Cross.* The stars: Claudette Colbert as Poppaea, "the wickedest woman in Rome," and Charles Laughton as an epically out-of-the-closet Nero. The musical interlude: a lesbian dance number of a lithe beauty billed as Joyzelle. The climax: a coliseum bloodbath: pygmies fight Amazons (the Amazons win), an elephant steps on a Christian's head, and crocodiles devour a blonde Christian martyr. For a topper, a gorilla

Paramount spiked sexuality into its horror films: Miriam Hopkins as Ivy in *Dr. Jekyll and Mr. Hyde* (1931).

Cecil B. DeMille's *The Sign of the Cross* (Paramount, 1932): horror at play in the Roman "games." The naked platinum blonde martyr is unidentified. The gorilla is either Charles Gemora or Joe Bonomo (who claimed he appeared in this film wearing Gemora's ape suit).

approaches a naked, bound-to-a-pillar martyr—this one with cascading platinum blonde hair—and presumably rapes her. The manager of the Princess Theatre of Albertville, Alabama, wrote to *Motion Picture Herald*: "This is a fine Biblical picture but is horrifying. You have to have good nerves to stay with this one, but the Good Book tells us these things happened. We had a few patrons that had to leave. This is another outstanding Cecil B. DeMille production."[3]

Then, come October of 1932, Paramount was shooting *Island of Lost Souls,* based on H.G. Wells' *The Island of Dr. Moreau* and directed with pace and punch by Erle C. Kenton. Charles Laughton was a whip-cracking, sado-maso Moreau, Bela Lugosi was a wildly hirsute Sayer of the Law ("Are we not men?"), and Kathleen Burke, winner of Paramount's "Panther Woman Contest" that attracted 60,000 hopefuls, was Moreau's "most nearly perfect creation." It was a role Wells had never imagined and a twist that would shock censors internationally: Laughton's Moreau wants to mate Burke's Panther Woman with Richard Arlen's human hero—despite the horror of her "stubborn beast flesh creeping back."

"This time I'll burn out *all* the animal in her!" raves Laughton.

Incidentally, the Paramount Panther Woman Contest came with certain definite stipulations as to desirability of the hopefuls. Among them:

- Must be not under 17 and not over 30 years of age.
- Must be in good health.
- Must be no less than 5'4" and no more than 5'8".
- Must have written endorsement of two citizens of good standing in the community endorsing her morality.

The last-noted requirement seems quite hypocritical—considering the nature of the sexed-up films that Paramount was producing at the time!

Paramount had entered a pitched battle for horror supremacy that Fall of '32 with Universal (who was then starring Karloff in *The Mummy*), Warner Bros. (then showcasing Lionel Atwill in *Mystery of the Wax Museum*), RKO (then preparing *King Kong*), and MGM (then starring Karloff, on his days off from *The Mummy,* in *The Mask of Fu Manchu*).

Monday, November 14, 1932: Grace Kingsley reports in the *Los Angeles Times*:

Murder having been committed in the kitchen, the pantry, the penguin pool and the washroom in our mystery stories of the screen, we aren't at all surprised to learn that it will now be accomplished in the zoo. At least if we are to believe the title of a Paramount picture just announced, which is *Murder at* [sic] *the Zoo*....

Friday night, November 18, 1932: Fredric March wins the Best Actor Academy Award for Paramount's *Dr. Jekyll and Mr. Hyde.*

Tuesday, November 29: Elizabeth Yeaman writes in the *Hollywood Citizen News*:

Every time a studio has a horror role to be cast, either Boris Karloff or Lionel Atwill is sought. Paramount has a juicy horror role in a coming picture, *Murders in the Zoo*. So Paramount has engaged Atwill for the featured character lead....

Lionel "Pinky" Atwill—already with *Doctor X* in release and *Mystery of the Wax Museum* and *The Vampire Bat* about to pounce on the public—will star as Eric Gorman, the sex-crazed villain.

The role is a splendid early Christmas gift for the new horror star: a mad sportsman who suspects his wife is a raging nymphomaniac and murders her various alleged lovers in outlandishly gruesome ways. Eventually he feeds his wife to alligators, lets loose an entire zoo of wild animals, and perishes entwined by a giant python.

The concoctors of this mayhem are scriptwriters Philip Wylie[4] and Seton I. Miller.

Wylie was co-author (with Edwin Balmer) of the science fiction novel *When Worlds Collide,* then in six-month serialization (September 1932 to February 1933) in *Blue Book* magazine. The buzz about the book had brought Wylie to Paramount, where DeMille was

"The *Mental* Lon Chaney" (as *Motion Picture* magazine dubbed him) meets the Panther Woman from Paramount's *Island of Lost Souls*: Lionel Atwill and Kathleen Burke invite you to join the kinky fun and games of *Murders in the Zoo.*

reportedly planning an epic film of *When Worlds Collide.* Meanwhile, Wylie had adapted *Island of Lost Souls* (sharing onscreen credit with Waldemar Young). As for Seton Miller, his credits included such films as *The Dawn Patrol* (1930) and *Scarface* (1932); he'll win an Oscar (with Sidney Buchman) for the screenplay for *Here Comes Mr. Jordan* (1941).

Wednesday, November 30: "Animal Trend Sweeps Films; 'Zoo' Pictures Turn Studios into Menageries," headlines the *Los Angeles Times.*

Saturday, December 10: "*Island of Lost Souls* Out-Frankensteins Frankenstein," acclaims the *Hollywood Filmograph,* after seeing a preview. The film will open in Chicago in time for Christmas, and in New York and Los Angeles early in the New Year.

Paramount sees the chance to claim the horror crown: If *Island of Lost Souls* proves all the studio hopes it will be, *Murders in the Zoo* will have to be a worthy follow-up.

Thursday and *Friday, December 22* and *23:* William H. Wright of Paramount Publix Corporation sends two copies of the script for *Murders in the Zoo* and some "substitute pages" to Dr. James Wingate at the Association of Motion Picture Producers in Hollywood, along with wishes for "a very merry Christmas!"

Also on December 23: Island of Lost Souls opens in Chicago, home town of Kathleen "Panther Woman" Burke. Universal's *The Mummy,* starring Boris Karloff, opens in the Windy City the same day. Both films do so-so business.

Tuesday, December 27: *The Hollywood Citizen News* announces that Paramount has added contractee Randolph Scott[5] to *Murders in the Zoo*. Scott beats competitors Stuart Erwin, Gordon Westcott and John Lodge for the part of the heroic toxicologist. Also cast: Gail Patrick, tall, brunette ex-law student from Alabama, and one of the three Panther Woman runners-up, as Scott's co-worker-girlfriend. Charlie Ruggles and John Lodge will play a comic zoo publicist and an Atwill victim.

The *Citizen-News* also notes that Edward Sutherland is set to direct. One of Mack Sennett's original Keystone Cops, director of such comedies as W.C. Fields' *Tillie's Punctured Romance* (1928), Sutherland faces a bleak posterity among classic film fans. Louise Brooks idolaters have never forgiven him for reportedly cheating on his "Lulu" spouse during their marriage (1926–28); Laurel and Hardy fans despise him for having remarked, after directing the team in *The Flying Deuces* (1939), "I'd rather have worked with a tarantula"[6] than with Laurel. Sutherland's engagement as director, along with Charlie Ruggles' casting, indicates that *Murders in the Zoo* will be at least as much comedy as it will be horror.

Wednesday, December 28: William Wright sends the censors the "Final White Script" and news that *Murders in the Zoo* had been set to start shooting the previous day, but had not. The same day, James Wingate writes to Paramount:

> From the standpoint of the Code we would like to call your attention to the expression "Good Lord" in Scene D-3.
>
> From the standpoint of official censorship it would be well for you to protect yourself on Scene F-98, where Gorman kicks his wife's hands loose and drops her into the pond, as some of the censor boards are strict with kicking scenes.

This objection is notable, since the scene concerned Atwill (as Gorman) kicking the hands of Burke (as Evelyn) while she's trying to save herself from the devouring alligators. The censor inference is that, while it's passable to feed a woman to alligators, kicking her hands is not!

Wingate's letter concludes: "In Scene C-21, some of the censor boards occasionally delete any action concerned with people asking the way to the toilet." This is in reference to the line of Peter Yates, to be played by Ruggles, after fainting at his proximity to a green mamba snake. More on that later.

Also on December 28: Grace Kingsley writes in the *Los Angeles Times,* "Paramount's greatest trouble right now in connection with animal pictures is to find a forty-foot boa constrictor for scenes in *Murders in the Zoo*."[7]

As *Murders in the Zoo* nears the eve of shooting, Paramount adds a special

Kathleen Burke as the Panther Woman in *Island of Lost Souls*.

dash of sensation and exploitation: Kathleen Burke, *Island of Lost Souls'* Panther Woman, will play Evelyn, Eric Gorman's epically ill-fated wife. Miss Burke had to compete for the role, eventually snaring it away from Adrienne Ames, Lona Andre (one of the Panther Woman runners-up), and Susan Fleming (who later became Mrs. Harpo Marx).[8] Clearly, Paramount figures this "animal picture" requires an "animal actress," and *Murders in the Zoo* posters will proclaim: **Kathleen Burke (The Panther Woman)**.

The final script bears the date January 4, 1933, and *Murders in the Zoo* is in production by Thursday, January 5, 1933—Eddie Sutherland's 38th birthday.

* * *

This Man is <u>More</u> *Dangerous Than—*
The Lions He Caged!
The Tigers He Hunted!
The Snakes He Trapped!
The Killers He Snared...
And Then Set Free to Run Amuck in a Zoo Crowded with Pleasure-Seekers!
—Publicity for ***Murders in the Zoo***

Murders in the Zoo naturally devotes much publicity to the animals, rented by Paramount from the Selig Zoo in Los Angeles. "Caged Beasts Move to Studio During Night,"[9] runs a headline in the *Murders in the Zoo* pressbook:

> Transportation of sixteen truckloads of wild animals and venomous reptiles ten miles through Los Angeles, from the Selig Zoo to the Paramount Studios, was accomplished recently with as much care and precision as an army moving munitions through a zone of fire....
> Ten of the trucks were loaded with cages of lions, tigers, leopards, panthers, pumas, hyenas, chimpanzees, and snakes. The remaining six ten-ton trucks, with trailers especially remodeled for their unusual load, were used to transport 50 alligators. The alligators were loaded during the darkest part of the night, when they could not see to snap at the trainers, and when the cold at that hour made them sluggish.
> The caravan passed through Los Angeles at about four o'clock in the morning, so that danger of automobile collision and resultant possible escape of the animals was most remote.

At least one animal isn't a resident of the Selig Zoo. His name is Oswald, and he's a 25'-long, 360-pound python who has come to Hollywood from the Texas snake ranch of "Snake" King. Reportedly Oswald won the role after his trainer convinced Paramount that Oswald had "a hearty streak of laziness, and wouldn't crush anyone's bones." Nevertheless, Oswald, perhaps suffering stage fright, puts up a hell of a fight when it comes time for his pre-film examination—a reported 20 men join forces to restrain the reptile.

Along with the animals come two superstar trainers. One is Olga Celeste, aka "The Leopard Woman," who'd performed daily at the Luna Park Zoo in Los Angeles from 1925 to 1931, as well as training leopards for the movies. (In 1938 she will direct the leopard "Baby" in RKO's Katharine Hepburn-Cary Grant comedy *Bringing Up Baby*.) Also engaged for *Murders in the Zoo* is John "Chubby" Guilfoyle, who'd personally taught his cat-control skills to the legendary Clyde Beatty, and who'd lost an arm to circus bears.

For Paramount, it's as if the circus is coming to town. *Murders in the Zoo* is becoming the joy of Paramount's publicity department, and one can only imagine the electric thrill when Kathleen "The Panther Woman" Burke meets Olga "The Leopard Woman" Celeste.

Yet topping Oswald, the gators and the whole menagerie and their trainers in show-

Oswald, the python of *Murders in the Zoo*, posing between scenes with director Edward Sutherland (left), an unidentified snake trainer, and a clearly agog Lionel Atwill (right).

stealing savagery is the star Lionel Atwill, immediately marking his territory as *Murders in the Zoo*'s cat-eyed king of the beasts.

The opening credits of many films of the early 1930s featured close-ups of the stars, their names below them. *Murders in the Zoo* raises this custom to novelty gimmickry: animals that morph into the members of the film's cast. A whiskered seal, clapping its fins, transforms into mustached Charlie Ruggles, clapping his hands. A black bear becomes grizzled Harry

Beresford, who plays the zoo curator. A dove and an owl turn into a beaming Gail Patrick and a grinning Randolph Scott, our heroine and hero. A duo of frisky jungle cats become Kathleen Burke and John Lodge, the film's allegedly adulterous lovers, not long for this world.

And climactically, as the music swells, a fierce-looking tiger evolves into a fierce-looking Atwill. Clearly relishing this anthropomorphic intro, the star suavely eyes the audience, drags on his cigarette—and casually blows smoke through his nostrils.

Murders in the Zoo opens in French Indo-China. Actually, the locale is the Paramount Ranch, out in the hills of Agoura, near Malibu. The ranch had recently served as the camp of the beast men in *Island of Lost Souls,* where whip-cracking Charles Laughton had presided over Bela Lugosi's Litany of the Law. We see Atwill as Eric Gorman, "millionaire sportsman," kneeling over a prone figure, who's pinned down by coolies.

"A Mongolian prince taught me this, Taylor," says Atwill. "An ingenious device for the right occasion. You'll never lie to a friend again ... and you'll never kiss another man's wife."

Atwill rises, puts his topee on over his toupee, boards an elephant, and rides away as the victim struggles to his feet. The bound "Taylor" (played by an uncredited Edward Pawley,[10] later a "toughie" in Warner Bros. melodramas) stands and lunges pitifully toward the camera. We see the terror in his pleading eyes ... and the stitches in his sewn-shut mouth. It's a grisly, still-shocking image that haunts the rest of *Murders in the Zoo,* despite the film's various swan dives into low comedy.

Of course, some of the comedy is perversely effective. Atwill returns to the firelit camp, where we first see Kathleen Burke as Evelyn Gorman. Foxy and feline, Ms. Burke makes a racy first impression in her jungle puttees and boots; Atwill certainly seems to think so, and kisses her passionately. He also informs her that Taylor has left the party.

Burke: What did he say?

Atwill: He didn't say *any*thing!

The actor tosses off the line, while lighting a cigarette, with superb comic aplomb, and *Murders in the Zoo* quickly makes its message clear: This is going to be a very nasty movie. Meanwhile, the coolies bring word about poor Taylor: "Tigers eat."

The film takes off, the characters sailing on the *S.S. Salvador* for America. We meet Evelyn Gorman's new boy toy, Roger Hewitt, played by Harvard Law School graduate John Lodge, blueblood grandson of Massachusetts Senator Henry Cabot Lodge. He's handsome and dapper, but reputedly has his troubles on this set, Hollywood columnist Jimmy Starr reporting that Lodge "is the cause of a flock of retakes for *Murders in the Zoo* at Paramount."[11] Lodge will fare better in politics, serving as governor of Connecticut from 1951 to 1954.

Back in the U.S., at the Municipal Zoo, we meet Jerry Evans (Gail Patrick) and Dr. Jack Woodford (Randolph Scott), our romantic toxicologists. Patrick seems pleased as punch with her new capped teeth, courtesy of Paramount, proudly showing them off with big smiles; Scott already has the lanky likability that will make him one of the all-time great Western stars. Indeed, the strapping Scott and tall, dark and lovely Patrick are slick and almost intimidatingly photogenic, providing *Murders in the Zoo* with a world-class pair of horror film ingénues.

Finally, we meet top-billed Charlie Ruggles as recovering alcoholic PR man Peter Yates, working for the Municipal Zoo. He mugs and stammers, now and then warbling the Bing Crosby favorite "Please" ("Lend Your Little Ears to My Pleas"). His comedy's a matter of taste, but his timing is undeniably excellent. He also now and then contributes to the movie's

Atwill and Burke in *Murders in the Zoo* (Photofest).

cruel humor, as when Gail Patrick tells Ruggles, who suffers from animal-phobia, about the financial woes facing the zoo:

Patrick: If we all don't pitch in and help here, the animals will go and starve!

Ruggles: Good!

Fascinating to watch is art-deco beauty Kathleen Burke, sloe-eyed, bee-stung-lipped, all adorned in Paramount finery, softly purring her lines. She sensually suggests the nympho-maniacal vamp that Atwill suspects her to be, even if the script leaves the true degree of her carnal appetites a mystery.

Yet Atwill supremely takes it all—and with a vengeance. Elegantly posing like the slightly-gone-to-seed Roaring '20s matinee idol that he truly is, endlessly smoking cigarettes, smiling like a predatory toddler, the star masterfully delivers his dialogue with bite, as when he tells Ruggles of his empathy for the animals he's trapped: "I love them! Their honesty, their simplicity, their primitive emotions. They love, they hate ... they *kill*."

A moment later, a lion nearly claws Ruggles through the bars of its cage. The scene plays as a sick, Paramount inside-joke homage to an off-screen disaster during the making of *Island of Lost Souls*: On location at Catalina, a tiger had reached through its bars, clawed one of the beast men, and nearly torn his arm from its socket.

The Municipal Zoo hosts a banquet—an idea hatched by Ruggles' PR wizard—and the diners sit by the caged animals. (One of the banquet guests, *sans* dialogue, is Jane Darwell,

"I'm not going to kiss *you!* You're going to kiss *me!*" Atwill clutches his not-long-for-this world spouse Kathleen Burke in this spicy scene from *Murders in the Zoo.*

seven years before audiences saw her Academy Award–winning portrayal of Ma Joad in *The Grapes of Wrath.*) The insanely jealous Gorman arranges for Evelyn and Roger to sit beside each other; he sits across from them, grinning and smoking. Suddenly Roger leaps and shrieks—he's suffered a fatal green mamba snake bite. The guests scream and flee, the Gormans return home, he pours her a brandy, and Atwill and Kathleen Burke play a pre–Code vignette that one must see and hear to believe:

Burke: You killed Roger Hewitt.
Atwill: Now, my dear, you're not yourself. Drink some of this.
Burke: That's why you sat right across from us.
Atwill (*chuckling*): Evelyn, you don't think I sat there all evening with an eight-foot mamba in my pocket, do you? Why, it would be an injustice to my tailor!
Burke: I don't know how it happened, but why was it he was struck and no one else?
Atwill: Why aren't you more concerned with *my* narrow escape? (*moving his hand up her arm*) I sat within two feet of the snake myself.
Burke: Don't touch me!
Atwill (*nearly touching her breast*): I never saw you look more beautiful....
Burke: Yes, Eric ... I know. Now you're going to make love to me....
Atwill: I never wanted you more than I do at this moment....
Burke: Oh, you're not human!

Atwill: I'm not going to kiss you. (*grabbing her and stroking her hair*) *You're* going to kiss *me!*
Burke: Kiss you? I hate you! Yes, Roger and I loved each other. I was going to leave you for him.
    Now will you let me go!
Atwill: My dear, why didn't you come and tell me? You know I have too deep an affection for
    you to ever stand in your way ... (*grabbing her, stroking her hair, and nearly touching her breast
    again*) What is it ... what is it that makes me love you so?
Burke: I *hate* you!

She eludes him. He lewdly chuckles, cat eyes gleaming as he watches her run and lock herself in her boudoir. "I'm coming back in five minutes," Gorman announces. "I expect to find this door open." However, the wily Evelyn sneaks out, peeks in a window, and learns her husband's secret: Gorman has a model snake's head—a truly obscene-looking weapon—loaded with green mamba poison, and has used this to "bite" Roger in the leg. She takes off to the zoo to tell the authorities. Gorman, after a great show of nearly suppressed hysteria as he realizes what's happened, pursues Evelyn, who's running toward the zoo as fast as her high heels will carry her.

It's *Murders in the Zoo*'s famous centerpiece: the nocturnal Eric and Evelyn episode, played on the zoo's footbridge ... and over the alligator pool. Atwill retrieves his snake head: "If I weren't willing to kill for you," he says, "I couldn't have expected you to go on loving me." He wants to take her home—and as is obvious by his leer, to bed—but Evelyn rants, promising to blow the whistle on him: "You're not human! ... They'll *electrocute* you! They'll *hang* you!"

So ... Eric forces Evelyn's head back over the bridge rail, and then tosses her into the pool. We see her bob briefly to the surface as the alligators move in for their midnight snack, the creatures growling, splashing, and seething. It's one of the most truly gruesome episodes in Golden Age Horror.

Actually, in its original form, the episode might have been even *more* horrifying. As noted, the script originally called for Evelyn to try to rescue herself from the pool, and Eric to kick her hand loose from the bridge. On March 10, 1933, three weeks before *Murders in the Zoo* opened on Broadway, the New York state censor sees the film and, among other excisions, demands to trim "half" of the footage of "Gorman as he chokes his wife and throws her into alligator pool." The censor also notes: "Eliminate view where he kicks her hand from bridge."

Apparently Paramount shot the scene as originally scripted, defying the early censor protest—then presumably trimmed the bit before general release. One can only imagine the visceral impact on audiences had they seen a drenched Kathleen Burke, trying to escape the alligators, grasping at the bridge as Atwill kicked her away!

Daylight. A child scoops a rag of Evelyn's dress from the alligator pool. In a bravura show of innocence, Atwill mournfully touches it, shivering as he identifies it. Evelyn Gorman's gator demise seems to be the last nail in the imperiled zoo's coffin and Gorman promises to sue Woodford for criminal negligence. Ruggles' Peter Yates takes work cleaning the cages, and in one of them uncovers the green mamba. He shouts, shrieks, faints, and after Woodford retrieves the snake, revives and delivers the censor-defying "bathroom humor": "Is there a good laundry in this town?" Ruggles asks Gail Patrick.

Meanwhile, Woodford discovers that the measurement of the teeth of the snake that killed Roger Hewitt doesn't match those of the retrieved mamba. He informs Atwill's Gorman. The villain, fearing exposure, attacks the hero with his trusty poison snake head, then

The horror centerpiece of *Murders in the Zoo*: Atwill feeds Burke to the alligators.

kills the mamba, placing its body on the fallen Woodford to make it appear that Woodford and the escaped snake have killed each other.

Jerry rescues Woodford—the two had developed an antidote. She escapes Gorman's clutches, the zoo sounds its alarm, and in a berserk climax, Atwill, pursued by the police, runs amok, releasing the zoo's animals from their cages and creating a battle among the menagerie.

It was here that Life imitated Art—disastrously.

Tuesday, January 17, 1933: In a festivity of Big Top–style publicity, Paramount invites the press, ASPCA representatives, and even its own stars—including Marlene Dietrich, Gary Cooper, Miriam Hopkins, Cary Grant, Frances Dee, and the Marx Brothers—to a luncheon to behold the shooting of the wild beast vs. wild beast finale from a platform above the arena. The spectacle offers the chance to see 19 jungle creatures set loose in a single enclosure.

The studio should have known better. During the recent shooting of *King of the Jungle*, starring Buster Crabbe, a tigress had escaped, a tiger had clawed the leg of an animal trainer, and elephants had almost stampeded a cameraman. Still, the showmanship potential of *Murders in the Zoo* is too flamboyantly savage to ignore. The stars and press indeed come, watching from perches safely above the stage floor, their refuge protected by "heavy wire fencing."

Lionel Atwill is on hand, at his most charming to greet the guests. To join him, who better than Kathleen "Panther Woman" Burke? Atwill's double is a veteran animal trainer who actually releases the animals. Olga Celeste and "Chubby" Guilfoyle are there, as are two more "expert animal trainers."

The result is a debacle.

"Savage Beasts Clash in Wild Film Melee," the *Los Angeles Times* will headline the next day—adding, with questionable humor, that the disaster "afforded Hollywood the greatest cat fight in its history."

As Atwill's double pulls the lever, lions, pumas, leopards, and panthers come storming into the enclosure, and a lion begins combat with what the press describes as "a husky puma." The other beasts howl and screech and run riot. Several vicious battles break out between the cats and a leopard leaps atop its cage.

"I'll betcha that leopard up there," jokes Groucho Marx, "never changes his spats."[12]

Few are laughing, other than the hyenas, who—spooked by the fighting cats and the four trainers firing revolvers and cracking whips—cackle madly in their cages. Women scream and faint, celebrities run for cover, and the ASPCA presumably shrieks along with the animals as a lion rips the neck of a lioness, two lions fight for mastery, and the lion and puma continue their death battle. A leopard actually escapes through the wire screen and Olga Celeste pursues it, finding it hiding under a heap of boxes. It will require four hours to retrieve the hysterical animals and corral them back into their cages.

All the while, the cameras keep cranking as Paramount captures *Murders in the Zoo*'s epic battle of the beasts on film. Meanwhile, the lion has ripped the puma to pieces. The trainers end its misery with revolvers.

The *Hollywood Citizen News* notes that "17 cats" had engaged in the mayhem and reports the death of the puma. The most compelling eyewitness account comes from Harrison Carroll of the *Los Angeles Evening Herald Express*. One of the most trustworthy of the Hollywood scribes, Carroll reports (January 18, 1933):

> Murders, holocausts, terrible accidents—I've seen them all, but the biggest shock came yesterday when a lion and puma staged a death-fight as an unprecedented climax to a motion picture scene at the Paramount studio.
>
> For two hours we had been waiting—having our pictures made looking through the wire barrier, crabbing to director Eddie Sutherland about the delay, wise-cracking about the docile-looking lions, the pumas lying on their backs like house-cats, the dozing leopards, the ludicrously grinning hyenas.
>
> What an anticlimax, jeered a voice, if the animals refused to come out of their cages when the doors were opened, when the half dozen cameras started grinding on the big scene for *Murders in the Zoo*.
>
> Then came Eddie Sutherland's call for lights, for action.

The murderer of the story dashed across the room, pulled a lever releasing all the doors of the line of cages.

A moment's tension. A lion climbed gingerly out. A leopard flashed into the aisle. Another lion. A puma jumped nervously.

For weeks these animals had been trained to work together, but something went wrong. A puma tried to slither by a lion. There was a snarl. Suddenly the two animals were coming headlong toward the cameras. The puma tried to pivot, slipped. The lion was upon him, seizing the middle of his back.

Vaguely we were aware of other movement—the wily leopards to the top of the cages, the hyenas cowering in their cells, the other pumas leaping nimbly, the lions falling over one another.

But with an awful fascination, the eyes came back to that silent deadly struggle.

Unable to avoid it, director Eddie Sutherland never allowed it to finish. Pistols—blank cartridges—roared in the lion's face. Men jabbed at him. Snarling, he backed away.

Murders in the Zoo **director Eddie Sutherland (left), Gail Patrick and Randolph Scott, up close and personal with a reptile (courtesy Ronald V. Borst–Hollywood Movie Posters).**

But the puma, its back broken, lay upon the floor. A merciful shot ended its suffering.

Subdued as we were, pasty-faced a few of us, as we came down from the platform after the animals had been driven back into their cages.

The mild thrill had turned out to be a tragedy, the cinema drama had turned real.

And I'm not so hard-boiled. I know that now.

For some time, the beastly bloodbath was the talk of Hollywood, despite Paramount's attempts to soft-pedal the incident. Philip K. Scheuer wrote in his January 22, 1933, *Los Angeles Times* column about "Wild animals at Paramount, all but stampeding 'the press' invited last week to witness the filming of scenes for *Murders in the Zoo....*" Paramount had a PR disaster on its hands, and its only hope was that, since this was a horror picture, the publicity would titillate the morbidly curious.

It was a very sad and shameful disaster.

Back to the film...

Atwill takes sanctuary in a cage that, unknown to the villain, is also the lair of ... Oswald. The giant python crawls through the shadows, hisses mightily, bites "Pinky" in the thigh, and then slowly, sinuously wraps itself around him. Publicity claims that Atwill, always delighted by the macabre, demands he play the scene with no double, but it's clearly a dummy-in-Atwill clothing for part of the episode. Nevertheless, the audience gets a gruesome payoff close-up of Atwill's anguished face, partially covered by the giant snake, to take home and sleep with before the episode fades out.

Randolph Scott recovers, Gail Patrick smiles. The zoo survives. And Charlie Ruggles, plastered again, hits a not-yet-retrieved lion on the nose, singing "Please" as he drunkenly wanders over the infamous alligator pool bridge.

The End

* * *

"I am a modern Richard III!"
—Lionel Atwill[13]

As *Murders in the Zoo* wraps up, it's a big time for Lionel Atwill. *The Vampire Bat* has opened at Broadway's Winter Garden Theatre on January 20, 1933, and *Mystery of the Wax Museum* has premiered at Warners Hollywood and Downtown Theatres February 9, 1933.

On February 11, 1933, *The Los Angeles Evening Herald Express* publishes an Atwill interview by W.E. Oliver. It follows in its entirety—evidence of how Atwill enjoyed presenting himself to the press, and how the press enjoyed presenting him:

Is that a real alligator that *Murders in the Zoo*'s Gail Patrick sits upon in this publicity shot?

This is the story of Lionel Atwill, an actor, who hides a deadly purpose. This man, for years, has nursed a dreadful obsession under an urbane mask. A man about town with the appetite of a werewolf!

A white lodge in the Hollywood hills is where the bizarre thespian lives. Discovered at last, the white edifice gleamed at me like a mausoleum in the moonlight. A Great Dane boomed sepulchral threats from his deep throat. The door opened and I found myself in the house of the sinister man. He is the actor who has played half of the mad doctor roles in Hollywood since the screen took up with the jitters.

Through the open window I saw Hollywood, spread out in the darkness like a jeweler's showcase. Cool sanity of the moonlight! Inside a somewhat stocky man advanced with a smile, his cultivated accent and sophisticated small talk designed to disarm me.

It was the diabolical hero of

Doctor X, of *Mystery of the Wax Museum* (now to be seen on the Warners' Hollywood and Downtown screens), of *The Vampire Bat* (on the Pantages screen), and *Murders in the Zoo*.

HEYWOOD BROUN PRAISES HIM

But although his talk was of Ibsen, in which on Broadway he earned the accolade of Heywood Broun's printed praises, sinister suggestion urged itself through his bland personality.

The eyes of two iron owls, holding up the logs in the fireplace, glared unblinkingly. The Hound of Baskerville, outside, bayed again. The tusked maw of a bear rug snarled at me. The black-beamed roof seemed to sink down an inch. Oil portraits glowered on the walls.

While the master of the white lodge spoke of his 27 years on the stage, seven of them starring with the late David Belasco, I saw a bookcase full of steins. A connection between these jugs and blood shook me. Hollywood's Doctor of Horrors paused to pick up a stick of stuffed celery and clip it with his sharp incisors. To break the spell of evil, I groped at a book on a table. My hand recoiled as if struck. It was Massillon's *Oraison Funebre*, which means death in any language.

WHITE LODGE MASTER LEERS

"Mr. Atwill, you have played Ibsen, Shakespeare, some of the most romantic stage heroes written and much sophisticated drama like *The Silent Witness*. Now, in Hollywood, I find you playing mad doctors, blood-lusting sadists, a sinister butcher who embalms women in wax. How does it happen?"

The master of the white lodge dropped his urbane mask. He almost leered.

"When I was a child my mother took me to see *Faust*. I wanted ever after to be Mephistopheles. But from that time I never got the chance. Always problem plays. Romantic heroes. Always sophistication.

"I came to Hollywood. Rufus Lemaire asked me to play Doctor X. It wasn't exactly the devil, but the next thing to it. I had such a good time frightening people that I have been playing mad doctors, almost ever since—that is, discounting such roles as *The Lady* [*The Secret of Madame Blanche*].

"I am a modern Richard III!" His wild laugh rang out across the lonely Hollywood hills. "I'm the most complete sadist, tiger-man, sensualist you can imagine—in my picture roles, of course," he hastened to reassure me.

But he couldn't. The Mephistophelean obsession rode me like a curse. His very next announcement sent me jibbering down the canyon road to the white lights of the town.

"Tonight, I'm going to watch Jim Londos wrestle Ray Steele," he gloated. "They put on a real show."

Always tortured muscles! Gnashing teeth! Agony of the flesh! Bruised beef!

The clean, normal night air of Hollywood was good to breathe again.

The End

* * *

> *HE KILLED FOR LOVE*
> *AND LOVED TO KILL!*
> *Jealousy Drives Him Mad!*
> *Hate Drives Him to Kill!*
> *Terror Stalks in a Zoo!*
> —Paramount publicity, **Murders in the Zoo**

Tuesday, February 28, 1933: Paramount previews *Murders in the Zoo* at the Alexander Theatre in Glendale. *Variety* reports (March 3, 1933):

A weak sister, *Murders in the Zoo* will have to battle for what it gets. For those who enjoy horror there's a woman being thrown to a flock of crocodiles, a man being fed to tigers, and the heavy being crushed by a giant python. For laughs, Charlie Ruggles walks through the picture with little connection to the story and gives a good example of what a comic can do to harm a film when allowed to run riot.

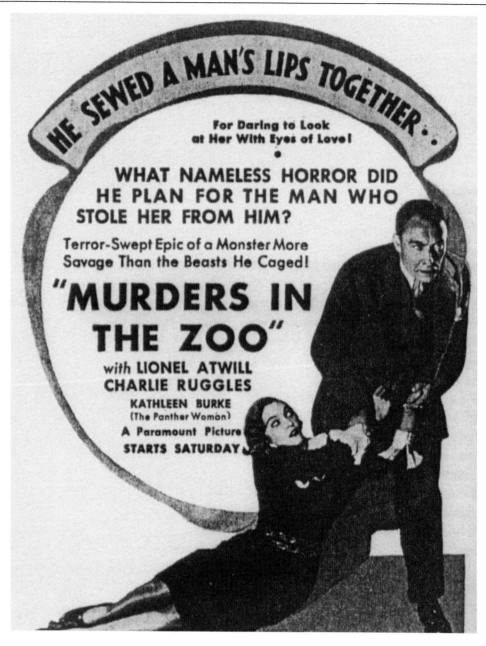

Publicity: Kathleen Burke appears hell-bent on pulling down Lionel Atwill's pants in this *Murders in the Zoo* pressbook display.

> Edward Sutherland's direction slipped up in allowing Lionel Atwill to become too heavy. Actor is sufficient of a menace to get along without a hideous laugh and a flock of withering looks.

Actually, Atwill unleashes no hideous laugh in *Murders in the Zoo*—he does give forth with a few lewd chuckles—but as the preview version ran 65 minutes and the release version 61 minutes, Pinky's cackle might have ended up on the cutting room floor. The hard-to-please *Variety* critic goes on to write that Kathleen Burke "fails to impress," that Gail Patrick is "no beauty" (but is "a refreshing personality"), that the film "will have to depend on the animals and horror to attract," and that "snakes get a bad reaction from the women in the audience, causing a few of them to walk out pale."

Meanwhile, the film runs afoul of the state censors. As previously noted, the New York censor has demanded the excision of the shot of Atwill kicking Burke's hand from the bridge and the March 10, 1933, report includes these cuts as well:

> Reel 1—Eliminate all close views of the man where his mouth is shown sewn together.
> Reel 7—Eliminate all close and distinct views of Gorman's body with snake coiled around it, and eliminate all close views of his agonized face as he is crushed to death.

In Massachusetts, the state censor insists on these cuts, dated March 20, 1933, although they only apply to Sunday showings:

> Reel 5—Eliminate scene showing the throwing of girl's body into pool.
> Reel 6—Eliminate dialogue:—"Is there a good laundry in this town?"
>   Eliminate scene showing the injection of the venom
> Reel 7—Eliminate scene showing snake snapping at man and coiling around him

The Pennsylvania state censor chimes in (March 23, 1933) with cuts deemed necessary for every day of the week:

> Reel 1—Eliminate all views of Taylor with his mouth sewed up.
> Reel 5—Eliminate views of Gorman throwing his wife, Evelyn, in alligator pool.
> Reel 6—Eliminate speech by Peter—"Is there a good laundry in this town?"
>   Eliminate views of Gorman wiping his fingerprints from stick.
> Reel 7—Eliminate semi-close-up of Gorman, on ground, with python coiled around him and close-up view of Gorman, on ground, with python coiled around his neck and of him gasping.

Friday, March 31: Murders in the Zoo opens at Broadway's Paramount Theatre. The studio provides a stage show with headliners Bob Hope and Patsy Kelly and places the accent on high-spirited lunacy: "IT's NUTS! CRAZY WEEK... As Cuckoo as a Clock! As mad as a March Hare! A show devised by the CRAZIEST guys in the world!" *The New York Times* reports of the film: "Lionel Atwill as the insanely jealous husband is almost too convincing for comfort and Kathleen Burke as the wife suggests the domestic terrors of her life capably...."

Thursday, April 6: Murders in the Zoo opens at the Paramount Theatre in Hollywood, also with a riotous stage show, featuring Lamberti (the "xylophone maniac"), radio's comedy team of Frank Watanabe and the Honorable Archie, Rube Wolf's orchestra, singer Max Lerner, Fanchon and Marco's Sunkist Beauties, and Martha Raye. The *Los Angeles Examiner* notes: "Roars, shrieks and cacklings of the wild animals on the screen at the Paramount Theatre yesterday were echoed to an amazing degree by the audience, at times driven to a mild state of hysteria by scenes of *Murders in the Zoo*...."

The Hollywood Citizen News writes that the crowd at the Paramount "enthusiastically greeted" Watanabe and Archie, "but their reception was mild compared with that which marked the exhibition of the new film.... Interest in the film so far as acting artistry is concerned centers entirely upon Atwill, who offers another of his striking and clean-cut performances." *The L.A. Illustrated News* tosses bouquets to Martha Raye, describing her as "a most excitable example of jazzomania" (and adding, "Wonder if she is like that at home?"), but praises *Murders in the Zoo,* hailing Atwill as "the new dean of terror" and "a genius in curdling blood."

Poster for *Murders in the Zoo* (1933).

However, as for box office... In its first six days at New York's Paramount, *Murders in the Zoo,* with its stage show prices, takes in $18,540,[14] where the high had been *Finn and Hattie* ($85,900) and the low *Hello, Everybody* ($15,600). In Los Angeles, the film brings in $14,000[15] in its one-week run at the Paramount, where the high had been *Beloved Bachelor* ($41,000) and the low *Tomorrow and Tomorrow* ($7,500).

Compare this to the box office for *Island of Lost Souls* which reaped $26,100[16] in its opening week at Broadway's Paramount, $23,000[17] at Hollywood's Paramount, and was considered, for all its ballyhoo, a box office disappointment. In the *Los Angeles Times,* Norbert Lusk filed this analysis of the New York box office:

> *Murders in the Zoo* holds forth at the Paramount, rating pretty good reviews on the whole, but with no enthusiasm wasted. The latter is difficult to understand for as horror films go this is more convincing and out of the ordinary than many and provides legitimate thrills.... However, in spite of these merits, the cast is not strong in box office names and because of this it may never achieve the success it deserves....

International censorship travails abound. In Ontario, a vituperative censor cuts the "bloody face and mouth sewn up" shot, totally eliminates Kathleen Burke's death scene via alligators, and all of Atwill's death scene via python—including "view of Gorman dead." The mutilated result will totally bewilder audiences. The British censor cuts the scenes of alligators "swishing through water" after Atwill throws Burke in the pool, shortens the scenes of the animals fighting each other, and eliminates several close-ups of the python killing Gorman.

Meanwhile, Germany, Sweden and Latvia reject *Murders in the Zoo in toto.* Quebec and Australia originally ban it as well, but then pass it with a variety of cuts. Australia cuts the usual—Taylor's sewn-up mouth, Evelyn and the alligators, and Peter's "Is there a good laundry in this town?" quip—but also snips the hot exchange between Atwill and Burke, which the censorship report paraphrases thusly:

> *Gorman:* I never saw you look so beautiful.... You know I have too deep an affection for you to ever stand in your way.
> *Evelyn:* Ugh.

As for Japan, the censor cuts the close-up of the man's lips stitched together, the liquid dripping out of the snake's head, the alligators after Evelyn's thrown into the pond, the python killing Gorman—and includes this aside: "Conflicts between human beings and reptiles, in which the former is killed or injured, are absolutely banned by the censors."

Meanwhile, back in the USA, exhibitor reports vary wildly. W.H. Brenner of the Cozy Theatre of Winchester, Indiana, writes to *Motion Picture Herald* that he "had the biggest Sunday business in three months. The picture deals with wild animals and science in an interesting and entertaining manner."[18] However, R.W. Hickman of the Lyric Theatre of Greenville, Illinois, warns his *Motion Picture Herald* fellow exhibitors: "[M]ost likely you'll starve to death with it. Don't believe that it will please a living soul. Too bad they continue to make this type of picture."[19]

Within a month and a half of *Murders in the Zoo*'s release, Paramount unleashes two more horror films. *Terror Aboard,* directed by Paul Sloane, has a *Beau Geste*–style opening of a derelict ship populated by corpses—victims of a serial killer played by John Halliday—and comic relief from Charlie Ruggles. *Supernatural,* directed by *White Zombie*'s Victor Halperin, stars Carole Lombard, her body possessed by an executed murderess's soul. As these films reach theaters in the spring of 1933, it's clear to Paramount's front office that neither *Island of Lost Souls* nor *Murders in the Zoo* has been a box office winner. Additionally,

Left to right: **Kathleen Burke, John Lodge and Charlie Ruggles on a *Murders in the Zoo* lobby card.**

Murders in the Zoo's bloody animal melee likely still haunts the studio. They probably realize that the success of *Dr. Jekyll and Mr. Hyde* has made them over-confident in the Hollywood horror contest.

Yet horror goes on at Paramount, even in its sex sagas. In *The Song of Songs* (1933), directed by Rouben Mamoulian, Marlene Dietrich weds a decaying old baron—played with bombastic lechery by Lionel Atwill—and endures a horrific wedding night in his spooky old chateau. In *The Scarlet Empress* (1934), directed by Josef von Sternberg, Dietrich weds badly again—this time to freakish Grand Duke Peter, played by a make-your-flesh-crawl Sam Jaffe.

Nineteen thirty-four sees several horror-fantasy-mystery films from Paramount: *Death Takes a Holiday,* directed by Mitchell Leisen, and starring Fredric March as Prince Sirki; *The Witching Hour,* directed by Henry Hathaway, and dealing with hypnosis; the rarely revived *Double Door,* starring Mary Morris as a horrible crone forever threatening to seal her sister (Anne Revere) in her mansion's airtight room; and *Menace,* directed by Ralph Murphy. Paramount ultimately gives up on horror, eventually and tentatively venturing back into the genre via the Bob Hope comedy *The Cat and the Canary* (1939) before unleashing *Dr. Cyclops* (1940), with Albert Dekker in the Technicolor, people-shrinking title role. As for *When Worlds Collide,* George Pal finally produces it at Paramount in 1951.

Meanwhile, on September 16, 1935, Paramount requests that censor Joseph Breen provide Reissue Code Seals for a number of pre–Code films, including *Island of Lost Souls* and *Murders in the Zoo*. On September 18, 1935, Breen replies, rejecting several of the films, including *Island of Lost Souls* due to "extreme horror," adding, "[P]lease note that the picture has been rejected *in toto by fourteen censor boards*." As for *Murders in the Zoo,* Breen approves re-release only with certain eliminations:

> *Murders in the Zoo*.... Eliminate close-up of man's lips stitched together... Eliminate line: "Is there a good laundry in this town?"[20]

* * *

> Short on running time but long on exotic thrills, classy production values
> and Lionel Atwill, ***Murders in the Zoo*** is a fascinating curio and
> a minor masterpiece of offbeat '30s horror.
> —*Fangoria* magazine

So ... where does *Murders in the Zoo* rate in the race for pre–Code Hollywood's most "notorious" horror film?

The two top contenders for the dubious prize have always been MGM's *Freaks* and Paramount's *Island of Lost Souls*. The former boasts Olga Baclanova's evil Cleopatra, director Tod Browning's nightmarish carnival atmospherics, and, of course, some classic horror set-pieces, including the "Gooble-Gobble" wedding feast and the bloodthirsty climax. However, the film's extensive pre-release cutting and Browning's muddled, ambivalent presentation of the "freaks" (alternately played as innocent "children," twisted monstrosities, and wisecracking burlesque comics) ultimately damages the film's overall impact. *Island of Lost Souls,* despite the fact (or maybe because of it) that the beast men of Charles Laughton's Dr. Moreau are actors in Wally Westmore makeup, is arguably superior. The Frankenstein-as-vivisectionist saga from H.G. Wells' original, the bravura vileness of Laughton as Moreau, the kinky glamour and bizarre but undeniable pathos of Kathleen Burke's Panther Woman, the "What is the Law?" droning of Bela Lugosi's Sayer of the Law—all slickly, sensually delivered by director Erle C. Kenton and cinematographer Karl Struss—give this remarkable movie a several-noses-ahead victory (in my opinion) over the competing *Freaks*.

So ... how does *Murders in the Zoo* stand up against *Island of Lost Souls*? Well, it doesn't, really. *Murders in the Zoo* has no mad scientist-playing-God motif, no army of beast men, no tropical island with a giant asparagus plant—it's basically a lurid story of a wife-killing pervert. Much of it, of course, is full-throttle comedy, Charlie Ruggles squeezing out the laughs, green-lighted by ex–Keystone Cop director Eddie Sutherland.

Yet there's something genuinely perverse in a film that asks you to chuckle with glee both minutes before and moments after alligators devour a beautiful young woman. *Murders in the Zoo* so merrily mixes Atwill's sex-charged lunatic, Ruggles' antic drunkard, Burke's alleged nympho, and the hungry alligators, fighting cats and giant python Oswald, that the film is both rampantly entertaining and virtually violating—or so it must have seemed to sensitive 1933 audience members. It creeps up on a viewer rather like Oswald creeps up on Atwill in the climax—a hissing serpent of a horror-comedy film. Universal's *The Old Dark House* (1932) had spiced comedy with horror, as had Warners' *Doctor X* and *Mystery of the Wax Museum,* and as would MGM's *Mad Love* (1935), but no film of the era did it as successfully, wickedly, or as brazenly as *Murders in the Zoo*.

Indeed, *Murders in the Zoo* is Hollywood's best—and perhaps only—pre-Code screwball comedy horror film ... and, indeed, a minor masterpiece.

* * *

Perhaps it's a comment on the times that, for all the rampant melodrama of *Murders in the Zoo,* the grim story recently played for real. On October 18, 2011, Terry Thompson, owner of an exotic animal farm in Muskingum County, Ohio, set loose his wild animals and then shot himself to death. The beasts ran wild and authorities had to hunt through a rainy night, shooting and killing one baboon, six black bears, eight lionesses, 18 rare Bengal tigers and more—a terribly tragic carnage, tallying the lives of 49 animals.[21]

One can only wonder if Terry Thompson had ever seen *Murders in the Zoo.*

Murders in the Zoo

Studio, Paramount. Associate Producer, E. Lloyd Sheldon. Director, A. Edward Sutherland. Screenplay, Philip Wylie and Seton I. Miller. Cinematographer, Ernest Haller. Art Director, Hans Dreier. Musical Director, Nat W. Finston. Original Music, Rudolph G. Kopp, John Leipold. Music Department, Karl Hajos, Sigmund Krumgold. Animal Trainers, John Branson, Olga Celeste, Chubby Guilfoyle, "Snake" King. Still Photographer, Sherman Clark. Incidental Music: "Please" (by Leo Robin and Ralph Rainger), "Look Who's Here" (by Harold Adamson and Burton Lane), "At the Bow Wow Ball" (by Edward Heyman and Boyd Bunch), "Roses from the South" (by Johann Strauss). Running time: 61 minutes.

Filmed at Paramount Studios and the Paramount Ranch in Agoura Hills, January 1933. New York City opening, Paramount Theatre, 31 March 1933. Los Angeles opening, Paramount Theatre, 6 April 1933.

Charlie Ruggles (Peter Yates); Lionel Atwill (Eric Gorman); Gail Patrick (Jerry Evans); Randolph Scott (Dr. Jack Woodford); John Lodge (Roger Hewitt); Kathleen Burke (Evelyn Gorman); Harry Beresford (Professor G.A. Evans); Edward McWade (Dan Baker, Zoo Guard); Jerry Baker (Little Boy at Zoo); Edward Pawley (Taylor); Ethan Laidlaw (Policeman Reardon); Bert Moorhouse (Apartment Desk Clerk); Edwin Stanley and Walter Walker (Doctors); Florence Wix (Ship Passenger in Deck Chair); John Rogers (Steward); Lee Phelps (Banquet Photographer/Zoo Guard); Syd Saylor (Banquet Photographer); Stanley Blystone, Syd D'Albrook, Eddie Boland (Reporters); Duke Green (Stevedore); Duke York (Seaman); Jane Darwell, Samuel S. Hinds, Cyril Ring, Phillips Smalley (Guests at Banquet); Oswald (the Python).

4

The Mystery of Lionel Atwill

An Interview with the Son of
the Late, Great Horror Star

It was a lingering mystery in the wildly colorful life of one of horror's greatest stars.

In 1944, Lionel Atwill—Broadway matinee idol of the Roaring '20s, and celebrated star of such classic Hollywood melodramas as *Mystery of the Wax Museum, Murders in the Zoo,* and *Son of Frankenstein*—had semi-emerged from the eclipse of the infamous "orgy" scandal that had crippled his career.

Friday, July 7, 1944: The 59-year-old actor married his fourth wife, a beautiful, blonde 27-year-old contralto named Paula Pruter in Las Vegas, and took her to live at his Pacific Palisades estate.

Sunday, October 14, 1945: Atwill and Paula became parents of a healthy baby boy, Lionel Anthony Guille Atwill, born at Cedars of Lebanon Hospital in Los Angeles.

Monday, April 22, 1946: Lionel Atwill died of bronchial cancer at his Palisades home, leaving his fortune to his wife and baby son.

Whatever happened to the widow? Whatever happened to the son? And, indeed, whatever happened to Atwill's ashes—reportedly unclaimed in vaultage at the Chapel of the Pines Mortuary in Los Angeles for over half a century?

The answers are here. Lionel Anthony Guille Atwill[1] spoke with me of the family history, and of his very unusual odyssey from the summer of 2003 (which he's developing into a book)—bringing to closure these mysteries.

* * *

Interview

After all my research on Lionel Atwill, it's remarkable to be talking with his son.

Right now I'm wearing his gold ring that he always wore, including in many of his films. I've worn it since I was 18—over 40 years now. If I had two starlets for each arm, I'd be set.

You were born in Los Angeles in the fall of 1945, at the time your father was acting in **House of Dracula.** *He died in April of 1946, so you were only six months old.*

Yes. The truth is, I've known very little of my father until the last few months, when I started researching his life for a book in which he will play a small role. I obtained a copy of

A proud Atwill holds his baby son (courtesy Lionel Anthony Atwill).

his will (through the Internet) and a copy of your book, *Hollywood's Maddest Doctors,* the same way. In fact, it wasn't until I'd read his will that I learned he'd left me a bequest of money in England. Wonder whatever happened to that?

Do you remember seeing him when Shock! Theatre *came on TV in the late 1950s?*

Yeah, I do ... and I think I probably remember seeing him before that, the occasional film. Before seeing him on television, everything I knew about him I learned through my mother. I'm just now realizing that was a strange relationship, because she was so much younger than he was and really not with him all that long.

What was your mother's surviving emotion about him?

She just idolized him. My mother was infatuated by him, obsessed really, into her 80s, which I guess is normal when a girl in her 20s marries a movie star who was almost in his 60s. Now that I'm approaching my father's age at the time of his marriage to my mother, I wonder how the hell he did it. But then I also wonder how he got married four times, too.

But yeah, I remember watching those horror movies, in sixth, seventh, eighth grade, on a little black and white TV. Good stuff!

There's this wonderful picture you sent me, of your mother with you as a baby, standing by your father's oil painting portrait, around the time of his death.

Yeah. Note my disgruntled expression. The son of one of Hollywood's most famous swordsmen, and they put me in a dress! I have that painting, by the way—which was done in the 1920s—here in my home in Vermont.

Were there other mementoes of your father around the house?

There was the life mask, made for *Mystery of the Wax Museum.* My mother had it for years. I don't know what happened to it, but I imagine it broke or deteriorated in one move or another, and she threw it out. I was fascinated by it as a kid, as I recall.

What particular memories of your father did your mother share with you?

There were two things. One was how much he adored me. I think her point was, here was a father in his 60s, who really enjoyed being a father. She said he constantly wanted to change my diapers, give me a bath, and put me to sleep—all those things considered by people in our generation to be what the well-rounded father does. The other thing she always said was how much she was in love with him. Those were the two things. And she never really talked about anything else.

Did she say anything about his film career?

Yeah, she said it was basically just a job. On days when my father was working in a film, he'd have to get up at five in the morning. My mother would make him breakfast, and he wouldn't get home until around 6:30 at night. I remember when I first asked my mother about my father, she said his advice to me was, "Never become an actor!"

Tell me about your mother.

She was very attractive, quite striking—tall, 5'9", with long blonde hair, as was the fashion in the '40s. She was strong-willed, amusing, very lively and entertaining. She'd moved with her mother to California in 1939 and worked here and there as a singer; her career was pretty much on track, from what I recall her telling me and little things I found in scrapbooks

Paula Atwill, Atwill's fourth wife, with baby Lionel about the time of Atwill's death in 1946. Paula's portrait is on the table. "The son of one of Hollywood's most famous swordsmen, and they put me in a dress," jokes "Tony" Atwill today (courtesy Lionel Anthony Atwill).

and the like, when she married my father. Her career was on the rise, certainly, and she sang on the radio and at the Hollywood Bowl. She was a classically trained contralto, not doing pop stuff, and sang for some movies, doing some voiceovers for non-singing actresses—what movies they were, I don't know. I could never pin her down—as she got older, I kept trying to get her to write the specifics. I kept pushing and sending her notes, saying, "Why don't you write the details down?" But what she would write would be purely emotional.

So she never gave anecdotes about their courtship, or marriage in Las Vegas?

No, she never did. I remember her telling me they were married in Las Vegas, and that was that. As much as I tried, I could never get anything else out of her. That whole generation's fairly tight-lipped—they didn't casually reveal things—but she was *particularly* tight-lipped.

So for a little less than two years, your mother was Mrs. Lionel Atwill, living at his Pacific Palisades estate with the pool and tennis court and all that acreage...

Right. The house was at the end of D'Este Drive and overlooked the valley below. There were orchards all around it. I remember once I visited there in '69, driving down the little narrow street with a divider with palm trees on either side. I actually knocked on the door and introduced myself to the people living there. They were very nice and said, "You know, we still have a poster of your father, from one of his movies, framed, downstairs in the play-room, if you'd like it." I said, "No, you keep it—you've got the house, you get the poster!" The house has been all redone now.

So your mother's love for your father was ongoing.

Oh yeah! He was the love of her life. She was truly infatuated.

After your father's death, when you were a little boy, was your mother working?

Yes, she was doing some writing for radio, and she was still singing a little bit. But I think she wasn't working much—didn't have to, at that point at least. For those five years— my father died in '46, and she remarried in '51, five years and some change—she'd sold the house on D'Este Drive and we were living in the house my father had owned on 407 7th Street, in Santa Monica. The house is still there, by the way—it hasn't changed at all. Anyway, my mother would talk about my father all the time. She'd talk about him in front of my step-father, which was always sort of embarrassing!

Tell me about your life.

In 1951 my mother married a wealthy ne'er-do-well and we moved east. I went to school in the city and the summers we vacationed on Lake Champlain in the Adirondacks of New York. I was sent off to boarding school in Pennsylvania [the Hill School in Pottstown] and then went to Duke, majoring in English and biology. After college—this was 1966—I served in Vietnam as a recon platoon leader with the 1st Infantry Division. [*Interviewer's note: Atwill won two Bronze Stars.*] After leaving the Army, I got married and returned to the Adirondacks, where I went to work for a start-up magazine called *Adirondack Life*. I ran that for six years, and then I eventually struck a deal with a New York City-based magazine called *Backpacker*, editing it from Vermont. After doing that for several years, I freelanced for anyone and everyone: *Yankee, Ski, Skiing, Esquire, Geo*, and the hook and bullet mags. That connection got me on the masthead of *Sports Afield*, where I worked quite happily for a dozen years. My goal then (and now) was not to take the publishing world by storm but

An aerial view of the Atwill estate, 13515 D'Este Drive, Pacific Palisades, with its pool and tennis court (courtesy Lionel Anthony Atwill).

to live a pleasant life in the country, which I've managed to do. Most recently I worked for *Field and Stream.*

I have a wonderful daughter, Amanda, who went to Brandeis in Boston and now works for a sports management company, which takes care of the finances of about 400 professional athletes. She's having a great time.

Does your daughter watch her grandfather in his films?

Yes! She used to get a great kick out of it when she was about 12 or 13—I had all these videotapes of my father's movies. Friends would come over to the house, they'd say, "Let's watch a movie," and Amanda would say, "Okay! I'll show you my granddaddy!" Just recently I was chatting with her and she told me that she and her boyfriend had rented *Murders in the Zoo* from her local Video Shack. Apparently the proprietor is an old movie buff, so he was all excited to meet my daughter.

A couple rather "tough" questions. First of all, did your mother ever allude to the story of the "orgies" that your father allegedly hosted in 1940 and 1941, several years before their marriage?

I first heard about that when a friend sent me a copy of *Hollywood Babylon II.* That book's over-the-top, breathless and purple, but it did present some of the facts, or most of the facts. My mother had obliquely referred to that incident, but her version was watered-down and very brief. The best I recall, she told the story that my father had tried to protect a friend of his who had gotten an underage girl pregnant—which could be the distilled version, I guess, of the story you tell in your book.

Errol Flynn and Charlie Chaplin all got into trouble at the same time. There might have been a political situation, trying to bribe celebrities—pay up, or...

Yeah, or we'll get something on you.... Well, the fact that they kept watering these things down until they finally got a confession to perjury—I mean, having blue movies is not exactly the worst crime in the world, even in the '40s. It did sound like there was more to it than what meets the eye, and I guess we'll never find out.

The other "tough" question ... it's been reported that your father was cremated at the Chapel of the Pines in Los Angeles in 1946, and his ashes never claimed. Can you talk about this?

That's a part of the basis of the book I'm writing. It was in the mid–90s that I found out my father's ashes remained unclaimed. I got a letter from a guy who told me his last name was Atwill, and he implied that there was a family connection in England, but it was all a little vague. Anyway, at the time he was attempting to start a scriptwriting company, and he said, "I've admired your father's work, and I think it's terrible that he is where he is, and I think it would be more appropriate if we rescued him from the shelf he's on and buried him in a fitting ceremony in Forest Lawn, or one of the celebrity cemeteries." It all made me a little suspicious, because I wondered, "What's in it for this guy?" (I'm sort of an Eastern cynic.) I thought he probably wants to be in the limelight of whatever minor ceremony this might involve, and get a little press, and make the connection, real or imagined, with my father.

Anyway, he'd given me the details on Chapel of the Pines, so I called them up, and they'd said he was sitting on a shelf, A26 or something. So I called my mother, and first I said, "This sort of comes as a shock to me, but apparently Dad is still sitting on a shelf in the mortuary!" And my mother said, "Damn! I kind of forgot! You know, in my grief, I just forgot about it!" Which is hard for me to imagine today, but maybe that's possible—she had a lot to contend with, she was selling the house, her mother was living with us, I was a baby, and given those circumstances I can perhaps understand. My mother never had a very strong religious streak, so I don't think there was great significance for her in putting my father in a cemetery. So anyway, I said, "Well, listen, if you're perfectly comfortable with this, I'm comfortable with it."

Still, I called the mortuary and quizzed them—you know, I didn't want him to be in a potter's field; I wanted him to be at least in a semi-dignified spot. I talked to this nice lady there, and I said, "Well, what's the 'neighborhood' like? Who are his closest, most intimate friends there?" She said, "I'm not at liberty to tell you names, but I can assure you that he's in the company of some notables." And I said, "That's probably not too bad," and rather than make a big to-do about the whole thing, I wrote them a formal letter that said that, 'I am his heir, and my wish is that he just stay there,' so that this other guy didn't do an end-run on me somehow and pull him out. I never did hear from him again.

My stepfather had died in 1992. My mother died in Florida in August of 2002. At that time, I decided to bring some continuity to her life—and perhaps to mine—by rejoining

Paula Pruter Atwill was a classical singer before her marriage to Atwill (courtesy Lionel Anthony Atwill).

A bare-chested Atwill and his beautiful wife Paula, probably shortly after their July 1944 marriage. He was 59 when they wed and she was 27. Note Atwill's dog and pipe (courtesy Lionel Anthony Atwill).

her remains with my father's. I did that in the summer of 2003, driving from my home in Vermont to Florida, and then to California. I got the notion to reunite my parents and along the way, do *Travels with Charley* in search of people from my past. I bought a camper for my truck, loaded up my two dogs (if I can't out-write Steinbeck, I can sure out-dog him), and we had a great trip. Seven weeks, 10,000 miles. I saw a dozen people whom I have not seen going back to 1959. So that was really, really fun. And now I'm weaving all this into a book.

I imagine the visits to claim the cremains were bizarre.

When I picked up my mother in Florida, her ashes were in a plastic bag inside a paper bag—like a little shopping bag. The girl said, "Now make sure you keep the paperwork with you, because should you be stopped by a cop, say for speeding, and he stumbles on this in a search of your car, he's going to think it's either explosives, cocaine, or anthrax!" [*Laughing*] And all I could think of was, "And which would my mother choose?"

And from there...?

Across America. After I picked up my mother in Florida, I visited my best friend from elementary school, my high school roommate, my battalion commander from Vietnam, Fort Benning, my first girlfriend (who along the way was in an Andy Warhol movie), and several more folks of dubious distinction.

Finally arriving in Los Angeles, and the Chapel of the Pines.

Yes, the "beautiful" Chapel of the Pines. I guess it was beautiful in its day. Your picture of the crematory in your book does it more than justice. I swear I saw bullet pockmarks in the faux marble columns [*laughing*], and I just loved the concertina wire on top of the walls surrounding the place. I knew it wasn't there to keep people *in!* The neighborhood has decayed substantially, but I'm afraid the residents of the Chapel have no options for moving.

It was kind of funny. First, I got ahead of schedule. So I called up the lady at the Chapel of the Pines to whom I had sent the paperwork and had given an estimated arrival time. I said, "Look, I hate to do this to you, but I picked up a week in my travels, I'm out there before I thought I would be, and I'd really appreciate anything you can do to retrieve my father and finalize the paperwork, and all that stuff." And you would have thought that I'd asked her to go out with a shovel and dig him up—"Oh my God, no! We have to get this cleared from the state, we've got to do this...." I thought, okay, I see—they haven't done anything up until now, and they're going to do everything the day before. So I turned on all the charm I could muster on a cellphone while driving on the 405 or wherever and I said, "Listen. I've got two dogs, and a truck, and a camper, I really don't want to just bang around Southern California for a week waiting for this, and I really appreciate anything you can do." She said, "Okay. Come tomorrow. I'll have him at one o'clock."

So I get there at 12:30, on a typical hazy, smoggy L.A. day, planning that I'll find some place to eat nearby. I start driving around and I'm thinking, "You know, I think I'll skip the meal, because I don't see too many hospitable restaurants out here, in this particular neighborhood." So I pulled into the Chapel of the Pines parking lot, went in my camper and made a peanut butter and jelly sandwich! While I'm sitting in the back in the parking lot of this crematorium, this little old guy walks out of the "serious business" room—you know, the one with the big chimney. I almost wanted to say, "Hey—want some lunch?"

Finally, at one o'clock, I went up and beat on the door. This black lady came out, and she was quite sweet. I gave her a can of maple syrup—I was playing Johnny Mapleseed all the way across the country, handing out maple syrup to people I stayed with, and I said, "You know, you were really nice"—I give her this thing of maple syrup, and she was just so taken with that. And I said, "This is a creepy place to work," and she said, "It's not that bad. I don't mind it here, I've been here nine years," and she gave me the whole story of her life. Well, meanwhile, here's my father—in this blue velvet bag that looks like it should contain a two-gallon jug of Crown Royal.

Did the Chapel of the Pines lady have any idea of who your father had been?

Yeah, she did, actually. It was kind of funny. She said, "You know, he's on our wall of fame." I said, "Oh, yeah?" She said, "It's outside here." So she takes me out there, and of course, we can't find his name there. And she said, "Well, *hell,* I *thought* he was here!" [*Laughing*]

Was there an urn inside the bag, with his name on it?

It wasn't even an urn. It looked like a classy, supersize, black 1940s shoebox—a cardboard box with a mailing label on the end. As it was bigger than a shoebox, I'd say it was designed for its purpose. Surely it was more dignified than the plastic bag in which my mother resided.

The inevitable question: Did you look in the box?

Yes. And my father looked like, with a little diligence and some Duco cement, you could almost put him back together again. The bones were in three- or four-inch pieces. They didn't pulverize the bones back then the way they do now. I think it's probably to avoid that shock of opening up the box and seeing Dad or Uncle Louis, you know, in recognizable pieces. So now they put them through a crusher that reduces everything to flour. I later

The Chapel of the Pines in Los Angeles: Lionel Atwill's ashes were in vaultage here until his son claimed them and buried them with the ashes of his mother Paula.

showed my daughter Amanda her grandfather. She'd been an archaeology major, and she said, "Hell, Dad, in three hours I could put him back together!"

So you brought the remains of your father and mother back to Vermont?

Right. Actually I was thinking of either putting them in the Pacific Ocean or in Pacific Palisades—if I could find some place I could do that without having the cops accuse me of distributing anthrax, cocaine, or explosives! Once in California, I decided that scattering their remains in Pacific Palisades would mean that they would be fill in a driveway in a few years, and throwing them in the Pacific would reduce them to little more than jock itch in some surfer's shorts. I looked at the Malibu coastal scene, and then I looked at the Pacific Palisades scene, and I said, "Nothing here lasts more than about 15 years"—it's such a tragic, funny world out there. There's so little here that was part of their lives, you know—so much has been torn down and replaced. So I brought both of them home with me, and have buried them together in a beautiful spot in the Vermont woods.

You wear your father's ring, as he wore it—the little finger of the left hand.

It's three intertwined bands of gold, and you can see him wearing it in your book in the stills from *Doctor X, Murders in the Zoo, The Man Who Reclaimed His Head, Mark of the Vampire, Son of Frankenstein,* and *The Ghost of Frankenstein.* It's an old Cartier ring.

A story about the ring: I wore it in Vietnam. We were operating in an area east of Saigon on an island appropriately dubbed VC Island. The land was flat, low and crisscrossed with canals and streams. We would rig a rope across the water and hand-over-hand pull ourselves across. It was a dicey maneuver because we each carried 50 to 70 pounds of ammo and gear and these rivers, canals would often be six or seven feet deep in the middle. I was up to my neck, holding the rope with my right hand and sculling with my left when I felt the ring come off. I swept my left hand down through the water to stabilize myself and felt something bump my palm. I closed my hand around it, pulled it out of the water, and there was my ring.

Any of his films make a special impression on you?

Oh, I love *Mystery of the Wax Museum.* I think that was probably as popular a film as any he made, at least in which he starred. So yeah, I used to watch that all the time.

Well, your father surely was a larger-than-life personality.

Exactly. And as far as his scandal goes, at least he was fairly straight and heterosexual, which isn't as bad as a lot of those other poor folks who've been dragged over the coals. At least he wasn't Fatty Arbuckle!

And what's the title for your upcoming book?

Hauling Ash.

* * *

Lionel Atwill Facts

- *Sunday, March 1, 1885:* Lionel Alfred William Atwill is born in Croydon, England.
- *Monday, Halloween, 1904:* Atwill makes his professional acting bow as "A Footman" in *The Walls of Jericho* at London's Garrick Theatre.

Left: Lionel Anthony Atwill, standing by his father's portrait in Vermont in 2004. *Right:* Note the ring on Lionel Atwill's finger in this portrait from *Son of Frankenstein* (1939). His son wears the same ring in the preceding picture. Both men wear the ring on the little finger of their left hand.

- *Tuesday, March 5, 1912*: Atwill scores a triumph in *Milestone*s, which opens at London's Royalty Theatre and runs over 600 performances.
- *Monday, January 8, 1917*: Atwill makes his Broadway debut in the title role of *The Lodger,* Marie Belloc-Lowndes' play about Jack the Ripper. The *New York Times* pans his performance as well as that of his leading lady Phyllis Relph, who is Atwill's real-life wife. They will have a son, John.
- *Thursday, October 11, 1917*: *Eve's Daughter* opens at Broadway's Playhouse Theatre. The red-haired, cat-eyed Atwill, playing the lascivious "Man-Siren" who seduces the play's star Grace George, becomes the talk of Broadway. Incidentally, Atwill's light red hair earns him a lasting nickname: "Pinky."
- *Monday, March 4, 1918*: Famous Players-Lasky releases the film version of *Eve's Daughter* with Atwill making his movie debut, reprising his stage role of the "Man-Siren." Billie Burke plays the female lead.
- *Thursday, December 23, 1920*: *Deburau,* based on the life of the French clown and mime, opens at the Belasco Theatre, directed by David Belasco, with Atwill in the title role. He scores a major triumph. "The greatest glory of the evening belongs to Mr. Atwill," hails Heywood Broun of the *New York Tribune,* writing that it's one of the greatest stage performances of recent years, second only to Barrymore's Richard III. Portraying the courtesan who breaks Deburau's heart: Elsie Mackay, who earlier in 1920 had wed Atwill, following his divorce from Phyllis Relph.

Tony Atwill and his dogs at his home in Vermont in 2004.

• *Monday, March 3, 1924*: *The Outsider* opens at New York's 49th Street Theatre, starring Katharine Cornell as a cripple and Atwill as the doctor who tries to save her with his miraculous "rack." The play and its stars are so shattering that, as George S. Kaufman will write in the *New York Times*, the opening night audience stays still and seated "for some five minutes after the final curtain."

• *Monday, April 13, 1925*: Shaw's *Caesar and Cleopatra*, staring Atwill and Helen Hayes, is the first attraction at Broadway's new Guild Theatre. On opening night, President Calvin Coolidge raises the curtain.

• *Thursday, December 17, 1925*: "How Lionel Atwill Saw Elsie's Love Fade," headlines the *New York Daily Mirror*. The story details how his wife Elsie Mackay had an affair with an actor, Max Montesole, while Atwill was directing them in the Broadway-bound play *Deep in the Woods*. Atwill's associ-

Matinee idol: Lionel Atwill on Broadway in the title role in *Deburau* (1920).

ate Claude Beerbohm claims Atwill considered "shooting" and "throttling" Montesole. Instead he invaded her "love nest" and sued for divorce. *Deep in the Woods* never opens.

• *Thursday, November 11, 1926*: *The Squall* opens at New York's 48th Street Theatre, directed by Atwill—one of seven Broadway plays he'll direct over the next several years.

• *Tuesday, March 8, 1927*: "Lionel Atwill parades as the mythical Ulysses," headlines the *Washington Post* as *The Adventurer* plays Washington's Belasco Theatre. Atwill stars *and* directs. "A pagan theme, the story gets pagan treatment," writes the *Post* critic John J. Daly; "so here are all sorts of outlandish and shocking scenes and situations—enough, in fact, to keep tongues wagging for many moons." *The Adventurer* never reaches Broadway.

• *Thursday, January 30, 1930*[2]: The *Los Angeles Evening Herald* announces that Atwill "comes to ye [*sic*] Gold Coast to portray the role of Sykes [*sic*] in *Oliver Twist,* which Lionel Barrymore will megaphone. Ruth Chatterton is also in the cast." Atwill would have been a splendidly wicked Bill Sikes, and Ms. Chatterton well-cast as the tragic Nancy; Barrymore's involvement creates the impression that MGM is preparing the film. Alas, it never happens.

• *June 1930*: Atwill marries his third wife, Henrietta Louise Cromwell Brooks MacArthur, ex-wife of General Douglas MacArthur. The bride is a multi-millionairess and they wed at her estate, Rainbow Hill (named after MacArthur's regiment), in Maryland's Green Spring Valley.

• *Monday, October 26, 1931*: *The Silent Witness*, a sex-courtroom melodrama, opens at the Belasco Theatre in Los Angeles. Atwill reprises his Broadway role of Sir Austin Howard, who claims he strangled a voluptuary—but is actually lying to save his son. Playing the volup-

Atwill and his third wife, Louise Cromwell Brooks MacArthur, at their 1930 wedding. She had been previously wed to General Douglas MacArthur.

tuary: Olga Baclanova (the evil "Cleopatra" of *Freaks*). Playing the son: Bramwell Fletcher (who just played in *Svengali* and will soon appear in *The Mummy*). Fox will film *The Silent Witness* with Atwill and Fletcher in their stage roles and Greta Nissen as the voluptuary. It will be Atwill's sound debut.

• *Wednesday, August 3, 1932*: *Doctor X* opens in New York City, starring Atwill, Fay Wray and Lee Tracy, and directed by Michael Curtiz. The two-color Technicolor mix of horror and comedy concerns a cannibalistic murderer who coats himself in synthetic flesh. Preston Foster plays the cannibal, but Atwill will steal the honors.

• *Tuesday, August 30, 1932*: Louella O. Parsons, in the *Los Angeles Examiner,* reports that *Doctor X* is a hit, playing to "capacity houses" and that Warners has signed Atwill for *Wax Museum.* "In the beginning," writes Parsons, "Lionel, who is an Englishman, and Michael Curtiz, who is a Hungarian, figuratively didn't speak the same language. Their battles were numerous, but they finally got together and made such a good picture that Warners are willing to risk putting the two temperaments together again."

• *Thursday, October 27, 1932*: Having visited the *Mystery of the Wax Museum* set, Louella O. Parsons writes that she "had a hard time recognizing Lionel Atwill in a weird makeup, enough to frighten innocent children and harmless old ladies. Lionel and Mike seem to have subdued the English and Hungarian temperaments and are getting along *tres elegan*t."

• *Saturday, November 19, 1932*: Majestic Studios completes *The Vampire Bat,* starring Atwill, Fay Wray, Melvyn Douglas, and Dwight Frye (as a bat-petting halfwit named Herman). As mad Dr. Otto von Niemann, Atwill rants the classic lines, "*Mad?* Is one who has solved the secret of life to be considered *mad?*"

• *Thursday, February 9, 1933*: *Mystery of the Wax Museum,* also in two-strip Technicolor, has its Los Angeles premiere at Warners Hollywood and Downtown Theatres. On opening day, the Hollywood Theatre has "the unveil-

Lurid poster art for *Mystery of the Wax Museum* (1933).

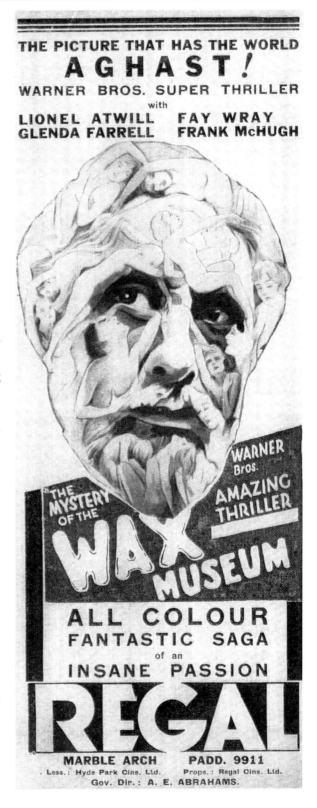

ing" of a wax museum in the outer lobby. "Is She Woman or Wax?" teases the promotional copy, beside a picture of Fay Wray in a negligee. "Lionel Atwill gives a splendid performance as the sculptor," reports the *Evening Herald Express*, "creating sympathy for the man despite the horrors that his mania drives him to."

• *Sunday, February 12, 1933*: "*SUCCESOR TO CHANEY SEEN, Lionel Atwill New Master of Makeup,*" headlines Muriel Babcock of the *Los Angeles Times*. She quotes Atwill:

> Give me a role in which the mental as well as the physical portrayal is important. Let me do a maniac, if you will, but let me express mentally as well as through physical makeup the flair of a tortured soul, the cackling and diabolical fiendishness of a crazed man. Let me have a characterization in which I may put something more than a surface portrayal and I am satisfied. All I want to do is act.

• *Wednesday, May 17, 1933*: The *Hollywood Citizen News* reports that Rouben Mamoulian, who'd recently directed Atwill as the decaying old baron who provides Marlene Dietrich a horrifying wedding night in Paramount's *The Song of Songs,* had hosted a dinner dance at the Ambassador Hotel. Atwill and his wife Louise attended and mingled with such guests as Dietrich, Claudette Colbert, Jean Harlow, Cecil B. DeMille, Gary Cooper, Katharine Hepburn, Fredric March, Miriam Hopkins, Myrna Loy, Karen Morley, Leslie Howard, Helen Hayes, Josef von Sternberg, Paul Lukas, Ralph Bellamy, Kay Francis, Alice Brady, Frank Capra, Louis B. Mayer, and many more.

• *Tuesday, May 30, 1933*: "Horror-Haunted Actor," headlines the *Los Angeles Record,* noting that Atwill has signed to star in Universal's *Secret of the Blue Room,* co-starring Gloria Stuart, Paul Lukas and Onslow Stevens. In her 1999 memoir *I Just Kept Hoping,* written after her Oscar-nominated "comeback" performance in *Titanic,* Gloria Stuart remembered *Secret of the Blue Room*:

> Dear Lionel Atwill—a still handsome late-fortyish ex-theater-matinee-idol-making-it-in-Hollywood! So! All of a sudden, one Saturday afternoon when our film was finished, I opened the front door. Lionel. I looked at him, he smiled at me, moments of silence, so I asked him to come in. We had never had more than lunch together in the Universal Studios commissary, in the company of various other actors. Why?
>
> He was, as we used to say, put away in a smashing gray tweed jacket, with a smashing vest and smashing gray flannel trousers, an ascot, and—I couldn't believe my eyes—smashing gray felt spats. Yes, spats! In Southern California!
>
> Into the living room. Sherry or port was the polite social drink then. Yes, he would have a sherry. The conversation was so hesitant, so stilted, so barren. I became impatient and lied, saying I had an appointment very soon with Percy Westmore for a makeup consultation.
>
> As he rose, and I rose, he very clumsily put his arm around my waist, and I very quickly disengaged him. He burbled something, we walked toward the front door. I let him out, and that was that.
>
> Spats?[3]

• *Thursday, May 9, 1935*: Paramount's *The Devil Is a Woman* opens at Hollywood's Paramount Theatre. Starring in this sado-maso love saga, directed by Josef von Sternberg: Marlene Dietrich, Lionel Atwill, and Cesar Romero. Cut from the film is a song, "If It Isn't Pain Then It Isn't Love." The Catholic Legion of Decency slaps *The Devil Is a Woman* with a "Condemned" rating anyway.

• *Saturday, May 1, 1937*: Louella O. Parsons writes: "Before the Lionel Atwills returned

Unusual attire for an unusual man: Lionel Atwill, in derby, tuxedo coat, tennis slacks and shoes ... and his monocle. The dog looks amused (courtesy Lionel Anthony Atwill).

Atwill and canine companion (courtesy Lionel Anthony Atwill).

from the continent, they were the guests of Mrs. Wallis Simpson at luncheon. Mrs. Atwill and Mrs. Simpson are old friends from Baltimore."

• *Monday, December 20, 1937*: Cecil B. DeMille's *Lux Radio Theatre* presents *The Song of Songs,* with Dietrich and Atwill reprising their roles from the 1933 film.

• *Summer, 1938*: 20th Century–Fox signs Atwill to a seven-year, four-way contract— actor-director-writer-associate producer—at a salary starting at $900 weekly, to escalate in the seventh year to $3,000 weekly.[4] Mysteriously, he'll only act in several Fox films, the studio never optioning his other services before dropping his contract in August 1940.

• *Saturday, August 27, 1938*: "Lionel Atwill catching the first tuna of the season of Catalina," reports Sally Moore in the *Evening Herald Express.*

• *Friday, January 13, 1939*: "One doesn't easily forget, Herr Baron, an arm torn out by the roots!" says Atwill as Universal's *Son of Frankenstein* premieres at the Hollywood Pantages. The stars: Basil Rathbone as Wolf von Frankenstein, Boris Karloff as the Monster, Bela Lugosi as broken-necked old Ygor, and Lionel Atwill as the monocle-sporting, wooden arm-saluting Inspector Krogh. The role, played with macabre humor and all variety of tricks with the "wooden" arm, will become possibly Atwill's best-remembered portrayal. "Lionel Atwill gives a standout performance in *Son of Frankenstein*," writes Ed Sullivan in his column three days later.

- *Wednesday, April 26, 1939*: The *Los Angeles Examiner* reports on the British Service Club's recent St. George's Day Dinner Dance at the Victor Hugo Restaurant, emceed by Alan Mowbray, with such guests as Atwill, Edgar Bergen, Martha Raye, and John Wayne. "Adia Kuznetzoff sang gloriously," writes reporter Ella Wickersham. Atwill will hear Kuznetzoff sing again when the Russian belts out the "Faro-La, Faro-Li" song in *Frankenstein Meets the Wolf Man*.

- *Wednesday, December 13, 1939*: Harry Crocker of the *Los Angeles Examiner* reports of a recent Lionel Atwill party: "Just imagine a rumpus room overflowing with 60 beautiful Earl Carroll girls!" Impresario Carroll's showgirls are reputedly "the most beautiful girls in the world," and Crocker writes that they "brought appreciative gleams of pleasure" to the guests. Meanwhile, Atwill and wife Louise have separated.

- *Friday, December 22, 1939*: Hal Roach transforms his Beverly Hills estate into a ranch to celebrate that night's premiere of the film version of John Steinbeck's *Of Mice and Men*, starring Burgess Meredith, Betty Field, and Lon Chaney, Jr. Among the 225 invited guests: Clark Gable, Carole Lombard, Errol Flynn, Bette Davis, Tyrone Power, Norma Shearer, James Cagney, Marlene Dietrich, Jeanette MacDonald, Basil Rathbone, Fay Wray, Deanna Durbin, and Lionel Atwill.

- *Yuletide, 1940*: Atwill hosts apparently several notorious parties.[5] One evening his Pacific Palisades house allegedly offers "wild revels by unclad guests on a tiger skin rug," as well as at least two pornographic films—*The Daisy Chain* and *The Plumber and the Girl*. The guests supposedly re-enact the pornography at the party. A grand jury will privately investigate the "revels."

- *Friday, March 28, 1941*: Universal releases *Man Made Monster*, in which Atwill transforms Lon Chaney, Jr., into an electrical freak. Atwill's famous line, leered to nightgown-wearing Anne Nagel: "You know, it's a curious fact that ever since my earliest experiments with rabbits and guinea pigs, I've always found the *female* of the species was more sensitive to electrical impulse than was the male!"

- *Saturday, April 26, 1941*: John Arthur Atwill, Atwill's son, dies as a result of enemy action in the RAF. Atwill receives a telegram two days later from the Secretary of State of the Air Ministry in London.

- *Monday, May 12, 1941*: A 16-year-old blonde rape victim named Sylvia Hamelaine appears in court at the trial of Cuban dress designer Virginia Lopez, who allegedly arranged the girl's rape. Lopez's lawyer, trying to portray Hamelaine as a degenerate, claims the girl has "cavorted in the nude at the home of Lionel Atwill." Sensational headlines ensue.

- *Wednesday, May 21, 1941*: Atwill appears in court, wearing a black armband to commemorate his son John's death. He denies the orgy saga, says the infamous tiger skin rug is actually "an old, moth-eaten bearskin," and swears under oath he owns no pornographic films.

- *Monday, June 2, 1941*: The jury decides Atwill's frolic was "just an innocent party."

- *Friday, January 23, 1942*: Universal opens a horror double feature, *The Wolf Man* and *The Mad Doctor of Market Street*, at the Vogue Theatre, 6675 Hollywood Boulevard. "STARS IN PERSON AT 9:00 TONITE!" proclaims a newspaper advertisement, with Bela Lugosi,

Warren William and Evelyn Ankers set to appear from *The Wolf Man* and Lionel Atwill, Claire Dodd and Nat Pendleton from *The Mad Doctor of Market Street*. Atwill, Lugosi and Ankers have just completed *The Ghost of Frankenstein*.

- *Friday, June 19, 1942*: Universal completes *Sherlock Holmes and the Secret Weapon*, in which Atwill is a splendidly diabolical Professor Moriarity.

- *Tuesday, June 30, 1942*: The Los Angeles Grand Jury indicts Atwill, accusing him of perjury in regards to his testimony in 1941. This time he'll claim he rented the pornographic films to entertain a visiting Northwest Mountie, but didn't watch them himself.

- *Tuesday, August 11, 1942*: The L.A. Grand Jury indicts Atwill again, accusing him of perjury in his recent testimony.

- *Thursday, September 24, 1942*: Atwill, with his lawyer Isaac Pacht at his side, confesses in court to Judge William McKay that he does indeed own *The Daisy Chain* and *The Plumber and the Girl.* "I lied like a gentleman to protect friends," says Atwill.

Newspaper ad for *The Wolf Man* and *The Mad Doctor of Market Street,* playing at the Vogue Theatre on Hollywood Boulevard in January 1942.

- *Thursday, October 15, 1942*: Lionel Atwill is convicted of perjury and receives a five-year probationary sentence. It's the fourth day of Universal shooting *Frankenstein Meets the Wolf Man*, in which Atwill plays the mayor. He fears Universal will fire him, and although the studio does not, this film will be Atwill's last for almost a year—Hollywood blackballs him.
- *Friday, April 23, 1943*: Judge William McKay exonerates Atwill of the perjury charge, claiming that his persecutors were not compelled "by a sincere desire to bring about justice" and that it would "constitute unusual punishment" to keep the actor from earning a living. "I am very deeply touched, your Honor," weeps Atwill.
- *Summer, 1943*: Atwill tours in stock productions of *The Outsider, The Play's the Thing,* and *My Dear Children,* hoping he'll get a Broadway stage offer. He doesn't.
- *Friday, June 18, 1943*: Louise Atwill obtains a final decree of divorce from Atwill.
- *Sunday, April 23, 1944*: *The New York Times* announces that Mae West, "the lady herself abursting for action," will bring her new play, *Catherine Was Great*, to Broadway under the production auspices of Mike Todd. The paper reports "Lionel Atwill, of Hollywood 'heavy' luster, may have one of the leading roles." The spectacle of Mae and "Pinky" together in this sex comedy would have been a show in itself—indeed, one wonders if Ms. West considered Atwill partly due to his recent "orgy" scandal. However, Atwill is not in the cast when *Catherine Was Great* opens at Broadway's Shubert Theatre on August 2, 1944, and runs 191 performances.
- *Thursday, April 27, 1944*: Atwill begins work on *House of Frankenstein*, which stars Boris Karloff as a mad doctor, Lon Chaney, Jr., as the Wolf Man, John Carradine as Dracula, J. Carrol Naish as a hunchback, and Glenn Strange as Frankenstein's Monster. Atwill has the small role of Inspector Arnz.
- *Friday, July 7, 1944*: Fifty-nine-year-old Lionel Atwill weds 27-year-old Paula Pruter in Las Vegas.
- *Wednesday, July 11, 1945*: Harrison Carroll of the *Evening Herald Express* writes, "The Lionel Atwills are expecting a baby in late September or early October."
- *Sunday, September 9, 1945*: RKO completes (shortly after midnight) *Genius at Work,* in which Atwill and Bela Lugosi menace the comedy team of Wally Brown and Alan Carney.[6] Best scene: Atwill in drag as a little old lady in a wheelchair, and a bearded Bela posing as his (her) husband.
- *Sunday, October 14, 1945*: At 6:51 p.m. Lionel Anthony Guille Atwill is born at Cedars of Lebanon Hospital in Los Angeles.
- *Monday, October 15, 1945*: Universal is starting the final ten days' shooting of *House of Dracula*. John Carradine has completed his scenes as Dracula; Lon Chaney and Glenn Strange are still working as Wolf Man and Frankenstein's Monster respectively, as is Jane Adams as a hunchbacked nurse. During this stretch, new father Atwill completes his role of Inspector Holtz, including his death scene as a mad doctor (Onslow Stevens) hurls him into electrical machinery.
- *Monday, February 4, 1946*: After three weeks' work on Universal's serial *Lost City of the Jungle,* Atwill, as the villain, is clearly too ill to continue, suffering from bronchial cancer.[7] Early that evening Universal, realizing the severity of Atwill's illness, shoots his death scene—perishing in a plane in an atomic blast—to provide closure for his role. Atwill never returns to the production and the studio will finish up with a new villain (John Mylong) and a double for Atwill (George Sorel), filmed from the back and/or with his hat pulled over his face.

An autographed picture of Lionel Atwill (courtesy John Antosiewicz).

- *Tuesday, April 9, 1946*: Harrison Carroll, *Evening Herald Express*: "You will hear denials, but the story is absolutely true about Lionel Atwill being seriously ill."
- *Monday, April 22, 1946*: Lionel Atwill dies at 7:10 p.m. at his Pacific Palisades home, age 61. The Chapel of the Pines in Los Angeles cremates the body three days later.
- *Monday, August 5, 1946*: *Film Daily* reviews *Genius at Work,* almost a year after Atwill had starred in it with Wally Brown, Alan Carney and Bela Lugosi at RKO. "Comedy and melodrama are mixed for the entertainment of easily pleased audiences.... It's evident there is no genius at work here."

5

James Whale, Colin Clive, Lionel Atwill and the Riding Whip
The Real-Life Horror Story of the Censorship of Universal's *One More River*

"I wish to join the Legion of Decency ... I condemn absolutely these salacious motion pictures which, with other degrading agencies, are corrupting public morals and promoting a sex mania in our land...."
—Pledge of the Catholic Legion of Decency, 1933[1]

"Under Particular Applications of the Code, Section 2, Subdivision 4, it is stated, 'Sex perversion or any inference to it is forbidden....'"
—Joseph I. Breen, Production Code chief, censorship letter to Universal regarding **One More River**, April 10, 1934[2]

"I'm a sensualist, if you like—a bit of an experimentalist—what does it matter? Sex naturally wanders from the paths laid down for it by morality."
—Sir Gerald Corven (played by Colin Clive), dialogue cut from the original script of **One More River**

"He seems to be quite a beast!"
—Dinny (played by Jane Wyatt) regarding Sir Gerald Corven, cut from the original script of **One More River**

"Did he tell you he used his riding whip on me?"
—Clare Corven (played by Diana Wynyard), **One More River**

* * *

Thursday night, May 3, 1934.

The Pantages Theatre in Hollywood hosts the premiere of Universal's *The Black Cat*. Stars Boris Karloff and Bela Lugosi are present for the festivities, as is leading lady Jacqueline Wells, and all behold the film's wildly baroque climax: Karloff, a modern Satan, hanging on a rack, stripped to the waist, arms stretched to his side and overhead ... Lucifer as Christ symbol.

Then Lugosi, onscreen, skins him alive.

It's blasphemous imagery, the topper in a film that also parades such perversions as incest, necrophilia, and a Black Mass. Although the Production Code's Joseph Breen had warned Universal—and the film's irrepressibly subversive director, Edgar G. Ulmer—that the film may not "become too gruesome or revolting,"[3] *The Black Cat* had merrily slinked

116

In *The Black Cat*, Karloff's crucified Lucifer is skinned alive by Lugosi's avenging angel.

past the Code and will somehow elude the wrath of the Catholic Legion of Decency. Indeed, Breen had even sent Universal a letter of congratulations "for the manner in which your studio and director have handled this subject!"[4]

Friday, May 11, 1934. Eight days after *The Black Cat's* premiere, Universal begins shooting *One More River,* based on Pulitzer Prize winner John Galsworthy's final novel, and masterfully directed by James Whale.[5] Unlike *The Black Cat,* the film has no profane Christ symbol, sacrilegious rites, or dead women posed on display in vertical glass coffins. It does, however, have a sexual sadist, played by Colin "Frankenstein" Clive, whose riding whip— although never even glimpsed in the film—will become one of the most infamously nasty props of 1934 cinema.

Result: Constant Universal vs. the Production Code battles, cuts, retakes, revisions, censorship "mutilation" all over the world, and a "Condemned" rating by the Legion of Decency. For between the May release of *The Black Cat* and the August premiere of *One More River,* movie censorship changed profoundly in America, both via the "new machinery" of the Production Code and the 12,000,000 members of the Legion of Decency—Catholics, Protestants, and Jews.

Indeed, according to the Bishops, a Catholic who attended a 1934 showing of *One More River,* knowing of its "Condemned" rating, might damn his or her soul to Hell for all eternity.

* * *

It's no horror film, of course—despite its original loss-of-soul potential. Nevertheless, *One More River* holds fascination for disciples of Golden Age terror.

- It's a major release from Universal during the studio's Golden Age, personally produced by "Junior" Laemmle, who was responsible for *Dracula, Frankenstein,* and virtually all the studio's early 1930s horror classics.
- It's a "special" from James Whale, who directed this film six months after the premiere of his *The Invisible Man* and six months before he began shooting *Bride of Frankenstein.*
- It presents, as noted, Colin Clive in a particularly vile starring role (with a caterpillar mustache, no less).
- It features Lionel Atwill, still fresh from starring in such horrors as *Doctor X, Mystery of the Wax Museum* and *Murders in the Zoo,* as Clive's divorce lawyer, sporting a periwig and a smirk in the Old Bailey climax.
- It has a script from R.C. Sherriff (who'd provided the scenario for *The Invisible Man*), cinematography from John J. Mescall (who'd shot *The Black Cat* and would film *Bride of Frankenstein*), art direction by Charles Hall (who designed the sets for the Universal horror classics), and special effects by Universal's legendary John P. Fulton.
- It even has a cameo by James Whale himself—whom we both see *and* hear.

The late, great film historian William K. Everson hailed *One More River* in 1975 as "James Whale's masterpiece." It's long been tough to determine if it truly is. A faded, ghostly-looking print played cable TV in the early 1980s. The movie then virtually disappeared, now and then re-surfacing at film conventions. However, on January 27, 2012, Turner Classic Movies broadcast a crystal-clear print in prime time as part of "James Whale Night," providing the 1934 film a showcase amidst other Whale works—*Frankenstein* (1931), *The Invisible Man* (1933), and *The Great Garrick* (1937)—for widespread evaluation.

Is *One More River* truly the director's "masterpiece?" Does it outshine the other Whale films telecast that night? Does it actually surpass Whale's all-hallowed *Bride of Frankenstein,* or his personal "pride and joy," the 1936 *Show Boat?*

One thing is certain: The production of *One More River* was a melodrama, a pitched battle in which James Whale the artist and Joseph Breen the censor each saw himself as the hero. Whale was trying to save his film from castration-by-censorship. Breen was trying to save Hollywood from itself.

The result: a flawed, compromised, but truly fascinating movie.

* * *

Part I: The Blueprint

"Burn the mill!"
—The villagers, as they burn the Monster in the windmill
in **Frankenstein** (1931), directed by James Whale

1934. The Hollywood censorship crisis might have seemed a strange echo from the climax of *Frankenstein*. The censors, churches, and civic groups were the torch-bearing "villagers." Film immorality was "the Monster."

The outraged masses were hell-bent on the foul creature's immolation.

Monday, February 26: James Whale returns to Universal City after a 12-week vacation in England. He's brought back R.C. Sherriff's script for *A Trip to Mars,* envisioned as a new Karloff vehicle. It soon vanishes from Universal's schedule.

Thursday, March 1: The Hollywood Reporter notes that Universal is negotiating for John Galsworthy's *One More River* and will produce it as "a special." If the deal is consummated, the *Reporter* claims, Sherriff will write the script in London and Whale will direct it at Universal. Actually, Sherriff has been working on the script for some time; he'll complete it on March 6 and dispatch it to Whale.

The Galsworthy novel (published after the author's January 31, 1933, death at age 65) is about many things: British social class, England's archaic divorce laws, women's rights. As pruned down by Sherriff, the story still touches on these concepts, with this focus:

Lady Clare Corven returns to England from Ceylon after her sadistic husband, Sir Gerald Corven, has sexually ravaged her. On the ship she meets Tony Croom, a gentle young man who falls in love with the emotionally shattered woman. Clare returns to her faithful sister Dinny and her family at their country estate, "Charwell," takes a job as secretary to Dinny's politician boyfriend David Dornford, and begins a platonic relationship with the smitten Tony. Meanwhile, Gerald returns, wants Clare back—and she absolutely refuses reconciliation. Sensitive about his social and professional standing, he only agrees to a divorce if *he* divorces *her.*

Shortly afterwards, Gerald rapes her.

Corven also hires a detective to tag Clare and Tony, who spend a sexless night in Tony's car after his headlights fail. Divorce court follows in the Old Bailey, where Clare attests, "It is against my wish to talk about my married life" and proudly refuses to specify Gerald's sadism. Gerald takes the stand and swears that he and Clare have resumed "marital relations," but Clare, realizing that rape is not "marital relations," vehemently denies it. Refusing to present herself as a victim, painted by Gerald's lawyer as an adulteress, Clare "loses" the case and the divorce goes through. Now a free woman and grateful to Tony for having defended her honor in court, she invites Tony to her flat and offers herself to him. However, Tony, imagining the perverted Gerald making love to Clare, flees the flat. Clare is alone.

It's a downbeat tale, to be sure, with its sparks of sadism and a singularly unhappy ending. Universal keeps an option on *One More River,* rather than making a purchase, for a very good reason: The studio fears the Production Code Administration—and Joseph Breen—will absolutely reject it.

* * *

Part II: The Censor

> *"The pest hole that infects the entire country with*
> *its obscene and lascivious moving pictures, must be cleaned and disinfected."*
> —Bishop John J. Cantwell, addressing his fellow bishops,
> November 1933, in a speech ghost-written by Joseph I. Breen[6]

Joseph Ignatius Breen is the man in the eye of the censorship storm. He's a Catholic and a former public relations man, dispatched to the film colony by the Production Code founder, Will B. Hays. After getting an eyeful, Breen had written to a Catholic priest that "paganism"[7] was amok in Hollywood and that "drunkenness and debauchery are commonplace."

Joseph Breen, czar of the Production Code—hell-bent on saving Hollywood from itself.

"Sexual perversion is rampant," wrote the outraged Breen, "and any number of our directors and stars are perverts.... They are, probably, the scum of the earth."

Angry that the producers have long mocked and skirted the Production Code, Breen has been crusading with an almost Messianic zeal, fighting to empower the Code, firing up the church and civic groups to reform Hollywood, instrumental in the late 1933 birth of the Roman Catholic Legion of Decency. The Legion's big gun weapon: the "Condemned" rating. The Legion has already "Condemned" Paramount's *Design for Living* (in which Miriam Hopkins shared a Paris flat with Gary Cooper and Fredric March and slept with both, though not at the same time), 20th Century's *Blood Money* (in which Frances Dee played, in her own amused words, "a masochistic nymphomaniacal kleptomaniac"), and MGM's *Queen Christina* (for which the Detroit Council of Catholic Organizations lambasted Greta Garbo as a "perverted creature").[8]

As Universal tinkers with the *One More River* script, two MGM films run afoul of the Legion of Decency:

Friday, March 30: Metro releases *Riptide,* starring Norma Shearer as a woman who bears an out-of-wedlock baby—before the story starts. Although she more or less behaves throughout the film, the Legion condemns it. In Argentina, a 15-year-old named Maria Eva Duarte (later known as Eva Peron) sees *Riptide* and decides she wants to be glamorous like Norma Shearer. *Riptide*'s profit: $335,999.[9]

Friday, April 6: MGM releases *Men in White,* starring Clark Gable, Myrna Loy and Elizabeth Allan, based on Sidney Kingsley's Pulitzer Prize–winning play. In the film, intern Gable and British student nurse Allan have a one-night stand; she becomes pregnant, gets an (implied) back alley abortion, and dies from complications. Her face fills with terror as she dies, as if she fears she's going to Hell for what she's done. The Legion of Decency will condemn it nonetheless. *Men in White's* profit: $790,212.[10]

"Condemned" movies are making big money anyway—at least when they star attractions such as Shearer and Gable—but Joseph Breen is undeterred. The real battle is just heating up. Meanwhile, Universal has finally braved sending the *One More River* script for Breen's approval.

Tuesday, April 10: Junior Laemmle, James Whale, Joseph Breen, Geoffrey Shurlock (Production Code censor), and Harry Zehner (Universal's assistant general manager) all meet at Universal City to discuss the script of *One More River.* In the eyes of Breen, the focus of the movie is crystal clear: It's "a film based upon sexual perversion." Breen follows up that day with a detailed letter to Zehner, and the news isn't good:

> As we told you this morning, the story of this play, based as it is upon sadism, is, in our considered judgment, a definite violation of the Code.
>
> Under <u>Particular Applications</u> of the Code, Section 2, Subdivision 4, it is stated, "Sex perversion or any inference to it is forbidden...."
>
> In the face of this quite definite prohibition, we in this office have no choice in the matter, except to say quite definitely, that any story based upon sadism, or suggestive sadism, or inference of sadism, is, in its very nature, forbidden by the Code.
>
> We can see no objection to your developing the character of Corven as that of a brutal man who has beaten his wife and thus compelled her to leave him, but we cannot allow any suggestion, directly or indirectly, referring to sadism.

Breen also includes a long list of dialogue that will have to be "carefully rewritten" to remove "suggestion of this perversion." Among them:

- Clare's line about Corven: "He's a sadist."
- Dinny's line: "He seems to be quite a beast!"
- Corven's line: "It was only an experiment. Some women adore it."
- Clare's line to Corven: "There are some things that can't be done to me, and you've done them."
- Corven's line to Clare: "I won't stand for another man having you" and his ensuing line, "You're a stony little devil."
- Clare's response: "I wish I had been."
- Corven's line: "I'm a sensualist if you like—a bit of an experimentalist—what does it matter? Sex naturally wanders from the paths laid down for it by morality. But everything works itself out. If Clare comes back to me—she won't even remember what happened in two years' time."
- Dinny's comeback: "You mean by that time you'll be experimenting with someone else?"
- Clare's lines to her mother as she discusses Corven: "I can only say there's a beast in him. I know it doesn't show but there *is,* Mother."
- Breen demands that the italicized words in the general speech, "I wish *to God* that I could understand this business" should be deleted, and Clare's line, "Did he tell you he used his riding whip on me?" will have to go.

Among many other objections, Breen cites the script's suggestion that Mr. Chayne, Corven's weasel of a private detective, "goes into the men's toilet.... Audiences do not react favorably to any screen action hovering in or near to lavatories." Also: "Care should be exercised in shooting the scene of Clare in the bathroom '*in her underclothes*.' We respectfully recommend that you *do not* show Clare thus attired."

However, aside from the sadism, the lavatory, and Clare's underclothes, Breen's major objections include two highly controversial sequences. One is the episode in which the audience learns that Corven has raped his estranged wife in her flat:

> We suggest that you play down as much as you can the definite inference that Clare and Corven have indulged themselves in Clare's apartment, to prevent the scene and dialogue being mutilated by censor boards.

Also, there's the courtroom climax, its references to "adultery," Tony using the expression "My God," Brough (Corven's lawyer) using the word "lovers" and "hell," Brough's use of the words "marvelous opportunity" in regard to Tony and Clare having spent the night together in a car, and Corven's taking the stand to testify that he and Clare had resumed sexual relations. Ultimately, there's the judge's response—"You mean that the marital relationship between you was re-established?"

These were—as Breen warned—"dangerous lines from the standpoint of public censorship."

Finally, there was the ending, in which Clare, a free woman, offers herself to Tony:

> [G]reat care will have to exercised, both in dialogue and action, to prevent this scene from becoming a highly censorable one, subject to severe mutilation. Specific attention is called to Clare's line ... "We're going to dine in" ... there is likely to be a definite unfavorable audience reaction which may manifest itself in the box office returns of the picture.

Whale likely smirks as he reads the letter: The Code is traditionally all bark, no bite. Nevertheless, the growing censorship crisis dictates that he takes this seriously, and he assigns William Hurlburt to tone down Sherriff's scenario and create a new ending.

Tuesday, April 17: Harry Zehner writes to Breen, noting that the studio is trying to fix the script "the best way we can," adding: "[We] wish to pass along to you the information that Mr. Laemmle Jr. feels that you have been a little hard on us in this matter. Nevertheless, as mentioned before, we are trying to work this out...."

Friday, April 20: Confident of a passable script, Universal closes the deal to buy the rights for $15,000. As spring unfolds in Hollywood, James Whale's fancy focuses on casting *One More River.*

* * *

Part III: The Casting

> *We have actually secured for the picture the services of Diana Wynyard, Colin Clive,*
> *and Frank Lawton, to play the leading roles, and as they are all really gentle folks I*
> *think our problem is already solved.*
> —James Whale, letter to Joseph Breen, May 5, 1934

Saturday, April 21: *Variety* announces the casting of one of the key roles in *One More River.* Significantly, it's the villain: Colin Clive will play Sir Gerald Corven.[11]

The casting is inspired—Henry Frankenstein as sex sadist. Since *Frankenstein*, Whale had wanted Clive for *The Old Dark House* as the cynical hero Roger Penderel (eventually played by Melvyn Douglas, as Clive was busy filming *Lily Christine* in London); he'd also considered him for *The Invisible Man* (before Claude Rains officially claimed the title role). For Whale, Clive and R.C. Sherriff, *One More River* is a happy reunion: All three had won fame and glory via the 1929 play *Journey's End* and its 1930 film version, featuring Clive's harrowing performance as the tormented, alcoholic Captain Stanhope.

Clive, sadly tormented and alcoholic in real life, is back in Hollywood after starring on Broadway with Katharine Hepburn in the disastrous play *The Lake*. Whale is excellent at delicately handling the hypersensitive, stage fright-suffering actor, and Clive signs for *One More River* at four weeks at $1,500 per week— total, $6,000.

Wednesday, April 25: Although Universal originally envisioned Margaret Sullavan as *One More River*'s star, *Variety* reports today that the role of Lady Clare Corven goes to

James Whale, director of *One More River*—hell-bent in saving his film from censorship castration.

Diana Wynyard.[12] This is a coup for Universal: On the night of March 16, 1934, Fox's film version of Noël Coward's *Cavalcade* had won the Best Picture Oscar and Wynyard, *Cavalcade*'s star, had been one of the Academy's three Best Actress nominees. (She lost to Katharine Hepburn for RKO's *Morning Glory*.) Under contract to MGM, Diana had made her film debut with John, Ethel and Lionel Barrymore in *Rasputin and the Empress* (1932), in which her character Natasha also suffered a rape—ravaged by Lionel's black-bearded Rasputin.

Tall, doe-eyed, and very much in the "ethereal" style, Diana, borrowed from Metro, gets solo, above-the-title star billing on *One More River* and a fee the Universal front office computes at four weeks at $3,000 per week, plus four-and-a-third weeks at $1,500 per week— total, $18,500. The budget papers also assure the *soignée* Diana that she'll parade through *One More River* in no less than a remarkable 19 costumes, including "Traveling Outfit" ($275), two different pair of "Lounging Pajamas" ($140), and "Underwear-Negligee" ($75).

Also on April 25: *Variety* writes that Frank Lawton will co-star in *One More River* as Tony Croom.[13] Lawton's casting is curious: in *Cavalcade*, Diana Wynyard aged in the story from 1899 to 1933, and Lawton (two years older than Diana) had played her grown son Joey, who dies in World War I. Now, in *One More River*, Lawton will be playing the wooing lover to an actress who'd just played his mother.

Lawton will star as the grown David in MGM's *David Copperfield* (1935). He'll also play romantic leads in the Karloff and Lugosi *The Invisible Ray* and Tod Browning's *The Devil-Doll*, both released in 1936. He has an engaging style, but the cherubic actor will seem

Diana Wynyard. Tall, British, and ethereal. In her brief Hollywood career, she endured two (off-screen) rapes: by Lionel Barrymore in *Rasputin and the Empress* and by Colin Clive in *One More River.*

to shrink beside Ms. Wynyard; indeed, in what seems a Freudian typo, one of the many censorship notes will refer to "Tony" as "Tiny." Lawton, fresh from the Broadway play *The Wind and the Rain,* signs on for *One More River* at five weeks at $1,500 per week—total, $7,500—plus a $1,000 bonus.

Whale incisively selects the featured players. Of special note is Mrs. Patrick Campbell, who was the original Eliza Doolittle in *Pygmalion* in 1914; in fact, George Bernard Shaw wrote the role specifically for her. "Mrs. Pat" is a dyed and ample 69 as she signs for *One More River* as *bon mot*—loving Lady Mont, at $3,000 per week with a two-week guarantee. It's widely believed that the actress, famed for her wit, originated the oft-quoted quip that seems especially appropriate for *One More River*: "It doesn't matter what you do in the bedroom, as long as you don't do it in the street and frighten the horses."

Making her film debut as Dinny, Clare's loyal sister, is 23-year-old Jane Wyatt, fated for Frank Capra's *Lost Horizon* (1937) and TV's *Father Knows Best* (1954–1960). Her fee is $850 per week for six weeks and the budget sheet affords her 14 costume changes.

Reginald Denny, recently in John Ford's *The Lost Patrol* (as Brown, who delights in taunting Karloff's religious lunatic Sanders), takes the role of David Dornford, at $1,100 per week on a two-week guarantee. Alan Mowbray joins the show as Clare's lawyer, Mr. Forsyte, at $650 per week for two-and-a-half weeks; the venerable C. Aubrey Smith contracts to play Clare's father, "The General," at $1,250 per week for four weeks; Henry Stephenson portrays Clare's Uncle Lawrence, set for $1,500 per week for three-and-a-half weeks. And E.E. Clive—who was policeman Jaffers ("'E's all eaten away!'") in *The Invisible Man* and will play the Burgomaster ("Monster indeed!") in *Bride of Frankenstein*—signs for *One More River* as snoopy, disguise-loving private detective Chayne. His contracted fee: $500.

Perhaps the most curious casting is Lionel Atwill, who will play Mr. Brough, Sir Gerald's divorce lawyer. Atwill had star billing in *Doctor X, Mystery of the Wax Museum,* and *The Vampire Bat,* and major supporting cast billing in such films as Marlene Dietrich's *The Song of Songs*. Indeed, the actor is very vain on this point—he'll bail out of Fox's *George White's Scandals of 1934* over a billing issue—yet he accepts sixth billing in *One More River.* Possible reasons: (a) he wants to work with "Jimmy" Whale (and will act in two more films for him), (b) he loves courtroom intrigue (a real-life hobby is attending murder trials), and (c) he likes the nature of the show.

Indeed, for Atwill—surely one of the most sexually idiosyncratic actors of Golden Age Hollywood—a film about sadism is irresistible. He signs at $2,000 per week for two weeks. One imagines he might have done it for nothing.

All in all, the budget for *One More River* will come to $344,125—about $50,000 more than the final cost of *Frankenstein*. The schedule is 36 days. Whale's weekly salary at Universal is now $2,250. He's delighted with his players and with Hurlburt's adjustments to the script, including the new happy ending: Although Tony still flees from Clare's seduction, he returns the next morning for a promising finale.

Thursday, May 3: As previously noted, Universal's Karloff and Lugosi *The Black Cat* premieres at the Hollywood Pantages. For whatever mysterious reasons—maybe because it's a horror movie—the Legion of Decency looks the other way.

Friday, May 4: RKO releases *Finishing School,* in which a rebellious teenage girl (Frances Dee) sleeps with her boyfriend on Christmas Eve and becomes pregnant. The Legion of Decency condemns it.

Saturday, May 5: With the start of shooting *One More River* less than a week away, James Whale writes a cheery letter to Joseph Breen:

> I am sending you herewith a revised script of *One More River*. You will notice that I have taken out, not only the subject of "sadism," but all references to it, so that now any dialogue references to the subject can quite easily be taken as meaning extreme cruelty and ill-temper. The end of the picture I have completely remodeled and trust it will meet your requirements.

Whale's aforementioned paragraph about the stars Wynyard, Clive, and Lawton being "really gentle folk" probably fails to ease Breen's suspicions. Clive, after all, created Frankenstein's blasphemous Monster. Producer Junior Laemmle had sat on a jury that had unanimously passed *Queen Christina* after Breen had demanded MGM trim a scene in which Garbo languished on a bed. And as for Whale ... Breen knows his reputation rests on *Journey's End* (in which the hero is an alcoholic), *Waterloo Bridge* (in which the heroine is a streetwalker), and *Frankenstein* (in which the hero is a monster maker).

Also, while Breen is likely above this, one wonders if he's making *One More River* a personal issue. Very aware of the Hollywood gossip, he probably knows that Colin Clive is an alcoholic ("Drunkenness and debauchery are commonplace") ... he's also likely aware that Whale lives openly with producer David Lewis ("...any number of our directors and stars are perverts")....

Tuesday, May 8: Breen, having reviewed the revised script, writes to Harry Zehner and reluctantly gives *One More River* the green light:

> However, particularly with regard to the element of sadism, we should like to say that our final judgment will depend pretty much on the manner in which the picture is shot. Sadism or any possible inference of it is a dangerous subject from a Code standpoint, and we urge you again to exercise great care to keep it absolutely free from any possibility of offense.

Thursday, May 10: Zehner writes to Breen, advising him that he's instructed Whale that, "wherever there is a likelihood of the dialogue or action implying sadism, he will shoot protection shots to be inserted in the finished picture." Jimmy Whale never intends to do any such thing. In fact, the director is defiantly determined to ignore virtually all of Breen's original objections, both major and minor, and shoot his movie precisely as he sees fit.

Friday, May 11: *One More River* begins filming.

* * *

Part III: The Shooting

> I thought *One More River* was a very good picture, but they shouldn't have paired Frank Lawton and Diana Wynyard because she looked like she could have been his mother.... She was never an ingénue, she was always a tall, wonderful-looking woman. And Frankie was tiny! So there wasn't any romance, there wasn't any tension. Frankie Lawton could be very good, but in *One More River* he was so wimpy—and Colin Clive was so much more attractive! He was strong and masculine, a macho kind of guy.
>
> —Jane Wyatt, "Dinny" in **One More River,**
> interview with Tom Weaver, *Starlog* magazine, 1990

The shoot of *One More River* will be remarkable for a variety of reasons.

First of all, there's Diana Wynyard. On a good day, the towering, wraith-like actress, with her strangely intense eyes, might have played a Botticelli angel; on a bad day, she might have been a very scary *Bride of Frankenstein*. She's alternately lovely and gawky in *One More River,* despite Whale having John J. Mescall photograph her almost reverently, nearly always capturing her preferred right profile. (Rarely in the film will we see her less-chiseled left side.)

She's uncompromising in her craft. The most famous story about Wynyard comes from

Oddly cast lovers: Diana Wynyard and Frank Lawton in *One More River*. Wynyard had played Lawton's mother in *Cavalcade*, Best Picture Academy Award winner of 1933.

the late 1940s, when she was playing the great Shakespearean ladies in England. Preparing to portray Lady Macbeth, Diana did her research and announced that sleepwalkers usually walked with their eyes closed—hence, she would play Lady Macbeth's famous sleepwalking scene just this way. No warning could change her mind. Result: She walked off the stage during a performance and fell fifteen feet.

By the way: She climbed back on stage and finished the performance. Diana's as persnickety as Whale, and they will clash during *One More River.*

Whale has more fun with Mrs. Patrick Campbell. The Great Lady minces through *One More River* rather like Oscar Wilde in drag, merrily tossing off lines such as "Oh! I have a pain ... I don't know whether it's flatulence or the hand of God." Whale allows her to bring her Pekingese "Moonbeam" to the set daily and indulges her, even as she spoofs Lady Macbeth, taking a candle upstairs to her bedroom, reciting, "What's done, cannot be undone... To bed... To bed...!"

Diana Wynyard has a star cottage on the Universal lot ... her co-stars have their cottages and bungalows too. Frank Lawton believes a black cat is good luck, received one as a gift when he arrived in Hollywood, and brings the cat along to the studio. Lawton's natural charm helps in his romantic scenes with his leading lady; still, a cynical viewer might surmise that Lawton's Tony never presses for intimacy with Wynyard's Clare because he knows very well she could flatten him.

Whale has created a Hollywood "England" that is both fanciful and realistic—an interior hall with a wall of diamond-paned windows ... a little country village under Universal's back lot mountain with a war memorial cross and a duck pond ... a restaurant orchestra that boisterously plays "The Daring Young Man on the Flying Trapeze" ... an English garden with a goat that mugs for the camera, rather like the owl will mug in Whale's *Bride of Frankenstein*. For the many British players in the film, the atmosphere Whale so charmingly captures likely gives them a sense of nostalgia—as do the daily tea breaks.

As noted, Jane Wyatt made her film debut in *One More River*. As she told Tom Weaver:

> I did have the jitters, I'm sure, but everybody was very helpful. James Whale was the most charming man—he wasn't a warm man, he was kind of austere. But he was great with Mrs. Patrick Campbell, who did have the jitters—she *really* had the jitters! He was wonderful with her, and he did beautiful things with the picture—he was a real artist. The interiors of the houses were just beautiful because they spent hours lighting them and getting the flowers just right.

Incidentally, Wyatt also well-remembered *One More River* due to legendary makeup artist Jack P. Pierce:

> I went into makeup at Universal for the first time, and the makeup man was little Jack Pierce, who was quite celebrated (which I didn't know at the time).... And he started pulling out all my eyebrows! I cried out, "Stop! Stop! I don't want you to pull out my eyebrows!" He said, "Listen, little girl: I have made up the greatest. Don't you tell Jack Pierce what to do. Look!" And he waved his arm toward all the pictures he had up on the wall. Well, they were not glamour pictures, they were Boris Karloff and Bela Lugosi and I don't know who else [*laughs*]! He was a wonderful little guy and I got to be very, very fond of him.

As Whale delights in capturing the British atmosphere, he perhaps revels in the film's dark sensuality even more so. Surely one of Whale's great joys on *One More River* is directing Colin Clive again, especially in so strikingly perverse a role. Although Breen had objected to the word "beast," it's truly a beast that Clive evokes as Whale provides him a deluxe, theatrically gothic introduction.

The scene is a *One More River* highlight. Wynyard wears a beautiful dark evening gown with a plunging neckline and a bare back. She's quite alluring and seems to be proudly aware of it—until she learns that Clive's Corven is in the house. Suddenly, almost child-like, she cowers, retreating and standing behind a chair. The obese butler (Robert Greig) announces, "Sir Gerald Corven," sinister music softly plays, the door opens ... and Clive enters in a tuxedo and mustache for three increasingly intense close-ups—just as Whale had introduced Karloff's Monster in *Frankenstein* and Rains' bandaged Jack Griffin in *The Invisible Man*. Colin's Sir Gerald suavely strolls in, poses for another close-up:

> *Clare*: What do you want?
> *Corven*: You!
> *Clare*: You can't have me.
> *Corven*: Don't be absurd!

He attacks, grabbing her, bending her back, trying to kiss her. Audiences who heard *One More River* had rape as a subplot probably expected to see one now. However, Clare escapes his arms, flees, and the scene continues:

> *Corven*: Some women like rough handling!
> *Clare*: You're a beast!

Notice the "beast" line that Breen had protested remained, as originally filmed. So did this dialogue, which had been cited for elimination:

Starlet Jane Wyatt (left) with Mrs. Patrick Campbell, the original Eliza Doolittle of *Pygmalion,* in *One More River.*

Corven: You're a stony little devil.
Clare: I wish I had been.

The scene plays with mounting tension, both players excellent:

Clare: Can't you understand? You killed all the feeling that I've ever had for you. I'll never come back.
Corven: And I say you will!

Again, the sadist attacks, more viciously than before, bending her back, nearly yanking off her dress and almost exposing her left breast, passionately kissing her. Then he laughs wickedly, proceeds to leave the room, and pauses at the door.

"*Au revoir,*" the villain says, and exits.

As directed by Whale and played by Clive, there's little doubt that Sir Gerald Corven is not only a sadist—he also belongs in a cage.

Indeed Whale, despite "playing nice" with Joseph Breen, is determined to make *One More River* all he originally intended it to be. Breen has asked Whale to cut Corven's dialogue in which he presents himself as rather a Jekyll and Hyde personality. Yet, as Corven rides with Dinny in her car, after he discovers Clare's apartment, he says: "What I want you to understand is that I'm two men. One, and the one that matters, has his work to do and means to do it. And the other man? Well, the less said about him, the better."

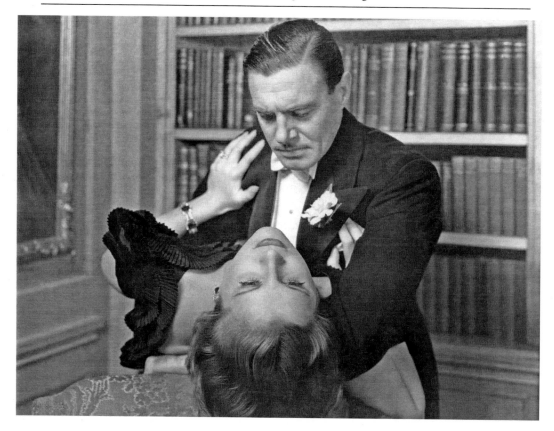

The beast about to strike: Sex sadist Colin Clive attacks estranged wife Diana Wynyard in *One More River*.

Whale defies Breen right down the line. Indeed, Chayne enters a café men's room (*Messieurs,* reads the door) although the inference is that he went in not to heed nature's call, but to put on a mustache as a disguise. Also, Whale shows Clare in the bathroom in her underwear—Wynyard standing in the loo, wearing a slip, her best side toward the camera.

This brings us to the Battle of the Brassiere. Diana shows up one day on the *One More River* stage and announces she's playing a scene without a bra. Whale, who seems to have a keen sensitivity regarding lingerie—he'll later make Anne Darling, the shepherdess in *Bride of Frankenstein,* change her "white, lacy panties" to "black, lacy panties," even though the panties never show—gets very angry.[14] In fact, for a time, he shuts down the set as he and Diana fight it out. As Jane Wyatt told James Curtis in his book *James Whale: A New World of Gods and Monsters,* "I don't remember if he ever got her into a bra...."[15]

Nevertheless, it's a happy shoot, Whale enjoying his story, actors, atmosphere and defiance. In fact, he's in such high spirits that, for the one and only time in his film career, he plays a cameo. At a political rally, we see Whale on profile in dark overcoat and hat; he removes the hat, turns his back to the camera, and yells, "Now, let's have a big cheer for David Dornford, MP for Condaford. Hip-hip...!"

And the crowd cheers, "Hooray!"

The film's climax, the divorce in the Old Bailey, is brilliant. The towering courtroom set with its high ceiling and diamond-paned window (diamond-paned window seems a motif in *One More River*) has almost an ecclesiastical effect, including the lofty perch of the God-like Judge (superbly played by Gilbert Emery) in his black robe and white periwig. Wynyard, striking an I-Am-Woman-Hear-Me-Roar pose, 1934 style, clearly relishes this episode in the witness box, her hat cocked over her left eye, resplendent in her furs, standing up to the judge and even her own lawyer Mr. Forsythe (Alan Mowbray).

Best of all, she bites back at Sir Gerald's lawyer, Mr. Brough—played with racy relish by Lionel Atwill. Posing, preening, raising sexual insinuation to high art, Atwill enjoys a *One More River* romp, providing a crackling, between-the-lines carnality. At one point he notes that, on the ship home, Tony visited Clare's room late one night and stayed for 20 minutes. Clare claims she merely showed Tony pictures:

Brough: Do you mean to say that nothing else whatever took place between you during those 20 minutes?
Clare: Nothing that could give you satisfaction!
Brough: How were you dressed?
Clare: I'm sorry to have to inform you that I was fully dressed.
Brough: Me Lord ... may I ask to be protected from these sarcasms?

As Colin Clive's "Gerry" takes the stand and claims he and Clare had resumed sexual relations, *One More River* takes on a perverse aura rare even in the rawest pre–Code movies. Again, this was in open defiance of Breen and the Production Code's warning. The scene is destined to haunt both audiences and James Whale—although in very different ways.

Meanwhile, as *One More River* continues, there have been ominous headlines:

Friday, June 8: Cardinal Dougherty of Philadelphia announces that his diocese will boycott all movies, calling them "perhaps the greatest menace to faith and morals today."[16]

Monday, June 18: "50,000 AT MEETING VOTE FILM BOYCOTT; Mass Gathering of Catholics at Cleveland Take Pledge of Legion of Decency," headlines the *New York Times.*

Friday, June 22: The Federation Council of the Churches of Christ in America recommends that Protestants join and support the Catholic Legion of Decency. Meanwhile, the Central Conference of American Rabbis beseeches Jews to back "the Catholic crusade."

Censorship has become a firestorm across America. The religious and civic groups, in their mania to "clean up" the movies, are threatening to boycott and destroy the entire film industry.

Tuesday, July 3: Whale completes *One More River.* The film is ten days over schedule. Before Breen and the revising Production Code can review it, very significant happenings develop with major repercussions for Hollywood in general and *One More River* in particular.

* * *

Part IV. The Retakes

Were the mothers of America aroused to the necessity of protecting their children from the moral defilement that lurks in every depraved motion picture, they would shun the place that presents it as they would avoid with horror a pesthouse.
—Letter from Cardinal Hayes, read at all Masses
in the New York diocese, Sunday, July 15, 1934[17]

Saturday, July 7: "BREEN MADE UMPIRE FOR FILM MORALS—To Put Official Stamp on Clean Pictures—Others To Be Banned," reads a Page One Headline of the *New York Times.* A new, empowered Production Code Administration is about to be re-born.

Monday, July 16: The new Production Code Administration now exists, and Breen begins his newly empowered post by viewing *One More River* again. He's already watched it at least twice.

Tuesday, July 17: The verdict comes down for *One More River*: Breen is demanding *over 30 cuts*. Although Whale had eliminated some of the more "colorful" dialogue (e.g., Corven's "I'm a sensualist..."), most of what Breen had originally objected to is in the movie.

Now Jimmy Whale must pay the price for his defiance. Otherwise, there will be no release certificate—and Universal will be stuck with a $350,000 movie that nobody can see.

One More River feverishly begins daily retakes. On July 21 *Variety* runs this headline: "U Is Disinfecting *1 More River.*"

Whale has to round up actors, revisit sets, and make all necessary changes in time to meet the deadline of a July 27 preview in Santa Barbara. Sometimes he'll shoot new scenes and speeches. For example, on the train to the country, Dinny has these new lines supposedly suggesting Gerald's "cruelty" rather than "sadism": "Clare, in your last letter you told me that Corven beat you—struck you across the face with the handle of his riding crop whip and kicked you. Is that true?"

Meanwhile, Clare's cryptic line about her husband's cruelties—"They're *that* kind"— came out, and she responded to Dinny with this new speech:

> But how? It's just my word against his. You see, my husband's attentions are without witnesses. Besides, how could I make a public show of that sort of thing? I couldn't. A plain divorce causes enough attention—this would be meat for a nine days' wonder. I can't even speak of it to anyone but you.

In other cases, Whale has to make adjustments for a single word. As Dinny strolled in the garden with Lady Mont, she said of Corven, "He seems to be quite a beast!" Whale loops in, "He seems to be quite a cad!" (Jane Wyatt's lips form "beast," although we hear "cad.") Clare's line to Corven, "You're a beast," becomes, "You're a brute" (in what looks like a retake). Also, in a scene between Clare and her mother, Clare said of Gerald, "I can only say there's a beast in him," and her mother replied, "You're sure it's not just the beast that's in nearly all men?" Once again, during the retake period, the dreaded "beast" becomes the acceptable "brute."

As for the rape scene, a memo from Maurice Pivar of Universal's editorial department notes:

> In the sequence where Corven comes to Clare's house in the Mews: Eliminate the cut of Tony standing outside and looking up. Also eliminate the close shot of the bed with the blanket turned up. As well as the pan shot of the darkened window as Dinny looks up at it.

Courtroom changes abound. Atwill as Brough had said, "He had *marvelous control*, hadn't he?—this young man who was in love with you." A looped line changes it to, "He *had beautiful* manners, hadn't he...?" Brough had also asked Tony, "You seriously expect us to believe that *after five months of longing*, you took no advantage *of that opportunity* but just went to sleep?"; a retake eliminated the italicized words. And so it goes.

In some cases, Whale refuses to make a change. Breen wants to cut Mrs. Patrick Campbell's "I don't know whether its flatulence or the hand of God"; Whale considers changing

The dramatic courtroom climax of *One More River*, as masterfully captured by James Whale: Diana Wynyard stands in the box. Gilbert Emery plays the judge.

"God" to "fate," but leaves it as originally shot. Breen wants to cut Clive's "Some women like rough handling"; Whale won't axe it. Nor will he cut Clare's line to her father, "Did he tell you he used his riding whip on me?" And as for the new ending ... Breen marks for excision Wynyard's lines, "You don't know how sorry I was this morning that I sent you away last night" and "...ashamed of myself for last night." Whale, again, refuses.

Finally, Whale absolutely will not eliminate what Breen had originally and most vociferously protested: the judge's line, "You mean that the marital relationship between you was re-established?" and Corven's reply, "Yes, my Lord." This had been among Breen's original, most firmly worded pre-shooting complaints, yet here they are in the rough print ... along with so many other previously registered objections.

Friday, July 27: It's the date of the preview. Breen and his staff attend a projection room showing of *One More River*. Breen, meeting Whale and company considerably more than half-way, writes later that day:

> Because, in our judgment, the changes and deletions made in the film get away definitely both from the subject of sadism as well as the frankness of the dialogue, it is our considered judgment now that the picture is in conformity with the Code, and we have so certified it.

Whale, Junior Laemmle, R. C. Sherriff and other Universal figureheads take the patched-together print of certified production #122 to Santa Barbara for the preview that night. Perhaps not surprisingly, the film, after its drastic surgery, seems to drag.

Saturday, July 28: Variety, reporting Breen's eleventh-hour approval of Whale's film, snidely headlines on page 1: "*One More River* Is Breenexed."

Monday, July 30: Variety notes that Junior Laemmle, Whale, and Sherriff "remained in Santa Barbara over the weekend for story conferences, following preview of *One More River* there Friday night." Whale decides to cut for pacing.

Tuesday, July 31: Universal previews the tightened *One More River* at the Ritz Theatre in Los Angeles. "This is strictly a class picture," critiques *Variety* the next day. "Acting and direction are superb."

Thursday, August 2: Harry Zehner writes to Breen, noting cuts made since the Santa Barbara preview: a village street sequence where Dornford makes a speech about English electors; a London club episode where Tony meets Sir Lawrence Mont and tells him he has met his niece Clare; a scene in which Dinny and Clare stroll with walking sticks, with dialogue about "the three p's"—pigs, poultry and potatoes; lots of dialogue while Tony and Clare sit in the car, including Clare's "There's never a moon when you want one"; a sequence where Clare, Dinny, Tony, the General, and Uncle Lawrence call on her lawyer, Mr. Forsyte, at his office; a scene with Dinny and Dornford on horseback; and other dialogue and pieces of scenes that slowed the story. Also, the whole episode of Clare and her mother talking about Corven being a "beast" (and later a "brute") has landed on the cutting room floor.

Zehner makes note that Whale has replaced Corven's line in the witness box, "We were husband and wife," with Corven saying, "My wife and I were reunited." Considering the angle of the shot of Corven in the witness box, Whale could have filmed this retake with only Clive present. Zehner also thanks Breen for his "constructive and helpful cooperation throughout."

Friday, August 3: Breen writes to the Honorable Will B. Hays in New York City, "*One More River* (Universal). We spent an immense amount of time with the studio in cleaning this up.... The element of sadism has, we believe, been satisfactorily eliminated, and some of the other questionable elements have been toned down...."

Meanwhile, the last-minute cutting has caused the film to miss its originally set August 2, 1934, premiere at the Hollywood Pantages Theatre. Replacing it is a double bill: Fox's *She Learned About Sailors,* starring Alice Faye and Lew Ayres, and MGM's *Murder in the Private Car,* starring Charlie Ruggles and Una Merkel (with Ray "Crash" Corrigan as "Naba the Gorilla").

Meanwhile, *One More River* has gone more than $20,000 over budget. The final negative cost: $366,842.24.

* * *

Part V. The Release, the Critics, the Censors and the Legion of Decency

> The Galsworthy story might easily have been made a cheap, daring and tawdry piece of sensationalism, but the discreet Messrs. R.C. Sherriff and James Whale ... never ceased to be rationalists, intent upon rendering an intensely human narrative humanly, sympathetically, and believably.
>
> —Nelson B. Bell, reviewing ***One More River*** in
> *The Washington Post,* August 12, 1934

Monday, August 6: *One More River* opens at Baltimore's Keith's Theatre. *The Baltimore Sun* critic Donald Kirkley praises the film as "one of the finest feathers in Junior Laemmle's cap. It is a suave and superior photodrama, steeped in English atmosphere, and following the best tradition of the stage ... *One More River* is one more tribute to the growth of the cinematic art in this country."

Thursday, August 9: After a preview the previous night, *One More River* opens at the Hollywood Pantages. Curiously, the same night, Colin Clive stars at the Hollywood Playhouse in a revival of *Journey's End*, directed by E.E. Clive (who also appears in the play as the cook, Mason). On August 10, Edwin Martin writes in his "Cinemania" column in the *Hollywood Citizen News*:

> The Boulevard at 11:30 p.m. ... breathing in gulps of fresh air after going over to see Colin Clive and an excellent company enact *Journey's End* ... and James Whale kept busy ... running back and forth from the Playhouse to the Pantages ... he was the original director of *Journey's End*, and is very interested in the production ... but he is also director of *One More River* at the Pantages ... he'd see one show for five minutes and then sneak across and see how the other was doing ... and both were doing splendidly, thank you, he said.

Elizabeth Yeaman of the *Hollywood Citizen News* catches both the press preview of *One More River* and the opening night of *Journey's End*. She reviews both, hailing Clive as "superb" in the play revival, and writing of *One More River*:

A trio you love to hate: Lionel Atwill as Sir Gerald's sinuous lawyer (standing, in robe); Colin Clive as Sir Gerald (seated, middle); and (at top) E.E. Clive as Sir Gerald's snoopy private detective, Mr. Chayne.

The Pantages Theatre may well be proud to show *One More River*.... Although there are suggestions of sadism, the picture is not morbid. It is, primarily, a beautiful and idealistic love story.... Director James Whale may stand as an authority on subtlety and artistic direction. He has handled *One More River* beautifully, giving the picture sincere, wholesome understanding and great artistry.

Also on August 9, *One More River* opens at New York City's Radio City Music Hall. *New York Times* film critic Mordaunt Hall will devote most of his Sunday column to it, hailing Whale and Sherriff as "that brilliant team" and the film as "a most stirring and impressive production."

One More River takes in $86,000 in its first week at Radio City Music Hall,[18] where the recent high had been *Little Women* ($109,000) and the low *Ann Carver's Profession* ($44,938). The *New York Times* calls this "unusually good business."

Meanwhile, the film reaps critical praise. Critic Mae Tinee (whose pen name was clearly designed to suggest "matinee") of the *Chicago Tribune* calls *One More River* "adult entertainment of worth," and offers an interesting aside: "Colin Clive rather gives you heartache. You hate to see him cast as the cad Sir Gerald is. Such a likable chap—and such a grand actor! Will you EVER forget him in *Journey's End*?"[19]

Friday, August 17: It appears that *One More River,* based on its early reviews and box office, will be a triumph. However, on this date, Joseph Breen writes to Junior Laemmle, with devastating news:

> I suppose you know that the Legion of Decency has condemned this picture as unsuitable for the Catholic patronage. This is the first picture passed under the recently set-up machinery to be so condemned. I suppose it is the divorce angle which brings down the condemnation of the Catholics; and I suppose that in the face of their very definite viewpoint on the subject of divorce, we are helpless under the circumstances.

This is disastrous. The national censorship storm is at its most violent and *One More River,* without a major box office star, will surely suffer the blow at the box office. Breen also attaches to his letter to Laemmle a list of cuts demanded by the State of Ohio Censorship Committee:

- 4th Reel: Where Dinny comes to Clare's apartment, eliminate underlined words in speech by Clare—"Hello, Dinny—*was it you who came before*?"
- Eliminate dialog—Dinny—"Yes, were you in?"
- Clare—"Sorry I couldn't let you in."
- Eliminate all scenes showing disarranged bed and of Clare and Dinny looking at it.
- Also eliminate italicized words in speech by Clare—"*Yes.* Jerry's been here. *He's only been gone ten minutes.*"
- 8th Reel: Eliminate italicized word in speech by Judge—"You mean that the *marital* relationship between you was re-established?"
- Eliminate italicized word in speech by Attorney—"Is it true that on the occasion of which your husband has just spoken, *marital* relationship was re-established between you?"

Breen makes his point with Junior politely but with I-told-you-so exasperation, regarding the "marital relationship" line:

> You will remember that we talked at considerable length, both with you and with Mr. Whale, about the danger from the censorship standpoint ... there is a very great danger involved in this

kind of dialogue. I think you will recall that I warned you that this speech was likely to be deleted by censor boards. I am sorry that it was, because it is going to make your picture a bit difficult to understand.

I am strongly of the mind that we ought to make the corrections here in Hollywood, and not risk the mutilation of so fine a picture as this by censor boards....

This is a radical suggestion, as it would require Universal to delay any further release and shoot more retakes. Junior rejects Breen's idea.

One More River continues in distribution. Censorship varies by state. Kansas cuts the view of the bed and Clare's line, "Yes—he was here." Pennsylvania cuts "all views whatsoever in which partly opened or partly uncovered bed or couch is seen," as well as Clare's line, "I pay my debts," and Tony's response, "*Debts*—Clare!" Massachusetts cut the infamous "marital relationship" lines, the scene showing the bed, and references to the word "adultery." It also scissors "the scenes showing Clare in obvious positions on couch." (As was the custom in Massachusetts, the cut version was "for Sunday showing only.")

Great Britain makes one cut: "Is it true that marital relationship between you was re-established?" Australia takes a big bite out of the courtroom scene, eliminating the entire sequence with the "marital relations" line. The film reaches Japan in late 1935, and the censor pounces—scissoring Sir Gerald kissing Clare, the visible bed in the boudoir, most of the night Clare and Tony spent in the car, Gerald's "My wife and I were reunited," both references to "marital relationship," Tony's imaginary vision of Clare and Gerald kissing, the close-up of Clare seductive on the divan, her line "I pay my debts"...

August 22: The Hollywood Reporter notes that Universal has picked up James Whale's option and given him a new, year-long contract.

Meanwhile, the big-city crowds like *One More River,* and although small town patronage is less enthusiastic, the film finds admirers there too. The manager of the Midway Theatre in Protection, Kansas, writes in the "What the Picture Did for Me" column in *Motion Picture Herald* (December 22, 1934): "We were afraid of this one because it was rated as a high-class picture. Everyone who saw it here went for it in a big way. We feel that the picture is good enough for any man's town. The box office was average."

Unfortunately, no financial figures are available regarding the box office profit or loss for *One More River.* The film fails to live up to Universal's expectations in London and eventually sinks into basic oblivion ... a relic from the Laemmle Universal era, when Junior Laemmle offered audiences classic monsters and films based on war carnage (*All Quiet on the Western Front*), prostitution (*Back Street*), race relations (*Imitation of Life*), and, in *One More River*'s case (and Joseph Breen's words), "sexual perversion."

The film becomes basically a sacrifice on the altar of censorship. Of course, Breen eventually mellows, the Production Code gradually relaxes, and times certainly change. On March 25, 1954, as Breen retires, the Academy awards him a special Oscar "for his conscientious, open-minded, and dignified management of the Motion Picture Production Code." As Mark Vieira incisively notes in his book *Sin in Soft Focus,* the industry would have provided Breen no such honor had he been merely a self-righteous fool.[20]

Still, one wonders what James Whale—long retired from films in 1954, basically forgotten in Hollywood at that time, and having never rated an Oscar or Academy nomination—thought of Breen's honor.

* * *

Part VI. The Film Today

One More River is quite possibly (and, in my view, almost certainly) James Whale's masterpiece. It is less known than many ... possibly less "entertaining" than his horror films ... [but] it represents the fullest flowering of Whale's unique, richly theatrical yet wholly cinematic style.

—William K. Everson, "Rediscovery," *Films in Review,* June-July 1975

So ... was Professor Everson correct in proclaiming *One More River* "Whale's masterpiece?"

It's all, of course, in the beholder's eye. However, Whale was at his most brilliant presenting lost souls ... Colin Clive's Stanhope in *Journey's End,* Mae Clarke's Myra in *Waterloo Bridge,* Claude Rains' Invisible Man ... and, of course, Karloff's lost "non-existing" soul in *Frankenstein* and *Bride of Frankenstein.* I'd give the "masterpiece" prize to *Bride of Frankenstein,* in which Whale prodigally unleashes Karloff's Monster and Elsa Lanchester's Bride, allowing his beloved monsters a lightning storm of emotions, climaxing the fantasy with Elsa's vainglorious hiss and Boris' heartbreaking tear.

One More River, by comparison, is a curio. After seeing how humanly, sympathetically, and even passionately Whale presents his monsters, here he is, dramatizing Galsworthy, trying to pinpoint the torment in characters whose behavior, in most cases, seems almost a *paean* to Victorian restraint. Whale has to capture the anguish of Clare Corven in a glance ... the way Diana Wynyard looks out her open window at the darkness of the summer night; she can't scream or hiss to make her bond with the viewer. Just so, Sir Gerald Corven, although coming close to molesting his wife onscreen, never fully unleashes "the beast" within; Colin Clive hints at it while taking his oath in court, saying "So help me God" with what seems both an agnostic contempt and a deep fear—as if frightened the Almighty, if He's really up there, might strike him dead for the perverse lie he's both living and telling.

It's a brilliantly polished, splendidly acted, beautifully photographed, and, of course, superbly atmospheric film.

Alas, real people date more noticeably than do monsters, at least in Whale's films, and *One More River* inevitably strikes many modern viewers as almost outrageously quaint. Some scenes play almost like a Carol Burnett skit mocking British propriety, so much so that one wonders if Whale slyly intended the satire. Case in point: the scene in which Dinny visits Clare and learns that Corven has raped her. First we see Corven accost Clare outside at her doorway and order her to go with him up to her flat. Then we see Dinny with her family, worried because Clare is late for dinner. Then Dinny takes a taxi to Clare's flat and looks up at the dark window. Then she goes to Corven's hotel and learns that he is out. Then she goes *back* to her family and learns that Clare *still* hasn't arrived. They express concern. Then Dinny goes *back* to Clare's flat, where Clare finally admits her.

Based on the time frame established—and Clare telling Dinny that Corven had left only ten minutes ago—Corven has presumably been ravaging Clare for hours. Nevertheless, the following post-rape conversation follows:

Clare: Have a cup of tea. I just made it.
Dinny: I'll say you had a headache.
Clare (with sugar): Two lumps?
Dinny: That's right.

Seduction! Diana Wynyard, her favored profile toward the camera, tempts a shocked Frank Lawton in the censor-defying finale of *One More River*.

Come the courtroom scene, and the film rips into life, largely due to Wynyard's pride, Clive's vileness, Atwill's bombast, and Whale's virtuoso direction, with a riotous variety of pans and close-ups. Yet here again, the Galsworthy story might exasperate a modern audience. Clare can easily sway the jury by revealing that "Gerry" has raped her—particularly after his shameful testimony that they've resumed "marital relations"—but she won't do so; it's simply against her dignity. Of course, one could hardly have expected the very laced-up Diana Wynyard to rip into an impromptu striptease while on the stand, revealing to the Old Bailey assemblage her riding whip welts; still, *One More River* cries out for a finale that doesn't let the kinky sadist villain off the hook, and provides Clare with more than her vanity, feminist pride, and a nebulously happy future with Tony. Indeed, a 21st century audience member might well wish that Clare had gone on a vengeance spree à la *The Girl with the Dragon Tattoo* and visited Corven one night with her taser, ligatures, and tattoo needle!

Yet again, the story is Galsworthy's, the people are the British upper middle class of the early 1930s, and this is what Whale provides—and often illuminates. Meanwhile, the film itself serves as a time machine, not just back to a bygone England but also the *very* bygone, almost other-worldly Hollywood of the summer of 1934.

And what remarkable ghosts they are.

Diana Wynyard, a sleek wolfhound of an actress, in what will be her final U.S. feature film ... fated to star unforgettably in the original British-made *Gaslight* (1940), largely forsaking movies ("I don't really want to be a film star") to embrace the London classical stage.

Colin Clive, Hollywood's Frankenstein, *One More River*'s "beast" (even if we never hear the word spoken), six months away from creating a Bride for his Monster, and only three summers away from his tragically early death. Lionel Atwill, representing a sex pervert in court, eight years away from a real-life court trial in which *he* was the sex pervert, branded as such, and facing disgrace the fictional Sir Gerald Corven never suffered.

And finally, there's James Whale at the peak of his power, all Universal City at his disposal, so delighting in his movie that he makes his one and only cameo. The film, as are so many fine films, is very much the personality of its director, and Whale himself played hard at seeming the British gentleman who showed little emotion—a luxury reserved for his monsters. For example, Whale refused to be a pallbearer at Colin Clive's funeral (Alan Mowbray, of *One More River,* did serve as a pallbearer); the director hated wakes, but also likely preferred to avoid the rampant emotion of a Hollywood funeral, even for so close and notable a friend.

It's sad to think that Whale, so very private a man, would die a suicide, drowning himself in his Pacific Palisades pool May 29, 1957, leaving a note to "All I love," and emotionally writing of his fear of illness and insanity. Not very "stiff-upper-lip British," perhaps ... but totally human, touchingly tragic, and finally brought to light in James Curtis' original *James Whale* book in 1982.

Clare Corven, had she truly existed, would surely have mourned so brilliant a man ... even if she would likely have favored the suicide note's perpetual suppression.

*   *   *

January 2, 1935: James Whale begins shooting his next film, *Bride of Frankenstein,* at Universal City. He lets his Swiftian nature run amok and again battles with Joseph Breen, who once more threatens to withhold a release certificate. Yet *Bride of Frankenstein,* even after pruning, emerges with Whale's humor and emotions unleashed—and even dares to present Karloff's Monster, virtually crucified by the villagers on a tall pole in the forest, as a bizarre, soulless Christ symbol.

Yet *Bride of Frankenstein* is, after all, a horror film ... and this time, as far as the Legion of Decency is concerned, Jimmy Whale gets away with it.

One More River

Studio, Universal. Producer, Carl Laemmle, Jr. Director, James Whale. Screenplay, R.C. Sherriff (and William Hurlbut, uncredited), based on the novel by John Galsworthy. Cinematographer, John J. Mescall. Art Director, Charles D. Hall. Music, W. Franke Harling. Editor, Ted Kent. Supervising Editor, Maurice Pivar. Special Effects, John P. Fulton. Makeup, Jack P. Pierce, William Ely. Hairdresser, Margaret Donovan. Gowns, Vera West. Sound, William Hedgcock, Gilbert Kurland. Assistant Directors, Harry Mancke, Joseph A. McDonough. Second Cameraman, Alan Jones. Script Supervisor, Helen McCaffrey. Jeweler, Eugene Joseff. Running Time, 88 minutes.

Filmed at Universal City, 11 May to 3 July 1934. Retakes, July 1934. New York premiere: Radio City Music Hall, 9 August 1934. Los Angeles premiere, Pantages Theatre, 9 August 1934.

Diana Wynyard (Clare Corven), Frank Lawton (Tony Croom), Colin Clive (Sir Gerald Corven), Mrs. Patrick Campbell (Lady Mont), Jane Wyatt (Dinny), Lionel Atwill (Mr. Brough), Alan Mowbray (Mr. Forsyte), Reginald Denny (David Dornford), C. Aubrey Smith

(The General), Henry Stephenson (Sir Lawrence Mont), Kathleen Howard (Lady Charwell), Gilbert Emery (Judge), E.E. Clive (Mr. Chayne), Robert Greig (Blore the Butler), J. Gunnis Davis (Benjy), Tempe Pigott (Mrs. Purdy), Snub Pollard (George), Billy Bevan (Cloakroom Attendant), Reginald Sheffield (Tommy), Doris Llewelyn (Vi), Arthur Hoyt (Perkins), Mary Gordon (Cook), Joseph North (Butler), Terry Spencer (Chauffeur at Ship), C. Montague Shaw (Guest), Frank Puglia (Waiter), Barlowe Borland, Luke Cosgrave, Stuart Holmes, Tom Ricketts, Hayden Stevenson (Barristers), Harold Nelson (Foreman of the Jury), James Whale (Cheerleader at Political Rally).

6

"Baby-Scarer!"
Boris Karloff at Warner Bros., 1935–1939

"Why did you have me killed?"
—Boris Karloff as John Elman, ***The Walking Dead***, 1936

"It not nice to make Fang mad!"
—Boris Karloff as General Fang, ***West of Shanghai***, 1937

"Are you suggesting that I'd drive a bayonet through my own hand?"
—Boris Karloff as Jevries, ***The Invisible Menace***, 1938

"My only crime was trying to save a life—if you call that treason!"
—Boris Karloff as Dr. Charles Gaudet, ***Devil's Island***, 1939

*"In approximately three minutes, this house,
with the entire British Cabinet, will be destroyed!"*
—Boris Karloff as Valdar, ***British Intelligence***, 1940

An arisen angel of death who resembles Frankenstein's Monster, and whose climactic death scene, to the mournful strains of "Kamenoi-Ostrow," reduces audiences to tears ... a Chinese warlord who speaks pidgin English, has an eye for the ladies and a date with a firing squad ... a red herring who's punched, stabbed, and shot ... a dashing French doctor who almost loses his curly-haired head to the Devil's Island guillotine ... and a German spy who sports a facial scar and a derby hat. These were Boris Karloff's star roles in (respectively) *The Walking Dead, West of Shanghai, The Invisible Menace, Devil's Island,* and *British Intelligence*—"Karloff's Warners Five."

Film history has basically smiled on these vehicles Karloff made for the brothers Warner between 1935 and 1939, where the star's dressing quarters neighbored those of James Cagney, Bette Davis, Paul Muni, Kay Francis, Edward G. Robinson, Humphrey Bogart, Ruby Keeler, Dick Powell, Olivia de Havilland and Errol Flynn. All the Karloff films provided top-billing showcases for the actor's versatility, all had Broadway openings (despite being "B" pictures), and all came packaged (more or less) with the super-slick efficiency of what was arguably Hollywood's most gutsy and colorful studio. Also, these films spanned a period when the horror blackout was at its darkest, keeping Karloff before the public at a time when Bela Lugosi lost his house and went on relief. Yet coverage has never fully focused on what happened *behind* the scenes of Karloff's Warners sojourn. In his three and a half years on a non-exclusive contract at Warners, the star (whom the trailer for *West of Shanghai* proclaimed as "Boris 'Baby-Scarer' Karloff") toppled from a prized, pampered attraction to a corporate liability, virtually tossed to the wolves by a studio desperately eager to dump him.

It's a genuine, colorful off-screen saga—and proof yet again that the true monsters in Golden Age Hollywood were often in the executive offices.

* * *

They are going to run the gamut from Rudy Vallee to Boris Karloff,
from Anthony Adverse *to* Shipmates Forever....
—*The Washington Post,* announcing Warner Bros.'
1935–1936 season, August 27, 1935

April 19, 1935: It's Good Friday, and Universal's *Bride of Frankenstein,* starring KARLOFF (as the studio bills him), makes its bow in San Francisco.

The star is at the peak of his popularity. On April 5, two weeks before, Karloff had completed *The Raven* with Lugosi at Universal. On April 20, the day after *Bride's* premiere, the *Washington Post* reports that Karloff, whose Universal contract allows for outside films, has signed for a picture for Gaumont-British Studios. And on May 6, Columbia Studios begins shooting *The Black Room,* starring Karloff as the good-and-evil medieval twins.

The Warner brothers, meanwhile, want a piece of the action.

The Warners lot, a socially conscious sin city of slick gangsters, sexy showgirls, and primed electric chairs, is just over the mountains of North Hollywood and Burbank from Universal, a Never-Never Land of gothic monsters, screaming heroines, and mad laboratories. "The Big U." is still under the wildly eccentric reign of 68-year-old studio founder "Uncle Carl" Laemmle and Junior Laemmle, his 27-year-old hypochondriac playboy son. If old man Laemmle evokes a royal hobgoblin, presiding over his mountain kingdom, 43-year-old Jack L. Warner suggests a gangster who wants to be a comedian (or vice versa)—slick, sharp and sometimes appallingly ruthless.

From 1930 through 1934, there's been a curious competition between Universal and Warners. Universal boasts a Best Picture Academy Award winner, *All Quiet on the Western Front* (1930); Warners has none. Warners has a thriving theater chain; Universal has none. Warners has a roster of popular stars; Universal has KARLOFF.

Wednesday, June 19: Warner Bros. announces that Boris Karloff is one of five stars signed "to make at least one picture during the new season for Warner Brothers and its affiliate First National." (The other four stars: Claudette Colbert, Charles Ruggles, Mary Boland, and Jack Oakie.[1]) It's all part of a wildly aggressive 1935–1936 campaign for Warners, which boasts that it "has spared neither expense, time or effort to set up the most ambitious program ever attempted."[2]

Actually, it's a sweetheart deal for both star and studio. Karloff had won acclaim at Warners as the perverted ex-preacher T. Vernon Isopod of *Five Star Final* (1931), a pre-*Frankenstein* triumph. (An isopod, incidentally, is a spiny parasite that attaches itself to deep sea fish.) He surely welcomes working for a studio as on-the-march as Warners after his travails at erratic Universal.[3] Meanwhile, Warners wants to score a hit in the horror genre; it hasn't since *Mystery of the Wax Museum* (1933).

The time is ripe. And indeed, as originally planned, Warners wants to unleash the most savage, bestial and bloodthirsty Karloff incarnation ever to stalk the screen.

* * *

Boris Karloff at home in Coldwater Canyon in 1938, during his Warner Brothers sojourn.

"the hideous creature" ... "that loathsome, hideous thing" ...
"the snarling, vicious thing" ... "the raging maniac" ...
"a jungle beast" ... "more like a monkey than a man" ... "the ape man"...
—descriptions of Boris Karloff's character in
the original script of ***The Walking Dead***

The supervisor of the new Karloff vehicle, *The Walking Dead*, is Warners' Lou Edelman. *Fortune* magazine will refer to him as "Lou (Red, White, and Blue) Edelman," and will write that he

> makes two types of movie, both usually low cost. One is the "service" picture, glorifying some branch of the uniformed forces of the nation: *Devil Dogs of the Air, Here Comes the Navy*.... Lou's other specialty is the headlines, which also give him ready-made plots. "Anything worth newspaper space is worth a picture," he says, and he keeps a scrapbook full of current clippings from six daily papers. He made *"G" Men* in eight weeks, starting with nothing but the title and the death of John Dillinger.[4]

Indeed, *"G" Men*, starring James Cagney and released May 4, has been one of Warners' 1935 super hits. Edelman finds at least three headline stories to inspire the new Karloff film:

- **Electric Chairs:** Consider the electric chair saga of unrepentant machine-gunner gangster Walter Legenza, who went "snarling" to his February 2, 1935, execution with two broken legs (guards had to wheel him into the chamber, lift him into the chair, and remove his plaster cast to attach the electrode). Defiant to the end, he refused 20 times to repeat the Salvation Army colonel's words, "God have mercy on my soul."[5] A second example is "Little Eva" Coo, a buxom blonde who'd murdered her crippled roadhouse handyman for insurance money. At her June 27, 1935, execution a matron safeguarded Eva's female vanity by standing in front of her so spectators couldn't see the guards adjust the electrode. "Goodbye, darling," said Eva to the matron just before the end.[6]
- **Dr. Robert Cornish:** In March of 1934, *Time* had reported that Dr. Cornish of the University of California had asphyxiated a fox terrier named Lazarus II and, six minutes after the dog's last heartbeat, placed its body on a seesaw-like teeterboard, injected a saline solution of oxygen, adrenalin, canine blood, etc., and brought Lazarus back to life. Unfortunately, the eight hours and thirteen minutes that Lazarus II lived again weren't happy ones for the dog—he whined, panted, barked, and behaved as if plagued by nightmares. Cornish followed up this experiment by pitching the idea of reviving executed criminals to authorities in Arizona, Colorado and Nevada. They declined. (Footage of Cornish and his experiments appear in the disastrous *Life Returns*, an indie released by Universal in 1935.)
- **The Lindbergh Heart:** A June 21, 1935, *New York Times* page one headline had extolled this artificial heart, which famed aviator Charles Lindbergh had researched with Nobel Prize–winning Dr. Alexis Carrel, as "one of the most sensational announcements in the annals of medicine." Lindbergh had become devoted to this concept after his sister contracted fatal heart disease in 1930; the method involved transplantation of an organ into a sterile chamber and its artificial feeding with nutrients—making it possible for the first time to experiment with human organs kept alive long after the donor was dead.

The original treatment of *The Walking Dead* is by Ewart Adamson—who, about the same time, scripts the Three Stooges' *Slippery Silks*. Karloff's character is named "Dopey";

Between scenes of *The Walking Dead*: leading lady Marguerite Churchill, Karloff (center), and Edmund Gwenn—the last destined for a 1947 Best Supporting Oscar as Kris Kringle in *Miracle on 34th Street*.

the star's Warner contract lists the role as "Creepy." At any rate, Dopey (aka Creepy) Elman is an alcohol- and drug-addicted musician who, as one gangster wisecracks, "likes his snow in summer as well as winter." Framed for murder by the hoodlums, Dopey-Creepy is a twitching mess before his electrocution, and after Dr. Beaumont brings him back to life, is basically a mad, rabid dog. As the original treatment introduces the resurrected Dopey:

> FADE IN on a Hospital Room. Nancy, in nurse's uniform, is sitting reading while Dopey, fully dressed, is lying on the floor asleep. A footstep hardly audible, is heard in the corridor and instantly Dopey springs half up and faces the door snarling. He is a repulsive, vicious thing, still without the power of speech, which makes one recoil in horror. Nancy speaks to him quietly as she would to a dog.... If it were not for her control of Dopey, they would have to keep him in a padded cell....[7]

At one point in the treatment, Nancy even pets Dopey on the head. Yet Warners goes beyond the mad dog motif. Piling on the sensation, the original *Walking Dead* treatment also presents Karloff's Dopey as a mute mix of Tarzan of the Apes, a human fly, and Frankenstein's Monster. He scales buildings, leaps from rooftop to rooftop, tears a throat, and snaps a spine. His face is "a bestial horror," and he lets loose with "savage roars."

Karloff is appalled. The original treatment survives in the Boris Karloff Script Collection at USC's Performing Arts Library, as do the star's notes (and editorial punctuation):

"He gets up like a dog bristling and pointing"—???????.... Dopey still too strong and Tarzanish ... no excuse for the torn throat and snapped spine.... Descriptions of Dopey sniffing the ground and following the scent, and of Dopey with arms hanging loosely from his shoulders like talons—would be very funny to audience....

Dopey's inability to talk is so identical to the "Monster" that it would be better to have him have complete loss of memory after he is brought back to life, but to retain the ability to speak....

Also, in the matter of makeup, no need to have him a hideous, vicious animal in appearance, because surely after electrocution a bad enough effect can be gained by a twisting of the body and by very dark—almost black skin—as if he had been completely scorched and burned....

Perhaps most significantly, it's Karloff who comes up with the idea of music triggering Elman's memory of his frame-up:

[H]is subconscious mind can react to certain types of music over the radio, which is in his hospital room, and which can be playing the piece which he played in Nolan's apartment the night the whole crime was planned. If Nolan could come into his hospital room for the first time, while his piece was coming over the radio, it could start a very hazy train of thought in Dopey's mind....

Dopey's addictions go, as does his bestiality. Playing in Karloff's favor in toning down *The Walking Dead* is the worldwide censorship storm then crashing over horror films. On September 26, 1935, Joseph I. Breen writes to Jack L. Warner:

Horror stories of all kinds are a precarious undertaking in these days ... I think you know that the British Board in London has indicated a disposition not to approve out-and-out horror stories; and a number of boards in this country, and in Canada, have already demonstrated their dislike for this type of story by mutilating a number of "horror pictures" which have been released in recent months....[8]

Breen demands there be no suggestion that the back-from-the-dead Dopey is "half-man-half-animal" ("this would be most offensive"), and insists that the murders have to be "suggested." As to the film's "metaphysical point," Breen writes Warners that they have "little to worry about," since Elman dies before describing "the other world"—which would be "a violation of nature's law and the usurpation of the powers of Deity."

Saturday, November 2: A Warners memo notes that Karloff will play "Creepy" in *The Walking Dead* at these terms:

$3,750 per week. Four-week guarantee. Artist's name shall be accorded first billing on the screen and in advertising and publicity under the control of the producer, and the name of no other member of the cast may appear in larger size type, and only the name of one female member of the cast may appear the same size type, as that used to display artist's name.[9]

Warner Bros. is dedicated to making its first Karloff vehicle a success—so much so that the studio provides its top director, the formidable Hungarian Michael Curtiz, who'd just completed the swashbuckler epic *Captain Blood*. He'd also expertly handled John Barrymore's *The Mad Genius* (1931) and Warners' early Technicolor chillers *Doctor X* (1932) and *Mystery of the Wax Museum* (1933), both starring Lionel Atwill and Fay Wray. The cameraman is Hal Mohr, who'd just performed the dazzling cinematography for Warners' *A Midsummer Night's Dream.*

Warners stocks the horror-gangster melodrama with a trio of its best in-house heavies: slick Ricardo Cortez as Nolan, the gang's smarmy mouthpiece; jowly Barton MacLane as gang boss Loder; and blonde, bullet-eyed Joe Sawyer as hit man Trigger Smith. As for the romantic leads, Marguerite Churchill (soon to be the heroine in Universal's 1936 *Dracula's Daughter*) is lovely as Nancy, the nurse who emotionally bonds with Elman, while Warren Hull (later the host of the TV game show *Strike It Rich*) is pleasant as Jimmy, the lab assistant who loves Nancy. Finally, Edmund Gwenn, who'd win an Oscar for playing Kris Kringle in 1947's *Miracle on 34th Street* (as well as play Dr. Harold Medford in Warners' 1954 *Them!*), is ideal as Dr. Evan Beaumont, the scientific genius who brings Elman back to life, only to become obsessed with learning what the man experienced in death.

Tuesday, November 5: The script is still very much in flux as Joseph Breen writes that he is "happy to note the great improvements" since the first draft, but still warning that the film must never be "a justification of progressive murder." The studio heeds Karloff's concerns and Breen's cautions and at least four more writers take cracks at the script as the shooting date approaches.[10]

Friday, November 22: Breen acknowledges he's received and reviewed "Part I" of the revised script, warning Warners to omit a close-up of Judge Shaw's corpse, the dimming lights during Elman's electrocution, and "any gruesome details" in the resuscitation scene.

Saturday, November 23: *The Walking Dead* begins shooting, with an incomplete script and an 18-day schedule, at the old Warner Studio, 5858 Sunset Boulevard, Hollywood. It's Boris Karloff's 48th birthday, and he isn't on call this first day as Curtiz works on the courtroom set.

Amazingly, considering the original story, *The Walking Dead* will come together splendidly—a haunting hybrid of horror movie, gangster melodrama, and religious morality parable. Indeed, rather than a horrific mix of Tarzan, mad dog and Frankenstein Monster, Karloff's John Elman (no longer nicknamed Dopey or Creepy) has become a gentle angel of death and divine retribution. Of course, the angel rather resembles the Monster—Warner rejects Boris's burn-him-black concept. The star wears a Monster-like heavy eyelid over his right eye, but basically conveys the risen Elman by twisting his body and holding one arm bent and stiff. It's Warners' executive producer Hal Wallis who suggests the back-from-the-dead "streak of white hair, running from the forehead back, in one narrow streak of white hair, and the rest of it should be the natural color of hair...."[11]

The shoot is a happy one. Karloff is great pals with Edmund Gwenn. Curtiz, infamous as a slave-driving director who overworks his actors mercilessly, respectfully honors (for the most part) the eight-hour day demands of Karloff (a Screen Actors Guild founder). Karloff will later refer to the director as "that grand fellow."

Several tidbits about *The Walking Dead*'s shoot:

• Production takes place at both of Warners' studios—the original on Sunset, and the First National 135-acre lot in Burbank, sometimes using both studios the same day.

• The jail cells and Death Row set, where Karloff walks the last mile to Old Sparky, is on Warner Bros. Stage One. The star powerfully delivers in this scene as, before the railroaded Elman enters the execution chamber, he looks up and says with moving faith, "*He'll believe me!*" Incidentally, on December 2, the same date Karloff is working on Warners' Death Row, the final two kidnappers and killers of the Tri-State Gang go to the electric chair at Rockview Penitentiary in Bellefonte, Pennsylvania.[12]

H.G. Wells visits Warner Bros. and the set of *The Walking Dead.* **Left to right:** **Warren Hull, a dapper Boris Karloff, Edmund Gwenn, Wells, a beaming Jack L. Warner, unidentified woman and the film's director Michael Curtiz.**

• The impressive laboratory set, with its arcs of electricity and rocking operating table (à la Dr. Cornish and Lazarus II), looms on First National Stage 3. No less than H.G. Wells pays a call to this set, escorted by a beaming Jack L. Warner. Karloff, out of makeup and costume that day, looks very dapper in his ascot, etc.—yet nevertheless receives a zinger from H.G. The "Lindbergh heart" used to raise the star from the dead in the melodrama is actually a chicken heart (or a turkey heart—sources differ). Wells gazes at the heart grotesquely glistening in the glass tube, looks at Boris, and asks, "And I suppose *that,* is your stand-in?"[13]

• The Music Room set, where Karloff plays the piano while giving the evil eye to the gangsters present, is on Warner Bros. Stage One—and Curtiz shoots the episode on Friday the 13th. The baroque vignette at the piano, as Karloff plays Rubinstein's "Kamenoi-Ostrow" while staring into the souls of his hoodlum foes, will be one of the star's great classic moments.

• The train yard episode, where Karloff's Elman terrifies Paul Harvey into running in front of a train, is shot Saturday night, December 14, on location at the Inglewood Railroad Depot.

• The wonderfully rainy and mournful graveyard "exterior" is actually an "interior," shot on First National's Stage 8. Karloff's death scene in the graveyard shed, advising Gwenn, "Leave the dead to their Maker. The Lord our God is a jealous God," is unusually powerful.

The Walking Dead: **Karloff escapes, heading for the cemetery.**

Indeed, Marguerite Churchill's weeping, the accompanying swell of the "Kamenoi-Ostrow" music, and the mournful final fade-out make *The Walking Dead* the most unusual and effective "tearjerker" of Golden Age horror.

Karloff finishes at 2:30 a.m., Saturday, December 21, after working that night on location in Griffith Park. Curtiz wraps up later that date at 4:15 p.m., six days over schedule. On January 6, 1936, he shoots scenes of cars and doubles in a location listed in the assistant director report as "Oak Grove, Pasadena," from 5:00 p.m. until 4:50 a.m. Gwenn and Churchill do retake work on January 7 and Curtiz fiddles briefly on January 8 with Karloff's double for a shot that's ultimately not used. A bonus will be the moving and uncredited score—the work of Bernhard Kaun, who wrote music for *Frankenstein* and *Doctor X*.

The Walking Dead's final cost: $217,000; Karloff's salary, $18,750; Curtiz's payday, $17,600.

Meanwhile, Warners has good news: The studio has made a profit in 1935, and a big one—$700,000. That same year, Universal has lost approximately $700,000. In fact, in November, a weary Laemmle Sr. had actually considered selling Universal to Warner Brothers. The deal collapsed when "Uncle Carl" demanded assured executive power positions for Junior and other relatives.

"Laemmle is keeping the world safe for nephews," wisecracks Jack Warner.

*   *   *

> "Boris Karloff Is Coming—The master of horror achieves his masterpiece in
> The Walking Dead, *Warner Bros.' Parade of Chills and Thrills.*"
> —Warner Bros. publicity, **The Walking Dead**, 1936[14]

Thursday, February 20, 1936: *The Hollywood Reporter* announces that Karloff has signed with Warner Bros. for two new pictures.

Monday, February 24: "Karloff Scores in Remarkable Role," headlines *The Hollywood Reporter* as it reviews *The Walking Dead*. Karloff, meanwhile, has set sail for England to star in *The Man Who Changed His Mind*.

The Walking Dead ships to exhibitors, the pressbook promising:

- This entire Campaign Plan has been created with all eyes on your BIGGEST PROMOTION IN MONTHS.
- It's your chance to go sensational with a picture that affords you more bally possibilities than a stageful of fanless fan dancers.
- Boris Karloff, long acknowledged as the master of mystery, turns in a performance that makes his "Frankenstein" seem like a cream-puff.

The pressbook offers a variety of what it calls "freak stunts," such as:

- Walking Skeleton—"This old bird is wearing tight-fitting outfit with skeleton painted on it in phosphorescent paint. He goes around at night handing out heralds to folks who don't faint."

The campaign book boasts that "this is the first film to depict the workings of Lindbergh's famous mechanical heart," and also makes this appropriate suggestion: "The film ends on a very somber note—and leaves an audience in no mood for jocularity. So don't follow this film with anything having a too-gay opening. Sharp change from a tense drama to comedy might not blend well."

Saturday, February 29: *The Walking Dead* opens at Broadway's Strand Theatre. "With a blaze of white streaking his hair, with sunken mournful eyes, hollow cheeks," writes the *New York Times,* "Karloff is something to haunt your sleep at nights." Meanwhile, between *The Walking Dead's* New York and Los Angeles openings, there are two significant events:

Thursday, March 5: The Academy Awards for 1935 celebrates its rites at the Biltmore Bowl. Warners' Bette Davis wins the Best Actress prize for *Dangerous* and, in accepting the award, asks Jack L. Warner to stand and take a bow. He does. More surprisingly, Hal Mohr, cameraman on *The Walking Dead,* wins the Best Cinematography Oscar for *A Midsummer Night's Dream,* and by write-in vote—the only write-in vote winner in Oscar history.[15]

Saturday, March 14: While Warners celebrates, the Laemmles mourn as Uncle Carl sees producer Charles Rogers and the usurping forces of Standard Capital gobble up the studio he founded. An era ends, and for the time being, the "New Universal" will maintain its Karloff contract.

Thursday, April 2: The Walking Dead opens at the Warner Bros. Hollywood and Downtown Theatres in Los Angeles. Ironically, the next day, Friday, April 3, Bruno Hauptmann, the convicted kidnapper and killer of the Lindbergh baby, goes to the electric chair professing his innocence at New Jersey State Prison. Here's *The Walking Dead,* a film about a convicted murderer claiming his innocence, going to the electric chair and resurrected by ... the Lindbergh heart!

The British Censor shortens Elman's "last mile" walk to the electric chair, cuts the pulsating heart in the test tube and three close-ups of Elman returning to life. At the end of the original movie Karloff and Gwenn each say "The Lord Our God is a jealous God," but the British censor excised the words "The Lord," so both actors say, "Our God is a jealous God." Australia demands several cuts and shows the film with a definite stipulation:

> SPECIAL CONDITIONS
> All publicity to prominently display the following words: "CENSORSHP WARNING; NERVOUS AND EXCITABLE PEOPLE SHOULD AVOID THIS HORROR PICTURE."
> The above warning to appear as a subtitle—at least 15 feet in length—at the beginning of each screening of the film.

Finland and Switzerland ban *The Walking Dead,* as does Singapore ("Because it is gruesome").[16] Nevertheless, *The Walking Dead* is a hit. It tallies a domestic rental of $273,000, plus a healthy foreign rental of $316,000, for a worldwide rental of $589,000. Estimated profit for Warners: $94,750.[17]

Boris Karloff's first Warner Bros. film scores a bull's-eye. His performance is both remarkably sensitive and sublimely eerie, and the film has nicely skirted the anti-horror factions. Warners, predicting lightning will strike, had picked up its option on Karloff's services even before the film's release.

Nineteen thirty-six will prove a big, booming year for Warners, with such hits as *Anthony Adverse, The Petrified Forest,* and *The Charge of the Light Brigade.* Karloff's *The Walking Dead* plays its part in contributing to the studio's walloping $3,200,000 fiscal profit.[18] Meanwhile, the 1936 *Film Daily Yearbook* features a full-page advertisement presenting portraits of the "Triumphant Warner Bros. Stars," among them James Cagney, Bette Davis, Errol Flynn, Edward G. Robinson, Ruby Keeler, Paul Muni and, nestled between Warren William and Olivia de Havilland ... Boris Karloff.

Karloff is delighted.

Karloff in the rainy cemetery climax of *The Walking Dead.*

* * *

It's curious that, as *The Walking Dead* is shooting, Warner Bros. recruits another Universal horror star: Claude Rains, who'd won fame in *The Invisible Man* (1933) and followed up at the studio in *The Man Who Reclaimed his Head* (1934) and *Mystery of Edwin Drood* (1935). The diminutive British actor starts on the Warner payroll December 2, 1935, beginning at $4,000 per week; as with Karloff, Rains is paid only for the weeks he works on a film, not on the usual 40-week deal.[19] However, unlike Karloff, Rains will primarily embrace featured player status and give indelible character performances in such classic Warner fare as *Anthony Adverse* (1936), *The Adventures of Robin Hood* (1938), *Now Voyager* (1942) and, of course, *Casablanca* (1943).

Claude Rains will stay at Warners on non-exclusive contract for over a decade, prospering there long after Karloff had departed the studio.

* * *

"How you do. I am Fang. I speak most dang bad English!"
—Boris Karloff in **West of Shanghai**

After two 1936 films in England—the delightfully offbeat *The Man Who Changed His Mind* and the unfortunate *Juggernaut*—Karloff comes home to Hollywood. He visits 20th

This *West of Shanghai* (1937) advertisement features Karloff as General Fang, "White Tiger of the North."

Century–Fox for *Charlie Chan at the Opera,* and in early 1937 makes his new Universal picture, *Night Key,* playing a kindly old inventor. Meanwhile, he's ready and eager to carry on at Warners.

Sunday, February 7, 1937: Before he can make a new Warners film, Karloff's face and form grace a new Warners cartoon as the studio releases Looney Tunes' *Porky's Road Race.* Porky's primary foe in the race is Borax Karoff, who resembles Frankenstein's Monster. When the villain spectacularly crashes, an ambulance arrives, loads the car on a stretcher—and leaves Borax in the grass. The cartoon also features likenesses of Clark Gable, Laurel and Hardy, W.C. Fields, Charles Laughton (as Captain Bligh), Edna May Oliver, George Arliss, Leslie Howard, John Barrymore, Elaine Barrie, and Freddie Bartholomew, as well as Greta Garbo's feet (very large, of course).

Wednesday, February 10: *The New York Times* reports that Warners is forsaking *Black Widow* ("the scheduled mystery yarn") that the studio had been preparing for Karloff, and has opted to star him in *China Bandit.* It's based on Porter Emerson Browne's *The Bad Man,* a play that had opened August 30, 1920, on Broadway and ran an impressive 342 performances. A 1923 film version saw Holbrook Blinn reprising his stage triumph as Pancho Lopez, the title character; Walter Huston inherited the juicy part in Warners' 1930 film version. Huston's version featured this tag line:

> When he laughs You laugh with him—When he kills You kill with him—When he loves You love him—THE BAD MAN IS GOOD!

Bryan Foy and his Warners "B" unit produce the Karloff version, inspired by the then-current Sino-Japanese conflict. The same *Fortune* magazine article that had extolled Lou Edelman refers to Foy as "a still more spectacular corner cutter"[20]:

> Foy learned to respect the dollar by being brought up in vaudeville (his father was Eddie Foy), and later became a shoestring independent producer of the most opportunistic stripe, with titles like *Sterilization, What Price Innocence?* and *Elysia* (made in a nudist camp) to his credit. He picked these subjects because he "needed something to take the place of Clark Gable." He boasts that he heard of technocracy on a Thursday, shot a short about it on Friday, and booked it on Monday. Such was Foy's training for his job at Warner, which is to produce no less than 26 features a year at a total cost of about $5,000,000. Foy, in short, heads up all Jack's "B" pictures, as he hates to hear them called, and thus guards the real backlog of the whole Warner program.

In the new version by Crane Wilbur (who will script Warners' 1953 3-D hit *House of Wax*), the locale changes to China and Pancho Lopez morphs into a Chinese warlord named General Fang. The premise—Fang holding missionaries and oil men hostage in a lonely China outpost—presents rich opportunity for melodrama and Karloff will be Pancho's new incarnation, the formidable Fang, aka "The White Tiger of the North." The star's fee: $5,000 per week on a four-week guarantee.

Ricardo Cortez, back from *The Walking Dead,* is smarmy as ever as greedy oil man Gordon Creed, whom Karloff shoots in the film—twice! Beverly Roberts plays Jane, Cortez's long-suffering "apprentice missionary" wife; Douglas Wood plays Galt, Creed's rival prospector; and Sheila Bromley takes the role of Lola, Galt's blonde glamour-girl daughter. Six foot five inch tennis pro Worster Von Epps—who's joined Warners as an actor and has changed his name to Willard Parker—is set to play prospector Jim Hallet, whom both Jane and Lola love, and Richard Loo will be a standout as Mr. Chang, Fang's poker-faced bodyguard, who speaks perfect English and knows American slang. Also, a curious by-the-way: playing the

Karloff is flanked by *West of Shanghai* leading ladies Beverly Roberts (left) and Sheila Bromley—and apparently enjoys it.

role of Fang's nemesis, General Ma, is Tetsu Komai, who was M'Ling, the faithful Dog Man of Charles Laughton's Dr. Moreau in Paramount's *Island of Lost Souls* (1932).

The director is 33-year-old John Farrow, who the previous September had wed Maureen O'Sullivan (Mia Farrow will be one of their eventual seven children). Farrow will later direct such films as *Wake Island* (1942) and *Hondo* (1953) and will win an Oscar for his writing work on *Around the World in Eighty Days* (1956).

Monday, March 1: Warners begins shooting *West of Shanghai* on an 18-day schedule.

Cortez, Bromley, and several other players are on call this first day on the Railway Station set on First National Stage 22, along with 50 extras and ten stock players.

Thursday, March 4: The Academy Awards banquet honoring 1936 releases takes place at the Biltmore, and this year a Warner star wins the Best Actor Oscar: Paul Muni, for *The Story of Louis Pasteur*. The studio wins an additional seven awards, including Best Supporting Actress (Gale Sondergaard in *Anthony Adverse*).

The same date: *The New York Times* announces that Warners is planning to film Edgar Allan Poe's *The Pit and the Pendulum*. Karloff isn't specifically mentioned as the star; however, the *Times* notes that, although Poe's tale had never been filmed, "the torture incident was once featured by Universal in one of Boris Karloff's horror films." (The film, of course, was 1935's Karloff-Lugosi vehicle *The Raven*.) Surely Karloff is the obvious choice to head Warners' Poe horror saga.

Saturday, March 6: *West of Shanghai* wraps up its first week on schedule. Karloff hasn't begun work yet. "Parker recast," reads the report; Willard Parker[21] had only worked Friday and Gordon Oliver[22] will replace him. Farrow will reshoot Parker's single day of footage.

Wednesday, March 10: Warners shoots makeup tests of Paul Muni for *The Life of Emile Zola* and Boris Karloff for *West of Shanghai* on First National Stage One. Perc Westmore designs both makeups.

Thursday, March 11: Karloff joins *West of Shanghai* on this tenth day of shooting, working on the Warner Ranch in Calabasas with the principals, 70 extras, 20 horses, eight mules, one dog, and six wranglers. The star instantly revels in the role of the sly, cigarette-smoking Fang and romps through the role with a wry, sardonic humor. Consider Fang's little soliloquy, in which he explains his rise to power from coolie to war lord:

> One day, the captain is killed. I become captain. Next day the major. I am major. By and by, the colonel. I become colonel. I kill the general myself!

Karloff especially sparks in his scenes with Sheila Bromley. When Fang takes over the missionary compound, the lascivious warlord eyes the ladies:

> *Karloff*: Only two women—too bad. This one—[*indicating Bromley*]—not so good.
> *Bromley*: What's the matter with me?
> *Karloff*: Hair like straw. Eye like frog. Have wide mouth of fish.
> *Bromley*: Well, you're no geranium yourself!

Karloff pronounces "frog" like "fog"—as Fang, he drops all his r's in his pidgin English. Later, he appears more receptive to Bromley's charms and decides he wants to take her away as a "souvenir":

> *Karloff*: You like go with me?
> *Bromley*: No thank you.
> *Karloff [suggestively]*: I make you very happy!
> *Bromley*: I'm afraid I couldn't stand so much happiness.
> *Karloff*: I am Fang!
> *Bromley*: I am Lola!

Fang decides he doesn't want her anyway—claiming he doesn't like a woman "who is tough guy!"

A surviving outtake from *West of Shanghai* reveals Karloff apparently feeling at home at Warners. After he blows one of his lines, he curses, "Oh, Jesus Christ!" *West of Shanghai* also offers Karloff a properly showy demise—death by firing squad.

The opening of *West of Shanghai* at New York's Criterion Theatre in October 1937 (courtesy John Antosiewicz).

Saturday, March 27: *West of Shanghai* wraps up this evening, six days over schedule. John Farrow has lost time reshooting Willard Parker's scene, and Beverly Roberts has been out sick for two and a half days. Karloff finishes at 6:00 Friday, Cortez at midnight; Sheila Bromley is the last player to go at 6:10 p.m. Saturday.

Friday, April 2: *West of Shanghai* begins three days of added scenes, directed by B. Reeves Eason, the famed second unit director who'd staged the chariot race in the original *Ben-Hur: A Tale of the Christ* (1925) and had just provided the climactic charge in Warners' *The Charge of the Light Brigade*.[23] Karloff works on First National Stage 18 Friday; on April 3, he goes to the Warner Ranch in Calabasas, where Eason shoots battle scenes with 122 extras. Eason wraps up on the ranch Monday, April 5. Even running a week over schedule and with three days of added scenes, the total negative cost of *West of Shanghai* is only $168,000.

Between *West of Shanghai*'s completion and release, there were some significant developments:

Friday, April 16: "The New Universal"—now agog over Deanna Durbin—terminates Boris Karloff's contract. He had been a Universal star virtually since the release of *Frankenstein*. (Karloff had walked out in a money dispute in the summer of 1933, but the studio had quickly wooed him back into the fold.) Warner Bros. is now the only studio with which he has a pact.

Wednesday, May 12: Jack L. Warner, at New York City's Waldorf-Astoria, announces Warner Bros.' ambitious program for 1937–1938, pledging to spend $5,000,000 for rights to books, stage plays, and original stories and screenplays. The studio proudly boasts the names of its contract attractions—including Boris Karloff, who, for all the fun he had in *West of Shanghai,* surely hopes the studio will now star him in more prestigious fare.

Tuesday, July 6: The Hollywood Reporter, reviewing a preview of *West of Shanghai,* praises the star: "Boris Karloff enjoys an actor's holiday as the bandit, giving probably his finest screen performance."

Karloff appears to be carving a niche at Warners as the "B" unit Paul Muni—a character star who revels in makeups, a Muni for the comic book crowd. Nevertheless, Warners will hold up the release of *West of Shanghai* several months, slating the new Karloff film as a Halloween time release.

Meanwhile...

* * *

> This is the desperate tale of the murder of Riley by crucifixion, hanging, beating, torture and the calling of bad names. In fact, Riley is one of the deadest men in seven counties when the curtain goes up on Ralph Spencer Zink's *Without Warning* ... Mr. Zink believes in brutality as well as mystery, and he has spread both of them on thick....
> —Brooks Atkinson, reviewing the play ***Without Warning*** in *The New York Times,* May 3, 1937

Monday, July 12, 1937: The New York Times announces that Warner Bros. has bought the play *Without Warning* as a vehicle for Karloff. A flop play (it opened May 1 and ran only 17 performances), *Without Warning* seems destined to be a flop film. In addition to its short Broadway run, it's inevitable that the censors will tone down its rather spectacular crucifixion brutality (in the film, Riley will be tortured to death via bayonet). The Breen Office is also sure to frown on the play's sexual comedy—namely, a pair of newlyweds returning to a military base on Powder Island and seeking a cozy locale to do the deed (although this plot element will remain).

At any rate, after all's stripped down, Karloff plays Mr. Jevries (the role acted in the play by Philip Ober), a gray, bespectacled civilian sad sack at the arsenal—"wasted," as Tom Weaver wrote in *Boris Karloff* (Midnight Marquee Actors Series, 1996), "as the pinkest of red herrings."[24]

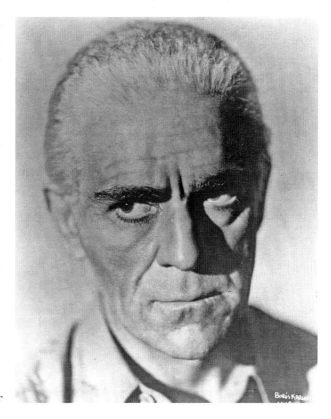

Karloff as a sadist's pin-up boy in ***The Invisible Menace.*** **In the course of the 54-minute film, the star is punched, stabbed and shot (courtesy John Antosiewicz).**

Tuesday, August 3: *Without Warning* begins shooting (under that title), Bryan Foy again supervising, John Farrow again directing, Crane Wilbur again scripting, and L.W. O'Connell again the cameraman. Karloff enjoys himself, especially delighted to be working with the blonde and very curvaceous Marie Wilson, who replaces Jane Wyman as the ditzy bride with hot pants.

"She was great fun!" Karloff exclaims of Ms. Wilson, a kewpie doll of an actress who makes her entrance in a duffle bag, smuggled onto males-only Powder Island by her soldier bridegroom. She turns 21 during the shooting and is a "discovery" of director Nick Grinde, who then manages her career and with whom she lives intimately (but reportedly never marries). Grinde later directs Karloff's *The Man They Could Not Hang* (1939), *The Man with Nine Lives* and *Before I Hang* (both 1940) at Columbia. Marie Wilson stars on radio, TV and film in *My Friend Irma* in the late 1940s and early 1950s. Sexist, perhaps, but maybe of interest is the fact that Ms. Wilson, whose measurements were 34.5–19–36 in her starlet years, will reportedly blossom to 39D–23–38 by 1952 when, understandably, she hits the apex of her popularity.

Back to the film... Eddie Craven reprises his Broadway role as the eager husband. Cameraman O'Connell provides some impressive night fog effects. A curio is the presence of heavy Cy Kendall, usually a villain, as the inspector called in to solve the killing. The first glimpse of Reilly's cadaver, trussed, gagged and hanging with a bayonet in the chest, is probably good for a squeal or two from 1937 audiences.

At any rate, it'll likely get more squeals than Karloff will in the picture. Tom Weaver's aforementioned write-up aptly described Karloff's Jevries in two words: a "punching bag."[25] Indeed, in the course of *The Invisible Menace*'s 54 minutes, Boris's punching bag is punched at least five times, shoved into a chair, pinned to a post with a bayonet through his left hand, and climactically shot, his stunt man toppling from a flight of stairs. There's also a flashback Haiti episode, where we see a hard-drinking Jevries cuckolded by Reilly (Harland Tucker) and Jevries' unfaithful, sloe-eyed wife (Phyllis Barry), who steal the company's money and railroad Jevries into prison. Of course, Karloff's long-suffering Jevries hasn't killed Reilly (although after seeing the flashback, we'd sure understand if he had). Seriously wounded by the actual murderer, Jevries at least appears to have a stab at survival as the film ends.

Saturday, August 21: *Without Warning* wraps up, precisely 18 days after it started shooting. A couple other curios: Playing Al, private of the guards, is Frank Faylen, who will achieve his major fame as Dobie Gillis' father, Herbert T. Gillis, on TV's *The Many Loves of Dobie Gillis* (1959–1963). Also: Carole Landis, later the "Ping Girl" blonde of the 1940s and a 1948 suicide, is then on stock contract to Warners, and appears early in the film with one line: "Can't I go with my Johnny?"

The film's total cost is only $138,000—nearly $100,000 less than the final tab for *The Walking Dead*. Obviously realizing what a sad and sorry programmer this "B" truly is, Warners will provide *Without Warning* a juicy new title: *The Invisible Menace*.

Thursday, October 28: *West of Shanghai* finally previews at New York City's Criterion Theatre. The star's reviews are outstanding, the *New York Times* writing:

> After all these humorless, if not outright horrendous years (even the advertisements proudly proclaim him a "baby-scarer"), Boris Karloff admirably acquits himself as a comedian in *West of Shanghai*....

The Invisible Menace. Left to right: **Karloff, Regis Toomey, Cy Kendall, and Charles Trowbridge.**

The domestic rental on *West of Shanghai* is $261,000; the foreign rental, $173,000; worldwide, $434,000. Profit: $57,500.

As for *The Invisible Menace*...

Tuesday, February 8, 1938: Swing Your Lady, a Warners comedy in which Humphrey Bogart promotes a match between wrestler Nat Pendleton and female blacksmith Louise Fazenda, opens simultaneously at the Warners Downtown and Hollywood Theatres. Bogart will consider it the worst movie of his career—even facetiously claiming he was never in it— it was just some guy, said Bogart, who *looked* like him!

Supporting *Swing Your Lady* on the bill is *The Invisible Menace.*

The new Karloff film is a Valentine's Day attraction at Broadway's Globe Theatre, and Rose Pelswick puts it quite pungently in her *New York Journal-American* review: "Mr. Karloff is neither invisible nor menacing in this picture. Customers who settle down expecting to be scared will find themselves feeling sorry for him."

Nevertheless, *The Invisible Menace* will make money. Domestic rental, $205,000; foreign, $105,000. Profit: $38,500.

After virtually indulging Karloff on *The Walking Dead,* soliciting his script changes and providing Michael Curtiz, Hal Mohr, and the splendid, power-packed Warner efficiency, the studio has dumped him into two "B" potboilers. The star had given an especially powerful performance in *The Walking Dead,* and his near–Monty Python approach had slickly saved *West of Shanghai.* There was little he could have done to salvage *The Invisible Menace.*

Meanwhile, Warners must decide whether or not to pick up Karloff's option to star in two more films.

Thursday, February 17, 1938: Louella Parsons reports in the *Los Angeles Examiner*:

Boris Karloff can't reform on the screen even if he wants to because the movie public won't have him in anything but eccentric characterizations. He had a year to go straight, but audiences all over the world turned thumbs down on a reformed Karloff. Jack Warner, in trying to decide upon a story for this difficult-to-cast actor, hit upon the idea of doing a Technicolor sequel to *Doctor X....*

Michael Curtiz will direct *The Return of Doctor X*, claims Louella, and Karloff's supporting cast will include Penny Singleton, Patric Knowles, and *West of Shanghai*'s Beverly Roberts.

Monday, February 21: Warners signs Karloff to a new "contract of employment." It comes, however, with a cutthroat stipulation: The star must agree to make each film for *half-price*—i.e., $10,000. The studio is basically getting a two-for-one deal for Karloff's services. Without any other film offers, Karloff desperately signs the contract.

Saturday, March 5: *The New York Times* notes: "Warners today (March 4) announces that Boris Karloff will appear in *The Witches' Sabbath*, the story of a German robber baron and his satanic operations in the seventeenth century. The legend is being put in script form by Anthony Coldeway and Dr. Manly P. Hall." (Dr. Manly P. Hall, the following year, will

In *The Invisible Menace*'s flashback to Haiti, Karloff appears with Phyllis Barry and Harland Tucker (center).

be pitching *The Witches' Sabbath* as a vehicle for his personal friend Bela Lugosi. He's also the man who will hypnotize Lugosi for the notorious publicity ballyhoo on Universal's 1940 Karloff-Lugosi flick *Black Friday*.)

Thursday, March 10: Oscar night comes again. The Best Picture of 1937 winner: Warners' *The Life of Emile Zola*. Jack L. Warner accepts the Oscar, so delighted with his acceptance speech that he'll pay to publish it in the trade papers.

Meanwhile, Warners reports its 1937 profit: $5,900,000. Karloff's three films for Warners had provided a profit of over $190,000. A Technicolor sequel to *Doctor X* could have a big payoff. So might *The Witches' Sabbath*. However, these films will never come to pass.

What happens instead is unforgivable.

The Warner files at USC infer that Jack L. Warner apparently has made a remark that he's embarrassed that his studio is making Karloff movies. Perhaps Warner has a swollen head: After an Academy 1935 Best Actress win, a 1936 Best Actor win, and a 1937 Best Picture win, he presumably feels that having Hollywood's bogeyman star on contract was beneath him and his studio—even at half price.

To be fair, Warner's "embarrassment" probably stems largely from the fact that censors are bullying him and the rest of Hollywood into bypassing horror films, hence keeping Karloff out of the genre in which he'd surely prove to be the most popular and profitable. Naturally, Warner wants to star Karloff in the field where he'd made his indelible mark, yet the festering problem remains: No studio in Hollywood is making horror films in early 1938. Even Warner Bros., the gutsiest of the bunch, lacks the nerve to buck the censors and women's groups and produce a horror film. The British ban had gone into effect in 1937. Horror seems cold and dead. And Warners has a contract with Karloff for two more pictures.

And so, in 1938, a banner Warner Bros. year where Errol Flynn magnificently wages an epic Technicolor sword duel with Basil Rathbone in *The Adventures of Robin Hood*, Bette Davis gives an Academy Award–winning performance as *Jezebel*, James Cagney goes screaming and crying to the electric chair in *Angels with Dirty Faces*, and Warners releases 52 feature films in 52 weeks while enjoying a $1,900,000 profit ... the studio screws Boris Karloff.

* * *

Boris awaits Warners' recall. He meanwhile has no film work. He fills in early 1938 on radio, singing (badly) with Bela Lugosi on *Seein' Stars in Hollywood* (March 13, 1938) and making five guest appearances on *Lights Out!* In April, the stage fright-suffering actor even plays vaudeville, delivering Poe's *The Tell-Tale Heart*. He also signs with Poverty Row's Monogram to begin the *Mr. Wong* series.

Saturday, May 28: *The New York Times* reports that Warners will star Karloff and Kay Francis in *I Spy*. It's a significant pairing: Warners is desperately trying to unload the high-priced Ms. Francis, who's vowed she'll keep her Warner contact "even if they put me in a bathing suit and have me walk up and down Hollywood Boulevard!" Francis might have been willing to parade in a bathing suit, but she absolutely refuses to co-star with Boris Karloff, and *I Spy* joins *The Witches' Sabbath* and *The Return of Doctor X* in the Warner nether region of unfilmed Karloff scripts. Kay Francis soon departs Warners.

Wednesday, June 8: The Coliseum in Los Angeles presents the Motion Picture Electrical Pageant and Parade of Stars. Mary Pickford is grand marshal, Jack Benny is master of ceremonies, and the studios provide their major attractions, waving from open cars. Appearing for Warner Bros.: Dick Powell, Anita Louise, Humphrey Bogart, Priscilla Lane, Pat O'Brien,

Rosemary Lane, and Hugh Herbert. Appearing for Monogram: Jackie Cooper, Jean Parker, John Carroll, Movita, and Boris Karloff.

Meanwhile, Warners provides Karloff with a new picture: *Devil's Island.* The studio blueprints the deal: Boris will receive $10,000 for 21 camera days. This comes to $3,333 per week. If he works beyond the 21 days, his fee will be pro-rated to $476.20 per day.

Karloff is frightened about his career longevity. He and wife Dorothy are expecting a baby in November. In a way, the financial sacrifice is worth it. *Devil's Island,* which the *New York Times* will salute as "savagely realistic," is a modest but meaty melodrama, presenting Boris perhaps his best sympathetic non-horror role of the decade: Charles Gaudet, a French doctor unfairly exiled to the infamous penal colony. The actor delivers stirring, defiant dialogue, operates and saves the life of the daughter of the wicked penal colony commander, leads a heroic escape, and climactically faces the guillotine—saved literally at the last second by his rebellious fellow prisoners. (It's a role that had supposedly been slated for George Raft.)

Even the makeup is a winner. Here we have a curly-haired Karloff (looking a bit like he did in *The Invisible Ray*), sporting a mustache (that vanishes once he arrives at Devil's Island, but comes back for the fade-out). Light years from the epic scope of Warners' *The Life of Emile Zola,* it's nevertheless a worthy, high-minded "B" with crusading pretensions, and Karloff, in effective Muni mode, clearly relishes his Cinderella-style casting from heavy to hero.

Bryan Foy again produces. The director is William Clemens, then 32 years old, who will direct various *Nancy Drew* films for Warners and *Falcon* films for RKO. There's evidence that Warners further tormented Kay Francis by originally assigning her to *Devil's Island;* at any rate, the leading lady is Nedda Harrigan, another of Boris's favorites. Ms. Harrigan had played the maid in the 1927 Broadway play of *Dracula* with Bela Lugosi, and had enjoyed working with Karloff in *Charlie Chan at the Opera.* As she remembered about the Chan film in Cynthia Lindsay's *Dear Boris:*

> [A] joy ... we occasionally broke up ... we were both opera stars—he played Mephistopheles—we had two genuine Italian opera stars dubbing the aria we were mouthing—Boris could never master the Italian so he bellowed away—"SAN FRANCISCO! SACRAMENTO! SANTA BARBARA!" Mephistopheles was a perfect part for him—he was full of the devil himself....

James Stephenson, the dapper, excellent British actor who was rather a bush-league Basil Rathbone at Warners in the late 1930s, plays *Devil's Island*'s cruel Commander Lucien, who suavely cuts the tip of his cigar in a miniature guillotine. And prominent in the supporting cast as Pierre, fated for a dramatic guillotine execution, is Adia Kuznetzoff, who'd play the Festival Singer ("Faro-La, Faro-Li") in Universal's *Frankenstein Meets the Wolf Man* (1943). The cameraman is George Barnes, who'd soon win an Oscar for his cinematography on *Rebecca* (1940). Barnes' seven wives included Warners' Joan Blondell, to whom he was married from 1932 to 1936.

Devil's Island proceeds on its 21-day schedule in defiance of the French government, who officially protests its production. France had boycotted Warners' *The Life of Emile Zola,* in which Joseph Schildkraut's Dreyfus (an Academy Award–winning performance) suffered on Devil's Island. Warners later claims it proceeds with *Devil's Island* because France had announced it would shut down the colony (which eventually saw service until 1953).

Wednesday, June 22: Karloff reports to the Interior Court, Palais de Justice set on First

Devil's Island poster.

National's Stage 22 for the first day's shooting of *Devil's Island*. There are 64 extras, as well as a group of stock players and "bits on day check" actors. Karloff sees some familiar faces from his terror past. Playing the president of the Assize Court is Frank Reicher, Karloff's victim Prof. Meiklejohn in *The Invisible Ray* (Reicher's most famous role was Captain Englehorn in *King Kong*); acting as the Advocate General prosecutor is Leonard Mudie, Professor Pearson in *The Mummy;* and serving as the jury foreman is Paul Panzer, a mourner in the opening of *Frankenstein* and a member of Karloff's satanic cult in *The Black Cat*. Karloff passionately plays his Palais de Justice scenes, protesting his innocence and impressing the company.

"You're condemning me for doing my duty—for the sworn obligation of every doctor to relieve suffering—save human lives!" he orates.

"[T]he courtroom stuff looked like it should be very interesting and exciting," reports unit manager Jack Saper to studio production manager T.C. Wright in a June 25, 1938, memo, "and if it continues in this manner this might prove to be a good picture."

Devil's Island takes 26 days to complete and Karloff works every one of them. A few notes about the shoot:

• The front office supersedes Karloff's SAG demands for an eight-hour day. On June 23, the second day of shooting, Karloff works from 9:00 a.m. until 10:20 p.m.; on July 7, 9:00 a.m. until 10:08 p.m.; on July 9, 9:00 a.m. to 9:20 p.m.

• On Thursday, June 30, the *Devil's Island* company goes on location to Sherwood Forest, far west in the San Fernando Valley near Malibu, to shoot the "Exterior Rocky Slope" episode where the carriage of Madame Lucien and her daughter runs wild. Karloff is there, as are Nedda Harrigan, Rolla Gourvitch (as the daughter, Collette), Adia Kuznetzoff and most of the "featured" convicts, as well as 37 extras, six stock players, four horses, two dogs, four animal handlers, one sled, and two wagons. One hundred forty lunches are served. The company works three days on the hot location.

• On Monday, July 11, the company reports to the Warner Calabasas Ranch, where Warners has provided the *Devil's Island* barracks and guillotine. In addition to stars Karloff, Harrigan and Stephenson on call this day, there are 238 extras.

• On Thursday, July 14, Karloff reports at 7:30 a.m. to leave the studio for the Calabasas ranch, where the company shoots his near-death at the guillotine. Then the star comes back to the First National lot, reports to Stage 3, and acts scenes in "Int. Gaudet's Condemned Cell" until 11:30 p.m.

• On July 19, Karloff puts in a 7:00 a.m. to 7:00 p.m. day with the second unit director Noel Smith on the exterior swamp–exterior road sets at the Santa Anita Rancho Forest.

Bob Ross (who replaced Jack Saper as unit manager) sends a July 22, 1938, memo to T.C. Wright that suggests the merciless pace of the shoot:

> Clemens company did not do so very good yesterday afternoon in Process with the long boat and I am telling him this morning that hot or cold he is to finish with Mr. Karloff and the rest of the cast before midnight tonight....

Clemens gets in just under the wire. On Friday, July 22, Karloff begins work at 9:00 a.m., completing his role in *Devil's Island* on First National's exterior lake at 11:40 p.m. The film comes in five days behind schedule.[26]

"[Karloff] knew he could break me up so he did—constantly," said Nedda Harrigan

Karloff in his most dynamic hero role, as *Devil's Island*'s Dr. Gaudet (courtesy John Antosiewicz).

who, at the time of *Devil's Island,* was wed to character actor Walter Connelly (and who after Connelly's death in 1940, married writer-director Joshua Logan). "I made two films with him and remember howling with laughter through both of them ... I loved him."

Thursday, August 4: The Regina Theatre in Los Angeles opens a triple feature—*Dracula, Frankenstein* and *The Son of Kong*—and the result is a sensation. Universal quickly

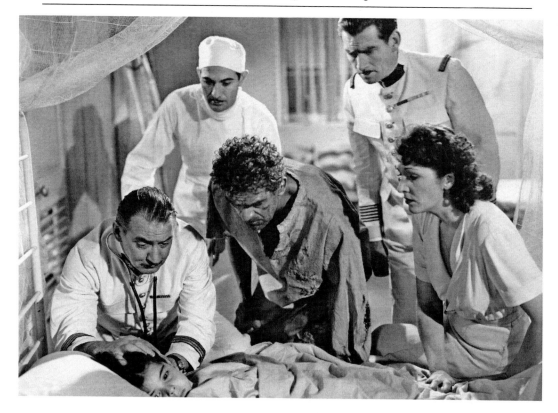

Devil's Island **players Rolla Gourvitch (as the young patient), Edward Keane (left), unknown actor as the doctor's aide, Karloff, James Stephenson, and Nedda Harrigan.**

decides to release *Dracula* and *Frankenstein* as a national double bill, and Boris Karloff is suddenly in a new, revitalized career position.

Wednesday, August 17: The *Los Angeles Examiner* reports on the Warner Bros. stag night party at the Vendome Restaurant, honoring sales managers from the United Kingdom. Jack L. Warner was toastmaster, the Dead End Kids sang their own version of "A Tisket, A Tasket" ("lusty, if not so harmonious," reports the *Examiner*), and among the many celebrities were Errol Flynn, James Cagney, Edward G. Robinson, Humphrey Bogart, Basil Rathbone, Claude Rains ... and Boris Karloff.

Tuesday, August 23: *Devil's Island* resumes shooting for two days of added scenes, without Karloff. The first day, the company encounters an unusual problem at Rancho Santa Anita when 5'2", 62-year-old British actor Will Stanton (as "Bobo") becomes ill and can't work from 2:00 a.m. until 5:00 p.m. due to what a production report cites as Stanton's "extreme nervousness." The next day Adia Kuznetzoff returns for some new shots and the film picks up scenes with him and several other players at Sherwood Forest, the Calabasas Ranch, and First National Stage 3.

The negative cost of *Devil's Island* will be $235,000—a considerably higher figure than *West of Shanghai* and *The Invisible Menace*, and about the same tab as that of *The Walking Dead*. The stirring music score will help, including a dash of the march from Prokoviev's "Love for Three Oranges," as well as the appropriately lugubrious "Song of the Damned" that the basso convicts sing on the eve of guillotine executions.

Monday, August 29: *The Hollywood Reporter* announces that Universal is wooing Karloff to a two-picture contract, the first to be a new Frankenstein saga. Universal's national release of the *Dracula* and *Frankenstein* double bill proves a tremendous box office draw.

Wednesday, November 9: Universal begins shooting *Son of Frankenstein*, starring Basil Rathbone as Dr. Wolf von Frankenstein, Karloff as the Monster, Bela Lugosi as broken-necked old Ygor and Lionel Atwill as one-armed Inspector Krogh. Rowland V. Lee produces and directs.

That same day: Warner Bros. (which has not yet released *Devil's Island* and still has a commitment from Karloff for another picture) announces in the *Hollywood Citizen News* plans for *two* Karloff vehicles. Karloff, after *Son of Frankenstein*, will report to Warner Bros. to play "a circus animal hypnotist" in *The Return of Doctor X* and "an actor who decks himself out in a disguise to do away with a man who has done him a great injury" in *The Dark Tower*. Claude Rains is to co-star in *The Dark Tower* as the detective who "trails the actor-murderer."

Friday, November 18: Warners writes to Karloff in regards to his next picture, communicating that the studio will require him to report December 19, 1938. Karloff, suddenly busy in films again, replies that he's still at work on *Son of Frankenstein*, which will go far over schedule, and that he will follow with his new Monogram *Mr. Wong* picture, to start on or about January 15, 1939. He naturally requests that Warners adjusts production of his next film there.

Wednesday, November 23: It's Karloff's 51st birthday—and the day that his daughter Sara Jane is born.

Tuesday, December 13: Warners' legal czar R.J. Obringer writes to Karloff, advising him regarding the studio's right to extend his contract to secure his services.

Wednesday, December 14: Obringer sends an Inter-Office Communication memo to Jack L. Warner regarding the studio's hopes of dumping three talents on contract: choreographer Busby Berkeley, songwriter Harry Warren, and Boris Karloff. The memo concludes:

> Boris Karloff's agent, Allen Simpson of the Hayward-McCormick Office, is talking to Karloff today, and will let me know on a mutual cancellation of the one remaining picture.

It's surely a shocker for Boris. With *Son of Frankenstein* still shooting and *Devil's Island* about to premiere, he probably believes his career is in an upswing. Now Warners wants to cancel its final picture on his contract rather than await his availability.

He's likely devastated. Warners has coldly sent Karloff down the studio food chain, cutting his salary in half—and now wants to dump him entirely!

Thursday, December 15: R.J. Obringer sends this Inter-Office Communication to Bryan Foy, with a copy to Jack Warner:

> I have made an effort to get out of our commitment for the remaining Boris Karloff picture. Karloff states he does not want to cancel on this picture, but is willing to do anything humanly possible to cooperate with you when you need him.
>
> As it now stands, his contract year, which will end March 31, 1939, will be extended for the period of time between December 19, 1938, and the date he finishes a picture for Monogram, following his present engagement for Universal, or approximately for a period of two months or until the latter part of May 1939. You must, of course, give him 30 days' notice starting date.

So, with Karloff demanding he complete his contract, Warners has at least several months to prepare *The Return of Doctor X, The Dark Tower,* or *I Spy* for him.

British Intelligence **stars Margaret Lindsay and a scar-faced Karloff.**

New Year's Eve, 1938: *The Hollywood Reporter* reviews *Devil's Island.* "Boris Karloff, in a sympathetic role, is very acceptable," notes their critic.

Saturday, January 7, 1939: Warners releases *Devil's Island,* still in defiance of French opposition.

Friday, January 13: *Son of Frankenstein* premieres at the Hollywood Pantages Theatre.

Wednesday, February 1: Karloff writes to Warner Bros. Pictures, Inc., via registered mail:

> Gentlemen:
> Referring to the second paragraph of your letter of December 13, 1938, please be advised that I completed my services for Monogram Pictures Corporation on January 31, 1939, and that I am available immediately.

Wednesday, February 8: *The New York Times* reports that Karloff's next film, *Witches' Sabbath,* will replace *The Dark Tower.* Certainly an all-out horror show from Warners in the wake of *Son of Frankenstein* now makes box office sense.

Thursday, February 23: It's Academy Awards night, honoring 1938.[27] Jack Warner hopes for a sweep: Best Picture (*The Adventures of Robin Hood*), Best Actor (James Cagney for *Angels with Dirty Faces*), Best Actress (Bette Davis for *Jezebel*), Best Supporting Actor (John Garfield for *Four Daughters*), Best Supporting Actress (Fay Bainter for *Jezebel*), and Best Director (Michael Curtiz for both *Angels with Dirty Faces* and *Four Daughters*). Davis and Bainter win.

Saturday, February 25: Fans arriving at Broadway's Globe Theatre for the New York opening of Karloff's *Devil's Island* are disappointed: The film (after having played many other areas of the U.S.A.) is mysteriously cancelled.

Tuesday, February 28: *The New York Times* reports that Warners has withdrawn *Devil's Island* because "the French government threatened to ban all Warner pictures for two months because of it." The report quotes an unnamed Warner representative: "We had no intention of showing the picture in France. But we are good sports and have withdrawn the picture entirely. It won't be shown anywhere from now on."

Monday, March 13: Warners begins shooting its new Karloff film: *British Intelligence*, based on Anthony Paul Kelly's play *Three Faces East* and twice filmed before, in 1925 and 1930, the latter with Erich von Stroheim. Bryan Foy is producer, Mark Hellinger is associate producer, Terry Morse (who will direct the U.S. footage for 1956's *Godzilla, King of the Monsters!*) is director, Margaret Lindsay is leading lady, and Sidney Hickox (who will be cameraman on Warners' 1949 Cagney classic *White Heat*) is cinematographer. The film, in fact, is apparently *I Spy,* which Kay Francis had refused to film with Karloff.

Boris's role: Valdar, a spy who sports a derby and a facial bayonet scar. Although *Son of Frankenstein* has empowered Karloff's box office potency, Warners still engages him for the contracted half-price fee of $10,000. That Warners tosses Karloff into this pitifully weak sister of a film, rather than starring him in *The Dark Tower, Witches' Sabbath, The Return of Doctor X,* or the apparently long-forgotten *The Pit and the Pendulum* when the public is hungry for a new horror, seems like corporate vengeance on Karloff for refusing to bow out of his contract.

Boris valiantly tries to save *British Intelligence.* He acts up a storm, limping, leering, hissing, glowering; one gets the impression he'd break out in a London music hall–style song-and-dance rendition of "Linda and Her London Derry-Air" if he thought it would help the cause. It's all for naught. The presence of such familiar horror faces as Leonard Mudie, Paul Panzer, Holmes Herbert (1931's *Dr. Jekyll and Mr. Hyde*), Lester Matthews (*The Raven*), and Lawrence Grant (*Son of Frankenstein*) is of little benefit, as is the lovely Maris Wrixon, who will star with Karloff in Monogram's *The Ape* (1940). Stock war footage abounds.

British Intelligence is, as Tom Weaver has expressed it, "near-total incomprehensibility."

Tuesday, April 4: Warners completes *British Intelligence.* Negative cost: $172,000.

Thursday, April 6: *The New York Times* runs this headline:

France Penalizes Warner Brothers
Bans Films for 2 Months as a
Rebuke for *Devil's Island*

Having coped for several years with a horror ban, Warners is now confronting a *Devil's Island* ban—and now pursues its own *Karloff* ban. In what may very well be an explosion of front office anger and badly timed international hypersensitivity, Karloff goes down in flames at Warners.

Meanwhile, Warners proceeds to produce *The Return of Doctor X* anyway—and without Karloff! The studio considers replacing Boris with Bela Lugosi or James Stephenson, finally casting no less than Humphrey Bogart (not as a "circus animal hypnotist," but a rabbit-petting, blood-seeking grotesque). Bogart's oft-quoted lament on this one:

British Intelligence **players Karloff, Lester Matthews, and Margaret Lindsay (courtesy John Antosiewicz).**

> I had a part that somebody like Bela Lugosi or Boris Karloff should have played. I was this doctor, brought back to life, and the only thing that nourished the poor bastard was blood. If it had been Jack Warner's blood ... maybe I wouldn't have minded as much.

And as if to add insult to injury, Bogart even wears a white streak in his hair à la Karloff's Elman in *The Walking Dead!*

Meanwhile, *British Intelligence* braves the public. "Karloff makes a juicy morsel of the German spy role," writes *Variety*. "He has a supposed bayonet wound on his face, walks with a limp and is the picture's menace because of his sheer trouping." Yet the story's a mess.

Tuesday, January 30, 1940: British Intelligence opens at the Metropolitan Theatre in Washington D.C. The next day, the *Washington Post* is direct in its review headline: "*British Intelligence* Is Screen at Its Lowest Ebb."

Saturday, February 10: British Intelligence opens at Broadway's Globe Theatre. "Boris Karloff, who usually haunts people, is just spying on them in *British Intelligence*," notes the *New York Times*, "but being spied on by Mr. Karloff is more terrible that being haunted by an ordinary bogeyman...."

The domestic rental will be $238,000, the foreign rental $130,000, and *British Intelligence*'s profit will be a respectable $44,000. As fate will have it, the film is the only one of Karloff's "Warners Five" to fall into the public domain.

Friday, July 12: *The New York Times* reviews *Devil's Island*. Almost two years after the film had completed shooting, Warners breaks its vow never to show it again—France is too busy fighting Hitler to squawk about a 62-minute "B" movie (released with a whitewashing foreword). The film plays Broadway's Globe Theatre and Warners naturally attempts to spark business by advertising the film as the "uncensored" version. *The New York Times* is impressed properly, noting, "Mr. Karloff contributes a sterling characterization...." There will be, however, no foreign release of the film.

Devil's Island eventually earns a domestic rental of $414,000, by far the largest of Karloff's five Warner films. However, with no foreign release, the film's profit is paltry: $15,500.

After *British Intelligence,* Warners had exercised no more options on Karloff's services; by the time *Devil's Island* finally played Broadway, Karloff had been away from the studio for 15 months. The star didn't suffer. Since *Son of Frankenstein,* Karloff had made *Tower of London* and *Black Friday* for Universal, continued his Mr. Wong potboilers at Monogram, and commenced his "Mad Doctor" series at Columbia. Shortly after *Devil's Island*'s second release, he starred in *The Ape* for Monogram and *You'll Find Out* for RKO. Six months after *Devil's Island*'s Broadway opening, Karloff was live on Broadway—as mad Jonathan Brewster in the super stage hit *Arsenic and Old Lace.*

The play's metamorphosis into film might have paved the way for Karloff to return to Warner Bros. in glory, but that's a story for the next chapter.

* * *

In retrospect, various issues worked against Boris Karloff at Warner Bros.: the international censorship protest against horror films, the studio's consequential reluctance to present Karloff in his trademark genre, Jack L. Warner's snobbery about "Karloff pictures," and the corporate exasperation about *Devil's Island.*

Yet Boris Karloff, forever upbeat, probably savored primarily happy memories of his work at Warners. *The Walking Dead* boasts one of his most moving performances, *West of Shanghai* offers his most wryly comic portrayal of the 1930s, and *Devil's Island* presents the star as handsome and heroic. The five films he made there certainly spotlighted his talent— indeed, he looks and acts markedly different in each of the five roles. He'd earned approximately $80,000, had fun working with Edmund Gwenn, Marie Wilson, and Nedda Harrigan, and for a time was an attraction at perhaps the most colorful studio in 1930s Hollywood.

Indeed, the lost opportunities probably annoy a Karloff fan more than they ever haunted the late-in-life Karloff himself.

Yet, strangely and mysteriously, the "Baby-Scarer" never made a feature film for Warner Bros. again. In January 1958, however, Karloff returned to the lot for eight days to shoot his scenes for *Frankenstein 1970,* but only because producer Aubrey Schenck had rented space there on the *Too Much, Too Soon* John Barrymore house set. (Allied Artists would release *Frankenstein 1970.*)

There's a sad postscript.

Warners' 1964 *Ensign Pulver,* a dreary and belated sequel to the studio's 1955 hit *Mister Roberts,* stars Robert Walker, Jr., as Pulver and Burl Ives as the unspeakable captain. In the film, the ship's crew is seen watching a movie, and we see clips from *The Walking Dead.* However, *Ensign Pulver* presents *The Walking Dead,* on which Warners had once upon a time so respectfully indulged and showcased Boris Karloff, as a travesty—and calls it *Young*

Dr. Jekyll Meets Frankenstein. The crew members show up to watch it only because they'll be placed on report if they don't.

"Every time I see this picture," exults the horrible captain, "the better I like it!"

The Walking Dead

Studio, Warner Bros. Producer, Jack L. Warner; Executive Producer, Hal B. Wallis; Production Supervisor, Lou Edelman; Director, Michael Curtiz; Screenplay, Ewart Adamson, Peter Milne, Robert Andrews, and Lillie Hayward (from a story by Ewart Adamson and Joseph Fields); Cinematographer, Hal Mohr; Art Director, Hugh Reticker; Music, Bernhard Kaun; Set Designer, Anton Grot; Makeup, Perc Westmore; Editor, Tommy Pratt; Costumes, Cary Odell; Assistant Director, Russ Saunders; Dialogue Director, Irving Rapper; Gowns, Orry-Kelly. Running Time, 66 minutes.

Filmed at the Warner Bros. Studios, Hollywood, First National Studios, Burbank and Griffith Park, Los Feliz, California, 23 November–21 December 1935. New York premiere, Strand Theatre, 29 February 1936. Los Angeles premiere, Warners Hollywood and Downtown Theatres, 2 April 1936.

Boris Karloff (John Elman); Ricardo Cortez (Nolan); Edmund Gwenn (Dr. Evan Beaumont); Marguerite Churchill (Nancy); Warren Hull (Jimmy); Barton MacLane (Loder); Henry O'Neill (District Attorney Werner); Paul Harvey (Blackstone); Robert Strange (Merritt); Joseph Sawyer (Trigger Smith); Eddie Acuff (Betcha); Addison Richards (Warden); Joe King (Judge Shaw); Ruth Robinson (Mrs. Shaw); Kenneth Harlan (Martin); Miki Morita (Sako); Frank Darien (Cemetery Watchman); Edgar Sherrod (Priest); Cris Corporal (Black Prisoner); Gordon "Wild Bill" Elliott (Announcer); Boyd Irwin (British Doctor); Jean Perry (French Doctor); Nicholas Kobliansky (Russian Doctor); Harrington Reynolds (English Doctor); Edward Piel, Sr. (Train Engineer); Alphonse Martell (Florist); Lucille Collins (Tough Girl in Courtroom); Isabel La Mal (Sob Sister); William Wayne (Trusty); John Kelly (Joe, Merritt's Bodyguard); Sarah Edwards (Female Physician); Nick Moro (Convict); Tom Schamp, Ed Carlie, Jim Pierce (Prisoners); Charles Sherlock (Broadway Type); Spec O'Donnell (Copy Boy); George Beranger (Nolan's Butler); James P. Burtis (Guard Who Answers Phone Too Late); Wade Boteler, Edward Gargan (Guards); Lee Phelps, Tom Brower, Harry Hollingsworth, Lee Prather (Bailiffs); Paul Irving, Brandon Beach, Malcolm Graham (Guests).

West of Shanghai

Studio, Warner Bros. Executive Producers, Jack L. Warner, Hal B. Wallis. Associate Producer, Bryan Foy. Director, John Farrow. Screenplay, Crane Wilbur (based on the play *The Bad Man,* by Porter Emerson Browne). Cinematographer, L. William O'Connell. Art Director, Max Parker. Editor, Frank DeWar. Costumes, Howard Shoup. Make-Up, Perc Westmore. Music, Heinz Roemheld. Dialogue Director, Jo Graham. Technical Director, Tommy Gubbins. Running Time: 64 minutes.

Filmed at Warner Bros. First National Studio, Burbank, and at Warner Bros. Ranch, Calabasas, CA, 1 March–27 March 1937; Additional Scenes, 2 April–5 April 1937. New York premiere, Criterion Theatre, 28 October 1937.

Boris Karloff (General Wu Yen Fang); Beverly Roberts (Mrs. Jane Creed); Ricardo Cortez (Gordon Creed); Gordon Oliver (Jim Hallet); Sheila Bromley (Lola Galt); Vladimir

Sokoloff (General Chow-Fu Shan); Gordon Hart (Dr. Abernathy); Richard Loo (Mr. Cheng); Chester Gan (Captain Kung Nui); Douglas Wood (Myron Galt); Tetsu Komai (General Ma); Eddie Lee (Wang Chung, the assassin); James B. Leong (Pao); Luke Chan (Chan, Abernathy's servant); Tom Ung (General Ma's Aide); Paul Fung (Station Master); Mia Ichioka (Hua Mei); Selmer Jackson (Harry Hemingway); Maurice Liu (Train Conductor); Daro Meya (Chinese Officer); Frank Tang (Chinese Merchant); Sammee Tong (Messenger).

The Invisible Menace

Studio, Warner Bros. Executive Producers, Jack L. Warner and Hal B. Wallis. Associate Producer, Bryan Foy. Director, John Farrow. Screenplay, Crane Wilbur (based on Ralph Spencer Zink's play *Without Warning*). Cinematographer, L. William O'Connell. Editor, Harold McLernon. Art Director, Stanley Fleischer. Original Music, Bernhard Kaun. Stock Music, Heinz Roemheld. Sound, Leslie J. Hewitt. Gowns, Howard Shoup. Assistant Director, Elmer Decker. Dialogue Director, Harry Seymour. Running Time: 54 minutes.

Filmed at Warner Bros., 3 August–21 August 1937. Los Angeles opening, Warners Downtown and Hollywood Theatres, 8 February 1938.

Boris Karloff (Mr. Jevries); Marie Wilson (Sally Wilson Pratt); Eddie Craven (Pvt. Eddie Pratt); Regis Toomey (Lt. Matthews); Henry Kolker (Col. George Hackett); Cy Kendall (Col. Bob Rogers); Charles Trowbridge (Dr. Brooks); Eddie Acuff (Cpl. Sanger); Frank Faylen (Al, private of the guard); Phyllis Barry (Aline Dolman); Harland Tucker (Ted Reilly); William Haade (Pvt. Ferris); John Ridgely (Pvt. Innes); Jack Mower (Sgt. Peterson); Anderson Lawler (Pvt. Abbott); John Harron (Pvt. Murphy); Willard Parker (Pvt. Booker); Emmett Vogan (Investigator in Haiti); John J. Richardson (Pvt. Nelson, Hackett's Orderly); Edward Keane (Officer at Dolman's Hearing); Henry Otho (Boat Loading Announcer); Jack Shea (Tough Soldier); Brick Sullivan (Guard Outside Tent); Jesse Graves (Servant); Sol Gorss (Guard); Carole Landis (Woman).

Devil's Island

Studio, Warner Bros. Producer, Bryan Foy. Director, William Clemens. Screenplay, Anthony Coldeway, Raymond L. Schrock, Kenneth Gamet and Don Ryan. Cinematographer, George Barnes. Editor, Frank Magee. Art Director, Max Parker. Sound, Robert B. Lee. Original Music, Howard Jackson. Stock Music, Max Steiner. Assistant Director, Arthur Lueker. Dialogue Director, John Langan. Technical Advisor, Louis van der Ecker. Running Time: 62 minutes.

Filmed at Warner Bros. First National Studio, Burbank; Warner Ranch, Calabasas; and Santa Anita Rancho Forest, 22 June–22 July 1938. Additional scenes filmed 23 August and 24 August 1938. Release date, 7 January 1939.

Boris Karloff (Dr. Charles Gaudet); Nedda Harrigan (Madame Helene Lucien); James Stephenson (Col. Armand Lucien); Adia Kuznetzoff (Pierre); Rolla Gourvitch (Collette Lucien); Will Stanton (Bobo); Edward Keane (Duval, camp doctor); Robert Warwick (Demonpre, Minister of Colonies); Pedro de Cordoba (Defense Attorney Marcal); Tom Wilson (Emil, a prisoner); John Harmon (Andre Garon, a prisoner); Richard Bond (Georges, a prisoner); Earl Gunn (Leon, a prisoner); Sidney Bracy (Soupy Hawkins, a prisoner); George Lloyd (Dogface, a prisoner); Charles Richman (Gov. Beaufort); Stuart Holmes (Gustav

LeBrun); Leonard Mudie (Advocate General); Egon Brecher (Debriac, LeBrun's henchman); Frank Reicher (President of Assize Court); Paul Panzer (Jury Foreman); Harry Cording (Guard accepting bribe); Alonzo Price (Capt. Fearreau, First Convict Ship), John Hamilton (Captain, Second Convict Ship).

British Intelligence

Studio, Warner Bros. Executive Producers, Jack L. Warner, Hal B. Wallis. Producer, Bryan Foy. Associate Producer, Mark Hellinger. Director, Terry Morse. Screenplay, Lee Katz (based on Anthony Paul Kelly's play *Three Faces East*). Cinematographer, Sidney Hickox. Art Director, Hugh Reticker. Editor, Thomas Pratt. Music, Heinz Roemheld, Bernhard Kaun. Makeup, Perc Westmore. Gowns, Howard Shoup. Sound, Stanley Jones. Assistant Director, Elmer Decker. Dialogue Director, John Langan. Running Time: 61 minutes.

Filmed at Warner Bros. Studios, 13 March–4 April 1939. New York opening, Globe Theatre, 10 February 1940.

Boris Karloff (Valdar); Margaret Lindsay (Helene von Lorbeer); Bruce Lester (Frank Bennett); Leonard Mudie (James Yeats); Holmes Herbert (Arthur Bennett); Austin Fairman (George Bennett); Lester Matthews (Henry Thompson); Maris Wrixon (Dorothy Bennett), Lawrence Grant (Brigadier General); Morton Lowry (Lt. Borden); Leyland Hodgson (Lord Sudbury); Winifred Harris (Mrs. Maude Bennett); Louise Brien (Miss Risdon, Bennett's Secretary); David Cavendish (Captain Lanark); Paul Panzer (Peasant); William Bailey (British Intelligence Agent); Crauford Kent (Cmdr. Phelps); Glenn Cavender (Under Officer Pfalz); Evan Thomas (Major Andrews); John Graham Spacey (Crichton, Intelligence Agent); Joe De Stefani (German Officer); Carlos De Valdez (Von Ritter); Frederick Vogeding (Baron Kuglar); Clarence Derwent (Milkman); Frank Mayo (Brixton, Intelligence Agent); Arno Frey (German Junior Officer); Frederick Giermann (Otto Kurtz); Carl Harbaugh (German Soldier); Sam Harris (Cabinet Minister); Stuart Homes (Luchow, German soldier); Willy Kaufman (German Corporal); John J. Richardson (Cockney Soldier); Ferdinand Schumann-Heink (German Officer); Hans Schumm (German Senior Officer); Robert R. Stephenson (Cockney Soldier); David Thursby (Agent Reporting Strangler's Identity); Leonard Wiley (Captain Stuart); Henry Zynda (German).

7

Libel and Old Lace

"He said I looked like Boris Karloff!"
—Boris Karloff as Jonathan, ***Arsenic and Old Lace,***
Broadway, 1941

"He said I looked like Erich von Stroheim!"
—Erich von Stroheim as Jonathan, ***Arsenic and Old Lace,***
Chicago Company, 1941

"He said I looked like Bela Lugosi!"
—Bela Lugosi as Jonathan, ***Arsenic and Old Lace,***
National Company, 1944

"He said I looked like Boris Karloff!"
—Raymond Massey as Jonathan,
Arsenic and Old Lace, film version, 1944

Monday, February 28, 1944: Baltimore's Ford's Theatre proudly presents the national company of *Arsenic and Old Lace,* publicized as the "Farewell Visit of This Sensational Comedy."

"BELA LUGOSI, In Person," heralds the ads.

It's the play's fourth visit to Baltimore in a little over three years. In December of 1940, *Arsenic and Old Lace* had braved the city for its pre–Broadway engagement. The star was Boris Karloff as mad Jonathan Brewster, a horrific serial killer whose face, refashioned by a drunken plastic surgeon, resembles ... Boris Karloff's. In March of 1941, after the show's phenomenal New York success, the Chicago company tried out here, starring Erich von Stroheim as Jonathan—looking, of course, like von Stroheim. In September of 1943, Karloff himself returned to Baltimore, trouping in the national company. Now in 1944, Lugosi—the script altered so Bela could make sport of himself—has replaced Karloff, who'd finally gone home to Hollywood.

The *Baltimore Sun's* second-string drama critic, who signs his (her?) column "E.T.B.," covers the opening. Come the final curtain, "E.T.B." has seen all "three of the theater's most fearful bogey men" in action as Jonathan—and files a comparison of interest to the ages:

Of the three, perhaps Mr. Karloff was the most fearful, despite overtones of conceivable gentlemanliness and even gentleness; Mr. von Stroheim, the most hateful; and Mr. Lugosi, the most comforting.

Mr. Karloff ... alone realized the maniacal personality written into the part by the playwright. Mr. von Stroheim was implacable, ruthless and cruel, but always viciously sane and logical. And Mr. Lugosi is almost too commonplace a killer, especially for Brooklyn, U.S.A., where killing as an art long ago outgrew the commonplace.

Boris Karloff as the original Jonathan Brewster of *Arsenic and Old Lace*.

In the motion pictures, at least since his famous *Dracula*, Mr. Lugosi has depended largely upon mysterious, flowing black cloaks and close-ups of his sinister eyes and devilish eyebrows for his projections of horror; in a shabby sack coat and with close-ups impossible, even for those in the $2.21 seats, his sanguinity is perceptibly diminished.[1]

If Lugosi reads the review, one seriously doubts he is pleased. ("Comforting? *Common-place*?!") Yet all three Jonathans—even Karloff, who'd won glory and made a fortune via

Left: **Erich von Stroheim, who played Jonathan in** *Arsenic*'s **national company. He replaced Karloff on Broadway in 1942 while Karloff and several of the original cast took over in the tour.** *Right:* **Bela Lugosi, who replaced Karloff in the** *Arsenic and Old Lace* **national company in 1944.**

Arsenic and Old Lace—have suffered disappointments. Indeed, with the touring company set to close in the spring of 1944 and the still-running Broadway version fated to shutter in June after 1,444 performances, Warner Bros. was preparing to release the film of *Arsenic and Old Lace* in September. The studio had shot the movie in the fall of 1941, directed by Frank Capra and starring Cary Grant as Mortimer. None of the trio of stage Jonathans immortalized their performance on film—the role had gone to Raymond Massey, made up to resemble Karloff.

Why did it work out that way? How did it go over then? How does it go over now? And how close did the film come to spawning a libel and right of likeness suit that might have rocked horror film history?

* * *

> *The Monster was in town last night.*
>   *People make faces at him. People say "Boo!" and try to scare him. It doesn't work. He's used to it. He's Boris Karloff, the creeping death, the mummy, the walking horror. He's Frankenstein's Monster.*
> —Donald Kirkley, *The Baltimore Sun*, December 23, 1940[2]

Yuletide, 1940. Baltimore, awaiting Santa Claus, meanwhile greets Boris Karloff, who's come to town to try out in the macabre three-act comedy *Arsenic and Old Lace,* his Broadway debut. On November 27, 1931, almost nine years previously, Donald Kirkley, who now reports Karloff's visit, had reviewed *Frankenstein*:

He who is not scared by *Frankenstein*, at Keith's Theatre, cannot be scared by a motion picture....
Pieced together with bits of bodies filched from graves and gallows, and fitted with the brain of
a criminal, this fiend is the embodiment of everything evil in human experience—violence, stupidity, lust, hatred, fear and cruelty. It will hold the spectator spellbound ... and afterward come
to him in nightmares....[3]

Now, "the embodiment of everything evil" is playing Santa Claus at a Baltimore charity
event, and preparing for his New York stage bow. He is, in his own word ... "terrified."

The legend goes that playwright Joseph Kesselring had whipped up *Arsenic and Old
Lace* after imagining the last thing his grandmother would do.[4] However, Kesselring's muse
was actually far more sinister: He presumably knew the saga of "Sister" Amy Archer-Gilligan,
a serial killer who ran the Archer Home for Aged People in Windsor, Connecticut. In his
book *The Devil's Rooming House* (Lyons Press, 2010), M. William Phelps tells how one could
arrange a lifetime stay in Amy's home for $1,000. To clear room for more, Amy, between
1908 and 1916, poisoned possibly no fewer than 40 resident oldsters and perhaps as many
as 64. Sister Amy's weapon: rat poison.

There were exhumed bodies (including that of Amy's second husband), autopsies, a
sensational trial ... and in the summer of 1917, a jury convicted Amy Archer-Gilligan of mass
murder. She faced the gallows, but a new trial saw her claiming insanity as a defense, as well
as a surprise revelation: Her 19-year-old daughter testified that Mom was "a drug fiend,"
hooked on morphine. Amy received a sentence of life imprisonment, but while incarcerated
at Wethersfield State Prison, behaved bizarrely—e.g., "playing funeral music on the piano
when on those rare occasions nobody had died recently." In 1924, declared "hopelessly
insane," she entered Connecticut Valley Hospital, an asylum in Middletown.

Amy was still there, working in the asylum cafeteria and praying with a Bible in her lap
when Joseph Kesselring came to Hartford, contacted Hugh Alcorn (who'd prosecuted Amy)
and asked him to help him write a drama about the murders. As Phelps writes,

> [T]he prosecutor gave Kesselring access to court documents. The dramatist went to work studying
> every nuance and detail of the Archer Home murders.

It is the 38-year-old Kesselring's third play—his most recent, *Cross-town*, had opened
on Broadway on March 17, 1937, and expired after only five performances—and he fortunately has found sponsorship by Howard Lindsay and Russel Crouse. High-spirited Broadway
pros, the duo had dramatized *Life with Father*, which had opened at the Empire Theatre
November 8, 1939, and became a colossal hit. Lindsay himself played Father (growing a han-
dlebar mustache for the role) and his wife Dorothy Stickney portrayed his wife Vinnie. In
fact, *Arsenic and Old Lace* had come to Lindsay's attention after Kesselring had sent it to
Stickney as a potential vehicle for her.

The original play, titled *Bodies in Our Cellar*, was almost *Springtime for Hitler*-style
awful, a tasteless mess complete with various references to the smell of rotting cadavers in
the basement and basically devoid of humor. Amused by its dreadfulness—and perhaps fearful that the very-much-alive Amy would hear of the play in the asylum and be still capable
of a lawsuit—Lindsay and Crouse extensively rewrote the show, taking no credit but privately
arranging to share royalties with Kesselring. The rewrite tells the tale of sweet Aunt Abby
and Aunt Martha, who live in an old Victorian house beside a Brooklyn cemetery. They poison lonely geezers with elderberry wine, believing they're performing a mercy. Their brother
Teddy, who thinks he's Teddy Roosevelt, roars "Charge!" as he runs up the stairway (which

he thinks is San Juan Hill) and disposes of the cadavers (whom he believes are yellow fever victims) in the cellar (which he believes is the Panama Canal). A nephew, Mortimer—a drama critic who hates the theater—becomes hysterical when he discovers his aunts' little secret, that there are no less than 12 bodies in the basement.

"This," he tells them, "has become a very bad habit!"

The play kicks into wicked speed when a second nephew, Jonathan, shows up one spooky night. An escaped serial killer with at least 12 victims all over the world, he travels with a drunken plastic surgeon, Dr. Einstein, who, while intoxicated, had given him a new face. As Jonathan explains the killing of one Mr. Spenalzo, whose body now resides in a rumble seat: "He said I looked like Boris Karloff!"

"You see, insanity runs in my family," Mortimer confesses to his fiancée Elaine. "It practically gallops."

Arsenic and Old Lace is Lindsay and Crouse's first time out producing together for Broadway. They line up *Life with Father*'s Bretaigne Windust to direct, and hatch a terrific showmanship plan: get Boris Karloff himself to play Jonathan!

May 1940. Russel Crouse comes to Hollywood—Lucey's Restaurant, near RKO Studios, specifically—to woo Karloff. The star gives him, as Crouse will remember, "the fastest no" he'd ever heard, arguing he'd only played the stage in "the sticks" and felt presumptuous starring on Broadway. When Crouse trots out his big gun line—"He said I looked like Boris Karloff!"—the star roars with laughter, delighted at the idea of lampooning himself. Still he demurs, saying he'll only brave New York if the play has three roles larger than his. There are precisely three larger roles—so Karloff agrees to make his Broadway debut at age 53.

Broadway dynamos Howard Lindsay and Russel Crouse—producers (and uncredited rewriters) of the play *Arsenic and Old Lace*.

For his trio of co-stars, Lindsay and Crouse secure top Broadway troupers. Fifty-four-year-old Josephine Hull wins the role of Aunt Abby; she is a veteran of 30 New York plays, including the 1937 Pulitzer Prize winner *You Can't Take It with You*. (She is, incidentally, sister-in-law to Henry Hull, star of Universal's 1935 *WereWolf of London*.) Ms. Hull had decided to become an actress in 1902; "One of my aunts stayed up all night weeping, thinking of all the dreadful people she knew I was going to meet."[5] Sixty-seven-year-old Jean Adair, as Aunt Martha, has acted in more than 20 Broadway shows, among them *Murder at the Vanities* (1933) with Bela Lugosi, and *On Borrowed Time* (1938), as the unspeakable Aunt Demetria. Forty-year-old Allyn Joslyn, as Mortimer, had won Broadway stardom in the screwball comedy *Boy Meets Girl* (1935) and is a comic timing dynamo, returning to the stage after such films as *Only Angels Have Wings* (1939) and *No Time for Comedy* (1940).

Stout and hearty John Alexander, whose previous Broadway play *Out from Under* (1940) had run only nine performances, lands the plum part of Teddy. Edgar Stehli, whose New York stage credits included playing the foppish Osric in John Barrymore's *Hamlet* (1922), signs on as Dr. Einstein. Elizabeth Inglise is set to make her Broadway debut as Elaine. Bruce Gordon, later gangster Frank "The Enforcer" Nitti on TV's *The Untouchables*, lands the small role of Police Officer Klein.

Saturday, December 7: Karloff completes *The Devil Commands* at Columbia Studios and takes an all-night plane from Los Angeles to New York to commence rehearsals. He is so scared he stutters. The company pretends not to notice. Mortified and terrified, Karloff wants to quit.

> I was rotten and I knew it. I wanted to say, "I can't go through with it—let me get back to Hollywood." And I almost did go back. I decided against it only after I'd taken a long walk alone up Fifth Avenue and wrestled it out of myself.[6]

He walks all night, gets back to the hotel at 5:30 a.m., catnaps and—resolute—reports to rehearsal. The stutters vanish but the nerves remain. "Everyone connected with the production was so kind and helpful," Karloff will remember. "Bretaigne Windust, the director, was wonderful—patient and understanding." As for Lindsay and Crouse, Karloff affectionately dubs them "the beamish ones."

Thursday night, December 26: *Arsenic and Old Lace* plays its first performance at Baltimore's Maryland Theatre. Karloff, his lucky silver dollar in his pocket, trembles in the wings. "The funniest play about murder in the history of the stage," rhapsodizes Donald Kirkley in the next day's *Baltimore Sun*, praising Josephine Hull, Jean Adair, Allyn Joslyn, John Alexander, Elizabeth Inglise, Edgar Stehli ... and Karloff:

> It is pleasant to be able to report that Mr. Karloff so far overcame his announced nervousness at the thought of facing that greatest theatrical monster of all—an audience—as to give a thoroughly composed and forceful performance, well-rounded and complete. It is his business to make Jonathan a formidable, dangerous fellow, and he does this to perfection.
>
> We have long suspected that the frightful makeup of Frankenstein's Monster concealed a first-rate stage actor, and Mr. Karloff's performance last night proved it. By way of parenthesis, it proved also that good actors can be made in Hollywood.

Although the show is a smash in Baltimore, Lindsay and Crouse are cautious. Kirkley had admired Elizabeth Inglise as "the most attractive leading lady seen hereabouts in too many seasons," but the producers decide she is "too English" as the Brooklyn fiancée and replace her with Helen Brooks.[7] There is concern that the rapturous Baltimore reception will prime Manhattan critics for an opening night kill. Additionally, Lindsay, Crouse and Kesselring have gleefully made the character of Mortimer a lethal satire on theater critics—a pretentious (but amusing) jackass who lapses into fourth estate clichés even while fighting with his fiancée:

> *Mortimer*: When we're married and I have problems to face, I hope you're less *tedious* and *uninspired*!
> *Elaine*: And when we're married, *if* we're married—I hope I find you *adequate*!

A major concern is the very essence of the play—a lighthearted look at two serial killers who bury their victims in the cellar. The final curtain falls on the aunts merrily committing their thirteenth murder. The humor is wildly subversive—will the New York critics righteously denounce it?

And as always, there is the gamble with the third serial killer—Karloff. Is the star actually *too* frightening in person? Act III presents a spine-tingling episode, played in candlelight, in which Karloff's bloodthirsty Jonathan binds and gags Joslyn's Mortimer in a chair, anxious to kill his brother via "the Melbourne method"—a lingering, two-hour vivisection. Sinuously putting on a black rubber glove, lovingly fondling glittering surgical knives, Karloff lisps and hisses:

> Mortimer, I've been away for 20 years, but never once in all that time—my dear brother—were you out of my mind. In Melbourne one night, I dreamed of you—When I landed in San Francisco, I felt a strange satisfaction—once more, I was in the same country as you.... *Now*, doctor, we go to *work*!

It is a chillingly macabre *tour de force*, truly worthy of the King of Hollywood Horror, frightening audiences into breathless silence. Is he *too* sadistic? And will Karloff hold up, artistically and emotionally, as he is still suffering so terribly from stage fright?

Arsenic and Old Lace leaves Baltimore, recklessly plunging into the belly of the beast in New York. There is a curtain call gimmick—12 old men, supposedly the victims of the aunts, come up from their graves in the cellar to line up and take a bow. Karloff, meanwhile, has his own special curtain call: He rises from the window seat, like a vampire arising from his coffin.

Come the New York opening, Howard Lindsay, who is performing that night in *Life with Father*, fatefully shakes hands with Russel Crouse, who will witness *Arsenic and Old Lace*'s premiere at Broadway's Fulton Theatre. "It is my studied conviction," says Lindsay to Crouse, "that we either have a very big hit, or we both will be run out of town."[8]

* * *

He proves that pure, unputtied Karloff is scariest of all.
—*Life* magazine, reviewing Karloff in
Arsenic and Old Lace, February 17, 1941

Friday night, January 10, 1941: Come the curtain call of *Arsenic and Old Lace*, Karloff, Josephine Hull and Jean Adair stand stage center, the tears running down their faces, the audience cheering, everyone on the stage and in the audience thrilled to be part of one of the most riotously triumphant evenings in Broadway history.

New York Times: "[S]o funny that none of us will ever forget it." *New York Journal-American*: "Mr. Karloff ... is overpoweringly sinister in a performance that would, I should think, scare the other actors out of their makeup."

The national press cheers too. "A violently funny and batty murder play... Loony, witty, timed to the split second..." raves *Time,* writing of Karloff: "Making his Broadway debut, without any of his usual horrific face putty or false hair, he is every bit as sinister as he was in *Frankenstein.*"

Yes, the Brewster girls are the true stars of the show—in fact, star-billed Karloff demands they receive the final curtain call. Yet Karloff is the powerhouse. For all their sophistication, New York audiences behold Hollywood's Frankenstein Monster himself, on stage and "in person," with a genuine awe. The star's wickedly potent presence seems to possess the Fulton Theatre, while still allowing the hilarity to romp; for all the "loony" comedy, it is the terrified movie bogeyman who truly makes the show. The line "He said I looked like Boris Karloff!" always brings down the house, and as *The Baltimore Sun*'s Donald Kirkley puts it, Karloff's "impersonating himself" on the stage becomes "one of the most clever coups in the history of the contemporary drama."

Boris Karloff is an overnight Broadway sensation. Indeed, as showcased live and in the flesh in *Arsenic and Old Lace,* he is—to use a colloquial modern-day term—a rock star.

Apparently, Lindsay and Crouse have believed all along this would be the case. They'd originally offered Karloff a chance to invest in the show and the star had cautiously declined. Now, with the play a resounding hit, they reveal they'd generously held out a $6,000 "piece of the action" for Karloff, who will reportedly earn it all back in three weeks. Karloff is reaping a salary of $2,000 weekly, plus ten percent of the house (which, at standing room only, takes in approximately $17,000 weekly). He also has a ten percent interest in the whole enterprise. He is the star of a show business phenomenon that promises to make him a millionaire.

As always, Karloff—now a gaunt, 147-lb. version of himself, still suffering the "terrors" of live theater and losing weight in "sheer fright"—regards himself with irreverence. He privately claims he had only one memory of the opening of *Arsenic and Old Lace*: "I had diarrhea for three weeks!"

* * *

Officer O'Hara: I never go to the movies. I hate 'em! My mother says the movies is a
    bastard art.
Mortimer: Yes, it's full of them!

—From Act II of ***Arsenic and Old Lace***

Wednesday, February 5, 1941: Only 26 days after *Arsenic and Old Lace* opens—and apparently about the time Karloff recovers from his gastro-intestinal distress—the *New York Times* announces that Warner Bros. has closed the deal to purchase the screen rights.

Reportedly every major studio had bid and Warners topped its major competitors, Paramount and Goldwyn, offering $175,000, plus 10 percent of the gross (or 15 percent— sources differ) for Lindsay, Crouse, Karloff and the other 20-plus investors.[9] Compare the cost to two previous Warner Broadway buys: *George Washington Slept Here* ($83,000) and *Old Acquaintance* ($75,000). Protective of the Broadway show, the producers arrange a release date of January 1, 1943, allowing the play a solid two-year run before the film will come to theaters. As it is, they underestimate.

The Warner news must intrigue Karloff. As noted in the "Boris Karloff at Warner Bros." chapter, there had been three profit-making Karloff vehicles for WB—*The Walking Dead* (1936), *West of Shanghai* (1937), and *The Invisible Menace* (1938)—before Jack L. Warner had forced the star to make *Devil's Island* (1939) and *British Intelligence* (1940) at half-price—$10,000 each. That Warner now has to pay so walloping a tab for a play Karloff stars in and partly owns surely provides the star a righteous chuckle.

Likely, Karloff happily imagines eventually returning in glory to Warner Bros. after his recent humiliations there, and starring in *Arsenic and Old Lace.*

* * *

*Mortimer, have you forgotten the things I used to do to you when we were boys? Remember
the time you were tied to the bedpost—the needles under your fingernails—?*
—Boris Karloff as Jonathan, ***Arsenic and Old Lace***

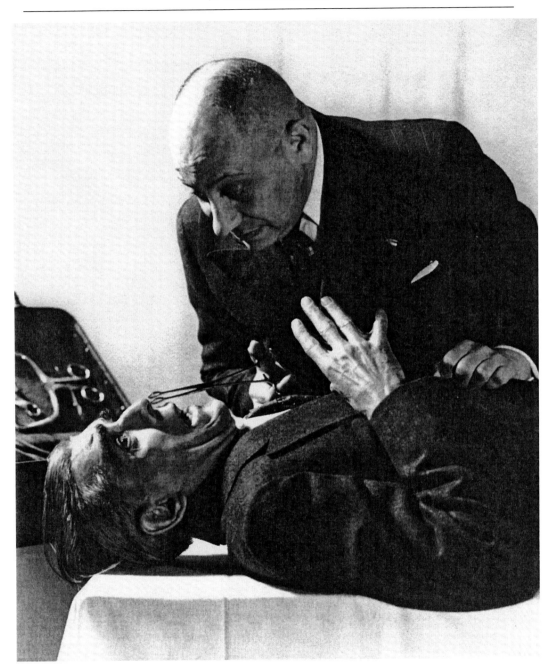

Two Jonathans: Karloff and Erich von Stroheim, doing some grisly clowning for publicity for *Arsenic and Old Lace*.

February 6, 1941: The *New York Times* runs this notice:

Erich von Stroheim may portray the Boris Karloff role in the Chicago company of *Arsenic and Old Lace*, opening there on April 1, it was learned yesterday. Mr. von Stroheim is discussing the idea with Russel Crouse, co-producer of the hit, with whom he recently saw the play. Bela Lugosi and Lon Chaney, Jr., also have been considered for the part.[10]

Lugosi has been feathering his nest in Hollywood, hoping to re-ascend to the number one horror star position Karloff had enjoyed ever since the release of *Frankenstein*. Chaney Jr., who'd triumphed as Lennie in *Of Mice and Men* (United Artists, 1939), has recently signed with Universal and had completed *Man Made Monster*, not to open in New York until March; *The Wolf Man* won't start shooting until October. Still, Lindsay and Crouse already see young Lon as a horror star. At any rate, von Stroheim wins the Jonathan role, and will score a triumph in Baltimore in March of 1941 before moving for a 12-week run in Chicago.

Meanwhile, several of Karloff's Hollywood acquaintances brave Broadway. On March 12, 1941, Elsa Lanchester, the Bride of Frankenstein herself, opens in the melodrama *They Walk Alone*, portraying a maniacal killer and providing a virtuoso display of what the *New York Times* calls "savage insanity." It folds after only 21 performances. More significantly, in light of what would later transpire, on March 11, 1941, Katharine Cornell opens in a hit revival of Shaw's *The Doctor's Dilemma*, flanked by two leading men who'd run afoul of Karloff at Universal in 1932: Bramwell Fletcher, who'd gone stark raving mad at the sight of Karloff as *The Mummy,* and Raymond Massey, who'd battled Boris's bearded butler Morgan in *The Old Dark House*.

Karloff happily settles into his *Arsenic and Old Lace* eight-shows-a-week routine. He also becomes a frequent visiting guest star to radio's *Inner Sanctum,* starting with the March 16, 1941, broadcast "The Man of Steel." That same date, the righteous wrath that *Arsenic and Old Lace* threatened to unleash emerged from one Jessie Wilcox of Brooklyn, whose letter appeared in the *New York Times'* "In the Drama Mailbag":

> [M]urder is not funny; insanity is not funny.... I feel it is an imposition on theater-loving people to ask them to spend two and a half hours in such an atmosphere.... The terrific success of the thing and the echoes of thoughtless laughter are to me no excuse for its being....

Allyn Joslyn himself responded in a letter to the *Times*: "[T]he play does not make fun of insanity.... The enjoyment is obtained by watching the effect the dearly demented have on the saner members of the cast." He added, rather profoundly: "Who in this day of uncertainty is as happy as 'Teddy' Brewster, whose future, with its exciting adventures and absolute security, is an open book where all may read?"

Of course, the play romps on, a terrific hit. On the same April 13, 1941, that the *Times* runs Joslyn's letter—Easter Sunday, by the way—the full cast of *Arsenic and Old Lace* visits West Point, offering a free performance for the faculty and cadets.

June 1941: A curious event will foreshadow major *Arsenic* events-to-come. Karloff is set to take a month-long leave of absence from the play to return to Hollywood and complete his Columbia contract in *The Boogie Man Will Get You,* a horror comedy clearly taking its cue from *Arsenic*'s success. Lindsay and Crouse consider a guest actor to fill in for the month, and even ponder simply closing down the play until Karloff returns. At last, unwilling to allow Karloff to leave, the play's producers arrange with Columbia to delay the film until February of 1942.

In an era when Broadway plays sometimes shut down for the summer months, *Arsenic and Old Lace* plays on, the Fulton Theatre kept comfortable by a brand new $15,000 cooling system. Meanwhile, the Fulton is neighbors with the Gaiety Theatre, a burlesque house— in fact, they adjoin and their back alleys abut. As warm weather arrives, the talents of both houses take breaks between acts in the alley. There one can see Karloff, having a smoke and chatting with the various strippers as the ladies cool off after a Gaiety bump and grind.

ARSENIC AND OLD LACE

Program for Broadway's *Arsenic and Old Lace* (1941).

* * *

"He said I looked like Edward G. Robinson!"
—Edward G. Robinson (had he played Jonathan
in the film of *Arsenic and Old Lace*)

Thursday, July 24, 1941: Douglas Churchill, Hollywood reporter, telephones this news to the *New York Times*:

> Frank Capra will produce and direct the screen version of *Arsenic and Old Lace*, for Warner Bros, the studio announced today.... Capra will supervise the property's adaptation to the screen.... Edward G. Robinson has been mentioned for the Karloff role.

Frank Capra is a three-time Best Director Academy Award winner: *It Happened One Night* (1934), *Mr. Deeds Goes to Town* (1936) and *You Can't Take It with You* (1938). His flair for casting is acute. So why is he originally considering Edward G. Robinson for Karloff's part of Jonathan Brewster?

Few clues will be forthcoming from Capra himself. In his best-selling but high-apple-pie-in-the-sky 1971 memoir *The Name Above the Title,* the great man will play footloose and fancy free with many of the realities of his career, including his producing and directing *Arsenic and Old Lace.* Capra will claim he saw the play in New York, fell in love with it, learned between acts that Warners owned the rights, ran backstage afterwards, and immediately offered Josephine Hull and Jean Adair $25,000 each and John Alexander $15,000 to recreate their roles in his movie. Then, wrote Capra, he convinced Jack L. Warner in Hollywood that he could produce and direct it in four weeks on a $400,000 budget. In fact, none of the three players earned half the salary Capra reported, the film's schedule was double what Capra wrote, and the budget was nearly triple what Capra claimed.[11]

Additionally, Capra will write that he made the film because he was about to enter the Army Signal Corps and wanted a profit-making film to keep the cash flowing for his family while he earned Army pay. "The way we lived," wrote Capra, "a major's salary of $250 a month wouldn't pay the phone bill." Capra did enter the Signal Corps in late 1941—while wrapping up *Arsenic and Old Lace*—but that summer he is telling the press he is making the film because his plan to become an independent producer-director for United Artists has collapsed.

In his excellent 1992 biography *Frank Capra: The Catastrophe of Genius,* Joseph McBride will provide some personal reasons why Capra fell under the spell of *Arsenic and Old Lace.* Capra's mother (who made her own wine) seemed a sweetie to her familiars, but Capra and family knew about her actual dark side—and feared it.[12] Additionally, Capra had an older brother who provided him much torment as a child, and grew up to be a criminal— shades of the sinister Jonathan Brewster.

Lindsay and Crouse had hoped that Rene Clair would direct the film version; they accept Capra, naturally aware that he is one of the few film directors whose name has box office power. Capra engages Warner Bros. script workhorses Julius J. and Philip G. Epstein, twins, to adapt the play; the Epsteins had been Oscar-nominated for Warners' *Four Daughters* (1938) and will win the Academy Award (along with Howard Koch) for the script of *Casablanca* (1943).[13]

At any rate, for the next three months, *Arsenic and Old Lace* will be a roller coaster of rampant rumors, madcap negotiations and ultimate compromises:

Friday, July 25: *The Hollywood Citizen News* reports, "Bela Lugosi will start a road tour soon, playing Boris Karloff's role in *Arsenic and Old Lace*." Apparently Lindsay and Crouse aren't totally satisfied with von Stroheim, and Bela gets the nod. However, Lugosi—sensitive about taking on a role created by his rival Karloff—backs out for the time being. "He really would have liked to play the part," his wife Lillian will recall, "but pride wouldn't let him."[14] The national company will begin a 35-week tour September 15, with von Stroheim as Jonathan.

Saturday, August 2: Allyn Joslyn gives his final performance as Mortimer in *Arsenic and Old Lace*. He will leave for Hollywood to join the cast of 20th Century–Fox's *I Wake Up Screaming*.[15] Earlier that week, on July 30, Joslyn and Karloff were honorary pallbearers at the Little Church Around the Corner funeral of William Parke, who'd created the role of *Arsenic*'s Mr. Witherspoon, the superintendent of Happy Dale Sanitarium—and the last victim of the old aunts. Parke had died of a heart attack at his home. Clinton Sundberg, who'd played Mortimer in the Chicago company, replaces Joslyn.

Monday, August 11: Warners announces that the star role of Mortimer in *Arsenic and Old Lace* will go to ... Richard Travis. He's a contract player, largely unknown, who'd just played the romantic male lead in *The Man Who Came to Dinner*. The news is decidedly anticlimactic. Capra had offered Mortimer to Bob Hope, who'd starred in Paramount's horror comedies *The Cat and the Canary* (1939) and *The Ghost Breakers* (1940), but Paramount had nixed a loan-out. Reportedly Capra also approached Jack Benny to play Mortimer, but Benny declines, eventually starring in Warners' *George Washington Slept Here*. Legend claims Capra also considered Warner star Ronald Reagan.

Capra does want Josephine Hull and Jean Adair for the film, and the play's producers are willing to arrange a leave of absence. For Teddy, Capra considers casting Andy Devine.

Meanwhile, Warners' idea of starring Edward G. Robinson as Jonathan fizzles. Robinson, a major Warners star and a top Hollywood heavy since *Little Caesar* (1930), has a flair for comedy, and is no beauty—so the line "He said I looked like Edward G. Robinson!" might have worked. Yet Capra and the Epsteins have discovered in developing the film script that *Arsenic and Old Lace,* with its bodies in the cellar and graveyard outside the window, clearly requires a bogeyman to tap its full potential. The film script introduces Jonathan thusly, in almost the same words as the play script:

> Jonathan enters. He is very tall. There is something sinister about him—something that brings a slight chill in his presence. It is in his walk, his bearing, and his strange resemblance to Boris Karloff.[16]

Jonathan's line "He said I looked like Boris Karloff!" remains in the script, and Capra realizes the film needs what the Broadway show has.

It needs Karloff.

Capra and Warners feverishly begin negotiations to sign Karloff for the film. One story claims Karloff, believing himself key to the film's success, demands too high a salary. Another theorizes that the star, bitter about the way Warners had treated him recently, refuses to work again for the studio.

All of this is nonsense. The reason Karloff can't get the green light to make the film of *Arsenic and Old Lace* is simple: Howard Lindsay and Russel Crouse won't release him.

Truly, if the hit play has so impressive an advance sale, why are Lindsay and Crouse so reluctant to give up Karloff, if only for two months? The fact is, both producers realize that

Karloff is the play's top attraction, and his temporary absence could cause the money train to jump the tracks. These men are making *Arsenic* fortunes—Karloff too—and are protecting their investment (and Karloff's) by keeping the star in a play that promises to be a record breaker.

Of course, the same men will eventually share in the profits of the film, and have reason to want the movie version to be as popular as possible. Lindsay and Crouse plead with Warners to delay the film until late June 1942, when Karloff will be free of his stage contract and the whole cast, in fact, will be available for the film.

Frank Capra, however, already has the wheels in motion.

Karloff, meanwhile, gallantly gives everyone the impression he'll be happy to stay in New York and keep the show going while Hull and Adair go to Hollywood. In fact, he deeply wants to do the film, and Lindsay and Crouse—now good friends with the actor and wanting to please him—realize it.

They make Warner Bros. a fascinating counter-offer.

* * *

> *"He said I looked like Humphrey Bogart!"*
> —Humphrey Bogart (had he played Jonathan
> in the play of ***Arsenic and Old Lace***)[17]

It seems a fair deal: Lindsay and Crouse will swap Karloff to Warners to make the film of *Arsenic and Old Lace* if Warners loans them Humphrey Bogart to play Jonathan in New York during Karloff's absence!

Bogart is having a great 1941 at Warners. The year had begun with the release of *High Sierra* and that summer he'd starred in *The Maltese Falcon,* which will open in New York October 18, 1941—just at the time Warners will start shooting *Arsenic and Old Lace.* Capra himself is enthused about this idea and tries to get Jack L. Warner to make it happen.

Meanwhile, more events:

Wednesday, September 10: John Huston completes a final day of retakes on *The Maltese Falcon.* Bogart has meanwhile started a new film, *All Through the Night,* which will keep him busy into early October.

Tuesday, September 30: Capra and Warner Bros. announce major news: Cary Grant will star as Mortimer in *Arsenic and Old Lace.* (Whatever happened to Richard Travis?) Grant makes a complex and generous arrangement with Warners: His fee is $160,000; of that amount, $50,000 will go to the Hollywood division of British War Relief of Southern California, $25,000 to the American Red Cross, $25,000 to the USO, and $10,000 to Grant's agent. Grant gets the remaining $50,000, which Warner arranges at $8,333.33 on a six-week guarantee.[18]

Meanwhile, with the Bogart-Karloff trade looking less than hopeful, Warner Bros. has a secret weapon. On contract is Raymond Massey, 45-year-old Canadian actor, who had powerfully scored as Lincoln in Robert Sherwood's Pulitzer Prize–winning play *Abe Lincoln in Illinois* (1938) and the RKO film version (1940), for which Massey received a Best Actor Academy nomination. Massey had been an effective villain in such films as *The Prisoner of Zenda* (Selznick–United Artists, 1937) and *Drums* (Korda–United Artists, 1938); for Warners, he'd played a powerful and frightening John Brown in *Santa Fe Trail* (1940), virtually blowing away co-stars Errol Flynn (as Jeb Stuart) and Ronald Reagan (as Custer). Indeed, Reagan will claim that when Flynn learned how large Massey's role was, he "stayed away four

Top: An autographed portrait of Raymond Massey. *Bottom:* Raymond Massey, seen here as Jonathan in the Warner Bros. screen version of *Arsenic and Old Lace,* directed by Frank Capra and released in 1944.

days" from the shooting, fearful that Massey would take the show.[19]

Massey is tall, dark, well-respected, had observed Karloff up close when both had played in *The Old Dark House*—and is under contract to Warners. "I tested for Capra and won this wonderful role,"[20] Massey will remember late in life—but it will come without the blessing of the play's producers. After Capra sends news of Massey's casting to Howard Lindsay and Russel "Buck" Crouse—asking at the same time to borrow John Alexander to play Teddy (he can't get Andy Devine)—Lindsay and Crouse fire off this telegram to Capra, dated September 30, 1941:

> Dear Frank: Feel we can promise you Alexander. Will let you know by end of week. Do not talk to his agent at any time. Casting of Massey very disappointing to us as it makes valueless the trick of resemblance to well-known villain which we consider important. We were happy about Bogart and will still trade Karloff for him. Confidentially Massey will not get comedy values of Jonathan. Kindest Regards,
> Buck and Howard[21]

A last stab at a Bogart-for-Karloff swap falls through. Massey arranges to play Jonathan at $5,000 per week on a five-week guarantee. The contract stipulates he'll work "two additional weeks free if required."

Meanwhile, Warners closes the deals for Josephine Hull and Jean Adair, both receiving $1,250 per week on an eight-week guarantee. Lindsay and Crouse also provide John Alexander, who signs for $700 per week on an eight-week guarantee.

Playing Elaine will be Warners' Priscilla Lane, who will receive her weekly $1,000 studio pay. Jack Carson, a $750 per week Warner contractee, joins the show as O'Hara, the comic cop who aspires to be a playwright.

A very happy addition: Peter Lorre as Dr. Einstein. Lorre, who'd just minced so memorably as Joel Cairo in Warners' *The Maltese Falcon,* signs at $1,750 per week with a six-week guarantee.

Arsenic and Old Lace gets the deluxe Warner treatment. The director of photography is Sol Polito, cinematographer of such WB classics as *Five Star Final, 42nd Street, The Adventures of Robin Hood,* and *Angels with Dirty Faces.* The composer is the legendary Max Steiner, whose work included the epic score for *King Kong,* the unforgettable one for *Gone with the Wind* and an Oscar-winning one for *The Informer.* Both Polito and Steiner will receive 1941 Oscar nominations for Warners' *Sergeant York.*

Final *Arsenic and Old Lace* budget: $1,220,000. Schedule: Eight weeks, i.e., 48 days.

So, come the week of October 13, Josephine Hull, Jean Adair and John Alexander all depart the New York play for Hollywood. Patricia Collinge takes over as Aunt Abby, Minnie Dupree as Aunt Martha and Harry Gribbon as Teddy. Capra films wardrobe tests of Cary Grant and Priscilla Lane the afternoon of Friday, October 17, and *Arsenic and Old Lace* will start shooting Monday morning, October 20, 1941.

Karloff stays on in New York with the new players, the SRO audiences and the neighboring strippers—counting his blessings, and never revealing to Lindsay and Crouse how heartbroken he truly is. Meanwhile, Capra assures the studio that, since Warners has bought the film rights, there's no cause for fear that Boris Karloff might sue Warner Bros. for illegal use of his likeness and for libel.

* * *

Capra started this picture yesterday in the INT. MARRIAGE LICENSE BUREAU on Stage 4. They obtained their first shot at 9:35 and finished at 6:10 p.m. covering 5 scenes, 2'40" in time, 22 set-ups and 3 pages of script.
—Eric Stacey, unit manager, Warner Bros. Inter-Office Communication to T.C. Wright, studio production manager, regarding *Arsenic and Old Lace,* October 21, 1941[22]

Week One: Monday, October 20, to Saturday, October 25, 1941

"This company progressed very nicely for their first day," reports Eric Stacey. On hand are stars Cary Grant and Priscilla Lane. (In the play, Mortimer and Elaine are engaged; in the film, they marry early in the show.) Spencer Charters is the marriage license clerk, Charles Lane is a reporter, and there are 42 extras. The company finishes the sequence on Stage 4 the next day. High spirits prevail. Capra will write in *The Name Above the Title:*

I couldn't have been happier. No great social document "to save the world" ... just good old-fashioned theater—an anything goes, rip-roaring comedy about murder. I let the scene stealers run wild; for the actors it was a mugger's ball.[23]

Josephine Hull and Jean Adair have both settled into the Chateau Elysee in Hollywood, and John Alexander has taken quarters at 2337 North Canyon Drive. All three report Tuesday to Stage 17 for wardrobe and makeup tests. Meanwhile, the company, working with a Revised Temporary Script, is skirting censorship trouble. The Breen Office, protesting the "sex frustration" of newlyweds Mortimer and Elaine, has nixed the idea of Elaine whistling for Mortimer to come to the parsonage while her father is away. Stacey explains in his October 21 report that Capra and the Epsteins have decided that the couple will leave right away for Niagara Falls. This means he (Mortimer) tells the Taxi Driver to wait, and apparently this Driver will be waiting outside the house throughout the entire action of the play waiting for the couple to leave ... they are going to write various scenes to fit this situation.

This is a boon for the actor playing the Taxi Driver, Garry Owen. Stacey notes that Owen's going rate is $600 per week; Warners, due to his long engagement, has managed to reduce his salary to $400 per week for seven weeks.

"Naturally," reports Stacey, "if we can get rid of him sooner, we will do so."

On Wednesday and Thursday, Grant, Lane, and Owen report to Stage 7, the Exterior of the Brewster house. Art Director Max Parker's Victorian Brewster abode is a Hollywood marvel, the exterior rolling away to reveal the interior, and there's even a next-door cemetery. The set virtually screams Halloween—precisely the time the film takes place; we'll see the old aunts giving Jack O' Lanterns to the neighborhood children. It's in this autumn leaves–covered graveyard that the bride and groom play a bizarre "romantic" episode, Grant pursuing Lane around the tombstones:

Elaine: But Mortimer, you're going to love me for my mind, too?
Mortimer: One thing at a time!

Hedda Hopper pays a call to the set and will write in her column:

Visited Cary Grant on the set of *Arsenic and Old Lace* the other day, which story, by the way, is so spiced with sex, intermingled with the "stiffs," that I hope Frank Capra got his O.K. from Will Hays before doing that hilarious scene in the graveyard....

Meanwhile, Capra is hatching comic ideas, as Eric Stacey notes in his daily report:

Mr. Capra is adding a routine in the house with the cat that is supposed to belong to the old ladies. This cat will be a running gag throughout the picture (when they carry the body thru the set at night they will step on its tail, and many other gags...).

Stacey enthuses that a deal is set for a "very good trained cat" for $35 per week, and "we only pay the handler on the days the handler actually works." Any fan of the movie knows there's no sign or sound of a cat in *Arsenic and Old Lace*; nevertheless, the cat and its trainer will show up almost every day for the next eight weeks, the feline doomed to the cutting room floor.

On Thursday, Josephine Hull and Jean Adair begin work. As the current plan is to finish Cary Grant's role in six weeks, Capra skips the aunts' first scenes in the film and picks up with them peeking coyly through a window, watching Mortimer's graveyard escapade with Elaine. The maiden aunts deliver dialogue not in the play version:

Martha (nostalgically): Remember—when we were young—and ran away from the boys?
Abby (wistfully): Yes. Sometimes I think we ran too fast.

It's cute dialogue—but it'll be cut from the release print.

Grant and Jean Adair have a happy reunion; about 20 years previously, Grant had contracted rheumatic fever on a theatrical tour and Adair had nursed him through his illness. However, both Hull and Adair, with very little film experience, are terribly camera-shy—and terrified. "There were times," Ms. Hull will recall of filming *Arsenic and Old Lace*, "when I sat in a corner of the stage on the verge of tears because I was so sure I had done everything wrong."

Morbid (but funny) love scene: Cary Grant as a frenetic Mortimer and Priscilla Lane as his bride Elaine on the terrific cemetery set of *Arsenic and Old Lace.*

On Friday, John Alexander as Teddy joins Grant, Hull and Adair. Alexander has appeared in several films, usually uncredited, most recently as Robert Todd Lincoln in the Warners short subject *The Flag of Humanity* (1940). His first filmed scene: appearing on the balcony in tropical clothes and helmet and with shovel, en route to "Panama." The day's work also includes Abby showing Mortimer a childhood picture of his brother Jonathan:

> *Abby (terror in her face):* Just the thought of Jonathan makes me afraid. (*shuddering*) Do you remember when he used to cut worms in two—with his teeth?

Saturday focuses on Jack Carson as Officer O'Hara and Ed McNamara as Officer Brophy, patrolling outside the Brewster home. Thirteen extras are on call. Carson is demanding time off today to bring his wife and newborn baby home. Capra excuses him from noon to 2:30.

Meanwhile, Raymond Massey has been en route to Hollywood from New York. Stacey's Saturday report notes: "Raymond Massey is expected in by train at Pasadena around the noon hour today, Saturday, and will report directly to makeup where Perc [Westmore] will personally supervise his makeup as 'Boris Karloff,' and spend most of the afternoon thereon. We will make a test, if everything is successful, to be shot by Polito, upon completion of the day's work."

Note the wording—"his makeup as 'Boris Karloff.'" Warner legal counsel Roy Obringer has serious concerns about a Karloff likeness, and Capra has assured him they'd use just suggestive makeup. In truth, however, Capra has ordered Westmore to make Massey resemble Karloff as much as possible—and Westmore has created a sponge "Karloff mask." Massey and Westmore are ready for a test by evening, shot from 5:50 to 6:05 p.m. Massey removes his mask-makeup and takes up quarters at 220 South Cliffwood in Brentwood.

The first week wraps up, *Arsenic and Old Lace* on schedule, the script still incomplete. Meanwhile back in New York, Sunday, October 26: Karloff guest stars on *Inner Sanctum* in "Terror on Bailey Street."

WEEK TWO: MONDAY, OCTOBER 27– SATURDAY, NOVEMBER 1, 1941

On Monday, as *The Wolf Man* begins shooting at Universal, Frank Capra starts his day on *Arsenic and Old Lace* at Warners by reviewing the tests of what Eric Stacey calls "Raymond Massey as 'Jonathan Brewster' in the 'Boris Karloff' makeup." Stacey writes:

> Mr. Capra saw these tests this morning, Monday, at 8:00 a.m. and expressed himself as being very well-pleased with the results, in spite of the fact that he told me he thought that the Makeup Dept. will be fiddling around all week with it....
>   Perc Westmore informs me that he wants to make one more test around Wednesday to improve the makeup a little more, and is also planning on taking Mr. Massey to a special dentist for certain piece work involving a gold band....

Capra shoots scenes of Grant, Hull, and Adair—the action following Mortimer's discovery of the corpse in the window seat, and the aunts' explanation. On Tuesday, Grant, Hull, and Adair carry on, Capra spending much of the day shooting close shots of what he'd filmed the previous day. They finish at 6:25 p.m.; at 6:45, Massey and Peter Lorre shoot a photographic and sound test.

Wednesday: Grant, Lane, Hull, and Adair work; so does 76-year-old Edward McWade as old man Gibbs, who almost drinks the elderberry wine before Mortimer hysterically stops him from becoming victim #13. Come the end of the day and Massey has *another* makeup test—his third in five days. Stacey reports:

> [T]hey made another makeup test of Raymond Massey for the "Karloff" part, which was viewed this morning [October 30] and the consensus of opinion is that the first test was the best, so we will probably go back to the original makeup.

Thursday, Friday (Halloween), and Saturday: The sequence continues with Mortimer and the aunts, as well as Elaine, Gibbs and the Taxi Driver. Incidentally, this episode includes dialogue the Breen Office had ordered cut: Aunt Martha's recipe for poisoned wine, which Breen feared that would-be poisoners in the audience might emulate:

> *Martha:* Well, Mortimer, for a gallon of elderberry wine I take a teaspoonful of arsenic, and add a half-teaspoonful of strychnine, and then just a pinch of cyanide.
> *Mortimer (appraisingly):* Should have quite a kick!

Meanwhile, Capra has Cary Grant giving a wild, hysterical, screwball performance—rather like the one Grant gave in Howard Hawks' *Bringing Up Baby* (1938), but multiplied by ten. Popped-eyes, funny sounds, violent "takes," whinnies, squeals, spritzes when he tries to whistle ... Grant looks and sounds as if he's having the time of his life. He isn't.

"I tried to explain to [Capra] that I couldn't do that kind of comedy—all those double takes," Grant will say in later years. "I'd have been better as one of the old aunts!"

Posterity will take aim at Grant's Mortimer. "Capra's hick jollity turns Grant into a manic eunuch," writes Pauline Kael in *5001 Nights at the Movies*. Grant, fearful he looks ridiculous, is prickly, complaining about the set, his role, and even the other players' costumes. Still, there's no denying the star's energy, crackerjack timing—and professionalism in accepting Capra's direction and trying to please him. Nevertheless, Grant's performance in *Arsenic and Old Lace* will be his personal least favorite of a long career.

There are tedious troubles with lighting effects; Priscilla Lane calls in sick on Thursday; and Capra, as Eric Stacey reports, is "panning people all around the room." Also, as of Saturday, Capra has decided to shoot the film "in strict continuity in the home"; he'll go back and shoot the first episodes in the house late in production. However, Warners has arranged the shooting to concentrate on Cary Grant, and as Stacey reports, if Capra shoots in continuity, there will be days Grant doesn't work. Grant, despite his discomfort in the film, makes no fuss about this and demands no additional salary.

The second week of *Arsenic and Old Lace* ends with the film two days behind schedule and the script still incomplete.

Week Three: Monday, November 3– Saturday, November 8, 1941

By this time, Capra has developed a pattern, which Eric Stacey will describe in one of his daily reports:

> His method of shooting is as follows: He times his work so that the last thing in the day he will stage, and photograph, [is] a master long shot of a sequence; then the following morning at 8:00 o'clock when he sees his dailies of the previous day's work, he will continue in that sequence and make changes while he is shooting closer shots of the same action, and as ideas develop he will sometimes go back and make close-ups again having the character read a different line, or have the character do a different piece of business.
>
> I do not see how anyone can control this since this is the way he works, and if any changes are to be made in the way Mr. Capra makes pictures I certainly do not feel that I am qualified to tell him what to do....

Wednesday: Cary Grant, Josephine Hull and Jean Adair report at 9 a.m. Raymond Massey and Peter Lorre start work two hours later as Jonathan and Dr. Einstein. ("There is something about him that suggests the unfrocked priest," notes the script of Einstein). Both Massey and Lorre are immediately effective:

> *Jonathan*: Come in, doctor. This is the home of my youth. As a boy I couldn't wait to escape from this house. And now I'm glad to escape back into it ... I hope there's a fatted calf awaiting the return of the prodigal.
> *Einstein*: Yeah, I'm hungry!

Thursday: Josephine Hull and Jean Adair start work at 9:00 a.m.; Massey and Lorre join them at 10:30. Eric Stacey reports:

> This morning, after looking at the rushes of yesterday's work, which involved the first photography of Raymond Massey who is playing the Karloff part, Mr. Capra was very disappointed with the way he looked.
> We had made three tests of Mr. Massey as "Karloff" and the first test made was decided upon. This was the makeup that he used yesterday, but Mr. Capra, after seeing the first day's work, decided that he was not gruesome enough and did not look enough like Karloff....

Raymond Massey as a scar-faced Jonathan and Peter Lorre as a pop-eyed Dr. Einstein in the film *Arsenic and Old Lace.*

Capra leaves the makeup as is on Thursday, but Friday begins with Massey undergoing a makeup adjustment that lasts from 9 to 10:45 a.m. Stacey reports:

> [T]his morning, Friday, they added a lot of scars on his face and removed his eyebrows, and he is looking much more the way Mr. Capra wants him.

The final makeup is wonderfully "Karloffian," and Massey sells it with his wild eyes—evoking a savage animal, with Karloff's face sewn and stitched to it. In an interview with James Bawden, Massey remembered *Arsenic and Old Lace*:

Everybody was convinced it would be a huge hit and we had such fun making it. I'd already played a disturbed man in my worst-ever play performance, *The Black Ace*, so as Jonathan Brewster, I simply played Randolph Calthorpe. I did not imitate Boris Karloff as some people charged (but never to my face).[24]

Whatever Massey's inspiration, the effect is genuinely frightening and works splendidly. Massey *does* come off as a macabre mix of Karloff and Frankenstein's Monster—and Peter Lorre, as Dr. Einstein, seems like his talking pet tarantula.

Capra retakes several key close-ups of Massey and proceeds with the shooting:

> *Jonathan*: Forget Mr. Spenalzo!
> *Einstein*: But we can't leave a dead body in the rumble seat! You shouldn't have killed him, Chonny. Just because he knows about us—what happens—[*he gestures strangulation*].
> *Jonathan*: We came to him for help and he tries to shake us down. Besides, he said I looked like Boris Karloff....

The scene ends with Lorre and Massey ad-libbing about the new face Jonathan will receive. "I just let them go," Capra will recall. "That one scene went about three or four minutes beyond the scene and it's all in the picture."[25] In fact, about 25 seconds of the ad-libs are in the picture.

Saturday: Hull, Adair, Alexander, Massey and Lorre work much of the day on scenes that will ultimately be cut, including Teddy entering from the cellar in his tropical attire, blowing his bugle, shouting "Charge!" and rushing up the steps past Jonathan and Einstein. "Jonathan draws his revolver," notes the script. "Einstein flattens himself up against the wall."

The third week of shooting ends. The script is still incomplete, the film still two days behind schedule.

WEEK FOUR: MONDAY, NOVEMBER 10– SATURDAY, NOVEMBER 15, 1941

Monday: The *Arsenic* company covers 6¼ pages—"by far the best day this company has had since the beginning of the picture," reports Stacey, "and everything is proceeding very nicely." It's the scene after the aunts have provided dinner for Jonathan and Einstein, and includes this memorable exchange:

> *Jonathan*: Teddy! I think it's time for you to go to bed.
> *Teddy*: I beg your pardon. Who are you?
> *Jonathan*: I'm Woodrow Wilson. Go to bed!
> *Teddy*: No—you're not Wilson. But your face is familiar. [*Jonathan stiffens*] Let me see. You're not anyone I know now. Perhaps later—on my hunting trip to Africa—yes, you look like someone I might meet in the jungle.

Stacey reports:

> [I]t is the general opinion of Mr. Capra that this show will run over by a week or ten days.... I believe that certain strict deals were made with the three members of the cast from New York ... and I am notifying you now that these artists will undoubtedly go beyond their original eight-week guarantee.... [I]f there is some legal work to be done to prevent them from being taken from us, or something, it should now be presented to Mr. Obringer.

Part of the reason for the possible run-over: Capra plans to retake and tone down some of Cary Grant's hysteria. Also, the film is now three days behind schedule.

Tuesday: The same principals work, as does Priscilla Lane. Capra shoots the memorable scene of Massey's Jonathan lunging through the window above the window seat—*Arsenic's* big Halloween "Boo!" moment.

Besides fearing an injunction from Lindsay and Crouse if Hull, Adair, and Alexander run over schedule, Stacey sees two other potentially serious problems:

1. Due to Capra proceeding in "direct continuity," Cary Grant hasn't worked for six days. If he isn't finished by December 1, "large penalties are to be exacted by Columbia Pictures," where Grant is due to start a new film. Grant has told Stacey not to worry—he doesn't believe Columbia will be ready for him on December 1, and Grant and Capra have a "personal" deal which will allow him to run over his original finish date. Stacey worries anyway.

2. Perhaps the most interesting "worry": "Also want to mention the possibility again of lawsuits arising from our use of Raymond Massey impersonating Boris Karloff."

It's a bombshell. Has Karloff, angry over not playing Jonathan in the movie and bitter about his treatment at Warners, hinted he'll sue Warners over this impersonation? Or is it all mounting panic on Warner Bros.' part—after multiple tests and retakes to make Massey as Karloffian as possible?

Wednesday: The company continues with "various complicated lighting effects." Stacey reports one lighting effect no one anticipated: a fire, caused by a light in the cellar. Stacey writes that the fire, although extinguished quickly, damaged the clothing of one of the electricians. "I presume we are to reimburse him for his loss," writes Stacey.

The question of how long Warners needs Hull, Adair and Alexander remains up in the air, since there's still no ending scripted. The most intriguing problem, however, remains the potential Karloff lawsuit, now genuinely haunting Warner Bros. On this day, November 12, Warners' legal eagle Roy Obringer charges into the fray, writing an air mail letter to Jack L. Warner, who's then staying at the Waldorf-Astoria Towers in New York City. Obringer relates that he and lawyer Morris Ebenstein

> have looked at four days' rushes involving scenes of Massey. The makeup of Massey (as checked with Perc Westmore) consists of a sponge mask and bears a very striking resemblance to BORIS KARLOFF. Likewise, Massey is wearing a wig, and although the hair is brown and Karloff's is white, nevertheless, the hair dress and parting of the Massey wig is similar to the hair dress and parting of Karloff's hair.
>
> In the dialogue, Massey makes the statement that Peter Lorre, portraying the role of Dr. Einstein, has performed an operation upon him with results that people are remarking that he (Massey) looks like Boris Karloff, and the identification of Massey with Karloff is further established by the fact that one of the characters says that Massey looks just like a character seen in motion pictures. Furthermore, the script, in describing the Massey character, specifically states that he should look like Karloff, and the name of Boris Karloff is found actually written into the script in a number of places. Other dialogue references are made to his (Massey's) personality having been seen or would most likely be seen in the jungle, which can raise only one inference, i.e., that Massey (in his resemblance to Karloff) looks horrible, and this may be considered by Karloff as libelous.[26]

Obringer reports that the Warner legals have even performed a test: taking stills of Massey in his *Arsenic* makeup and showing it to "one or two persons who have no knowledge of our purpose." The "spontaneous impression": "it was a photograph of Karloff." Additionally, Obringer notes that Massey had visited his office only the previous day to "to finally sign his contract"; Obringer asked him about his makeup, and Massey replied, "I'm supposed to look like Boris Karloff." The letter continues:

Massey in Jonathan Brewster makeup, on the *Arsenic and Old Lace* set (Photofest).

I checked further with Westmore, who stated that he was specifically instructed by Frank Capra to effect a makeup on Massey to resemble Boris Karloff as closely as he possibly could, and, as a matter of fact, he used still portraits of Boris Karloff to get the physical features in creating a mask for Massey.

As such, Obringer notes, Perc Westmore and Raymond Massey, if called upon to testify, would both benefit a Karloff lawsuit, as would the film script.

Therefore, it is the opinion of both Morris and myself that this is a very definite risk which you will have to decide to take or, as an alternative, to approach Karloff for some kind of a release. Keep in mind that Karloff could claim that his name was used and that he was being represented in our picture. Likewise, the reference to his jungle episode and other references might well be considered by Karloff as libelous.

On the right of privacy angle, should Karloff bring an action in New York State and it be held that his privacy rights were invaded, it would be mandatory upon the court to grant him an injunction of the showing of the picture. In other states where they may possibly not have privacy statutes, Karloff could claim unfair competition, claiming that his physical features were his livelihood and that livelihood was being damaged or prejudiced by our unfair copying of his visage; or Karloff could possibly go into Federal Courts of New York State and secure jurisdiction covering all other states from an angle of unfair competition.

Obringer attaches a release form to submit to Karloff. He writes that Warner will have to decide whether or not to pursue it, noting that Lindsay and Crouse might "prevail" upon Karloff to sign it, as Karloff was getting royalties from the play. He adds that Capra too might be "sufficiently influential" to coax Karloff into signing the release, but advises against it, candidly doubting Capra's "sincerity," since Capra had been untruthful to Obringer about the "definite Karloff mask." The lawyer closed that Capra's contention that Warners had bought the play and thereby had freedom to use the Karloff lines "is not a fact":

[W]hatever rights Lindsay and Crouse may have in the play or whatever activity Karloff may have therein do not pass to us upon the purchase of the right to make a motion picture based upon the play, as the rights of libel and privacy are still personal to Karloff and do not pass with the picture rights.

Accompanying Obringer's letter is this legal release, dated November 12 and addressed to Warner Bros. Pictures, Inc.:

Gentlemen:

It is my understanding that in the motion picture now being produced by you and directed by Mr. Frank Capra, based upon the stage play *Arsenic and Old Lace*, the actor who is portraying the role of "Jonathan," which is the same role I am now portraying in the stage version of said play, has been made up to resemble me, and that reference to such resemblance is made in the dialogue of the picture.

Please be advised that I consent to the foregoing.

Yours very truly,

———————

BORIS KARLOFF

It's fun to imagine Jack L. Warner coming to the Fulton Theatre, hat and legal release in hand, trying to charm Karloff into signing the release after Warner had forced Karloff to work for half-pay in his last two Warner Bros. films. Karloff might have fantasized terrorizing "J.L." and his studio with a major lawsuit, but this would surely have been contrary to his own interests, as he stood to share in the fortune the film promised to earn. It also would have been at definite odds with the "Dear Boris" persona.

Jack Warner presumably gets his Karloff release. Meanwhile, back in Hollywood:

Thursday, November 13, and Friday, November 14: Cary Grant returns to the show. The episode—Jonathan attacking Elaine, who's come to the house, and the aunts and Mortimer intervening—originally had dialogue missing from the movie. "Good grief!" exclaims Mortimer when he first sees Jonathan. "What's that—a Halloween mask?"

Abby: It's your brother Jonathan. He's had his face changed. Dr. Einstein performed the operation on him.

Mortimer: I wouldn't care if he were Boris Karloff! C'mon, beat it...!

Saturday: Grant, Hull, Adair, and Massey all work this morning; Lorre and Carson join them in the afternoon. The company is having trouble scheduling Carson, who's simultaneously working on *Larceny, Inc.*, starring Edward G. Robinson and directed by Lloyd Bacon.

Week four ends with the film now three to four days behind schedule. With no ending yet scripted, the studio isn't able to schedule new actors for the final part of the film.

WEEK FIVE: MONDAY, NOVEMBER 17– SATURDAY, NOVEMBER 22, 1941

Monday: A shocker shows up in the production report: Capra finally admits he'd released the Epstein brothers while the *Arsenic* script was still incomplete, and Jack Warner has assigned them to another project.

The reason for this seemingly ridiculous situation seems obvious: Capra wants to be the *auteur* of his film. (Debate about whether the true genius of his films is Capra or his former chief writer Robert Riskin will plague Capra until his death in 1991.) The director likely believes he can come up with a finale himself, but his ideas so far are no better than the capers of the comic cat, which still shows up on the set with its handler every day.

Warner is still in New York. Capra agrees to send him a wire asking for the Epsteins. Meanwhile, Capra wants James Gleason to play Lt. Rooney and Edward Everett Horton for Mr. Witherspoon of Happy Dale Sanitarium. Both will be available around November 26.

Tuesday, Wednesday and Thursday: Capra completes six pages of script Tuesday, four pages of script Wednesday. Thursday is Thanksgiving.

Friday and Saturday: Capra is still being mysterious about the script. Eric Stacey writes that with the present temporary script, they only have about four to six days of work involving the actors they're concentrating on—Grant, Hull, Adair, and Alexander. Meanwhile, the lack of script continues contagiously complicating Jack Carson working in *Larceny, Inc.* Stacey asks studio manager T.C. Wright to contact Warner executive producer Hal Wallis regarding the "gravity" of this script situation.

Also, the episode where Jonathan and Einstein tie up Mortimer in a chair has become a problem child. A frazzled Stacey reports about Saturday's shoot:

> They had quite a poor day again.... due to a lot of mechanical problems in the scene, such as tying up Cary Grant with the curtain cords, gagging him, and also light effects.... Also, the sequence itself Mr. Capra does not like very much, and whenever that happens he always shoots a lot of film. In fact, most of Saturday was spent in taking over Friday's work....

Stacey adds that Capra was hoping "to get some script by next Thursday," and notes that it's "impossible to concentrate on any one person in the cast without wasting the others."

Week Five ends. The film is now five days behind schedule and still has no ending.

Sunday, November 23: Boris Karloff celebrates his 54th birthday.

WEEK SIX: MONDAY, NOVEMBER 24–
SATURDAY, NOVEMBER 29, 1941

Monday: Grant, Massey, Lorre, John Alexander and Jack Carson work on basically the same sequence Capra's been shooting for three days now. The director makes 30 set-ups of Grant being tied up and gagged. With Capra so maddeningly vague about the script, Stacey has personally spoken to the Epstein brothers, who "hope to have something on paper" by Thursday.

Tuesday: Massey and Lorre get a day off as Capra again hits his stride, shooting four and three-quarter script pages: scenes in the Brewster home, as well as the cemetery and exterior of Elaine's home. Chester Clute joins the show as Dr. Gilchrist, who's prepared to commit Teddy after the latter takes him on a stroll through the cemetery ("Arlington is beautiful this time of year, is it not, doctor?"). Also shot is the scene where Mortimer—afraid his family's insanity will pass on to their children—tells Elaine, "I love you so much, I can't go through with our marriage":

Elaine: Now, just because Teddy—
Mortimer: No, it goes way back. The first Brewster—the one who came over on the *Mayflower*. You know, in those days the Indians used to scalp the settlers—he used to scalp the Indians.

Wednesday: Clute finishes his role. Edward McWade, as Gibbs, comes back for an added scene as he flees the house. Meanwhile, the unit learns the script *won't* be ready by Thursday, as anticipated.

Thursday: Grant, Massey, Lorre, Carson, Edward McNamara (as Officer Brophy) and John Ridgely (as the cop Saunders) work in the scene in which the police apprehend Jonathan.

Friday and Saturday: Capra returns to the early part of the film and the first sequence inside the Brewster home. Josephine Hull, Jean Adair, John Alexander, Jack Carson and Edward McNamara report to Stage 7, as does Grant Mitchell, beginning work as the sneezing Rev. Harper, Elaine's father. Capra moves smoothly and this scene plays nicely—great "takes" between Alexander's Teddy and Carson's O'Hara, and the bit in which the grandfather clock chimes at odd moments.

Week Six ends. There's still no completed script. Meanwhile, Capra

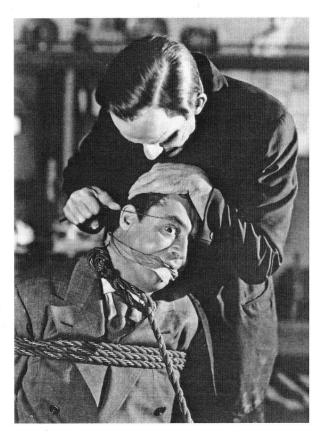

The Melbourne Method! Massey and Grant in *Arsenic and Old Lace*.

promises to finish Hull, Adair and Alexander by Sunday, December 21. This is hardly reassuring, as all three are supposed to back in the play in New York on December 22.

Week Seven: Monday, December 1–Saturday, December 6, 1941

Monday and Tuesday: The early sequence continues. Grant Mitchell wraps up his Rev. Harper role Tuesday at noon.

Wednesday: Capra shoots various close-ups and 31 set-ups, including a riotous fight sequence with doubles for Massey, Carson and McNamara. The rest of the script is now coming in gradually.

Thursday and Friday: James Gleason joins the show as Lt. Rooney on a two-week guarantee at $1,500 per week. Gleason eventually gives his close friend Karloff his copy of the *Arsenic and Old Lace* film script.

Saturday: Starting *Arsenic and Old Lace* today is Edward Everett Horton, who has signed on at $5,000 per week on a two-week guarantee to play Mr. Witherspoon.

The company finally has the rest of the script. They go home Saturday night, of course unaware of the world history about to happen the next morning.

Week Eight: Monday, December 8–Saturday, December 13, 1941

Monday and Tuesday: On the harrowing day after Pearl Harbor, Grant, Hull, Adair, Alexander, Lorre, Gleason and Horton work. Capra keeps things moving, shooting over ten pages Monday and Tuesday. The United States is now at war and Capra is eager to finish up everything. He decides against retakes of Grant's most over-the-top scenes.

Wednesday: James Gleason finishes as Lt. Rooney. The film script, after all the delays, ends the same way as the play, despite Breen Office objections: Aunt Abby and Aunt Martha, in a dead heat with Jonathan at 12 murders apiece, top their now-arrested nephew by poisoning ... Mr. Witherspoon. Also, one of the great laugh lines of the play had come when Mortimer, learning he was actually illegitimate and hence not carrying the Brewster brand of insanity, exulted, "I'm not a Brewster! I'm a bastard!" Due to censorship, the Epsteins changed the line to "I'm not a Brewster! I'm a son of a sea cook!" The altered line will also get terrific audience response.

Friday: John Alexander finishes his role as Teddy; Garry Owen (as the hapless Cabbie) and John Ridgely (as policeman Saunders) finish too. Frank Capra officially joins the Signal Corps, which will allow him time to complete and edit *Arsenic*.

Saturday: Cary Grant, Josephine Hull, Jean Adair, and Edward Everett Horton's Witherspoon all finish. Vaughan Glaser, as Judge Cullman, starts and completes his single scene.

Capra has finished with the New York players a full week earlier than he'd recently anticipated.

Week Nine: Monday, December 15, and Tuesday, December 16, 1941

Monday: Speed is of the essence: The call is 8:00 a.m. Jack Carson's Officer O'Hara and Edward McNamara's Officer Brophy finish. Massey and Lorre play a memorable scene in the cellar set on Stage 11, where Jonathan expresses his desire to kill Mortimer via the "Melbourne Method." Capra has especially enjoyed working with Lorre; in Stephen D. Youngkin's biography of Lorre, *The Lost One,* the author quotes Capra as considering Lorre "fully one-third" of *Arsenic and Old Lace:*

> He was a remarkable innovator ... he himself built his part with little tricks that were almost indiscernible, with his eyes, with his face, with his body.... Each of these built a character and built up a love in the director for that person who's thinking of things that he should be thinking of. You're so grateful to him.... That is acting before your eyes![27]

Lorre makes a dynamic suggestion: In the cellar, Lorre's idea was for Massey to appear on the wall as a monstrous shadow, while the camera focuses on Lorre's face and his horrified response. The suggestion sounds a bit like camera-hogging—and Lorre makes the most of his close-up—but it also works splendidly for Massey, a great, dark, bogeyman shadow on the cellar wall.

Tuesday: The call again is 8:00 a.m. Massey and Lorre play another scene in the cellar, where they plan to bury Mr. Spenalzo. Priscilla Lane joins them at 9:00 for a pick-up shot where Jonathan and Einstein accost Elaine; she wraps up her role at 10:30 a.m. Massey and Lorre then go back to Stage 11 and play a scene in Grandfather's Lab, high in the Brewster house. As the script describes it, the only light is "the moon streaming in through the window"; there are "cobwebs in profusion," as well as "an old-fashioned operating table, sinks, faucets, test tubes.... There is a large picture of Grandfather on the wall. He was not a handsome man."

> *Jonathan* [*looking around*]: Yes, just as it was—even to the jars of poison on the shelf. Grandfather made them himself.
> *Einstein* [*pointing to the picture*]: And dot, I suppose, is Grandfather? [*Jonathan nods grimly*] I could have done a good chob on him.
> *Jonathan*: Look, doctor—an operating table. A little moth-eaten, perhaps, but entirely serviceable.
> *Einstein*: Yes. I operate on you here.
> *Jonathan*: Only on me? That would be selfish. Doctor, we could make a fortune here! This laboratory—there's a large ward in the attic—ten beds, doctor—and Brooklyn is crying for your talents.

The scene continues, Jonathan announcing that "practically everybody in Brooklyn needs a new face" and that the house "will be our headquarters for years." As for the aunts objecting:

> *Einstein*: And if they say no?
> *Jonathan* [*the moonlight on his face adds menace*]: Doctor—two helpless old women—?

Very regrettably, this scene—filled with macabre atmosphere, and revealing Jonathan's master plan—will fall on the cutting room floor, along with the antics of Capra's cat. At any rate, Massey finishes at 3:45 and Lorre at 3:50.

PRODUCTION FINISHED AS OF TODAY, TUESDAY, 12/16/41 reads the Daily Production and Progress Report. With Capra working as energetically and patriotically as possible this last week, the film, which had been running as many as five days behind, ends up only one day behind schedule.

Monday, December 22: Josephine Hull, Jean Adair and John Alexander rejoin Karloff and the Broadway company of *Arsenic and Old Lace.* The next day, Karloff plays Santa Claus at the Beekman Hospital in New York's Lower East Side for 200 children between ages five and 12. New York Governor Alfred E. Smith accompanies him. The children charge Karloff's Santa for gifts, the *New York Times* reporting that this stampede "upset the gaily lighted Christmas tree."

"The usual hospital staff was supplemented by four policemen from the Oak Street station house in maintaining order," reports the *Times*.

* * *

Hail! All hail! To Lindsay and Crouse
We're loyal backers, we never grouse
Once a month we shout their praise
As those lovely checks slide down our ways...
Long yell for Karloff, Kesselring too,
Erich von Stroheim will pull us through...
—"Doggerel" found in Boris Karloff's estate papers, 2008,
written by an ***Arsenic and Old Lace*** backer, circa 1942[28]

Come the 1942 New Year and *Arsenic and Old Lace* continues playing to SRO houses. In February, when the time comes for Karloff to take a leave of absence for Columbia's *The Boogie Man Will Get You,* Lindsay and Crouse once again successfully bargain to postpone the film. Karloff stays on in the play, paying guest visits to radio's *Inner Sanctum* and *Information Please.*

Saturday, June 27, 1942: Karloff plays his final Broadway performance of *Arsenic and Old Lace.* Josephine Hull, Jean Adair, John Alexander, and Edgar Stehli are set to leave too and join Karloff in the national company. Lindsay and Crouse reportedly condone the cast playing tricks on each other this night. As noted, Karloff takes his curtain call lifting the lid and rising from the window seat. He can position himself into the seat via an off-stage side entrance. Come his curtain call on the night of June 27, and some prankster has nailed down the lid. Karloff, basically buried alive in the window seat, tries to escape as the actors, according to *Variety,* "roared" with laughter.[29] He finally gets out the side of the window seat and takes his bow. The audience, as is usually the case when this type of shenanigan rears its head on stage, has no idea what's happening.

Monday, June 29: Erich von Stroheim replaces Karloff in the cast.

Tuesday, July 7: Columbia begins shooting *The Boogie Man Will Get You,* starring Karloff and Peter Lorre—the latter receiving reimbursement from Lindsay and Crouse for the time he forfeited due to the postponements. Karloff plays a wacky mad doctor, and the film tries for *Arsenic*-style humor while basically falling flat. The two stars, both pals, surely perceive the *Arsenic* rip-off and wince together.

Monday, August 17: The road company of *Arsenic and Old Lace* opens in Los Angeles, starring most of the original cast members. Karloff will head the national tour for 66 weeks. The Broadway production meanwhile continues at the Fulton.

Wednesday, December 23: *Arsenic and Old Lace* opens in London. Despite the Blitz, it's a huge hit and will run 1,337 performances, becoming the longest-running American play on the London stage to that time. Edmund Willard plays Jonathan.

Friday, January 1, 1943: The date arrives that Warners had set as the release of the film *Arsenic and Old Lace.* However, the Broadway show is still running, so the film stays on the shelf.

Monday, January 4: Joseph Sweeney (whom some will remember as old "Juror No. 9" in 1957's *Twelve Angry Men*) takes over the Jonathan role in *Arsenic and Old Lace* in New York, replacing Erich von Stroheim, who leaves for Hollywood to play Field Marshal Rommel in Paramount's *Five Graves to Cairo*. Sweeney had previously replaced Edgar Stehli as Dr. Einstein.

Thursday, March 25: "Boris Karloff is having a field day on the road in *Arsenic and Old Lace*," reports the *New York Times*. The national company is about to play a week in Seattle, where the advance sale already is beyond a staggering $20,000.

Thursday, August 5: Another company of *Arsenic and Old Lace* opens in San Francisco. Starring as Jonathan: Bela Lugosi, who's failed to become Hollywood's top horror star since Karloff's absence, falling under the additional shadow of Lon Chaney, Jr. After San Francisco, Bela stars in *Arsenic* at the Music Box Theatre in Hollywood for five weeks.

Monday, September 6: *Arsenic and Old Lace* pays its third visit to Baltimore. "Mr. Karloff is even better than he was when he first appeared in this city, some 1,000 performances ago," reports the *Baltimore Sun*'s Donald Kirkley.

Late January 1944: Boris Karloff plays his final performance of Jonathan Brewster in the national company of *Arsenic and Old Lace*. "I wept the night I had to quit," says Karloff, who heads to Universal City on a two-picture, $60,000 contract. Bela Lugosi replaces him on the tour.

Tuesday, February 1: Universal begins shooting *The Climax,* a Technicolor clone of the studio's *Phantom of the Opera*. Susanna Foster, Turhan Bey and Karloff are the stars.

Tuesday, February 15: Karloff begins a new radio show, *Creeps by Night*.

Thursday, February 17: "Karloff Heads to Legit" headlines *Variety* on page 1. The report claims he'll return to Broadway in a "mystery comedy" written for him by Howard Lindsay and Russel Crouse. It doesn't happen.

Tuesday, April 4: Universal starts filming *House of Frankenstein,* in which Mad Doctor Karloff unleashes the studio's classic goblins. Lugosi's tour in *Arsenic and Old Lace* is just long enough to keep him from joining the film, and John Carradine plays Dracula. Lon Chaney is the Wolf Man, Glenn Strange is Frankenstein's Monster and J. Carrol Naish is a homicidal hunchback.

Thursday, May 18: Karloff signs with Val Lewton's horror unit at RKO, where he'll star in *The Body Snatcher, Isle of the Dead* and *Bedlam*. Bela Lugosi will also appear in *The Body Snatcher* as a Karloff victim.

Saturday, June 17: *Arsenic and Old Lace* finally plays the last of its 1,444 performances in New York, where it had moved to the Hudson Theatre. Josephine Hull is back playing Aunt Abby after the national tour, Effie Shannon has inherited Jean Adair's role of Aunt Martha, and Joseph Sweeney is still playing Jonathan. Only *Life with Father* had surpassed *Arsenic*'s longevity. The play has earned Lindsay, Crouse, Karloff and its other 28 investors $2,000,000, plus an additional two million in national companies. Royalties will keep coming in from productions all over the world.

At last, Warner Bros. can release the film, which has already played for the troops overseas—and has morphed a bit over the past 32 months. Preview audiences didn't like the aunts killing Edward Everett Horton's Mr. Witherspoon, nor did the Breen Office. Consequently, the release version simply lopped off the finale—unfortunately eliminating Jonathan's exit, the police taking him away as he taunts the aunts that their score of victims will stay even, 12 to 12. (The trailer will feature footage of Horton about to drink the wine.)

The aunts merrily kill one last victim—Edward Everett Horton, superintendent of Happy Dale Sanitarium—in the originally filmed finale of *Arsenic and Old Lace*. Warners cut the episode before release.

The last scene shows Cary Grant, Priscilla Lane and the Cab Driver, outside the house by the cemetery:

> *Mortimer*: No, no, I'm not a Brewster! I'm a son of a sea cook! [*He throws Elaine over his shoulder and runs through the cemetery*] *Chaaarge!*
> *Cab Driver*: I'm not a cab driver, I'm a coffee pot!

Fade Out, swell of music, THE END, Cast of Characters.

As noted, pruned was the vignette in the laboratory with Massey and Lorre, as was a scene of the two aunts in their beds. Added was the opening riot at the baseball game—presumably directed by someone other than Capra at some time unspecified in Warner Bros. production reports (and largely composed of actual baseball game newsreel footage). The final version runs 118 minutes and comes in at a final tab of $1,164,000—more than $50,000 under budget.

Finally, by the time *Arsenic and Old Lace* is released, two of its players have died, both in 1943: Edward McWade (who'd played Old Man Gibbs) and Spencer Charters (the Marriage License Clerk), the latter a suicide.

* * *

Wait 'til you see Raymond Massey...
he makes FRANKENSTEIN Look like a GLAMOUR BOY!
—Trailer, ***Arsenic and Old Lace***

Monday, August 28, 1944: Warners hosts a special trade showing of *Arsenic and Old Lace* at Warners Hollywood Theatre. *Variety* hails the film as "a hilarious witch's broth of entertainment."

Friday, September 1: The movie opens at Broadway's Strand Theatre to enormous business—and mixed critical reception. Archer Winsten of the *New York Post* praises Josephine Hull and Jean Adair, but critiques that, considering the outrageous plot, it was "unwise to belabor the points with excesses of performance, noise and furious action":

> Cary Grant ... careens around the house with acrobatic energy rather than critical insight. Raymond Massey, the bad, mad Brewster with a face like Boris Karloff, refuses to act like a pogo stick, but his makeup is enough to constitute a major distraction.

Winsten notes that audience response will depend on one's individual taste in "lunacy" and writes, "A similar effect might be achieved if Abbott and Costello found themselves in a Sherlock Holmes feature."

Saturday, September 30: Donald Kirkley, who'd reviewed the play's pre–Broadway tryout in December of 1940, reports on the movie version in the *Baltimore Sun*:

> The epic, macabre humor of *Arsenic and Old Lace* has been fully retained in the screen version.... In some ways the film is superior. The company as a whole is much better, and the action, freed from the space restrictions of a single set, is smoother....
>
> Josephine Hull and Jean Adair ... shine brightly in the roles they have made peculiarly their own. They are perfect. Cary Grant is no better than Allyn Joslyn but, being a bigger star, has acquired more importance in the story, and profits accordingly....

Surprisingly, Kirkley, who had so praised Karloff in the play, writes that "the most pronounced improvement" the film offers is Raymond Massey as Jonathan! The critic notes that Karloff as Jonathan had been "excellent showmanship," but one with "a theatrical ring."

> Mr. Massey, on the other hand, is doubly delightful: first, as the terrifically menacing villain of the piece; second, as the author of a satire on the Monster. When, in the play, Boris Karloff turned to the drunken physician who, through plastic surgery, has changed his face, and said: "You made me look like Boris Karloff!" it was funny, but it didn't ring true. In the film Mr. Massey really does look like Mr. K. as the latter appeared [as] "Frankenstein's Monster."

Kirkley adds that Peter Lorre "has never done anything quite so good," and opines that the play "is one of the funniest things ever to grace the American stage. The film is just as funny."

The movie is a smash. On November 4, 1944, Warner Bros. announces in *Motion Picture Herald* that *Arsenic and Old Lace* "is breaking holdover records in key cities," noting that it's currently "in its fifth week in Seattle and San Francisco, fourth week in St. Louis, Oakland and Washington, and third week in more than two dozen situations."

However ... one can't please all the people all the time. *Arsenic and Old Lace*'s offbeat humor sets off righteous anger with some audiences. Various small town exhibitors vehemently write to the *Motion Picture Herald*'s "What the Picture Did for Me" column:

> ...We had a number of walkouts and very severe comments were overheard. I am sorry that I played this film because such pictures sort of undermine faith in the movies. (Leonard J. Leise, Rand Theatre, Randolph, Nebraska, February 3, 1945)
>
> This is the poorest Warner picture I have ever played. Warners would do the show business a favor if they took this picture and burned it up. Many walkouts. (O.E. Simons, Roxy Theatre, Menno, South Dakota, March 31, 1945)
>
> This was really poison at the box office, and I'm not trying to be funny. (R. Covi, Covi Theatre, Herminie, Pennsylvania, January 12, 1946)

Nevertheless, *Arsenic and Old Lace* proves a gigantic hit: Domestic rentals: $2,836,000; foreign rentals: $1,948,000; profit: $2,074,000. The only person unhappy is Frank Capra, who claims in his memoirs that his first percentage check for *Arsenic and Old Lace* came to $232,000, and federal and state taxes took $205,000 of it.

February 1945: Boris Karloff, "homesick" for his play and eager to help the war effort, plays in a G.I. version of *Arsenic and Old Lace* in the Pacific. His cut of the film's profits must have been hefty too—hopefully enough to assuage his regret at not appearing in it.

* * *

"He said I looked like John Carradine!"
—John Carradine as Jonathan, summer stock, 1946

Fate smiles on many of the prime movers of Broadway's *Arsenic and Old Lace*.

Wednesday, November 1, 1944: Less than five months after she closed in *Arsenic*, Josephine Hull opens at New York's 48th Street Theatre in *Harvey*. Playwright Mary Chase will win the Pulitzer Prize and the play will run 1,775 performances. As such, Ms. Hull will have two back-to-back stage hits that keep her employed for eight years. Additionally, she'll reprise her role in the film version of *Harvey* (1950) and win an Oscar.

Wednesday, November 14, 1945: *State of the Union*, produced and written by Howard Lindsay and Russel Crouse, opens at New York's Hudson Theatre, starring Ralph Bellamy and Ruth Hussey. Lindsay and Crouse win the Pulitzer Prize and the play runs 765 performances. One of the happy investors: Boris Karloff. When *State of the Union* becomes a film in 1948, starring Spencer Tracy and Katharine Hepburn, Frank Capra directs it.

Monday, August 5, 1946: John Carradine plays Jonathan in *Arsenic and Old Lace* with the South Shore Players of Cohasset, Massachusetts. The actor will revive the role in stock over the years.

Monday, November 25, 1946: Karloff plays Jonathan on radio's *Lady Esther Screen Guild Theatre's* "Arsenic and Old Lace," a 30-minute version with Eddie Albert as Mortimer.

Summer, 1947: Bela Lugosi tours in stock in *Arsenic and Old Lace*. He will perform in various stock revivals of the play as late as 1954, two years before his death.

Monday, April 11, 1949: TV's *The Ford Theatre Hour* presents *Arsenic and Old Lace* with several members of the original Broadway cast: Karloff as Jonathan, Josephine Hull as Aunt Abby, and Edgar Stehli as Dr. Einstein. Ruth McDevitt portrays Aunt Martha, William Prince is Mortimer, and Bert Freed is Teddy.

Sunday, July 6, 1952: Radio's *Best Plays* presents a 60-minute "Arsenic and Old Lace" with Karloff as Jonathan, Jean Adair as Aunt Martha, Evelyn Varden as Aunt Abby, Donald Cook as Mortimer, and Edgar Stehli as Dr. Einstein.

Wednesday, January 5, 1955: TV's *The Best of Broadway* presents "Arsenic and Old Lace" with a cast to die for: Karloff and Peter Lorre as Jonathan and Dr. Einstein, Helen Hayes as Aunt Abby, Billie Burke as Aunt Martha, Orson Bean as Mortimer, John Alexander as Teddy, and Edward Everett Horton as Mr. Witherspoon.

Thursday, March 21, 1957: Karloff performs *Arsenic and Old Lace* in Alaska for the Anchorage Community College Theatre Workshop. Part of the lure is to check on oil wells in which he's invested. Still, he has a grand time and turns over his percentage of the performance's profits to help the group build its own theater.

Monday, February 5, 1962: TV's *The Hallmark Hall of Fame* present a 90-minute

Arsenic and Old Lace. Seventy-four-year-old Karloff is a vital, high-spirited Jonathan, Dorothy Stickney (Mrs. Howard Lindsay, who'd brought the play to her husband's attention over 20 years before) and Mildred Natwick are Aunt Abby and Aunt Martha respectively, Tony Randall is Mortimer, Tom Bosley is Teddy, and George Voskovec is Einstein.

Monday, April 23, 1962: Only two and a half months after the aforementioned telecast, "Sister" Amy Archer-Gilligan, the serial killer who apparently inspired *Arsenic and Old Lace,* dies in the Connecticut Valley Hospital, which she'd never left after her 1924 incarceration. Her reported age is 89.[30] It's a safe bet she never received a dime in *Arsenic and Old Lace* royalties.

* * *

Wednesday, April 2, 1969: The 90-minute TV *Arsenic and Old Lace* is a curio. Helen Hayes is back as Aunt Abby, with Lillian Gish as Aunt Martha, Bob Crane as Mortimer, David Wayne as Teddy, and Sue Lyon—sexpot star of *Lolita* (1962)—as Elaine. Portraying Jonathan Brewster: Fred Gwynne, the erstwhile Herman Munster of TV's *The Munsters.* Dr. Einstein is now called "Dr. Jonas Salk" and is played by Jack Gilford; Richard Deacon plays Mr. Witherspoon.

The telecast comes precisely two months after Boris Karloff's February 2, 1969, death in England. The venerable star was 81 and worth over $2,000,000; surely a respectable part of his fortune came via *Arsenic and Old Lace.* He was a parsimonious man, but one wonders what percentage of his millions Karloff would have forfeited for the chance to have played in the *Arsenic and Old Lace* film version.

By the time Karloff died, many of the vital forces of the original play were gone. Jean Adair, the original Aunt Martha, had died May 11, 1953. She'd enjoyed Broadway hits in *Detective Story* (1949) and *Bell Book and Candle* (1950); her final role had been Rebecca Nurse in Arthur Miller's *The Crucible,* leaving the play due to illness ten weeks before her death. Josephine Hull had died March 12, 1957, having racked up another late-in-life Broadway hit, *The Solid Gold Cadillac* (1953). Russel Crouse died April 3, 1966, and Howard Lindsay, February 11, 1968. Their phenomenally successful partnership had continued, including winning the Tony Award for writing the book for the Rodgers and Hammerstein musical *The Sound of Music.*

And as for Joseph Kesselring ... his next Broadway play was *Four Twelves Are Forty Eight,* which opened at the 48th Street Theatre on January 17, 1951. The title and comic plot—wildly politically incorrect, even in 1951—referred to three generations of American Indian girls who became unmarried mothers at age 12. The stars were Britisher Ernest Truex as a foul-mouthed Osage Indian named Uncle Snake Tooth and blacklisted Anne Revere (Best Supporting Actress Oscar winner for 1944's *National Velvet*) as an Indian matriarch named Nellie Bawke. Brooks Atkinson of the *New York Times* wrote that Revere had "never had a worse role in Hollywood" and noted that while she wore red makeup on her face opening night, her legs were white ("Not full-blooded, apparently," wrote Atkinson). Otto Preminger, of all people, directed the incredibly lame comedy and Pat Crowley was the ingénue lead. Atkinson wrote that all the "malicious gossips" who had claimed Howard Lindsay and Russel Crouse were truly responsible for the success of *Arsenic and Old Lace* via their uncredited rewrite of Kesselring's play need only see *Four Twelves Are Forty Eight* to prove their point; he also called it "one of the sorriest episodes of the season." The disastrous show ran only two performances and ended Kesselring's Broadway career. He died November 5, 1967, at age 65.

*   *   *

"He said I looked like Boris Karloff!"
—Abe Vigoda as Jonathan,
***Arsenic and Old Lace**, Broadway, 1986*

Thursday, June 26, 1986: *Arsenic and Old Lace* has a Broadway revival at New York's 46th Street Theatre. The stars come from TV sitcoms: *All in the Family*'s Jean Stapleton as Aunt Abby, *Alice*'s Polly Holliday as Aunt Martha ... and *Barney Miller*'s Abe Vigoda as Jonathan. "The years have not been kind to Mr. Kesselring's farce," writes Frank Rich in the *New York Times,* panning Brian Murray's sluggish direction (claiming the first act "seems to go on for about three weeks"). As for the new Jonathan Brewster,

> Mr. Vigoda plays a goon who's constantly mistaken for Boris Karloff—a joke that must have been hilarious when Karloff originated the role. Although Mr. Vigoda's visage is almost as formidable as Frankenstein's Monster's, his performance is merely heavy, when it's a comic heavy that's required.

The production runs 221 performances, during which time there are several key cast changes: *WKRP in Cincinnati*'s Gary Sandy replaces Tony Roberts as Mortimer, *Happy Days'* Marion Ross takes over for Polly Holliday as Aunt Martha, *F Troop*'s Larry Storch replaces William Hickey as Dr. Einstein, and Jonathan Frid—Barnabas Collins of TV's gothic soaper *Dark Shadows*—succeeds Abe Vigoda as Jonathan.

*   *   *

*I still can't believe that this play happened to me. It is one of
the luckiest things that ever happened to an actor.*
—Boris Karloff re: ***Arsenic and Old Lace**, 1943*

The Frank Capra film of *Arsenic and Old Lace* is a classic today, despite the traditional critiques. Cary Grant certainly never made peace with it. Shortly before his death in 1986, I saw Grant make a personal appearance at Johns Hopkins University in Baltimore, where he answered questions from the audience. An attractive young woman approached the microphone, told Grant how much she loved *Arsenic and Old Lace* and how she admired his performance in it. Grant, while not rude, made absolutely no response and looked at the woman as if she'd just said she was visiting from Mars.

Seventy-three years have passed since *Arsenic and Old Lace* both shocked and delighted Broadway with its macabre comedy. As Frank Rich noted over 25 years ago, the play creaks now, the "shock" level long diluted by familiarity and the changing times. However, Capra's film version still works—the "bits," the "shtick," the lightning pace, all serve the piece handsomely, the Misses Hull and Adair merrily unruffled in the eye of the slapstick storm. And yes, Raymond Massey is a splendidly sadistic, stitched-together Jonathan, the show's irreverent homage to Karloff and Frankenstein's Monster perhaps best delivered via third person, rather than by the King of Horror himself.

Still, one wonders about an "alternate" *Arsenic and Old Lace,* had Universal Studios won the film rights. Perhaps they would have waited until the summer of 1942 to shoot the film, as Howard Lindsay and Russel Crouse had hoped, when the Broadway cast was available. Maybe, in a moment of brilliance, Universal would have brought back a then-in-exile James

Whale to direct, adding the same eccentric touches he'd so brilliantly given *The Old Dark House* and *Bride of Frankenstein*. Josephine Hull and Jean Adair would recreate their roles, of course; if Universal couldn't afford Cary Grant as Mortimer, perhaps they'd have cast the play's Allyn Joslyn. Peter Lorre would have been available as the perfect Dr. Einstein—in the summer of '42, he played in *Invisible Agent* for Universal. Since Priscilla Lane was on contract to Warners, Universal's own Evelyn Ankers would have served nicely as Elaine. John Alexander, naturally, would be back as Teddy ... although Universal might have unleashed Lon Chaney, Jr., to roar "Chaaaarge!" and stampede up the stairway.

And it seems certain—considering the history of star and studio—that Universal would have surely starred Boris Karloff as its one-and-only choice as Jonathan Brewster.

Arsenic and Old Lace—The Play

Producers, Howard Lindsay and Russel Crouse; Author, Joseph Kesselring; Director, Bretaigne Windust; Setting, Raymond Sovey; General Manager, Carl Fisher; Press Representatives, Richard Maney, Ted Goldsmith; Stage Manager, Walter Wagner; Assistant Stage Manager, Margaret Joyce; Production Assistant, Carmen Lewis; Electrician, Sam McIntosh. Scenery Builders, William Kellam Construction Company, painted by Robert W. Bergman Studio.

New York opening: Fulton Theatre, 10 January 1941.

The Original Cast (in the order in which they speak): Josephine Hull (Aunt Abby); Wyrley Birch (The Rev. Dr. Harper); John Alexander (Teddy Brewster); John Quigg (Officer Brophy); Bruce Gordon (Officer Klein); Jean Adair (Aunt Martha); Helen Brooks (Elaine Harper); Allyn Joslyn (Mortimer Brewster); Henry Herbert (Mr. Gibbs); Boris Karloff (Jonathan Brewster); Edgar Stehli (Dr. Einstein); Anthony Ross (Officer O'Hara); Victor Sutherland (Lieutenant Rooney); William Parke (Mr. Witherspoon).

Arsenic and Old Lace—The Film

Studio, Warner Brothers; Executive Producer, Jack L. Warner; Associate Producer and Director, Frank Capra; Screenplay, Julius J. Epstein and Philip G. Epstein, based on the play by Joseph Kesselring; Cinematography, Sol Polito; Editor, Daniel Mandell; Music, Max Steiner; Musical Director, Leo F. Forbstein; Orchestrator, Hugo Friedhofer; Sound, C.A. Riggs; Art Director, Max Parker; Costumes, Orry-Kelly; Makeup, Perc Westmore, George Bau, John Wallace; Hair Stylist, Anita De Beltrand; Special Effects, Robert Burks, Byron Haskin; Props, Lou Hafley; Second Prop Man, Kefe Maley; Assistant Prop Men, Alfred Williams, Levi C. Williams; Assistant Director, Russell Saunders; Second Assistant Director, Claude Archer; Production Manager, Steve Trilling; Unit Manager, Eric Stacey; Still Photographer, Mickey Marigold; Script Clerk, Wandra Ramsey.

Filmed at Warner Brothers Studio, Burbank, CA, 20 October to 16 December 1941. New York opening: Strand Theatre, 1 September 1944.

The Cast: Cary Grant (Mortimer Brewster); Priscilla Lane (Elaine Harper); Raymond Massey (Jonathan Brewster); Jack Carson (O'Hara); Edward Everett Horton (Mr. Witherspoon); Peter Lorre (Dr. Einstein); James Gleason (Lieutenant Rooney); Josephine Hull (Abby Brewster); Jean Adair (Martha Brewster); John Alexander (Teddy Brewster); Grant Mitchell (the Reverend Harper); Edward McNamara (Brophy); Garry Owen (Taxi Cab

Driver); John Ridgely (Saunders); Vaughan Glaser (Judge Cullman); Chester Clute (Dr. Gilchrist); Charles Lane (Reporter); Edward McWade (Gibbs); Spencer Charters (Marriage License Clerk); Sol Gorss (New York Pitcher); Hank Mann (Photographer at Marriage License Bureau); Lee Phelps (Umpire); Leo White (Man in Phone Booth); Spec O'Donnell (Young Man in Line); Jean Wong (Young Woman in Line).

8

Production Diaries

Cat People and *The Curse of the Cat People*

Dress a woman wearing a formal evening gown and a cat head mask and
have her walk down the streets of your town.... Have her visit food stores,
department stores and others of a similar nature....
—From the pressbook for RKO's **Cat People**, 1942

Baltimore, late January 1943.

Cat People has opened at the Hippodrome Theatre, playing with a racy stage show, *The Earl Carroll Vanities of 1943.* Accompanying the bill is a bizarre presence: a "Cat Woman," slinking up and down Eutaw Street these raw winter nights. She's blonde and willowy, wearing a black evening gown, long black gloves, and a Halloween cat mask complete with fangs. She carries a shopping bag, with printed words approximate to what the RKO pressbook has suggested:

M-I-A-U!
I'm bound to see Simone Simon in *Cat People*.
Hippodrome Theatre

She's mysteriously silent, undoubtedly per the Hippodrome's orders—although some claim they'd heard her purr "M-i-a-u" now and then as she prowls the streets and shops, only a few blocks from Westminster Church, where Edgar Allan Poe lies buried. Her identity is a secret, and the locals enjoy guessing who she might be. A hard-up local actress or model? A stand-by showgirl in the *Vanities*?

Some feel sorry for her; no doubt the feline lady is counting the hours until she can get out of the cold, take off her tight gown, high heels and that damned cat mask, and enjoy a stiff drink. Yet others find her a strangely unnerving spook—a sexy yet scary lure for a smash hit horror movie that reportedly causes screams and nightmares as few films have ever done.

As a mother with her little girl walk near the Hippodrome this night, they encounter the Cat Woman. The mother laughs, reassuringly. The Cat Woman purrs "M-i-a-u," softly.

The screaming child runs up Eutaw Street, hysterically.[1]

* * *

I am a fugitive from EVIL THINGS ... I must keep myself from loving you—
lest I turn and claw you to shreds! For I am marked with the curse of those
who slink and strike at night ... I AM ONE OF THE "CAT PEOPLE!"
—RKO publicity, *Cat People*

215

Dress a woman wearing a formal evening gown and a cat head mask and have her walk down the streets of your town carrying a large shopping bag with copy such as suggested in the illustration. Have her visit food stores, department stores and others of a similar nature during shopping hours.

Pressbook cartoon of a Cat Woman.

Cat People, Val Lewton's premiere title-tested horror movie, was actually a *noir* sex tragedy—and a show business sensation. It cost only $141,000, ran just 73 minutes, boasted perversely calculated shock scenes, and featured a trio of bizarrely sensual females:

• Auburn-haired Simone Simon, notorious for her Ooh-La-La allure and a 1938 Hollywood sex scandal that had run her back to Paris, played Irena—a foreign Jekyll-Hyde bride, adrift in New York City, fearful her passion will transform her into a snarling beast who will rip her rosy-cheeked, 4-F husband to shreds.

• Blonde Jane Randolph, an RKO starlet, was Alice, sashaying a tightrope between appealing All-American heroine and predatory glamour girl phony, her wild, screaming, damsel-in-distress hysteria in the pool playing as a sado-maso crowd-pleaser.

• Ash-blonde Elizabeth Russell, an arch fashion model, was the original "Cat Woman," looking like a mad mix of fairy tale evil princess and 1942 sex dominatrix, "coming on" to Irena on her wedding night so slyly that Lewton received letters of congratulations for "introducing lesbiana to films in Hollywood."[2]

It all takes place in a wickedly enchanted 1942 New York City, where a leopard screams at night in the Central Park Zoo ("like a woman," says Irena). Seventy-two years after its shoot, *Cat People* still seems chillingly *alive,* a dark, sleek feline of a film, purring with Lewton's two pet fetish fears—cats, and being touched.

The official release date when this dark, sexy and subversive movie pounced on the U.S. public: Christmas, 1942.

Part I: Production Blueprint

*I cannot hear the soft fall of snow ... without
    remembering the animal steps that once
    followed me one dark early winter night.
I cannot dive into a swimming pool without
    a horrible dread that some evil thing may
    splash into the water and drag me down*

below the surface.... And I never, not even at the
height of day, take the transverse walk through Central Park.
—From DeWitt Bodeen's May 1, 1942, story treatment
for *Cat People,* as narrated by the character of Alice[3]

Thursday, May 8, 1941: RKO-Radio Pictures' *Citizen Kane* has its Hollywood premiere, after battles with its alleged inspiration, William Randolph Hearst. Among the 3,000 people inside and outside the El Capitan Theatre: *Kane's* producer-director-star-co-writer Orson Welles and his lover Dolores del Rio, John Barrymore, Charles Laughton and Elsa Lanchester, Bud Abbott and Lou Costello—and Simone Simon. Hearst's vengeful refusal to run RKO publicity costs the studio dearly: *Citizen Kane,* in its initial run, will lose $160,000.[4]

Wednesday, March 4, 1942: "Koerner Subs for Joe Breen" reads *Variety's* headline. Charles Koerner is the general manager of RKO Theatres, with a flair for exploitation. Joe Breen, former Production Code chief, has been operating the financially imperiled studio since May of 1941. Koerner is set to replace Breen until the latter returns from vacation on April 6.

Monday, March 16: A tall, burly, 37-year-old writer named Val Lewton, whose credits run from novels to poetry to pornography, joins RKO. Formerly story editor for David O. Selznick, Lewton is a "discovery" of Koerner, who observed Lewton raconteuring at a party. In the low-budget league of the studio's *Falcon* and *Mexican Spitfire* series, Lewton will produce title-tested horror films that will hopefully keep desperate RKO afloat. Lewton, who has a devoted wife, daughter and son, settles into work at his second floor office at 780 Gower Street in Hollywood.

Tuesday, March 17: RKO previews Welles' *The Magnificent Ambersons* at the Fox Theatre in Pomona. The crowd jeers. One audience member describes the film on his (her?) preview card as "a horrible distorted dream." Welles will refuse to reshoot the ending.

Val Lewton is finding his way in a highly politicized studio hothouse where heads are about to roll. Hypersensitive, he's keenly aware of it.

Friday, April 3: *The Ghost of Frankenstein,* Universal's big horror special of 1942, opens at Broadway's Rialto Theatre. Lon Chaney, fresh from *The Wolf Man,* plays the Monster, and the film features horror favorites Bela Lugosi and Lionel Atwill, Universal's new "Scream Queen" Evelyn Ankers, and the usual Brothers Grimm atmospherics. Meanwhile, Lewton and his writer, 33-year-old DeWitt Bodeen, screen Universal horrors—to decide what to *avoid*.

Monday, April 6: Joe Breen, set to return as RKO general manager, does not. Charles Koerner continues and Breen goes back to his job as Production Code head.

Approximately at this time: "No one's done very much with cats," Koerner tells Lewton and Bodeen. Koerner, who has audience-tested the title *Cat People,* is enthusiastic; Lewton is appalled. "Val *hated* cats!" remembers his widow, Ruth, over 50 years later. She claims he actually feared felines—possibly a psychic scar due to grisly nighttime fairy tales told him as a child by his old nurse in Russia.[5]

Thursday, April 23: "RKO Plans Unique Film, *The Cat People,*" headlines Edwin Schallert in his *Los Angeles Times* column:

> This studio is planning to do a unique original, developed right within the company itself by DeWitt Bodeen, writer, and Val Lewton, producer.... The treatment will be essentially modern and doubtless in some respects the film will compare with, say, a *Frankenstein*. RKO has often gone in for the historically unique like the *Kong* features....

The Hollywood premiere of RKO's *Citizen Kane* (1941). The film's producer-director-star-co-writer Orson Welles sits beside his lover at the time, Dolores del Rio. On the other side of del Rio is John Barrymore. The expense and notoriety of *Kane* will usher Val Lewton into RKO Studios.

Lewton and Bodeen have contacted with two ghosts from Lewton's literary past: *Panther Skin and Grapes,* a book of verse he wrote and published in 1923, and "The Bagheeta," a story he wrote for *Weird Tales* in 1930. The latter was a florid tale of a teenage boy, sent by his village into a forest to kill a leopard woman. This morphs into the legend of the Cat People, but Lewton takes no credit; he wants Bodeen to get the glory. He's also always neurotically ashamed of his own work.

Friday, May 1: Bodeen dates his 50-page treatment, written as a short story and as told by Alice Moore, the film's "heroine." The most compelling characters are female: Irena Dubrovna, the Serbian-born fashion designer who suffers the curse of the Cat People, and her rival and target, Alice. This isn't surprising: The most dominant figures in Lewton's life as he grew up in the Sleepy Hollow area of New York were his mother Nina and his aunt, the legendary actress Nazimova. His father, a wastrel, had abandoned the family when Val was a boy. There's a significant difference in the original story from the screenplay: The "Cat Woman" is actually a "Cat Man," bearded and all in black.

Wednesday, May 20: Jacques Tourneur, Lewton's good friend and personal choice to direct *Cat People,* arrives at RKO. The 37-year-old Tourneur, son of legendary French director Maurice Tourneur, had co-staged (with Lewton) the "Storming of the Bastille" sequence of

MGM's *A Tale of Two Cities* (1935) during Lewton's tenure with Selznick. Tourneur has been directing Bs at MGM, and shorts in that studio's *Passing Parade* series.

Tuesday, June 30: Edwin Schallert writes in the *L.A. Times*: "Here's interesting news. Simone Simon is being dealt with again for a leading part in *The Cat People.* I don't know if this is complimentary or not, but they want femmes that look like felines for this film...."

Part II: The Star

> *"She was like a cat ... as long as you smoothed her, she purred; when you stopped ... she scratched!"*
> —Simone Simon's secretary Sandra Martin, accusing Simon of hosting orgies, 1938[6]

Monday, May 2, 1938: After midnight.[7] James Richard Pacheco, a busboy from Rhode Island on the eve of his 18th birthday, celebrated in a curious way: He climbed a telephone pole, hoping to see through the boudoir window of 347 Conway Street in West Los Angeles, and get a glimpse of Simone Simon in her nightgown—or less. The butler, Philip De Dyne, saw the voyeur, got a revolver and called the police, who ordered Pacheco to abandon his Peeping Tom perch.

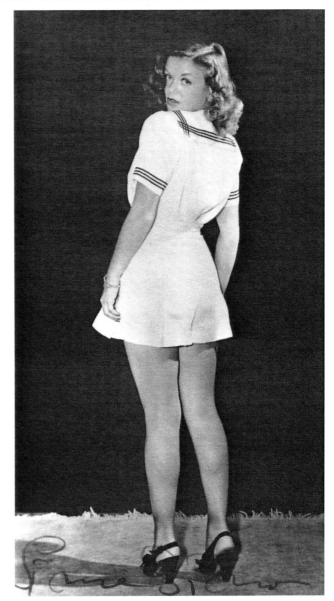

Simone Simon, in an autographed pose typical of her allure. After Hollywood scandal and exile in France, she was the star of *Cat People.*

Police found Pacheco's pockets stuffed with publicity pictures of *La* Simon. The boy claimed he'd fallen in love with the actress the moment he'd seen her picture.

"I came west to meet her," said Pacheco. "I have been trying to see her for a long time."

Result: "Mentality tests" for Pacheco. The young man vowed he'd wanted to save Mlle. Simon from "kidnappers" and confessed he'd hoped she'd loan him money to study witchcraft in South Africa. He ended up in a psychopathic ward. Incidentally, at least one newspaper reported Simon's attire during Pacheco's peek-a-boo: "a silk nightie."

RESIDENCE OF SIMONE SIMON

BEVERLY HILLS, CAL. X300

Scene of scandal: A postcard of Simone Simon's Los Angeles house in the late 1930s, where she was allegedly an orgy hostess, unleashing the infamous "Gold Key Scandal."

As police apprehended Pacheco at dawn, May 2 held more drama for Simone Simon. Later that day, 20th Century–Fox's "Tender Savage" went to court, where she testified regarding 18 counts of grand theft and forgery against her secretary, Sandra Martin, who lavished the embezzled money on a penthouse, jewelry, and fancy lingerie.[8] Martin retaliated by claiming that she had an audio recording of the star, hostessing an orgy that would "blow the lid off Hollywood." Martin's defense lawyer went on the offensive—painting Simone as a lascivious voluptuary and questioning her about two 18-karat gold keys to her home that she gave to an unnamed lover. The lawyer demanded the lover's name.

"You'll never know!" said Simone on the stand.

Hence, "The Gold Key Scandal"[9]—all part of the legend and lore of the tempestuous Simone Simon, whose film career would never be the same. That summer when Fox previewed *Josette*, in which Simone sang in "moanin' low" style, Hedda Hopper sniped in her June 11, 1938, column: "If S.S. intends to continue singing, she'll have to pay more attention to her music lessons and less to gold keys."

Fox dumped Simone. Jean Renoir cabled her to come to Paris and star in the Emile Zola adaptation *The Human Beast*. As she headed for the ocean liner *Normandie* in New York Harbor, a posse of snubbed autograph seekers chased her, screaming insults, and the IRS cornered her on the ship, demanding back taxes of $4,000.

"I think I *never* come back here!" yowled Simone.[10]

Hitler scared her back here, and she won the featured role of the Witch Girl in RKO's *The Devil and Daniel Webster*. From there it was personal appearances. When RKO's *Mexican Spitfire at Sea* played Boston, Simone sang on the vaudeville bill.

Val Lewton, meanwhile, is a Simone Simon fan. He's instructed DeWitt Bodeen to write the role of Irena with Simon in mind, intent on this daredevil casting.

Monday, July 6, 1942: *The Hollywood Reporter* announces that Simone Simon will cut short a personal appearance tour in the east and head to Hollywood for *Cat People*. Not publicized is her startlingly low salary: $4,500, or $1,500 per week for three weeks' work.[11] This very modest fee reveals at least two realities: (a) Simone still hasn't won respectability in Hollywood, and (b) she's desperate for a starring role. RKO magnanimously tosses in an additional $400 for round trip train fare from New York.

Hollywood gossips predict that Simon, once in Hollywood, will claw and screech as she stars in a "B" horror movie. As such, the publicity boys bait her—complete with a cat mask they want her to wear for PR photos. In 1994, via long distance from Paris, Mlle. Simon, 83, blind, wealthy and still tempestuous, alternately purred and scratched as she reminisced about her arrival at the L.A. train station:

> I had a reputation of being temperamental—I never knew why—but this became part of my temperamental legend, because when they said, "Will you please, Miss Simon, put that on your face?" I said, "I certainly will *not* put that on my face! If you want, you can photograph me with it in my *hand*." So they said, "Oh, there she goes again!"[12]

Part III: The Snake Pit

> *The script presents three difficulties....*
> —Joseph I. Breen, censorship letter to RKO
> re: *Cat People*, July 13, 1942[13]

Thursday, July 2: "Orson Welles Evicted from Offices by RKO" headlines page 1 of *Variety*. Welles is actually in Brazil, shooting the never-to-be-completed *It's All True,* but his Mercury Productions staff members get the boot.

Friday, July 10: RKO releases *The Magnificent Ambersons,* with new scenes and a happy ending. (The "ghost" directors: Robert Wise, Fred Fleck, and Jack Moss.) There are many cuts from Orson Welles' original version. The film will lose $620,000.[14] Mark Robson, who was Welles's editor, recalled that RKO "punished" anyone associated with Welles—including Robson, who was banished to the "B" unit:

> I was assigned to Val's unit as an editor: to show him something about film and to help guide that department.... He thought of his unit—and he had his own little horror unit—in terms of the producer, the writer, the director, and the editor; a kind of team in which we all worked extremely closely together.[15]

Lewton has an affectionate nickname for his own unit: "The Snake Pit."

The *Cat People* company—Lewton, Tourneur, Bodeen, Robson, and Lewton's attractive, well-read secretary Jessie Ponitz—have great fun refining the startlingly morbid story. Lewton is personally investing his personality into the project—the fear of cats and his dread of being touched (even hating handshakes). The result: the story of a woman who fears she'll transform into a savage cat if a man makes love to her. Lewton's having fun but he's also deeply stressed: Will this actually get past the censors?

Monday, July 13: Joseph I. Breen, back at the Production Code office, reviews the *Cat People* script. He writes to RKO executive William Gordon, citing the script's "three difficulties":

the overemphasis on the fact that Oliver and Irena are not consummating their marriage; the unacceptable suggestion, on page 57, that Irena is illegitimate; and the gruesomeness and horror angles which should be minimized if the finished picture is to be approved by us....

Breen has other concerns, such as Irena's blessing herself when she sees the Cat Woman—"the making of the 'sign of the Cross' will be deleted in England," warns Breen. In front of his Snake Pit pals, Lewton laughs at the censors. Privately he's in agony. He stays in his RKO office late into the night, anguishing over every detail.

Friday, July 24: RKO completes its budget sheet for *Cat People,* listing the grim realities of low-budget production.

- Total approved budget, $118,948. To place this figure in perspective, it's more than $100,000 less than Universal will spend on *Frankenstein Meets the Wolf Man,* which will start shooting October 12. Then again, it's over $97,000 more than the $21,371.45 that Poverty Row's PRC Studios had spent producing *The Devil Bat* (1941), starring Bela Lugosi.
- Shooting schedule: 17 days. *Frankenstein Meets the Wolf Man* would have a schedule of 24 days.
- Salary for screenplay writer DeWitt Bodeen: $1,600. Bodeen, who celebrates his 34th birthday the weekend before *Cat People* begins shooting, will work on the film as dialogue director.
- Salary for director Jacques Tourneur (or "Jack" Tourneur, as the budget sheet lists him): $3,000.
- Salary for Val Lewton: $3,575.

Meanwhile, there has been another setback for Lewton. He wants to borrow from David O. Selznick a brunette, 23-year-old actress named Jennifer Jones to play Alice. Selznick, while wishing his former story editor well, has big plans for Ms. Jones and refuses to loan her. Lewton has to turn to the RKO stock player roster to find an Alice.

Monday, July 27: Simone Simon reports to the still gallery, striking various sultry poses with her leading man Kent Smith. There's a full moon that night, and the following morning, RKO Production #386 begins shooting.

Part IV: The Shooting

WEEK ONE: TUESDAY, JULY 28, TO SATURDAY, AUGUST 1, 1942
BOY MEETS CAT WOMAN

Tuesday: Filming of *Cat People* begins at 9 a.m. The locale is the Interior Irena's Apartment set, Stage 11, on RKO's Pathé lot, an annex located at 9336 Washington Boulevard, Culver City.

It's a locale rich in Hollywood history: Cecil B. DeMille had built the castle of Jerusalem here for *The King of Kings* (1927), Boris Karloff had acted twin brothers in the Tyrolean village here in *The Black Room* (1935), and David Selznick had burned "Atlanta" (actually the "Great Wall" from *King Kong*) here in *Gone with the Wind.*

On call: Simone Simon and Kent Smith. Rumors that Mlle. Simon will prove the French kiss of death for Lewton's premiere movie seem groundless. Assured in her sexpot notoriety, she sets loose her bedroom eyes and baby doll voice, trying to bewitch the males in the company. Bodeen will remember her as "lovable." Others in the company, especially female ones, will quickly disagree.

Thirty-five-year-old Kent Smith, an RKO contractee, has a fine Broadway background, playing such roles as "The Bastard of Orleans" to Katharine Cornell's title character in *Saint Joan* (1936). His screen presence is bland, if likable—perfect for Ollie, Irena's hopelessly upstaged husband. Smith has his compensation: his $5,000 *Cat People* salary exceeds his leading lady's.

Also on the set that day are a kitten, a canary, and a dog. Animals and their treatment are of considerable concern, and on this first day, Lewton receives an Inter-Department communication from RKO executive William Gordon:

> It is essential that Mr. Richard C. Craven, Western Regional Director of the American Humane Society, be contacted so that he may be personally present or send a representative when all shots in which the leopard will be photographed are taken. The same will obtain [to scenes] in the pet shop and those involving the killing of the canary and the throwing of the canary into the leopard's cage. These precautions are taken in order that we may receive a certification from Mr. Craven that no animals were mistreated. Said certifications are imperative for British release and certain other markets....

The set includes a practical fireplace that, as the call sheet noted, "will work" and the apartment house staircase is a leftover from Welles' *The Magnificent Ambersons*. Tourneur works the company until 6:55 p.m. completing 15 set-ups. Shot this first day: Irena's soliloquy about the Cat People, hauntingly delivered by Simone Simon:

> When King John drove out the Mamalukes, and came to our village, he found dreadful things. People bowed down to Satan, and said their Masses to him. They had become witches.... King John put some of them to the sword, and some—the wisest, and the most wicked—escaped into the mountains ... their legend haunts the village where I was born.

Simone Simon "la-las" a few bars of "Do-Do," a lullaby à la Stravinsky or Debussy, which will become Irena's haunting motif in both *Cat People* and *The Curse of the Cat People*. She'll reprise it briefly in *The Curse of the Cat People*, with a few French lyrics.

At least one first day problem occurs. Lewton wants an impressive statue of King John slaying a Mamaluke to decorate Irena's apartment—a major prop related to her Cat Women superstition. An irate worker in the studio Plaster Shop files a complaint that the picture that served as the model for the statue wasn't delivered until late afternoon and the prop statue was needed the next morning. The worker submits the bill for the Statue of King John: $60; actual cost with overtime and 27.5 percent overhead: $82.

Wednesday: On call at the Irena's Apartment set are Simone Simon, Kent Smith, a canary, a kitten, a dog ... and Jane Randolph, playing Alice, Ollie's fellow draftsman (draftswoman). The RKO starlet has studied with Max Reinhardt, been on stock contract at Warner Bros., and even served as an ice-skating model for Disney's *Bambi*. RKO had already cast her prominently in *The Falcon's Brother* and *Highways by Night*.

Jane is blonde, leggy, 26 years old, and a complete departure from the winsome, rather vulnerable-looking Jennifer Jones. With the dry delivery of a star-billed stripper and a pirate's flair for hats, she's a lovely, lethal, almost swaggering Alice, serving nicely as *Cat People's* horror heroine and (in Alice's own words) "the new kind of other woman." She's also determined to prove a formidable rival for Simone Simon, onscreen and off.

On her first day on the set, Jane Randolph, in a slinky dress and a smashing hat, joins

Simon and Smith in a scene doomed to the cutting room floor: Alice visits Ollie and his bride-to-be Irena for cocktails at the latter's apartment. Ollie has exchanged a kitten (which didn't like Irena) for a canary—which resolutely will not sing for her. Upon Alice's arrival, however, the bird bursts into song. A moment later, as they raise their martini glasses, the trio hears the "eerie scream" from the Central Park Zoo. "It's the panther!" gasps Irena.

It's a nicely prophetic scene, underscoring the rivalry of the two ladies, Irena's feline nature, and the kinship of the caged panther. At least one still survives of this scene.

The company works this day to 7:45 p.m.

Meanwhile, in one of those happy accidents that come into play on movie sets, animosity erupts between the two leading ladies. In 1989, over 40 years after her final film *Abbott and Costello Meet Frankenstein* (1948), Jane Randolph, a wealthy, globe-trotting widow based in Switzerland, paid a visit to Los Angeles and chatted with me about *Cat People*. She quickly described Simone Simon in one word: "Terrible!"[16]

Jane Randolph, an RKO starlet, played Alice in *Cat People*, clashing with Mlle. Simon onscreen ... and off.

Miss Randolph went on how *Cat People* came close to turning into *The Simone Simon Follies,* recalling Simone as a terror in the makeup department and a diva on the set: "She was always upstaging me. Jacques Tourneur really bawled her out, in French ... and she didn't like that either. She was very difficult with everyone!"

A cat fight seems to loom on the horizon. Meanwhile, Miss Randolph knows enough French to relish the day Tourneur, his initial attraction to his star diminished, shouts at Simone, "*Chienne!*"

Thursday: The star trio works on the same set until 8:10 p.m.

Friday: The morning presents a major crisis. *Cat People* has fallen one day behind schedule—and executive producer Lou Ostrow, after seeing the first three days' work, wants to can Jacques Tourneur. As Tourneur later admitted:

> It was very embarrassing. Mr. Koerner was in New York when we started shooting. Lou Ostrow was the executive producer and after he saw three days of rushes, he called in Val and said: "We're going to fire the director...." Val called Koerner but he was still in New York. The next day, he got back, looked at the rushes and said: "Leave Jacques alone. He's doing fine."[17]

Saturday: With the studio chief behind him, Tourneur continues at RKO Pathé on the Interior Irena's Apartment set with Simon, Smith, and Randolph. The company works from 9:00 a.m. to 7:55 p.m. Come the end of week one, the film is still one day behind schedule.

Within the first week, and before any of the shock sequences have been shot, Lewton and Tourneur have done marvelous things with *Cat People*. As the late Joel Siegel will write in his landmark 1973 book *Val Lewton: The Reality of Terror*:

> Throughout, the film is tinged with the kind of moral and intellectual ambiguity which characterizes Lewton's best work. Alice is not a sweet, innocent rival for Oliver's affections, but a woman whose sexual hostility towards Irena is made obvious at several points. Oliver is a thoughtless dolt whose stolidity generally serves to increase his wife's fear about herself ... Irena, fighting what turns out to be an actual curse, is more sympathetic than any other character in the film, and is certainly more sinned against than sinning.

Lewton, meanwhile, is purring over his leading lady. Val Lewton, Jr., an art restorationist, remembers his father at the dinner table, agog over Simone Simon, telling his wife, daughter, and son how the star makes jokes on the set about her falsies.

WEEK TWO: MONDAY, AUGUST 3,
TO SATURDAY, AUGUST 8, 1942
HORROR CHEESECAKE, AN UNSAFE ZOO,
AND A BAD BATHING SUIT

Monday and Tuesday: The *Cat People* company continues on Stage 11 on the Irena Apartment set. Simone Simon, Kent Smith and Jane Randolph work Monday from 9:00 a.m. to 8:00 p.m. acting scenes in the middle and later part of the film. Despite the long day, the company, by Monday night, is *two* days behind schedule.

Filmed Tuesday is one of *Cat People*'s most memorable shots. As the script describes it:

INT. IRENA'S BATHROOM—NIGHT
CLOSEUP of the base of an old-fashioned bathtub that has foot supports of ornamental balls with tiger claws extending from over the tops. Over the scene comes the broken sobbing of Irena.
CAMERA MOVES UP, and we see Irena in the tub. She sits very still in the still water, but her glistening shoulders shake as she tries to control the storm of her hysteria.

Implied is that Irena is recovering from stalking Alice in Central Park and attacking the sheep. It's a bizarre image, a splash of horror cheesecake for Mlle. Simon (shot from the back), both sexy and heartbreaking.

"Tub will be practical—hot water," notes the day's call sheet.

Also on Tuesday, a new actor enters: RKO's Tom Conway as the enigmatic Dr. Judd. Conway has just inherited the role of "The Falcon," having co-starred with his real-life brother George Sanders and Jane Randolph in *The Falcon's Brother*. Jane recalls Conway as "an angel"—indeed, he'd saved her from brother George's smarmy advances on the Falcon film. Conway replaces the originally announced Carl Brisson.[18]

Watching *Cat People* today, Conway's silky-smooth performance seems all the more impressive, considering his well-publicized alcoholic downfall—found in 1965 as an alcoholic derelict, estranged from brother George Sanders, living in a $2-a-day flophouse in Venice Beach, California. Conway died in 1967.

Wednesday: The *Cat People* company reports to the RKO Hollywood lot, working on Stages 5 and 9. Simon, Smith, and Randolph are all on call, as is a kitten. Tourneur shoots scenes in the hotel lobby, in the swimming pool locker room, and in a phone booth; all of these take place before and after the famous swimming pool episode. This includes the superb

Haunting horror cheesecake: Simone Simon as Irena, weeping in her bathtub after killing lambs in Central Park.

use of shadow by Tourneur and cameraman Nicholas Musuraca—slyly insinuating that Irena the cat is stalking Alice the fox.

It also includes one of *Cat People*'s most famous lines. As Mary Halsey (as Blondie, the hotel desk clerk) hands Jane Randolph's Alice her robe after the latter emerges from the pool, she looks at the robe and marvels, "Gee whiz, honey. It's torn to ribbons!"

There's a new problem, or revelation. Apparently Jane Randolph has been wearing a girdle under her *Cat People* frocks. Now squeezed into a bathing suit that looks like a dime store corset, she appears a bit portly. There's little anyone can do now about this delicate problem, and Simone Simon is likely delighted. Years later, recalling the pool sequence, Jacques Tourneur rather ungallantly remarked: "My only complaint about the scene was that the girl threatened in the pool wasn't feminine or diminutive enough. She was built like a wrestler! Too bad!"[19]

The company works 9:00 a.m. until 6:50 p.m. and completes an impressive 24 set-ups but now is *three* days behind schedule.

Thursday: Tourneur shoots exterior scenes in the Central Park Zoo, actually housed on RKO's Stage 7. Simone Simon, Kent Smith, Jane Randolph, Tom Conway, and Alec Craig (as the zookeeper) are all there, as are 30 extras, and several animals.

There's another crisis. As *Variety* reports the next day:

Efforts to get more life in caged animals being used for a scene in RKO's *Cat People* yesterday resulted in a free-for-all between a black panther, an Indian leopard, and a South American puma

Mary Halsey as Blondie and Jane Randolph as Alice—the latter in her iron maiden of a bathing suit—regard her robe, "shredded to ribbons," in the crowd-pleasing payoff of *Cat People*'s classic pool episode. Note Blondie's sharp fingernails!

that tore out the wire netting between bars separating the felines. Shooting was stopped and repairs hastily made to keep cats from stealing the show from players. Cats were aroused into action, which went beyond director Jack Tourneur's expectations with air hoses and sticks, after they persisted in lying quietly in the cages during scene showing Simone Simon sketching at Central Park Zoo.[20]

The August 6 production report confirms this near-disaster, although it makes no mention of a puma; it does mention a panther, a leopard, a lion ... and a dog. The crew strengthens the cages with wire mesh, and the emergency causes the company to begin shooting late—11:25 a.m. They work until seven p.m. The sequence originally features Jane Randolph's Alice, but after editing, we only see her from the rear in the background, recognizable by her blonde hair and black chapeau. Due to the delay with the cages, Tourneur completes only nine set-ups. *Cat People* is now *four* days behind schedule.

Incidentally, the song the hurdy-gurdy player provides in the opening zoo episode is von Flotow's aria "Heaven Protect Thee"—an appropriate choice, considering the story. Also, an early draft of the script had intended this scene in this episode:

Shot 5. Ext. Terrace Garden Table—Park—Afternoon.
Close shot of the Cat Woman... The woman looks like a cat. She has a round tabby face and a

pompadour which somehow suggests the roundness of a cat's head. The eyes, slanting, large, very light in color, fringed with sweeping lashes, are completely feline. She turns the great luminous eyes in the direction Oliver and Irena have taken.

Lewton, preferring to limit the Cat Woman to a single scene, had excised this flourish from the script.

Friday: It's back to the zoo on Stage 7—Simon, Smith, Randolph, Conway, Craig, ten extras, a puma, a panther and a leopard. Work goes on to 7:10 p.m. Included is Judd's addressing Irena's "psychic need to loose evil upon the world" and her desire for death—themes that will dominate time and again in Lewton's horror films.

The script originally had a fascinating cage-side soliloquy here for Irena, remembering when she was 13, and her mother died in Serbia—a panther woman:

> I held her hand when she died. That hand ... even as I held it ... turned to the black paw of a panther. I felt the coarse hair, the sharp talons, the pads ... I felt them ... I saw her lying, black ... I saw that.... The priest would not come into our house when he saw what was on the bed.

The speech will be cut—probably because it's too literal in its horror content.

Saturday: A long day and night—9:00 a.m. to 11:20 p.m.—including work on the Zoo set on Stage 7 and the Transverse Walk set on Stage 4. Simon, Smith, Randolph, Conway, and Simon's stunt double Linda Finn are on call, as are ten extras, four stand-ins, one panther, one leopard, and one puma. On this 11th day of shooting, Tourneur films the climax of *Cat People*—Irena at the zoo, having been stabbed by Dr. Judd's sword cane, the sword protruding from her shoulder, unleashing the panther upon herself. Joseph Breen had warned: "It should be quite clear that Irena is not committing suicide where she enters the panther's cage."

Lewton defies Breen—the suicide is clear. The script had offered this denouement, which the prospective audience will surely be waiting to see:

> Under Irena's fur coat is a black leopard's body, the leg and paw in the same attitude her arm and hand had taken, and the broken blade that had once protruded from Irena's gleaming shoulder is now rooted in the black form of the panther.

"Gruesomeness and horror angles should be minimized," Breen had admonished, noting that this scene was "especially questionable." Lewton has Tourneur comply, but not to placate Breen. The producer is clearly infatuated with Simone Simon's Irena, who has become rather his dark side's fantasy pin-up girl. He can't bear to reveal her beastly carcass, so he actually jettisons *Cat People*'s big climactic moment ... and leaves the finale shrouded in mist.

The film needs a finale "button" and Lewton will ask DeWitt Bodeen to add a verse to close the film. Bodeen finds it in John Donne's *Holy Sonnets V*:

> But black sin hath betrayed
> To endless night
> My world, both parts, and
> Both parts must die.

WEEK THREE: MONDAY, AUGUST 10, TO SATURDAY, AUGUST 15, 1942
SUPERMAN FIGHTS A PANTHER, THE STALK, SKINNED CALF HEADS, AND A ZOOMORPHIC VAMP

Monday: As the third week of shooting begins, Tourneur photographs all the scenes in Dr. Judd's office on RKO's Stage 9. The company works 9:30 to 6:45. A memorable shot this day: Simon's face, aglow in a single spotlight as Irena, under a trance, murmurs, "I have no peace."

Tuesday: It's back to the Pathé lot, Stage 11, and the Int. Irena's Apt. set. Famed stunt man Paul Stader, who doubled such stars as John Wayne, Johnny Weissmuller, and Cary Grant (and will be Kirk Alyn's double for the title role in the *Superman* serial of 1948), joins the principals from 12 to 2:20 to observe Tom Conway, whom he'll be doubling this evening.

After the company departs the set at 6:40, a second unit reports to Pathé's Stage 11. Edward Donahue, who had been first assistant director on *Citizen Kane* and will later be associate producer of the 1957–1958 season of TV's *Adventures of Superman,* is the director. Frank Redman, RKO cameraman later active on TV's *Perry Mason,* is cinematographer. Mel Koontz, on hand with a lion and a leopard, is the animal trainer. The second unit shoots Dr. Judd's fatal battle with the leopard—Paul Stader doubling Conway. The company works from 7 to 12:20 a.m., serves 37 "midnight meals," and resume until 2:20 a.m. Director, cameraman, and stunt man will receive no onscreen credit for the dangerous night's work.

Wednesday: The company finishes up the late-in-the-film scenes in Irena's apartment building on Pathé's Stage 11. Then they move to RKO's Stage 4 and Tourneur shoots one of the great suspense and horror vignettes of film history: Irena nocturnally stalking Alice through Central Park.

The company works on the Exterior Transverse Walk and Exterior Park Entrance, and between 3:30 p.m. and 6:50 p.m. Tourneur brilliantly captures the first part of the classic episode.

> MED. SHOT—a street lamp on transverse. It throws a circular pool of light. Alice emerges from the darkness, crosses the area of light, and continues on into the darkness. The soft click of her heels fades into the distance. Even as the sound of her steps fades, the sound of Irena's steps comes into the scene. Irena comes from the darkness, crosses the area of light, and continues on after Alice into the darkness.

There's an almost viscerally pleasing devilment in the scene: Jane Randolph's Alice, all gussied up in her long beige coat and stylish 1942 black chapeau, sashaying through the park, her high heels clicking on the street, and Simone Simon's Irena, following in human form, looking vindictive, tormented—and hungry. The twisted Lewton magic works, and one actually starts rooting for Irena to catch up with her prey, pounce, and bite her in the girdle.

Donald Kerr plays a taxi driver and there are six extras. The same day, Hedda Hopper runs this tidbit in her column:

> On the *Cat People* set they have three dangerous animals in cages—a black panther, a spotted leopard and a cougar. Also on the set are a trained monkey, a chicken and a couple of cats. Simone Simon says script calls for her to get in the cage with the panther but trainer says it's absolutely impossible. They haven't decided what to do about it yet....

Either Hedda made it up or Simone was telling fairy tales.

Thursday: A 12-hour day—9 a.m. to 9 p.m.—includes more shots of the stalk:

> CLOSEUP of Alice's feet as they walk along, the heels clicking on the wet pavement.
> CLOSEUP of Irena's feet as they walk along, her heels likewise clicking on the pavement....
> SHOT of Alice, as she peers more closely into the darkness. She is troubled. The silence is ominous. She frowns apprehensively, turns, and starts to walk on a little faster. She turns her head

Jane Randolph's Alice in Central Park, wearing one of her stylish hats—is there a leopard stalking her?

slightly, but does not dare look behind her. She increases her pace and walks very rapidly through the next area of light and on into darkness. The sound of her own steps is loud, and she begins to run. She reaches the next pool of light, stops stock still, panic-stricken, afraid to move. Outside the circle of light is only blackness and silence. Alice's frightened eyes peer into the darkness. She shrinks against the lamp post. Sheer terror crosses her face....

And then comes the scene's classic payoff climax:

> Suddenly there is a roaring sound that fills the soundtrack.... A pattern of light cuts across Alice's face.... There is a hissing, screeching sound.
> SHOT of a transverse bus, as with a hiss of air brakes it stops directly alongside Alice. She grasps the platform rail to steady herself. The doors open.
> BUS DRIVER: Climb on, sister.

This is the legendary Lewton "bus." Editor Mark Robson receives the credit for the concept, and the "bus"—a surprise sight and sound at a tense moment, calculated to jolt the audience—becomes a Val Lewton trademark. Charles Jordan, who plays the bus driver, lands a part a few months later at Monogram as Detective O'Toole in Bela Lugosi's *The Ape Man*.

The company continues work on Stage 10 and Exterior Building G. Simone Simon is on hand for the entire 12-hour stretch.

Friday: Little wonder the star is ten minutes late after her marathon the previous day. She joins Jane Randolph on RKO Stages 10, 12, and 7—Interior Office Building, Exterior Office Bldg., and the Exterior Street near Irena's apartment. There are six extras and work goes to 6:30 p.m.

Saturday: The company shoots a new shock sequence: the snowy wedding night meeting at the Belgrade Café with the Cat Woman.

The exterior and interior of the Serbian restaurant are on RKO's Stage 14. The restaurant window offers a glimpse of skinned calf heads—a nicely macabre touch—and the crew has snow ready to fall before the 9:00 a.m. call. Celebrating Irena's nuptials, along with newlyweds Simone Simon and Kent Smith, is Jane Randolph, in another glamorous hat, worn at a jaunty angle.

There are two new players. Jack Holt, once a top Paramount star and the inspiration for Dick Tracy's "Fearless Fosdick," plays "The Commodore"—the ship designing company boss of Ollie and Alice. Holt has an old contract with RKO and agrees to play this role, a virtual bit, for $2,500. (It had originally been budgeted for only $300.) A short time after *Cat People,* Holt, fearful of a Japanese coastal invasion, will sell his Pacific Palisades ranch to Val Lewton. Also joining the cast as "Doc" Carver, Oliver and Alice's co-worker, is 6'5" Britisher Alan Napier, fated for celebrity as Alfred the butler on TV's *Batman.* Napier will claim he got the part simply due to his friendship with Lewton; less than nine years later, he'll deliver Lewton's eulogy. The shooting call includes eleven extras and three sideline musicians.

The true star attraction this day, however, is Elizabeth Russell as the "Cat Woman." Elizabeth's zoomorphic vamp, in a killer black gown and with an ebony bow in her blonde coiffure, will surely be one of *Cat People*'s top sensations.

A former New York City model and Paramount player, Elizabeth is now a freelancer, sharing a Beverly Hills house with Maria Montez (about to become Universal's Technicolor "Queen of Kitsch" in *Arabian Nights*). She has the "willowy angel" look that the Depression public had loved, but 1940s Hollywood sees the actress as a fallen angel—a female Lucifer. Elizabeth had just played in Monogram's *The Corpse Vanishes* as "The Countess," witchy wife of Bela Lugosi; Bela keeps her young by kidnapping brides and injecting their spinal fluid into the evil crone.

"Don't touch me, you *gargoyle!*" she hatefully hisses to dwarf Angelo Rossitto as Bela serenades her at the organ with "Ave Maria."

Elizabeth Russell, who will play the original "Cat Woman" of *Cat People,* in a 1936 Hollywood publicity shot.

As for her oddball *Cat People* casting, Elizabeth will remember that she and Montez were on a double date—Maria with writer Peter Viertel (who later wed Deborah Kerr), Elizabeth with Austrian refugee Friedrich von Ledebur (who will play Queequeg in 1956's *Moby Dick*). Viertel mentioned that his friend Val Lewton was seeking a woman who looked like a cat for a film he was producing at RKO, and suggested Elizabeth go see him.

"You mean you think *I* look like a *cat*?"[21] asked Elizabeth, who was no fan of felines.

At any rate, she went to see Lewton, who cast her on the spot. The August 15 assistant director report notes, "Reasons for Delay: Waiting for Miss Russell...," and one presumes this was due to makeup trying to create as feline a look as possible. The scene is, as the show biz lingo put it, "a Wow"; as bride and groom laugh, the Cat Woman turns at her table, looks, rises, sashays over to the couple, and poses for a haunting, spine-chilling but incredibly glamorous close-up. As DeWitt Bodeen's script reads:

> Irena laughs, and turning around, looks up at the Cat Woman. The smile fades from her face. She stares at the woman with a kind of haunted fascination. The Cat Woman takes a step closer, never removing her eyes from Irena. She smiles and speaks. (Note: Irena's voice is to be dubbed on the sound track when the Cat Woman speaks.)
> CAT WOMAN: Moja sestra.
> Irena blanches and shrinks back into her chair. She makes the sign of the Cross. The Cat Woman smiles and repeats the words. (Note: Scene without the sign of Cross to be made for England.)
> CAT WOMAN: Moja sestra.

And the Cat Woman, having called Irena "my sister," elegantly places a fur over her shoulders—a nice bestial touch—and strolls out into the night and the snow.

Lewton loved mixing beauty and horror; in Elizabeth Russell, he had cast a beautiful woman who was strangely scary on screen. The strangely violating way that the Cat Woman smiles at newlywed Irena—slyly, lasciviously—is the real "Wow" of the scene. In the fairy tale take on *Cat People,* Irena has seen a fellow Cat Woman, who in greeting her, has cursed her, but in subliminal Lewton, the Sapphic inference is there—a perverse woman "coming on" to a bride on her wedding night.

Although it seems crystal clear that Lewton and company knew precisely what they were insinuating, not all of them saw it that way—or at least would admit it. Oscar Wilde called homosexuality "the love that dare not speak its name," and the *Cat People* pack had crafted a homosexual scene that they'd dare not admit to the public—or apparently, even each other. Bodeen recalled the letters RKO received in response to the vignette, many actually praising Lewton for his "boldness":

> [Val] was indignant when he called me into his office, demanding to know if I had deliberately written the scene with that meaning. I saved myself by saying, "Val, if you write a scene between two strange women and one says to the other in a foreign language, 'My sister,' you can bet your ass that there will be those who say, 'Ah, lesbians.'" He cooled down then, and laughed....

It's very difficult to believe that sophisticate Lewton was in the dark as to the lavender *double entendre* of the scene. Consider (a) Lewton's famous aunt, Nazimova, was a "notorious" lesbian, (b) Lewton surely co-existed peacefully with lesbians during his colorful New York days, where he reported on everything from cosmetics to stigmata sufferers, and (c) *The Seventh Victim* (1943), Lewton's fourth RKO thriller, is virtually a Gay Pride Parade, with a least *five* female characters inferred to be homosexual. Lewton likely had a panic attack when the letters came in, fearing his sophisticated inside joke had been too overt—and worrying about the possible wrath of the RKO big shots.

At any rate, Bodeen in later years admitted he'd written the Cat Woman scene with this intent:

> Actually, I rather liked the insinuation, and thought it added a neat bit of interpretation.... Irena's fears about destroying a lover if she kissed him could be because she was really a lesbian who loathed being kissed by a man. It was a nice meaning, in the full sense of the word "nice."

Supporting the original inference is dialogue in the script that was never shot or perhaps shot and not used. After Ollie asks Irena, "What did she say, darling?" he receives this response:

> Irena (*slowly, seriously*): If this were any night but my wedding night ... if you were any man but my husband ... I would not tell you.

As for the "Cat Woman" herself, Elizabeth Russell—a divorcee in 1942, raising a young son—will also be sensitive in her late years about the lesbian interpretation, claiming that she had just tried to give "the impression of mystery." Also, she wasn't happy that Lewton and Bodeen had decided—probably for purpose of seeming Serbian kinship—to have Simone Simon dub Elizabeth's "Moja sestra."

"Do you know," said Elizabeth, "Val Lewton later told me that was the biggest mistake he ever made—letting her dub my line!"

Meanwhile, Simone Simon apparently has a regret or two about Elizabeth Russell. "I remember Elizabeth Russell, naturally," Simon told me, "because she was so striking!" Yet on that memorable shooting day in 1942, Simone—possibly jealous that Elizabeth is stealing the attention, maybe feeling blown away by a feline presence that exceeds her own, perhaps just devilishly eager to wrap up the scene—pulls a star stunt. Jane Randolph will remember:

> We were sitting at a table in a café and Simone deliberately took her drink, and just spilled it down the front of her whole pale blue silk suit. Well, that stopped production.... She'd do things like that!

Incidentally, another possible reason that Simone purposefully spilled the drink was that she didn't want to deliver the "sobs of hysterical laughter" that the script called for as the scene ended.

At any rate, Tourneur dismisses the company from the cafe set at 5:55 p.m. and moves Simon, Smith and Randolph (all in new outfits) to Stage 7, for shots in the museum—including the memorable shot of Irena standing by a statue of Bubastis. There's been no dinner break. They work briskly and finish at 7:55 p.m.

Meanwhile, this same Saturday, the second unit with director Edward Donahue and cameraman Frank Redman are at work on RKO Stages 4, 6 and 7, filming shots of the Exterior Sheepfold in Central Park, the Exterior Arched Bridge, and Exterior Fifth Avenue. The story infers that Irena, having failed to snare Alice, had sated her bloodlust by slaughtering sheep in Central Park. Murdock MacQuarrie plays the shepherd, Bud Geary (as a mounted policeman) and Eddie Dew (as a street policeman) are on call, and so are five extras, 15 sheep, a horse and a taxi. They work from 9 to 4:15.

For all the artistry, the labor of two units and a total of 31 setups—an amazing day's work—week three ends with *Cat People* now *five* days behind schedule. This is the day the film was originally scheduled to wrap. Lewton is hyper-tense. He's also infatuated with another *Cat People* actress—Elizabeth Russell. "Val was a darling man," said the actress. "He liked me, and I liked him":

> We were never lovers; we might have been, but since we were not, there was a closer bond. Val told me he had never cheated on his wife since they had been married. I wasn't about to dispel that sanctity.

By the way, how did Elizabeth Russell, whose moment of time in Hollywood was playing "The Cat Woman," respond when asked her true feelings about felines?

"I can't stand them!"

A scene cut from *Cat People*: Jane Randolph's Alice gets acquainted with Simone Simon's Irena and one of her talents. Kent Smith's Ollie observes.

Week Four: Monday, August 17, to Friday, August 21, 1942
Screams in the Pool

Monday: A big day in horror film history as Jacques Tourneur directs Jane Randolph and Simone Simon in the legendary swimming pool episode of *Cat People*. The company goes on location to the Royal Palms Hotel, 360 South Westlake in downtown Los Angeles, where RKO has rented the pool in the basement for $35. DeWitt Bodeen remembered: "It was a one-time elegant apartment house ... in an area near Westlake Park that had once been fashionable; in fact, it was near the bungalow court where William Desmond Taylor had been murdered."

Jane Randolph wriggles again into that body girdle bathing suit and dives into the pool as Simone Simon watches from the shadows. The sequence is sensually, perversely fascinating. The shadows created by cameraman Nicholas Musuraca make the pool seem a flooded tomb, or mausoleum. We watch voyeuristically as glamour girl Alice, makeup off, hair wet, bobs helplessly in the water as devilish shadows flicker and cat screeches echo all around her until she becomes a wild, screaming hysteric. Again, we almost enjoy the sight and sound of the foxy Alice, looking increasingly helpless and terrified, suffering this manic meltdown. Bodeen's script precisely blueprinted every sight and sound:

Alice, as she hears the water, is afraid that the thing may have slipped into the pool. She looks around her in terror. She begins to scream. Her cries race around the empty room, echo back at her from the dark end of the pool, and are thrown back at her from the high, domed ceiling.

SERIES of THREE QUICK SHOTS, over which are the echoes of Alice's voice screaming for help.

First, the empty dark room.

Then, the black surface of the pool.

Then, the high, beamed ceiling.

SHOT of Alice, as she thrashes about in the water, screaming, the sound track filled with the sound of her voice and the mocking echoes.

The payoff: Simone Simon's Irena, looking like a million dollars in her fur coat and high heels, suddenly turns on the lights, steps out of the shadows, and flashes a glowingly bitchy grin.

"Is anything the matter?" she coos.

"The gruesomeness and horror angles," Joseph Breen had forewarned, "should be toned down as to Alice's fright in the swimming pool room." Lewton and Tourneur have gleefully thumbed noses at his request. Tourneur will insist the "cat" shadow on the wall was his fist. The cat sounds come later and are apparently a mix: Actress Dorothy Lloyd earns $60 for providing "cat noises"; additionally, the crew records cats roaring and growling at the Goebel's Lion Farm in Camarillo, California. An "overage" report dated October 23, 1942, notes Sound labor for scoring effects had tallied a tab of $795: "special animal noises that had to be recorded at lion farm. In addition 2 days were spent reverberating tracks to obtain special effects necessary to the picture."

RKO had provided telephone lines to the Royal Palms at a cost of $37.50 so the studio and company could stay in touch. Sixty box lunches are served, and Tourneur wraps up the episode at 1:40 p.m.—crafting one of the great sequences of horror in half a day.[22]

"Jane Randolph acted beautifully," said Simone Simon in 1994. "She was wonderful in that scene!"

There's a 20-minute trip back to RKO, and Simone Simon and Kent Smith meet at Stage 14 to shoot the Pet Shop episode. In this scene early in the film, the animals in the shop become wild and restless when Irena enters. The shop owner (Elizabeth Dunne) remarks, "The last time they did that was when an alley cat got in and ate up one of my nice white finches!"

Works ends that Monday evening at 8:45. Tourneur has shot two brilliant episodes on the same day.

The film's top shock sequences—the Central Park stalk and the swimming pool hysteria—are now complete, as is the wedding night party with the Cat Woman, the pet shop vignette, and the zoo climax. Yet there's much yet to do, and the film's still five days behind schedule.

Tuesday: Tourneur and company work on RKO Stages 7, 8, and 3. They shoot the scene in which Irena and Ollie come home from the wedding party and stand in the snow, discussing Irena's fears of consummating the marriage. Tourneur also shoots exterior scenes of the panther cage, Sally Lunn's Tearoom, and the transverse walk. The company uses three extras and the director completes 14 set-ups before dismissing everyone at 7:15 p.m.

Also today: Simone Simon finishes her role. Jane Randolph isn't sorry to see her go.

Wednesday: The company works in "Sally Lunn's Tea Room" on Stage 3 and the Interior Drafting Office on Stage 12, from 9 to 7:20 p.m. Kent Smith, Jane Randolph, Tom Conway,

Jack Holt, and Alan Napier are on call; so is black actress Theresa Harris, who plays Minnie, the waitress, in refreshing, non-stereotype style. Joe Breen even had concerns here:

> The drinking at this point should be minimized, and we suggest that Oliver be shown drinking beer instead of scotch highballs.... It might be better to show them sitting at a table, rather than at the bar, and also be having some sandwiches.

There are also seven extras, one black kitten, and one cat. All the principals are closed out now, except for Kent Smith and Jane Randolph.

Thursday: The couple works from 9 to 8:15 in the drafting office. There are eight extras and one cat.

Friday: Under great pressure to finish, Jacques Tourneur completes an amazing 30 set-ups. Included is the drafting room scene in Stage 12 in which Irena in panther form stalks Ollie and Alice; joining the actors on call are one panther (whose name is Dynamite), one cat, one dog, and one chicken. This episode had been another Breen censorship concern:

> The business of Oliver holding the T-square in front of him like a crucifix will undoubtedly prove offensive to many persons of sincere religious convictions. This business should be omitted. At this point, we request also that you omit Oliver's two uses of the phrase, "In the name of God."

Again Lewton defies Breen: The T-square as crucifix remains, as does "in the name of God." The company also films some pick-up shots, such as the cat in the swimming pool locker room.

Kent Smith finishes at 10:45 p.m. Jane Randolph, 11:15 p.m. The assistant director marks the daily production chart, "Picture Finished."

* * *

PART V. PROMOTION AND RELEASE

*SHE KNEW STRANGE, FIERCE PLEASURES
THAT NO OTHER WOMAN COULD EVER FEEL!*
—RKO publicity, **Cat People**

Val Lewton has seven weeks to fine-tune *Cat People* for a preview. Meanwhile, he's preparing his next film, *I Walked with a Zombie,* and blueprinting others, including *The Leopard Man.*

Monday, October 5: C. Bakaleinikoff, who had conducted Franz Waxman's brilliant score for *Bride of Frankenstein* in 1935, conducts Roy Webb's masterfully moody score for *Cat People,* recorded on RKO's Stage 2A. The film previews later that week at the RKO-Hillstreet Theatre in Los Angeles. Lewton, Bodeen, Simone Simon, and Jane Randolph are all there. The evening begins with a cartoon about a pussy cat, and when the title *Cat People* appears on the screen, the raucous crowd howls with laughter and makes cat sounds.

"Oh God!" gasps Lewton.

Simone Simon, who attends with a lady friend, nervously pinches the lady repeatedly. "I was so afraid the people would laugh at me," she recalled. The movie terrifies Jane Randolph—"I thought I was terrible," she remembered—and afterwards she sneaks out of the RKO-Hillstreet, frightened somebody might recognize her.

The audience, as Bodeen put it, was "enchanted."

Monday, October 26: Lewton starts shooting his new film, *I Walked with a Zombie,* Jacques Tourneur directing.

Friday, November 13: RKO has a new corporate motto—"Showmanship in Place of Genius," clearly a harpoon aimed at Orson Welles—and the trade papers provide Friday the 13th reviews for *Cat People. The Hollywood Reporter* writes:

> In his first show for RKO, Lewton has come through with an attraction that showmen can make count at the box office, something fresh and new in the "psychological" horror field. *Cat People* can make exhibitors sit up and purr over the cream of its profits. Yet it has to be sold as smartly as it was made....

Due to the "subtly done" horror, RKO prepares a deluxe horror campaign for *Cat People,* packed with purple prose tag lines:

> IT'S SUPER-SENSATIONAL! ... a beautiful woman soul-tortured by a dire obsession, hurtling to a stupendous emotional disaster.

There are radio blurbs:

> BEWARE! Of kissing strange, young women. One, now at large, changes into a panther and destroys lovers. Suspected of several crimes. Watch out! She may be one of the CAT PEOPLE.

Suggested PR gimmickry includes:

> Build a circular cage about six feet high. Inside place a cut-out of Simone Simon.... A placard at the cage was to warn, "For Safety's Sake! Keep Away from This Alluring Creature.... She is one of the CAT PEOPLE...." Another angle would be to have a real girl, dressed in evening gown and masked, seated in the cage.[23]

Saturday, November 28: With all final costs added, RKO prepares a final cost sheet for *Cat People*: $141,659.88—$22,711.88 over budget.

Saturday, December 5: *Cat People* braves the East Coast, opening at Broadway's Rialto Theatre. It's the home of the Universal horrors, where *The Wolf Man* had howled the previous December, and where *The Mummy's Tomb* had been the popular 1942 Halloween attraction. Bosley Crowther of the *New York Times* snidely reports:

> The strangely embarrassing predicament of a lady who finds herself possessed of mystical feline temptations, especially one to claw people to death, is the topic pursued at tedious and graphically unproductive length in RKO's latest little chiller, *Cat People* ... Miss Simone's cuddly little tabby would barely frighten a mouse under a chair.

Nevertheless, *Cat People* will pack the Rialto for two weeks, taking in $17,000.[24] (Universal's *The Wolf Man,* the previous December had earned $19,500 at the same theater.)

Monday, January 4, 1943: Simone Simon starts her first film job since *Cat People*: Republic's *Tahiti Honey*. She lands it after originally starred Ruth Terry leaves to have a baby.

Thursday, January 14: *Cat People*'s true potency takes hold at the Hawaii Theatre, 5939 Hollywood Boulevard, where RKO's *Citizen Kane* had moved after its El Capitan premiere and had been a powerhouse attraction. The Hawaii is also a horror salon, and it had recently offered a Universal double feature, *The Mummy's Tomb* and *Night Monster*—complete with an actor dressed as a Mummy, stalking up the theater aisle and causing kids to flee screaming to the lobby. Supporting *Cat People* is Warner Bros.' *The Gorilla Man*. Despite the bestial harmony of the titles, the latter film is a commandoes vs. spies potboiler.

Friday, January 15: "*Cat People* Lukewarm Film Thriller at Hawaii," headlines Edwin Schallert's *L.A. Times* review: "*Cat People*, per all advance heralding, is supposed to be some punkins as a thriller. But for my money, whatever that may amount to, it isn't a breeze let alone a shiver."

The result, however, becomes an L.A. phenomenon: The kinky, *noir* sexuality of *Cat People* becomes the talk of the town. Ironically, the cashier in the Hawaii's ticket booth is 18-year-old Marilyn Harris—who eleven years earlier played Little Maria, the child drowned by Karloff's Monster in *Frankenstein*. "A cat's head covered the cashier booth," remembered Ms. Harris of the Hawaii's *Cat People* ballyhoo, "and the change for the customers went down the tongue of the cat."[25]

The first week's take at the Hawaii tallies a hefty $9,600—short of the $10,000 *Citizen Kane* drew in its first week (October 10–16, 1941), but exceeding the $8,200 reaped by *The Mummy's Tomb* and *Night Monster* (December 10–16, 1942).[26] It's a certified holdover hit.

Saturday, February 13: Hedda Hopper reports in her column: "Seeing is believing, says I. *Cat People* ... well on its way to gross over a million, will be followed by a sequel, *Curse of the Cat People*.... Too bad they killed off Simone Simon in the first."

* * *

Cat People plays at the Hawaii for a remarkable 13 weeks. Folklore will claim it broke the record run of *Citizen Kane*, but Welles' masterpiece had stayed at the Hawaii for 17 weeks.

Also, some sources claim *Cat People*, in its original release, grossed $4,000,000. The RKO files report a far more conservative figure:

Domestic Rentals: $360,000
Foreign Rentals: $175,000
Worldwide Total: $535,000
Profit: $183,000[27]

"Rentals" does not mean "gross," and if one estimates the split between the theaters and the studio at 50–50, the film takes in over a million dollars. This is truly excellent business, although hardly the walloping sum legend provides. For perspective, *Cat People* easily out-performs RKO's *The Falcon's Brother*, which has worldwide rentals of $361,000 and a profit of $128,000. On the other hand, *Cat People* does less than one-sixth the business of 1943's *Hitler's Children*, which

Build a circular cage about six feet high. Inside place a cut-out of Simone Simon. Use copy as suggested in the illustration. Another angle would be to have a real girl, dressed in evening gown and masked, seated in the cage.

A masked feline beauty in a cage: pressbook exploitation ballyhoo for *Cat People*.

will become RKO's biggest money-maker to that time, with worldwide rentals of $3,355,000 and a profit of over $1.2 million.

Nevertheless, Lewton's *Cat People* gloriously exceeds expectations. Undoubtedly many who see it leave with a newly developed fear of Central Park, busses, and swimming pools. Some probably suffer nightmares about a cat-faced woman crashing their wedding night. And one can only imagine the effect the film has on the sex lives of the more unfortunately impressionable.

Now, a sequel will go into the works.

Had *Cat People* come from the hallowed gates of Universal, there might have been a truly horrific approach: Perhaps Elizabeth Russell's Cat Woman, slinking one moonlit night into a cemetery (a pet cemetery?), purrs witchcraft spells over Irena's grave. Rising from the dead is a clawing, raving creature, part female cadaver, part panther carcass, hell-bent on avenging herself (*itself*) on the ex-husband who'd rejected her, the woman who'd stolen his affection ... and their child. After all, hadn't Irena deserved cinema damnation by the almighty Breen Office for having killed Dr. Judd—and hadn't she also committed the unforgivable mortal sin of suicide?

Yet Lewton will resurrect Irena not as a monster, but as a transfigured, singing angel. Even more subversively, she becomes a loving guardian for a little girl who finds herself in a cursed world of her own as the only child of Oliver and Alice in their new life by the Hudson.

The sequel will feature a brilliantly novel twist—and prove both a triumph and a torment for Val Lewton.

The Curse of the Cat People
Part I: Production Blueprint

> The news today is of *Cat People*—and *Hepcat People*.
>
> RKO has decided to go ahead with its sequel to the phenomenally successful *Cat People*.... Simone Simon, the central character, will again depict the girl under the evil spell, and will again be aided, though not abetted, by Kent Smith and Jane Randolph, the sweethearts of the original.
>
> Val Lewton, who will repeat as producer, has been promised a budget double that of the first eerie work. The director will be Gunther Fritsch, whose short subjects for MGM have won him a couple of Academy Awards. The sequel's title is *Curse of the Cat People*.
>
> —Philip Scheuer, *Los Angeles Times*, August 14, 1943

The Hepcat People, Scheuer assures his readers, is "no gag." The Republic film will be a murder mystery about "jitter madness," dealing, as Scheuer writes, with "a super swing piece called 'Rhythm to Kill' which possesses its listeners and drives them to frenzied acts. The climax is a jam session in a zoo." The film never comes to be, but perhaps gives Val Lewton a good laugh. He can use one: Within the past twelve months, he's completed *Cat People* and produced four more films.

I Walked with a Zombie: lyrical, poetic, masterfully directed by Jacques Tourneur, a hauntingly beautiful horror film. *The Leopard Man*: also directed by Tourneur, stocked with three vivid, chillingly atmospheric, almost voyeuristic scenes depicting the murders of young women. *The Seventh Victim*: As Tourneur rises at RKO, Mark Robson makes his directorial bow with this exquisitely morbid curio; Jean Brooks stars as Jacqueline, a devil worshipper in a Cleopatra wig, targeted for assassination by a satanic cult.

The Seventh Victim has yet to be released; Lewton is now completing *The Ghost Ship*, starring Richard Dix as a psychopathic captain of a ship. *The Curse of the Cat People* will follow, but Lewton probably wonders how Philip Scheuer got certain things right and other things so very wrong in his column. The August 2, 1943, original budget sheet reveals the facts about RKO production # 435:

- Of course, Lewton wants Simone Simon to reprise her role of the heavenly Irena, and she signs for *The Curse of the Cat People* for a salary of $10,000—over double her fee for *Cat People*.
- Kent Smith and Jane Randolph are indeed back as Ollie and Alice, now living in Sleepy Hollow, New York, and blessed with a beautiful child. Smith has boosted his RKO stock by playing in both *Cat People* and the studio's mega-hit *Hitler's Children*, and now rates a $7,500 tab for the sequel. Jane Randolph has left RKO and the studio tracks her down to her grandmother's in Ohio. Her salary for the film: $1,050.
- Gunther von Fritsch, a 37-year-old from Austria-Hungary, makes his feature debut as *The Curse of the Cat People*'s director. Despite Scheuer's report, von Fritsch has not won any Oscars—although his 1943 Pete Smith "specialty" *Seeing Hands*, which deals with industry hiring the handicapped, will be Oscar-nominated as Best Short Subject of 1943 (but won't win). With Tourneur now an "A" director and Mark Robson still working on *The Ghost Ship*, Lewton gambles on von Fritsch. The director's salary: $2,500.
- The budget is by no means double that of *Cat People*. It's $147,315—about $30,000 more than *Cat People*'s budget and very close to the original film's final cost. The shooting schedule is 24 days—seven days more than *Cat People*'s.

DeWitt Bodeen had enjoyed a post–*Cat People* business-and-pleasure trip to New York City, researching *The Seventh Victim* (which he co-scripted with Charles O'Neal) and actually visiting a devil worshiper society on the Upper West Side ("I would have hated to be Hitler with all the spells they were working against him"). He also gathers material for *The Curse of the Cat People*:

> I went up to the Washington Irving country—Sleepy Hollow, etc.—and got a lot of good atmosphere. The screen story was told from the viewpoint of a middle-aged female "Down Easter" housekeeper in the Oliver Reed household, and deals, finally, with exorcism and a lot of other things ... but I was to follow a much-revised storyline....[28]

Indeed, the story will morph drastically under Lewton's intense supervision. As the producer gets passionately involved in the script, it becomes virtually autobiographical, daubed with the producer's own childhood experiences and obsessions. The major characters, in fact, are variations on Val Lewton:

- Amy: As the child who sees her father's dead first wife as a heaven-sent playmate, Amy is the lost-in-fantasy child Lewton had been. The setting is accurate: Lewton had grown up in Sleepy Hollow country at "Who Torok," the cottage of his aunt, actress Alla Nazimova. He even has Bodeen draft an episode in which Amy places her birthday party invitations in a "magic mailbox tree"—something Lewton himself did in his childhood with the invitations to his sister Lucy's birthday party. There will be belief in the Lewton family that the producer also fashioned Amy after his own daughter, 13-year-old Nina, who was as defiantly romantic as her father.

At age seven, Ann Carter gave an amazing performance as Amy in *The Curse of the Cat People.*

• Oliver Reed: Here Lewton cast himself in a double role—both lost child and intemperate, impatient but surely loving father. Lewton and Nina have a turbulent relationship. He named her after his mother (and named his yacht after both mother and daughter); he also will throw a glass of water in his daughter's face at dinner one night in front of guests. Both Lewton and Nina will die at the age of only 46, and both from heart trouble.

More Lewton *doppelgangers* take on major roles in the script. Julia Farren, the mad old Shakespearean actress, represents Lewton the scaremonger; just as Julia frightens Amy in her spooky old mansion with her soliloquy about the Headless Horseman, so does Lewton frighten the masses in darkened movie houses. The lonely, haunted Barbara Farren, unloved by her mother Julia (who refuses even to acknowledge she's her daughter), epitomizes Lewton's profoundly dark side—a scary, witchy spinster, and what Amy might become if she never resolves her traumas with her father. Indeed, one can see the role of Barbara as Lewton's almost cruel warning to his daughter Nina: "This is what you'll become, a spooky, unloved witch, if you fail in your relationship with me."

Part II: The Song of the Cat Woman

With the basic concept for his sequel in play, Lewton proceeds to finalize casting—and steer the show in a new, provocatively subversive direction.

Wednesday, August 18, 1943: Eight days before shooting is to start, von Fritsch films a test on RKO's Stage Four of Julia Dean as the old actress Julia. DeWitt Bodeen had suggested Ms. Dean "audition" by having Lewton and von Fritsch to tea on a silver service; she'd passed that test with flying colors, and now wins this one, returning to films after a 25-year absence. There are three girls playing Amy in the test; one of them is Sharyn Moffett, who will later portray the crippled Georgina in Lewton's *The Body Snatcher.*

Miss Moffett and the other two contenders that day ultimately lose out to blonde-haired, seven-year-old Ann Carter. Ann had recently appeared in *I Married a Witch* (1942) as daughter of "witch" Veronica Lake, complete with a peekaboo bang. She joins *The Curse of the Cat People,* set to work 23 of the production's 24 days, at a salary of $250 a week.

And as for Barbara Farren ... Lewton casts Elizabeth Russell, his original Cat Woman from *Cat People.* She'd worked for Lewton again as the dying, suicide-by-sin prostitute Mimi in *The Seventh Victim* and signs on for *The Curse of the Cat People* at $400 per week. Lewton is still infatuated with Elizabeth—and has cast her in the role that perhaps fascinates him most deeply.

Lewton changes Bodeen's "Down Easter" to a Jamaican, played by Sir Lancelot, who'd performed so memorably in Lewton's *I Walked with a Zombie*—"This was an innovation I very much liked," said Bodeen. The editor is Robert Wise, who'd worked for Orson Welles on *Citizen Kane* and *The Magnificent Ambersons*. Wise has quickly found Lewton to be "a marvelous man" and "a truly creative producer," and is delighted to be part of the Snake Pit.

Bodeen, back on the RKO payroll August 4 through August 24, revamps his original script to Lewton's specifications; he'll also work on the film as dialogue director, as he had on *Cat People*. The exorcism Bodeen had originally imagined for the film is long-gone from the script, but a new one is in place: The exorcism of Val Lewton's haunted childhood.

Finally, there's an influence no one in the Lewton unit ever acknowledges. During the spring and summer of 1943, 20th Century–Fox has been producing *The Song of Bernadette*, based on Franz Werfel's novel about Bernadette Soubirous and her visions of the Blessed Virgin at Lourdes. Jennifer Jones (Lewton's original choice for Alice in *Cat People*) is starring as Bernadette, Linda Darnell is appearing unbilled as the Virgin, and the film has proceeded with venerable publicity. In a twist that seems indicative of Lewton's subversively irreverent nature, he clearly patterns *The Curse of the Cat People* after *The Song of Bernadette*: Amy, the neurotic, disturbed child is our Bernadette, and Irena, the death-by-suicide Cat Woman, is our Virgin.

The Song of Bernadette as horror film: It seems a mockery, a blasphemy, and Lewton likely enjoys private chuckles over his decidedly unorthodox approach. However, the producer will supervise his "B" film with the same delicacy and sense of profound faith that will mark the 20th Century–Fox epic—and in doing so, he'll basically pull off a Hollywood miracle.

Part III. The Shoot, with Gunther von Fritsch as Director

WEEK ONE: THURSDAY, AUGUST 26, TO SATURDAY, AUGUST 28, 1943
A HOLY VISION, FALLING STARS, CORNFLAKES AS SNOW, A PILGRIMAGE TO LITTLE MARIA'S, AND A WITCH IN HIGH HEELS

Thursday: One year and five days after *Cat People* had wrapped up, *The Curse of the Cat People* begins shooting on RKO's Stage 7. The company assembles at 9:00 a.m. on

In a still for *The Curse of the Cat People*, Simone Simon's Irena, now a heavenly vision à la *The Song of Bernadette*, hovers over Jane Randolph's Alice and Kent Smith's Oliver.

the Amy's Bedroom set. The emotional scene shows Irena's ghost bidding farewell to the tearful Amy.

The assigned cameraman, Nicholas Musuraca, who's been on *Cat People* and *The Seventh Victim*, is still working on *The Ghost Ship*, so Frank Redman starts the picture. It's a night scene, calling for wind to blow and snow to fall outside the bedroom window. The first player on call is Ann Carter. Ann, who died in 2014, had recently enjoyed a "comeback" via Tom Weaver's *Video Watchdog* interview and her appearance in the Martin Scorsese documentary *Val Lewton: The Man in the Shadows*. She told me in March of 2008:

> Gunther von Fritsch was very soft-spoken, did not raise his voice and was patient. He must have been patient with me! He was quite young, quite slim, and had thinning dark hair. As I always remember Val Lewton on the set in a suit and tie, I remember Gunther Fritsch in slacks, white shirt and tie.[29]

Simone Simon punctually arrives for her call at 10:00 a.m., adorned in her Irene-as-angel costume, coiffure and makeup. In an early but discarded script idea, Amy saw a beautiful fairy princess in a storybook and imagined the princess as her friend. Rather than jettison the "look," Lewton retains it for his religious motif that will develop throughout the shoot. The costume will backfire in some circles: James Agee, playwright and critic who hailed Lewton's work, will joke that the gown makes Simone's façade look like "a relief map from *What Every Young Husband Should Know.*"

At any rate, the effect is certainly striking. Simone Simon, long perceived in Hollywood as a French sex fiend, now resembles a holy (if provocative) vision out of *The Song of Bernadette*. Ann Carter vividly remembered her first glimpse of this "vision":

> Oh, the dress! I was so impressed with her dress. It was a blue-gray chiffon dress with silver, metallic paper stars of different sizes—they weren't sewn on, they were glued on, and they'd fall off—and everywhere she went there were stars! So I'd pick them up, and thought it was very important that I'd give them back to her! She had a lot of makeup, and she was beautiful—and extremely nice to me.
>
> So there we were on the first day of shooting, and I'm crying, "Don't leave me!" and Simone Simon's stars are falling off her gown—and the men in the catwalks are dropping untoasted corn flakes for snow!

However beatific she appears, Simone Simon is unhappy. "Well, they better have tried to make me beautiful," said Mlle. Simon in a 1994 interview, "because I had nothing else to do! Good God!" Seymour Nebenzal (of *Hitler's Madman* fame) has offered her the role of the vixen Olga in *Summer Storm*, warning Simone, "If you do another 'B' picture, you're through with 'A' pictures." Simone nevertheless loyally accepts *The Curse of the Cat People* and Linda Darnell will boost her stardom as Olga. Oddly, Nebenzal has wanted two actresses recently employed as "Visions" for a sexpot role; at any rate, Simon told me:

> I was so grateful to Val for *Cat People* that I couldn't let him down ... but I don't regret it. I couldn't have said to Val, "Sorry, boy—you gave me this beautiful part in *Cat People*, but now I will let you down to do an 'A' picture." He would have understood, but he never knew. I never told him.

Lewton, sensing Simone's mood, tries to appease her. The dramatic scene today, not in the original script, is presumably a last-minute addition for Simone's benefit. Lewton possibly wrote it himself. The company wraps up at 5:25 p.m. Gunther von Fritsch has shot seven set-ups. Jacques Tourneur had averaged 17 a day his first week directing *Cat People*.

Friday: The company goes on location to Arthurs Ranch in Malibu to shoot the script's first scene—Eve March's Miss Callahan, Amy's teacher, leading Amy and a dozen singing children on a sunny pastoral field trip in Sleepy Hollow. The locale, with its bridge over the water, is lovely, and neighbors a hallowed site of horror film history: the locale where Boris Karloff's Monster threw Marilyn Harris's Little Maria into the lake in *Frankenstein*. Von Fritsch and interim cameraman Redman overcome challenges with the lighting continuity to provide a charmingly mystical and—yes—almost heavenly look. The company completes seven set-ups.

Saturday: It's another location day, this time to 900 West Adams Street in Los Angeles. The locale represents the old haunted Farren house. If the previous day, at pastoral Malibu, presented a metaphor for Heaven, today's metaphor, as conveyed by this old mansion, is Hell. Ann Carter, Julia Dean, and Elizabeth Russell are on call, as are three other children. Ann is proving a revelation, her expressions and body language wonderfully effective. Julia Dean provides only her voice for now, calling from high in the house as she tosses Amy a "magic ring."

And as for Elizabeth Russell ... as the lonely, haunted Barbara, she instantly evokes an attractive fairy tale witch in 1943 frock and high heels—just what Lewton desires. If Simone Simon is an angel, Elizabeth Russell is a devil, and Lewton will revel in the iconography.

The location trip serves 70 lunches as von Fritsch improves his completed number of

The spooky Farren house. Old Julia Farren signals Amy and throws her a ring.

set-ups today: 12. It's been only a three-day week for the company, but after today, *The Curse of the Cat People* is already officially one day behind schedule.

WEEK TWO: MONDAY, AUGUST 30, TO SATURDAY, SEPTEMBER 4, 1943 A RED WIG, SCARY CHEEKBONES, A SIGNIFICANT BUTTERFLY, AND THE RKO RANCH

Monday: Nicholas Musuraca, having finished his work on *The Ghost Ship,* joins *The Curse of the Cat People.* Von Fritsch devotes the day to Simone and Ann Carter only, and augments what was shot on August 26.

Tuesday: The company reports to Stage 12, the interior of the Farren house. The players on call are Carter, Russell, and Julia Dean, arriving for her first day of on-screen work. The original script describes Julia (surely a homage to Lewton's famed actress Nazimova) as "a fabulous creature, with a painted, rouged and powdered face, a wig of outrageously red hair, and scarlet lips...." In the 1990 colorized version, the wig is gray, but Ann Carter recalled:

> Julia Dean's wig was red—oh yes! A very weird red—a light, theatrical, strawberry-blonde, fiery red—a color nobody's hair ever was. She was pleasant between scenes, and I remember all that jewelry—ropes and ropes and ropes of stuff—and her black velvet dress. She was very overwhelming when she got going!

Von Fritsch and Musuraca provide a grand tour of the spooky old house in true fairy tale style. Carter remembered:

> Did you see all the different decorations that were so dark and evil-looking? And the stuffed cat eating a bird? Ech! They didn't scare me, but they got my attention—oh yeah!

Perhaps the most frightening spectacle is Elizabeth Russell as the witchy Barbara. Indeed, she's *so* witchy, one almost expects her to cackle and toss Amy into a fiery oven. Carter said:

> Elizabeth Russell—just to look at her! She was tall and thin, and the way she was lighted—her cheekbones—she was scary-looking, although she never did anything on the set to frighten me. I think she probably purposefully, for the good of us all, kept a certain feeling between us that wasn't really warm or fuzzy. She kept it as it was in the movie a little bit—you know, the distance.

Von Fritsch is paying for this meticulously rich work: After the company wraps up today, following an impressive 22 set-ups, the production is two days behind schedule.

Wednesday: Stage 11 provides an "Ext. River Bank" set as Carter plays her early scene with the butterfly. The butterfly originally has great significance in the story, although cuts made in the script during shooting will reduce it. Eve March and several child actors join her. There are retakes on some work from day two. Come afternoon, Simone Simon reports for more work on the Amy's Bedroom set. The day ends at 6:15 after only six set-ups.

Thursday and Friday: The company works on the RKO Ranch in Encino. It's a fascinating Never-Never Land of old sets, including the gothic exteriors from 1939's *The Hunchback of Notre Dame,* which Lewton will later use in *The Body Snatcher.* The ranch provides *The Curse of the Cat People*'s Sleepy Hollow exteriors (except for the Farren house which, as noted, is near downtown L.A.). Carter is there, as is Eve March and several child actors. The ranch will be demolished in the mid–1950s.

Thursday is the first day's work for Kent Smith, Jane Randolph, and Sir Lancelot. Smith, fated for knocks from many fans who attack Oliver's obtuse parenting, actually delivers the complex failure of a father Lewton wants—a man tormented by the fear that his child may go insane, as had Irena. Sir Lancelot is an appealing, intelligent "minority figure" as the singing servant Edward, and Jane Randolph is attractive as she reprises Alice, now a high-heel-wearing housewife. Domesticity has reduced Alice's swagger—and she'll wear a hat in only one scene.

Jane quickly senses "a big problem" on the set. This time it's not due to Simone Simon, whose role is small, Jane believes, because of her temperamental antics on *Cat People*. Nor, in her opinion, was it due to von Fritsch: "They had made so much money with *Cat People*," she will say, "that they wanted to do a sequel right away":

> There was a big strain at RKO at that time; they were having financial problems, and, boy, the producers would walk on the set and everybody would get pretty nervous. If you were overtime, you worked at night, and they were always worried about everything....

Meanwhile, Ann Carter fits in well with her new screen "family"—"I felt like I belonged," she says—and especially enjoyed Sir Lancelot, whom she called Mr. Sir Lancelot. "He was no nice, relaxed, warm and fun, and sang occasionally between scenes."

Saturday: Carter, Julia Dean and Elizabeth Russell return to Stage 12 for more shots inside the Farren house. The film is now three days behind schedule. Lewton is keeping Bodeen frantic, rewriting the script.

More and more, *The Curse of the Cat People* is emerging as a spiritual striptease of Val Lewton.

WEEK THREE: TUESDAY, SEPTEMBER 7,
TO SATURDAY, SEPTEMBER 11, 1943
THE HEADLESS HORSEMAN RIDES
AND THE MAGIC MAILBOX TREE

Monday: There is no shooting because of the Labor Day Holiday.

Tuesday: Work resumes on the Amy's Bedroom set. Carter and Simon act together that morning. Jane Randolph reports at one and Simone is dismissed at three—the two hours is one of the rare occasions Jane is on the shoot with her on- and off-screen nemesis from *Cat People*. Jane's performance as Alice has a strange subtlety: Early in *The Curse of the Cat People*, Oliver muses that the moody Amy could almost be Irena's child, and Alice indeed seems almost a kind stepmother to Amy rather than her natural mom.

Wednesday: It's back into the shadows of the Farren house: Ann Carter, Julia Dean, and Sir Lancelot work, and Dean delivers her wonderful Headless Horseman soliloquy:

> At the hour of midnight, down the road that goes through Sleepy Hollow, across the bridge, he goes galloping, galloping...!
> ...His great cloak sweeps around you, he swings you to his saddle bow, and you have to ride forever ... always his arms around you ... forever you must ride and ride and ride with the Headless Horseman!

It becomes even more magical via Roy Webb's music. Von Fritsch comes through this day with 25 set-ups.

Thursday: Ann Carter, Kent Smith, Jane Randolph and Sir Lancelot work on Stage 7, on the exterior Reed backyard set. Included in the day's work is the "magic mailbox tree" scene, which von Fritsch directs with special sensitivity. Ann Carter says:

> On the movie, perhaps the outstanding thing for me was that particular set. I can't even describe properly how it changed from season to season—all of them so pretty. For example, they made icicles in the winter—and all on a soundstage. There were people up there on the catwalks who dropped leaves, and as I'd mentioned, untoasted corn flakes for snow! It was absolutely beautiful—and just overwhelming for a kid.

This is the shoot's twelfth day, and the company is halfway through the 24-day schedule. The director is still three days behind, but Jacques Tourneur finished *Cat People* five days over schedule and there's hope Gunther von Fritsch can stay on top of all the demands.

Friday: Simone Simon, Ann Carter, Kent Smith, Jane Randolph, and Sir Lancelot work again on the Reed Backyard set on Stage 7. Included is the lovely scene where Amy sits by the pond with Julia Farren's magic ring and says, "I wish ... for a friend." Also shot is the almost celestial entrance of Simone as Irena's ghost, carrying Amy's ball. Carter's close-ups as she beholds this miracle are exceptionally touching, and both players movingly play the scene:

> *Amy*: I've wanted a friend.
> *Irena*: I've wanted a friend too. I've been lonely.
> *Amy*: But where do you come from?
> *Irena*: You wouldn't understand. I come from great darkness and deep peace.

Von Fritsch handles this challenging material with delicacy, but it takes time—he completes only ten set-ups. After shooting wraps at 6:00 p.m. Simone records the French Christmas carol she'll sing in the movie. The film is now *four* days behind schedule.

Saturday: Stage 7 hosts Simone, Carter, Smith, Randolph and Sir Lancelot as von Fritsch films the scene in Oliver's workshop where the father gives his daughter a model boat he's built for her, then scolds her for not playing with other children. It's very "Lewtonesque"—Lewton has a workshop on his ranch in the Pacific Palisades, where the yachtsman also tries to live up to his own Hemingway image by keeping watch at night, with bow and arrow, for coyotes!

Oliver's clash with Amy is a gut-wrenching scene, aided again by Ann Carter's reactions. Von Fritsch also devotes more time this day to refining the scene of Irena's entrance. The RKO front office thinks he's *too* meticulous. *The Curse of the Cat People* is now *five* days behind schedule.

Week Four: Monday, September 13, to Saturday, September 18, 1943
"You Called Me By My Name!"

Monday: Von Fritsch focuses on Simone and Carter in the Reed backyard. The film is now *six* days behind schedule.

Tuesday: The company shoots more scenes of Simone and Carter in the backyard, including the Halloween vignette where Irena burns the leaves. The film is now *seven* days behind schedule.

Wednesday: There's a crisis on Stage 12, as Gunther von Fritsch shoots a pivotal scene between Julia Dean's Julia and Elizabeth Russell's Barbara. The snowy night was to find the gray-haired Julia, her red wig beside her on its stand, the ancient actress quoting from Shakespeare's *King Lear.* Brackets mark critical dialogue cut from the release version.

> *Julia:* [Don't you like the wind, Regan? Or is your name Goneril?
> "Blow winds, and crack your cheeks!
> Rage! Blow!
> Now rain, wind, thunder, fire are my daughters..."
> [*smiling*] Oh, I could be Queen to King Lear tonight!]
> *Barbara:* Oh, I hate the storm. I hate it.
> *Julia:* I don't hate the storm. It blows beyond me. It was on such a night like this that Barbara died.
> *Barbara:* But I am Barbara. I didn't die.
> *Julia:* My Barbara was killed. [I killed her. Yes—it was my fault.... They warned me not to drive from the theater. There was a raging storm that night. Sleepy Hollow Bridge was covered with snow and ice. The car overturned. Barbara was killed.]
> *Barbara* [*interrupting, pleading*]: No, no. You were out of your mind. You didn't know anybody—you didn't remember anything. [And then, when your memory returned, you called for me, and I came to your bedroom. You expected a little girl. But I was sixteen—ten years older than when you last remembered me. You said I wasn't your daughter, that we were playing tricks on you—that your daughter was a little girl. I loved you. I wanted you for my mother. But you denied me.] Look at me, mother. Look into my eyes. Say that I'm Barbara.
> *Julia:* No, no. It's not true. Everything you say is a lie. You're a poor, lost woman. You're not my Barbara.

An alternate of this line in the script reads, "You're a poor drunken woman." At any rate, Elizabeth Russell will remember the day as "disastrous"; she'd avoided memorizing the lines because Lewton had told her he was changing them. However, no new lines come, Elizabeth doesn't know her original lines—and as she tries to learn them on the set, "suits" from the front office visit the stage and take note of the problem. As Elizabeth would recall:

> What shook me was that someone finally told me Val was in the hospital—and neither the director, nor anyone else, knew what he had told me about not memorizing my lines! They thought I was making up an excuse!

Indeed, the September 15, 1943, edition of *The Hollywood Reporter* writes that Lewton is in Hollywood Hospital due to a sinus problem. In fact, his hypersensitivity over *The Curse of the Cat People* has worn him down, and the mortified Elizabeth is without an ally. The actress learns the lines on the set and von Fritsch completes the scene without falling another day behind schedule.

Perversely, it's all for nothing. For whatever mysterious reasons, only a few lines, as noted, survive from this scene in the release print; the rest of this richly dramatic exposition will fall to the cutting room floor.

Also on Wednesday: A second unit shoots some scenes on Stage 7. The shots include Amy slapping the little boy for killing the butterfly, and Irena's spirit teaching Amy to make numbers by comparing them to fairy tale characters: "One is like a tall princess..." etc. (The number forming, incidentally, is another Lewton personal touch—the way Lewton and his wife Ruth taught daughter Nina and son Val to form their numbers.) Directing these 12 setups: *The Curse of the Cat People*'s 29-year-old editor, Robert Wise.

Gunther von Fritsch is at a major disadvantage. The hospitalized Lewton, who had championed Jacques Tourneur and Mark Robson in battles with the front office, isn't here to fight for him. The pressure is snowballing.

Thursday: All the principal actors gather on Stage 12 for the snowy night climax in the Farren house. Crossed out in Robert Wise's script is a very significant bit: "Barbara, with a half drink in her hand, stands looking down at a butterfly case in which there are a great many beautiful insects mounted on Victorian backing." Eliminated was this hint of Barbara's alcoholism, as well as—most unfortunately—the "butterfly connection" between Barbara and Amy.

Also crossed out is Julia humming a song from Shakespeare's *Cymbeline* and Barbara recognizing it. "I was singing it, just like you said, the night of the accident...," says Barbara, who now sings:

> Fear no more the heat o' the sun,
> Nor the furious winter rages.

With apparently no shooting of the butterfly case or the singing Barbara, von Fritsch directs the remainder of scene 193—in which Julia Dean's Julia and Elizabeth Russell's Barbara have a near-miraculous reconciliation.

Barbara: Tell me about little Barbara. What was she like?
Julia: She was like an angel. Somehow I never felt she belonged to this world. A bright and lovely child, with a serious, lonely little face. Her hair was like Amy's. In the sunlight it was pale, like shadowed gold. When I touched it, my fingers sang.

Clearly these lines fully underscore the Amy-Barbara "hook," and the script details what is to follow: "Quietly, Barbara bends over and presses her cheek against Mrs. Farren's face. The woman's soft hair tumbles down upon Mrs. Farren's shoulder and against her neck. The old lady fondles the tumbling locks and as she does so it kindles a dead memory."

Julia [*whispering*]: Barbara. My baby.
Barbara [*in an awed whisper as she comes around the chair*]: You called me by my name! [*She drops on her knees before her mother, clinging to her*] Promise me that you won't forget. That tomorrow will be the same. That you'll remember always... [*rising*]: There's another promise you must make. That little girl who comes here ... she mustn't ever come to see you again. Promise me you won't see her.
Julia: No, my child. I shall never see her again.
Barbara [*whirling around clinching her fists, to herself*]: If that child comes here, I'll kill her. Yes, I'll kill her.

Once again, all the artistry is for nothing. Virtually all of the reconciliation and the preceding dialogue will be cut, all the way to and including Julia's "No, my child. I shall never see her again." In the release print, there will be a "looped" line from Barbara—"You're always worse when that little girl's been here"—followed by Barbara's, "If that child comes here again, I'll kill her. Yes, I'll kill her."

Also filmed, but destined never to be seen by the public, is the crux of the snowy night climax. Julia (as in the final version), trying to hide Amy from Barbara, dies before her eyes on the staircase. The sight of death terrifies Amy. However, as originally shot, there is another sensation frightening the child—the sound of the insane, now demonic Barbara, locked in her room, trying to escape to kill Amy. "Let me out!" the madwoman screams and howls. Meanwhile, Irena comforts Amy by Julia's body:

Irena: Don't cry, Amy. She's dead. [*Amy shrinks away. Irena reaches for Amy's hand, takes it. With her other hand, Irena reaches down and touches the face of the dead woman.*] You mustn't be afraid.

Elizabeth Russell as Barbara and Julia Dean as her mother Julia have a snowy night reconciliation in the original ending of *The Curse of the Cat People.* **Val Lewton later discarded it and created a new ending.**

Amy [*sobbing*]: But she's dead.

Irena: But Death is good. It is our endless childhood. We go back to death, Amy. It is our home in peace forever. [*Amy pulls away in repulsion. Irena turns the child to her.*] But Amy. Look at me. I am dead. It's like you and me, Amy—playing in the garden all day. But we never tire. We never sleep, and the day never ends. [*Amy looks at her friend, and a slow smile forms on her face. Irena bends down beside her and brushes the tears from her smiling face.*] You're not frightened now, are you?

Von Fritsch this day also shoots scenes of Amy's snowy night arrival at the Farren house, Julia's welcoming of her, Irena's appearance to her, and Oliver, Alice, Miss Callahan, and Edward rescuing her. Also on call: Erford Gage (who'd played the poet in *The Seventh Victim*), here in a bit as a state trooper. (Gage was a casualty of war, fated to die in the Philippines in 1945.) The day ends at 6:40 p.m.

Friday: Von Fritsch continues with the shooting of the snowy night climax at the Farren house—19 set-ups plus a re-take of scene 65 where Amy returns the ring to the Farren house and Barbara admits her. It's superb work, but von Fritsch doesn't complete all the shots for the climactic episode and *The Curse of the Cat People* is now eight days behind schedule.

Also on Friday, *The Seventh Victim* opens at the Rialto in New York City. *The New York Times* sneers it's so bad that the projectionist probably ran it upside down and backwards.

Saturday: The company reports at 9 a.m. to the Reed Backyard Set on Stage 7—Carter, Simone, Smith, Randolph, March, and Sir Lancelot. Prop snow covers the set as von Fritsch shoots the Christmas Eve scene in which Irena, in a Yuletide cape and hood, carols in the backyard. Amy gives her a present, and Irena creates a magical scene to captivate Amy. The effect is charming, the magical lighting of Ann Carter and Simone Simon enchanting.

The company takes its lunch 12:30 to 1:30. Unbeknownst to von Fritsch or the company, another lunch is taking place—and Val Lewton, out of the hospital, and Sid Rogell, executive producer of the "B" unit, have invited editor Robert Wise to join them. Wise has been campaigning to direct—he'd done a bit of "ghost-directing" on *The Magnificent Ambersons* and *The Fallen Sparrow*, as well as Wednesday's second unit work on *The Curse of the Cat People*:

> I got a call to go over to Lucey's restaurant, cattycorner across from RKO, to see Val Lewton and Sid Rogell. They were at the table and said, "Well, you've been asking for a chance to direct ... we can't seem to speed Gunther up." It's not that they were dissatisfied with Gunther's work, he just couldn't go fast enough.... They said, "He's going to have to go, so we want you to take over Monday morning."
>
> I was thrilled, but I had a moment's hesitation, because I was scheduled to go back that night on the stage with Gunther ... he was shooting some stuff with special effects and he wanted me there.... I felt uncomfortable about going back and working with him and knowing I was going to take over Monday. I guess Rogell sensed this hesitation on my part, and he was not a man ever to mince words. He said, "Now listen, Bob. Somebody else is going to be there Monday morning. It's going to be you or somebody else."
>
> So I said, "As long as you put it that way, I'll be there!"[30]

Von Fritsch and the company work until six and take a dinner break until 7. Simone Simon returns to Stage 7 and von Fritsch, aided by his crew—including an uncomfortable, secret-keeping Robert Wise—shoots her final scenes in the backyard, including what will be the film's fade-out shot. It is the star's last work on the film—or so she presumes—and she finishes up at 10:10 p.m.

What Gunther von Fritsch has done—under Val Lewton's meticulous supervision, of course—has been extraordinary. He's shot most of *The Curse of the Cat People's* key scenes in 20 days. He's created a striking storybook imagery, as if a child's eyes were behind the camera, seeing Simone Simon as a beautiful fairy tale princess and Elizabeth Russell as a slinky, cat-faced witch. He'd even daubed it with the spiritual touch his producer wanted—Simone the angel vs. Elizabeth the devil—and delivered both the delicacy and the dashes of terror the film demanded.

Yet the film has been shooting 20 days on a 24-day schedule and is nowhere near finished. There is no greater mortal sin on a "B" movie. Sometime between 10:10 Saturday night and early Monday morning, Gunther von Fritsch will learn that RKO has given him the axe—and replaced him as director of *The Curse of the Cat People*.

Part IV: The Shoot, with Robert Wise Directing

WEEK FIVE: MONDAY, SEPTEMBER 20,
TO SATURDAY, SEPTEMBER 25, 1943,
"NERVOUS AS A CAT"

Monday: "I was nervous as a cat!" remembered Robert Wise. He greets Ann Carter, Kent Smith, Jane Randolph, Eve March, and Sir Lancelot on Stage 7, as *The Curse of the Cat People*'s new director. The cast is uniformly friendly and supportive—the only potentially temperamental player, Simone Simon, checked out Saturday night. Lewton presents Wise with a gift, Shaw's *The Art of Rehearsal*. J. R. Whittredge replaces Wise as editor. Ann Carter remembers a very smooth transition:

> I never thought anything about it. It was like, "Okay, this person has done what he's going to do, and now we have this person." I didn't question why or anything—it was just what it was.

Wise shoots a variety of scenes on the snowy Reed Backyard set, including the Christmas carolers who, probably to Lewton's joy, look oddly dark and sinister. By 6:25 p.m. Wise has completed 19 set-ups—almost three times as many as Gunther von Fritsch shot the first day. Lewton is very proud of him.

Tuesday: Wise moves to Stage 12 and the Farren house set, shooting Amy's visit to Julia with a Christmas gift. Elizabeth Russell, a disciple of astrology, forecasts that Wise will have a great career as a director. "I'm glad she called it right!" said Wise over 50 years later.

Wise shoots a scene also doomed to the cutting room floor. Julia, with no gift for Amy, tells her the story of Herne, the Huntsman:

> *Julia*: [T]here's a wild huntsman who scours the forest with his dogs and his men.... Everywhere he passes, the animals are slaughtered and lie dead beneath his trampling feet. If he should catch up with anyone walking in the wood, forever and forever they would have to hunt with Herne, the Huntsman.... Hear his horn?
> *Amy*: Does he kill people?
> *Julia*: No, not people—just deer and game, but the people he catches can never be free again. They too must kill and kill, covering themselves with blood.

The terrible tale is another nice showcase for Julia, à la her Headless Horseman soliloquy, and might even have tempted the audience to believe the scary Barbara is one of the Huntsman's killers. But the footage will not survive into the final cut.

Meanwhile, never filmed is an episode in which Irena and Amy admire a doe in the snow: "It is wildness and freedom. No one can touch it," Irena was to say of the doe. Later, on the way home from the Farren house, Edward and Amy find in the night "lying upon the snow in a pool of blood the mangled body of the little deer." Edward presumes a car has killed it and a deeply distressed Amy asks of the doe, "But where has it gone? Where's all the strength and the quickness?" The episode powerfully sets up Amy's fear of death, which is the centerpiece of the original ending—but it runs the risk of traumatizing sensitive audience members. Probably for this reason, Lewton never shoots it.[31]

Wednesday: Wise works again on the Farren house set, shooting new scenes for Amy's first visit and new shots of Barbara's mania in the climax. Director and cameraman improve Amy's original entrance into the Farren house, as the new shot shows Amy and Barbara caught in a mirror—playing up the thematic fact that they are reflected images of each other.

The new director also photographs the shot of Barbara from Amy's angle, the light chillingly playing on her satanic face. Wise clearly understands perfectly what Lewton wants and what von Fritsch has established, and his pace is impressive—13 set-ups today.

Thursday: Wise completes the original climax which von Fritsch had started. It's startlingly different from what will appear in the release print. After the rescue of Amy, the state trooper releases the wildly insane Barbara, described in the script as "hysterical with rage and drink," from her locked room:

> *Barbara*: Who turned the key in the lock? I heard the voice of my mother and the voice of that child, and when I tried to get out, the door was locked. *Who turned the key and locked me in?*

Barbara sees Julia's body on the staircase and kneels by her corpse. "You did it!" screams Barbara at Amy. "You stole her love! Thief... You thief!" She swoops down the stairs ("in a terrible fury," notes the script) to attack Amy, the troopers restrain her, and they lead Barbara off—likely to an asylum. Amy reconciles with her family and we realize it was Irena, Amy's guardian angel, who had locked the raving Barbara in the room and saved Amy's life.

Ann Carter remembered the harrowing climax:

> In the original ending, the question was, "Who locked the door?"—and it had been Irena. I remember Elizabeth Russell as Barbara, locked in her room. She was screaming and clawing at the door and she was just ... insane. Totally out of control. And the men came and took her away.

Wise then reports to Stage 4, and in a complete change of mood, shoots more of the Christmas episode in the Reed house.

Friday and Saturday: Wise is very busy on the Reed house interior on Stage 4. Meanwhile, on Friday, assistant director Harry D'Arcy returns to 900 West Adams Street with a second unit and shoots more exteriors of the Farren house with Ann Carter, Sir Lancelot, and Elizabeth Russell. As such, *The Curse of the Cat People* will actually contain the work of *three* directors. Wise finishes the week without the film falling any further behind schedule.

This week RKO reports a profit of $3,220,583 for the first 26 weeks of 1943, as compared with a loss of $643,000 for the same period in 1942.[32] The desperation Jane Randolph recalled at the studio was apparently for nothing. Lewton's horror releases to date have surely played a part in the financial boom.

Week Six: Monday, September 27, to Saturday, October 2, and the Last Day's Shooting, Monday, October 4, 1943

Monday and Tuesday: "Bobby" Wise (as the call sheet calls him) spends these days shooting the wonderfully snowy night scenes of the Exterior Bridge and Meadow and the Exterior Post Road, all on Stage 7. This includes the famous "bus" episode, where Amy fears she hears the Headless Horseman—which turns out to be a jalopy. The call sheet orders a Model-T Ford and two bloodhounds. Wise works rapidly and resourcefully, shooting 22 set-ups each day.

Wednesday: He shoots 18 set-ups on the Interior Reed home set.

Thursday: On the 30th day of shooting, the company works on Stages 7 and 12 and five different sets—the Ext. Reed Back porch, the Bridge and Meadow, Amy's Bedroom, the School, and the Farren hallway. They work with no dinner until 8 p.m.

Friday, Saturday, and Monday: The big push is on to complete this problem child production. As of Friday night, the film is now nine days behind schedule—Wise has finally lost a day—and all the scenes take place on the Int. Reed home set on Stage 4. Wise completes 15 set-ups Friday and 20 on Saturday, working until 9:45 that night.

Monday is a marathon. Company call is at 9. Ann Carter finishes at 4, Sir Lancelot at 5; there's an hour off for dinner, then Kent Smith, Jane Randolph and Eve March work until 11:25 that night. There have been 24 set-ups. After 33 days, the 24-day-scheduled production has wrapped up and the assistant director report sheet finally bears the words *Production Finished.*

The pronouncement, however, is premature.

Part V: The Retakes

> *Val asked me to have lunch with him, during which he told me*
> *his idea for the revised climax ... I didn't like it at all....*
> —DeWitt Bodeen

For Val Lewton, *The Curse of the Cat People* had been an emotional wringer. The trouble-plagued production's story haunts him ... and he can't leave it alone.

Wednesday, November 3: Shooting begins on Lewton's new film *Are These Our Children,* a juvenile delinquent saga fated to be released as *Youth Runs Wild.* Mark Robson directs and such Lewton "Snake Pit" players as Kent Smith, Jean Brooks, and Elizabeth Russell have roles.

Meanwhile, while busy on *Youth Runs Wild,* Lewton becomes hell-bent on shooting a revised ending to *The Curse of the Cat People.* The concept: As Barbara (no longer locked in her room by Irena) stalks Amy, the terrified child somehow sees Irena appear (via a special effects dissolve) in the place of Barbara. "My friend," she cries, and hugs her. Barbara, touched by the little girl's warmth, cannot bring herself to strangle her.

Bodeen is working on a treatment for RKO's *The Enchanted Cottage* when Lewton proposes his idea for a new climax. As Bodeen will remember, he's frankly unimpressed:

[I] told him that in my opinion, it smacked too much of Saki's "Sredni Vashtar" and several other short story horror classics. Val was indignant and said rather testily that at least, since I was already busy on a new assignment, I wouldn't be submitted to writing something I didn't approve of, that he himself would write the revised ending. This he did, and it was shot as an added scene, and all the original film was scrapped. I don't think Val ever forgave me, not for disapproving of his revised ending, but for recognizing its source. *The Curse of the Cat People* was the last screenplay I did for Val and, as with *Cat People,* I had also worked as dialogue director for the production—but I did not work in any capacity on the revised final scenes.

Thursday, November 18: Lewton signs a budget sheet to cover two days of retakes on *The Curse of the Cat People.* The full tab is $3,704. Ann Carter will collect $83.33 for two days, Eve March $58.33 for one day, and Elizabeth Russell $66.67 for one day.

Saturday, November 20: Forty-seven days after production originally wrapped, Carter and Russell report again to the Farren house set on Stage 12 with Harry Wild at the camera. (Wild will be cinematographer of Lewton's 1944 *Mademoiselle Fifi,* as well as RKO's 1944 *noir* classic *Murder, My Sweet.*) They shoot Lewton's new ending. Elizabeth's Barbara is truly spine-chilling as she nightmarishly ascends the staircase, Amy is pitifully frightened, and the pay-off—the teary-eyed Barbara, touched by the child's affection and unable to kill her—is strangely, powerfully affecting.

Wise works from 9:00 a.m. to 7:10 p.m. fully capturing the fairy tale horror—a wicked witch, scaring a pretty, terrified child—as well as creating an almost stained glass window religious iconography of an angel cherub, beholding the devil (in this case a female one). Roy Webb's beautifully moody music will powerfully accent the episode, and the scene is classic Lewton.

Why the revised climax? Having scrapped much of the Barbara and Julia backstory, Lewton perhaps decided that Barbara requires more sympathy—she still probably faces an asylum, but only after the audience has seen her touched by Amy and with tenderness in her eyes. As Amy reconciles with her parents, Elizabeth Russell's Barbara—who began as the witch of *The Curse of the Cat People*—becomes, via a dash of Val Lewton black magic reshooting and the man's empathy for his darkest character, *The Curse of the Cat People*'s most pitiful, haunting lost soul.

There is perhaps an additional reason for the gentler fate: After all, Barbara is Lewton's nightmare image of his own daughter Nina, grown and unloved—and as such, perhaps he can't stand what he's done to her in the original film.

Yet the new ending has sacrificed the film's true sense of the supernatural. Lost is the pay-off that a miracle has occurred (the trooper captain stating in the original that whoever locked the door "saved the life of that child"), and the inference that Ollie and Alice, based on Amy's rescue, must now be believers too. The retakes have confined Irena to Amy's imagination. And also lost are Irena's beautiful words about death—which might have been truly comforting to World War II audiences.

Which ending was better? Ann Carter said:

> The new ending was very different, and I think the original ending was more powerful. The new one was okay, but it just sort of tapered off. It's hard for me, at this time of my life, to imagine Alice and Ollie would have changed a lot, the way it now ended. I just think that the new ending was weaker and other one would have been better.

A haunting close-up of Elizabeth Russell, in the revised finale of *The Curse of the Cat People*.

Monday, November 22: Wise, now with cameraman Harold Stine, shoots new scenes on the Exterior River Bank set on Stage 12. Ann Carter, Eve March, and some child actors report, and there's a livestock call for ... one cat. Reason: RKO had noted the absence of cats in *The Curse of the Cat People*. Hence Wise shoots a scene of a cat in a tree, while a boy, in a nice wartime touch, pretends he's machine-gunning it. Wise also shoots new footage of Amy's butterfly. Carter, March, the children, the cat, and the butterfly are all finished by 5:30.

Tuesday, December 21: *Youth Runs Wild* wraps at RKO.

Monday, December 27: Twenty-six musicians gather on RKO's Stage 2A to record Roy Webb's score for *The Curse of the Cat People*.

Tuesday, January 4, 1944: Forty-three days after the cat-in-the-tree day of shooting, and over four months after *The Curse of the Cat People* began, Ann Carter and Simone Simon meet again for what the assistant director report lists as "Dubbing and Retakes—Black Velvet Shots." These likely relate to Irena's apparition in the climax. Robert Wise completes the work with Harold Stine at the camera.

Now, it's indeed finally over. Budgeted at $147,315, *The Curse of the Cat People*, according to the expense sheet of February 26, 1944, tallies a final cost of $209,348.03. More than $60,000 over budget, the film must prove a winner for Val Lewton.

Part VI: The Previews and Release

> *The Black Menace Creeps Again!*
> —RKO publicity for ***The Curse of the Cat People***

RKO, naturally, is appalled at what Lewton has wrought. As noted, wholesale cuts ensue. And there are various reasons to worry over the reception that awaits *The Curse of the Cat People*.

On Christmas Day 1943, *The Song of Bernadette* had premiered in Los Angeles to rapturous critical and popular response. On January 26, 1944, the film opens in New York City, again to great acclaim, and 20th Century–Fox prepares a road show release. If RKO perceives that Val Lewton had ripped off *The Song of Bernadette* in fashioning his over-budget, tawdry-titled horror movie, the fallout could be considerable.

Thursday, February 10: Fifteen days after *The Song of Bernadette*'s New York opening, RKO previews *The Curse of the Cat People* in New York. *Weekly Variety* reports:

> [H]ighly disappointing ... such an impossible lightweight that it will have trouble even on the lower half of twin bills.... Two directors worked on *Curse of the Cat People*, suggesting production headaches.... Many episodes are unbelievably bad.... Miss Simon, appearing as the spirit of the dead mother [*sic*], does almost a bit, a silly characterization.... Elizabeth Russell is standout.... Ann Carter does all right as the dream world kid, but probably wondered what all the fuss was about....

The trade papers are primarily negative, although Ann Carter wins praise—*Daily Variety* hailing her as "outstanding."

Thursday, March 2: The Academy Awards ceremony takes place at Grauman's Chinese Theatre in Hollywood. *The Song of Bernadette* loses to *Casablanca* as Best Picture, but Jennifer Jones wins the Best Actress prize for her Bernadette. It's also her 25th birthday. Shortly afterwards, she'll announce she's divorcing her husband, actor Robert Walker. In 1949, she will marry David O. Selznick.

Friday, March 3: With the newspapers filled with photos of a jubilant Jennifer Jones, *The Curse of the Cat People* opens at the Rialto, the horror salon of New York City theaters. The critical insults come—the *New York Journal-American* snipes that Simone Simon's ghost has "nicely tinted fingernails." Yet John T. McManus, whose reviews for *New York Newspaper PM* were often the most sophisticated in Manhattan, protests the film's "accursed title" and writes:

Have you ever expected thunder and lightning, then waked to find it the loveliest of days, with the last hint of the stars disappearing over the horizon? It's like that with *The Curse of the Cat People* ... the whole production is a novel and entrancing flight in film. Don't miss it.

Even the *New York Times,* which usually ate Lewton's films for breakfast, praises *The Curse of the Cat People* as "an oddly touching study of the working of a sensitive child's mind." The crowds come to the Rialto, as *Variety* reports *The Curse of the Cat People*'s take as a "very fine" $12,300 the first week and an "oke" $7,500 for the second week.[33] This was $300 more than the two-week take for both Universal's *The Wolf Man* and RKO's *I Walked with a Zombie,* and over $4,000 more than the Rialto took in during the two-week run of *The Seventh Victim.*

Thursday, April 27: The Curse of the Cat People opens at the Hawaii Theatre in Hollywood, where *Cat People* had shattered records. However, it serves only as the support feature for RKO's *Action in Arabia,* starring George Sanders. Philip K. Scheuer of the *Los Angeles Times* notes the hook to *The Song of Bernadette,* but doesn't belabor it:

> Simone Simon does turn up again in *The Curse of the Cat People*, but only as a kind and beneficent spirit with about as much malice in her make-up as Bernadette's vision. (That's the trouble with the studios—always developing a positive affection for their monsters and menaces and allowing them to go sissy on us.) ... [N]othing much that an expectant audience can get its teeth into—teeth that ought to be chattering, but probably won't be.

The double feature bill of *Action in Arabia* and *The Curse of the Cat People* draws $9,205 at the Hawaii,[34] only $395 less than the first week's take on *Cat People*. A valid comparison of the Hawaii business is difficult, since the sequel is on a double bill (and ticket prices have risen since 1943); at any rate, *Action in Arabia* and *The Curse of the Cat People* have a good Hawaii run of five weeks and six days (compared to *Cat People*'s 13 weeks).

The official RKO financial figures on *Cat People* and *The Curse of the Cat People* will speak volumes:

Cat People: Worldwide rentals, $535,000; profit, $183,000.
The Curse of the Cat People: Worldwide Rentals, $370,000; Profit, $35,000.

It is the least successful of Lewton's horror films to that time. (*The Seventh Victim* had made a profit of $59,000; all the other Lewton horrors up to that point had profits of over $100,000.) It's also the most sensitive "horror movie" ever produced, transcending its curse and surviving as Val Lewton's noble, flawed and poetic masterpiece.

Yet punishment for Lewton is sure and swift: He soon finds himself working with a new producer overseer: Jack Gross, formerly of Universal. "Jack was much like his name," laughed Robert Wise. It's Gross, demanding classic horror flourishes, who engineers Boris Karloff coming to RKO and the Lewton unit. Lewton, initially aghast, comes to love Karloff, while Karloff calls Lewton "the man who rescued me from the living dead and restored my soul." The happy result will be a trio of Lewton classics: *The Body Snatcher, Isle of the Dead* and *Bedlam,* with *The Body Snatcher* (directed by Wise) tallying the biggest worldwide rental of any Lewton film, $547,000.

* * *

The Curse of the Cat People *is, more than any other Lewton production, an oeuvre
in the true sense of the word. Everything that was Val was all through this picture.*
—DeWitt Bodeen

Thursday, September 7, 1944: The Hollywood Writers Mobilization Group and the Los Angeles Council of Social Agencies host a special seminar, "The Treatment of the Child in Films." There is a screening of *The Curse of the Cat People,* and Lewton and Wise join the discussion after the showing. Wise saves in his script a copy of a letter to RKO chief Charles Koerner from Hollywood Writers Mobilization, that reads in part:

> The Hollywood Writers Mobilization wishes to thank RKO Studios, and Messrs. Lewton and Wise for making this seminar possible. We know that many constructive things came out of it, not the least of which was the feeling on the part of those outside the industry, that by and large motion picture producers do realize their responsibility to the public and approach difficult problems with good measure of honesty and competence.

Lewton and Wise have been in good spirits at the seminar. Wise faces a celebrated director career, with Best Director Oscars for *West Side Story* and *The Sound of Music* awaiting him. Val Lewton faces professional heartbreak and has less than seven years to live. Remembered by DeWitt Bodeen as the most "desperately unhappy" individual he had ever known, losing "all faith in himself,"[35] Lewton dies Wednesday, March 14, 1951, following a heart attack. He is only 46 years old.

Part VII: The Legacy

> Sometimes he felt that his wings had been so clipped that he would never fly again. But nothing could ever quiet that restless spirit of creation. To the end, Val was soaring aloft on the wings of his creative imagination—wings that have carried him now beyond our ken to a rarer atmosphere, where they can no more suffer the crippling and bruising of our clumsy, insensitive world.
> —From Alan Napier's eulogy for Val Lewton, St. Matthew's Church, Pacific Palisades, California, March 1951[36]

In 1952, the year following Val Lewton's death, RKO re-releases *Cat People* and earns an additional $65,000 in profit. There is a 1957 re-release as well (financial figures not available) before the film begins its new life on TV.

In the mid–1960s, DeWitt Bodeen submits a *Cat People* TV series. He pitches the show to Greenway Productions, which produces such shows as *Batman* and *The Green Hornet,* and cites the enduring Late Show popularity of the 1942 film:

> As the story basis for a television series, it holds every promise of being a unique and profitable venture. Through its fame as a motion picture, it would find among the dyed-in-the-wool horror fans a pre-sold audience; its attraction to a younger audience would be immediate.
> Psychologically, its appeal is universal.[37]

Bodeen tries to sell the series as "a serious treatment" of TV's *Bewitched* and plans to bring back the original film's major characters: Irena, Oliver, Oliver's "assistant" (Alice), Dr. Judd, and "the mysterious Cat Woman." As Bodeen writes:

> This projected series of *Cat People* could grow into one of television's biggest series shows. Cat-lovers are worldwide, and the cat as a photographic subject is sure-fire. The domestic cat understands better than a human the menace behind one of the Cat People. Cat-lover, seeing a cat withdraw and arch its back, when in the proximity of one of the Cat People, would smile and say, "You see, it knows. It's smarter than we are."

But is the heroine, Irena, one of the Cat People? Or isn't she? See our next show. You may find out.

At any rate, Greenway Productions passes on the proposal. After all, they already have their "Catwoman"—Julie Newmar on *Batman*.

Many are familiar with Paul (*Taxi Driver*) Schrader's 1982 remake of *Cat People,* a hybrid from Universal and RKO (actually out of business since 1957). It offers Natassja Kinski as Irena Gallier, residing in New Orleans with Malcolm McDowell's Paul Gallier, her incestuous cat man brother. The erotic effort (Ms. Kinski displays a few flourishes of frontal nudity) revives *Cat People*'s three big sequences. The "My sister" scene with the Cat Woman (Neva Gage) falls completely flat. The stalk through a park becomes a forgettable jog for Alice (Annette O'Toole), although it indeed climaxes with a "bus" homage. A bit more effective is the pool scene, with a topless Ms. O'Toole bobbing and screaming in her black panties, the episode daubed with shadows and sound effects very similar to the original's. The finale (Spoiler Alert!): Irena's obsessed zoo curator boyfriend Oliver (John Heard), aware she's a cat woman, ties the willing Irena to a bed, has intercourse with her, then keeps the emerged panther in his zoo, where he visits her and feeds her tasty tidbits.

Coming on the heels (paws) of such state-of-the-art man-into-beast films such as *An American Werewolf in London, Cat People* cost $18,000,000. Its U.S. gross: only $7,000,000.

*   *   *

Most of the talent from *Cat People* and *The Curse of the Cat People* enjoyed long lives and careers. Jacques Tourneur's distinctive career included the British-made (and "Lewton-esque") *Night of the Demon* (1957); he died in 1977. Gunther von Fritsch weathered *The Curse of the Cat People*'s storm; he directed montage scenes for the boxing classic *Body and Soul* (1947), as well as the Vienna sequence of *This Is Cinerama* (1952) and many TV episodes, including *Cheyenne*

Poster of *The Curse of the Cat People.*

and *77 Sunset Strip.* Von Fritsch died in 1988. So did DeWitt Bodeen, whose later screenplay credits included *I Remember Mama* (1948) and *Billy Budd* (1962). Elizabeth Russell died in 2002, Simone Simon and Robert Wise in 2005, and Jane Randolph, the last survivor to have played in both movies, died in 2009, a still-attractive 93-year-old. All three female principals of the original *Cat People* had outlived Val Lewton by over 50 years, and remembered him with great affection. Ann Carter died in 2014 at age 77.

Of course, *Cat People* reigns today as one of the great horror classics, while *The Curse of the Cat People* survives fully vindicated, a Lewton masterwork of haunting delicacy, sensitivity and darkness. For this author, there are two poignant experiences associated with both films.

One is a telephone chat one night in 1993 with Ruth Lewton, Val's widow, then living in a retirement community in San Jose, California. Her husband had been dead for over 40 years and Ruth had never remarried. That night she spoke of what she called the stress, the darkness that had hastened her husband's early death. Ruth had paid tribute to her husband in an intensely moving way: She worked for many years with disturbed children, trying to save them from this darkness that nearly overcame the fictional Amy and eventually overwhelmed Ruth's real-life husband. "I thought that stress was a wicked thing," said Ruth Lewton.

Finally, there's Elizabeth Russell. In 1990, Elizabeth, white-haired but still felinely distinctive, was a guest at the FANEX convention in Baltimore. There was a Sunday showing of *The Curse of the Cat People,* and I was to interview her afterwards. I watched the long-retired actress as she watched the old film's climax, those unforgettable shots of Elizabeth's Barbara Farren, rising on the old house's gothic staircase like a vampy witch from Hell. She sat transfixed, motionless, the image of her from 46 years before seemingly hypnotizing her. Amy called Barbara "my friend," the Reeds rescued Amy, the music swelled, the film ended...

... and Elizabeth Russell ran.

Eighty-four years old at the time, she literally *ran* from the screening room, across the upper level of the lobby area of the Sheraton Hotel, chased by me all the while. She reached the lower level and kept running, out of the building, only stopping when safely in the sunlight, far from the apparition that had spooked her upstairs in the dark room and on the movie screen. She laughed a bit but offered no excuse for her escape, still rattled, eventually calming down and returning for the interview. Surely part of her unnerving came from seeing herself in her youth, and she expressed surprise that the ending she remembered—crying, screaming and locked in her room—had given way to a finale she no longer remembered ever shooting.

Nevertheless, I believe the cause of Elizabeth's response was due at least partially to *how* she was seeing herself—transfigured by Lewton, beautifully and chillingly representing the darkness that tortured him ... becoming, in the climax of *The Curse of the Cat People,* the "wicked thing" incarnate.

To have been a part of the Val Lewton magic must have been a rare privilege. To have beheld oneself as part of the magic again—after so many years, and in so bewitchingly haunting a form—must have been overpowering.

Cat People

Studio, RKO-Radio. Producer, Val Lewton. Executive Producer, Lew Ostrow. Director, Jacques Tourneur. Screenplay, DeWitt Bodeen. Cinematographer, Nicholas Musuraca. Editor, Mark Robson. Music, Roy Webb. Musical Director, C. Bakaleinikoff. Art Directors, Albert S. D'Agostino, Walter E. Keller. Set Decorators, Darrell Silvera, Al Fields. Gowns, Renie. Sound Recordist, John L. Cass. Assistant Director, Doran Cox. Photographic Effects, Vernon L. Walker, Linwood G. Dunn. Orchestrations, Leonid Raab, John Liepold. Russian Lyrics, Andrei Tolstoi. Dialogue Director, DeWitt Bodeen. Animal Trainer, Mel Koontz. Second Unit Director, Edward Donahue. Second Unit Cameraman, Frank Redman. Running Time, 73 minutes.

Filmed at RKO Studios, Hollywood, and the Royal Palms Hotel, Los Angeles, 28 July–21 August 1942. New York City premiere, Rialto Theatre, 5 December 1942. Los Angeles premiere, Hawaii Theatre, 14 January 1943.

Simone Simon (Irena Dubrovna); Kent Smith (Oliver Reed); Tom Conway (Dr. Judd); Jane Randolph (Alice Moore); Jack Holt (The Commodore); Alan Napier ("Doc" Carver); Elizabeth Russell (The Cat Woman); Mary Halsey (Blondie); Alec Craig (The Zookeeper); Elizabeth Dunne (Miss Plunkett); Dot Farley (Mrs. Agnew); Theresa Harris (Minnie); Charles Jordan (Bus Driver); Murdock MacQuarrie (Shepherd); Steve Soldi (Organ Grinder); Donald Kerr (Taxi Driver); Terry Walker (Hotel Attendant); George Ford (Whistling Cop); Betty Roadman (Mrs. Hansen); Connie Leon (Neighbor who calls police); Henrietta Burnside (Sue Ellen); Lida Nicova (Patient); John Piffle (Café Proprietor); Bud Geary (Mounted Policeman); Eddie Dew (Street Policeman); Paul Stader, Louis Roth (Stuntmen); Dorothy Lloyd (Cat Sounds).

The Curse of the Cat People

Studio, RKO-Radio. Producer, Val Lewton. Directors, Gunther von Fritsch, Robert Wise. Screenplay, DeWitt Bodeen (and Val Lewton, uncredited). Cinematographer, Nicholas Musuraca (and Frank Redman, Harry Wild, Harold Stine, uncredited). Editor, J.R. Whittredge. Music, Roy Webb. Musical Director, C. Bakaleinikoff. Art Directors, Albert S. D'Agostino, Walter E. Keller. Set Decorators, Darrell Silvera, William Stevens. Costumes, Edward Stevenson. Makeup, Mel Berns. Assistant Director, Harry D'Arcy. Sound Recordist, Francis M. Sarver. Sound Re-recordist, James G. Stewart. Songs: "Ruben Ranzo," "It Came Upon a Midnight Clear," and "Shepherds Shakes Off Your Drowsy Sleep." Running Time, 70 minutes.

Filmed at RKO Studios, Hollywood, the RKO Ranch, Encino, 900 W. Adams Street, Los Angeles, and Malibou Lake, Agoura, CA, 26 August–4 October 1943. Retakes, RKO Studios, 20 and 22 November 1943; 4 January 1944. New York City opening, Rialto Theatre, 3 March 1944. Los Angeles opening, Hawaii Theatre, 27 April 1944.

Simone Simon (Irena); Kent Smith (Oliver Reed); Jane Randolph (Alice Reed); Ann Carter (Amy Reed); Julia Dean (Julia Farren); Elizabeth Russell (Barbara Farren); Eve March (Miss Callahan); Sir Lancelot (Edward); Joel Davis (Donald); Juanita Alvarez (Lois); Charley Bates (Jack); Sarah Selby (Miss Plumett, Caroler); Erford Gage (Captain of the Guards); Mel Sternlight (State Trooper); Nita Hunter (Lois Huggins); Edmund Glover (Card-playing Guest); Gloria Donovan, Ginny Wren and Linda Ann Bieber (Little Girls).

9

Frankenstein Meets the Wolf Man Revisited

"The Greatest Selling Title in a Century of Shock Showmanship!"
—Advance publicity, Universal's Exhibitors Manual,
for **Frankenstein Meets the Wolf Man** (1943)

Thursday night, March 26, 1942: A ceremony takes place at the Hollywood Pantages Theatre, where the attraction is Universal's *The Ghost of Frankenstein*.[1]

Four of the film's stars are onstage, "in person." The audience applauds as Lionel Atwill, Evelyn Ankers and Bela Lugosi present Lon Chaney, Jr., son of the long-dead "Man of a Thousand Faces," a plaque, awarding him his own *soubriquet*.

It reads, "The Screen's New Master Character Creator."

Chaney had portrayed the title character in *The Wolf Man*, following as the Monster in *The Ghost of Frankenstein*, and now Universal affords him this fulsome honor. The actors also perform this "stunt," as *Variety* labels it, this night at the RKO-Hillstreet Theatre, where *The Ghost of Frankenstein* plays as well.

Atwill, a celebrated stage star of the Roaring '20s, had enjoyed his ballyhoo as the silent-era Chaney "Successor"[2] when he'd starred in Warner Bros.' *Mystery of the Wax Museum* (1933); vain and assured, he likely sees Chaney Jr. as merely a burly bully boy, hardly in his polished league. Ms. Ankers, leading lady in *The Wolf Man* and *The Ghost of Frankenstein*, thinks "The Screen's New Master Character Creator" is a drunken lout[3]; he's victimized her with crude practical jokes and calls her "Evelyn Shankers"—a shanker being a syphilis sore.

Perhaps the most conflicted, or *should* be, is Bela Lugosi. The actor has spent a decade eclipsed by Boris Karloff—or KARLOFF, as Universal top-billed him—who's currently starring in Broadway's super-hit *Arsenic and Old Lace*, leaving the Hollywood horror arena wide open for Lugosi. Now, the 36-year-old Chaney has come a-lumbering along, complaining about his makeups, drinking on the set, smashing his dressing room to pieces, yet enjoying a PR bonanza far surpassing anything Lugosi had received in the wake of *Dracula*. And so, sentenced by Universal to featured status in both *The Wolf Man* and *The Ghost of Frankenstein*, Lugosi must endure this night's consecration of a new, supreme Universal Horror Star.

It's all setting the stage for a Frankenstein movie to come ... perhaps the most infamously troubled production in Universal's horror history.

* * *

The off-screen sagas of *Frankenstein Meets the Wolf Man*, and its wild-and-wicked shoot at Universal City during the Halloween season of 1942, are real-life Hollywood melodrama:

263

- Boisterous Lon Chaney, Jr., in his most angst-ridden Wolf Man portrayal, reprieved at the eleventh hour from Universal's original razzle-dazzle brainstorm of starring him as both werewolf *and* Monster.
- Humbled Bela Lugosi, notoriously playing the Monster role he'd proudly scorned in 1931 ("I will not play a scarecrow!"[4]), collapsing on the set, mercifully unaware of the mutilation awaiting his portrayal in the editing room.
- Scandalized Lionel Atwill as the mayor, gallantly acting with bravado after receiving five years' probation for perjury regarding his Yuletide "orgies," painfully aware this might be his final film.
- Sexy Ilona Massey, in her blonde Bavarian braids and revealing negligee, enjoying Universal top-billing despite MGM having blackballed her after an in-house scandal.
- Wizened Maria Ouspenskaya, suffering an on-set accident that tosses her out of a carriage and out of the film.
- Pallid Dwight Frye, looking ill as a benign villager—or does he seem so because we realize he had only a year left to live?
- Pop-eyed Adia Kuznetzoff, Russian basso, merrily belting out the "Faro-La, Faro-Li" song.
- Meticulous Roy William Neill, masterfully directing, trying for genuine terror and tragedy before the 24-day schedule forces the film into near-kitsch.
- Salty Curt Siodmak, the film's scenarist, fated to make controversial remarks about both Chaney and Lugosi.
- The mysterious specters of uncredited stuntmen, leaving historians debating who doubled the Wolf Man and Monster in what Universal heralded as "the beast battle of the century!"

Need proof of the film's power to compel? Blast off into cyberspace and take a (very) long look at the Classic Horror Film Board, managed by David Colton and Kerry Gammill, and its "*Frankenstein Meets the Wolf Man*: Dissection Version" thread. As of June 25, 2013, there were 8,329 "replies" and 205,387 "views."

Fascination, passion, obsession ... it's a mania worthy of Colin Clive's Frankenstein himself. All the while, the film's production papers remain almost mystically elusive, leaving historians to often eccentric, far-flung research. Revisionist theories abound. Writer-researcher Scott Gallinghouse is currently at work on a full-length book on the film.

Meanwhile, this chapter commemorates the 70th anniversary of the release of *Frankenstein Meets the Wolf Man,* providing a variety of new discoveries, expanded theories ... and a tribute to the most retrospectively popular Universal horror classic of them all.

Part I. The Blueprint

> "I, Ygor, will live forever!"
> —The Monster, speaking in Ygor's voice
> in *The Ghost of Frankenstein* (1942)

Thursday, January 15, 1942: Universal completes *The Ghost of Frankenstein.* The climax: Mad Dr. Bohmer (Lionel Atwill) places the evil brain of old Ygor (Bela Lugosi) into the skull of Frankenstein's Monster (Lon Chaney). Bohmer has bungled, the Monster goes blind, the sanitarium burns down ... **The End.**

Thursday, February 26: Curt Siodmak, who scripted *The Wolf Man* (1941), is already at work on a treatment for *Wolf-Man Meets Frankenstein*, a sequel to both *The Wolf Man* and the not-yet-released *The Ghost of Frankenstein*. A page from Siodmak's treatment, dated this day (and discovered by writer-researcher Bob Furmanek[5]), refers to the Monster as both "Monster" and ... "Igor" [*sic*]. Siodmak, after reading the *Ghost of Frankenstein* script and/or seeing a pre-release screening, clearly has some confusion about whether the revived creature is now Ygor, as it's his brain, or the Monster, as it's his body.

Over 70 years later, horror fans will refer to this Ygor-Monster hybrid as "Ygorstein."

Sunday, March 29: The United Hungarian-American Defense Federation holds its first Red Cross benefit at Los Angeles' Polytechnic High School. Among the Hungarian émigré sponsors and performers: future *Frankenstein Meets the Wolf Man* stars Ilona Massey and Bela Lugosi.

Tuesday, March 31: Siodmak completes his script for *Wolf-Man Meets Frankenstein*. There's no longer any mention of Ygor, although the Monster, still blind and speaking, boasts of being the recent recipient of "a clever brain." Meanwhile, Siodmak, in the wake of *The Wolf Man*, asks for a Universal raise. It's denied. He does enjoy a Universal "perk": a secretary who, as Siodmak remembered with relish, cools down on hot nights by typing in only her bra.[6]

Wednesday, May 6: "Double Horror," headlines *Variety*:

Universal is playing a double-header in spinal chills. Studio is tossing its *Wolf Man* and *The Ghost of Frankenstein* into one horrendous grapple. Lon Chaney, Jr., ... is slated to clinch with himself in a duplex monstrosity titled *Wolf Man Meets Frankenstein*. General idea is that two monsters are better than one when they work on the same salary, even though there are no priorities on monsters....

Wednesday, June 3: As Universal begins shooting *The Mummy's Tomb*, Chaney takes on yet another monster, the funky Kharis. He bitches about the makeup and, so legend persists, gets through the shoot with a flask tucked in his costume.

Friday, June 19: Director Roy William Neill, who will direct *Frankenstein Meets the Wolf Man*, completes Universal's *Sherlock Holmes and the Secret Weapon*, starring Basil Rathbone, Nigel Bruce, and Lionel Atwill (as Moriarity). Neill wraps up the 68-minute movie in 16 days—five days ahead of schedule. Also on Neill's résumé: *The Black Room* (Columbia, 1935), in which he superbly directed Karloff's good and evil medieval twins. His speed, stylistics, and experience directing a star in a dual role is definitely a plus for the upcoming Frankenstein film.

Wednesday, July 1: "LIONEL ATWILL INDICTED ON PERJURY" headlines the *Los Angeles Examiner*. The perjury is in regard to the orgies Atwill (whose nickname is "Pinky") allegedly hosted at his Pacific Palisades house during Yuletide 1940, during which he reportedly showed the pornographic films *The Plumber and the Girl* and *The Daisy Chain*. Atwill claims he's the victim of a "sinister extortion syndicate," vowing to defame him if he fails to pay money. Universal, which employs Atwill regularly, watches the headlines.

Monday, July 6: Katherine Marlowe, an actress allegedly present at an Atwill "orgy," throws gasoline on the fire, claiming she's received threatening phone calls, one from an individual whose voice she recognized (but does not identify). Miss Marlowe tells the *Examiner*:

I received a telephone call at 8:44 p.m. on July 3 telling me that I "know too much" and that I would be healthier if I left town. I got one call at 3 o'clock in the morning previous to that. I have lost sleep, weight and my boyfriend over it and my mother is near a nervous breakdown.

Roy William Neill directs Boris Karloff and Marian Marsh in *The Black Room* **(1935) at Columbia Studios. His flair for atmospherics made him a fine choice to direct** *Frankenstein Meets the Wolf Man.*

I was not at the party in the Atwill house at which sex pictures were allegedly shown and I know nothing about it. I do know Atwill, however, and have been in his home on several occasions.

I am NOT leaving town. I AM getting my telephone number unlisted and I intend to respond if called as a witness and tell the truth. These threats won't stop me. I am from Texas and Texans don't scare easily.

Also on July 6: Despite the lurid newspaper reports, Universal casts Lionel Atwill in *Night Monster,* which starts shooting this date. Atwill and Bela Lugosi receive top billing, but appear as red herrings. Atwill will later admit that, but for Universal's "courage and magnanimity," he'd have been "a dead egg."

Wednesday, August 5: Monogram starts *Bowery at Midnight,* starring Bela Lugosi. It's Lugosi's third 1942 film for the bottom-of-the-barrel studio.

Wednesday, August 19: Ilona Massey, whose reputation in Hollywood is notorious, separates from her spouse of 17 months, actor Alan Curtis. She'd previously been mistress to Sam Katz, a producer at MGM, the studio that had hailed her as "a singing Garbo." Scandal erupted, and MGM had fired her and blackballed her as she began an affair with Curtis and married him. She'll claim that Curtis liked to drink and argue, and her sec-

Convicted: Lionel Atwill looks haggard in this courthouse photograph. On October 15, 1942, the fourth day's shooting on *Frankenstein Meets the Wolf Man,* the court found Atwill guilty of perjury and sentenced him to five years' probation.

retary will testify that Ilona emerges from these clashes "looking very haggard and ten years older."[7]

Thursday, August 20: *Variety* reports:

Bela Lugosi trains for Chicago Sunday, opening Sept. 4 in *Dracula* at the Cohan Grand Opera House. While doing the four-week Chicago run in the stage piece, Lugosi will also make personals in film houses there playing Monogram features in which he appears.... After the Chicago engagement, play goes on the road with a New York opening scheduled for early winter.

For unknown reasons, the tour and New York opening fall through. Lugosi will remain in Hollywood. He has no immediate film offers.

Friday, September 4: The *Los Angeles Times* writes that RKO is seeking Lon Chaney to star in *The Leopard Man,* to be produced by Val Lewton. Lewton's first film, *Cat People,* is not yet released, and Lewton himself is reportedly negotiating with Universal for Chaney's loan-out. Since he protests the use of "overt" horror stars, Lewton is probably relieved when Universal refuses to loan its "Master Character Creator." When *The Leopard Man* starts shooting in February of 1943, James Bell will play the heavy role presumably envisioned for Chaney.

Also on September 4: Maria Ouspenskaya, who played Maleva the Gypsy in *The Wolf*

Blackballed: Ilona Massey in November 1941. MGM had blacklisted the actress-singer after a sex scandal in 1940. Universal was basically defying MGM by starring her in *Frankenstein Meets the Wolf Man.*

*M*an and will reprise the mystical role in *Frankenstein Meets the Wolf Man,* needs the work. On this date, the Income Tax Bureau files a lien against her for $2,763.[8]

 Wednesday, October 7: Another Bob Furmanek discovery: Curt Siodmak provides Universal a *revised* script for *Wolf-Man Meets Frankenstein,* only five days before shooting is to begin. Siodmak, perhaps aware that trouble lies ahead for a talking Monster, has trimmed some of the creature's purple prose dialogue. Note this speech by the Monster, brackets marking the excised lines:

Die? Never! Dr. Frankenstein created this body to be immortal! His son gave me a new brain, a clever brain. [I shall use it for the benefit of the miserable people who inherit the world, cheating each other, killing each other, without a thought but their own petty gains.] I will rule the world! [I will live to witness the fruits of my wisdom for all eternity!]

George Waggner, who produced and directed *The Wolf Man*, produced *The Ghost of Frankenstein*, and is producing *Frankenstein Meets the Wolf Man*, sends the script to Joseph Breen for a censorship office green light. He doesn't get one.

Friday, October 9: Breen responds:

While the basic story can be approved under the provisions of the Production Code, there is an unacceptable attitude toward "mercy killings" ... which, even in a fantastic story such as this, could not be approved by us.

The censor cites the script's "gruesomeness," "drunkenness," and "suggestion of cruelty to animals." This objection also bears mention:

[C]are should be exercised as to the manner in which Rudi and his wife withdraw from the dancers. There must of course be no suggestion that they are leaving the group for sexual purposes.[9]

What most seriously concerns Breen, however, is the "mercy killings" aspect. In this exchange between Elsa and Maleva, brackets mark what will be missing in the release version:

Elsa: But [what about Talbot?] He's insane!
Maleva: Insane? He's not insane... He simply wants to die... [that is all he asks of the Doctor—
Elsa: Are you asking Dr. Mannering to kill a man?
Maleva: It would not be murder.... It would be an act of grace to deliver this unfortunate soul from his suffering.... My powers have failed ... but my prayers will be answered!]

Breen demands that Mannering, after Elsa begs him to destroy her father and grandfather's "monstrous creation," alter his response (note the brackets):

Mannering [hoarsely]: All right. Tonight—I'll drain out the Monster's artificial energies. And I hope I'll bring peace to both of them: [the insane murderer, who wants to die—and the inhuman thing, that wants to live forever...].

In fact, Breen even righteously suggests that Dr. Mannering *not* plan to kill the Wolf Man or Monster: "[H]e should make it quite clear that he hopes to cure these men rather than kill them."

Waggner trusts (rightly, as it turns out) that Breen will cut the film some slack when it's completed. There's no time for an extensive rewrite. The film starts shooting Monday.

While there's no precise information on the budget, the final cost of *The Ghost of Frankenstein* was $211,000.[10] The budget for *Son of Dracula*, which will begin shooting January 7, 1943, will be $207,750.[11] As *Frankenstein Meets the Wolf Man* had production values and shooting schedules (24 days) comparable to both these films, its budget is likely about $200,000. (Average cost of a feature film in 1942: $336,600.) Universal is both reaping publicity and saving money by starring Lon Chaney as both Wolf Man and Monster.

That plan is about to change.

George Waggner, producer of *Frankenstein Meets the Wolf Man,* as he appeared circa 1943 with Jane Farrar, who played in *Phantom of the Opera* and *The Climax.* Waggner produced both those films and also directed *The Climax* (courtesy John Antosiewicz).

Part II. The Thorny Shoot Begins

"I thought the dead were stiff!"
—Tom Stevenson as one of the grave robbers
in ***Frankenstein Meets the Wolf Man***

Monday, October 12: Shooting starts on *Frankenstein Meets the Wolf Man*. The still numbers indicate the first episode shot: the grave robbers (Cyril Delevanti and Tom Stevenson) robbing the Talbot mausoleum in Llanwelly Cemetery, and opening Lawrence Talbot's coffin ... on the night of a full moon.

Frankenstein Meets the Wolf Man's opening is arguably the most frightening scene in all Universal horror films: the desolate cemetery, the blowing leaves and cawing birds, the fouling of the Talbot tomb, and the moon-shrouded corpse of Chaney's Lawrence Talbot, covered in wolfbane in his coffin ... and with very long fingernails. Hans J. Salter's musical score will add to the chills. Meanwhile, *Variety* announces this morning:

> Patric Knowles draws the romantic lead opposite Ilona Massey in Universal's *Frankenstein Meets the Wolf Man*, in which Lon Chaney toplines in the dual roles. Picture rolls today.

Despite the Chaney publicity, there have been negotiations, and...

Tuesday, October 13: "LUGOSI PLAYS MONSTER IN U CHILLER FILM" headlines *Variety* on page six. The report is brief:

> Bela Lugosi goes to Universal to handle monster role in *Frankenstein Meets the Wolf Man*, which started yesterday with Roy William Neill directing. Studio originally had idea of having Lon Chaney portray both Frankenstein and the Wolf Man, which he has portrayed in recent chillers, but finally tabbed Lugosi for the former character.

The same day, *The Hollywood Reporter* headlines "One Monster Is Enough, So Lugosi Does Other," citing the "terrific physical strain" of Chaney playing both creatures as the reason for the eleventh hour casting. Unpublicized are Chaney's heavy drinking, rambunctious personality, and time bomb temper in Jack P. Pierce's makeup. These indelicacies probably also forced this decision, as did the challenges of the trick photography.

At any rate, George E. Phair finds it all rather funny in his *Variety* "Retakes" column of October 15:

> *Frankenstein Meets the Wolf Man*, originally designed as a double header for young Lon Chaney, is so horrendous that Lon is afeard to meet himself in a dark alley. So Bela Lugosi is called in from the bullpen to pitch the last half, with Lon batting, and vice versa. You can't run a horror picture nowadays without a supercharger.

There's irony aplenty, of course, in Lugosi now playing the Monster. Universal folklore is already rich in the saga of Bela turning his nose up at the role in 1931, unleashing Karloff upon the world and himself. Why play it now, four sequels later?

Here are ten good reasons:

1. Lugosi is available, his *Dracula* stage revival plans having collapsed.
2. He's living in his "Dracula House," with its tower, arched window, and pond, at 10841 Whipple Street, North Hollywood, very close to Universal City; it's an easy commute.
3. He'd score points with Universal by honoring this emergency call, which might lead to better studio treatment.

   4. He could potentially show up Karloff.
   5. He'd add the Frankenstein Monster to his résumé. Karloff had never played Dracula.
   6. Any film with Universal carries more prestige than one from Monogram.
   7. Roy William Neill is a very fine director, and Bela will likely do well by him.
   8. The Monster is blind, and thus the role is more of a challenge.
   9. The Monster now has dialogue; Bela had originally objected to the role in 1931 largely because the creature didn't speak.
   10. He'd loved playing Ygor, and now he'd be playing "Ygorstein," with Ygor's brain in the Monster's body.

It's nice to imagine Bela approaching the job with positive vibes, but he might not have even been aware of points eight, nine, and ten when Universal's emergency call came. In fact, his wife Lillian (who died in 1981) was outspoken to me (in 1974) as to the only reason why Bela agreed to play Frankenstein's Monster: "Money."[12]

Universal won't need Lugosi until the following week. Neill finishes up on the cemetery opening and moves on this week to the Llanwelly Police Station and Queens Hospital. Patric Knowles meanwhile has made his entrance as Dr. Frank Mannering. Audiences well remember this tall, handsome, credible actor in such blockbusters as Warner Bros.' *The Adventures of Robin Hood* (1938) ... and horror fans recall him as the gamekeeper in *The Wolf Man*.

Neill continues daubing the film with rich atmosphere—watch those shadows that follow Knowles, Dennis Hoey (as Inspector Owen), and Doris Lloyd (as a nurse) at Queens Hospital. He also shoots a sequence cut before the film's release, wherein Inspector Owen and an assistant examine the clothes in which Larry Talbot had been buried ("Material expensive, cut by a first-class tailor"):

> *Owen*: Rotten—as if they'd been buried for years! Have a look at these moldy spots [*pointing*] and the shoes—the leather is slimy...
> (*He picks up the shirt, which falls apart at his touch, as if it were woven of spiders thread....*)[13]

Thursday, October 15: On *Frankenstein Meets the Wolf Man*'s fourth day of shooting, Lionel Atwill goes to court. The verdict: guilty of perjury. Despite his claiming that he'd behaved "like a gentleman," he receives a sentence of five years' probation. He's officially a felon and it seems likely that Universal will fire him. The studio doesn't.

Atwill will be a very merry mayor, a tribute to his superb professionalism after what must have been a personal trauma in the courtroom. It grimly appears that *Frankenstein Meets the Wolf Man* will be Lionel Atwill's cinema swan song.

Surely buoying Atwill's spirits is Ilona Massey, who as *The Hollywood Reporter* will curiously write in its *Frankenstein Meets the Wolf Man* review, "would look naked even in a fur coat."[14] She's wearing a black bonnet, a beige, hip-hugging Vera West suit and black heels, and comes complete with her natural beauty mark. Ilona probably attracts wolf-whistles as she sashays to the stage for her first scene with Chaney and Atwill. Chaney is certainly all-eyes when they meet on-screen in the mayor's office. Ilona responds by giving Lon one of the sexiest up-and-down glances in 1940s cinema, and Atwill gets in on the act, providing his own racy spin on things:

> *Talbot*: Do you mind if I speak to the baroness alone, please?
> *Mayor* (*wide-eyed, suggestively*): Why, certainly, certainly!

Indeed, Atwill responds to this seemingly innocent exchange as if Lon asked if he could invite Ilona to Lionel's house for a showing of *The Daisy Chain*. Lionel "Pinky" Atwill ... still irrepressibly off-color, even as a convicted felon!

Sunday afternoon, October 18: The Los Angeles Coliseum hosts the Comedians vs. Leading Men Football Game.[15] Edgar Kennedy coaches the Comedians, including Jimmy Durante, Buster Keaton, Jack Oakie, Wallace Ford and Billy Gilbert; Randolph Scott coaches the Leading Men, boasting Broderick Crawford, Anthony Quinn, Cesar Romero, Allan Jones, and ... Lon Chaney. Betty Grable and Rita Hayworth are the two team captains, Milton Berle is one of the announcers, and the game benefits the USO and Mount Sinai Hospital.

"Leading Men 'Win' Gag Grid Battle," reports the *Hollywood Citizen News* the next day, the score Leading Men, 94, Comedians, 79. The article notes:

> Unfortunately, the game got off to a bad start when one of the players was injured by the oversized toss-up disc which fell on his toe. When a bevy of beautiful nurses was rushed by Jeep to the scene, all of the players took sick in need of the comforting of the gorgeous nurses.
>
> In the first play of the game, the score was brought to a 66–66 tie. The way it was done was simple—everyone had a ball. Things were going along fine until the screen lovers refused to come out of a huddle. The reason was discovered when a curvaceous starlet came skipping out of their midst.

As the *Hollywood Citizen News* concluded:

> Most stupendous play of the day was the 100-yard "creep" made by Lon Chaney, Jr. (alias Frankenstein), when he paralyzed everybody on the gridiron, including the refs, and then chased the whole screwy game to the showers.

Lon was in full Monster makeup, as Karloff had been when he played in a Celebrity Baseball Game in L.A. in August 1940. *Silver Screen* magazine (July 1943), describing the game, wrote that Lon "stopped the show."[16]

So, during this week, Lon Chaney really *did* play both the Wolf Man and the Monster!

Part III. The Monster Enters

It's the Monster ... the Monster!
—Dwight Frye as Rudi
in ***Frankenstein Meets the Wolf Man***

Monday, October 19: Business is booming at Universal. Also shooting at Universal this week: *Pittsburgh*, starring Marlene Dietrich, John Wayne and Randolph Scott; *It Ain't Hay*, starring Abbott and Costello; Alfred Hitchcock's *Shadow of a Doubt*, starring Teresa Wright and Joseph Cotten; and Deanna Durbin's *The Amazing Mrs. Halliday*.

Tuesday, October 20: Bela Lugosi has his 60th birthday.

Also on October 20: Universal will hire 474 extras, which, according to *The Hollywood Reporter*, is "the heaviest atmosphere call for the studio in weeks." Fifty-six of these extras will report to Soundstage 28, "The Phantom Stage," to caper in *Frankenstein Meets the Wolf Man*'s "Festival of the New Wine."

Originally built for the 1925 *The Phantom of the Opera*, the Phantom Stage had been the site of a December 1940 ceremony, dedicating the stage in Chaney Sr.'s honor; Chaney

A Wolf Man's best friend: Lon Chaney with his faithful dog Moose.

Jr. had been present in *Man Made Monster* makeup. Now looming in the soundstage is a huge replica of the village of Vasaria. The old exterior European Village, which appeared in the first four Frankenstein films, still stands on the back lot, but wartime restrictions regarding lit-up areas at night causes the studio to use an interior set as an exterior one. It also spares the company from being at the mercy of the weather and filming night-for-night shots into the wee hours.[17] Adia Kuznetzoff's Festival Singer merrily belts out the "Faro-La, Faro-Li" song (music by Hans J. Salter, lyrics by Curt Siodmak).[18]

Wednesday, October 21: The Hollywood Reporter writes, somewhat inaccurately:

Kuznetzoff Traps "Wolf"

Adia Kuznetzoff, internationally known Gypsy singer, gets a featured role in Universal's *Franken-stein Meets the Wolf Man*. Kuznetzoff plays himself in pic, chanting mysterious songs that prove to be a warning of murder—or worse.

Kuznetzoff has been touring California with a USO show, headed by British character actor Alan Mowbray. The troupe also includes such attractions as June Havoc, Diana Lynn, Peggy Ryan ... and Don Barclay, who plays *Frankenstein Meets the Wolf Man*'s ever-drunken villager, Franzec.

Also on October 21: Ilona Massey informs gossip columnist Louella Parsons that she and husband Alan Curtis (who will co-star with Patricia Morison and John Carradine in the independently produced *Hitler's Madman,* which starts shooting the following week) are divorcing.

Meanwhile, competing for the "Hottest Vasaria Babe" prize is Martha MacVicar, later known as Martha Vickers, here in her film debut. The shooting script specifies that Margareta, glimpsed in the tavern, standing on a table and lighting candles, is the daughter of tavern keeper Vazec (Rex Evans)—hence his vengeful mania after the Wolf Man kills her. No such inference will be in the release version, although Vazec, carrying the "dead" Margareta through the street, seems a homage to Ludwig (Michael Mark) carrying the corpse of Marilyn Harris's Maria through the village in *Frankenstein*.

Martha Vickers is fated to appear in Bogart's *The Big Sleep* (1946) as Carmen, a thumb-sucking nympho, and to become the third of eight Mrs. Mickey Rooneys.

The evocative casting of the villagers of Vasaria, calculated to remind audiences of Universal Horrors and Fantasies of long and recent past, features Beatrice Roberts, as Varja; she'd played the evil Queen Azura in Universal's 1938 serial *Flash Gordon's Trip to Mars*.[19] Harry Stubbs is Guno, the constable; he'd been in a number of Universal horrors, notably as the police chief murdered by the title character in *The Invisible Man,* and as the priest in *The Wolf Man*.

Most movingly, there's Dwight Frye as Rudi, Vasaria's newlywed tailor. The previous month, he'd labored at Poverty Row's PRC Studios, playing Zolarr, a hunchbacked assistant to vampire George Zucco in *Dead Men Walk;* Frye's performance in that shoddy film seems a heartbreaking self-homage to his glory days as fly-eating Renfield in *Dracula* and hunch-backed Fritz in *Frankenstein*. Pitifully reduced professionally, Frye earns his primary income at this time as a tool designer at Douglas Aircraft in Santa Monica. He's also dying of heart disease. A Christian Scientist, he avoids medical care and keeps the attacks he suffers at work a secret from his family. He'll die at the age of only 44 on November 7, 1943, almost precisely a year after acting in *Frankenstein Meets the Wolf Man*.

What classic horror disciple wouldn't have loved to have been among those 56 Festival extras? Singing to the feedback of "Faro-La, Faro-Li?" Soaking up the Phantom Stage atmospherics? Watching to see if Ilona Massey adjusted a stocking? Noting that Lon Chaney had brought his German Shepherd "Moose" to the set? Enjoying Lionel Atwill's mayor, with his arm tightly around the waist of Massey's Elsa as they dance at the Festival? Keeping vigil for the arrival of Lugosi's Frankenstein Monster?

Well, an alumna of that scene has turned up, although she admits the day held little magic for her. Her name is Sonia Darrin, only a teenager in 1942, fated a few years later to play the vampy Agnes in *The Big Sleep* (1946), with Humphrey Bogart, Lauren Bacall—and Martha Vickers. In 2012, the vivacious Ms. Darrin remembers the job only vaguely, with no specifics about Chaney or Lugosi:

Martha Vickers, then known as Martha MacVicar, with impressive canine company in this candid still from *Frankenstein Meets the Wolf Man*.

Frankenstein Meets the Wolf Man—Oh, for God's sake! I was 16 years old, being paid as an extra, maybe $2.50 per day, bored to death ... and they could never find me! I was always hiding out, reading or writing poetry! In that Festival scene, everybody had his or her arms raised up, "Ray-Ray!" and there I was with a stupid expression and my hands on my hips.

So there was an excited crowd, soon to be intimidated by the Monster, and I was unenthusiastic ... and waiting for them to call lunch.

It was silly of me. After all, who doesn't love Frankenstein?[20]

Colorful featured players: Adia Kuznetzoff as the Festival Singer (holding lantern); Don Barclay as Franzec (in hat and walrus mustache); Rex Evans as Vazec (center in glasses); Harry Stubbs as Guno (in constable's hat); Beatrice Roberts as Varja (second from right); Dwight Frye as Rudi (far right). Playing a dead Margareta: Martha Vickers.

Incidentally, Sonia is the mother of former child actor-celebrity Mason Reese, today the owner of a popular New York City sports bar.

Lugosi's first scene shot for *Frankenstein Meets the Wolf Man* is the Monster's crashing of the Festival and the ensuing riot. Screams, shrieks, overturned decorations, a rather startling shot of a woman writhing on the street in hysteria and held tightly by another woman, and finally a chase as Talbot climactically rides off in a carriage, the Monster aboard, kicking wine barrels at his pursuers. It's the first use of a double for the Monster on the film. (Some historians believe the stunt man to be Bob Pepper, who later doubled Chaney as Kharis in *The Mummy's Curse*.) Instantly, Bela's Monster is an interesting interpretation—the posturing, the stiff-legged walk, the outstretched arms. He's clearly working at inferring the creature's blindness and illness.

A curious anecdote about this episode ... *Movieland* magazine (June 1946) will profile Universal's professional screamer, Sara Swartz. The actress provides the reporter this story:

It would be presumed that Bela Lugosi, the Sheik of Shudders, would remain oblivious to a leaping larynx. Yet, during the filming of *Frankenstein Meets the Wolf Man*, he lost his poise entirely.... Miss Swartz was scheduled to scream, which she did to such effect that Mr. Lugosi jumped perceptibly and allowed both consternation and dismay to cross his face. Since the implacable camera recorded these reactions—entirely out of character for Mr. Lugosi—the scene had to be shot over again.[21]

"I don't want to live eternally!": Adia Kuznetzoff is the Festival Singer, sorry he sang to Lon Chaney as Talbot, who seizes him during the Festival of the New Wine. Ilona Massey, at table, observes. Note Dwight Frye in the center of the crowd (white arrow). The young lady in the black hat behind Kuznetzoff and to the right of the violinist is Sonia Darrin, who might be, as of this writing, the film's only survivor.

As work continues this week, Maria Ouspenskaya joins the show, the only Oscar-nominated player in *Frankenstein Meets the Wolf Man* (with Best Supporting Actress nominations for 1936's *Dodsworth* and 1939's *Love Affair*) as Neill shoots village street scenes, tavern scenes, and the chase into the hills after the Wolf Man.

Saturday night, October 24: Appropriately, there's a full moon over Universal City as week two wraps up on *Frankenstein Meets the Wolf Man*.

Part IV. The Monster Talks! ... and Talks ... and Talks...

> *I was afraid you'd run away....*
> —Bela Lugosi as the Monster, in a scene
> cut from *Frankenstein Meets the Wolf Man*

Monday, October 26: It's the third week of the shoot and the spotlight is on Bela Lugosi as the Monster.

Fast forward to 1963. Lon Chaney, in an interview with Hollywood columnist Bob Thomas, reminisces about *Frankenstein Meets the Wolf Man*:

Lon Chaney as Larry Talbot, the Wolf Man, and Bela Lugosi in *Frankenstein Meets the Wolf Man*.

> Poor old Bela Lugosi was playing Frankenstein's Monster, and it was evident after the first day or two that he didn't have the physical strength to handle the role.
>
> So I played them both. I'd do a scene one day as Frankenstein talking to the Wolf Man, using the back of another actor's head. The next day I'd do the same scene as the Wolf Man.[22]

Few take Lon Chaney's claim seriously. At any rate, during the third week of shooting, in the Frankenstein ruins, castle and laboratory, Lugosi delivers a lot of "Ygorstein" dialogue—all of it doomed to the cutting room floor. Might Chaney at some point have doubled the Monster in these scenes—the excision of which makes analysis impossible?

And what of Bela's dialogue? Did he speak in his raspy "Ygor" voice, as most suspect? The dialogue in the surviving shooting script helps us imagine how he acted and sounded. Lugosi was probably impressive in his "I will rule the world!" emoting. But much of the dialogue presents the Monster as a ninny, bullied by Talbot. Consider this exchange, in which Talbot promises to be the Monster's friend if the creature will provide him with Frankenstein's diary:

Larry: You've got to trust me! The diary will tell how to cure you—how to give you back your strength—your eyesight. You're weak—you couldn't defend yourself if the people from Vasaria attacked you again—

Monster [*disdainfully*]: They can't kill me...

Larry desperately tries to make the Monster believe him:

Larry: But if they catch you—chain you and bury you alive—with tons of earth on your body—
   where would your power be then? ... Where is that diary?
(*The Monster gets up clumsily, walks toward the door, groping his way*:)
Monster: Come with me...

Then there's the scene, in which Larry finds a strongbox[23] supposedly containing the diary,
and runs off with "the precious box in his hands." "Wait! Don't leave me—wait!" shouts the
Monster, who follows "clumsily."

Larry opens the box with hammer and chisel. In the edited film, we see Lugosi enter
the scene and open his mouth, about to say this line before it ended up on the cutting room
floor: "I was afraid you'd run away...."

Meanwhile, there's *Frankenstein Meets the Wolf Man*'s "mystery still"—unnumbered,
and showing Lugosi and Chaney wrapped in blankets in the ruins. It's a scene that follows
the Monster crashing the Festival, and it takes place in the underground study of the Frankenstein ruins, early morning. The script writes:

> On the ground, propped up by pillows and covered with blankets (found in Frankenstein's closet)
> lies the Monster, motionless. Only his labored BREATHING is HEARD.

Larry is throwing a log on the fire in the fireplace, which casts "a flickering light through
the room." He demands of the Monster: "Why did you come down to the village? Now
they'll hunt us again—"

(*The Monster turns his face toward the fire, beads of sweat on his forehead*:)
Larry [*bitterly*]: You think you're so clever—Frankenstein gave you a cunning brain, did he? But
   you're dumb! You've spoiled our only chance—
Mannering's voice: Talbot! ... Talbot!
(*Larry runs to the exit—but the Monster says, fearful*:)
Monster: Don't leave me—don't go!

There's much more dialogue than space allows, but as the aforementioned verbiage shows,
Bela Lugosi spoke (and whined) as the Monster this week ... a lot. If there's any truth at all
in Chaney's claim that he doubled Lugosi as the Monster, it had probably been during this
stretch of shooting.

Saturday, October 31: Universal begins shooting *White Savage,* starring Maria Montez
Jon Hall, and Sabu, in Technicolor. Arthur Lubin is director and George Waggner is producer. Waggner's attention is now divided as *Frankenstein Meets the Wolf Man* starts its final
ten days of shooting.

Also of note: On this Halloween of 1942, Chaney and Lugosi are likely working in the
Frankenstein ruins and/or laboratory. Of all the eight films in the Universal Frankenstein
canon, *Frankenstein Meets the Wolf Man* will be the only All Hallow's Eve where the Monster
was amok on the Universal lot.

Part V. All Hell Breaks Loose...

> *Horror pictures are growing so horrible that Bela Lugosi*
> *passed out during one of his own scenes.*
> —George E. Phair, "Retakes," *Variety,* November 8, 1942

Monday, November 2: It's the final scheduled week and Neill has a lot to finish, including the ice caverns scene, the climactic battle and the lab explosion.

Stills 52, 53 and 54 represent the moody episode where Talbot finds Maleva and they talk in the Gypsy camp. Lon and Madame are at their best and Neill captures a terrific atmosphere, including Torben Meyer's chilling reading of "He has the sign of the beast on him!" and those two rather wild-looking Gypsy ladies whom Ouspenskaya shoos from the tent. Also present: Lon's dog Moose, here playing the camp's dog Bruno.

By mid-week, Neill probably starts the mad lab sequence, leading to the climactic fight. Ilona Massey delights the company when she reports in her blonde braids and negligee, looking like a catalogue cover girl for Frederick's of Vasaria. Bela registers his great close-up of the Monster grinning on the operating table. Original inference: The creature has his sight back, hence Bela's "hubba-hubba" smile as he gets a load of Ilona.

The Kenneth Strickfaden lab equipment sparks and buzzes. Still number 60 shows doubles for Chaney and Lugosi on the operating tables. The doubles are probably in service due to the danger of the electricity.

Thursday, November 5: Bela collapses.

"Bela Lugosi Does Fainting This Time," headlines the *Wichita Daily Times* (November 6, 1942), writing that Bela "lost consciousness while strapped to a surgical table." Also on November 6, the *Hollywood Reporter* blames the collapse on Bela's "packing around the 35-lb. Monster makeup designed by Jack Pierce." Universal sends Lugosi home to recuperate.

The same day: Neill films scenes of Chaney and Ouspenskaya on the two-wheel carriage. The carriage overturns and Madame goes to the hospital. As *Variety* reports on November 6:

> Maria Ouspenskaya was taken to Cedars of Lebanon hospital yesterday with a broken ankle, received in accident on the set of *Frankenstein Meets the Wolf Man*. Character actress was riding in horse-drawn wagon with Lon Chaney on the Universal back lot and was tossed out when wagon hit a large stone.

She will not return to complete her role (per the script, arriving in her problematic carriage to rescue Elsa and Mannering from the flooded ruins).

Indeed, November 5, '42 has been a *very* bad day on the set.

Saturday, November 7: Bela's back, as proven by an autographed Universal commissary menu (also signed this day by Chaney, Abbott and Costello, Deanna Durbin and other Universal stars).[24] It would have been this day that Neill films the scene in the ice grotto; stills 61, 62 and 63 all present Bela and Lon in the ice. In still 61 particularly, Bela appears not to be wearing all of his Monster padding—a concession, perhaps, to his collapse? Shot 62 proves Bela was originally in the ice (or behind it); in the release version, we see Gil Perkins in the ice, but more on that mystery later.

It's now, very late in the shoot, that Lugosi delivers the first scripted scene of Monster dialogue, as Monster and Talbot chat in the catacomb, Talbot having built "a couple of small fires from the driftwood in the cave," the Monster sitting on "the stony ground." He holds out his "weak hands" toward the fire while "trying to focus his vision on Larry," and says, "Where are you?"

> Monster [*trying to get up*]: Help me to get up...
> Larry goes over to the giant and helps him to his feet.

Monster: Once I had the strength of a hundred men... It's gone... I'm sick...
(*He stands with Larry's help, and supports himself against the wall.*)

The scene moves to the interior of the Frankenstein catacombs:

Larry: How did you get here?
Monster [*laboriously*]: The village people burned the house down.... But I fell into that mountain
    stream.... I lost consciousness. When I woke up...
(*He points toward the wall of ice in horror:*)
Monster: I was frozen into that block of ice—
(*Larry stops and looks at the Monster, aghast:*)
Larry [*terrified by his memory*]: Buried alive! ... I know—
(*Larry identifies himself and tells the Monster he's hiding in the ruins, "the same as you."*)
Monster [*eagerly*]: Then you are my friend... We can help each other—
(*They look together for the laboratory:*)
Monster [*groping around again, half-blind*]: The laboratory must be behind the ice.... No! Up
    there! I remember now...

And they build a platform of logs and driftwood to reach the hole in the roof. All of
this, of course, will become long-lost footage.

Part VI. Overtime

> *I carried the real gal ... I had the* real *Ilona Massey!*
> —Gil Perkins, interview with the author, 1991

Monday, November 9: The film is now behind schedule. The final numbered stills are
a mixed bag. Still 69 shows the Wolf Man in the ice cavern, while still 70 shows him ready
to pounce on the constable in Cardiff (an early episode, after escaping his room at Queens
Hospital).

It's also during these final days that the director films long shots of the battle. Still 72
shows Australian stuntman Gil Perkins (or so many believe) doubling the Monster and carrying Massey; stills 71 and 73 show Massey in her negligee and on her cot, awakening to the
sound of the machinery.

In 1991, Gil Perkins, in a telephone chat with this author, claimed he doubled the Monster while bit player-stuntman Eddie Parker doubled the Wolf Man in the battle. Members
of the Classic Horror Film Board have exhaustively examined the battle scene to try to ascer-
tain Perkins' claim and identify the doubles. Although some claim Perkins did all the Monster
doubling, it appears to me that it's Parker as the Monster part of the time, including the shot
of the Monster carrying (and dropping) Elsa. It's also definitely Parker (the double-dimpled
chin a dead giveaway) as the Monster bursts the straps off the operating table.

On probably the production's last day, the company blows up the laboratory—still 79
showing the doubles for Massey, Knowles and Chaney, and still 80 showing the doubles for
Chaney and Lugosi, with fire in the background. It must have been quite a spectacle, the
flood water cascading on the stuntmen and the set. Meanwhile, the trick unit has been shooting miniatures of the dam exploding, Wolf Man transformations, and other material.

Wednesday, November 11: *Frankenstein Meets the Wolf Man* wraps. It's Patric Knowles'
31st birthday. Abbott and Costello's *It Ain't Hay*, directed by Erle C. Kenton (director of
The Ghost of Frankenstein), finishes up at Universal the same day.

Ilona Massey in braids and negligee—one of the sensations of the climax of *Frankenstein Meets the Wolf Man.*

Ilona Massey joins Fred Astaire on a war bond sales tour. Dwight Frye has landed a bit as a prisoner in Fritz Lang's *Hangmen Also Die!* Lionel Atwill is jobless. (Exonerated of his legal woes in April of 1943, Atwill won't work again in films until that October, as evil Dr. Maldor in Republic's *Captain America* serial.)

Friday night, November 13: Adia Kuznetzoff and Don Barclay appear with Alan Mowbray's USO troupe at Lake Norconian; Kuznetzoff, meanwhile, has won a role in Paramount's *For Whom the Bell Tolls.*

Friday, November 20: Roy William Neill starts shooting Universal's *Rhythm of the Islands,* starring Allan Jones and Acquanetta.

Monday, November 23: Universal starts Abbott and Costello's *Oh! Doctor* (released as *Hit the Ice*), with Patric Knowles prominent in the cast. A week later, *Variety* notes that Eddie Parker has joined the show. His role: an ambulance driver.

Friday, December 11: Exactly one month after *Frankenstein Meets the Wolf Man* wrapped up, Universal begins shooting *Captive Wild Woman,* starring Acquanetta ("a sensation in savagery") in the title role, Evelyn Ankers as heroine, and, as the mad doctor, an actor for whom Universal plans a horror star campaign: John Carradine.

Wednesday, December 16: Monogram starts shooting *The Ape Man,* starring Bela Lugosi, whose contract with Universal expires.

Thursday, January 7, 1943: Eight weeks after *Frankenstein Meets the Wolf Man* wraps, Universal starts shooting *Son of Dracula* with Lon Chaney in the title role.

The posters will read, "The Screen's Master Character Creator."

Part VII. Retakes and Editing

We filmed for about six weeks and after we finished, we did some retakes.
— Ilona Massey, interview with James Miller, *Varulven* magazine

In her apparent one-and-only late-in-life interview about *Frankenstein Meets the Wolf Man,* Massey remembered that, after the film was finished, "we did some retakes." It's significant that Ilona definitely recalled retakes. It's maddening that she wasn't asked for specifics.

At any rate, the areas where retakes are of the most interest are (a) the ice grotto scene where Talbot finds the Monster, and (b) the climactic Monster vs. the Wolf Man battle.

A nagging mystery ... why does Gil Perkins (or is it Eddie Parker?) appear as the Monster in the ice, when it's obviously *Bela* in the ice in still 62? A theory: Based on still numbers, Lugosi's scene in the ice cavern came very late in the shoot and probably after his November 5 collapse. He still might have looked ill when he returned (he looks a bit dazed in shot 61), and as this scene presents the Monster's introductory close-up, Universal perhaps decides to do a retake with Perkins (or Parker) to provide a more potent first impression. Don Glut had originally proposed this sensible explanation in his excellent 1973 book *The Frankenstein Legend.*

So ... was it Gil Perkins as Monster and Eddie Parker as Wolf Man, as Perkins told me in 1991? Eddie Parker as both in alternating shots? Why does it appear to be Perkins in Monster makeup in some shots, and Parker in others?

Massey recalled retakes, so she likely was in them. It's possible Universal decided to beef up the battle scene after shooting officially closed. It certainly appears that Perkins picks up Ilona ... but maybe a *retake* of Eddie Parker as the Monster, carrying Ilona and attacked by the Wolf Man, also ends up in the final version.

At any rate, the mystery remains, and unless detailed production papers emerge, it will endure. In fact, the Monster and Wolf Man makeups are so heavy, and most of the battle filmed in such long shots, that one could argue it's Evelyn Ankers as the Monster and Deanna Durbin as the Wolf Man, catfighting in the flooded Frankenstein ruins. A ridiculous conjecture ... but without the production reports, who can definitively prove it isn't so?

In goes the wonderful Hans J. Salter musical score ... out goes Lugosi's Monster dialogue. Why this major, drastic surgery on the completed film? Curt Siodmak told me in 1980 that the Universal powers-that-were, watching the film's rough cut, laughed uproariously when they saw and heard Bela's Monster emoting—"It sounded," said Siodmak, "so Hungarian funny...!" Others, in defense of Lugosi, scoff at Siodmak's account, suggesting the cuts came on the eve of national release, after preview audiences were uncomfortable with a talking Monster.

Monday, December 21: A censorship analysis chart (presently on file at the Academy's Margaret Herrick Library) reviews *Frankenstein Meets the Wolf Man* as to its content of liquor, violence, and religious ceremonies. It clocks the film at 6,688'—approximately

Patric Knowles, Ilona Massey, Maria Ouspenskaya arrive at the ruined castle.

74 minutes and 20 seconds. There's no mention of a talking Monster in the analysis's synopsis.

Meanwhile, the Turner Classic Movie Archive in 2013 gives *Frankenstein Meets the Wolf Man*'s release print footage as 6,601'. This computes to approximately 73 minutes and 20 seconds, precisely the length of the release version. As such, it's possible that about one minute was cut from the print the censor saw in December '42 (maybe the scene at the hospital, where Inspector Owen examines Talbot's burial clothes); it's also possible that the math was slightly off. At any rate, add to this fact that Lugosi's various dialogue scenes would certainly have run more than one minute, and it's clear that Universal had scissored the Monster's dialogue *prior* to December 21, 1942.

Incidentally, the liquor-violence-religious ceremonies analysis chart, rating the characters, lists only "Wolf Man" and "Young Doctor" as "Prominent" roles. As for "Frankenstein's Monster," the chart describes him as "minor," "unsympathetic," and "straight." ("Straight," by the way, suggested no indication of the Monster's sexual proclivity, but means he wasn't "comic" or "indifferent.")

Conclusion: Universal was quick to cut Lugosi's dialogue and the references to the Monster's blindness.[25] Was the editing really necessary?

The fact that Universal ordered the cuts so quickly after the film's completion would indicate the studio's immediate concern. At any rate, let's examine five likely reasons why Universal made its legendary cuts in *Frankenstein Meets the Wolf Man*:

One of the emergency cuts made in *Frankenstein Meets the Wolf Man*: Lugosi's Monster and Chaney's Larry Talbot share blankets in the Frankenstein ruins.

1. Universal's Frankenstein's Monster traditionally was mute. In *Bride of Frankenstein*, Karloff's dialogue ("The Monster Talks!") was a PR novelty hoot. In *The Ghost of Frankenstein*, Lugosi's Ygor voice coming from Chaney's Monster ("I am Ygor!") was a climactic jolt.

2. The Monster was supposed to scare audiences. Lugosi's Monster had such lines as "I'm sick," "Help me to get up," "I was afraid you'd left me," and "I was afraid you'd run away." Additionally, Talbot calls the Monster "weak" and "dumb." Universal's most celebrated creature hardly rated such insults.

3. As noted in the shooting script excerpts, the Monster "gropes" too damn much.

4. Curt Siodmak's dialogue for the Monster was not only too purple, it slowed down the pace. The running time of *The Ghost of Frankenstein* was 67 minutes. The running time of *Frankenstein Meets the Wolf Man*, even after the cuts, will be 73 minutes.

5. Cutting the Monster's crybaby dialogue and the references to his blindness bolstered the impression of a powerful creature—and here, sadly but truly, Lugosi needed all the help he could get. Of course, the script had called for an enfeebled Monster, so Bela didn't register the whirlwind power of Karloff's Monster, the marble rock power of Chaney's Monster, or the elephant-uprooting-a-tree power of Glenn Strange's Monster. Elsa Lanchester's Bride could easily scratch out his half-blind eyes and hiss in his face, while Bela's Monster was still saying, "Help me to get up."

The Curt Siodmak story, long derided, rings true. One can imagine Universal "suits" viewing a projection room screening of *Frankenstein Meets the Wolf Man*, amazed and appalled by a blind, sick, yakety-yak Monster with a Hungarian accent, eventually succumbing to gales of laughter.

Yet it wasn't the actor's fault. For Bela Lugosi hadn't played Frankenstein's Monster— he'd played the *ruins* of Frankenstein's Monster.

The first time we see (and hear) Lugosi (not a double) in the release print of *Frankenstein Meets the Wolf Man*, he's stumbling through the destroyed sanitarium, arms outstretched, bats (!) flying about him. He stalks into a piece of debris, grimaces, and lets out a sound that sounds like both an old man's gag and a crow's squawk. This spastic, freakishly diminished Monster is what Siodmak had originally envisioned and what Lugosi had played—a sick, blind, decaying creature with a new, festeringly evil brain, vaingloriously lusting to "rule the world" even as he's physically falling into pieces. Such an interpretation might have been a truly creepy twist in Universal's Frankenstein series—especially in contrast to the seeing, seething, freshly supercharged Monster of the climax.

"I can't destroy Frankenstein's creation," says Patric Knowles' Dr. Mannering. "I've got to see it at its full power!"

Indeed, one glimpses a vivid peek at this unholy metamorphosis in the climactic battle scene close-up of Lugosi, arms stretched to his side, grinning wickedly, triumphantly exulting in his restored Monster strength.

So it was this bizarre conception of Frankenstein's Monster that had so disastrously misfired—not Lugosi's performance, and not even Siodmak's often-blamed dialogue. The tragedy was that Universal apparently didn't see it that way. Lugosi had collapsed on the set, required at least two doubles, and possibly given a performance that, physically, verbally and dramatically, struck the front office as a disaster.

Maybe, the powers-that-were figured they'd have been better off following the original plan ... and starring Lon Chaney in both roles...?

At any rate, Edward Curtiss will rate a Best Editing Oscar nomination (but doesn't get one) for his remarkably smooth emergency surgery on what Universal had diagnosed as a critically sick picture. Only in the scene in the ruins where Talbot and the Monster find Elsa's picture do we see, for a fleeting moment, Bela's mouth move, forming erased-from-the-soundtrack dialogue. Yet the overall damage to the performance is severe and inevitable.

Considering the role Bela Lugosi had played in defining Universal Studios, it's also unforgivable.

Part VIII. Release, Box Office and Censorship

> FRANKENSTEIN MEETS THE WOLF MAN OPENED ASH WEDNESDAY BREAKING ALL HOUSE RECORDS INCLUDING HOLIDAY AND WEEK-END BUSINESS AND THEN BROKE NEW RECORD ON FOLLOWING SATURDAY NOW IN SIXTH DAY AND BUSINESS IS TERRORIFIC ON THIS HORRORIFIC
> —Telegram from the manager of the Trans Lux Theater
> in Boston to Universal Studios, Monday, March 15, 1943

Final cost of *Frankenstein Meets the Wolf Man*: $238,071.79.[26]

Thursday, February 18, 1943: Universal previews *Frankenstein Meets the Wolf Man*. *The Hollywood Reporter* and *Variety* run favorable reviews the next day.

Friday, March 5: *Frankenstein Meets the Wolf Man* opens at the 594-seat Rialto Theatre in New York City. Despite rain on Saturday and a blast of cold weather on Monday, the crowds are big. "Exactly what the doctor ordered for his small seater," reports *Variety* on March 10; "over $15,000 in view, socko." The film exceeds the prediction—the first week's take will be $15,500.[27] In its four-week sojourn at the Rialto, *Frankenstein Meets the Wolf Man* will bring in (according to *Variety*) a walloping $42,000, and the Rialto will stay open from 8:30 a.m. to 4:00 a.m. to accommodate the crowds.

A giant horror hit, *Frankenstein Meets the Wolf Man* surpasses such 1943 Rialto contenders as Universal's *Son of Dracula*, starring Lon Chaney ($41,000); MGM's *Hitler's Madman*, starring John Carradine ($28,500); RKO's Val Lewton chiller *The Ghost Ship* ($28,100); and Lewton's *I Walked with a Zombie* ($19,500).

Thursday, July 22: *Frankenstein Meets the Wolf Man* opens at both the 3,389-seat Los Angeles Paramount Theatre and the 1,451-seat Hollywood Paramount Theatre, supported by Universal's *Captive Wild Woman* ("2nd THRILL HIT! Can You Take It?"). Despite a one-day trolley car strike and temperatures in the 90s, business is remarkable. In its first week at the Paramount Downtown, the film draws $28,000[28]; at the Hollywood Paramount, $12,000. The combined take equals the September 1942 first-week business of Paramount's acclaimed Best Picture Academy nominee *Wake Island*, starring Brian Donlevy (who, in 1966, will marry Lillian Lugosi). The horror double bill is a holdover, with $11,000 in its second week at the Downtown Paramount and $5,500 at the Hollywood Paramount.

Not everybody's happy. The state censor in Ohio itemizes a cut:

> Reel 1 (section B)—Where Wolf man attacks Officer, allow only flash where he jumps on him and eliminate entirely scene of him choking him, digging his teeth in his neck and continued scene of him biting him.

Ontario and New Zealand demand the same cut. Pennsylvania has problems with Vazec blowing up the dam: "Eliminate close view of Vazec's hands about to light fuse and lighting fuse."

Reviews are primarily snide—few 1943 critics will regard a film titled *Frankenstein Meets the Wolf Man* with anything but cavalier condescension. Typical is this review from *Newsweek* (March 8, 1943), which Jack P. Pierce pastes into his scrapbook, despite the irreverent tone:

> [The film is] a double-barreled field day for those with either a rampant sense of humor or a facility for goosepimpling at the drop of a mangled corpse...
> Involved in this horrific hugger-mugger are Frankenstein's seductive daughter (Ilona Massey) and a rather simple-minded English doctor (Patric Knowles), both of whom might have blushed unseen if an objectionably stuffy rumpot hadn't thought of blowing up a strategically located dam. As it is, both Monster and Wolf Man are electrocuted, mangled, and drowned, but it's getting so you can't trust the movies. Next thing you know, Frankenstein and the Wolf Man will be meeting Universal's Deanna Durbin.

Also, a number of small town exhibitors write to *Motion Picture Herald*, complaining that the film was a dud, their patrons wanting no part of "the beast battle of the century." Perhaps the most damning review comes from the manager of the Jackson Theatre in Flomaton, Alabama: "Lugosi not a very impressive Monster; nothing to compare with Karloff. Hope Universal quits making this series."

From a Universal Exhibitors Manual, an early advertisement for *Frankenstein Meets the Wolf Man*. From its inception, the studio planned to star Lon Chaney as *both* the Wolf Man and the Monster.

Part IX. Curt Siodmak and the Hitler "Weenie"

Bela Lugosi could never act his way out of a paper bag...
Lon Chaney was a confused homosexual....
—Curt Siodmak, interview with the author, 1980

Late in his life, Curt Siodmak delighted in spicing up his interviews with salty quotes, such as those aforementioned. Having fled Nazi Germany in the early 1930s, he lived late-in-life on a ranch near Sequoia National Park, regaling any and all listeners with this zinger: "I wake up every morning and say 'Heil Hitler,' because if it weren't for that son of a bitch, I wouldn't be in California—I'd still be in Berlin!"

During my 1980 interview with him, Siodmak reminisced about concocting what he called *Frankenstein Meets the Wolf Man*'s "weenie" (i.e., its gimmick or twist): The Wolf Man wants to die and the Monster wants to live. However, there might have been another "weenie"—a Frankenstein's Monster whose "I will rule the world!" lust for power evokes that "son of a bitch" ... Adolf Hitler!

In the early months after the U.S. had entered World War II, Siodmak perhaps had created a macabre spoof. Surely it would have amused the émigré to personify Der Fuehrer as a blind, sick, bolt-necked, vainglorious monstrosity, stitched together from corpses, stalking and stumbling in castle ruins and an ice cavern, battered in battle with the Wolf Man, washed

Curt Siodmak, at age 90, signs autographs at the *Famous Monsters* Convention in Crystal City, Virginia, in 1993. Siodmak wrote the scripts for *The Wolf Man* and *Frankenstein Meets the Wolf Man* (photograph by the author).

away by the waters of an exploded dam. And Lugosi's Monster walk does resemble a "goose-step"....

In my interviews with him about *Frankenstein Meets the Wolf Man,* Siodmak never mentioned a Hitler "weenie" (no wonder, considering how horrible that sounds). And it's way too late to ask him now—he died in 2000 at the age of 98, having earned enmity from many of the faithful for his aspersions on Lugosi's talent and opinions on Chaney's sexuality.

Anyway ... the Monster-as-Hitler "weenie" was probably too audacious (or silly) to succeed, and the pruned Monster dialogue in the final script gives evidence that Siodmak and producer George Waggner were already shying away from the Third Reich concept.

Perhaps they realized what an insult they were directing at Frankenstein's Monster.

Part X. Posterity

The reason for *Frankenstein Meets the Wolf Man*'s popularity with horror fans might be the personal off-screen melodrama has bequeathed the film a special angst of its own. Blackballed Ilona Massey, scandalized and convicted Lionel Atwill, injured Maria Ouspenskaya, and dying Dwight Frye. Lon Chaney, flanked by Moose and agog at Ilona, playing with power and star quality he'd never top at Universal. Roy William Neill, trying to direct a "silk purse" out of what was in essence a "sow's ear." Edward Curtiss, challenged to edit and save a horror epic that, in Universal's eyes, had emerged as a pants-cracking comedy.

And most of all, there's Bela Lugosi, desperately accepting a role he'd dismissed as worthy of "a half-wit extra," forced to follow Karloff, giving his all as "Ygorstein," collapsing on the set, gutted in the cutting room. All the revisionist theory in the world won't alter the shattering damage this creature did to the Lugosi legacy—both when he *didn't* play it in 1931, and when he *did* play it in 1942.

A mystery: What did Bela Lugosi personally think of *Frankenstein Meets the Wolf Man,* and his disastrously altered portrayal? As he rarely went to his own films, was he even aware that the editing had taken place? Did anyone at Universal ever tell him of the editing decision, and why they made it?

Probably somewhere along the line, Lugosi became aware of the cuts; he certainly became aware of Universal's response to his Monster performance. As noted, Universal starred Lon Chaney in *Son of Dracula* (1943), and then cast John Carradine as Dracula in *House of Frankenstein* (1944) and *House of Dracula* (1945). World War II Universal shut the gate on Bela, who, after *Frankenstein Meets the Wolf Man,* would not return until 1948 and Universal-International's *Abbott and Costello Meet Frankenstein.*

Lugosi's oft-quoted remark allegedly made between scenes of *Frankenstein Meets the Wolf Man* regarding the Monster's growl—"That *yell* is the worst thing about the part. You feel like a big jerk every time you do it!"[29]—suggests a certain arrogance toward the role. Lillian Lugosi's insistence he did the part only for the "money" implies a possible apathy.

However, correspondence has recently come to light that perhaps gives telling insight into Lugosi's emotions about *Frankenstein Meets the Wolf Man.* Ford Beebe was a Universal director whose credits included the Lugosi serial *The Phantom Creeps* (1939) and the Lugosi-Atwill feature *Night Monster* (1942). Beebe died on his 90th birthday, November 26, 1978; that March 19, he'd written a letter to Richard Bojarski, author of *The Films of Boris Karloff*

(1974) and *The Films of Bela Lugosi* (1980). Bojarski died in 2009 and the letter is now in the archives of collector John Antosiewicz, who graciously sent me a copy. Beebe's never-before-published memory of visiting Bela "near the end of his contract with Universal" dates it to the time of *Frankenstein Meets the Wolf Man,* maybe even during it. As Beebe wrote:

> I never enjoyed working with any actor more than I enjoyed working with Lugosi. He was not only a finished craftsman, but he was a gentleman in every sense of the word. Oddly enough I lived within half a block of his residence on Whipple Street in North Hollywood, but not being much of a partygoer, I never visited him but once, and that was at his request. It was near the end of his contract with Universal and he seemed to be afraid that he had outlived his usefulness with the studio and he wanted some assurance to the contrary. As a matter of fact, Bela was a bit unsure of himself, so I answered his call for help....

Beebe wrote that he received "the surprise of my life" when he arrived at Lugosi's house: "It was exactly what one would have expected of Dracula, not Lugosi, to live in." The wood was dark, the blinds drawn, and as Beebe wrote, "It wouldn't have surprised me to see a slinking 'undead' lady creep out of the shadows and dissolve into the woodwork." He continued:

> I'm not at all certain that I was able to assure him as to his standing with the studio, but if not, it was not because of my lack of trying, for I knew exactly how he felt. Like many people in show business, I, too have an inferiority complex. And Bela was such a consummate artist that he couldn't bear to think he might not have lived up to his illusion he had been trying to establish.

That Universal Studios in general, and probably his Monster performance in particular, made the immensely talented Bela Lugosi "afraid he had outlived his usefulness" and gave him an "inferiority complex," is surely the most frightening thing about *Frankenstein Meets the Wolf Man.*

Frankenstein Meets the Wolf Man

Studio, Universal. Producer, George Waggner. Director, Roy William Neill. Screenplay, Curt Siodmak. Cinematographer, George Robinson. Original Music, Hans J. Salter. Makeup, Jack P. Pierce. Art Director, John B. Goodman. Set Decorator, Russell A. Gausman. Costume Designer, Vera West. Editor, Edward Curtiss. Visual Effects, John P. Fulton. Associate Art Director, Martin Obzina. Associate Set Decorator, Edward R. Robinson. Sound Director, Bernard B. Brown. Sound Technician, William R. Fox. Assistant Director, Melville Shyer. Song: "Faro-La, Faro-Li," music by Hans J. Salter, lyrics by Curt Siodmak. Running Time, 73 minutes.

Filmed at Universal Studios, 12 October–11 November 1942. Opened at the Rialto Theatre, New York City, 5 March 1943. Opened at the Paramount Los Angeles and Hollywood Theatres, 22 July 1943.

Ilona Massey (Baroness Elsa Frankenstein), Patric Knowles (Dr. Frank Mannering), Lon Chaney (Lawrence Talbot/The Wolf Man), Lionel Atwill (Mayor), Bela Lugosi (The Frankenstein Monster), Maria Ouspenskaya (Maleva), Dennis Hoey (Inspector Owen), Rex Evans (Vazec), Don Barclay (Franzec), Dwight Frye (Rudi), Harry Stubbs (Guno), Adia Kuznetzoff (Festival Singer), Beatrice Roberts (Varja), Doris Lloyd (Nurse), Cyril Delevanti (Freddy Jolley, Grave Robber), Tom Stevenson (Grave Robber), Torben Meyer (Gypsy), Martha MacVicar (Margareta), David Clyde (Llanwelly Police Officer), Jeff Corey (Cemetery Caretaker), Charles Irwin (Constable), Sonia Darrin, Lance Fuller (villagers), Eddie Parker, Gil Perkins (stunts).

10

Horror Propaganda
Hitler's Madman

"Sensational!"
—MGM's teaser line for ***Hitler's Madman***

John Carradine was *Heydrich ... a Shakespearean actor, with a reputation*
of going overboard. A lot of Nazis behaved like Shakespearean actors.
—Douglas Sirk, director of ***Hitler's Madman***[1]

"If P.T. Barnum had ever been swept by a wave of righteous indignation, the result might not have been greatly different from *Hitler's Madman*," writes the *New York Times* after the film premieres at Broadway's Rialto Theatre on August 27, 1943.

The *Times* critique is cold and clear. *Hitler's Madman* is a lurid circus, a midnight carnival, a risqué peep show of Nazi atrocity. In its depiction of the assassination of Reinhard Heydrich and Hitler's barbaric revenge on the village of Lidice, it's hardly in the league of such World War II epics as *Mrs. Miniver* and *Wake Island,* or even of *Hangmen Also Die!,* the previously released saga of Lidice, directed by Fritz Lang. It's trite melodrama.

It is, in fact, a horror movie.

Actually, there's plenty to spark this claim—or accusation:

- John Carradine, sporting a false nose that makes him resemble a California condor, plays the satanic Heydrich, gleefully presiding at gynecological exams for Czech girls he recruits as prostitutes, blasphemously wiping his boots with sacred cloth—and viciously slapping an old priest.
- Patricia Morison, fated to appear at Universal as the acid-throwing murderess in *Calling Dr. Death* (1943) and the vampy villainess in the Sherlock Holmes entry *Dressed to Kill* (1946), portrays the heroine, complete with a heart-wringer death scene.
- Elizabeth Russell, fresh from her cameo as the Cat Woman in *Cat People,* mournfully haunts the film as a feline, black-clad widow, looking hell-bent on clawing Heydrich to death.
- The pastoral Lidice seems to be nestled right over the Hollywood Hills from Universal's Vasaria, the site of *Frankenstein Meets the Wolf Man,* shooting simultaneously.
- The apocalyptic climax, in which the ghosts of slaughtered patriots rise from Lidice's flames and ashes, imploring the living to avenge their deaths as a choir of angels sings over the carnage, places the bizarre film into the realm of the supernatural.

Even the theater helps stick on the terror tag: The Rialto is Broadway's horror salon, home of the Universal fright-fests and Val Lewton's RKO chillers. The overall inference is crude, if apt: Heydrich's ghost has arisen as a Hollywood bogeyman—joining the mythology of Frankenstein's Monster, the Wolf Man, and the Cat Woman.

Yes, this strange, passionate film, based on one of history's most shocking bloodbaths, plays like a sex and horror movie, and MGM virtually sells it as such. The eccentricities are many, including 20-year-old Ava Gardner in a bit as a "Sacrificial Daughter of Lidice" and 74-year-old vaudevillian Al Shean, real-life uncle of the Marx Brothers, as the doomed priest. Packaged by Jewish émigrés, produced independently in Hollywood when such projects are almost unheard-of, the film survives a new leading lady at its eleventh hour, and fights a pitched battle against United Artists' *Hangmen Also Die!*, filmed at the same time. MGM had gobbled up *Hitler's Madman* for release and added finishing touches, including a censor-defying sex episode that very nearly cost the film its release certificate. When, over a year after Lidice, *Hitler's Madman* opens at Grauman's Chinese Theatre, it's as a supporting feature for the Fred Astaire RKO musical *The Sky's the Limit*.

Yet few movies of the war years capture the true evil genius of Hitler's madness as does this admittedly erratic, deeply moving, sadly forsaken film. In an era when Hollywood produces inexcusably specious propaganda, *Hitler's Madman*, for all its sensationalism, resonates with spirit, gallantry and outrage.

In its uncompromising attack on the terrors of the Nazis, it makes us believe in monsters.

* * *

"And may God defend the right!"
—from the final scene of **Mrs. Miniver** (1942)

Thursday, June 4, 1942: MGM's *Mrs. Miniver,* the saga of a British family caught in the drama of Dunkirk, premieres at Radio City Music Hall. The star is Metro's red-haired diva Greer Garson and the film will win six Oscars, including Best Picture, Best Actress (Garson) and Best Director (William Wyler). Worldwide rentals will total $8.8 million[2] and Winston Churchill, a *Mrs. Miniver* fan, will write to Louis B. Mayer that the film is "propaganda worth a hundred battleships."[3]

Behind the scenes, things had not been as rosy: Thirty-seven-year-old Garson had been having an affair with her 25-year-old onscreen "son," Richard Ney. Mayer had demanded the romance stay secret until after *Mrs. Miniver*'s release. The couple will wed in 1943 and divorce in 1947, the ensuing rancor including Ney bitterly revealing to friends Garson's true age. (Of course, it's unfair to pick on Greer Garson. After all, 4-F Errol Flynn is Warner Bros.' World War II hero during the same era that he goes to court for statutory rape!)

The problem with *Mrs. Miniver* is not in its star. Wyler will later attack his own film as "synthetic" in its depiction of the wartime British family. In 1970, Garson, appearing at a screening of *Mrs. Miniver* in Annapolis, actually will apologize for the film: "We really thought we were doing something important at the time," she will plead.

They *are* doing something important—enormously so. The noble pursuit is to defeat Hitler and Hirohito, and Hollywood has become a 24–7 propaganda factory. Wartime inspiration is essential, and expertly played Axis villainy is at a premium. Notably, *Casablanca*, shooting that summer at Warners, hires Conrad Veidt to play Nazi Strasser for $25,000—the same salary being paid to Ingrid Bergman as Ilsa![4]

Ironically, on June 4, 1942—the day *Mrs. Miniver* opens in New York—Reinhard Heydrich, the Reichsprotektor of Bavaria and Moravia, dies of wounds from an assassination attempt. Six days later, Hitler enacts a horrid revenge that shocks the world.

* * *

Nazis Blot Out Czech Village;
Kill All Men, Disperse Others

By The Associated Press

Berlin, June 10 (from German broadcasts recorded in New York)—All men in the Czechoslovak town of Lidice have been shot, the women sent to concentration camps, the children placed in "educational institutions" and the town itself "leveled to the ground" on the charge that the population gave shelter and assistance to the slayers of Nazi leader Reinhard Heydrich, the Berlin radio announced tonight.

—*The New York Times*, Page 1, June 11, 1942

Reinhard Heydrich had a variety of gothic nicknames: "The Hangman," "The Blonde Beast," "Himmler's Evil Genius," "The Butcher of Prague" and "The Lord Over Life and Death" among them. Himmler referred to Heydrich as "Genghis Khan," while Hitler had his own *soubriquet* for Heydrich: "The Man with the Iron Heart."

With the eyes of a fox, an epic Aryan nose and cropped blonde hair, Heydrich looked and acted the role of the Nazi Superman. He'd become an SS major in 1931, later serving in the Luftwaffe, flying nearly 100 missions and finally shot down by Russians. He'd chaired the Wannsee Conference of January 20, 1942, where he masterminded the Final Solution, planning the deportation and transportation of 11 million Jews worked to death or killed outright. And he reigned as the Reichsprotektor of Bavaria and Moravia, announcing, "We will Germanize the Czech vermin."[5] Heydrich so seemingly believed in his destiny and invulnerability that he rode about Prague in an open car.

Historian Helmutt G. Hassis, who will refer to Heydrich as "the young, evil god of death," sees in the man "an almost erotic lust for extreme danger." If this indeed was the Hangman's pet perversion, it would prove his downfall.

The assassination plan: *Operation Anthropoid.*[6] In his excellent book *Heydrich: The Face of Evil,* Mario R. Dederichs relates that locksmith Josef Gabcik and chimney builder Jan Kubis, both lieutenants in the former Czech army,

Reinhard Heydrich, "The Hangman," fated for assassination in 1942.

were the choices of the Czech Government-in-Exile to assassinate Heydrich. They trained in the British Isles, and the RAF parachuted both men into Pilsen on December 29, 1941. The Prague underground hid them.

Wednesday, May 27: Heydrich left his base at Prague Castle, planning to fly to meet Hitler later that day, expecting a promotion. He approached the tram stop at Klein-Holeschowitz Street in his open, dark green Mercedes 320. Gabcik stepped out, removed his gun from under his coat and aimed at "The Hangman." The gun failed to fire. Gabcik had been keeping the gun dismantled in the same pocket where he kept greens for his rabbits—and the gun had jammed with rabbit food.

Kubis threw a bomb. It fell short, and bomb splinters struck Kubis in the face. Kubis escaped by bicycle, his face bleeding, Heydrich's chauffeur in foot pursuit. Heydrich, wounded in the back by the blast, drew his pistol and chased Gabcik, but as he fired at him, he collapsed. The clumsy but earnest assassins escaped and Heydrich fell near the tram stop, where a female passerby recognized him.

"Heydrich!" she screamed. "Jesu Maria!"

The Hangman might have survived, but the nervous doctor cut the surgical hole too large; additionally, horsehair stuffing from the Mercedes seat complicated the infection. On the morning of June 4, eight days after the attack, Heydrich died of septicemia. In a dash of the occult that some Nazis so favored, Dr. Bernhard Wehner, a police investigator of the assassination, claimed Heydrich's facial expression as he passed from earth (his "death mask") betrayed "an uncanny spirituality and entirely perverted beauty, like a Renaissance Cardinal."[7]

There are two elaborate state funerals in Prague and in Berlin, complete with a torchlight procession, flaming sconces, and blasts of Beethoven and Wagner. In Berlin, both Himmler and Hitler deliver eulogies, Der Fuehrer posthumously presenting "my dear comrade Heydrich" the highest state of the German order. Privately, Hitler would be more candid to his inner circle, calling Heydrich's showboating in his open Mercedes "a stupidity of no use to the nation."

Reinhard Heydrich is laid to rest in Invaliden Cemetery in Berlin—and Hitler unleashes what historian Andrew Curry will call in his article "The Heydrich Equation" in *World War II* magazine (September-October 2011), "an orgy of revenge."

Wednesday, June 10: Accusing the people of Lidice of having harbored the still-at-large assassins—and there's no evidence that they had done so—Hitler's SS Gestapo invades the small coal-mining village. According to Dederichs, the SS executes all 184 men—all males over 15. The mass execution takes all night and most of the next day. The 198 women go to Ravensbruck, the infamous women's concentration camp in northern Germany. As Andrew Curry will report:

> Fifty-three died by the end of the war. A few of Lidice's 104 children were given to SS families for "proper upbringing"; 82 of them were gassed. The SS then torched the town, dynamited its houses, school and small church, excavated the town's cemetery, and even re-routed the small stream that ran through it. By early July, there was literally nothing left.

The massacre is, in the words of the Czechoslovak government, "the most dastardly German act since the Dark Ages."[8]

Assassins Gabcik and Kubis, tormented by the slaughter, consider confessing and dying in a "blaze of glory." Instead, they take sanctuary in the crypt of St. Cyril and Methodius

Cathedral in Prague. At 2: 00 a.m. on Thursday, June 18, eight days after the horrors of Lidice, the Gestapo surround the church and invade it just after 4:10 a.m. with guns and grenades, battling the assassins in the choir stalls. The wounded Kubis fatally shoots himself in the head. Gabcik and the surviving patriots take refuge again in the crypt. The Nazis flood it, finally blasting into the area with dynamite, discovering the final four all have shot themselves. The Gestapo decapitates all four, hanging their heads on stakes and ordering their families to identify them. They also shoot the priests who'd afforded Gabcik and Kubis sanctuary.

A Hollywood Jew, incensed by the horrors of Lidice, decides to dramatize the barbarism for the entire world to see—and to produce the saga independently.

*   *   *

> *A friend of mine, maybe the finest producer in Europe at the time,*
> *Seymour Nebenzal, came to America…. [H]e was what I considered*
> *the Selznick of Europe. He was a man of exquisite taste….*
> —Edgar G. Ulmer, interviewed by Peter Bogdanovich,
> published in *Kings of the Bs* (1975)

In the summer of 1942, Seymour Nebenzal, 43-year-old German émigré producer, is preparing the release of his new film *Prisoner of Japan*. Poverty Row's PRC will release the potboiler, which had cost all of $22,186.86.[9]

It's a far cry from his glory days in Germany, when the New York–born Nebenzal was the *wunderkind* of Nero Films. He'd produced the sensational *Pandora's Box* (1929), directed by G.W. Pabst and starring Louise Brooks as Lulu, a prostitute slaughtered by Jack the Ripper at Yuletide. Then there was *People on Sunday* (1930), fashioned by a coterie of young talents destined to make a mark in Hollywood: directors Billy Wilder, Fred Zinnemann, Curt Siodmak, Robert Siodmak, Edgar G. Ulmer, and cinematographer Eugen Schufftan.

Arianne Ulmer Cipes, Edgar's daughter, a former actress who spearheads the Edgar G. Ulmer Preservation Corporation, will recall in 2010:

> These men were of the same "tribe," as it were—a "mix," all intertwined, who went back a long way together…. They all came from the same culture—different cities, but from the Austrian-Hungarian Empire—Jews deeply under Catholic influence.[10]

Nebenzal's productions had been usually quirky, often opulent and sometimes legendary. There was *M* (1931), directed by Fritz Lang and starring Peter Lorre as the child killer, hunted down by the Berlin underworld…. Lang's *The Testament of Dr. Mabuse* (1933), starring Rudolf Klein-Rogge as the mad Mabuse, ruling a crime empire from an insane asylum….

Meanwhile, Josef Goebbels had recognized *The Testament of Dr. Mabuse* as anti–Nazi propaganda. Nebenzal fled Germany and settled in Paris, where he produced the classic romance *Mayerling* (1936). By 1940 he was in Hollywood, producing MGM's *We Who Are Young,* starring Lana Turner, but clashed with the Metro powers-that-were and decided to become independent. At PRC, he headed his own Atlantis Pictures Corp., coping with that company's bargain basement resources and limited distribution, finding the style of better-to-reign-in-Hell-than-serve-in-Heaven freedom he desired.

During the World War II years there are two major independent producers in Hollywood: David O. Selznick and Samuel Goldwyn. Each has impressive contract talent, access to major financing, and distribution of their prestigious product via United Artists. UA warns all prospective producers not to bother with a sales pitch unless they have a budget of at least a half million dollars, and as gossip viper and movie colony observer Hedda Hopper reports:

> Even so, more pictures are announced for United Artists release any year than two majors can make. But there's many a slip between announcement and production. Most of them die a-borning. More these days than ever....[11]

Monday, June 8: Only four days after Heydrich's death and two days before the atrocity begins at Lidice, *Variety* runs this notice:

Figuring Far Ahead

Atlantis Pictures is shaping up yarn out of current headlines, "Himmler's Hangman," for August production for Producers Releasing Corporation.

Nebenzal, of course, is by no means in the big money league for United Artists. Nor is PRC in any shape to finance the Heydrich saga he envisions, nor release the film on a large enough scale that a vast audience would see it. Hence, Nebenzal's Angelus Productions, with headquarters at 9138 Sunset Boulevard in West Hollywood, will proceed totally independently with a three-pronged plan: (1) personally raise the money for the production, (2) film it with PRC staff, and (3) seek a distributor.

Tuesday, June 30: "Nebenzal Will Film *Hangman*," headlines *The Hollywood Reporter*, only 26 days after Heydrich's death.

It's a wildly reckless gamble in the Hollywood of 1942, where everything rests on studio resources, protection, and assured distribution. Meanwhile, advising Nebenzal at the time is Edgar G. Ulmer, who'd directed Universal's devilishly perverse *The Black Cat* (1934), the first teaming of Boris Karloff and Bela Lugosi. Ulmer has also directed such curios as the Yiddish *Green Fields* (1937) and the all-black *Moon Over Harlem* (1938) and is now with Nebenzal at PRC, where he'd scripted *Prisoner of Japan* (as well as directing the final two days in place of Arthur Ripley[12]) and directed *Tomorrow We Live*.

Nebenzal devoutly commits himself to this project; as he finds his ragtag team, he raises his money. The majority comes from one man: Dr. Erwin O. Brettauer, a Swiss businessman and émigré, living in Los Angeles. Brettauer had financed some of Nebenzal's films in Germany, including *M* (for which, by the way, Ulmer had designed the sets). Haunted by Lidice and believing in Nebenzal, Brettauer personally provides $150,926.33 in financing. Additionally, $80,682.07 comes via the California Bank, and $7,193.85 from RCA Manufacturing Co., Inc. Nebenzal now has over $230,000 to produce his picture.[13]

He also finds a scriptwriter: German émigré Emil Ludwig, best-selling biographer of subjects ranging from Napoleon to Jesus Christ to Stalin, but with no film credits. Ludwig works on the script with Albrecht Joseph, later an editor on TV's *Adventures of Superman* and the feature *The Incredible Shrinking Man* (1957). The July 21 *Variety* notes that Ludwig "winds up" his treatment that week, but he soon becomes a liability, as Ludwig will arrogantly tell the *Los Angeles Daily News*:

> I wrote it with my little finger. When you see this picture on the screen, it won't be my story anyway. Some Hollywood specialist, who knows nothing about the subject, will have rewritten it.[14]

Thursday, July 23: *Variety* reports that Angelus Productions wants Erich von Stroheim to play Heydrich. However, von Stroheim had replaced Boris Karloff in Broadway's *Arsenic and Old Lace* the previous month and is committed to the play.

Friday, July 24: George E. Phair writes in his "Retakes" column in *Variety*:

Football players used to "die for dear old Rutgers," and actors sometimes suffer a fate worse than death for their Art. The big idea is to find a thespian courageous enough to play the role of Heydrich the Hangman.

Nebenzal, meanwhile, will consider Francis Lederer for Heydrich—Lederer having worked for him in Germany in *Pandora's Box*.

Wednesday, July 29: A major problem suddenly looms. *Variety,* taking its cue from the song "I'll Be Glad When You're Dead, You Rascal You," runs this report:

Now That Rascal's Dead
They're Fighting Over Him

Hollywood, July 28

Protest against use of the film title, *Heydrich the Hangman*, by United Artists was filed with the Hays office and the Screen Writers Guild by Angelus Pictures, Inc., new company headed by Dr. Edwin Brettauer. Complaint was caused by a recent announcement that Arnold Pressburger would produce a picture of that title for UA release. Angelus claims priority for its own story, *The Hangman*, written by Emil Ludwig and now in preparation to start in six weeks, with Seymour Nebenzal producing.

Aside from a title adjustment, there's little that Nebenzal and Brettauer can do to stop Pressburger; the Heydrich assassination and Lidice tragedy is, of course, public domain. Now battling a rival production, Nebenzal selects *The Hangman*'s talent force:

Monday, August 24: "Sirk Pilots *Hangman*," headlines *Variety*. Edgar Ulmer would seem the logical choice for director, but later claims he personally recruited Douglas Sirk, a German émigré who'd been a brilliant Weimar Republic theater director, as well as a promising talent at Ufa Studios. The 45-year-old Sirk is a perfect choice, for he has a vividly stark history with the Nazis: His first wife, Lydia Brinken, had denounced Sirk to Hitler, noting that Sirk's second wife, actress Hilde Jary, was a Jew. Frau Brinken had also managed to arrange that Sirk would never see their son, Claus Detlef, who became a Hitler Youth and the major child star in German cinema. Finally surrendering hope of getting his son out of Germany, Sirk and Hilde arrived in Hollywood circa 1940, where he'd worked on an unproduced remake of *The Cabinet of Dr. Caligari*. As Douglas Sirk will remember in Jon Halliday's book, *Sirk on Sirk*:

I was offered the picture, which was to be shot at some speed: I was given one week's shooting time. It was specifically presented to me as a very low-budget film, not even a B-feature, but a C- or D-feature. I realized that it was both a chance and a danger. It could be useful and it might launch me. Or it could stick me as a B-feature director. And when this happens to you, no matter how good you are, you can just get stuck. Ulmer, for example, I think is a very good director, but he got stuck with B-features all his time in Hollywood.[15]

Sirk's Nazi nightmares spark his passion—and his decision to direct *The Hangman*.

Eugen Schufftan, another refugee from Hitler, becomes *The Hangman*'s cinematographer. He's a virtuoso who ironically can't gain entry into the Hollywood cinematographers' union. As such, *The Hangman* will bill him as "*Technical Director.*" Since Nebenzal's cameraman is legally unable to shoot a frame of film, the camera credit will go to PRC's card-carrying union member Jack Greenhalgh.[16]

The script, meanwhile, is a problem. Ulmer will claim that the Ludwig-Joseph collaboration on *The Hangman* is "horrible." Ulmer, his wife Shirley and what Ulmer called

John Carradine as Heydrich, suggestively revealing his dagger.

his "gang from the Yiddish picture" all revamp it, the final script cobbled together by at least five writers, and it takes the path of one of Ulmer pet fascinations: good vs. evil. Arianne Ulmer Cipes remembers:

> With Dad, it was very often the Faust concept—he had a fascination with Catholic iconography. We had shadow boxes of the martyr saints on display in our home. Dad had a thing for blonde angelic women ... always the angel. A woman was either a Madonna, blonde and ethereal, or a whore, brunette and evil. This was something he'd taken from Murnau, with whom he'd worked

on *Sunrise* [1927]. In *The Hangman*, there'd be the heroine, Jarmila, a blonde angel, and Heydrich—the devil himself.

As for the Catholic sensibility ... the script for *The Hangman* presents as its iconic talisman a statue of St. Sebastian, the martyr traditionally believed to having been killed *twice* by Roman Emperor Diocletian—first shot full of arrows, and then, after miraculously surviving, beaten to death and tossed into a sewer. In a decidedly baroque touch, the statue's "voice" is to speak to the audience in the opening and closing of the film, proclaiming how conquerors pass away and free men will win victory. To get approval for this and other Catholic imagery in the script, Nebenzal sends a copy to Fr. John J. Devlin of St. Victor's Church in West Hollywood. Fr. Devlin's October 10, 1942, reply:

> [M]y only criticism is the voice of the Saint. To be perfectly frank with you it has a phony quality, particularly in the fadeout of the picture. I suggest that you eliminate the Saint's voice entirely....[17]

The *voice* will go, although the statue stays. Meanwhile, the casting reflects the Good vs. Evil approach, especially in the key role.

* * *

> *"Carradine Heydrich in Indie* Hangman.*"*
> —*Hollywood Reporter* headline, Tuesday, October 13, 1942

John Carradine, notorious screen villain and member of John Ford's famed stock company, is ideal casting as Heydrich, the evil "Lord Over Life and Death." The actor is so infamous that a crowd had recently booed him and thrown debris at him when he'd ridden in a Hollywood parade. Carradine is freelancing, having just left 20th Century–Fox, and has been actively raising money in New York, hoping to star on Broadway as Richard III.

Vowing to portray Heydrich as despicably as possible, Carradine sees *The Hangman* as almost a sacred patriotic duty to the war effort. The 36-year-old actor had desperately wanted to fight and had tried to enlist in the Navy, but was rejected, reportedly due to his teeth. "What do you expect me to do?" he demanded. "*Bite* the Japs to death?"[18]

As it was, the actor joined the "Coast Watch" early in the War, sailing his yacht *The Bali* at night off Santa Monica, keeping his eyes peeled for Japanese ships. He's also been selling war bonds, auctioning off his shirt and suspenders for money and a kiss (from the female bidders, of course).

Nebenzal and Ulmer are thrilled: In John Carradine, *The Hangman* truly has its Devil incarnate.

Having signed its star, director and cinematographer, and having stitched together a script, *The Hangman* still needs a distributor. Meanwhile, Nebenzal continues running afoul of the rival production. It's more threatening than ever—for it's to be produced and directed by a fellow émigré and Hollywood big-leaguer that many in *The Hangman* company know all too well.

* * *

> *He sits with all the airs of a dictator and old movie hand behind his boss-desk, full of drugs and resentment at any good suggestion, collecting surprises, little bits of suspense, tawdry sentimental touches and falsehoods, and takes licenses for the box office.*
> —From the journals of Bertolt Brecht, describing Fritz Lang while
> Brecht wrote the story for their film ***Hangmen Also Die!*** (1943)

Fritz Lang is a genius—as well as "a sadist," recalled Edgar Ulmer, "of the worst order you could imagine." The title of Patrick McGilligan's superb 1997 biography of Lang will be apt: *Fritz Lang: The Nature of the Beast.*

Lang has long been in Hollywood, having escaped Germany, and most recently has been with 20th Century–Fox, where he'd directed the taut anti–Nazi *Man Hunt* (1941). Now he has announced his own film about Lidice, tentatively titled *Never Surrender.* It too, in a sense, is an independent production, Lang co-producing with Arnold Pressburger, but assured of United Artists distribution. Determined his project will be neither a horror film about Heydrich nor emotional propaganda, Lang oddly distances himself from the volatile story and later says:

> If I had felt intense hatred, I would have made the picture differently. As it is, I do not even show the attack on Heydrich. There are no atrocities shown in the picture. We filmed no torture scenes.... We did not make this like any other war pictures. The love story, for example, is incidental.[19]

The accent is to be on the Czech people, honor-bound to protect Heydrich's assassin despite massive executions. Lang recruits Brecht, pillar of Berlin's leftist avant-garde theater—and a man Lang had helped flee Germany—to collaborate with him on the story. The two men quickly clash, Brecht intimidated by Lang's Hollywood fame, fortune, and undeniable arrogance.

For the fictional assassin[20] Dr. Svoboda, Lang signs Brian Donlevy, whom Hedda Hopper hailed as "the hottest thing in town" after he'd starred in Paramount's just-released *Wake Island.*[21] As Heydrich is to be only a minor player in the film, Lang holds off casting the role. The situation is strange and surely intimidating: Lang, by far the most famous and successful of the Nebenzal coterie to flee Germany, is making a film about Lidice that will boast a popular star, a top budget, and United Artists distribution.

Never Surrender powerfully threatens to bury *The Hangman.*

*   *   *

> *Heydrich's line, "...A pretty girl like you can serve so much better*
> *entertaining our courageous German soldiers with her feminine charms..."*
> *should not be over-emphasized in the reading.*
> —Joseph I. Breen, letter to Seymour Nebenzal
> regarding the script for **The Hangman**, October 19, 1942

In Bohemia, Czech patriots tell themselves Heydrich had fallen under the curse of the crown of King Wenceslaus. As *The Hangman* proceeds toward production, it seems to do so under its own curse.

Monday, October 19: It's an especially eventful day and night for *The Hangman.* The morning presents promising news, via *The Hollywood Reporter,* that Republic Studios is "on the verge" of taking on distribution of *The Hangman.* Republic, whose primary fame rests on Gene Autry, John Wayne, Roy Rogers and slam-bang serials, will eventually do a deal in which Consolidated Laboratories—an interest of Republic president Herbert J. Yates—will handle the film processing. If Nebenzal finds a major distributor within 60 days of *The Hangman*'s completion, Republic will share in the profits; otherwise, Republic will distribute the film itself.

The same day: Joseph I. Breen, censorship czar of the Motion Picture Producers and Distributors of America, having reviewed the script, writes a letter to Nebenzal, citing 15 specific trouble areas. Among them:

- A scene showing Lidice villager Bartonek and his wife Maria in bed together: "[P]lease have in mind that the British Board of Film Censors deletes scenes of men and women in bed together, even though they be married."
- Catholic ritual: "The business of the priest making the sign of the cross will probably be deleted by the British Board of Film Censors.... The British Board of Film Censors has usually deleted the 'Our Father.' This latter caution applies to all points in the script where the 'Our Father' is used."
- Heydrich and his (presumably fictitious) mistress, Brigitte: "The greatest care should be exercised.... [We ask] that the business of the girl snuggling against Heydrich and his pulling her closer be eliminated." (The film will eliminate Brigitte altogether.)
- Jarmila and Karel spending a night together: "As now written, these scenes are *unacceptable,* since they suggest that your heroine and hero are on the verge of indulging in a sex affair. They may be shown as sweethearts, but nothing more...."
- Regarding the dying Heydrich's cries for morphine: "Some political censor boards delete such references ... it would be well to substitute another word, such as 'sedative.' ..."
- The execution of the men of Lidice: "Gruesomeness should be avoided.... We urge and recommend that you keep all these scenes in *long shots,* as to get away from close scenes of unacceptable gruesomeness."
- The aftermath of the executions: "[K]indly omit the business of the soldier 'starting to vomit.'"

Pruned during early conferences with Breen had been "the rather definite suggestion" that Heydrich was procuring Czech girls as "prostitutes or white slaves for the German armies in Russia." Eventually the MPPDA permits some dialogue in the classroom by Heydrich to the effect that some girls were being secured for the German troops as "entertainers."

The same day: Nebenzal is closing a deal to sign Frances Farmer, who'd scored in the Group Theatre's *Golden Boy* (1937), to star in *The Hangman* as Jarmila, the doomed Lidice heroine. Ulmer believes she's ideal for the blonde, angelic martyr. Farmer is blonde, but her recent off-screen behavior has been hardly angelic: She'd just departed Paramount amidst rumors of wildly erratic behavior and heavy drinking. Gene Tierney, who'd acted with Farmer in 20th Century–Fox's *Son of Fury* (1942), recalled that Farmer had tantrums on the set, threw things and "literally snarled"[22] at people. Ulmer has encouraged Nebenzal to cast her, despite the Hollywood grapevine reports that Farmer is mentally ill and/or an alcoholic.

That night, 10:30 p.m. EST: NBC Radio in New York City presents Paul Muni leading a cast reading Edna St. Vincent Millay's poem "The Murder of Lidice," backed by NBC's symphony orchestra.

At almost the same time, Frances Farmer is en route to a party at Deanna Durbin's house, driving intoxicated with her lights on through a black-out area in Santa Monica. Frances is abusive to the arresting police—"You bore me," she allegedly tells them—and a night court judge tosses her into Santa Monica City Jail.[23]

Tuesday, October 20: Ironically, the next morning, as the gossip about Farmer circulates through the film colony, *The Hollywood Reporter* headlines, "*Hangman* Gets Farmer." Nebenzal is terrified: Shooting of *The Hangman* is to start in precisely one week! The producer can hardly risk a leading lady who's receiving such bad press. Ulmer, who bristles when anyone used the word "crazy" or "insane," characteristically champions Farmer.

"Cancelled," reads the word beside Frances Farmer's name on *The Hangman*'s production records. The film suddenly and disastrously has no leading lady.

The same day: Edith Gwynn writes in her "Rambling Reporter" column in *The Hollywood Reporter*: "John Carradine sold a heck of a lot of war bonds by kissing the gals with each purchase, but he's not too much of a romantic type to get the lead role of Heydrich in *The Hangman*...."

Thursday, October 22: George Phair writes in his *Variety* "Retakes" column:

> John Carradine draws the most highly prized heavy role of the year as *Heydrich the Hangman*. There is a part wherein the actor is permitted to chew all the scenery in sight, artificial and natural, including all the inhabitants thereof.

Sunday, October 25: The Allied world marks Lidice Memorial Day.

Monday, October 26: *The Hangman* begins shooting, during the week of a full moon. The company works at the Fine Arts Studio, 7324 Santa Monica Boulevard in Hollywood. Contrary to what Douglas Sirk will remember or was perhaps initially told, *The Hangman* has a five-week schedule, and its budget of over $250,000 is literally over ten times the cost of the producer's recent *Prisoner of Japan*.

Tuesday, October 27: Nebenzal signs his new leading lady. She's Patricia Morison, a cinema *femme fatale* who'd made her debut as a gun-toting Bonnie Parker clone in Paramount's *Persons in Hiding* (1939). Ms. Morison is a fiery-looking, auburn-haired movie siren, blessed with the longest hair in Hollywood (39") and looking, frankly, far more the evil voluptuary of Ulmer's fantasies than the blonde angel he favors. He protests, but to no avail. "I was only five years old," Arianne Ulmer Cipes recalls, "but I remember being at the dinner table at our house in Hollywood while Dad and Nebenzal had the big argument. It was really quite something!"

Like Frances Farmer, Morison, who's fated to win Broadway stardom in the Cole Porter musical *Kiss Me Kate* (1948), has just departed Paramount, unhappy at playing heavies. ("I over-ate my way out of the Paramount contract," she'll remember.[24]) She's recently returned from a USO tour of the British Isles with Al Jolson, Merle Oberon and Frank McHugh. Meanwhile, an angry but faithful Ulmer agrees to do second unit work on the picture, and insists his wife Shirley stay on as script supervisor.

"Dad and Nebenzal were still friends," says Arianne Ulmer Cipes.

Then, suddenly, Nebenzal seems destined to receive a great (and overdue) break. Late that week, Fritz Lang's *Never Surrender* is set to start filming. Washington passes a wartime law placing a ceiling

Patricia Morison in a typical vamp pose, showing off the longest hair in Hollywood.

on salaries, meaning that Brian Donlevy, having already earned big money in 1942, will have to star in *Never Surrender* for a very small salary, or maybe none at all. As such, he has the legal right to abandon the film. If he does, the entire project will be stuck with no leading man, likely fall through—and *The Hangman* will have lost its competitor.

Hedda Hopper probably isn't guilty of too much hyperbole when she reports the hysteria as the *Never Surrender* forces await Donlevy's decision:

> The turmoil on the set and in the offices of the head guys was indescribable. Stockholders tore their hair. Lawyers cajoled, argued, threatened.... The Screen Actors Guild advised Brian to do it. He agreed....[25]

It's good news for Lang but very bad news for Nebenzal. The big-budget rival, with a major star and Fritz Lang's direction, will proceed and begins shooting October 31, based at the General Service Studio.

Meanwhile, as Halloween arrives, there's plenty of horror amok in Hollywood. At RKO, Christine Gordon is slinking as the zombie wife in Val Lewton's *I Walked with a Zombie.* At Universal, Lon Chaney is the lycanthrope and Bela Lugosi is the Monster in *Frankenstein Meets the Wolf Man.*

For true Evil, however, John Carradine reigns supreme as *The Hangman.*

* * *

> John Carradine was a "grand" actor, of that "classical" style. It wasn't put on—he was just naturally that way. He spoke like that in everyday conversation! He was from another time in a way, another era, the classical era....
>
> There was Carradine's presence. I mean, you couldn't *not* look at him! Some people fade away on screen, even good actors, but when Carradine was on the screen, even when he wasn't doing anything, you *had* to look at him.... We have a lot of good actors in film today, but very few have that screen charisma that knocks you out. Some people have it, whether they're playing heroes, or sexpots, or villains—and John Carradine had it.
>
> Of course, I didn't have many scenes with Carradine personally in *Hitler's Madman.* We worked together in the Angeles Forest, in the snow and the mountains. I killed him—Alan Curtis and me!
>
> —Patricia Morison, interview with the author, 1998[26]

The Hangman begins wistfully, almost in fairy tale fashion, an off-screen narrator reciting the early verses of Edna St. Vincent Millay's "The Murder of Lidice." This is a *coup*—Fritz Lang had wanted to use the poem for his Lidice film, but Nebenzal gets the rights. As the poem proceeds, we see a pastoral Lidice, its water wheel, its church steeple, all under Smetana's *Die Moldau*—PRC's Budapest-born Karl Hajos providing the stirring score.[27] There's Lidice's statue of St. Sebastian, standing in a pose of proud anguish, wearing a halo and protruding arrows. The first interior shot focuses on a crucifix.

Along with this statue of a saint and the figure of the crucified Christ, we soon behold Lucifer—in flesh and blood. As Heydrich, John Carradine, parading about in full Nazi regalia and a vulture's beak of a false nose, chillingly transforms the make-believe into cold, bitter reality. As Douglas Sirk will say:

> In fact, John Carradine *was* Heydrich ... a stage actor, and more particularly, a Shakespearean stage actor, with a reputation of going overboard. A lot of Nazis behaved like Shakespearean actors.... [H]e was excellent for the part. He had a certain dry theatricality, which is just what I wanted.

The makeup department toned down Patricia Morison's glamour for *Hitler's Madman*; still, that's a lot of lipstick for a Czechoslovakian village girl.

Sirk also had an advantage: He'd met Reinhard Heydrich. In Jon Halliday's book *Sirk on Sirk,* the director will recall:

I did not know Heydrich well, but I had met him at a party in Berlin. It must have been one of the awful parties Ufa was always throwing.... [B]eing a very optical man, I got a good impression of his face, and it was very interesting. The thing was that Heydrich had been in the German Navy.... I started out at the German Naval Academy at Murwik.... Heydrich had been there, too— but I think he was younger than I was.... He must have heard I'd been to Murwik, and so he came over to me at this party. He was in mufti, but he had the Nazi button.... [H]e looked and behaved just like Carradine.[28]

A sculptor, Carradine creates a bust of Heydrich, fashioning his false nose for the role. The *Screen Guide* (March 1943) feature "Villains Aren't So TOUGH!" will give ample coverage to Carradine's Heydrich nose, showing the actor personally whipping up the appendage in a pot on a stove and noting:

First step in the transformation of amiable John into vicious, ill-tempered Reinhard Heydrich, onetime head of the Gestapo, is the preparation of a gelatinous substance made from gum, sugar and formaldehyde! This is poured into a plastic mold, allowed to cool. The new nose is held in place by spirit gum.... John's next job is to blend the false skin with his own. The success of this operation determines the life-like quality his character makeup assumes. John has no trouble here. Heydrich, the arch fiend, comes to life!

To assure readers Carradine is actually benign, the feature runs a picture of him reading *Robinson Crusoe* to son John (aka David) and stepson Bruce.

Morison effectively plays Jarmila, actually capturing the sad angel quality Ulmer had desired; she wears her flowing dark hair in a bun that, à la the St. Sebastian statue, almost seems to have a halo around it. In 1942, Morison—who turned 99 in 2014—was living near the ocean in Pacific Palisades, where she'd pass the gun emplacements as she walked the beach:

I remember very well *The Hangman*'s original backer, Brettauer.... The interesting thing was that, at this time of Hitler, Dr. Brettauer was Jewish, but his little wife was a true German peasant girl with blonde braids around her ears—I'll never forget her! Long after we made the film, and after I'd sold my house in the Palisades, they lived near me in the Hollywood Hills at the top of La Brea, and I used to see them walking their two little dachshunds. They were charming!

For Karel, the fictional assassin, Nebenzal and Ulmer have selected Alan Curtis, mustached former model who'd recently appeared in Bogart's *High Sierra*. In 1941, Curtis had married Ilona Massey, MGM's blonde Hungarian opera star—who'd walked away from being mistress to a Metro producer to marry Curtis. MGM had vindictively dumped Massey, blackballing the newlyweds; as Curtis signs for *The Hangman,* La Massey stars in Universal's *Frankenstein Meets the Wolf Man.* At any rate, the two stars have separated, Massey blaming her hard-drinking husband.

Ralph Morgan (brother of Frank Morgan of *The Wizard of Oz*), wearing a walrus mustache, portrays Hanka, Jarmila's father. Morgan has just played the title role in Universal's *Night Monster,* flanked by Bela Lugosi and Lionel Atwill; in the spring of 1942, he'd starred as Mayor Orden in the Broadway play version of John Steinbeck's *The Moon Is Down.* As Hanka, the always excellent Morgan evokes a grizzled apostle, transforming from pacifist to avenger who joins in the assassination plot. Although Jews produce *The Hangman,* the look and feel—as envisioned by Ulmer and captured by Sirk—is very much Catholic prayer book.

Alan Curtis, Ralph Morgan and Patricia Morison as the heroic assassins of *Hitler's Madman*. Note the crucifix on the wall—the film is rich in Catholic iconography.

Horror devotees will immediately recognize Ludwig Stossel, fated to die agonizingly in Ulmer's *Bluebeard* (PRC, 1944) and in *House of Dracula* (Universal, 1945), although many others will remember him as "That Little Ole Winemaker, Me!" from the Italian Swiss Colony Wine commercials of the 1960s. Respected by Ulmer for his stage work with Max Reinhardt, the short, plump Stossel is a standout as the cowardly Burgomaster Bauer, who cooperates with the Nazis, only to be later arrested by them and scream for mercy.

"Mamma!" he cries to his wife. "They are taking me... Heil Hitler! Heil Hitler!"

Effectively cast as Maria Bartonek, soon-to-be-widowed villager, is Elizabeth Russell, darling of the Val Lewton RKO horror films. She sadly slinks through *The Hangman,* suggesting an all-in-black Madonna, an unnerving presence despite the sympathetic nature of her role. Elizabeth's big scene: joyfully preparing supper for her husband (played by Richard Bailey), whom the Nazis have promised to return home after questioning. Come the knock on the door, and two men bring him home—in a coffin.

For all these horror episodes, a surprising number of comic character actors appear in *The Hangman,* all in dramatic roles. Indeed, the first actor to sign for the film (on September 24, over a month before shooting started) had been bald, blustery Edgar Kennedy, "King of the Slow Burn," well-remembered for his work with Laurel and Hardy and clearly relishing his heroic part of Nepomuk, a marauding mountain hermit.[29] Bespectacled, 74-year-old Al Shean, of the famed vaudeville team of Gallagher and Shean, has signed on as Fr. Semlanik, possibly the most Semitic-looking priest in film history. Strangest of all, Hobart Cavanaugh, a weak-chinned stooge in many comedies, cops the role of the sinuous Heinrich Himmler. Such casting is a definite eccentricity of *The Hangman,* as the comic players threaten to remind audiences of a pie fight.

Yet grim, fervent conviction wins the day—and *The Hangman* is John Carradine's show all the way. As Morison remembers, the actor "took himself terribly seriously" as Heydrich, and set a baroque tone of Nazi lechery and depravity. We first see Heydrich in his office, seated at his desk, signing execution papers, learning of sabotage:

> Another ammunition train blown up. This must stop. I know what's wrong. We've been shooting them *after* they commit sabotage. We must catch them *before*—get the organizers, the intellectuals. They're the ones. We'll teach them. Intellect is poison!

Heydrich and his Gestapo crash the University, where an aged professor (Tully Marshall) is lecturing on Kant and the credo that "sufficient pressure would be able to destroy its own counter-pressure, but this is not necessarily true. Force and violence destroy only bodies, never the essence of the opposing force." The Reichsprotektor, recognizing the subversive political message, takes the professor's place, sits, places his foot up on the desk and proceeds:

> Intelligence is a great thing, backed up by force.... As your Protector, I feel it is my duty to offer you the necessary counterbalance for intellect in the stimulating climate of bombs and shells. I ask you to form a labor legion for the Russian front. All those in favor, please raise their hands! [*Pause*] Very regrettable! Not even one!

With no volunteers, Heydrich plans to send the male students to a concentration camp, and then casts his lecherous eye on rebellious female student Clara (Jorja Curtright, aka Jorja Rollins):

> Naturally, I am not sending ladies to concentration camps. They will go to the Russian front instead of the men, not, of course, to dig trenches. No, lovely one, I would never think ... of that. A pretty girl like you can serve so much better, entertaining our courageous German soldiers!

The Hangman moves from lechery to sacrilege and its most strikingly haunting episode: the Blessing of the Fields. It opens on sunny wheat fields waving in a gentle wind, the faithful worshippers singing an Alleluia, altar boys, men carrying a statue of Christ, burning candles, and old Father Semlanik presiding. Then, from the point of view of the bell tower, we see Heydrich's speeding open car. "What sort of carnival is this?" demands Heydrich.

His car drives wildly into the procession, scattering the crowd, the men running, the women screaming. Heydrich confronts the priest, Carradine looming over Al Shean, as if hungry to pick his bones. Ralph Morgan's Hanka tries to make peace:

> *Priest*: Quiet, Hanka. Turn the other cheek.
> *Heydrich*: So that's what you do, eh? Turn the other cheek?
> *Priest*: So it is written.

And Heydrich slaps the priest! The imagery again is iconic: Satan himself violating a man of God. Hanka lunges to the priest's defense, but Father Semlanik holds him back:

> *Priest*: Out of the dust Man rises and to the dust he shall surely return ... and when the day comes, you shall be judged less than the dust which covers your boots.

The shocking "Blessing of the Fields" episode: John Carradine, as Heydrich, confronts Al Shean as the village priest.

> *Heydrich*: So you think I can't provoke you? [*snatching the cloth off the litter that holds the Christ statue and wiping his boots with it*] How is this, my holy sufferer?
> *Priest*: That's sacred cloth!

Fr. Semlanik tries to grab the cloth and Heydrich's bull-necked bodyguard Muller (John Merton) shoots him—three times! The crowd gasps and Heydrich casually tosses the profaned cloth atop the dead priest:

> *Heydrich*: So I couldn't provoke him, eh?

A woman falls to her knees to pray. A little girl asks, "Mother, are they going to kill us *all?*"

The episode, with its blasphemy, sadism and payoff cold-blooded murder, is still a shocker today, as it must have been for the original audiences. Indeed, upon the film's release, the Pennsylvania state censor will demand a cut: "Eliminate views showing Heydrich's boots actually being dusted with sacred cloth."

While on the pastoral location site, the lead players, aware of the overwhelming grimness

Opposite, top: **Carradine's Heydrich profanes the sacred cloth, wiping his boots with it...** *Bottom:* **... then sneers over the priest who'd fatally tried to stop the sacrilege.**

of the episode, afford the company a bit of escapist entertainment: Al Shean, in priest attire, performs his old Gallagher and Shean vaudeville act, while John Carradine, in full Nazi regalia, recites a soliloquy from Shakespeare's *Richard III.*

The sequence naturally primes audiences for the exciting assassination scene, filmed in the picturesque Angeles Forest in the San Gabriel Mountains. Morison's Jarmila rides her bicycle in front of the open car of Carradine's Heydrich. "A beautiful girl means a beautiful day!" leers Carradine as only he can. Alan Curtis's Karel opens fire. Ralph Morgan's Hanka throws a grenade. The car crashes quite spectacularly, the assassins escape, and as an SS trooper on motorcycle approaches the scene, he falls too, shot down by Edgar Kennedy's Nepomuk. It's a good "button" to a scene that has very little to do with the actual assassination, but plays as a truly visceral crowd-pleaser.

Major death scenes follow—one of them our heroine's. Nazi pursuers shoot Jarmila as she and Karel escape the village; she dies in a mountain hut. "You're crying!" she says to Karel; "No I'm not," he lies. Morison has portrayed her heroine with beauty and bravery, and the sight of Jarmila's grave in the forest as Karel sadly continues his escape, is yet another intense moment in *The Hangman.*

As for Carradine's own magnificently baroque death scene: It will be reshot at MGM,

The slaughter: Elizabeth Russell (from *Cat People* and *The Curse of the Cat People*) and Blanche Yurka face the climactic atrocity of *Hitler's Madman*.

so this chapter will cover it later. The film's climax—Hitler's revenge, the Gestapo marching into Lidice, the women screaming as the Nazis herd them into trucks, the children crying, the men singing the Czech national anthem "Where Is My Home?" as the Nazis machine-gun them against a church wall—is heartrending. The singing male victims might seem pure Hollywood, but the event is reportedly historically accurate, and Sirk captures the final defiance touchingly and brilliantly.

Explosions. Fire. Flames of Hell imagery. And in a denouement far better seen than described, angelic voices sing "Where Is My Home?" as the specters of dead patriots rise from the carnage. There's a moment's temptation to smirk at the theatricality, but you can't—the anger, passion and depth of sincerity of the director and actors are all too intense. The ghosts approach the camera, addressing the audience, reciting verses from "The Murder of Lidice." The last to appear is Richard Bailey's Bartonek. The singing swells. Sirk and Schufftan create a truly beautiful final imagery, the statue of St. Sebastian, with its halo and arrows, still standing, seemingly mournful but proudly inviolate. Bells ring. The light and clouds are magnificent, as if Heaven itself is weeping of this atrocity. The end title appears.

* * *

Tuesday, November 10: "Carradine Wraps Up One," headlines *The Hollywood Reporter*, adding: "John Carradine completed his role in *The Hangman* and starts in *Never Surrender* for Fritz Lang Nov. 15."

Apparently, the star of *The Hangman* is joining the competition! Although the role isn't mentioned, presumably Carradine will play Heydrich again in *Never Surrender*, the way Bobby Watson played Hitler and Martin Kosleck played Goebbels in several films.[30] However, the November 13 *Hollywood Reporter* lists Hans von Twardowski in the cast of *Never Surrender*, and it will be von Twardowski—who'd acted in *The Cabinet of Dr. Caligari* and for Lang in *Spies* (1928)—who'd portray Heydrich in Lang's film.

Nebenzal and Sirk continue work on *The Hangman* through November and into December. Carradine, meanwhile, reports to Universal, playing a mad doctor who transforms a gorilla into brunette starlet Acquanetta in *Captive Wild Woman*, which begins shooting December 11.[31] The former Heydrich is starring in a horror movie that will strike some then (and many today) as rabidly racist Nazi propaganda: Hitler had called the Negro "a half-born ape," and in her *Captive Wild Woman* transformation, Acquanetta—before turning into an ape woman—turns black.

Perhaps the strangest irony will follow in January 1943. Carradine signs to play yet another Nazi in Monogram's *I Escaped from the Gestapo*. The leading lady: Frances Farmer, who during shooting, slaps a hairdresser, knocking her down and dislocating her jaw. As Carradine will remember:

> We were shooting a scene and all of a sudden she stood against a pillar and started singing dirty songs. She refused to stop and the studio wanted to call the police. I said, "The police! What this girl needs is a doctor." But the really frightening thing is the next morning they had already recast Mary Brian in the role.[32]

A sad scrap of film showing a dazed-looking Frances Farmer, pulling a shawl over her head, remains in *I Escaped from the Gestapo* in a montage sequence. More widely seen are real-life photographs of a policeman violently wrestling with a hysterical Farmer in court. Her famous descent into asylums follows, her pitiful legend later filmed as *Frances* (1982) with Jessica Lange in the title role.

* * *

"Hangman Sold to MGM for Release"
—*The Hollywood Reporter,* Page 1 headline, February 4, 1943

Records indicate that Nebenzal tinkers with *The Hangman,* hiring actors as late as December 19. One suspects he might do this to extend his chances for major distribution, as Republic's option is set to expire February 15. On January 29, 1943, *The Hangman* officially receives its certificate of approval, no. 9121, from the MPPDA.

Then a virtual miracle comes to pass for Seymour Nebenzal: Metro-Goldwyn-Mayer announces it will acquire and release *The Hangman.* It's a Cinderella story, Hollywood studio-style. On Thursday, February 4, *The Hollywood Reporter* notes:

> Reports yesterday were that MGM may put it back into work for a few added scenes and additional production outlay.... Made independently, Angelus gave Republic an option on the picture, expiring Feb. 15, but kept a free rein to negotiate a bigger deal if it could.

Based on studio records, MGM's payment barely covers Nebenzal's negative cost of $280,000. Meanwhile, Republic, per its original deal with Nebenzal, is entitled to a share of any profits MGM will earn releasing *The Hangman*—and is very angry at Nebenzal for jumping the gun on its option. Still, it's major news in Hollywood, and a triumph for Nebenzal and independent production.

Friday, February 5: "Refugees Gambled and Won with *The Hangman*" headlines *The Hollywood Reporter:*

> Behind the sale of *The Hangman* to MGM is the amazing story of a group of refugees who gambled their money in producing a picture without a release—and hit the bulls-eye....[33]

MGM meanwhile assures Nebenzal he'll have approval of the changes to come, and that Douglas Sirk will direct the new scenes. Assigned to *The Hangman* is Howard Emmett Rogers, a prolific MGM contract writer whose work had included an adaptation of *Tarzan and His Mate* (1934), the screenplay for Jean Harlow's *Libeled Lady* (1936) and, most recently, the story for Judy Garland's *For Me and My Gal* (1942). He's a trusted in-house talent, whose home studio pays him 52 weeks per year rather than the usual 40. Rogers' job is to analyze *The Hangman* and add scenes and touches that will help the film appear more in the league of MGM product.

Saturday, February 27: Rogers (who will be uncredited) has completed a 42-page script noted "Retakes," its cover bearing a typed stamp of approval: "Script okayed by Mr. Nebenzal."

The Hangman will receive polish, promotion, and distribution from the most powerful studio in Hollywood. This seeming salvation is well-timed: Fritz Lang is about to release his Lidice film, now titled *Hangmen Also Die!*

* * *

"Lang was an absolute monster to me!"
—Anna Lee, remembering ***Hangmen Also Die!***[34]

Fritz Lang's Lidice movie has proceeded with considerable misery—especially for the leading lady.

Playing the gallant heroine is Anna Lee, fresh from John Ford's 1941 Academy Award–

winning Best Picture, *How Green Was My Valley.* (Horror fans best remember her as Boris Karloff's leading lady in *The Man Who Changed his Mind* [1936] and *Bedlam* [1946].) In 1991, Ms. Lee, during her long, happy run as Lila Quartermaine on TV's *General Hospital,* spoke with me about *Hangmen Also Die!* and recalled that the banks financing his film had rejected Lang's girlfriend, Virginia Gilmore, for the lead. Lang then subjected Lee to a reign of terror, forcing her to remove her high heels, claiming she was too tall—then stomping on her bare feet in his "big Prussian boots." He also has demanded that she punch her hand through a real glass carriage window—and when she didn't cut herself, he demanded she repeat the scene until she did.

"I really got a bad cut," said Ms. Lee. "My whole wrist was cut open. It could have been quite dangerous if I'd hit that main artery, but fortunately I didn't." Lang—who, as Lee recalled was then "a sick man, obviously on drugs "—ogled her cut wrist and then, like a vampire, began lapping up the blood.

Lang's cast is impressive. Three-time Academy Award winner Walter Brennan plays against type as the heroine's father, a Czech professor, and Gene Lockhart is the treacherous "Quisling," framed for Heydrich's assassination by Czech patriots and shot down on the steps of a church. As for Heydrich ... Lang has stuck to his guns about showing neither his assassination nor the razing of Lidice, but does present Heydrich in an early scene, as played by Hans von Twardowski. As Heydrich, Twardowski enters sporting a monocle, fondling a riding crop, and swaying his hips, instantly giving an impression of perversion, screaming and shrieking his lines in German, leaning almost seductively back on a desk to pose luxuriantly under a giant portrait of Hitler. The role is virtually a cameo, but it powerfully resounds throughout the 135-minute film.

The shoot has become especially unhappy for Bertolt Brecht. When Brecht wrote a non-dialogue role of a vegetable seller for his actress wife Helene Weigel, Lang spitefully cast another actress, Sarah Padden, in the part. But most bitter is the fight Brecht will wage with John Wexley, who will receive the solo screenplay credit; Brecht is only credited as co-writer of the story with Lang. In what seems almost absurdist today, Brecht even faces the indignity of having his name on the credits "Americanized" to "Bert Brecht."

Lang's film has its exciting moments, captured by the masterful cinematographer James Wong Howe. But overall, Lang has directed with a curious detachment, almost as if afraid of becoming too emotionally obsessed by the genuine horror of his subject. And speaking of horror, a curio: Playing a bit as an imprisoned Czech is Dwight Frye, Renfield of *Dracula* and Fritz of *Frankenstein,* and fresh from his role as a villager in *Frankenstein Meets the Wolf Man.* It will be one of Frye's final films before his untimely death.

Meanwhile, as *Hangmen Also Die!* faces its United Artists release and *The Hangman* prepares for an MGM makeover, a sleeper emerges from RKO: *Hitler's Children,* based on Gregor Zeimer's novel *Education for Death.*[35] The film tells of the love affair of Hitler Youth Karl (Tim Holt) and American-born Anna (Bonita Granville). It also features Otto Kruger as evil Nazi Henkel, and offers sensation aplenty. Perhaps its most notorious scene presents a clinic where the Nazis sterilize women deemed unfit to bear German children.

Hitler's Children opens February 24, 1943, soaring to become the highest grossing film in RKO's history, surpassing both *King Kong* and *Top Hat.* Cost: $205,000; worldwide rentals: $3,355,000; profit: $1,210,000.

Can either *Hangmen Also Die!* or *The Hangman* match *Hitler's Children* in box office potency?

The rival production: Hans von Twardowski as Heydrich in the opening of *Hangmen Also Die!*, directed by Fritz Lang.

*   *   *

"New Hangman scenes for MGM"
—headline in *The Hollywood Reporter,* March 1, 1943

Monday, March 1: MGM starts retakes on *The Hangman* this week.[36]

• Some retakes are minor, simply to add polish. For example, in the original, Ralph Morgan's Hanka leaves his house early in the film, telling his family he'll tend to the horses. The film then cuts to the plane from which assassin Alan Curtis parachutes. Howard Emmett

Rogers adds an "exterior" to sharpen the transition: Morgan "outside," hearing the plane and looking up at it. It's actually a process shot filmed on a stage, and Rogers notes in his Retakes script: "Use as PROCESS PLATE the stock shot from *Florian* [a 1940 MGM release], showing the farm house with the horses in the foreground."

• A new scene shows Curtis observing a raggedy band of Czech laborers, marching and guarded by Nazi soldiers. "My side—it is paining!" says an ill laborer. "You Czechs are always complaining!" says a soldier. "Get back in line!" Playing the ailing laborer, incidentally, is Michael Mark—Maria's father in *Frankenstein* and a familiar bit player in many horror films.

• The script calls for stock shots of a "mountainside" and exterior shots of Prague—again for transition.

• Rogers reworks and expands Jarmila's love scene with Karel and beefs up Karel's exhortations to the villagers to help in sabotage. Off-screen voices are added, spouting lines such as "Karel Havra is right!"

• There are new scenes in Gestapo headquarters. Playing Lt. Buelow—Hans von Twardowski, who'd just portrayed Heydrich in *Hangmen Also Die!*

• A new sequence has German soldiers come to Hanka's house after the assassination— unaware he was one of the assassins—and press him into service.[37]

However, the most notable new scene is, to use a Hollywood ballyhoo term of the time, a "socko-boffo." Aware of the stir caused by the sterilization scene of *Hitler's Children,* H.E. Rogers has written an episode in which Heydrich leers at various Lidice village girls, preparing to send them to the Russian front as prostitutes—and subject them to gynecological examinations for venereal disease. Carradine will ogle MGM's most luscious starlets in a sensually vile vignette fashioned to out-shock *Hitler's Children,* inspire all variety of word of mouth, and surely lure the morbidly curious masses to see *The Hangman.*

Wednesday, March 3: Joseph Breen is amazed and appalled. Reviewing the draft of the scene, he fires off this letter to Louis B. Mayer:

> We regret to report to you that it is our considered and unanimous judgment that all of this action ... dealing with Heydrich's interest in procuring Czech girls as prostitutes for the German army on the Russian front, together with the showing of the room where they are examined by physicians for this assignment, is completely and entirely unacceptable under the provisions of the Production Code....

Thursday, March 4: MGM scores at the Academy Awards, *Mrs. Miniver* enjoying its six–Oscar triumph. (Best Director winner William Wyler that night is reportedly filming a bombing raid over Germany.) In this post–Oscar euphoria, MGM ignores Breen's dictate.

The result is a true curio, due to the various MGM starlets as the "Sacrificial Daughters of Lidice," the carnal nature of the scene, and the diabolic lechery that Carradine—truly earning his $2,500 per week—so vividly provides. The ladies stand on a platform, as in a line-up, under bright lighting and relatively unadorned; according to the pressbook, technical advisor Felix Bernstein, in reviewing the starlets, made sure that "fingernail polish, rouge and lipstick were barred. High heels, silk stockings and jewelry also went the way of the cosmetics."

The camera suggestively focuses on Carradine's hips and thighs as he straddles a chair. His bodyguard Muller stands by as a guard introduces each girl. Among them:

Guard: Eliza Cermak, age 16.

The infamous new scene: John Carradine (seated) as Heydrich, and the "sacrificial daughters" of Lidice. This censor-defying episode almost prevented the release of Hitler's Madman. In the line-up of ladies, Frances Rafferty is second from left; Vicky Lane, fourth from left; Ava Gardner, fifth from left.

Playing Eliza is Metro's Frances Rafferty, previously a member of the Hollywood Bowl Ballet Company and a drama student of Maria Ouspenskaya. She'd played a showgirl in *Presenting Lily Mars,* and is destined to achieve her top fame on the TV sitcom *December Bride* (1954–1959). Frances' Eliza wears glasses, which her persecutors snatch away:

Eliza: But I need them for reading! Please! Please don't take my...

Heydrich: Tsk, tsk, tsk... There, you see, Muller? Nothing but misled daughters of Eve.... Well, Eliza Cermak, you will not need your glasses any more. We might send her to the army headquarters....

Eliza [*shocked*]: Oh!

Heydrich (*with a sardonic smile, remembering the professor's lecture*): She could lecture about ... [*suggestively*] ... "pressure creates counter-pressure." Wasn't that it? Next one!

Incidentally, Carradine reads the "counter-pressure" line so lasciviously that the Ohio state censor will cut it!

Guard: Katy Chotnik, age 17.

Playing Katy is raven-haired Vicky Lane, also a showgirl in *Presenting Lily Mars.* Vicky has played the sexpot assistant to the Devil (Edward Arnold) in the MGM short *Inflation*

(1943) and will later lurk as Paula the Ape Woman in Universal's *The Jungle Captive* (1945). From 1948 to 1950 she will be the wife of Tom Neal, star of *Detour* (1945), who will eventually go to prison for murdering his later wife.

> *Heydrich*: Katy is very beautiful ... indeed! She should be popular. What a very cold stare, Katy! Well, our brave German soldiers on the Russian front are used to conquering the cold, I guess. Next one!
>
> *Guard*: Franciska Petrick, age 17.

And there's a full-bloom, 20-year-old Ava Gardner, in the midst of her 16-month run as Mrs. Mickey Rooney and then playing MGM bits such as Perfume Girl in *DuBarry Was a Lady*. Ava's an eyeful, but simply cries and has no dialogue; MGM will soon farm her out to Monogram to star with the East Side Kids and Bela Lugosi in *Ghosts on the Loose*.

> *Heydrich*: Very lovely. Too bad she's a Czech. Next one.

Eventually we see again Jorja Curtwright as Clara Janek, the rebellious student from the university:

> *Heydrich*: Ahh, my little friend Clara!

And we soon get a glimpse (with a blast of ominous music) of the examination room. As the Retakes script describes it:

> The room beyond, which has overhead lighting, is a large high-ceilinged room with four delivery tables (such as are used by gynecologists to examine women) visible. Groups of white-robed doctors and assistants are standing by the tables. Eight or ten girls have already gone into the room.
>
> *Clara*: Don't go in there! We'll be examined as if we were cattle—then we'll be sent to the Russian front!!

The scene climaxes with Clara, fatally defiant, tears running down her face, taking a last stand on a window sill. Joseph Breen had cautioned MGM that Clara's "glorified suicide" was unacceptable, but she jumps to her death anyway. We don't see her jump, the camera only showing the shocked faces of the other ladies.

> *Heydrich*: There, you see, Muller? Another victim of the intellect!

Heydrich's death scene is also an MGM retake, and masterfully played and directed: Heydrich in a baroque bed, wailing, "I'm bleeding to death! ... If I don't get morphine, I'll have you shot. I'll have you *all* shot!" (Note the morphine reference stayed, despite Breen's objection.) MGM had deleted the Himmler performance by Hobart Cavanaugh, reporting he was "excellent" but that his familiarity as a comic player made him unsuitable to play Himmler. Howard Freeman, the new Himmler, plump and prissy, waddles in to keep a deathbed vigil as Carradine acts one of the great scenes of his almost 60-year film career:

> *Heydrich*: We'll be the only ones to lose.... We were too weak! That's it! Every day I had them shoot thirty—it should have been three hundred, Himmler! Three thousand! Day for day! ... I should have done away with them all—all of them—all of them.... Kill them if you want to be safe, every day, all of them. Shoot them! Shoot them! Kill!

And he expires. Perhaps the story had spread, but the lighting by Sirk and Schufftan of Carradine's "death mask" suggests the "entirely perverted beauty, like a Renaissance Cardinal," that the investigator who had witnessed Heydrich's death had reported. At any rate, the death scene will inspire fervent cheers wherever the film will play.

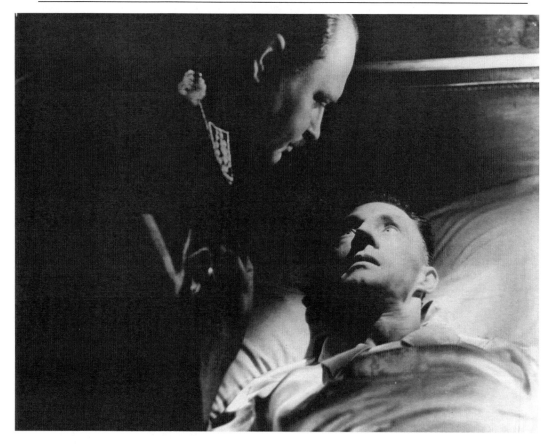

Heydrich's death scene: "Shoot them ... shoot them!" John Carradine as Heydrich, Howard Freeman as Himmler.

At last it's finished—again. MGM's final negative cost on *The Hangman,* after the purchase from Nebenzal and retakes: $405,678.81.[38]

Monday, March 22: Fritz Lang's *Hangmen Also Die!* previews in Los Angeles. "Grimness Shouldn't Hinder Box Office," headlines *The Hollywood Reporter,* praising the film as "in many ways, a masterpiece of its kind."

Friday, March 26: "Repub, Angelus In *Hangman* Tangle," runs a *Hollywood Reporter* headline, noting that Republic has officially protested Nebenzal selling *The Hangman* to MGM and that arbitration will follow. "Dispute is between Angelus and Republic, with MGM involved only as a third party," according to the article. Judge Lester Roth will represent Republic, attorney Jules Cove will fight for Angelus, and Jerry Geisler—who later in 1943 will defend Errol Flynn in the star's rape trial—will sit "on the outside." No outcome will be announced. At the very least, Nebenzal has taken on new legal expenses.

Tuesday, April 13: The Motion Picture Producers and Distributors of America sees what MGM has retitled *Hitler's Hangman,* which includes the episode of Heydrich and the Czech girls that Joseph Breen had axed. Result: outrage. "The present version represents some changes from the original," C.R. Metzger of the MPPDA writes in a report: "Much of the charm and originality of the Angelus production has been eliminated." Metzger gives a summary of the film's censorship history, and then takes aim at MGM:

> When Metro bought this finished production, they sent in added scenes dramatizing the selection and procurement of these girls by Heydrich, which dramatization we disapproved.... Metro also re-inserted the glorified suicide of one of the girls, Clara, which we likewise disapproved. Upon receipt of our letter of March 3, Mr. Al Block, of Metro, telephoned the undersigned and stated that the producers assigned to this story at Metro had seen the "clinical" sequence of the picture, *Hitler's Children* (RKO), and were determined to include a similar sequence in their re-editing of *The Hangman*. Mr. Shurlock, who had reviewed *Hitler's Children*, called attention to the fact that the clinical sequence in that picture dealt with the sterilization of girls believed unacceptable as mothers of the future German race. The present clinical sequences of *The Hangman* seemed to suggest only an examination for possible venereal disease, and whether these Czech girls should be acceptable as prostitutes for the German soldiers.

MGM, determined to upstage *Hitler's Children* in sensationalism, refuses to cut the episode as legendary studio manager Eddie "Bulldog" Mannix prepares for battle. Result: The MPPDA withholds a certificate of release.

Nebenzal's noble endeavor, for which he and his company had worked so passionately, is suddenly in a Hollywood Limbo.

Joseph Breen, in New York and having missed the screening of *Hitler's Hangman*, learns of the firestorm and responds by telegram:

> Impossible without having seen Metro opus to pass any judgment. I suggest that here again extenuating circumstances of war have important bearing on general acceptability and suggest staff examine picture and advise Mannix of decision.

Thursday, April 15: The decision comes quickly. On the same day *Hangmen Also Die!* opens at the Capitol Theatre in New York, Breen informs MGM that the original certificate for *The Hangman*, no. 9121, "will apply as to this re-edited version." The world will see an uncut *Hitler's Hangman*—sacrificial daughters of Lidice included.

Tuesday, June 8: Two days before the first anniversary of the Lidice slaughter, MGM hosts a tradeshow of *Hitler's Hangman* in Los Angeles. The result, for the most part, will be a critical slaughter.

Wednesday, June 9: The *Hollywood Reporter* brutally pans *Hitler's Hangman*, claiming the screen treatment is "in no manner commensurate with the importance of its subject" and calling most of the cast "embarrassingly bad." The same day, *Daily Variety* also gives a thumbs down, noting, "Cast, text and treatment will confine it to secondary billing."

Saturday, June 12: *Showman's Trade Review* sees much to admire:

> Well, here it is in picture form—the visualization of an act that will go down in history as one of the most barbaric crimes ever committed. For the squeamish, this will be hard to take.... Scenes like the separation of mothers and children and the lining up of all men against a wall, will tear the heart out of most people and will be long remembered.... [I]t should be seen by every American, for one is left with a sense of horror and hatred at the cruelty of man-against-man and a desire to pitch in and help rid the world of such vile creatures.... The most outstanding portrayal is John Carradine's. You hate him with such vehemence that you actually forget he's an American playing a role....

Monday, June 14: *Film Bulletin* calls *Hitler's Hangman* "too grim, morbid and depressing," and adds, "Aside from a striking characterization of Heydrich by John Carradine, the cast, the playing, the dialogue are well below Metro standards." The overall trade reviews convince MGM that *Hitler's Hangman* is surely not what Louis B. Mayer had hoped it would be. Indeed, it might very well prove a livid embarrassment.

MGM apparently suspected as much. Metro has decided to sell the film as a horror movie, giving it a third title—*Hitler's Madman*—and the pressbook suggests exhibitors try these sideshow stunts:

> A giant transparent skull, illuminated by a red flasher light and with the line "I Am Violent Death!" drenched in lurid red paint, will certainly bring your patrons up short ... use real rope with a hangman's noose and suspend from a real wooden crosspiece.... A real skeleton borrowed from medical society, will secure the ultimate in horrifying appeal when displayed on your advance lobby.... As an advance screen flash, throw a picture of a horrible-looking hangman's noose on the screen together with the shocker—"Coming! To Chill You with Terror! *Hitler's Madman*!"

The bloodthirsty PR campaign for *Hitler's Madman* is easily the macabre match of any Karloff and/or Lugosi horror epic:

> • Hanging Hitler in effigy ... a socko stunt for *Hitler's Madman*. Get the cooperation of newspapers on behalf of the USO, Army and Navy Relief.... Arrange for the hanging of Hitler or his madman in the town square or in front of your theater.... Ask the mayor to officiate at the event....
> • Exhibitors who have a weakness for "coffin" exploitation on horror pictures ought to have a field day with *Hitler's Madman*. Place a dummy figure in a real coffin to be borne about your streets by "pallbearers." Also display the "victim" of Nazi cruelty in your lobby. Stunt must be explained by lurid and sensational signs connecting the picture title.
> • Hang a giant noose from your flagpole, top of theater building or over marquee. Use it as an advance teaser stunt, explaining it thusly: "Hitler Gave His Madman Enough Rope to Hang Himself. See What Happened to This Monster...."

Posters offer variations on a sprawling woman in a torn dress, cowering under a whip. The film's one word teaser: "Sensational!" And thus does MGM release Seymour Nebenzal's passionate paean to the victims of Lidice.

MGM rates its own films as "AA," "A," "B" and "C" attractions. *Hitler's Madman* is a "C" as it plays engagements that summer of 1943, usually to savage reviews. Perhaps the most heart-breaking critique comes from the War Department. This little-known archive of Hollywood history resides today at the Library of Congress—reviews of Hollywood films, solicited under War Department auspices, written by critics—many from the trade papers— who aided the war effort by analyzing films as to the potential wartime impact and sensitivities they might create. Elisabeth Z. James sees *Hitler's Madman* and writes her analysis July 16, 1943. She notes in "Personal critical information":

Acting: No belief. Very poor
Script: Stiff, lifeless, and pretentious
Art Direction: Papier mache quality. Cheap
Architecture and Set dressing: Same
Costume Design: Theatricalized peasant—incredible

As for "Impressions," Ms. James writes:

> There is nothing in this film to indicate that its producers thought for one minute that the events it portrays did or could actually happen. The picture is a stiff theatricalization—false from beginning to end. It lacks even the diversion of trash: the vulgarity itself lacks life.[39]

Opposite: **Poster for *Hitler's Madman*, MGM, 1943.**

Horror show: Pressbook publicity for *Hitler's Madman*.

Friday, August 27: *Hitler's Madman* finally arrives in New York City, playing at the Rialto, Broadway's House of Horror. The Rialto had previously hosted such 1943 features as Universal's *Frankenstein Meets the Wolf Man* and RKO's *I Walked with a Zombie*. Albert Mayer, the theater's manager—nicknamed "The Merchant of Menace"—is famous for "tarting up" the front of his theater with carnival-like displays. This is ideal for *Hitler's Madman*'s promotional imagery of John Carradine pointing a bayonet at Patricia Morison's neck.

In yet another case of the film's bad luck, Warners' *Watch on the Rhine,* based on Lillian Hellman's play and starring Paul Lukas and Bette Davis, opens on Broadway the same day.

Praising the Warner film (for which Lukas would win the Best Actor Oscar), the critics—likely alienated by *Hitler's Madman*'s "Sensational!" campaign—have few bouquets to toss it. *The New York Telegram* notes the film's problems but writes, "In spite of all the shortcomings in cast and timeliness, the picture has a final impact likely to leave you shaken and silent." *The New York Sun* review, however, is more typical:

> The Rialto's new feature, *Hitler's Madman*, is a lurid piece.... The film's exciting but not terribly believable. John Carradine plays Heydrich with leer and sneer. Patricia Morison poses prettily, even in her death scene ... *Hitler's Madman* is still no better than its title.

Amazingly, many of these critics, only 14 months after Lidice, are sadly, almost pathetically missing the point. Lidice *was* a horror show. A lot of Nazis *did* act like Shakespearean actors. In their calling for a more restrained approach, the critics are forgetting the totally unrestrained ferocity of Heydrich and the barbaric mania of Hitler's revenge. Perhaps the critics fear the intensity of the subject, afraid that a full-blooded depiction of Lidice is inadvisable ... and that madness lies that way. Indeed, what could possibly do the story of Lidice justice ... *except* a horror film?

Hitler's Madman has thrown itself into the belly of the beast. For all the lurid theatricality and despite the hybrid final product, the film retains its nobility and passionate sincerity, and audiences respond powerfully. The film plays three weeks at the Rialto, tallying an impressive total of $28,500.

Meanwhile, MGM, desperate about what to do with *Hitler's Madman*, incongruously sticks it as a support feature for several of its big-budget musicals. In Detroit, it's on the bill with *Du Barry Was a Lady;* in Kansas City, with *Best Foot Forward;* in Denver, with *Presenting Lily Mars.* At Grauman's Chinese Theatre in Hollywood, *Hitler's Madman* is second feature for RKO's *The Sky's the Limit,* starring Fred Astaire and Paulette Goddard. *Variety* reports the first week's take as a "sky-high" $16,000.

The film excites and moves many audiences. The manager of the Luna Theatre in Battle Creek, Iowa, writes to *Boxoffice* (October 23, 1943):

> Did not expect to do anything on this one and imagine my surprise when they came in droves, thereby giving one of the best grosses in years on a Thursday, Friday, Saturday, Sunday. Younger folks came to the show expecting to see something rather risqué and sensational and they were not disappointed. Older patrons came for the same reason.... Summing it up, *Hitler's Madman* turned out to be one of the top sleepers of the year in this locality....

Nevertheless, MGM, obviously ashamed of its adopted, dressed-up, freakish "C" movie, officially yanks it from distribution—no reason given in the studio archives.[40] The withdrawal date is listed as October 7, 1943, but the film will still play engagements late into the year. On December 13 at the Home Theatre in Washington D.C., it again supports the MGM Technicolor Lucille Ball musical *Best Foot Forward*—a bizarrely eclectic Yuletide attraction.

How does *Hitler's Madman* officially fare in its David vs. Goliath battle against *Hangmen Also Die!* at the box office? The numbers aren't really fair, considering that MGM pulled *Hitler's Madman* from distribution prematurely. Nevertheless, here are the totals;

Hangmen Also Die!	*Hitler's Madman*
Domestic rentals: $845,210	Domestic rentals: $305,000
Foreign rentals: $738,568	Foreign rentals: $202,000
Worldwide rentals: $1,583,778	Worldwide rentals: $507,000

The Fritz Lang film earns over a million dollars more in rentals than does Seymour Nebenzal's hapless project. While no information on *Hangmen Also Die!*'s profit-loss is now available, the MGM archives record a loss for *Hitler's Madman* of $95,000.[41]

* * *

> Even today I still dream about my husband nearly every night. He wants to separate himself from me. He wants to leave me. I reproach him that he has deserted me. Almost every night it is the same.
> —Mrs. Lina Heydrich, widow of Reinhard Heydrich,
> in an interview with *Jasmin Magazine,* 1969

Reinhard Heydrich has been a plum role for various actors over the decades. Among them was Kenneth Branagh, who won an Emmy for playing Heydrich in TV's *Conspiracy* (2001).

As for Seymour Nebenzal, his Angelus Productions packaged the well-received *Summer Storm* (1944), based on Chekhov's "The Shooting Party" and starring George Sanders, a very alluring Linda Darnell, and *Hangmen Also Die!*'s Anna Lee. He produced another half-dozen films, including a 1951 remake of his own *M*. Incidentally, despite the troubles on *Hitler's Madman,* the love between Nebenzal and Edgar Ulmer (who went on to direct such PRC gems as 1944's *Bluebeard* and 1945's *Detour*) had never lessened. Arianne Ulmer Cipes recalls:

> In 1961 I married in Italy. Dad and Mom were in Paris, developing a Jeanne Moreau version of *Mata Hari*. Meanwhile, Nebenzal and his wife Elsie had moved back to Munich, and he did his last film there, *The Girl from Hong Kong*. Dad and Mom left Paris when they realized Nebenzal was dying, and went to Munich so Mom could be with Elsie and Dad could be with Nebenzal—who literally died in Dad's arms.

Seymour Nebenzal died in Munich September 22, 1961. He was 62 years old. Ulmer died in Los Angeles on September 30, 1972, age 68.

Eugen Schufftan, *Hitler's Madman*'s cinematographer who couldn't get into the ASC union, eventually won the Oscar for Best Black and White Cinematography for *The Hustler* (1961). He died in New York City September 6, 1977, at age 84.

Douglas Sirk went on to big box office and a certain cult fame with his Universal-International deluxe soap opera hits *Written on the Wind* (1956) and *Imitation of Life* (1959). *Hitler's Madman* possesses Sirk's wonderful stylistics of light and shadow. Sirk died in Switzerland January 14, 1987, age 89.

Over the past 70 years, *Hitler's Madman* has won its admirers. In his fascinating and often dead-on book, *Alternate Oscars,* Danny Peary opines that John Carradine should have been among 1943's Academy Award Best Actor nominees for his chilling Heydrich. In 1992, on the 50th anniversary of the Lidice massacre, the TNT network ran *Hitler's Madman,* although it actually aired at 3:05 a.m. EST on June 11. Turner Classic Movies has frequently shown the film in recent years, as well as *Hangmen Also Die!*, and it's fascinating to compare and contrast the two films. "Lidice: The Mark of the Beast," the *Washington Post* had headlined June 15, 1942, as the bloodbath shocked the world, and it's the "Beast" that *Hitler's Madman* so passionately presents.

In Prague today there is a 30'-tall monument commemorating the site where the assassins attacked Reinhard Heydrich. Josef Gabcik and Jan Kubis are Czech heroes, and the church where they died so violently now has a museum in the crypt in their honor.

John Carradine as the Nazi Heydrich, seemingly baying at the moon in this publicity still from *Hitler's Madman.*

What of Heydrich's family? In his book *Heydrich: Face of Evil,* Mario R. Dederichs writes that neither Heydrich's widow Lina nor their children have ever addressed the terror the man so horribly unleashed. The widow's grave marker in St. Georg Rural District New Cemetery on the island of Fehmarn in the Baltic Sea reads, "Lina Manninen, widow of Heydrich, *nee* von Osten, 1911–1985." There's a rumor that, buried with Lina in her vault, along with various relatives, is the husband she always honored, Reinhard Heydrich. The wooden cross marking Heydrich's grave at Invaliden Cemetery in Berlin vanished after the war, and some believe that SS men, at Lina's request, exhumed Heydrich's corpse and secretly delivered it to Fehmarn. Dederichs notes that the Gardens and Cemeteries office of Berlin-Mitte district told him that "bones are present" in Heydrich's original grave, but "some uncertainty remains as to whether, in the confusion of the immediate postwar period, somebody interfered with the bodies." In 2001 Heydrich's descendants renounced "forever" any interest in connection with the grave at Invaliden.

So there's a chance that Reinhard Heydrich—whose truly evil essence Hollywood couldn't touch, even in its most lurid propaganda—might have enjoyed a posthumous last laugh on history. And this is truly, in the most genuine sense of the word ... horrific.

Hitler's Madman

Production Company, Angelus Pictures, and Metro-Goldwyn-Mayer. Producer, Seymour Nebenzal; Associate Producer, Rudolph Joseph; Director, Douglas Sirk; Story, Emil Ludwig and Albrecht Joseph (suggested by "Hangman's Village" by Bart Lytton); Screenplay, Peretz Hirshbein, Melvin Levy and Doris Malloy (and, uncredited, Edgar G. Ulmer, Shirley Ulmer, and Howard Emmett Rogers); Verses from "The Murder of Lidice" by Edna St. Vincent Millay; Director of Photography, Jack Greenhalgh; Technical Director, Eugene Schufftan; Production Designer, Edgar G. Ulmer (uncredited); Art Directors, Fred Preble and Edward Willens; Editor, Dan Milner; Music Score, Karl Hajos (and, uncredited, Mario Castelnuovo-Tedesco and Nathaniel Shilkret); Sound Engineers, Percy Townsend and W.M. Dalgleish; Production Manager, Ralph Slosser; Second Unit Director, Edgar G. Ulmer (uncredited); Assistant Director, Mel De Lay; Technical Advisors, Felix Bernstein, Paul Elbogen; Publicity, Jack Kelly. Running Time, 84 minutes. PCA Certificate Number, 9121.

Filmed at Fine Arts Studio, Hollywood, 26 October-mid-December 1942; Retakes and Additional Scenes at MGM, Culver City, March 1943.

Trade Show, Los Angeles, 8 June 1943. New York City Opening: Rialto Theatre, 27 August 1943.

Patricia Morison (Jarmila Hanka); John Carradine (Reich Protector Reinhard Heydrich); Alan Curtis (Karel Vavra); Ralph Morgan (Jan Hanka); Howard Freeman (Heinrich Himmler); Ludwig Stossel (Mayor Herman Bauer); Edgar Kennedy (Nepomuk); Jimmy Conlin (Dvorak); Blanche Yurka (Mrs. Anna Hanka); Jorja Rollins (Clara Janek); Al Shean (Father Semlanik); Victor Kilian (Janek); Johanna Hofer (Mrs. Marta Bauer); Wolfgang Zilzer (Colonel); Tully Marshall (Professor); Elizabeth Russell (Maria Bartonek); Richard Bailey (Anton Bartonek); Richard Nichols, Betty Jean Nichols (Bartonek Children); Lora Lane (Minna); Johnny Good (Rupert Hanka); Emmett Lynn (Germak); Ben Webster (Old Man Masaryk); Nellie Anderson (Old Lady Masaryk); Arthur Thallasso, Dan Duncan (Gendarmes); John Merton (Muller, Heydrich's Bodyguard); Dick Talmadge (Chauffeur); Frank Hagney (Engineer); Hugh Maguire (Boy); Hans Von Morhart, Ray Miller, Charles Marsh (Soldiers); Peter Van Eyck, Richard Ryen, Otto Reichow, Sigfrid Tor (Gestapo); James Farley (Town Crier); Solvig Smith (Milkmaid); Budd Buster (Conductor); Chet Brandenburg (Linesman); Ernst Hausman, Sam Waagenaar (Sentries); Dan Fitzpatrick, Frank Todd (Coffin Bearers); George Lynn (First Officer); Wilmer Barnes (Second Officer); Carl Neubert (Third Officer); Dennis Moore (Orderly); Lester Dorr (Sergeant); Edgar Licho (Doctor);

Fred Nurney (Captain); Lionel Royce (Captain Kleist); Hans Von Twardowski (Lt. Buelow); Louis V. Arco (German Sergeant); Michael Mark (Czech Laborer); Frances Rafferty (Eliza Cermak); Vicky Lane (Katy Chotnik); Ava Gardner (Franciska Petrick); Mary Elliott (Anna Parsek); Natalie Draper (Julia Petschek); Walter Bonn (Military Doctor); William McCormick (Assistant Doctor); Betty Jaynes, Celia Travers (Nurses).

11

John Carradine and His "Traveling Circus"

I must be cruel, only to be kind.
—*Hamlet,* Act III, sc. 4.

Monday, October 18, 1943[1]: Poverty Row's Monogram Studios is shooting its new horror opus, *Voodoo Man.* During the week that follows, the macabre spectacles will abound—most notably that big, climactic crowd-pleaser of a voodoo ceremony.

There's Bela Lugosi as Dr. Marlowe, with goatee and flowing wizard's robe, miraculously maintaining his dignity as he tries to energize his long-dead wife. "Death ... to life!" he intones.

There's George Zucco as Nicholas, high priest of Ramboona, wearing a hat crowned with feathers, his face streaked with warpaint, chanting at the ceremony: "Ram ... *boo* ... naaaaa!"

Starlets (all Caucasian) play Lugosi's zombie posse, dressed in angelic gowns, lacquered with makeup and lipstick, staring blankly, and probably wondering what the stock gals at MGM are doing today. William Beaudine's stark direction registers, capturing all the movie magic in one fleeting, hastily under-rehearsed, who-the-hell-cares take.

Yet most striking of all—arguably—is John Carradine as Toby, Dr. Marlowe's hire-the-handicapped goon henchman. Rarely has mental enfeeblement come to the screen in so rawly realistic a fashion. The back story on Toby is lost to the ages, but one imagines he'd been a carnival geek, biting off the heads of live chickens before escaping his freak show pit and running away to the Voodoo Man for a new lease on life. Alas, Bela's Dr. Marlowe hardly treats him with liberal tolerance.

"He'll beat me!" moans Carradine's Toby.

The actor wears his long hair over one eye. He runs about with little bouncy baby steps, like some horrific toddler. His voice is warped, like a damaged record played too slowly, or a 1960s biker on impure acid. He leers at the female zombies. "Gosh, you've got nice pretty hair!" he tells one of the girls, stroking her tresses.

And come that climax, as goateed Lugosi prays, and war-painted Zucco chants, and those my-girdle-is-killing-me zombies look as if they know their Hollywood futures have just crashed and burned, Carradine's Toby the Terrible, slack-jawed and bug-eyed, beats a hell of a mean bongo, providing percussion for *Voodoo Man*'s apex of emotion.

* * *

Sunday night, October 24: Within days of wrapping up *Voodoo Man,* "John Carradine and His Shakespeare Players" open in *Hamlet* at San Francisco's Geary Theatre.

It is, perhaps, the greatest night of his life.

The magic of *Voodoo Man.* **Bela Lugosi (center), George Zucco (top), and John Carradine (left of center). Seated facing each other: Wanda McKay (left) and Ellen Hall. Louise Currie stands at the right.**

* * *

Bela Lugosi used his *Voodoo Man* paycheck to keep the wolf from the door of his North Hollywood home. George Zucco spent his on animals for his Mandeville Canyon ranch.

For John Carradine, however, *Voodoo Man*—along with many of the other questionable films in which he starred at the time—was a way to make a dream come true. Here was Carradine as Hamlet, madly in love with the blonde and beautiful actress playing Ophelia, winning an ovation, set to follow in repertory as Shylock and Othello. After the performance, Carradine stepped out of the Geary into the San Francisco night, dressed in his black cape and fedora, holding his cane, confident in his dream of premiering his company on Broadway on Shakespeare's 380th birthday—April 23, 1944—and vowing he'd never make another movie.

In fact, he'd make about another 150 of them—quite a few far worse than *Voodoo Man.*

The short-lived Shakespeare triumph was kind, only to be cruel—indeed, virtually everything about John Carradine's dream-come-true eventually morphed into a nightmare. First of all, it destroyed his marriage. His Ophelia soon became wife number two, bore him three sons, but eventually broke his heart and became, according to Carradine himself, "a Hollywood bag lady." In addition, his stage status, despite various triumphs over the decades, ultimately tarnished so that, in his very late years, he joined a traveling bus tour with falsetto singer Tiny Tim and a trained chimp.

Yet perhaps more than anything else in a 63-year career, John Carradine and His Shakespeare Players defined the man, at least in his own mind. Cruel, indeed, that Carradine had to serve a professional sackcloth penance for his success almost until his death ... 45 years later.

*   *   *

Let Hercules himself do what he may,
The cat will mew and dog will have his day.
—***Hamlet***, Act V, sc. 1

1930: Hollywood-at-large figures John Carradine belongs in a madhouse, not in the movies.

He's a scarecrow in cape and black fedora, a virtual vagrant marching up and down Hollywood Boulevard at night, waving a cane and roaring Shakespeare—a specter both funny and frightening, a mad mix of classical actor and circus wild man. Come midnight, and it's a terrifying spectacle to behold the Bard of the Boulevard,[2] a ranting, raving Richard III:

> I have oft heard my mother say
> I came into the world with my legs forward...
> The midwife wonder'd, and the women cried,
> O! Jesus BLESS us, he's BORN with TEETH!
> And so I was; which plainly signified
> That I should snarl and bite
> And play the dog....[3]

Legend claims that the "dog" scared away Peter the Hermit, another Hollywood curio, who fled into the Hills—probably hyperbole, but after all the decades, who's to say? After storming the streets, the Bard heads for the Hollywood Bowl and develops his voice by reciting to the 15,000 empty seats. Director John Ford, who lives in the area, hears him doing a one-man *Othello*—and sics the police on him.

Why the act? He's a brilliant young man who claims he actually knows all of Shakespeare by heart. He also has the show-off flair of a carnival barker. But perhaps most of all, Richmond Reed Carradine—born in New York City in 1906, having arrived in Los Angeles as a freight train "banana messenger" after acting in stock in New Orleans, a vagabond actor who also survives as a painter and sculptor—idolizes John Barrymore. Like fans of 21st century rock stars who emulate their idols' excesses, Carradine passionately emulates Barrymore's.

He drinks.

By Carradine's later account, it's probably 1930 that he hikes up Tower Road in Beverly Hills, finally reaching Bella Vista, John Barrymore's magnificent estate, Fate decreeing that he meet his *beau ideal*, hoping to petition Barrymore's advice on playing Richard III. Carradine is bedecked in his stock wardrobe, including cardboard spats. Barrymore wears a robe.

"I am going to play Richard III!" says Carradine.

"Let's have a drink!" says Barrymore.[4]

It will be one of Carradine's all-time favorite days, memories and stories. The visit baptizes his idolatry. He is a friend of John Barrymore. One day, he believes, he will be the *new* Barrymore.

Eventually, Carradine becomes "legitimate." He plays bits in the movies ... Cecil B.

DeMille's *The Sign of the Cross* (1932) ... James Whale's *The Invisible Man* (1933). In the Karloff-Lugosi *The Black Cat* (1934), he's a Black Mass organist; in *Bride of Frankenstein* (1935), he pops up as a hunter, crashing the peaceful idyll of Boris Karloff's Monster and O.P. Heggie's blind and holy Hermit. Carradine wears his black hat at a jaunty angle, pops his eyes, and roars, "This is the fiend who's been murdering half the countryside!" as if he's in the Globe Theatre—as if the Bard of the Boulevard got lost in Hollywood and has ended up in Universal's soundstage forest.

There's stage work too—notably at the legendary Pasadena Playhouse.[5]

Tuesday, June 27, 1933: Carradine makes his Playhouse debut in *Foolscap,* a comedy which presents Bernard Shaw (Carradine) and Pirandello (Frank Puglia) in a private insane asylum in England. They write a play for the inmates, who believe themselves to be such personages as Shakespeare, Cleopatra, and Judas. Carradine will recall that the opening night performance ran three-quarters of an hour longer than the dress rehearsal due to the audience laughter.

1935: The Pasadena Playhouse presents all of Shakespeare's history plays, and John Carradine joins the festival.

Monday July 1: He plays the title role in *King John.* The audience is pleased as punch when Carradine's treacherous monarch meets his end via poison from a monk.

Monday, July 8: Carradine is Hotspur in *The First Part of King Henry IV,* fighting a quite spectacular sword duel with Richard Carlson's Henry.

Monday, July 29: He is Richard in *The Second Part of King Henry the Sixth.*

Monday August 5: A night of climax: Carradine stars as Shakespeare's "foul lump of deformity," *Richard the Third.* "A horse, a horse, my kingdom for a horse!" roars Carradine magnificently.[6]

There are several Barrymore connections to this triumph. Michael Strange, Mrs. Barrymore from 1920 (shortly after his *Richard III* in New York) until their divorce in 1928, plays Lady Anne. Also, Blanche Yurka, Barrymore's Gertrude in *Hamlet* in 1922, is in Hollywood, portraying Madame DeFarge in MGM's *A Tale of Two Cities*; she catches a performance of *Richard III* and publicly praises Carradine.

Tuesday, February 11, 1936: It's the eve of Abraham Lincoln's 127th birthday, and *The Prisoner of Shark Island* premieres at Grauman's Chinese Theatre in Hollywood. John Ford has directed the 20th Century–Fox saga in Passion Play

An early portrait of John Carradine as Iago in *Othello,* signed with his original stage name, "John Peter Richmond," circa 1930.

style. For allegedly aiding John Wilkes Booth after Lincoln's assassination, Warner Baxter's Dr. Mudd goes to the Dry Tortugas—Hell. There he meets Carradine's snarling Sgt. Rankin—Satan. Wild-eyed, whiskered, crowing, "Hi'ya, Judas!" at Mudd, Carradine evokes a mad Shakespearean actor, suffering from lycanthropy. The actor takes his bride Ardanelle to the festivities. As the couple departs after the show, the crowd vehemently boos Carradine. Ardanelle is horrified, but 20th Century–Fox is delighted. As Eleanor Barnes writes in her review of *The Prisoner of Shark Island* in the *Los Angeles Daily Illustrated News*:

> Screen fame has come to John Carradine as the villain, a new type of actor.... Carradine is a sadistic prison guard, a man with a fantastic gleam in his eyes and a voice that carries venom, ugliness and sincerity.
>
> No doubt Carradine will be another of the Peter Lorre and Charles Laughton or perhaps Boris Karloff brand of monster, who scares women and children and makes strong men reach for their revolvers.[7]

Even as *The Prisoner of Shark Island* was still shooting, Fox had awarded Carradine a seven-year, 40-weeks-per-year player's contract that started January 2, 1936, at the following weekly terms:

First six months, 1936: $200	1939: $750
Next six months, 1936: $250	1940: $1,000
1937: $350	1941: $1,300
1938: $500	1942: $1,750[8]

Additionally, John Ford makes him a member of his famous stock company. The Bard of the Boulevard has arrived. Great films follow, sometimes on loan-out: MGM's *Captains Courageous* and *Of Human Hearts,* with Carradine in the latter a very moving Lincoln; RKO's *Mary of Scotland* and UA's *The Hurricane,* both for Ford.

The "dog" is indeed having his day.

*   *   *

> *The villainy you teach me, I will execute;*
> *and it shall go hard but I will better the instruction.*
> —Shylock, **The Merchant of Venice**, Act III, sc. i

Naturally Carradine celebrates—flamboyantly. He buys a Duesenberg. He attends premieres in top hat, cape, and diamonds. He smokes long Russian cigarettes. He drinks and, as his wife Ardanelle complains, kisses other women at parties.

And always, there's Shakespeare.

Summer, 1938: Carradine arrives by train in Pineville, Missouri, to play Bob Ford, the man who shoots Tyrone Power's title buckaroo in the back in *Jesse James*. He departs the train ("with a dapper tilt to his Panama hat," reports the publicity) and announces to the awaiting crowd of 5,000, "I am here for a sole purpose—to kill Jesse James!" Then he launches into Shakespeare. This reportedly appalls the Ozark mob, many thinking he's speaking a foreign language or babbling in tongues.[9]

Summer, 1939: Carradine joins John Ford's *Drums Along the Mohawk* on location at Cedar Breaks National Monument, 11,000 feet up in the Utah mountains, playing the Tory villain in cape and eye patch. Every night there's a campfire, and Carradine performs Shake-

Carradine in his most famous villainous performance: as Bob Ford in *Jesse James* (1939).

speare. "He was magnificent," the late Kay Linaker, a co-player in *Drums Along the Mohawk*, will remember. "He could recite whole plays, do the different characters... I never heard anybody do 'Tomorrow and tomorrow and tomorrow' as well until I heard Ian McKellen do it."[10]

John Carradine has succeeded—having become a dark, ascetic, almost mystical figure in some of the greatest films ever made. Perhaps what we recall most vividly are his death scenes. In *Stagecoach* (1939), Carradine is the mysterious Hatfield, a notorious Southern gambler—the only victim to perish in the movies' most famous Indian attack. In *The Grapes of Wrath* (1940), he's Casy the preacher, the character so vivid a Christ figure that John Steinbeck had actually given him the initials J.C. Indeed, Carradine is very Christ-like when in *The Grapes of Wrath,* he stands in a stream under a bridge, transfigured and glowing in the night in the strike breakers' flashlights, crying, "You don't know what you're doing!" before a lout smashes his skull with a club. And in *Blood and Sand* (1941), he dies in Academy Award–winning Technicolor—arms stretched at his sides, now naked from the waist up, looking very much like the gaunt figure on the crucifix that hangs above his death bed.

Always, there's the hero worship—or anti-hero worship—of John Barrymore. Carradine is one of the Bundy Drive Boys[11]—Barrymore, artist John Decker, W.C. Fields, Errol Flynn, Thomas Mitchell, Anthony Quinn, writer Gene Fowler—who carouse epically at Decker's home-studio, 419 North Bundy Drive in Brentwood. As Errol Flynn will reminisce late in life:

> Barrymore, John Carradine and I used to go three or four days without sleeping. We'd start out in some bistro at noon and a week later find ourselves in Mexico or in a yacht off Catalina with a dozen bottles on the floor and a gaggle of whores puking their guts up all over the place....[12]

Carradine sits with Barrymore in the decaying Bella Vista, reading Shakespeare throughout the night. He performs his cackling, snorting, awesomely profane Barrymore impression before the great man himself, once at a November 21, 1941, art show for John Decker. On that night, the Hollywood celebrities also include Lionel Barrymore as Carradine recites Gene Fowler's brilliantly bitter poem "The Testament of a Dying Ham":

> To the wenches who trumped up a passion,
> And held a first lien on my cot,
> To the simpering starlets and glee-ridden harlots
> Whose sables were masking their rot...

Flynn will call it the "sheer zing of existence," but something darker is at play here too: a masochistic self-demolition. Over the previous 11 years, Carradine has witnessed Barrymore almost blasphemously destroying himself—and in his idolatry, has embraced the darkness with the light.

Still, John Carradine has done himself proud. He's settled into a home at 5433 Ben Avenue, far out on the frontier of the San Fernando Valley, with Ardanelle, her son Bruce (whom Carradine has adopted), and their son Jackie—later known as David and whom his parents call "Pooky." (David will claim that a "pooky" is German for a "little fart.") The actor has acquired a yacht, the *Bali,* sailing to Catalina. David will vividly remember a storm at sea, his father in his glory, daringly sailing the *Bali* right into the eye of a tempest as the family, all terrified, literally hang on for dear life. Meanwhile, John Barrymore publicly hails Carradine as one of ten "extremely fine actors worth watching for pointers."[13]

By December of 1941, Carradine is one of the top character actors in Hollywood, earning $1,300 per week at 20th Century–Fox. Then, in January of 1942, Fox declines to pick up Carradine's option and boost his weekly salary to $1,750. He arrives in New York City in February, announcing plans to raise $50,000 to mount a production of *Richard III.* As the *New York Times* reports:

> No longer under rigid contract to the films, Mr. C thought the other day he would produce the revival either this Spring or—if various people who think the time too late have their way—in the early Fall. He will play the title role; he has played it before, in the South and the West, where his Shakespearean repertoire also included such items as *Othello* and *The Merchant of Venice.*

Friday, February 20, 1942: Carradine guest-stars on radio's *Information Please,* along with Boris Karloff. The host, Clifton Fadiman, tosses Carradine an interesting question:

Fadiman: Mr. Carradine, who killed Jesse James?
Carradine: I did!

Sunday, March 8: The *New York Times* reports that Carradine claims to have "half the necessary money" in hand for his *Richard III,* with "the rest in view."

Tuesday, March 10: Carradine is among the celebrities at the Navy Relief Show at Madison Square Garden with such stars as Tyrone Power, Myrna Loy, Edgar Bergen and Charlie McCarthy, Kate Smith, Boris Karloff, and Vincent Price (the latter two "in drag" as Floradora Sextette ladies). Joining the celebrities are chorus girls from Broadway musicals, all performing before an SRO crowd of 21,000.

Saturday March 28: Carradine hosts the radio show *This Is War—It's in the Works,* written and directed by Norman Corwin. John Garfield, Frank Lovejoy, Henry Hull, and Katherine Locke are also on the 30-minute show, which begins airing on 12 different networks at seven p.m., and then airs again at 12:05 a.m. on another network, then 12:45 a.m. on two other networks. After the first broadcast and late in the evening, Carradine becomes wildly drunk—requiring an emergency replacement literally seconds before air time.[14]

News comes he's postponing *Richard III* to September. Carradine returns to Hollywood.

Monday, May 11: Carradine plays the sly, hunchbacked Louis XI in *The Vagabond King* at the Los Angeles Philharmonic Theatre.

Friday, May 29: John Barrymore dies at age 60 after a decade of virtual suicide-by-debauchery. John Carradine mourns—loudly.

Sunday, May 31: Laird Cregar cancels an appearance on Edgar Bergen and Charlie McCarthy's *Chase and Sanborn Show,* and Carradine pinch-hits for Cregar. The program jokes about the actor's screen villainy, offering badinage between Carradine and Charlie:

Carradine: Why, I'm considered the elite of the better class monsters. In my last picture, I made everyone hate me.
Charlie: Well, the picture's over, bud—don't overdo it![15]

Tuesday, June 2: Carradine is present among the invited guests at the Barrymore funeral at Calvary Cemetery in Whittier. "The first thing I saw when I walked in," producer-writer Nunnally Johnson will recall, "was old John Carradine sitting there, rocking back and forth and keening so you could hear him all over the church."[16] They inter John Barrymore in a marble crypt at Calvary Cemetery, and Lionel Barrymore personally carves "Good Night, Sweet Prince" on his tomb.

John Carradine vows it is time that he does Barrymore—and himself—proud.

For a time he still hopes for a Broadway *Richard III,* announced for December of 1942, then put off until the next season. The reason: "Mr. Carradine's film commitments."

Summer: He makes two movies at MGM, playing a Nazi in *Reunion in France* and a villain in *Northwest Rangers.* He also plays Bret Harte in Warner Bros.' *The Adventures of Mark Twain,* appearing in the episode of "The Celebrated Jumping Frog of Calaveras County," begging his bullfrog Daniel to jump with the promise, "Flies!"

October: He is superb as Heydrich in the independently shot *Hitler's Madman* (see Chapter 10).

December: Universal, which has announced a big studio build-up for Carradine as a horror star, casts him in *Captive Wild Woman* as a mad doctor who transforms a gorilla into starlet Acquanetta.

January 1943: He's another Nazi in Monogram's *I Escaped from the Gestapo.*

Monday, March 8: Carradine joins Ray Milland and Paulette Goddard on Cecil B. DeMille's *Lux Radio Theatre* in "Reap the Wild Wind." Also that month: retakes at MGM for *Hitler's Madman.*

April: He stars as a lusty sea diver in *Isle of Forgotten Sins* at PRC and menaces Roy Rogers in *Silver Spurs* at Republic.

May: He stars in Monogram's *Revenge of the Zombies* as a Nazi mad doctor in the American South, preparing a zombie army.

Meanwhile, there are problems at home. On one occasion, five-year-old David has tried to hang himself by jumping off the bumper of his father's Duesenberg. Carradine saves him, punishing the child for his intended suicide by burning his comic books.[17] Also, as David will write in his 1995 memoir *Endless Highway*, Ardanelle has secretly undergone "two illegal kitchen-table, more-or-less wire-hanger abortions," and his father

> was furious. She was killing his babies. When Dad got angry about something, there was no question of resisting him. After a lot of yelling and a lot of tears, it was agreed they would start another child forthwith, one he could keep, no buts about it. They got right down to the task that very night.

Saturday, May 29: Hedda Hopper writes in the *Los Angeles Times*: "John Carradine, who's boasted he'll play a Shakespearean repertoire on the New York stage, has cried 'Wolf' too often. I'll believe it when I see him do it."

That Hedda Hopper's dare comes on the one-year anniversary of John Barrymore's death probably isn't lost on Carradine. Meanwhile the Carradines make a pact: They'll patch up their marriage, Ardanelle will bear another child, and John will now pursue his dream goal of forming his own repertory company. He will be star, producer, director, and sole owner. He will play Hamlet, Shylock, and alternate as Othello and Iago.

It will be "John Carradine and His Shakespeare Players."

* * *

> *The devil hath power*
> *To assume a pleasing shape.*
> —*Hamlet*, Act II, sc. 2

Carradine needs money, so he signs for RKO's *Gangway for Tomorrow*, playing an intellectual hobo (à la Barrymore, naturally) who finds World War II patriotism by working in a factory.

He needs a theater and persuades the Pasadena Playhouse, which respects Carradine—indeed, he'd been the guest speaker at the 1941 graduation—to book his troupe.[18] The Playhouse is then presenting a summer festival of Booth Tarkington plays and possibly as part of his deal, Carradine stars in *Colonel Satan*, playing the title role—aka Aaron Burr. The play opens July 6, 1943, and the cast also includes Playhouse stalwart director-actor Onslow Stevens and 26-year-old Raymond Burr.

He needs a set and is thrilled to buy the surviving "Elsinore" from Barrymore's 1922 *Hamlet*, designed by the legendary Robert Edmond Jones. With its tall, twisting staircase, it will serve as the unit set for *Hamlet, The Merchant of Venice* and *Othello.*

He needs finances to transport the set and design the costumes. On August 9, 1943, *Variety* writes that the government has slapped Carradine with a lien for back taxes amounting to $3,094.[19] Undaunted, he mortgages his San Fernando Valley home and sells the *Bali*.

And, of course, he needs actors. As David Carradine would write:

> His biggest problem was to find an actress who could play Ophelia in *Hamlet*, Portia in *The Merchant of Venice* and Desdemona in *Othello*; three of the juiciest and most demanding roles ever written for a woman.
> What walked in the door was Sonia Sorel.

Sonia Sorel is 22 years old, a rapaciously attractive blonde, a leggy mix of angel and voluptuary. In certain light and angles, she appears a great beauty; in others, a sly witch.

She's a 1942 graduate of the Pasadena Playhouse, where she's played an impressive array of roles, including aristocratic Tracy Lord in *The Philadelphia Story* (the Katharine Hepburn role, March 9, 1942) and vampy Crystal Allen in *The Women* (the Joan Crawford role, December 9, 1942). She can be scary, too: On Valentine's Day, 1943, she portrayed the maniacal, man-killing, organ-playing Emmy in the melodrama *They Walk Alone* (the role Elsa Lanchester had so chillingly played on Broadway in 1941).

As David Carradine, who later admitted "falling in love" with Sonia at age seven, will write in *Endless Highway*: "She was young, she was beautiful, and she could *act*. You couldn't trust her any farther than you could throw her...."

Her real name (and the one she is still using in the summer of '43) is Sonia Henius. Born in Milwaukee on May 18, 1921, she comes from a wealthy family of brew masters, and has nicely feathered her nest at the Pasadena Playhouse by becoming the mistress of the aforementioned actor-director-nudist, Onslow Stevens.[20] Besides acting with Carradine in the recent *Colonel Satan,* Stevens had played the Ghost of Henry VI in Carradine's *Richard III* in 1935. In Fox's 1936 *Under Two Flags,* Stevens, as Sidi-Ben-Youssiff, sentenced Carradine, as mad Foreign Legionnaire Cafard, to a spectacular death scene: trampled by horses running north, south, east and west.[21]

Sonia instantly captivates Carradine. As David Carradine will remember:

> To make it tough on her for her audition, Dad had her read the Queen in *Hamlet*; a difficult role for a young girl. Well, she made him cry, and that was probably *it* right there; though for the moment, Dad kept his pants on. He hired her, and went home to Mother and the kids.

Saturday, August 21: Carradine guest stars on radio's *Stars Over Hollywood* in "The Devil's Laugh."

Monday, August 23: Universal begins shooting *The Mummy's Ghost,* with Lon Chaney as the Mummy and Carradine as the evil high priest Yousef Bey.

Thursday, August 26: The actor is on the radio again, a guest on *The Joan Davis Show.*

Meanwhile, Carradine cast the rest of his company—and a rather unusual lot they are:

• Announced to play Queen Gertrude in *Hamlet* is Alice Crawford, a London actress who once upon a time had been Sir Herbert Tree's leading lady.

• C. Montague Shaw, 61-year-old Australian actor, wins the title role of Antonio in *The Merchant of Venice,* Brabantio in *Othello* and Polonius and the First Grave Digger in *Hamlet.* Shaw has played in such films as *Rasputin and the Empress* (1932), *The Mask of Fu Manchu* (1932), *Les Misérables* (1935), and *A Tale of Two Cities* (1935); he's also acted in such serials as Republic's *Daredevils of the Red Circle* and *Zorro's Fighting Legion* (1939).

- Houseley Stevenson, the British-born, 64-year-old father of Onslow Stevens, a respected Pasadena Playhouse director-actor, as well as a small-part player in such films as *Crime Doctor* (1943), signs on as the Duke of Venice in *Othello,* Old Gobbo in *The Merchant of Venice,* and the Ghost of King Hamlet.
- George Pembroke, whose film credits include Monogram's *Invisible Ghost* (1941) and *Black Dragons* (1942), both with Bela Lugosi, as well as Republic's super serials *Adventures of Captain Marvel* (1941) and *Perils of Nyoka* (1942), lands several minor roles: Montano in *Othello,* Tybal in *The Merchant of Venice,* and the First Player and the Priest in *Hamlet.*

In the grand old tradition of Edwin Booth and Henry Irving, Carradine decides he'll alternate as Othello and Iago. To share the roles with him, he hires 28-year-old Alfred Allegro, who has appeared in several Broadway plays, including the 1938 hit *Haiti* and the 1939 musical-ballet flop *Adelante.*[22] (Allegro soon changes his name to David Bond; 20 years later, he'll play Jack the Ripper in the *Twilight Zone* episode "The New Exhibit," April 4, 1963.)

Among the young hopefuls in the company are Dean Goodman who, on August 23, had made news by marrying Marlene Dietrich's daughter Maria. In 1996, Goodman, who by that time had become a noted actor and a San Francisco drama critic (and who would die in 2006), would speak with me about his half-century-before casting:

> John was *very* supportive. Of course, that was wartime, and it was hard to get a good company of male actors together. I myself had been in the service, but had left under a Civilian Disability Discharge. I just heard about the Carradine company... I took a chance, went over there to the Pasadena Playhouse, and auditioned for him. He was most receptive and anxious to have me in the company, but a lot of the roles had been cast. John was very apologetic that he could only offer me Lorenzo in *The Merchant of Venice* as a chief role. But it was my first Equity job and I was thrilled to do it.
>
> As for juggling his acting and directing, John was fine—he knew very well what he wanted. He knew what the actor's process is, and he was very good that way, and kind to his actors.
>
> John was reviving the tradition of the actor-manager of the 19th century and the first 20 years of the 20th century. By the 1940s, it had died out—and doing three plays in repertoire, in a commercial theater atmosphere, was rather a daring thing to do.

Carradine also assigns Goodman to understudy Laertes and Cassio. Goodman is so delighted that he tries to persuade his bride, Maria, to audition for Carradine. It surely would have been a PR boon to have Marlene Dietrich's daughter in the company, but Marlene nixes the idea. As Goodman would quote Maria's words: "No. Mummy doesn't want me to do it. She says the Carradine company is going to fail. It's bad enough for one of us to be involved in it."[23]

Saturday, September 4: "Shakespearean Series Will Star Carradine" headlines Katherine Von Blon in the *Los Angeles Times:*

> John Carradine, who was a Shakespearean interpreter before motion pictures claimed him, brings his own company to the Pasadena Playhouse for a feast of Shakespeareana, opening Sept. 27. *Othello* will be the initial play with Carradine carrying the leading assignment. *The Merchant of Venice* follows with the actor assuming the role of Shylock. As a strong climactic piece, *Hamlet* is marked for October 12.

Thursday, September 9: Eighteen days before *Othello* is set to open at the Playhouse, Universal completes shooting *The Mummy's Ghost.* Carradine pours as much of his Universal paycheck as possible into his troupe.

Meanwhile, Ardanelle suffers a miscarriage—a boy—and she almost dies. The doctor says her previous abortions have damaged her so badly that attempts at having another baby would probably kill her. As David will remember: "This was shattering news for Dad. That word 'never' was a killer; he had been planning on a baseball team. He went unsteadily back to rehearsals, his world in shambles; and there was Sonia to stroke and comfort him...."

The Carradine home has become the stage for its own tragedy: Ardanelle, apparently haunted by her abortions, begins sleepwalking, à la Lady Macbeth, prowling at night through the Ben Avenue house. According to David Carradine, "She would wander around in her nightgown, looking in corners, intoning, 'Where are my babies?' She had an idea they were all in a basket behind a door or something."

Rehearsing, planning, dreaming, swordplay, costume fittings, wig fittings ... Sonia. Dean Goodman remembers the festering attraction Carradine harbors for his leading lady:

> Sonia was still having an affair with Onslow Stevens. But John—he loved blondes [*Laughing*], and he had a fixation on Sonia. She was very buoyant, very sparkling, bubbling with personality, and John thought she was going to be the Ellen Terry of this age! He was bound and determined that he was going to get her, or die trying!

All the while the Pasadena Playhouse is *simpatico* to Carradine's Shakespearean company dream and affords every production benefit possible. As Carradine is rehearsing as both Othello and Iago, Alexander Gill actually directs *Othello*. Carlo Caiati, formerly of *La Scala*, designs the sets. And, as a special favor, Gilmor Brown, the Playhouse's managing producer, arranges for Playhouse favorite Onslow Stevens (rather than the relatively unknown Alfred Allegro) to play Othello at the weekend performances to Carradine's Iago.

*   *   *

Damn her, lewd minx! O, damn her, damn her!
—**Othello**, Act III, sc. iii

Monday, September 27: The Pasadena Playhouse is packed. Carradine is Othello, Alfred Allegro Iago, Sonia Henius Desdemona. Dean Goodman thinks Carradine's Othello "all wrong":

> Othello is mad with jealousy. But John, being a tall, slender man, had the theory that the Moors were highly cultivated people and intellectual, and he approached it that way. I think there was a certain logic in his contention, but it didn't work for that specific play as well. His Othello was very reserved.

Nevertheless, come the Act V climax and Othello's mad murder of Desdemona, Carradine delivers in blood-and-thunder style:

> *Desdemona*: O, banish me, my lord, but kill me not!
> *Othello*: Down, strumpet!
> *Desdemona*: Kill me tomorrow; let me live tonight!
> *Othello*: Being done, there is no pause.
> *Desdemona*: But while I say one prayer!
> *Othello*: It is too late!

As Shakespeare wrote, "He stifles her." Moments later, Othello, aware of Desdemona's innocence and the horrific murder he's committed, gives his final soliloquy, "Of one that loved not wisely but too well":

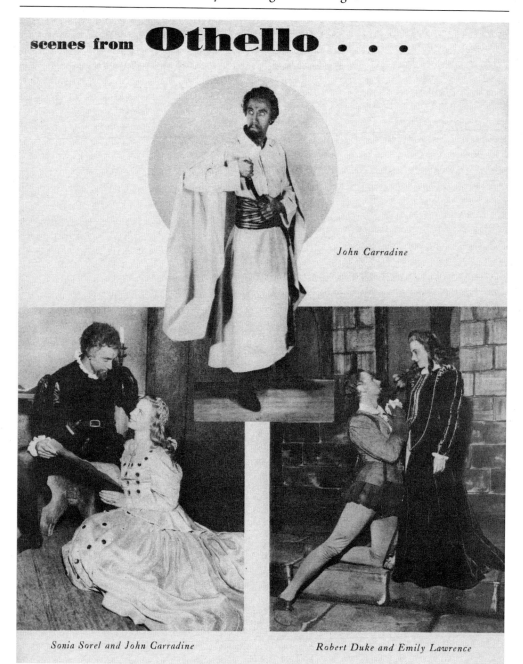

scenes from **Othello** . . .

John Carradine

Sonia Sorel and John Carradine

Robert Duke and Emily Lawrence

Scenes from *Othello*.

...Set you down this;
And say besides, that in Aleppo once,
Where a malignant and a turban'd Turk
Beat a Venetian and traduced the state,
I took by the throat the circumcised dog
And smote him, thus.

He stabs himself. Carradine will always be proud that, come the curtain, there is no applause initially—the audience is numb, overwhelmed by the tragedy and performance they'd just witnessed.

Tuesday, September 28: The *Los Angeles Times* runs its review of the "handsome and lavish" production:

> John Carradine, featured in the name part, gives an interesting and vivid performance.... It is an intellectual reading that he gives. However the passion of the primitive man grows as his doubt continues. Carradine allows his emotional power full reign during the later moments....
>
> Alfred Allegro was a spirited, playful villain.... Sonia Henius was a lovely, flower-like Desdemona, and acted with grace and sprightliness.

Friday, October 1: A bizarre thing happens. As arranged, Onslow Stevens plays Othello, and Carradine acts Iago. It's a heady mix of Shakespearean tragedy and Pasadena Playhouse soap opera: John Carradine as Iago, wickedly insinuating to Onslow Stevens as Othello, that his love, Desdemona, is unfaithful—Desdemona, of course, played by Stevens' mistress Sonia, whom Carradine is himself madly pursuing! The dynamic of these particular performances of October 1, 2, and 3 must possess a twisted, sensual energy, and audiences love it.

Also on October 1: Monogram Studios is shooting *Return of the Ape Man*. Bela Lugosi is Prof. Dexter, who thaws a hairy cave man (i.e., "ape man") out of arctic ice (actually Monogram cellophane); Carradine is Prof. Gilmore, Dexter's assistant, whose brain Dexter later transplants into the ape man; and George Zucco is originally cast as the ape man. A still survives of Zucco in cave man rags, wild wig, beard and bulbous false nose, looking lividly mortified; Frank Moran replaces him in the actual film after Zucco presumably storms off the shoot.[24]

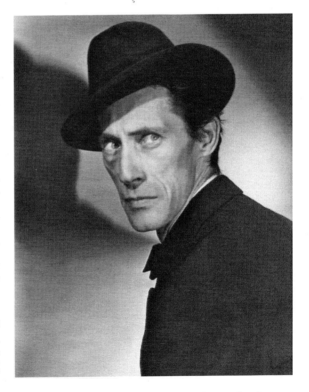

At any rate, here's John Carradine, cavorting in Monogram madness by day, playing his beloved Shakespeare by night. His energy is epic—and his proposed tour requires every bit of the princely $3,000 weekly pay Monogram is providing him.

Carradine's Shakespeare Company is enjoying a wildly successful start. Columnist Lee Shipley took in *Othello* and writes in the *L. A. Times*:

> Ever since the opening last week the house has been jammed and turning away cash customers unable to find seats. I went Sunday night and was amazed by the eternal timeliness of Shakespeare.[25]

Tuesday, October 5: *The Merchant of Venice* premieres. Carradine's Shylock looks like he has crept out of a Shake-

A Monogram portrait of John Carradine, when he was acting at Monogram by day in *Return of the Ape Man* and at the Pasadena Playhouse by night in Shakespearean repertory.

speare first folio—tall, gaunt, with a long gray beard, and seeking that grisly pound of
flesh:

> If you repay me not on such a day,
> In such a place, such sum or sums as are
> Express'd in the condition, let the forefeit
> Be nominated for an equal pound
> Of your fair flesh, to be cut off and taken
> In what part of your body pleaseth me.

Dean Goodman will consider Shylock the best of Carradine's repertory portrayals:

John's Shylock was very moving, especially when he discovered that his daughter Jessica has run
off with Lorenzo. There was a sadness about his portrayal, a pathos; it never got overly sentimental,
but it was there.

Sonia is an eyeful as Portia, in black costume, a bonnet over her blonde hair and her
legs on ample display in black tights. Meanwhile, during *The Merchant of Venice*'s week's
engagement, Carradine labors at Monogram, still stooging for Lugosi in *Return of the Ape
Man.*

Tuesday, October 12: The engagement climaxes with *Hamlet,* performed the week of a
full moon. The production has, in the words of the *Los Angeles Times,* "all the shock and
magnificence" of "the full chord of the Renaissance." Carradine is, as Dean Goodman will
recall, "a very virile Hamlet," superb in his soliloquies, including John Barrymore's favorite,
the "Now I am alone" speech:

> ... bloody, bawdy villain!
> Remorseless, treacherous, lecherous, kindless villain!
> O, vengeance!

"Brilliant Production of *Hamlet* Given," headlines the *Los Angeles Times,* and Katherine
Von Blon praises the star:

John Carradine, as the Melancholy Dane, painted a poignant and tragic picture of the lonely intro-
spective youth, beset with so many conflicting emotions. He somehow seemed to stress the piercing
medieval note of doom in his moving revelation of the pathos and travail of the human soul.

The critic finds one flaw in Carradine's performance: "his voice, which in certain passages
rang with fine resonance, and in others rendered the text more or less obscure." As for the
leading lady (who now has changed her stage name):

Sonia Sorel goes on record as one of the most fragile and appealing Ophelias seen in many a day.
All the finer cadences of the delicate creature were revealed with heartbreaking pathos. She received
a well-deserved ovation.

Alice Crawford of Sir Herbert Tree fame has bailed out somewhere along the way, and
there are two alternating Gertrudes: young Maxine Chevalier (who resembles, in Ms. Von
Blon's words, "an early Florentine painting") and Kay Hammond. The latter had played
Mary Todd Lincoln in D.W. Griffith's *Abraham Lincoln* (1930), but hasn't been in a film
since *Way Down East* (1935).

Thursday, October 14: Dorothea Eiler reviews Carradine's *Hamlet* in the *San Mateo
Tribune*:

Carradine's performance as Hamlet after his success as Shylock and Iago proves him one of the
outstanding Shakespearean actors of our time. In the opinion of this reviewer he far surpasses

scenes from **Merchant of Venice**

Sonia Sorel and John Carradine

Scenes from *The Merchant of Venice*.

Maurice Evans in understanding the subtleties of the role. His ease and grace on the stage are marvelous to behold, and he reads the lines as if they were extemporaneous. He is not the Shakespearean actor portraying Shakespeare's greatest character; he is Hamlet, living a tragedy.

Sunday, October 17: *Hamlet* plays its final performance at the Pasadena Playhouse. Carradine's three-week run reportedly has shattered all Playhouse records for Shakespeare, despite gas rationing, with 250 people turned away each week.[26]

The dream is coming true. The official premiere in San Francisco is only a week away.

Monday, October 18: The day after *Hamlet* closes, *Voodoo Man* starts shooting at Monogram.

Wednesday, October 20: Frederick C. Othman, United Press Hollywood correspondent, files a story with the headline:

"Actor Trades Movies
for Shakespeare Tour—
Carradine, Fed Up with Hollywood,
Hopes He'll Never Have to Return"

Othman writes that *Voodoo Man*'s Lugosi, Carradine, and Zucco "carve the souls out of beautiful women and in so doing turn them into zombies. Then Carradine puts his blonde zombies into coolers and makes love to them through plate glass windows." The reporter paints an evocative picture of the *Voodoo Man* set: producer Sam Katzman, cracking "I call this a moron picture," boasting about his fancy house and swimming pool, while "the $3,000-per-week half-wit practiced voodoo rhythm on Monogram Studio's idea of a Haitian drum."

Meanwhile, Carradine crows to Othman about his "excellent" advance sale in San Francisco and that he has "every hope of never coming back to the movies"—minimizing the fact that he's already played in some of the greatest films in Hollywood history:

> I never did like 'em. Occasionally I got to play in a good one. But mostly I have been in pictures that never got anywhere and never settled anything; that only caused the patrons to waste an hour and a half of their valuable time.
>
> Of course, if I don't succeed in Shakespeare, I'll be back to make some more pictures. After all, I do appreciate all the money Hollywood's paid me.

The arrogant words are ill-chosen, and probably alienating to the film studios; they seem to be so to Othman, who writes, "So much for Carradine and Hamlet, and good luck to 'em both." Surely the actor has a lot on his mind—getting his troupe to San Francisco and preparing for what he sees as his first, best destiny. Still, he just keeps giving the finger to the film colony.

"If this goes over," Carradine vows, "I'm through with Hollywood forever!"[27]

* * *

I am very proud, revengeful, ambitious;
with more offences at my beck than I have thoughts to put them in...
What should such fellows as I do crawling between heaven and earth?
—**Hamlet**, Act III, sc. i

Sunday night, October 24: Carradine and his Shakespeare Players open in *Hamlet* at the Geary Theatre, providing San Francisco what *Time* magazine calls "its biggest Shakespeare premiere of modern times."[28] *Variety* reports the opening night to be a sellout, with the $1,800 box office reportedly holding $400 more than it had the night Maurice Evans' record-breaking *Hamlet* had opened in San Francisco several years previously.[29] There is only one empty seat—beside Ardanelle Carradine, and reserved for John Barrymore.

"Jack always said he wanted to see my opening," says Carradine. "I don't know whether he saw it or not."

It is Carradine's night of triumph. His Hamlet is a classical powerhouse—awesome, inspiring ... unstoppable. Come the second night and a three-minute earthquake hits San Francisco, rattling the Geary's chandelier and spooking the audience. A lesser actor would

Risqué flyer for John Carradine and His Shakespeare Players, October 1943.

flee to the wings. Carradine merely speaks louder. Finally, some sailors, entranced by the performance, restore order: "Shut up, everybody!" they shout.[30]

Tuesday, October 26: Variety reviews *Hamlet*:

> Venture is first legit for Carradine who financed the show, and while he was slightly nervous as the star he landed solidly following the first act. The supporting cast, despite its general lack of experience, gave a good account of themselves in the production which was bought from the Barrymore estate. Present indications are that gross will hit around $13,000 for first week. The play had a handsome reception with no advance publicity, thus killing local wiseies who asked, "Who is Carradine?"

Actually, there has been advance publicity, and it causes controversy. Carradine has produced a "John Carradine and His Shakespeare Players" flyer, sketched in the style of Aubrey Beardsley. It presents Carradine in Shakespearean bonnet and garb, playing a lute, flanked by a trio of vampy, Elizabethan, bare-breasted, nipples-showing beauties. Two of the females wear sheer apparel, presenting pubis. It's surely an eye-opener, and critic Wood Soanes of the *Oakland Tribune* protests that the flyer reeks of "burlesque."

Nevertheless, the opening is a thrill for the actor. Perhaps the most eloquent praise for Carradine's Hamlet will come decades later in Leonard Wolf's book *A Dream of Dracula* (1972). Wolf, a professor at California State University in San Francisco who taught an accredited course in vampirism, had seen Carradine as the woeful Dane, and set the scene:

> Claudius and Polonius had just walked off a stage otherwise empty except for a single chair. Hamlet entered, sniffed the air, as if he knew who had preceded him. Then he began to pace with a questioning, nervous intensity. He appeared to be looking for something ... something he needed to get his hands on ... something he had forgotten ... or lost. Something as vital as it was unseizable, which, if it could be found, would affect destinies. He ranged across the stage, back and forth, like an injured animal whose misfortune it was to be also a prince in whom speech and loss were raging. His hands sought the air; his head twisted. When he walked he was a knife; he was a wound. Finally, he caught up the lone chair, swung it around and sat down. It was done with an abusive dance movement, as the last protest that a prince and a beast and a mind could make together against the world before they were required to focus on:
>
> "To be, or not to be; that is the question..."
>
> It was a very great Hamlet. Pretty nearly an overwhelming one. Whenever Carradine appeared, there was a sense of danger and of grief. I wanted to weep, but he was too nobly tall to be pitied; I wanted to cry out, but he was in too much pain to be disturbed. I do not know when I have been gladder to see a Hamlet die, so I could stop caring what happened to him.[31]

Wolf added that this memory would later and forever cause conflict as he watched Carradine as a Hollywood Dracula: "When Carradine stalks through a catchall film like *House of Frankenstein* or the slightly (but not much better) *House of Dracula* to share his genius with the Wolf Man and the Frankenstein Monster, I feel a tide of trouble rising in me, though I am not always sure whether the swell of feeling is for him—or for me."

Carradine embraces his triumph. He does so, as Dean Goodman will remember, with "bawdiness," a "ribald sense of humor," and "a flamboyance which sometimes bordered on bad taste":

> This was John's dream—this is what he really wanted to do, to be the 19th century actor-manager, à la Sir Henry Irving and Johnston Forbes-Robertson, and to take over the John Barrymore mantle. He played the actor-manager role constantly—and to the hilt! Oh, yes! When we were on tour, John dressed the part offstage—wearing a cape and a big fedora, and flourishing a cane, striking deep, sonorous tones all the time.

scenes from **Hamlet**

Sonia Sorel

John Carradine

Maxine Chevalier   *Emily Lawrence*   *Sonia Sorel*

Scenes from *Hamlet* from Carradine's Shakespeare program.

Poor John ... I think he was born about 50 years too late [*laughing*]—if he had been active at the end of the 1800s, he would have been in his element. He was very much in the "grand manner"—yeah!

All of us in the company regarded John and his shenanigans with amusement. He was a lot of fun, and we enjoyed being part of his traveling circus.

Saturday, October 30: *The Merchant of Venice* follows *Hamlet* at the Geary. Hazel Bruce reviews the play in the *San Francisco Chronicle*, noting that, in this era of World War II restrictions, "the richness and color of the piece were almost in the nature of a miracle."

> Major interest in the play lies naturally with Shylock and with Portia. John Carradine was one of the most convincing-looking Shylocks I have seen. His leanness, his slight stoop, the richness of his "Jewish gabardine," made him a dominating figure the moment he stepped onto the stage.
>
> John Carradine's psychological understanding of the character was also apparent from the start. The arrogance, the coolness of mind, the candidly admitted avarice ... they stood there outlined like a strong line drawing. But for two acts the listener was almost maddened by catching only key words in long familiar lines, and by a hurried diction and swallowed endings.
>
> The third act, when Mr. Carradine gives a magnificent performance, when he spoke clearly and vibrantly and without any apparent haste, merely proves that unless he overcomes this habit of haste and clarity, it is going to go hard with him when he takes his repertory company to Broadway. It cannot be carelessness because Mr. Carradine loves Shakespeare only less than his breath.

As for Sonia Sorel, Ms. Bruce writes that she is "excellent" and plays Portia with "refreshing jets of comedy."

Tuesday, November 2: The Sonia situation becomes stranger. On this day the *San Mateo Times* reports that Ardanelle Carradine "will be a house guest for a few days" at the San Mateo home of Mr. and Mrs. Henry Henius, Sonia's parents. Presumably, while Carradine chases their daughter, Mr. and Mrs. Henius house his wife.

Wednesday, November 3: "Carradine's *Hamlet* Sock $14,000 in Frisco," headlines *Variety*. The trade paper judges this money to be "excellent." While critic Wood Soanes has his reservations about Carradine's acting—and "burlesque" flyer—he applauds the actor's achievement: Carradine has "conquered San Francisco and made Shakespeare a box office attraction."

Thursday, November 4: *Othello* follows *The Merchant of Venice* at the Geary. The company finishes its two-week engagement, business building each week, and such is the demand for tickets that the company could remain at the Geary for an additional three weeks. However, the Geary has booked a stage production of *Jane Eyre*, starring Sylvia Sidney and Luther Adler (who were married at the time), so Carradine and his troupe must vacate after the final November 6 performance.

Wednesday, November 10: The Carradine company opens at the Seattle Metropolitan Theatre with opening night receipts of $1,700 and an advance sale of $10,000.

Tuesday, November 22: "Carradine Reaping," headlines *Variety,* reporting "a big $21,000" in Seattle, where the company plays 13 performances in 11 days to "turn away trade." While in Seattle, Carradine is again stingingly candid in regard to Hollywood: "Since quitting pictures—and for good—I find that at last I'm really working and earning an honest living."[32]

The barnstorming continues in Oregon, as does John's passionate pursuit of Sonia, as does the ribald humor. Dean Goodman will remember a lunch in a Portland restaurant with John and Sonia where John, "with a curl of his lip," condemns his entrée.

"Am I supposed to eat this," Carradine asks the waitress, "or *did* I?"

* * *

> *... as prime as goats, as hot as monkeys....*
> —**Othello,** Act III, sc. iii

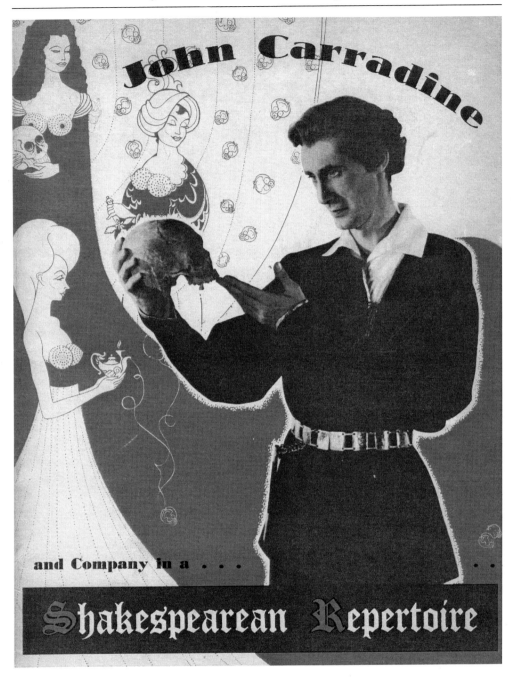

Cover of the program for "John Carradine and His Shakespeare Players," 1943.

Monday, December 6: After touring the West Coast, John Carradine and his Shakespeare Players return to Los Angeles and move into the Biltmore Theatre for a two-week run, opening with *The Merchant of Venice.*

Competing theatricals are of the racy variety: *Ken Murray's Blackouts of '43* at the El Capitan, and *Maid in the Ozarks* at the Belasco. The big horror movie attraction in town is a Universal double feature at Hollywood's Hawaii Theatre: Lon Chaney in *Son of Dracula*, George Zucco in *The Mad Ghoul,* and Evelyn Ankers in both.

"And a glorious revival it is!" rhapsodizes Gladys Stevens in *The Hollywood Citizen-News,* reviewing *The Merchant of Venice*:

> John Carradine, as Shylock, is magnificent ... he consciously and sincerely brings to the foreground the thoughts, frustrations and vengeance of the downtrodden people that Master Shakespeare realized and revealed even in his time. Carradine's miser is not altogether a cruel, mercenary man, but a pitiful example of an old fellow, embittered, maddened, and materialistic because of the racial discriminatory scorn cast upon him.
>
> Sonia Sorel, portraying Portia, who tempers mercy with justice, might easily be the clever, vivacious lady of today. Her interpretation is perfect—that of a lovely, devilish coquette striving to save the happiness of the man she loves, through her initiative and wit.

The *Los Angeles Times* comes to review the play and Edwin Schallert calls Carradine's Shylock "the thoughtful portrait of a studious actor." Apparently Carradine has improved his diction since San Francisco, as Schallert notes his speeches are "meticulously rendered." As for Sonia, she possesses "great charm."

Harrison Carroll of the *Los Angeles Evening Herald-Express* is less impressed:

> In a vacation from screen horror roles, John Carradine last night donned the beard and robes of Shylock ... Carradine's portrayal ... lacks the quality of magnetism that emanates from real stars, be they of the stage or the screen. All the great Shakespearean performers have had it. Carradine, a good sound actor, simply doesn't have it.

Carroll finds Sonia Sorel to be "a voluptuous Portia" and notes that the audience, come the finale, awarded the company "several curtain calls." Meanwhile, John's marriage to Ardanelle is still hanging together; when David turns seven on December 8, his dad and the company give him a party on the Biltmore stage.

Saturday, December 11: Hamlet opens at the Biltmore. Carradine, as he surely had hoped, wins his finest praise for this performance. Edwin Schallert writes in the *Los Angeles Times*:

> John Carradine assumed the Shakespearean mask of deep tragedy with marked success Saturday at the Biltmore Theatre. Hamlet is probably due to become his finest portrayal.
>
> It needs polishing as yet, but it is ironical, colorful and brilliant ... his Prince of Denmark is a solid achievement.... The famous soliloquies are well individualized in his reading. The "To Be or Not to Be," especially, is given a unique interpretation.
>
> Carradine has sought novelty in the Hamlet role—probably more than anyone except John Barrymore, and avoidance of old styles and traditions will probably be an added lure for many people.

Jean Irving of the *Hollywood Citizen-News* critiques:

> Too much that is commendable could not be said for Carradine's portrayal of the hapless prince of Denmark ... Carradine is Hamlet, gentle and sensitive, driven to the violence of revenge by his murdered father's ghost.
>
> The clean sharp knife of tragedy finds its way home when, tortured by the dilemma of fate, Hamlet cries out. "The time is out of joint; o cursed spite, that ever I was born to set it right!" Carradine's actions are suited to the word; he speaks his words trippingly on the tongue; he is superb.

Wednesday December 15: "Carradine's Bard Pays Off at $10,000 in L.A." headlines *Variety,* reporting:

Biltmore patrons are finding John Carradine and his Shakespearean players to their liking, coming across with $10,000 for the first week and the same for current and final stanza....

Thursday, December 16: Othello opens. Again, Carradine's Moor plunges the audience into eerie silence. Grace Kingsley of the *L. A. Times* hails the star:

John Carradine seems to have discovered in the character of Othello more than do many other actors of the role. He brought to the part last night at the Biltmore Theatre a sensitive and brilliant understanding....

He shows Othello as naïve, simple, a little vain, stern, ruthless, passionate, yet full of dignity, nobility, tenderness with flashes of delicacy of feeling, together with a certain shrewd Oriental reserve....

Carradine's portrayal of mounting jealousy in his drama of the cruel passion is skillfully limned. The scene in the death chamber is memorable for its mingled tenderness, heartbreak and contrasting ruthlessness.

By this time, Alfred Allegro has left the company to appear in a play called *The Face*. Robert Duke has replaced him as Iago, giving in Ms. Kingsley's words a "truly brilliant performance." As for Sonia, she is "lusciously lovely."

Saturday, December 18: Carradine's Othello murders Sonia's Desdemona, moments later stabbing himself. The curtain falls; the Los Angeles engagement is over. As David Carradine will write:

He and this goddess of an actress were together every night on stage, wowing the public, and the excitement between them was at a fever pitch. The inevitable happened; had already happened. They succumbed, of course. How could he help it? How could she?

Variety will give the final figure as $21,500 for the fortnight engagement.[33] The plan is for the company to play Salt Lake City, Kansas City, St. Louis, and then four weeks in Chicago; from there, New York for Shakespeare's April 23 birthday.

Sadly, it all will come to naught. David Carradine will write that the Shuberts offer to book the tour, but the stage manager takes the call, wants to go home for Christmas, and turns down the offer without ever telling Carradine.

"That's Dad's story," David Carradine will remember.

Dean Goodman (who has come back to L.A. to discover that wife Maria has deserted him after less than four months of marriage, leaving makeup caked in the apartment sink and the "plumbing clogged in the tub and in the toilet"), will provide a more believable account:

The problem was, when we got back to the Biltmore in L.A., John tried to get the United Booking Office to book us—and they wouldn't do it. They didn't think the tour was enough of a blockbuster, that John wasn't quite a big enough name at that time, I guess. So the company disbanded, and that was the end of John's dream for a Shakespearean company. He never got the company back together after the Biltmore.

The critical praise, the ovations, the financing, the masterful overcoming of so many challenges ... it all seems to count for nothing. In the eyes of the theater-at-large, John Carradine is a supporting actor in movies. Indeed, he's becoming a bogeyman in movies. Now that he's back in town, maybe Monogram will invite him to the opening of *Voodoo Man*.

* * *

O, horrible! O, horrible! Most horrible!
*—**Hamlet**,* Act I, sc. v

Monday, December 20: *The Hollywood Citizen News* reports Carradine has signed to appear in Universal's The *Merry Monahans*. Presumably he's set to play the has-been matinee idol role eventually portrayed in that Donald O'Connor musical by John Miljan.

The letdown must be overwhelming. He's back on Ben Avenue with Ardanelle and the two boys for what promises to be a very downcast Christmas. No more tours, no April 23 New York opening … no Sonia. So, Carradine reportedly gives the out-of-work Sonia lodging in the family home. It isn't the first time Carradine has brought a fellow player into the house; David Carradine will recall a very-late-in-life John Barrymore living with them for a time on Ben Avenue, his mother desperately and unsuccessfully trying to hide the household liquor from the Great Profile.

Friday, New Year's Eve, 1943: It's John and Ardanelle's eighth wedding anniversary. The explosion finally comes. Carradine, who's spent the evening, significantly, reading *Good Night, Sweet Prince*—Gene Fowler's best-selling biography of John Barrymore—suddenly tells Ardanelle, "I'm madly in love with Sonia and I want to be divorced from you to marry her. All I want are the clothes on my back."[34]

Out he goes. But now Sonia—either in a genuine act of good conscience, or to bait the hook more cunningly—suddenly disappears before her erstwhile Hamlet-Shylock-Othello-Iago can claim her. She goes to work in a bomb factory ("hard hat and all," recalls David Carradine). In a scene prophetic of the crowd-pleasing finale of *An Officer and a Gentleman*, Carradine finds her and retrieves her.

Thursday, January 6, 1944: Ardanelle Carradine announces she's seeking "an early divorce."

Monday, January 10: Universal begins shooting *The Invisible Man's Revenge*. The studio reassigns Carradine out of *The Merry Monahans* into this horror show as Dr. Drury, who walks an invisible Great Dane on a leash.

Thursday, January 27: *Variety* reports:

> Final accounting of John Carradine's recent 8-week tour of six Pacific Coast cities with his own Shakespearean company revealed net profit of $12,000. Strangely enough, only city in which company did not fare well was Los Angeles, where $4,000 loss was run up for 2-week engagement. In Seattle, city ordinarily good for three or four days of Shakespeare at best, company played to 75 percent capacity audience for eleven days. Weekly nut was $7,100, with Carradine presenting trio of plays, *Hamlet, Othello*, and *The Merchant of Venice*. As soon as actor completes current role in Universal's *The Invisible Man's Revenge*, he will take troupe, with slightly different personnel, to South for extended tour.[35]

Wednesday, February 2: Columbia starts shooting *The Black Parachute*, starring Carradine as a Nazi general. The tour of the South has obviously fallen through.

Friday, March 17: PRC starts *Waterfront*, starring Carradine as yet another Nazi.

Meanwhile, Carradine has moved into the notorious Garden of Allah, a colony of Spanish villas surrounding a pool shaped like the Black Sea, at 8152 Sunset Boulevard in West Hollywood. It's the former abode of stage and screen legend Alla Nazimova. Sonia has joined Carradine in his villa. Having failed to approximate John Barrymore as a Shakespearean stage star, Carradine appears hell-bent on approximating his legend as a hard-drinking screwball.

As Carradine roars Shakespeare, Sonia chases him around the pool, brandishing her high-heeled shoe as a weapon. The actor keeps a bust of himself by the pool, claiming he wants it to get a nice tan. One night he tries to walk across the pool, announcing he is Jesus.

Neighbor Marc Connelly, the famed playwright, makes bets with the neighbors that Carradine will make it. As Sheilah Graham writes in her book *The Garden of Allah,* "He lost his bet."[36]

If Carradine believes this living-in-sin showboating will make Hollywood think he's a genius, he's wildly mistaken.

Wednesday, April 12: Monogram, spending a bundle (for them), begins shooting Jack London's *Alaska,* hiring Carradine to play pretty much what is Hollywood's perception of him: a drunken Shakespearean actor with a long-suffering wife. The script affords him a noble death—saving the hero from a fire—and he dies from smoke inhalation, shuffling off his mortal coil slowly, slowly, ever so slowly, reciting: "To be, or not to be, that is the question..."

Sunday, April 23: On the night he had dreamed of opening "John Carradine and His Shakespeare Players" on Broadway, the actor is at the Garden of Allah, a few days away from starting work in *House of Frankenstein.* Rather than officially becoming the country's top classical actor, Carradine is now Universal's new Count Dracula, joining Boris Karloff's Mad Doctor, Lon Chaney's Wolf Man, J. Carrol Naish's Hunchback, and Glenn Strange's Frankenstein Monster.

For $3,500 per week on a two-week guarantee, John Carradine has just sold his soul to Hollywood.[37]

Saturday, May 27: Carradine guest stars on radio's *Stars Over Hollywood* in "The Ghost of Hamlet."

Wednesday, May 31: PRC starts shooting *Bluebeard,* with Carradine superb in the title role. Jean Parker is his leading lady; Sonia plays one of his victims. Edgar G. Ulmer, the director, allows Carradine and son David to live at his house at 1659 North King's Road, up the hill from the Garden of Allah, when Ardanelle dispatches authorities for money her ex-spouse owes her.[38]

Summer: Carradine, overwhelmed by divorce, money woes, and fights with Sonia, drinks 12 double Scotch and sodas at the Garden of Allah one night, goes berserk, and tries to drown himself in the pool. Three male nurses, alerted to the emergency, rush to the Garden and restrain him.[39]

Sunday, August 13: Carradine and Sonia wed in Nevada, following his Mexican divorce from Ardanelle. The state of California rules the marriage illegal.

Saturday, October 28: Carradine guest stars on *Stars Over Hollywood* in "Frankenstein and the Monster."

Wednesday, December 6: Carradine begins his final engagement at the Pasadena Playhouse. The show is *My Dear Children,* the tawdry sex comedy in which John Barrymore had starred on Broadway in 1940, peppering the play with ribald ad-libs and asides. Carradine plays the Great Profile's role of Allan Manville, performing his riotous Barrymore impersonation. His leading lady, naturally, is Sonia Sorel as Cordelia, the part Barrymore's last wife Elaine had played in New York. The big scene: Manville placing Cordelia over his knee and spanking her.

Sunday, March 25, 1945: Carradine and Sonia wed—again. They cut the wedding cake with Hamlet's sword. David Carradine will remember their home in the Hollywood Hills, up the hill from the Garden of Allah, as the "den of iniquity."

Friday, June 29: Police arrest Carradine for back alimony. He goes to jail, where the press photographs him suavely posing behind bars. Sonia comes to provide the $2,000 bail. They go to Coney Island to appear in a stock production of *My Dear Children.*

"O, horrible! O, horrible! Most horrible!" Carradine as Dracula, hamming it up between scenes with Anne Gwynne and Peter Coe on the set of *House of Frankenstein* (1944).

Thursday, September 20: Carradine, back in Hollywood, resurrects Dracula in Universal's *House of Dracula*. Playing the miracle-working doctor who tries to cure his vampirism is Onslow Stevens, formerly Othello to Carradine's Iago—and formerly Sonia Sorel's lover. In the course of the melodrama, which includes Lon Chaney's Wolf Man, Glenn Strange's Frankenstein's Monster, and Jane Adams' hunchbacked nurse, Carradine injects parasitic

John "kills" his real-life lover Sonia in Edgar G. Ulmer's *Bluebeard* (1944).

blood into Stevens and turns him into a rabid creature of the night. The convincing grin on Carradine's face while he performs this perfidy is probably simply due to good acting; ditto the look of satisfaction on Stevens' face when Carradine's Dracula turns into a skeleton.[40]

Meanwhile, David and Bruce, Ardanelle and John's sons, encounter a future in various boarding schools. Having a fleeing father who played Dracula and left his wife and sons has its impact on David "Pooky" Carradine:

> In terms of Pooky being affected by his daddy's line of work; I remember a recurrent dream that scared the hell out of me; my daddy, dressed up in a Dracula cape and a black hat, coming at me on a red tricycle with wings.

* * *

> *I will chop her into messes: Cuckold me?*
> —***Othello***, Act IV, sc. i

The John and Sonia marriage will produce three sons: Christopher (born January 1947), Keith (born August 1949), and Robert (born March 1954). Meanwhile, there's plenty of theater:

Saturday, December 15, 1945: *Murder Without Crime,* starring John and Sonia, and Broadway-bound, folds in Boston.

Montage: John Carradine in jail after his arrest for back alimony in June 1945. Upper left: Sonia comforts John after his release. Below: Ardanelle Carradine, the actor's first wife.

Wednesday, December 19: *Variety* reports that *Murder Without Crime*'s producer, Theodore Ruskin, "is preferring charges with Equity against John Carradine, alleging the latter wouldn't follow director Hale McKeen's suggestions and that Ruskin 'found it impossible to get from Carradine the cooperation usually accorded a producer by an actor.'"

Summer, 1946: Carradine flees Hollywood to avoid jail time for alimony contempt. If he comes back, he faces arrest.

Tuesday, October 15: John and Sonia make their Broadway debuts at the Ethel Barrymore Theatre in John Webster's Jacobean horror play *The Duchess of Malfi*. It stars Elisabeth Bergner in the title role, with John as the evil Cardinal and Sonia in the small role of Julia. The play runs 38 performances.

Summer, 1947: The Carradines play stock in *Hamlet*.

Summer, 1948: They play stock in *20th Century,* acting the roles played in the 1934 screwball comedy film by John Barrymore and Carole Lombard.[41]

Monday, December 27: After several Broadway flops, John finally enjoys a success as the Ragpicker in *The Madwoman of Chaillot* starring Martita Hunt at the Belasco Theatre. Sonia has a small role as "A Lady." The play will run 368 performances.

Saturday, February 3, 1951: Sonia plays Estelle in Tennessee Williams' *The Rose Tattoo*

Sonia Sorel and John Carradine, poolside at the Garden of Allah in Hollywood, circa 1944.

which opens this night at the Martin Beck Theatre, starring Maureen Stapleton. The play runs 306 performances.

The hits are rare. It's an erratic and often impecunious living. Finally, in 1953, the Carradines come back to Hollywood—where, indeed, John is arrested for back alimony and briefly serves jail time. John lands roles in movies—*The Egyptian* (20th Century–Fox, 1954), *The Ten Commandments* (Paramount, 1956), *Around the World in Eighty Days* (Michael Todd, 1956), as well as horror schlock such as *The Black Sleep* (United Artists, 1956), joining

Sonia and John arrive east for summer stock in 1945.

Basil Rathbone, Lon Chaney, and a very frail Bela Lugosi in the latter. There is also plenty of TV. Sonia turns up in an episode of TV's *Ramar of the Jungle* ("Urn of Destiny," January 23, 1954).

The Carradines move to an old ranch in Calabasas, where they live with their three boys. John buys Sonia a horse named Smoky. According to David Carradine, Smoky, a white,

Moab, semi-castrated stallion is "always horny."[42] One day when Sonia comes to the barn during her period, Smoky kicks his way out of his stall, chasing her into the house, beating on the door with his hooves. Sonia hides in the upstairs bathroom while John controls the wildly violent horse.

Blissful domesticity is not to be.

Monday, May 6, 1957: Sonia wins a Reno divorce, charging Carradine with "extreme cruelty."

Saturday, May 11: Sonia weds artist Michael Bowen, who, at 19 years old, is exactly one year younger than David Carradine. Bowen must present a legal affidavit signed by his father so he can wed Sonia, who is ten days away from turning 36. She is also three months pregnant.

Tuesday, June 11: The court finds Sonia and Bowen guilty of contributing to the delinquency of minors, fines them $200 each and places them on three years' probation. John Carradine becomes legal guardian of the three boys.

Friday, August 30: John Carradine weds Doris Rich, a blonde fashion show commentator, in Minden, Nevada. He now has a new stepson, Mike.

December 1958: Sonia loses a bid to win back custody of Christopher, Keith, and Robert. She leaves court crying with husband Michael and 13-month-old baby Michael.

Keith Carradine, caught in the mess as a small boy, later says:

> My dad was very private.... He just didn't talk. What my dad did was tell stories. Unless he got drunk. Sometimes then he'd have conversations with my mother—although she wasn't there—asking how she could have hurt him so much. I just listened.... What you experience as a kid sometimes takes a long time to get over.[43]

As for Sonia, she at times schemes for a comeback. Dean Goodman will recall:

> About 20 years after I was in John's Shakespeare company, I directed him in a production of *The Merchant of Venice* in Palo Alto. Sonia got John's first wife (with whom she was friendly, interestingly enough) to call me and ask me if she could play Portia with him! Well, I brought it up with John, and he was very diplomatic—he said, "Well, Dean, you're the director, and if you want her, why of course, I'll work with her—but I'd just feel a little uncomfortable." So I decided not to go that way.

Tuesday, May 18, 1971: Doris Rich Carradine is found dead of asphyxiation after a fire in her beachfront apartment in Oxnard, California. She is estranged from Carradine at the time of her death.

Thursday, July 3, 1975: Carradine marries for a fourth time, to Emily Cisneros, mother of four.

Monday, March 29, 1976: The actor is in the audience at the Dorothy Chandler Pavilion in Los Angeles the night Keith Carradine wins an Oscar for his song "I'm Easy" from *Nashville*.

Sunday, January 4, 1981: John Carradine opens—and closes—in Broadway's *Frankenstein*, playing the old Hermit who befriends the Monster. At a loss of $2,000,000, it's the biggest flop to this time in Broadway history.

Also in 1981: He joins a bus tour of Roy Radin's Vaudeville Show, touring the boonies with Tiny Tim, the Harmonica Rascals, a fire eater, and Zippy the Chimp. Tiny Tim tells the *New York Times* that Carradine "recites Shakespeare and he gets a very respectful reception." Then, after making sure that Carradine isn't nearby, Tiny Tim adds, "I often wonder what goes through his mind when we're on the bus."[44]

*   *   *

That it should come to this!
—**Hamlet**, Act I, scene 2

John Carradine nears 80. His hands are long horribly twisted by arthritis ("and my feet don't look like feet at all," he admits). He nevertheless amazes everyone with his professionalism, and wins a 1985 Daytime Emmy for the TV Movie *Umbrella Jack*.

"That's the only award I was ever up for and the only one I ever got," says Carradine. "I guess it's because the industry thinks, 'That poor guy. We never did anything for him. We better do something before he kicks off.'"

Tuesday, June 18, 1985: Keith Carradine and his wife Sandra become parents of a baby girl. In an obvious honor to Keith's mother, they name the baby Sorel.

John Carradine carries on. For over 40 years, through all the alimony, financial straits, lost homes, and various deprivations, he's somehow found the money to keep his Robert Edmond Jones Shakespeare set in storage. Only a few years before his death, he finally misses a payment—and loses the set.

The man's financial need to keep acting is desperate, but probably not as severe as his emotional need. "I keep pretty busy all the time, or I'd go nuts," Carradine confesses. Director Fred Olen Ray employs him whenever possible, in such fare as *Death Farm* (1986) as "the Judge of Hell." ("The old goat couldn't look any sadder," notes film historian Tom Weaver.[45]) John Carradine's final movie: *Buried Alive*, as a cackling geezer in a wheelchair. He has to go all the way to South Africa for the job.

He doesn't make it home alive.

Sunday, November 27, 1988: John Carradine dies this night in Fatebenefratelli Hospital, Milan, Italy, at the age of 82. The legend goes that he'd climbed the 328 steps of the gothic cathedral tower of the Duomo—the elevator was out of order—and suffered a heart attack. He reportedly dies in the hospital's paupers' ward, supposedly in the arms of David, who later tells friends his father had actually died of malnutrition.

Friday, December 2: The funeral for John Carradine at St. Thomas the Apostle Episcopal Church, 7501 Hollywood Boulevard, is appropriately macabre. David will write that the undertakers had given the cadaver "a demonic, artificial grin ... like nothing I had ever seen him do in real life, except in a horror film."[46]

The sons speak in tribute. David breaks down. Later, he decides to give his father a final drink, has trouble getting the drink into the corpse's sewn-together mouth, and pours champagne all over the cadaver.

Carradine's last wife, Emily, from whom he was estranged, reportedly skips the ceremony. Ardanelle is there—and so is Sonia, who, in David's words, has long-suffered from "real functional lunacy" and has become "an unhappy, crazy and desperate old woman."[47] According to Fred Olen Ray, the majority of the family basically ignores her.

John Carradine receives a burial at sea, in the Santa Monica Channel, a flag-draped coffin honoring his service in the early days and nights of World War II when he had sailed the *Bali* as part of the coast patrol.

Ardanelle dies shortly after John, in January of 1989. Sonia Sorel lives almost 16 more years. Late in life, Carradine had told acquaintances that Sonia had become a bag lady in Hollywood. This might seem unlikely, since she had two celebrity sons (Keith and Robert), a son who was an executive at Disney (Christopher), a celebrity stepson (David), and an actor son by her marriage to Michael Bowen (also named Michael Bowen).[48] However, it was presumably true. In 1996, Dean Goodman told me:

> I haven't seen Sonia for a while, but she went downhill after her divorce from John. In fact, the sons, Keith and Robert, have practically disowned her. Oh, yes. Well, she got to drinking too much, and she married somebody who was 20 years younger than she was, and was living almost like a hippie in the woods. She let herself go physically, and she put on an awful lot of weight. She was beautiful, attractive and very charming as Portia, Desdemona, and Ophelia, but it was very sad what happened with Sonia.

She had refused my 1989 request for an interview—"I don't want to talk to *anybody!*" she told Fred Olen Ray, who'd asked on my behalf. She wanders; on at least one occasion, she is found a vagrant in Hemet, the mountain pass town above Palm Springs. If ever anyone, in Othello's words, "threw a pearl away richer than all his tribe," it was Sonia Sorel, the brilliant leading lady of "John Carradine and His Shakespeare Players," who tossed out her talent for a life of epic squalor.

Friday, September 24, 2004: Sonia Sorel dies in Los Angeles at the age of 83.

*   *   *

> *There's a divinity that shapes our ends*
> *Rough-hew them how we will.*
> —***Hamlet**, Act V, sc. ii*

The Carradine family survives, the news sometimes sad—and tragic. David Carradine, who, as noted, had tried to hang himself when he was five, managed to succeed at age 72 on June 3, 2009, in a hotel room closet in Bangkok. The probable theory: accidental asphyxiation while masturbating. In *Endless Highway,* David had written of the first time he realized his daddy was an actor—in 1942, when Ardanelle had taken the five-year-old to see a stage production of *The Vagabond King* in Los Angeles:

"That's my dad!" David had cried out jubilantly, standing on his seat.[49]

Meanwhile, Sorel Carradine, beautifully blonde like her grandmother, has advanced in her career, appearing in such films as *The Good Doctor* (2011, with Orlando Bloom) and *The Happy Sad* (2012). She's been romantically linked with actor Chris Pine, whose grandmother was Anne Gwynne—who played the heroine seduced by John Carradine's Dracula in *House of Frankenstein.*

Of the family's many achievements, few remember "John Carradine and His Shakespeare Players," although the troupe's brief blaze of glory was surely the proudest era of Carradine's life and career. On rare occasions, a program from the company shows up on eBay; at least once, a flyer did, with its racy Aubrey Beardsley caricature. There can be no Turner Classic Movies' resurrection of the troupe—stage actors "carve in ice," as the expression goes—and the artistry and passion of a triumphant, inspired, madly-in-love John Carradine are sadly lost to the ages.

Tuesday, December 6, 1988: Four days after Carradine's funeral, *The Hollywood Reporter* runs a full-page tribute, with a photograph of John Carradine as Hamlet from the 1943 tour. "John Carradine—1906–1988," reads the words atop the page, and below are the lines Horatio had spoken over the dead Hamlet:

> Good Night, Sweet Prince,
> And Flights of Angels
> Sing Thee to thy Rest

The classical words are gloriously appropriate. However, one might have added these words from Prospero in *The Tempest,* that relate so powerfully to what John Carradine, his Shakespeare Company, and his erratic life and career were truly all about:

> Our revels now are ended. These our actors,
> As I foretold you, were all spirits, and
> Are melted into air, into thin air....
> We are such stuff
> As dreams are made on; and our little life
> Is rounded with a sleep.

John Carradine and His Shakespeare Players—Repertory

The cast lists below are those that appeared in the playbill for the Geary Theatre, San Francisco, 24 October to 6 November 1943:

John Carradine (Producer and Director); Michael Jeffrey (Associate Director).

Mr. Carradine's Staff: Jack Brandt (General Manager); Jacque Pierre (Press Representative); Dorathi Bock Pierre (Lecturer); George Ramsey (Stage Manager); Philip Raiguel (Technical Director); Carlo Caiati (Art Director); William Yancie (Head Electrician); C.A. Smith (Master of Properties); Frank Barnett (Master Carpenter).

Hamlet. Performed October 24, 25, 26, 27, 28, 29, 1943.

The Cast (In Order of Appearance): Philip Baker (Francisco); Dean Goodman (Barnardo); David Powell (Horatio); James Logan (Marcellus); Houseley Stevenson (Ghost); Kevin Kemble (King Claudius); Kay Hammond (Queen Gertrude); C. Montague Shaw (Polonius); Robert Duke (Laertes); John Carradine (Hamlet); Mauritz Hugo (Rosencrantz); Eldredge Clarke (Guildenstern); Sonia Sorel (Ophelia): George Pembroke (First Player); Emily Lawrence (Second Player); Philip Baker (Third Player); Thomas Leffingwell (Fourth Player); C. Montague Shaw (First Clown); George Ramsey (Second Clown); Ralph Brooke (Osric); George Pembroke (A Priest).

The Merchant of Venice. Performed October 30 (matinee and evening), October 31, November 1, 2, 3, 1943.

The Cast (In Order of Appearance): C. Montague Shaw (Antonio); Eldredge Clarke (Salerino); Mauritz Hugo (Salanio); David Powell (Bassanio); Dean Goodman (Lorenzo); Robert Duke (Gratiano); John Carradine (Shylock); Ralph Brooke (Launcelot); Houseley Stevenson (Old Gobbo); Maxine Chevalier (Jessica); Sonia Sorel (Portia); Emily Lawrence (Nerissa); Thomas Leffingwell (Balthazar); Kevin Kemble (Morocco); Houseley Stevenson (Duke of Venice); George Pembroke (Tubal); James Logan (Servant); Philip Baker (Servant).

Othello. Performed November 4, 5, 6 (matinee and evening on the 6th), 1943.

The Cast (In Order of Appearance): Kevin Kemble (Roderigo); Alfred Allegro (Iago); C. Montague Shaw (Brabantio); John Carradine (Othello); Robert Duke (Cassio); Houseley Stevenson (Duke of Venice); Sonia Sorel (Desdemona); Emily Lawrence (Emilia); George Pembroke (Montano); Thomas Leffingwell (Senator Lodovico); Houseley Stevenson (Gratiano); James Logan (Gentleman).

12

Shock! Theatre, The "Half-Witch and Half-Fairy" and Dr. Lucifer

Oh, we had such a time making the scene! When dear Boris jumped in that window,
how I screamed and carried on! I carried it off with such flair ... such style...
—Ottola Nesmith, pretending to be a madwoman
pretending to be Mae Clarke,
as she hosted *Nightmare! Theatre,*
Los Angeles, October 1, 1957

I damn near destroyed the studio one time!
—Richard Dix, remembering his nights
as Dr. Lucifer of *Shock! Theatre,* Baltimore, 1957–1959

Fall, 1957: Screen Gems releases to TV a 52-film sensation titled *Shock! Theatre. Dracula, Frankenstein, The Mummy, The Invisible Man, The Wolf Man* ... all these hallowed Universal goblins live again, making a pouncing, mass market comeback. The old classics, dispatched from TV towers, fly through the late night sky like witches on broomsticks, captured by rooftop antennas, haunting living rooms across the country. Many of the sequels come too, as do such horrors as the Karloff-Lugosi *The Black Cat.* A few oddities, such as *Chinatown Squad* (a slinky Valerie Hobson disguised as a Chinese "woman in black," 1935) and *Danger Woman* (an oomphy Patricia Morison in a negligee out to nab atomic secrets, 1946) pad the package for a year-round different film-a-week.

By mid–November of 1957, Screen Gems has sold the *Shock!* package to 78 markets, the revenue exceeding $8,000,000. "It's the biggest selling item in syndication," reports *Variety,* "and sponsorship on the local level is a sell-out. Ratings have also topped network shows in many locations."

Enough time has passed—26 years since the release of *Dracula* and *Frankenstein*—that a romantic quality comes with the horror classics, a nostalgia for these relics of the Depression and World War II. Yet they are still scary. Bela Lugosi's Dracula attacking Frances Dade's Lucy in her darkened boudoir ... Boris Karloff's Monster reaching for seven-year-old Marilyn Harris's Maria to drown her in the mountain lake ... it's all unsettling enough to prove titillating and almost subversive fascinations for 1957's "I Like Ike" America.

Indeed, for some, they are *too* subversive.

Wednesday, November 20, 1957: Variety writes that that the Television Code Review Board of the National Association of Radio and TV Broadcasters has met in Beverly Hills and has decreed that *Shock!* is "bad programming," apt to cause an "injurious effect on children." The Board has drafted an edict that will ban the shockers from appearing on its members' stations—more than 300 of them. The ban will be a "sweeping" one, and woe to the channels that dare defy it. As *Variety* reports:

> Failure to abide by such a ruling would result in offending stations being denied use of NARTB seal of good practice and the more serious setback of defending their nonconformity before the FCC when the time comes for license renewal. Stations signatory to the code could kill off the current fad by refusing to buy or show the tabooed pictures.[1]

Fortunately, the censorship fails—the fact that many of the stations show *Shock!* late at night saves it from extinction. Had the ban succeeded, the films would have gone back into the vaults—and one shudders to imagine their fate if Universal and Screen Gems had deemed the films forever unmarketable.

Of course, quite a few of the most dynamic *Shock!* prime movers are no longer here to see the revivals. James Whale, director of *Frankenstein* and *The Invisible Man,* had drowned himself in his Pacific Palisades pool the previous May. Bela Lugosi had died in 1956, and many who watch *Dracula* remember the gothic news that he now rests in L.A.'s Holy Cross Cemetery, buried in his Dracula cape. Lionel Atwill, so vividly aberrant in such *Shock!* fare as *Son of Frankenstein* (as one-armed Inspector Krogh) and *Man Made Monster* (as ravingly mad Dr. Rigas), had died in 1946. Dwight Frye, a revelation to viewers who behold him as the giggling Renfield of *Dracula* and the hunchbacked Fritz of *Frankenstein,* is totally forgotten-and had died in 1943. The star who's been gone the longest: Colin Clive, the anguished *Frankenstein* himself, who'd died in 1937, 20 years before *Shock!* premieres on TV.

Happily, Boris Karloff, the most celebrated of horror stars, still lives and prospers in 1957, a busy character actor and inspiring success story. He recently sang and danced on Dinah Shore's Halloween show (October 27, 1957). In fact, on the same date that *Variety* reports the potential *Shock!* ban—November 20, 1957—Karloff ironically appears as the guest of honor on *This Is Your Life.*

Lon Chaney, Jr., is then co-starring as a grizzled Chingachgook on the Canadian-filmed TV series *Hawkeye and the Last of the Mohicans.*

The newspaper promos ... the TV coming attractions ... the magical word "melodrama" in the *TV Guide* listings. For many children in 1957 (including this author, then six years old), fairy tales, in a wonderfully exciting, spine-chilling way, have just grown up.

Along with the package comes a promotional book packed with pictures, plot synopses for TV listings, and publicity blurbs on everyone from Evelyn Ankers (who is a guest star on TV's *Cheyenne* on January 28, 1958) to George Zucco (then in a sanitarium near Los Angeles). *Shock!* is such a hit that *Son of Shock!* follows in the spring of 1958, adding titles strangely missing from the first package (such as *Bride of Frankenstein, House of Frankenstein* and *House of Dracula*), and providing Columbia chillers that are excellent (*The Black Room*), fair (*The Man They Could Not Hang*) and dismal (*The Soul of a Monster*).

Finally, for better or worse, *Shock!* spawns its own creature, who will forever haunt thereafter the underbelly of U.S. showmanship ... the TV horror host.

Granted, Maila Nurmi, aka Vampira, had appeared in Los Angeles, making her official debut on May 1, 1954, creating her own folklore. However, the films she showed were not the Universals, and she's been off the air for over two years by the time *Shock!* appears. *Shock!* truly sires the horror host breed, and what follows is an account of two different players who become local phenomena as they emcee the classic horror films in 1957.

One becomes rather a legal phenomenon as well, inspiring one of the more peculiar lawsuits in film history. Another becomes a friend of mine late in his life, and I dedicate this chapter to his memory.

*   *   *

Tuesday, October 1, 1957, 9:30 p.m.: KTLA, Channel 5 in Hollywood, was offering the Los Angeles TV premiere of *Frankenstein.*

Rather than title the show *Shock! Theatre,* KTLA had opted for *Nightmare! Theatre.* The TV station had also engaged a horror hostess, 67-year-old veteran actress Ottola Nesmith. A ravishing brunette beauty of the World War I era, she'd appeared in several Broadway plays, including Oscar Wilde's *A Woman of No Importance* (Fulton Theatre, April 24, 1916, 56 performances). She was married to Leon d'Usseau, who'd directed such films as *Fury of the Wild* (starring Ranger the Dog, 1929); he was also one of the six writers of the famous serial *The Lost City* (1935) and executive producer of the dreary *Revolt of the Zombies* (1936).

By 1957, Ottola had a real-life "witchy" look, an especially "witchy" voice, and a résumé that included scores of films, including such prestigious fare as *Becky Sharp* (1935) and *Mrs. Miniver* (1942). She'd acted a number of times for Cecil B. DeMille, most recently in the Best Picture Oscar winner *The Greatest Show on Earth* (1952), and had just played in Billy Wilder's *Witness for the Prosecution* (1957).

Perhaps more of interest to KTLA was the gaggle of horror films Ottola had graced. Monogram's *Invisible Ghost* (1941) had cast her as the mournful Mrs. Mason. Universal's *The Wolf Man* (1941) used her effectively as Mrs. Bally, one of the coven of dark-clad village women who blame Lon Chaney Jr.'s Larry Talbot for the full moon slaughter of Jenny (Fay Helm). In 1943 she'd worked twice for Val Lewton's RKO horror unit: as Senora Contreras, whose daughter is murdered in a cemetery in *The Leopard Man,* and as Mrs. Lowood, the rather sapphic headmistress in *The Seventh Victim.* At Columbia, she was a governess on the watch against Lugosi's bloodsucker in *The Return of the Vampire* (1944) and a nurse in *The Son of Dr. Jekyll* (1951).

Meanwhile, Nesmith had a KTLA ace in the hole: Her son Loring was directing *Nightmare! Theatre.* In fact, Ottola had two sons. Arnaud d'Usseau had scripted such films as *Lady Scarface* (1941, starring Judith Anderson) and co-authored the 1943 Broadway play *Tomorrow the World,* starring Ralph Bellamy (Ethel Barrymore Theatre, April 14, 1943, 500 performances). The play became a 1944 film starring Fredric March. Arnaud was blacklisted after a 1953 bout with the House Un-American Activities. Second son Loring, then 26, provided his mom a juicy *Nightmare! Theatre* role: "the Lady Ghoul," a spooky old derelict who, while watching the horror films, madly imagines herself the leading lady.

If nepotism played a part in her hiring, it was nevertheless ideal casting. Ottola was a sparkling-eyed, high-spirited, out-on-the-edge actress, still very flamboyant—and ready for anything.

KTLA was an ace at razzle-dazzle, carnival-style promotion. As the premiere of *Nightmare! Theatre* approached, the station launched a doozie—although it wasn't directly related to *Nightmare!* On Sunday afternoon, September 15, 1957, a "Mystery Tower Sitter," as he became known in Southern California, had climbed the 150' KTLA tower at Sunset Boulevard and Van Ness Avenue in Hollywood, perching up there from noon to midnight for 31 days and nights.[2] Based on clues, contestants had to guess who the celebrity was, and the sender of the first postmarked postcard correctly guessing his identity would win a new car.

Ottola Nesmith, hostess of Los Angeles' *Nightmare Theatre* **in 1957.**

As clues came, and KTLA hawked the premiere of *Nightmare! Theatre* and *Frankenstein,* the vast majority of contestants guessed that the masked celebrity roosting up there day and night was the venerable 69-year-old Boris Karloff. The second-biggest vote-getter: Lon Chaney, Jr.

Come the night of October 1, the "Mystery Tower Sitter" was atop the KTLA tower, waving to the faithful. It was a big night for television. At 9:30, the Los Angeles public could choose from such fare as the debut of CBS's *Assignment Foreign Legion,* starring Merle Oberon; ABC's *Telephone Time,* offering "The Gadfly," starring Thomas Mitchell as Socrates; and NBC's *The Bob Cummings Show.*

Meanwhile, KTLA, Channel 5, premiered *Nightmare!*[3]

Ottola Nesmith, in makeup and costume as *Nightmare*'s hostess, looked as if she'd arrived at KTLA on her broom. The surviving script—which comes from the personal effects of Mae Clarke, who'd later obtained a copy from KTLA[4]—describes what Southern Californians beheld that memorable night:

Open On: Long Shot of Alley, Empty.
   Super Titles
   "KTLA Presents: "*Nightmare!*"
   Announcer: [*On Above*] [*Low, Close*] KTLA Presents ... *Nightmare!* And tonight's tale, the great classic of Terror and Suspense... Boris Karloff in ... *Frankenstein.*
   Change Slide: To *Frankenstein* on Above.
   The titles dissolve. For a moment we see the lonely, shabby empty alley. Then far off, at the end of the alley, the figure of a woman appears. She looks about furtively, then starts down the alley toward us. She shuffles toward us, stopping to investigate some of the refuse along the way. There's a touch of decay about her, with a touch of madness ... and pity, too.
   As she reaches a door on her left, she stops, glances about furtively to see if anyone is watching [*she knows people are always watching!*].... Secure that she is alone, she takes out a hairpin, does something to the electric box by the door, and a dim light appears. She laughs with self-satisfied pleasure ... then sees a name on the door.
                    Ottola Nesmith
   Ottola: [*anger*] Ridiculous! How dare they ... [*she turns to the alley and shouts*] How dare you do that! That's not my name! I've told you that! I've told you! I'm not Ottola Nesmith, I'm not! I'm ... I'm ... [*confused ... searches ... then brightens*] I'm ... Mae Clarke... [*softens, low, smiles*]. That's who I am. Mae Clarke. [*She takes out a soft pencil, crosses out the name of "Ottola Nesmith" and writes under it, "Mae Clarke." Then she glances up at light.*] And the electric company ... think they're so smart ... well, I fooled them.... [*Goes in*]
   Cut to Interior of Room:
   [*As she locks the door*] Turn off the power, indeed! How dare they ... [*whines mockingly, in imitation*] "Pay the bill, pay the bill," Hrump! Electricity is free, it's in the air ... all around us! [*Thunder clap. She rushes to window and throws open drape*] ... Oh, another lovely summer evening ... [*confusion*] Or ... is it winter... [*Puts her hand up to her eyes*] I do get so confused... [*She looks up and sees picture of Karloff in silhouette, from rear, goes to it, reads inscription*] "It was fun in Sarajevo, ... love, Boris." [*We see inscription*] Boris ... dear sweet Boris... [*glances slyly at audience*] Boris Karloff, you know... Ah, those were the days.
   [*Starts to move about grandly, theatrically as she removes her cape and gloves, fixes her hair grandly but in half-hearted way*]
   Belasco ... Frohman ... Dillingham ... all at my feet ... that's when stars were really great ... not like the silly young things today with their sweaters and skirts and ridiculous names ... in my day, an actress had to have grandeur ... stature ... a name ... David Belasco presents: Miss Ottola Nesmith... [*Savors it a moment, then turns suspiciously*] Who said that? Ottola Nesmith, indeed! That's not my name. I'm Mae Clarke, I told you that. "Mae Clarke starring in *Frankenstein*, supported by Boris Karloff." [*Turns to picture*] I'm sorry Boris, but it's true ... that's the way it should have been. [*Starts to make tea*]
   But that's not the way it goes ... up and down ... back and forth ... a turn of the wheel and here you are... Like now. I'm sort of ... between engagements, you might say. The fact is, I've had to take in roomers. Oh, yes it's true! Not that I'm ashamed of it, of course. Paying guests, call them. But it's strange. I seem to have trouble keeping them. I wonder why? I don't understand it. They come and stay awhile ... and then, well ... they just seem to disappear...
   [*Looks up suddenly*] Sheba? Sheba? Where is that naughty dog! [*Goes to window, calls*] Sheba ... where are you? [*Laughs*] That naughty, naughty dog ... into mischief, I dare say! [*A clock chimes*] Oh, it's time ... it's time. The music hour ... time to rest ... and dream ... now, where did I put those records? [*Searches about, finds them*] Oh! Here they are ... now let's see, what shall it be tonight... [*Hums to herself*] Oh, oh, yes ... this should be fine. Mary Shelley ... Part I of *Frankenstein* ...

Frankenstein poster.

lovely, lovely recording... [*Cranks machine and puts on record*] I've played it so many, many times ... but I never tire of it, such a charming beginning. A lonely graveyard, at night ... of course ... and then that man, hanging from a gibbet ... oh, lovely ... lovely...

[*Sits in great expectation and looks at set*]

Cut to Opening of Film.

It was, really and truly, a terrific prelude to *Frankenstein,* a nicely Gothic mix of Grand Guignol and *Sunset Blvd.* Meanwhile out in Los Angeles, the real Mae Clarke was watching.

* * *

While her own show business career hadn't been as Halloween-esque as the one Ottola Nesmith was pretending to have suffered, it had indeed presented its share of humiliations—and even actual horror.

Once upon a time, in the summer of 1931, Mae Clarke had been Queen of Universal. James Whale ("always the plu-perfect gentleman, and the *genius,*" remembered Mae[5]) had directed her superbly touching performance as Myra, the doomed streetwalker of *Waterloo Bridge,* one of the great sex tragedies and star portrayals of pre–Code cinema. "Jimmy" then requested her for *Frankenstein,* where Colin Clive fascinated her (she had a crush on him, *and* felt he had "the face of Christ"), Dwight Frye terrified her ("He'd scare the hell out of everyone!"), and Boris Karloff enchanted her ("That scene with the skylight ... like looking at God!"). A third film for Whale at Universal, *The Impatient Maiden* (1932), was a failure, but major stardom had seemed to loom on Mae's horizon.

In early 1932, Universal cast a trio of its most popular stars—*All Quiet on the Western Front*'s Lew Ayres, *Frankenstein*'s Boris Karloff and Mae Clarke—in *Night World* (1932), a racy mix of comedy, melodrama, and music. Ayres was a hard-drinking rich boy, Boris was a speakeasy kingpin named "Happy," and Mae was a revelation in both her acting and her hoofing in Busby Berkeley-choreographed dance numbers. She'd barely finished her role in *Night World* when tragedy came.

"MAE CLARKE, ACTRESS, IN SANITARIUM" headlined the March 5, 1932, *Los Angeles Times.*

Mae had suffered a nervous breakdown, her parents blaming it on overwork. She later revealed she'd undergone horrible shock treatments at the sanitarium that nearly killed her. She rallied, only to break her jaw and cut her face in a 1933 car accident while on a date with allegedly intoxicated actor Phillips Holmes. She claimed to be "permanently disfigured" but again resumed her career, only to enter a sanitarium once more in the summer of 1934.

When James Whale directed *Bride of Frankenstein* in early 1935, he brought back Karloff, Colin Clive and Dwight Frye, but cast Universal contractee Valerie Hobson as Elizabeth. In a flowing wig and looking and acting like an angel on the edge of hysteria, the willowy Valerie proved a far more stylized and colorful Elizabeth than Mae's original.

It seemed a cursed career—and a jinxed life. If she were remembered at all by the late 1930s, it was as the moll whom James Cagney pie-faced with a grapefruit in Warner Bros.' *The Public Enemy* (1931), filmed before Mae's success at Universal. It was a kitschy infamy that infuriated her.

By the late 1940s she'd married and divorced three times. There were no children. She was in and out of films; in 1949, she showed up as the overage heroine of the Republic serial *King of the Rocket Men.* She landed bits in such MGM films as *Annie Get Your Gun* (1950) and *Singin' in the Rain* (1952). She enjoyed a very dramatic role on TV's *Medic* ("When

Mae Clarke as she appeared in James Whale's *Waterloo Bridge* in spring 1931.

I Was Young," October 24, 1955) and had hopes of a revitalized career as a character actress.

In 1957, Mae had been a guest on at least six television shows. On the "Killer's Pride" episode of *Jane Wyman Presents the Fireside Theatre* (January 29, 1957), a co-player was *King Kong*'s scream queen Fay Wray, and the director was Robert Florey—who had adapted *Frankenstein* and had been set to direct the film before James Whale claimed it.

For all her history of rising and falling in Hollywood, Mae Clarke was only 47 years old. There was still a chance for steady work and some recognition.

Then came *Nightmare!*

Shades of Orson Welles' 1938 *War of the Worlds* radio broadcast, when many listeners feared Martians were actually invading, and Billy Wilder's 1950 film *Sunset Blvd.,* when many audiences were convinced that Gloria Swanson really was mad-as-a-hatter Norma Desmond, many people watching KTLA that night came to believe what they heard and (in this case) saw—Mae Clarke was now a batty old lunatic who lived in an alley. As *Frankenstein* rolled on that night, Ottola Nesmith returned several times, merrily reinforcing that impression.

* * *

Classic horror: Boris Karloff and Mae Clarke in *Frankenstein*.

The first interruption came right after Colin Clive's classic "It's alive!" hysteria in the laboratory:

Ottola: [*Happily*] Oh, I'm so glad. It's alive! Wonderful, wonderful. It's so nice to see a young man succeed. Hard work ... concentration will do it every time ... that's what I always say...
　　[*We hear a distant knock on the front door. She is frightened.*]
　　What's that? [The knock is repeated] It's someone at the door ... the front door. [*To camera*] I never answer the front door. I never use it. I haven't opened it in twenty years ... I don't trust the people out there. All the children, all those people who get up in the morning and go to offices and factories... [*with almost dread*] The "Day" people ... that's what I call them... [*Goes to window*] Go away ... Go away, I say! ... You're from the electric company, I know ... well, it's no use ... [*turns away angry*] Hrump! Try to turn the power off on me, will they? Well, they won't get away with it ... not while I have a hair pin left. [*Sees Victrola*] Oh ... the music ... I must get another record ... [*to camera*] ... Be back in a moment... [*Exits*]

There followed a 90-second commercial break, then:

Cut to: Ottola
　　Enters from Hall, Humming Gaily, Carrying Record, Goes to Victrola
　　Reads Label Then Puts It Down.
　　Ottola [*Reads*] "Part II of *Frankenstein*... Oh yes, I remember this... It's where Dr. Frankenstein's father enters upon the scene. Baron Frankenstein, of course. Such a dreadful man! So pompous, so lacking in understanding. He really didn't encourage the poor boy in his scientific research at all, you know. Just like my father. [*Becomes very Southern*] Ah, poor Papa, may he rest in peace... Always talking about honor ... and the family ... and always walking up and down on the veranda of our plantation. "Scarlett," he'd say to me, "Scarlett, you got to remember that family's the only thing that counts." And Mama, poor Mama ... she was always sort of sickly; she'd always be up in her room with the curtains closed and the door locked. Papa from the outside of the door, you know. Mama ... Mama was sort of strange ... she'd carry on and ... well, you know what I mean. [*Goes to Victrola*] Well, Baron Frankenstein was just the same. Here his boy has made this wonderful invention and all he talks about is family... [*Starts record*] Well ... you'll see....

Part II of *Frankenstein* began after Nesmith had added *Gone with the Wind* to her satire. The film played until the Monster's killing of Edward Van Sloan's Dr. Waldman—then it was back to Ottola's alley:

Ottola: Well, what do you think of that? Of course ... you really can't blame him, poor creature ... he did so want to be free and out in the sun and air. And after all, Dr. Waldon [*sic*] wasn't up to any good, you know. That most certainly wasn't a vaccination he was about to give the poor thing. Self-preservation, that's what I call it ... he who lives by the sword, dies by the sword ... as they say, justice always triumphs.... Where is the dog? [*Starts out hall*] Where is that silly creature? [*Calls as she exits*] Sheba ... Sheba... [*Fades Out*]

A 90-second commercial break followed, and then:

Cut to: Ottola
　　Ottola [*Carrying bridal veil*] Sheba! Sheba! [*A wolf's howl*] [*She laughs*] Oh, there you are ... you silly thing. Well, play nice ... and don't go too far from the house. [*Turns from window smiling happily as we hear repeat of wolf's howl, dog fading in distance*] [*Suddenly realizes what she's carrying and holds up veil and looks at it critically*] Oh dear, it most certainly could use a stitch or two ... but then it's been through so much. I wore it when I played Elizabeth, you know. [*Tries it on and prances about*] Oh, we had such a time making the scene! When dear Boris jumped in that window, how I screamed and carried on! I carried it off with such flair ... such style..., [*Goes to Victrola and turns record*] Part III of *Frankenstein* ... this is the part I was telling you about ... and it starts so happily too. The wedding, and all of that ... the happy bride ... the laughing peasants dancing in

the street and all the gentry up at the manor house drinking champagne.... Ah me, little did they know what was in store. Such screams and cries and shouts! Strange figures at windows, and all the running up and down the stairs ... and the locking of doors ... oh wonderful, wonderful....

The spectacle of Ottola "prancing" in her *Frankenstein* bridal veil must have been high Hollywood Gothic, especially for viewers who had come to believe this was truly Mae Clarke. Strangely, Mae herself, when interviewed in later years about *Frankenstein,* enjoyed telling the story of how she nearly became hysterical during the Monster-in-the-boudoir scene, and how Karloff calmed her by wiggling his upstage little finger during the filming to remind her, "It's just Boris in makeup."

Frankenstein resumed, up to the villagers' pursuit of the Monster. Then came another break with the make-believe heroine of the film:

[*Excited, moves about hurriedly, excitedly*] [*Lead in on segment*]
   Ottola: Oh glorious, glorious! Fire, and flame and blazing torch! [*Change*] Oh ... but that poor creature... I so do hope he escapes. It's so unfair ... all so [*sic*] angry men against him. He doesn't have a chance. After all, it isn't his fault. As for Dr. Frankenstein, he brought it all on himself. A fine way for a father to act, I must say. Well, then, if he's not the creature's father, what is he? Oh dear, dear ... I'm so upset.

There was a minute-and-a-half commercial break, then:

Cut to: Ottola
   She is putting on record.
   Ottola [*upset*]: Well, here it is ... the last part. It's all so sad. I never did care for it... Mob violence, that's what it is. Remember what I said before. "Day People" that's what they are ... you look on them... [*Sits*] [*Sadly*] Well ... here we go. Fire and flame ... fire and flame....

And the climax of *Frankenstein* played on. Monster and Monster Maker battled, the flames devoured the windmill, and Ottola returned after the final credits:

Ottola: What an end! What a magnificent end! Such grandeur! Such flamboyance! Of course, that's really not the end, you know ... there's more ... that impetuous young man, Dr. Frankenstein, recovers and marries Elizabeth and lives happily ever after ... which is more than he deserves. As for the poor brute ... well ... devoured by flames. [*Smiles slyly, looks about, then to camera, confiding, low*] ... or was he? ... more about that another time. [*Goes to record album*] Oh ... I have such wonderful records here ... so many cozy ... restful ... dreamy hours ahead.... Next week, we have one all about pets... [*Reads*] ... *The Werewolf of London* ... yes ... shall we hear a bit of it? ... Let's!
   Cut to: Trailer for *WereWolf of London*
   Cut to: Ottola
   Ottola: And here's a bit of another... [*Looks about, then to camera*] *The Mummy's Tomb*... [*Shivers deliciously*]
   Cut to: Trailer for *The Mummy's Tomb*
   Cut to: Ottola
   Ottola in chair, leaning back
   Ottola: Oh yes ... charming ... charming ... charming... [*Long Pause*]
   [*Then, in the distance we hear a clock strike midnight*]
   Ottola: It's midnight ... all the stores are closed: time to go shopping!
   [*Bustles about, puts on her hat, cape, gloves, parasol, etc.*]
   Tempest Fugit ... tempest fugit ... as Dr. Frankenstein says ... or was it Dr. Frankenstein... Oh dear, I do get so confused... [*Looks up at picture*] ... Good night, Boris... [*Holds a moment, then bustles out the door*]
   Cut to: Alley

She looks about, then checks door and makes a noise of approval that all's well.
The following is done as afterthoughts... She starts up the alley, then stops and turns back....
Ottola: Remember what I said ... about the rooms ... they're very nice; so if you're interested drop around and we'll have a cup of tea. After dark, of course ... oh yes ... and no "Day People," please... [*Starts up and stops again*] ... and remember ... the back door....
     [*She shuffles up the alley and disappears from sight*]

*   *   *

I saw my whole career destroyed, all I had done, all I had worked for, all my future earnings swept away in one and one-half hours.... I wasn't poverty-stricken, I'm not an old has-been, I don't want pity and I don't want to be laughed at ... I want to die with my boots on.
                              —Mae Clarke, testifying in court, July 16, 1958[6]

On Thursday, October 3, 1957, less than 48 hours after the *Nightmare!* telecast, Mae Clarke signed an arrangement with Barry S. Scholer, attorney at law, to represent her litigation. The letter stated:

It is understood and agreed that your fee will be entirely contingent and will be equal to one-third (⅓) of any and all recoveries you make before trial, or forty percent of any and all recoveries made at least an hour after trial has begun. It is understood that if no recovery is made, I will be billed for nothing but court costs.
     It is further understood that you may resign from the case if at any time hereafter your investigation discloses that my case is without merit.[7]

Meanwhile, on Monday night, October 14, 1957, the "Mystery Tower Sitter" ended his gig at midnight. The next day, he revealed himself: It was Glenn Strange, 6'4", 58-year-old Western heavy, who'd played Frankenstein's Monster in *House of Frankenstein, House of Dracula,* and *Abbott and Costello Meet Frankenstein.* Reportedly 21,799 contestants had mailed in their guesses, and 301 had been correct.[8]

Two days after Strange's unveiling, October 17, 1957, the *Los Angeles Times* headlined, "TV Suit Filed by Mae Clarke Asks Million." The story came complete with a picture of Mae with hair stylist Jacques Martin. Mae, who'd invited the press to photograph her at a beauty shop "before, not after, treatment," was suing both Paramount Television Productions *and* Ottola Nesmith, claiming they'd portrayed her as a "broken-down, has-been actress, poverty-stricken, slovenly attired and ill." She told reporters:

I am neither dead nor a has-been. I am a working actress who is still paying her own way. I have a terrific sense of humor and the ability to laugh at my own self when I have done something funny.
     But I think it's unfair for any actress to face today's critics on the basis of work done 26 years ago. As to today's actresses, many are as good or better than the stars of the old days.

As Barry S. Scholer prepared Mae's case, *Nightmare! Theatre* and Ottola Nesmith carried on at KTLA. She had the distinction of being the only named-and-pictured horror host in issue #1 of *Famous Monsters of Filmland,* published in February of 1958, and was featured with several others of her late night ilk in the May 26, 1958, *Life* magazine feature "Night Harbingers of Horror." Also in May of 1958, Ottola gave up her *Nightmare! Theatre* gig.

Tuesday, July 15, 1958: Ottola appears as the Soothsayer on the *Shirley Temple's Storybook* TV episode "The Little Lame Prince."

The same day: The Mae Clarke trial is proceeding in Los Angeles in the courtroom of

Superior Judge Fredrick F. Houser. Testifying is David Hyman, a hairdresser who had watched the show and presumed he was seeing the real Mae Clarke. Hyman testifies that he was regaling a customer about the show the day after its telecast: "In the movie she looked so glamorous. I thought she really must have lived it up, or drank a lot ... to have changed so much."[9] He adds that he made some "very unflattering remarks" and then suffered the painful discovery that the customer he was entertaining was the *real* Mae Clarke.

"I could have crawled under a hole if I could have found one," says Hyman.

The real show, however, is Ottola Nesmith. She appears in court that day and, as directed, reads the words "I am Mae Clarke" from the *Nightmare!* script. The *Los Angeles Times* notes her "exaggerated gestures" and "stage-like voice." She poses for the press—gladly.

"Ottola Nesmith Gets Her Cue and Puts on Her Act," reads the caption for a *Los Angeles Herald and Express* feature that gives the dominant upper space to Ottola and the subordinate lower photo to Mae. (Both ladies wear white gloves.) The *Herald and Express* writes:

> Waving the script in one hand, gesturing dramatically with the other, Miss Nesmith read her lines with all the histrionic flair she could muster—reproduced, in fact, the scenes just as they were included in the TV program, minus costumes and sets.

The defense claims there was no intention to steal Mae's identity, but only to create the proper mood for the show.

Wednesday, July 16: Mae takes the stand. "I was shocked," she tells the jury. "I was just shocked to think anyone in my profession would do this to me." She says that Ottola's impersonation inferred that "I hadn't worked since I played in that picture" and dramatically expresses her humiliation: "How am I going to make a living? I've now entered my older, more mature—richer, I think—years. I would like to die with my boots on."[10]

Monday, July 21: It's the most colorful day yet. Nesmith comes barnstorming into the courtroom, fully adorned in her *Nightmare!* "lady ghoul" costume. The *L.A. Times* will report the next day:

> As she waved her flame-colored fan, the actress described for the jury her mid–Victorian black faille cape edged with ruching; a "just too young" tulle picture hat; the tan satin gown dripping with lace and fringe and beads. She gestured with a little blue-ruffled parasol.
>
> "It was an actor's dream role," she declaimed. "She could fancy herself young and beautiful. She could say 'I'm Napoleon.' She was half-witch and half-fairy."

Friday, July 25: It appears that Mae is no match for Ottola's high-spirited showmanship. The jury votes nine-to-three against the plaintiff. As a public figure, Mae Clarke has no right of privacy and damages are denied. "Well, it's God's will," says Mae.[11]

Wednesday, January 21, 1959: "Mae Clarke $1,000,000 Suit Settled," headlines the *Los Angeles Examiner*. Mae has sued again but, rather than the million dollars, she receives an unpublicized $7,000. Late in life she will tell her close friend Doug Norwine that she'd used the money for a vacation in Hawaii.

July 1958: Mae Clarke in Superior Court, suing KTLA and Ottola Nesmith.

Both ladies resume their careers. Ottola Nesmith makes a trio of guest visits to Boris Karloff's TV show *Thriller.* "The Hungry Glass" (January 3, 1961) casts her as old Laura Bellman, a horrid crone who spends her life staring at the mirror and seeing a reflection of a beautiful young woman (Donna Douglas). "Yours Truly, Jack the Ripper" (April 11, 1961) presents her as Rowena, a bohemian artist. Her best-remembered *Thriller* visit is "Pigeons from Hell" (June 6, 1961) as Eula Lee Blassenville, aka "The Zuvembie." The last is widely celebrated as one of the most frightening episodes in TV history.

Thriller associate producer Doug Benton will tell film historian Tom Weaver:

> Ottola Nesmith was a tiger.... [S]he was a very good actress. Do you remember a playwright, Arnaud d'Usseau? ... He was a blacklisted writer, and she was his mother. She used to talk about him, she used to talk about working in London, she was very garrulous ... I just remember her because she was so vivid and full of beans at that late age!

Leon d'Usseau, Ottola's husband, dies on June 6, 1963, age 77. Ottola appears as nutty hospital inmate Maggie Lafarge on "The Night of the Howling Light," an episode of *The Wild Wild West* (December 17, 1965), and as witch Enchantra on "The Trial and Error of Aunt Clara," an episode of *Bewitched* (February 2, 1967). Her final documented TV appearance is on *Ironside* (October 23, 1969) as a charwoman; her final film, *The Comic* (1969), unbilled as a housekeeper. Ottola Nesmith dies in Hollywood on February 7, 1972, at the age of 82.[12]

Mae Clarke's life and career remain erratic. Alcohol plagues her. She shows up as "Woman in Office" in *Thoroughly Modern Millie* (1967), playing the bit at Universal where she'd once been the top female star. Eventually she settles at the Motion Picture Country

A 1983 shot of Mae Clarke at the Motion Picture Country House, where she resided late in life.

House, where she rides about on a three-wheeled bicycle with an *E.T.* doll in her basket. Interviewers who come to see her could find her bitterly antagonistic or totally charming. When I meet her in May 1983, she is fortunately (after a rocky start) charming. The day is unforgettable as my wife Barbara and I sit in her cottage and Mae remembers *Frankenstein,* talking about Karloff, Clive, and Whale and dramatically acting out the Monster's walk and discovery of light.

Mae Clarke died on April 29, 1992, at age 81. She's cremated and buried with her parents in Valhalla Cemetery in North Hollywood. Her final effects include a letter she had received from no less than Ottola Nesmith herself, mailed after Mae's successful second trial. Dated January 25, 1959, Ottola's handwritten missive reads:

> My dear Miss Clarke:
> Ever since the announcement of your settlement I've wanted to write and congratulate you and say I, too, was pleased to hear it.
> By a strange coincidence, I saw you on the late show that night in an old picture. You gave such a convincing performance and looked so pretty. And, a few weeks prior to that, we "caught" you on *The Loretta Young Show.* My husband said, "No one could have been better in the part."
> I trust, one of these days we may work together—outside of a Court Room!
> I do hope some day when you're in Hollywood you'll give me a ring and we can have a visit over a cup of tea.
> May the best of luck attend you and all good wishes from
> Yours sincerely,
> Ottola Nesmith

*   *   *

Monday, October 7, 1957: Six days after Ottola Nesmith's *Nightmare!* had made its debut in L.A., John Zacherle begins hosting *Shock!* in Philadelphia. His character name is Roland (accent on the *-land*) and he becomes the epitome of his show business breed, with macabre humor and the then state-of-the-art gimmick of cutting away from the film to a shot of him clowning while the film's audio continues. In 1958, he moves to New York and officially became Zacherley.

Saturday, November 9, 11:15 p.m.: It is the premiere night of Baltimore's *Shock! Theatre* on WBAL-TV, Channel 11, and the film is *Frankenstein.* The author is in the second grade. Everyone on the school bus has been chattering about the odds of their parents allowing them to stay up and see *Frankenstein.* My beloved parents allow me, and both of them keep vigil with me to see it ... but as the show begins, I chicken out...

... and reject the hospitality of *Shock!'s* host, Dr. Lucifer.

His real name is Richard Dix—the same name as the film star who died in 1949. Dix is a tall, wavy-haired actor, a native Baltimorean who'd served as a B-17 gunner in World War II. He'd worked in the scenery and lighting department at Baltimore's WMAR Channel 2, and had been in military intelligence at Fort Holabird, Maryland, during the Korean War. Dix also acted in many plays and every summer starred in *The Common Glory,* a "symphonic drama" by Paul Green that told the story of the Declaration of Independence and played at a 3,500-seat amphitheater in Williamsburg, Virginia. There were horses on stage, battleships on a lake behind the stage, and cannon firing at the stage. "It was," as Dix remembered, "a spectacular production!"[13]

After his military service ended, Dix joined WBAL, then located at 2600 North Charles Street in Baltimore. He has presence, vitality and a big booming voice. Every weekday afternoon he appears on Channel 11, playing Officer Happy, who has a lilting Irish brogue, and shows episodes of *The Little Rascals*.

In 1993, the weekend before a major Baltimore blizzard, Richard Dix will sit in his home, the same one he'd occupied while hosting *Shock!* 36 years previously, and reminisce:

> Officer Happy was five days a week—no writers, and telecast live! I was on my own, whatever I could come up with and do, as long as it didn't cost anything, or next to nothing. The objective primarily was to think of nice, pleasant ways to lead into the comedies and at the same time, to give little homilies. "Do your homework," "Pay attention to the police"—trying to reinforce what we thought was going on in the schools at the time.
>
> Once, we had a Story-Telling Lady on the show. The kids were getting shots, and we wanted to do it on the air, to encourage children to get their shots. Officer Happy would get a shot, every kid would get a shot, and we wanted the Story-Telling Lady to get a shot. Well, she was trying to avoid it! I was trying to egg her on to get the shot; she kept saying, "In a minute..."
>
> Well, when we went to the film, I said, "What's the matter with you? Let's get this shot!"
>
> And she said, "It's against my religion!"
>
> And I said, "Oh!"
>
> She was Quaker, I think, or some religion that did not believe in this sort of thing. So when we came back from the film, the nurse was pulling back the hypodermic needle from the Story-Telling Lady, who didn't mind *pretending* she'd had the shot!

Officer Happy becomes a beloved Baltimore figure, making many personal appearances. Nancy Lee Dix, Richard's actress wife, will recall: "Our son Don was born at Mercy Hospital while Richard was doing Officer Happy, and Mercy's PR man got in a camera crew. It was great—Officer Happy's baby was born in *his* hospital!"

Richard Dix is WBAL's actor-in-residence in 1957, hence the natural choice when the station wants a horror host. Dix creates the role of Dr. Lucifer, and Nancy will join him as Mrs. Lucifer, whose first name, incidentally, is Grace. As Dix will remember:

> My inspiration for Dr. Lucifer was Charles Addams. Both Nancy and I are fans of Addams; we had all his cartoon books, and liked his approach and sense of humor. Actually, in some instances, I'd take a cartoon he'd done and stage it; we'd visualize and animate the actual Addams cartoons.

Dix chuckles affectionately as he recalls his macabre alter-ego, always elegant in his goatee, formal dress, and (sometimes) cape and top hat:

> Dr. Lucifer was the serious, sedate scientist, who could never do anything right. He saw himself as a "quality" scientist—he drank tea, he did all "quality" things and he liked working on "quality" projects. But he had no "quality" at all—the results of his experiments were always disastrous! It was a lot of fun.

As for his ghastly spouse, Nancy Lee Dix remembers:

> Mrs. Grace Lucifer, too, came out of the Charles Addams books. She was a loving wife—a kooky lady, but nice and very much in love with her husband. The makeup, the wig, and the costuming were the facade of the character, but in fact she was a nice person and an everyday housewife—who just happened to cook bunny rabbits!

In fact, the affection of the Lucifers is prophetic of the sexual chemistry of Carolyn Jones' Morticia and John Astin's Gomez on TV's *The Addams Family*, which will come along seven years later.

The *Shock! Theatre* ratings in Baltimore are terrific. "It was much better received than I think the station ever thought it was going to be," Dix says. November 16 offers *The*

Mummy, November 23, *The Wolf Man.* I finally get up the courage to watch the night of November 30, when *Shock!* presents *Frankenstein Meets the Wolf Man.* It's a weird sensation for me to realize that Dr. Lucifer is the same man that I enjoy every afternoon as Officer Happy.

Dr. Lucifer and *Shock!* are the overnight talk of the town.

Monday, December 9: Two days after *Shock!* has shown *Dracula,* Donald Kirkley, veteran film critic of the *Baltimore Sun,* fires off a broadside at the old horror classics:

> They cater to the same deplorable human traits which were exploited much more effectively by the Romans in their circuses and, long before that, by primitive tribesmen who took delight in watching the torture of captive enemies....

Nevertheless, Kirkley praises Dix's "excellent satire," and *Shock!* appears to be here to stay. In fact, WBAL adds *Horror!* after the *Tonight Show* Friday nights and after *Shock!* on Saturday nights, such is the voracious appetite for the films. Dr. Lucifer remains confined to the Saturday night *Shock!* Every show is live—no tape in 1957. Dix recalled the basically *ad hoc* way the show comes together weekly:

> Those shows were scripted. The films would arrive in the studio on Thursday. I would look at the film, and sometimes the director (such as Lennie Levin) would look at it with me, which always helped. Sometimes we would see something in the film we could fine-tune into a running gag; if we didn't find that, we'd try to pick up something that maybe had no connection with the film. Or sometimes one of us would come in and say, "Hey! I've thought of something that might be funny," and we'd sit down and start talking.
>
> We'd rough it out—no dialogue, nothing written, just an idea of what was going to happen. Fifteen minutes before we went on the air, we'd rehearse the first little shtick. Then while the film was running, we'd rehearse the second little shtick. So that's the only way we kept going, and we were always just a half-a-step ahead of where the film was.

There are ghoulish props festooning the *Shock!* set, and Dix will remember this macabre anecdote:

> Those bones you saw, the skulls and things—they were real! We got them from Johns Hopkins, various places like that, and there were people who had human bones in their house they didn't want—and brought them in to us! So those bones had been people at one time. And when the show went off the air, we had an awful time getting rid of them! We couldn't just put them in a dump!
>
> Along the way, we had acquired an honest-to-God mummy—some Hopkins professor had it in his possession and for a few bucks, we were able to get it. So we had a mummy, with no death certificate, and the bones, and we couldn't get rid of them. I think the Baltimore Museum, after a lot of legal work, finally took possession. I guess it's a little sacrilegious; these people lived—and they ended up as props on a stupid horror show!

Actually, Richard and Nancy take care to make sure *Shock!* is never "stupid." It's fun and crazy, but treads a very fine line, as Dix will recall:

> The show was funny, but it wasn't slapstick, or ridiculous, or ludicrous. Things had to have a reason and we tried to be very serious about it. Today when I see an occasional horror show host (and there are one or two still floating around), I can't identify with them. In theater, you're supposed to have characters—whether people hate the character or love the character, they should have some identification with the character. So that's what we were trying to do ... we wanted it to be funny and enjoyable, so people would watch it, enjoy it—and identify with it.

From Baltimore's *Shock! Theatre*: Richard Dix as "Dr. Lucifer," Nancy Lee Dix as Mrs. Lucifer, and their daughter Landra.

The show becomes a Dix family affair, as Nancy will remember:

We had our daughter, Landra, on the show, as the Lucifers' daughter Lucretia, and even our Weimaraner dog, the "Grey Ghost" dog! We would have brought our baby son on too, but the studio was so hot in those days. So we talked about the fact I'd given birth, although you never saw the baby. We referred to him as Baby Borgia!

Dr. Lucifer "borrows" Zacherley's popular trick of appearing in the movies:

Looking back, we did some good things, difficult things. Sometimes we would insert Dr. Lucifer into the film: two-way phone conversations became three-way phone conversations. And they had to cut to us, insert us into the film, and that took a lot of effort on the part of the crew. Today, it would be a very simple thing to do—we can split a screen—but then it took a lot of time. But the crew enjoyed working on the show; they had a good time. It was a lot of fun!

Meanwhile, Dix also enjoys the films and will eventually meet some of their stars in the theater:

As to favorite stars of the old horror genre, I would have to include Mr. Karloff, because of the original *Frankenstein*, which, to this day, I think, is still a good movie. And next, because I later had the pleasure of meeting him, Lon Chaney, Jr. I was rehearsing a show in Chicago, I think his show was going out, so I got to meet him. He was a huge man, a monster of a man, hands the size of hams! But very nice, gentle and interesting. He told me his horror stories about working on *The Wolf Man* and all that kind of stuff.

Under similar circumstances, I met John Carradine. A very *dramatic* individual! That song— "Hi Diddle-Dee, An Actor's Life for Me"—Carradine seemed to *live* that, with cape and hat. He actually dressed the part of an old actor. I was only in his presence a short time, but he came in— and took over the room! He worked the room *very* well!

Although Dix makes many personal appearances as Officer Happy, he's determined to keep Dr. Lucifer within the studio to preserve the illusion. An exception:

Thursday, August 14, 1958: Dr. Lucifer is "Monster of Ceremonies" at Baltimore's Stanley Theatre to promote Vincent Price's *The Fly*. Nancy is there as Mrs. Lucifer, and local actors play Dracula and the Wolf Man.

Thus does madness reign Saturday nights in Baltimore. At Yuletide, Dr. Lucifer sets a bear trap to catch Santa Claus, to prove he exists; naturally, Lucifer catches himself. Then there's the memorable night Dr. Lucifer hosts a race.

I damn near destroyed the studio one time! We were doing a race on the show and one of the guys said he had a little miniature cannon, which they used to start regatta races; he was in a yacht club. He brought it in and charged it; he had a silk stocking with just a little bit of black powder that he rammed down into this thing. At the proper moment on the show, I was to light the fuse and it would go off.

Well, we lit the fuse, it went off—and a ball of compressed air shot out of the cannon, across the studio, and destroyed nine lamps. They blew up! And the big plate glass window, where the director and technicians could look down into the studio—that plate glass window was *bending*, and everyone was running for cover! *Bang*! Right on the air!

The audience never saw it, they didn't know what happened, but that was the closest we came to having a serious accident. After that, we were a little more careful with explosives in the studio!

Eventually, a real monster stalks into WBAL—new management. They fail to renew the contract for the *Shock!* films and the show goes off the air in the spring of 1959. The package moves to WTOP, Channel 9 in Washington, D.C., where *Shock!* follows the late Saturday night movie (with no host). The faithful in Baltimore—at least those with powerful TV antennas—pull in the old films from there and *Shock!* continues throughout the 1960s. Come the early 1970s, Channel 9 hires a Friday night horror host, Sir Graves Ghastly, and the shockers get a whole new lease on life.

For a time, Dix (a director for Baltimore Children's Theatre and the president of Bal-

At the Stanley Theatre in Baltimore, August 1958: Promoting *The Fly* are Richard Dix as Dr. Lucifer; Nancy Lee Dix as Mrs. Lucifer; Joe Bandiera as Dracula; George Goebbel as Wolf Man.

timore's AFTRA) stays on at the new WBAL. It is not, however, an amicable relationship. One fateful morning, Dix has "sign-on" duty. In one of those strange things that happens for no seeming reason, Dix reads Channel 11 as a Roman numeral "2." Channel 2 is one of Channel 11's rivals, the other being Channel 13. The WBAL powers-that-be promptly can him.

Baltimore's finest actor is suddenly out of work.

It's devastating for a man with a family, but Dix decides to make the best of it and become a full-time professional theater actor. "I figured as an actor, a man could be out of work at least some of the time, and it would be considered okay," he would joke. It was what he always had truly wanted to do—"So, really, WBAL did me a favor."

His acting résumé grows. Locally, Richard and Nancy both become favorites at Baltimore's Oregon Ridge Dinner Theater and Garland Dinner Theatre. They act at Baltimore's Center Stage (I see Richard there as a very bloodthirsty Casca in *Julius Caesar* in 1973) and D.C.'s Arena Stage. Richard acts with the American Shakespeare Theatre, the Old Globe Theatre, the Guthrie Theatre, and indeed, all over the world, including the Moscow Art Theatre, the Pushkin Theatre of Leningrad, and the Jerusalem Theatre in Israel.

Richard and Nancy both play in the Universal TV film *Vanished* (1971) and Richard appears in various other films, including Joseph Wambaugh's *The Black Marble* (1980).

Naturally, Richard aspires to play Broadway, and does so twice. In *Othello* (Winter Garden Theatre, February 3, 1982, 123 performances), starring James Earl Jones and Christopher Plummer, Richard plays Gratiano. In *Show Boat* (Uris Theatre, April 24, 1983, 73 performances), Richard is Windy and understudy to Donald O'Connor in the role of Cap'n Andy.

Nothing survives from Baltimore's *Shock!* The shows had been live and there were no tapes. Once, when the Dixes had wanted to take a vacation, Richard persuaded WBAL to make a short film to play on *Shock!* during his absence. "They wouldn't pay for sound, so I recorded a little acetate disc; it was like a monologue, a dream sequence. I later gave it away to a man writing a book on Baltimore television—that was the only film clip."

* * *

My meeting Richard and Nancy Lee Dix will come by strange chance. In 1993 I attend a Nostalgia Convention on a cold Saturday in Baltimore and learn only after getting home—and looking at the program I'd picked up—that the Dixes are attending the convention with other Baltimore TV personalities.[14]

I kick myself for missing them—I've never met them and presume at the time they live in New York or California. Gary Svehla, the convention's host, informs me that they are right in Baltimore, less than an hour's drive from my home in Pennsylvania, gives me their number, and I arrange to interview them for Gary's magazine, *Midnight Marquee*.

Richard, with his mustache, mane of white hair and booming voice, looks and sounds like he'd just bounded out of a Shakespeare folio. Nancy is still attractive, slender and charming. Although they'd been warmly received at the convention, they are both surprised and flattered by my interest.

We become friends. In 1994, both come to see me perform in *Lend Me a Tenor* at the Cockpit-in-the-Court Summer Theatre. It's a bit daunting to realize that Officer Happy-Dr. Lucifer and Grace Lucifer are there at that matinee, but I carry on, and they are kind and generous in their remarks about my performance. Afterwards, we go to dinner. At the restaurant, Dix says, "Table for four, please." The young hostess takes one look at him, hears him speak only those four words, and asks him, "Are you an actor?"

Richard Dix dies in September of 1998; his wife Nancy dies soon afterwards. I was very fortunate to have met them, to have heard their stories, to have told them how much I enjoyed their work, how it really and truly had an influence on my own life and work.

Bravo to you both.

* * *

The *Shock!* nights, over half a century ago, now seem as bygone as the "old" films the show presented. It's odd to think that horror

Richard Dix, circa 1993.

hosts still haunt TV. It's strangely reassuring to realize that on those shows, after all the years, somebody is seeing *Dracula* or *Frankenstein* for the very first time, and perhaps falling under the thrall of Bela Lugosi and Tod Browning, or Boris Karloff and James Whale.

The magic continues. And as Ottola Nesmith used to say on *Nightmare! Theatre,* "Fire and flame ... fire and flame...."

13

Junior Laemmle, Horror's "Crown Prince" Producer

It's Hollywood's Golden Age of Horror, and Carl Laemmle, Jr., appears to have the greatest dream job of all time—general manager of Universal City, California.

At age 22, he produces *Dracula;* at age 23, *Frankenstein.* He goes on to produce *Murders in the Rue Morgue, The Old Dark House, The Mummy, The Invisible Man, The Black Cat,* and *Bride of Frankenstein.*

He's Universal's 5'3" "Crown Prince," reigning from his "throne room" over his 230-acre kingdom in the San Fernando Valley, having the run of such hallowed horror sites as the Phantom Stage, the back lot European Village, Jack Pierce's makeup bungalow, and the cavernous Stage 12, home of *Dracula's* Transylvania castle and *Frankenstein's* tower laboratory.

He's prime mover on several milestones in classic horror. He approves the 11th hour casting of Bela Lugosi as Dracula. He referees the various summer of 1931 battles over *Frankenstein,* passing judgment on the legendary Robert Florey-directed test of Lugosi as the Monster, ultimately turning the film over to James Whale, and signing off on Whale's personal choices of Colin Clive as Frankenstein and Boris Karloff as the Monster. He is, at various times, officially the "boss" of Whale, Karloff, Lugosi, Clive, Tod Browning, Dwight Frye, Karl Freund, Helen Chandler, Mae Clarke, Zita Johann, Claude Rains, Edgar G. Ulmer, Elsa Lanchester, Valerie Hobson, Henry Hull, Frances Drake, Gloria Holden....

Of course, he builds his reputation on more than horror. In November of 1930, Junior had won the Best Picture Academy Award for having courageously and lavishly produced *All Quiet on the Western Front.* He produces such acclaimed films as *Waterloo Bridge, Back Street, Counsellor at Law, One More River, Imitation of Life* and *Show Boat.* His films boast stars such as John Barrymore, Jean Harlow, Irene Dunne, and Claudette Colbert.

Then, come March of 1936, new management overthrows the Laemmle regime. Junior's career is virtually over at age 28. And despite his product, which would seem to speak for itself, no "mogul" will ever receive such rampant disrespect from cinema historians.

He had come to power, of course, as the son of Carl Laemmle, Sr., legendary film pioneer and founder of Universal. Hollywood had seen his general manager–at–21 post as the climax of Laemmle's infamous nepotism, and nothing Junior could do would reverse the judgment. Junior is reputed to be a joke, a fool, a hypochondriac, a spoiled scion; "Everyone liked Junior," gossip vulture Louella O. Parsons would write, "but we all thought of him as a pampered rich young man who enjoyed bad health and preferred blondes." He's a notorious playboy, gambler, and terrorizer of starlets who don't succumb to his advances. He never produces

Autographed portrait of Junior Laemmle, Universal's "Crown Prince" (courtesy Neil Lipes).

another film after leaving Universal, despite a berth at MGM in 1937, seemingly "proving" he'd have never been a producer without his father handing him the job. Over the years, various announcements that he's back in business fail to impress anybody.

He becomes one of the most colossal has-beens in Hollywood history.

In the autumn of 1957, when *Shock! Theatre* is a late night TV sensation, many of the talents of these old horror films are long dead. Junior Laemmle is only 49 years old. Yet the fact that he had begun the classic horror cycle and had produced many of the key melodramas in the *Shock!* package will do absolutely nothing to bring him back into the spotlight.

He languishes, ill and forgotten, at his home above Beverly Hills. And when Junior Laemmle dies on September 24, 1979—ironically, the fortieth anniversary of his father's death—apparently no film historian had ever successfully interviewed him at length about his legendary seven-year rule at Universal City.

* * *

There are mysteries about all this, of course. The sad fact is that Junior Laemmle, having experienced an epoch of Hollywood history at such a very young age, basically overdosed on it, took much of it for granted—and remembered relatively little. Not long before Junior's death, writer-historian Paul Jensen attempted to interview Universal's erstwhile "Crown Prince"—who lamented he'd never "starred Karloff and Lugosi together in the same film." Jensen gently reminded him of *The Black Cat*.

"No," replied Junior. "That was just Karloff."

It seemed he had little to offer regarding what had been one of the most daring, colorful and fascinating reigns in cinema history. His father's bullying, the failure of Universal to earn steady profits during his tenure, the jeers and sneers of Hollywood, the illnesses both real and imagined, the professional disappointments, the personal heartbreak at losing the two great loves of his life (his father had forbidden the marriages), the politics, the parasites—one could argue that all these pressures had effectively pulverized Junior long before his demise.

It may have seemed a dream job, but as Junior Laemmle himself said late in life, "It wasn't worth it."

* * *

It seems almost fantastic that, in addition to his seemingly enviable job, Junior had a lady friend of nearly 40 years who was the stand-in and body double for Marilyn Monroe.

She was Evelyn Moriarty, and at the time she'd met Junior, long before the Monroe connection, she'd been a chorus girl in the stage revue *George White's Scandals*. Evelyn became a ravishing Earl Carroll showgirl and eventually doubled Monroe in *Some Like It Hot* (1959), *Let's Make Love* (1960), *The Misfits* (1961) and the never-completed *Something's Got to Give* (1962), from which Monroe was fired shortly before her mysterious death.

Evelyn Moriarty died May 20, 2008, in Los Angeles. Fifteen years previous, I'd chatted with her about Junior. What follows is a transcript of the interview, with annotations regarding some of the people and events she remembered.

* * *

Interview[1]

Many dramatic and conflicting stories circulate about Junior Laemmle. You knew him for over 40 years.

Yes. He was very sweet. He was very *good*.

A little background about yourself—how did you come to Hollywood?

I came here with *George White's Scandals*. I was underage!

Note: According to the Internet Movie Database, Evelyn was born November 16, 1926. Her memory was that she came to L.A. in early 1940, which means she would have been only 13. Even if she knocked off a few years as she grew older, she was clearly very young when she arrived in Hollywood.

And how did you become an Earl Carroll showgirl?

I needed a job and I didn't know how to do anything! I was about the right height and type in those days. Earl Carroll's was near Sunset and Vine, a little up from Vine. It later was the Aquarius, and Ed McMahon had his talent show there. I think that was the happiest time of my life. Everybody went there, every night of the week.

Incidentally, a newspaper clipping says that you were a witness in the Lionel Atwill orgy trial!

What it was ... somebody asked me if I wanted to go swimming, out in Malibu, one day, one Sunday, a weekend, and we went to this beach house, and really went swimming. It was when I first came here, and I'd only been here a short time ... around 1940. It was kind of a cold, nasty, dreary day in May or June. Then we went out and got something to eat, and the next thing I know, about six months later, I'm subpoenaed to the grand jury ... with Lionel Atwill!

Evelyn Moriarty, Earl Carroll Girl and Junior Laemmle's longtime lady friend (courtesy Evelyn Moriarty).

It seems Atwill was supposed to have shown stag pictures or something like that. Well, to this day, I've never seen stag pictures, I have no use for them and I didn't see any. I was actually out in the water, swimming.

Note: The Atwill "orgy trial" of 1941 and 1942 claimed the actor was hosting these notorious evenings at his Pacific Palisades home during the Christmas season of 1940. He also owned a beach home at Malibu. Evelyn's story infers he was hosting such parties that spring and at that home as well. A news clipping of the era reports Atwill had invited the entire troupe of Earl Carroll's showgirls to his Palisades house for a tennis match.

Well, I was only a kid! I wasn't 16 years old, and it scared the hell out of me! I was afraid I'd be put in jail! I took a cab [*laughing*], and I went up to this room and I said to the grand jury, "No, I didn't see any stag pictures, I was swimming." I added, "If they *did* show pictures, I wouldn't have seen them anyway, because I can't see—I'm very nearsighted and I didn't have my glasses!" [*laughing*] And they looked and laughed and let me go! And I asked, "Will you please pay the cab bill?" I remember there was something in the paper..." What Earl Carroll Beauty went to the grand jury and demanded to have her taxi cab paid?" The whole thing was crazy!

Did you meet Junior at Earl Carroll's?

No. I came out here in *George White's Scandals* and we were working at the Biltmore. As I told you, I was underage and could have gotten into a lot of trouble, but I didn't know any better and everybody was very nice to me. Around that time Harry Ritz, of the Ritz Brothers, told me that Hollywood would groom me and if I got in any trouble he'd give me the money to go back home to New York, Long Island, where I belonged. So I was sort of protected.

Anyhow, I met Junior. I was doing *Scandals,* I was only here a couple of days, and some publicity men took me to a nightclub called the Little Troc. I didn't know one name in Hollywood, I didn't know what a producer was, I didn't know what a director was—very uneducated. The Ritz Brothers were there. I was dancing with Harry Ritz, and this little guy with this big smile is sitting there with the governor's son. They stopped at the table and introduced me to Carl Laemmle, Jr. I couldn't pronounce his name, let alone remember it! They said he was a producer. I didn't know enough to play up to him because he was a producer; I just went on my merry way. Then the governor's son came over to our table and I said, "Well, I met the president's son—Roosevelt Jr.!" (I had met him one day backstage in New York.)

Anyway ... I was invited up to Carl Laemmle, Jr.'s house to go swimming. (Oh, swimming [*laughing*] when I say swimming, I think of that Lionel Atwill thing!) The next day, a publicity man picked me up and drove me up Benedict Canyon, next door to where Harold Lloyd lived. We went up this private driveway, and up to this big place—and I thought Junior was sort of the manager of the place! This big estate—I thought he was the *manager* or something—I didn't think he owned the big estate! And they got a kick out of me, because I was unaffected! So that's how I met him.

What struck you about him right away?

Nothing very much!

So he didn't take offense, or feel a big need to impress you?

I don't think he had to go out of his way to impress anybody. Everybody was out to get what he or she could from him.

This was 1940, so he had left Universal...

And MGM. He was about 32—and already retired!
Note: The Laemmles had lost Universal to creditors in March of 1936. Junior joined MGM in the spring of 1937, leaving by fall without having produced any pictures.

He was living at the old Laemmle estate in Benedict Canyon—"Dias Dorados?"

Yes.
Note: The estate, formerly owned by film producer Thomas Ince, was truly palatial, even boasting its own zoo. Laemmle Sr. had died there on September 24, 1939.

What about Junior's personality?

Well, I think he was shy ... I just remember that I used to call him "Poor Little Rich Boy." I felt sorry for him. Even though I told you I was uneducated, and didn't know much, I did know that all these people were out to clip him.

The trouble with Junior was that he was too honest ... and another thing about him was that he was used to having complete control. When they sold Universal, he went over to MGM, and he had to do what somebody told him to do. He couldn't take it. He had very good ideas, but you know how people are, people with ideas—other people try to pull them down and don't want them to do well.

Did he realize people were out to "clip" him?

Yes and no. He only put out so much—they could only get so much, and that was it. You see, I wasn't there to clip Junior or anything. I was real. I didn't "yes" him. If I thought something was wrong, I'd see somebody and I'd say to Junior, "Ah, he's a phony."

I imagine this won you a lot of trouble from the people out to clip him!

Well, with a lot of people, I was an outsider. I was "the showgirl." I was "the gold digger." But believe me, I gave more to Junior than he gave to me! *(Laughing)*

Were you ever officially engaged to him?

No.

But you were friends until he died?

Uh-huh.

What was he doing in his retirement? Did he have hobbies?

He went to the racetrack. He was a big gambler.

Was he much for nightlife?

He was before he got sick. He went to a lot of theaters and a lot of movies. And places to eat, like Perrino's. He didn't like nightclubs so much, because he didn't like the air-conditioning. He would have it turned off!

You mentioned "he got sick." Various reports claim he was ill the last ten years of his life.

The last *twenty* years.

His hypochondria was supposedly legendary.

Yes, he was known as a hypochondriac. I think his father was, too—I read that his father was. And Junior would always be with the doctor. If someone coughed in the room with him, he would go check out the doctor—he wouldn't let anybody with a cold around him. He thought he had sinus trouble, wouldn't have flowers....

In the beginning, when this first happened to him, he had some friends who were dying of heart attacks, so he started walking kind of funny—I went through this thing with him—instead of bending his legs when walking, he'd walk with his legs real stiff—like a goosestep. Well, what happened was, he used to fall. He went into a hospital, had a check-up, came home, got a private nurse—and for 20 years, he was in bed.

Was he still in Dias Dorados in Benedict Canyon at this time?

No. They had sold the place, in the 1950s I think, when a million dollars was a lot of money. They sold it, tore down the original house, sold the glass that had silver in it, and the beams, and subdivided the property. So, while Junior was waiting for a house to be built on the top of Tower Grove Drive, above Beverly Hills, he lived in one of George Cukor's houses, on Cordell Drive. Cukor had three houses built on his property. Spencer Tracy had

Evelyn in her showgirl finery. She later became the stand-in and devoted friend of Marilyn Monroe (courtesy Evelyn Moriarty).

one of the houses, and the man who was the head of an automobile company had another one, and Junior had the third one—he rented it—then moved to Tower Grove.

Junior should have never moved out of Benedict Canyon, because there he had to walk down the steps! [*laughing*] The Tower Grove house was one story.

What kept the two of you close during all those years?

Well, you see, I came from the other side of the tracks. I didn't know how to eat; I didn't know anything. Junior *watched me grow up*. Junior was very good to me. He was always there if I needed anything. I remember one time when I first was around Hollywood, and Mervyn LeRoy saw me at the racetracks, doing some charity work for Warner Brothers, and he came into Earl Carroll's and said he was going to make a star out of me. He sent the car from MGM to come get me, and I went to his office.... Well, I told Junior everything. So Junior called LeRoy and said, "You leave her alone, she's a good girl!" He *protected* me.

Junior bought me a dog when I got a divorce—he was a very good friend. I had these little poodles—a family of poodles—and he used to babysit them! You know I was connected with Marilyn Monroe and people are always asking me about Marilyn—she was the most wonderful girl who ever lived. When we went to Reno to do *The Misfits* [1961], my dogs used to stay up at Junior's house. And he wrote me *letters* from the *dogs!* The *poodles!* So Junior was very sweet. He was just *good*.

By the way, Junior wanted to produce *Rain* with Marilyn. He wanted to do things—people were always after him for something, but then when he wanted to acquire a project for himself and needed distribution or stuff, nobody wanted to help him.

So he did express interest in resuming his career?

Yes. At one point he had the option on the book *BUtterfield 8,* for which Elizabeth Taylor won an Oscar. About the time of *Bonnie and Clyde* [1967], maybe before it, he'd written to Jack Warner and thought they ought to put their two heads together and make *Son of Rico* or something.

Note: Rico was the role Edward G. Robinson had played in Warner Bros.' Little Caesar (1930).

Junior loved gangster pictures! And then, toward the end, he hired the man who wrote *The Fly* to come over and they were writing a play, *The Invisible Woman,* because Junior had done the film *The Invisible Man.* But it didn't go anyplace.

Note: The Fly had two credited writers—George Langelaan (1908–1969), who wrote the original short story published in Playboy in 1957, and James Clavell (1924–1994), who wrote the screenplay. Langelaan died ten years before Laemmle. Clavell wrote the novel Shogun, winning an Emmy for the famed 1980 TV mini-series. It would appear Evelyn was referring to Clavell, but with such credits as The Great Escape (1963) and To Sir with Love (1967), it seems unlikely Clavell would be "hired" by Junior at this time.

Do you think that, with different doctors, Junior might have rallied?

Oh, he was waiting for Dr. Salk to find a new vaccine for him. And these doctors would come, but what they did, they yessed him to death and he wasn't doing anything to help himself. Like, he didn't *try* to walk. He said, "I can't walk, I can't walk." And I remember one doctor saying, "If you don't use your muscles, then they're going to deteriorate, and other things are going to get bad with you." And that's something he wouldn't do.

When he first got sick, he'd go to this clinic at Cedars. It was Cedars of Lebanon then and they used to put him in the pool. He'd get mad at this doctor because he wanted somebody to *pick* him out of the pool—he didn't try to get out himself. So he stopped going. He wouldn't *try*. He was waiting for a miracle drug.

Junior was such a hypochondriac that he would send himself flowers—even though he thought flowers made him sick! He was almost like Howard Hughes! It was a real strange situation, now that you make me think of it!

How was his mental state in his final years?

He was clear, but he lost interest in a lot of things. I used to—and it was almost like a job with me—I used to go up there to Tower Grove, and I was like his Saturday night date. And he'd come to the table, and then he would go back into his bedroom and go to sleep. He would lose interest. The only way people could keep his interest was to talk about the older times. Now a lot of people who had worked for him at Universal, they used to talk about the different things that happened.

And he enjoyed that?

Yeah. Lew Ayres, from *All Quiet on the Western Front*, used to come up at the end. And Lewis Milestone, who directed that picture—Junior called him "Millie." And Paul Kohner, but he was another phony. And John Huston. Junior gave John Huston his first job. Walter Huston came to Junior and said, "John needs a job," and Junior said, "Okay, he starts tomorrow." Junior was a very *kind* man.

But Junior ... he lost confidence in people. He once told me that, in the old days, he couldn't get up in the morning and pee without Mervyn LeRoy calling, but after he didn't have a studio, Mervyn LeRoy didn't talk to him! Jean Renoir was one of Junior's best friends until Renoir died [in 1979], but he didn't meet him at Universal. What a darling little man Renoir was, and a very *simple* man.

Did Junior ever reminisce with you about his Universal years?

No. But when he used to lie in bed, I used to tell him he was just like the Mummy in his picture! He used to put the covers right up to his neck and tuck them in, beneath the sheets! I don't know how he moved in that bed! At the end, Junior had a housekeeper, who was really a German housekeeper... Are you Jewish?

No.

I used to tell Junior that, with his housekeeper, that it was another case of a German killing a Jew! She thought she owned the house! And you know these old German people, or European people, the men come first. They sit at the table and all that. Oh golly, the whole thing was *weird!*

So the German housekeeper dominated?

More or less. When she first moved up to the house, she had a room in the back, the maid's room. Then she moved up front—and finally, she decided to lock Junior in his room! And I said to him, "What if you have a heart attack?" She'd lock him in his room, and sit on the couch near his door. And then she used to tell awful stories about me. When I say "tell awful stories," I was the outsider, but if I stayed away, he called. He had his television in his room, and he used to watch television there. And I used to sit there and watch television too. That's *all* I was doing, believe me. And she went around telling some strange stories. I told her that if she didn't shut up, I was going to tell Junior what I'd heard!

She intimated things of a lewd nature?

Yes, yes, yes! Before she came, his bedroom was like everybody's living room, and he entertained in his bedroom. People would come up and he'd talk to you, he didn't feel like getting up. He'd be in bed. That was his way.

Why would she lock him in his room?

I do not know! The whole thing was *bizarre*, believe me! I used to tell people, "It's like *Sunset Blvd.!*"

What can you tell me about Junior's death and funeral?

It was disgraceful.

I hadn't gone up the weekend before, because I was told he was sick and didn't want to see anybody. He'd had a stroke, and he was pretty sick. His niece Carol, his sister's daughter, had moved up to the house, to watch things. When he died, she called me. I didn't see the body, because I was working. I attended the funeral. But I understand he was buried in a T-shirt that I had bought for him. I used to go out and buy him cotton T-shirts because, in the end, the last few years of his life, he didn't wear shirts. He was a terrific dresser at one time, but they used to just put these T-shirts on him. So I used to go out and buy him these pretty blue ones and yellow ones, colored ones, to give him more color. And I understand he was buried in a T-shirt, and a scarf wrapped around his neck!

Why?!

I don't know.... I don't know.

What happened at the funeral?

Rabbi Magnin officiated at it. There was a very small crowd. Carol gathered all the flowers that were there and took them in the limousine.

Note: The legendary Rabbi Edgar F. Magnin (1890–1984), the spiritual leader of B'nai B'rith and the Wilshire Temple, had delivered eulogies at the epic funerals of Irving Thalberg in 1936 and Carl Laemmle, Sr., in 1939. The Laemmle Sr. funeral, at the Wilshire Temple, had drawn nearly 2,000 mourners.

Did Rabbi Magnin speak well of Junior?

Oh yeah, but as Rabbi Magnin said, the Junior that they knew wasn't here any more, he'd gone before. And Rabbi Magnin was one of the trustees or something, but at the end, Rabbi Magnin didn't want any part of it. There was too much fighting going on.

Where is Junior buried?

It was out at Home of Peace, that cemetery where his father is ... in East Los Angeles ... a Jewish cemetery.

What happened to the Academy Award Junior had won for* All Quiet on the Western Front*?

It disappeared! I don't know whether the Oscar disappeared while he was still alive, around the time he died, or whether it disappeared later ... but they couldn't find his Oscar. It used to be over with the books. A lot of times I'd pick it up.

That's the way it was. He always had people around, and they ignored everybody here but played up to him, to see what they could get out of him. I used to go there one week and I'd see something—and the next week, it would disappear!

Note: Various stories circulate about what happened to the Oscar. One account reports that it's buried with Junior.

You mentioned fighting about his estate. As he hadn't worked since 1937, and had received his share of the Laemmle fortune after Carl Sr.'s death in 1939, was there still much left?

He didn't have very much. Some paintings. There was a lien on the house. If he hadn't died, he might have ended up being homeless, or at the Motion Picture Relief Home.

It seems he deserved a lot more than he got.

Yes, Junior was good. The last present he ever gave me—Junior got me a little Shih Tzu that I just buried last week. He said, "You have to have a dog, you have to have a little dog!" I think it was because he knew damn well I'd stay home and take care of the dog instead of going out! And he used to like to see her, and I'd take her up there, and he used to throw food at her! I used to tell him that if he didn't stop, I was never going to bring her up there again, because he used to buy the dog filet mignon!

Everybody here gets hurt. I was. If something was wrong at the studio and I was unhappy, he knew it. I wouldn't have to say anything to him. And he would always ask, "Was it a Jewish person or a Christian?" And if it were a Jewish person, he'd buy me a present! And if it were a *Christian* person, he'd buy me a present! It didn't matter who did it, he always did something to make up for what somebody did. Really!

So he was always there for you.

Yes, he was.

Junior Laemmle Timeline[2]

Tuesday, April 28, 1908: Julius Laemmle is born in Chicago. His father, Carl Laemmle, is a 41-year-old immigrant from Laupheim, Bavaria, who, fascinated by nickelodeons, had founded the Laemmle Film Service in 1906.

1909: Carl Laemmle forms the Independent Motion Picture Company in New York. This is in defiance of the Motion Pictures Patents Company, established by Thomas Edison—who eventually slaps Laemmle with no less than 289 lawsuits.

Saturday, June 8, 1912: Laemmle starts Universal Pictures. He moves to California, partly to elude Edison. (He can escape into Mexico if Edison pursues him.)

Monday, March 15, 1915: Carl Laemmle presides as he officially opens Universal City, located on an old chicken ranch under the mountains of the San Fernando Valley. Ten thousand people attend the festivities. Six-year-old Julius Laemmle is there with his camera.

Wednesday, January 11, 1922: Universal releases *Foolish Wives,* starring and directed by Erich von Stroheim. Profligate in his spending, von Stroheim built Monte Carlo on the studio back lot and spiced the film with flamboyant depravity. "Uncle Carl," shocked, nevertheless promotes the film as "The First MILLION DOLLAR PICTURE." Meanwhile, Universal primarily produces cheap westerns and comedies.

Thursday, September 6, 1923: Universal releases *The Hunchback of Notre Dame,* starring Lon Chaney. The cathedral built on the back lot remains there until destroyed in the mid–1950s.

Sunday, November 15, 1925: Universal releases *The Phantom of the Opera,* starring Lon Chaney. Soundstage 28, built to house the Paris Opera set, still stands in 2014 and is still known as the Phantom Stage.

Monday, November 8, 1926: Universal releases the first entry of *The Collegians,* a series of 44 two-reelers depicting college life over a four-year period. Junior writes and produces most of them.

Carl Laemmle, Jr., and Carl Laemmle, Sr., during Junior's young years (courtesy Neil Lipes).

Sunday, April 28, 1929: Carl Laemmle, Jr., turns 21. He's now officially general manager of Universal City. Hollywood-at-large sees this promotion as a folly of nepotism and predicts disaster for Universal.

Monday, May 27, 1929: Universal releases the musical *Broadway*, which Junior personally produces. Spending a reported $1,000,000 on the film, he had approved the building of Universal's Stage 12, known as the *Broadway* Stage. It's the largest stage on the lot (believed to be, in 2014, the seventh largest soundstage in the world); it comes to be after director Paul Fejos masterminds the *Broadway* Crane, which Fejos developed and refined with the help of cameraman Hal Mohr. The giant crane, which provides dazzling opportunities for cinematography, required a steel floor to support it (most sound stages then are made of wood). Junior gave the green light for the stage's steel construction. He also approved *Broadway*'s Technicolor sequences.

Junior is determined to produce "A" films that make Universal a true competitor with major studios; he figures the low-budget "B"s will pay for the "A"s. His lavish expenditures worry his father.

Friday, March 21, 1930: Junior takes his new production *The King of Jazz,* a musical revue starring Paul Whiteman and his Band and shot entirely in Technicolor, to San Bernardino for a secret preview. Jimmy Starr, columnist of the *Los Angeles Record,* reports the next day that the movie "is by far the finest film revue and most sensational production yet to be made! Junior Laemmle has more than proved his ability." Junior has spent an estimated $2,000,000 on the picture, which will flop. Universal later gets unflattering publicity when, unhappy about its losses, it sues the corpulent Whiteman, claiming he ate too much in the commissary while shooting the picture.

Monday, April 21, 1930: All Quiet on the Western Front, personally produced by Junior, has a gala premiere at Los Angeles' Carthay Circle Theatre. It's precisely one week before Junior's twenty-second birthday. He's spent $1,448,863[3] filming the Erich Maria Remarque novel and the opening night audience (and guests at the party Junior hosts afterwards at the Embassy Club) includes Louis B. Mayer, Charlie Chaplin, Douglas Fairbanks, Mary Pickford, Gary Cooper, Lupe Velez, Cecil B. DeMille, D.W. Griffith, Tod Browning, Marlene Dietrich, and many more. The film is a triumph.

Tuesday, April 22, 1930: Jimmy Starr, covering the "thrilling party" at the Embassy, reports that Junior was with actress Alice Day. Laemmle Sr. had previously demanded Junior stop seeing Day because she was a Gentile. "Wonder if this past romance is building again?" ponders Starr.

Monday, September 29, 1930: Universal begins shooting *Dracula,* despite the objections of Laemmle, Sr., who feels the story is "morbid." Junior, who champions the film, has selected Bela Lugosi to reprise his stage role; Lugosi later jokes that he got the part in the film only after "Old Man Laemmle" tested all his relatives and "the pets of their pets." Tod Browning, who'd directed many of the hits of the recently deceased Lon Chaney, is Junior's choice to direct.

Wednesday, November 5, 1930: All Quiet on the Western Front wins the Academy Award as Best Picture. The film has enjoyed worldwide acclaim, will take in a remarkable $3,000,000 in international rentals, and will earn Universal a profit of $516,741. Junior doesn't accept the Oscar—Laemmle Sr. does, although he'd originally and vehemently opposed the film's message and expense.

Thursday, November 13, 1930: "Carl Laemmle, Sr. Delighted with Success of Jr.," headlines Elizabeth Yeaman in the *Hollywood Daily Citizen.* "All credit goes to Junior," says Laemmle Sr. Unpublicized is the fact that "Uncle Carl" is apoplectic about *Dracula.*

Tuesday, December 2, 1930: Elizabeth Yeaman announces that actress Sidney Fox, "a diminutive little creature with the charm and poise of a veteran," arrived in Hollywood the previous day, under contract to Universal. Junior had signed her after seeing her in the Broadway play *Lost Sheep.* According to the rumor mill, Junior and Sidney are lovers and their relationship wins her preferential treatment at the studio.

Junior Laemmle with a boom crane on Universal's back lot (courtesy Neil Lipes).

Monday, December 15, 1930: Jimmy Starr reports in the *Los Angeles Evening Express* that Bette Davis "arrived in town Saturday for work as a featured player at Universal." Davis later claims that Junior invited her to his "throne room" office, looked at her legs, and closed the door in her face. Legend relates that Junior laments that Davis "has as much sex appeal as Slim Summerville."

Thursday, January 8, 1931: Elizabeth Yeaman announces that actress Rose Hobart arrived in Hollywood yesterday, "in the midst of the downpour," signed by Junior to a Universal contract. Hobart (who will score in Paramount's 1931 *Dr. Jekyll and Mr. Hyde*) will fight with Junior and, decades later, claim that as a producer, "Junior didn't know his ass from a shotgun!"[4]

Thursday, February 12, 1931: *Dracula* opens at New York City's Roxy Theatre. It's the baptism of classic horror and a giant hit. Bela Lugosi becomes a star. Junior Laemmle has sired a genre that will be Universal's lasting distinction. Laemmle Sr.'s face-saving remark on the film's popularity: "I knew it was good, but I didn't know it was *that* good, even after seeing it in the projection room."

Saturday, May 23, 1931: *Waterloo Bridge,* based on Robert Sherwood's play and starring Mae Clarke as the tragic prostitute Myra, begins shooting. Making his Universal directorial debut is James Whale, whom Junior Laemmle has signed to a contract after admiring Whale's work on Tiffany's *Journey's End*. Clarke, who will act in three films for Whale, will refer to him late in her life as "a genius." As for Junior, she will describe him as "retarded."[5]

Tuesday, June 16, 1931: Robert Florey begins directing a two-day test for *Frankenstein* with Bela Lugosi as the Monster. Junior is in New York City. When he returns, he looks at the Florey-Lugosi test. Decades later, Junior tells writer Rick Atkins, "I laughed like a hyena!"

Thursday, July 2, 1931: The *Los Angeles Examiner* announces that Lugosi has departed *Frankenstein* and will star in Universal's *Murders in the Rue Morgue*. Meanwhile, Junior has taken *Frankenstein* away from Robert Florey (who will direct *Murders in the Rue Morgue*) and given it to James Whale. While Junior might have "laughed like a hyena" at Lugosi's test, it's likely Bela's gone because Whale wants a different Monster.

Monday, August 24, 1931: *Frankenstein* begins shooting. Whale has selected Colin Clive, whom he directed in the London stage and Hollywood film versions of *Journey's End,* for the title role, and has chosen Boris Karloff to play the Monster. Junior approves this casting, even though Lugosi is a star after *Dracula* and Karloff is basically unknown. Junior's oft-quoted remark: "Karloff's eyes mirrored the suffering we needed."

Wednesday, October 21, 1931: Elizabeth Yeaman in the *Hollywood Daily Citizen* reports that Junior, "following a week of rest at [Lake] Arrowhead, has gone to the Cedars of Lebanon Hospital for treatment of hay fever."

Thursday, October 29, 1931: *Frankenstein* previews in Santa Barbara.

Monday, November 2, 1931: Ms. Yeaman notes that Junior, after two weeks at Cedars, is now recuperating "at a desert retreat." Word spreads that Junior is a hypochondriac.

Friday, November 6, 1931: *Strictly Dishonorable,* a sex comedy based on the play by Preston Sturges, has a gala premiere at the Carthay Circle Theatre. Junior personally produced, John Stahl (who, along with James Whale, is one of Universal's top two directors) directed, and Sidney Fox has the coveted star role. The next day, Jimmy Starr of the *Evening Express* writes of Junior's protégée: "Sidney Fox, pretty newcomer, suffers from the lack of close-ups.... There is also an obvious avoiding of full-shot scenes with Miss Fox. One tiny glimpse disclosed her somewhat overweight. Don't eat starchy foods, Sidney."

Laemmle Sr. and Laemmle Jr. grace the cover of this Universal program, during a very special time in the studio's history: The summer of 1931 (courtesy Neil Lipes).

Friday, December 4, 1931: *Frankenstein* opens at the RKO-Mayfair Theatre in New York City. It's a smash hit and a sensation. Boris Karloff now has a Universal star contract.

Wednesday, February 10, 1932: *Murders in the Rue Morgue* opens at the RKO-Mayfair in New York. Sidney Fox, as the heroine, gets top-billing over Bela Lugosi, as mad Dr. Mirakle. Broadway audiences laugh at the finale in which Lugosi's gorilla lugs Ms. Fox over Paris rooftops. Still, the film is a tepid success.

Tuesday, April 5, 1932: Jimmy Starr reports in the *Evening Herald Express* that Junior was a guest at "the big social event of the weekend," a buffet hosted by Mr. and Mrs. Richard Rodgers. According to Starr, Junior "bounced in and sorta admitted his weakness was Constance Cummings." Junior is very serious about the actress, but—again—Laemmle Sr. vows to disinherit him if he weds a Gentile.

Summer, 1932: *Variety* reports that worldwide rentals for *Dracula* have reached $1.2 million, *Frankenstein*, $1.4 million. The prestige of *All Quiet on the Western Front* and the phenomenal success of the horror films is a combination that should assure Junior of respect in Hollywood. It doesn't. Additionally, Laemmle Sr., while publicly extolling his son, fights him bitterly over many studio decisions.

Thursday, August 4, 1932: *Back Street,* based on the Fannie Hurst novel about a woman who sacrifices everything for a married man, premieres at the Carthay Circle Theatre. Junior produced, Irene Dunne and John Boles star, and John Stahl directed. The film's so popular that Universal will produce 1941 and 1961 remakes.

Wednesday, August 10, 1932: The 1932 Summer Olympic Games are in Los Angeles, and Junior has engaged the All-America Football Team of 1931 to appear in the film *The All American.* On this evening, at Dias Dorados, the Laemmle estate in Benedict Canyon, Junior hosts a farewell dinner and dance for the team. Among the Universal stars dining at the buffet and dancing on the lawn: Boris Karloff, Sidney Fox, Lew Ayres, Gloria Stuart, Tom Mix, Tala Birell, and Paul Lukas. Uncle Carl, of course, is there too.

Thursday, October 27, 1932: Universal's *The Old Dark House,* based on the J.B. Priestley novel, directed by James Whale, starring Boris Karloff, and produced by Junior, opens at the Rialto in New York City.

Friday, December 23, 1932: Universal's *The Mummy,* starring Boris Karloff and directed by Karl Freund, opens in Chicago. Junior was in New York when it began production, and although his name is on the credits, the actual producer is Stanley Bergerman—husband of Junior's sister Rosabelle. The posters herald the star as "KARLOFF the Uncanny."

Tuesday, January 17, 1933: Universal celebrates Uncle Carl's 66th birthday, honoring him with a 66-pound cake. Junior is at his side; KARLOFF and James Whale are among those paying homage. The same day, *The Hollywood Reporter* announces that Universal will shut down temporarily in February. Financial peril is severe and the studio will remain closed for several months.

Friday, November 17, 1933: Universal's *The Invisible Man,* produced by Junior, opens at the Roxy Theatre in New York City and sets a three-year record for attendance. Claude Rains stars as "The Invisible One"; James Whale is director. The film will place number nine on the *New York Times'* Ten Best list of 1933.

Thursday, December 7, 1933: Universal's *Counsellor at Law,* produced by Junior, opens at Radio City Music Hall. John Barrymore stars, William Wyler directed. Many believe Barrymore's performance as the Jewish lawyer to be his best screen work.

Wednesday, February 28, 1934: *The Black Cat,* supposedly based on Poe's tale, begins shooting at Universal City. Junior has engaged KARLOFF (as the studio now bills him) to star as the modern incarnation of Lucifer, and Bela Lugosi to co-star as his avenging angel nemesis. Edgar G. Ulmer, 29-year-old crony of Junior's, directs. The film concerns incest, necrophilia and devil worship, and Junior, who's been bitterly battling with his father, privately hopes the film will scare the hell out of him.

Thursday, May 3, 1934: The Black Cat premieres at the Hollywood Pantages. Karloff, Lugosi, and leading lady Jacqueline Wells are there for the festivities. The film, despite Uncle Carl's apoplexy, will be Universal's big moneymaker of the season.

Friday, May 11, 1934: James Whale begins shooting *One More River,* based on the John Galsworthy novel. The film concerns a sex sadist (Colin Clive) who beats his wife (Diana Wynyard) with a riding whip and, after their estrangement, rapes her. Junior, who champions the film, will have all-consuming battles with the Production Code. One can imagine Uncle Carl's response.

Friday, October 19, 1934: Uncle Carl, his daughter Rosabelle, and Rosabelle's husband Stanley Bergerman host an afternoon party at Dias Dorados, honoring Junior, who's preparing to embark on a three-month trip to Europe and Africa. One hundred seventy friends attend, including Irving Thalberg, James Whale, Jean Harlow, Irene Dunne, and Claudette Colbert.

Thursday, November 29, 1934: "*Imitation of Life* Breaks a Film Taboo," headlines film critic Donald Kirkley in *The Baltimore Sun.* The movie, based on the Fannie Hurst bestseller, has opened at Baltimore's Keith's Theatre, and concerns race relations. Claudette Colbert and Louise Beavers star, John Stahl directed, and Junior produced (although Henry Henigson was the actual supervisor). The film's an unabashed tear-jerker, but as Kirkley writes, "When a studio, no matter how, or why, finds the courage to break a taboo, as in *Imitation of Life,* it is big news, and an occasion for rejoicing." The film becomes one of 1934's biggest moneymakers and gets an Academy Best Picture nomination (losing to Columbia's *It Happened One Night*).

December 1934: Laemmle Sr., outraged that his son the past year has made films about race relations, sex sadism, and devil worship—and likely jealous of the success Junior has achieved—makes his move. As Junior leaves for a vacation in Europe, Uncle Carl, ready and willing to sacrifice Junior, seizes control, redefining the studio he founded. Son-in-law Stanley Bergerman, his right hand man, has become Universal's executive producer.

Monday, December 10, 1934: Harrison Carroll of the *Evening Herald Express* writes: "It sounds too fantastic but Junior Laemmle has received a good offer from another company and has, at least, given it consideration. The young boss of Universal says he is going to Europe but still hangs on in New York, where he is running up record telephone bills talking to the coast. It's a pretty general rumor that Junior is none too pleased with the developments at Universal since he left on his holiday. Worn out as he is, he may let them be until his return from Europe, but many of his pals are predicting an early return to the studio, and the offer from the other major company is too nice to laugh off."

Thursday, December 20, 1934: Jimmy Starr writes in the *Evening Herald Express:*

A new bombshell exploded on the Universal lot, and fires flamed for another shake-up—not an uncommon inter-office blast at this particular studio. First rumblings of the new rumpus started when Carl Laemmle, Jr., young production boss of the plant whose production record is indeed enviable, stepped aboard an eastbound train on the first lap of a many-times postponed European vacation.

Unfortunately, or maybe it is most fortunate (for Universal), Junior was taken ill in New York and missed his steamer. Since Junior's departure, Carl Laemmle, Sr., has had full sway at the studio operating reins, and dissatisfaction has loomed among the ranks of associate producers, directors and story department heads.

The latest development: Junior Laemmle is definitely foregoing his vacation to return to the studio and rearrange studio matters....

Monday, December 24, 1934: Starr reports that Junior "will be here today to straighten out some Universal Studios matters." There's no peace or good will between Senior and Junior this Yuletide as they battle about Universal's future.

Wednesday, January 2, 1935: *The Return of Frankenstein,* fated to be retitled *Bride of Frankenstein,* starts shooting at Universal. KARLOFF is back as the Monster, Colin Clive returns as Frankenstein, Elsa Lanchester plays Mary Shelley and the Bride, and James Whale directs. Junior personally produces.

Tuesday, January 8, 1935: Jimmy Starr reports a Universal settlement: Junior is now second vice-president of Universal, and will be an independent producer within the studio, producing "six super-special films" in 1935, including *Show Boat* and *Dracula's Daughter.* Laemmle Sr. will supervise "all the affairs of the studio," while Bergerman remains executive producer. "And once more the little dove of peace sails over Universal," writes Starr, "and everybody is happy!"

Monday, January 28, 1935: Universal begins shooting *WereWolf of London,* starring Henry Hull. Stuart Walker directs. Stanley Bergerman produces.

Saturday, April 6, 1935: Harrison Carroll writes that Junior will produce a remake of *The Hunchback of Notre Dame.* The three leading candidates for the title role: Boris Karloff, Conrad Veidt, and Claude Rains. Junior never produces the remake.

Saturday, April 20, 1935: *Bride of Frankenstein* opens at the Hollywood Pantages. James Whale presents audacious flourishes—e.g., Karloff's Monster, hanging on a pole like the crucified Christ—that surely appall Uncle Carl and somehow elude the censors. A macabre masterpiece, it's the climax of Universal horror.

Wednesday, April 24, 1935: *Variety* headlines on page one, "Unit Plan for U with Bergerman Leaving." In an outrageous display of family feuding, Stanley Bergerman, still functioning at Universal as executive producer, had refused to green light any of Junior's proposed projects for 1935–36, only approving those of producers Jerry Sackheim, Leonard Speigelgass, Edmund Grainger, and himself. When Laemmle Sr. ordered Bergerman to deal with Junior, Bergerman refused and walked out of Sr.'s office. Meanwhile, the giant hit of *Bride of Frankenstein* at the Pantages, personally produced by Junior, makes a fool of Bergerman and starts rumors that Junior will nab Bergerman's executive producer post. Bergerman leaves the studio and prints his letter of resignation in the evening edition of an April 23, 1935, newspaper.

Thursday, April 25, 1935: Elizabeth Yeaman reports the latest corporate news at Universal: Uncle Carl is developing "a system of unit production." He will oversee all, and Junior "will not again become director of production, but will remain as one of the unit producers, handling the bigger pictures, first of which will be *Show Boat* with Irene Dunne." Stanley Bergerman, executive producer at the studio for the past eight months, has resigned.

Friday, July 12, 1935: Universal begins shooting *Magnificent Obsession,* directed by John Stahl. He runs perilously over schedule and budget; when the film finally wraps in the fall, the cost is nearly $1,000,000. Irene Dunne's salary alone tallies $145,000—$50,000 more than the entire cost of *The Black Cat.* Meanwhile, the studio, which will suffer a 1935

The Laemmle family: Uncle Carl with son Junior, daughter Rosabelle, and son-in-law Stanley Bergerman (courtesy Neil Lipes).

corporate loss of almost $700,000, is preparing two elaborate productions: *Sutter's Gold* and *Show Boat*. Laemmle Sr. needs money for these pictures to float.

  Friday, October 25, 1935: Elizabeth Yeaman of the *Hollywood Citizen News* announces, "Uncle Carl Laemmle has raised a huge cash loan and is going to retain his Universal Studios...." She doesn't disclose the terms. Laemmle Sr. eventually negotiates with Standard Capital for a $750,000 loan; as collateral, he gives Standard Capital the option to buy Universal within 90 days for $5.5 million. Always the gambler, Uncle Carl bets Standard Capital can't raise the money.

Tuesday, November 19, 1935: Sutter's Gold goes into production, James Cruze directing, Edward Arnold starring.

Monday, December 9, 1935: Show Boat begins shooting, Junior personally producing, James Whale directing, Irene Dunne starring. The financial drain on the studio as this elaborate musical proceeds is staggering—so much so that Laemmle Sr. can't gather the money to pay back Standard Capital.

Saturday, January 25, 1936: Sutter's Gold completes shooting. The film shapes up disastrously. Costing $773,144.87 (more than $79,000 over budget), it will be a flop.

Wednesday, March 11, 1936: James Whale completes *Show Boat.* Final cost: $1,275,000.

Saturday, March 14, 1936: Uncle Carl loses his bet: Standard Capital buys Universal.

Wednesday, April 15, 1936: Elizabeth Yeaman writes in the *Hollywood Citizen News:* "The name of Laemmle will soon vanish from the executive roster at Universal. Uncle Carl is gone, having sold the studio for $5,500,000, and today it became known that Carl Jr. has handed in his resignation at the studio. He was scheduled to produce *My Man Godfrey,* with William Powell and Carole Lombard, a picture which starts immediately. But his resignation becomes effective on Saturday."

Tuesday, May 12, 1936: Show Boat has a gala premiere at the Hollywood Pantages Theatre. Preceding it is a parade down Hollywood Boulevard, James Whale among the celebrities. "The Laemmle's *au revoir* to Universal is brilliantly achieved in *Show Boat,*" writes Louella O. Parsons in the *Los Angeles Examiner.* The musical will be one of 1936's big hits, although "The New Universal," with Charles R. Rogers at the helm, reaps the benefits.

Thursday, May 6, 1937: Elizabeth Yeaman writes, "Carl Laemmle, Jr., finally has signed that long-rumored contract to produce at MGM." He will stay several months and produce no films.

Sunday, September 24, 1939: Carl Laemmle, Sr., dies of a heart attack at Dias Dorados at age 72. Junior shares in the $5,000,000 estate. He's paid dearly for the honor by having given up Alice Day and Constance Cummings. He will never marry.

Thursday, January 22, 1942: Louella O. Parsons writes: "What will Carl Laemmle, Jr., do with all his assorted pills (said to be the largest collection in the world) now that the Army medicos have examined him and declared him 100 percent fit?" Junior becomes an Army private and spends most of his World War II military time stationed at the Plaza Hotel in New York City.

Monday, March 5, 1945: Louella O. Parsons writes in the *Los Angeles Examiner:*

> This I call big news. Carl Laemmle, Jr., is coming back into the movies and with a property that is both interesting and fascinating. He plans to film the life story of Julian Eltinge, famed female impersonator. Julian, whom I first met in Paris in 1920, could make up as the most beautiful woman in the world, and yet the very fact that he could play a character of that kind ruined his life. He was a normal, red-blooded man and he fell in love with a girl. They became engaged, but her family objected, refusing to let her marry a female impersonator.
>
> His mother, 85, is still alive and lives here, and has given her consent to putting Eltinge's story on the screen. There'll be only a few scenes showing him as a female impersonator, and most of the picture will be his story of the good old theatrical days, showing all the famed people who were his friends.

The film is never made.

Fall, 1957: *Shock! Theatre* becomes a TV sensation, showcasing the old Universal horror classics. The popularity does nothing to revitalize the life and career of Junior Laemmle, who'd basically introduced the horror genre.

Monday, September 24, 1979: At 5:00 p.m. on precisely the 40th anniversary of the death of Carl Laemmle, Sr., Carl Laemmle, Jr., dies at age 71 at his home, 1641 Tower Grove Drive, above Beverly Hills. He's suffered for years from multiple sclerosis; the cause of death is a stroke. Stanley Bergerman, Junior's brother-in-law who fought with him for control of Universal in the mid–1930s (and who also had never produced another film after leaving Universal), is informant for the death certificate. (Bergerman will die in 1998 at the age of 94.) The death certificate lists Junior's last employer as Metro-Goldwyn-Mayer, where he'd worked for several months 42 years previously. Malinow and Silverman Mortuary handle the arrangements.

Wednesday, September 26, 1979: Laemmle Jr. is laid to rest at Home of Peace Memorial Park in Los Angeles, entombed in a crypt room with his father, mother, and other family members.

* * *

In the late 1970s, Neil Lipes of New York developed a novel idea that involved Universal Studios and the long-retired Carl Laemmle, Jr. As Mr. Lipes wrote to me:

Movies, Monsters, the Laemmles, & Universal Pictures ... a lifelong love. I have been intoxicated with motion pictures from the earliest days of my childhood in Brooklyn, New York. Back then we were not so formal, referring to those reels of projected emulsion simply as "the movies." Most weekends were fraught with excitement, as Saturday and Sunday were the two days during the week when I would be given my "allowance" ... which "allowed" me to attend "the movies" at either of the following neighborhood theaters ... the Midwood, the Kent, the Elm, and the Leader. The aforementioned were my go-to theaters, as I could walk to them from my house.

Those early theaters were a delight, as the architecture just seduced one upon paying the princely sum of 15 cents and entering a world of magic and mystery. Once seated with a box of Bon-Bons or other confections, the dual curtains would begin to draw back ... first the heavy velvet one, followed by a sheer one, to finally reveal that magic expanse of white ... the screen ... and spilling upon it that pencil beam of light, emanating from the projectionist's booth.

My fascination with horror and Universal Pictures actually started thanks to a local former DJ from Philadelphia, now on local NYC independent TV station WOR-TV channel 9. His name was John Zacherle, or fondly referred to as Zacherley.

It was Zacherley who with studio hijinks showed all manner of horror films from Universal Pictures. The program was on late, and I had to feign that I was sleeping, only to get up and put the TV on, and hopefully not wake my sleeping parents!

This set the stage for what was to continue for my entire life.

Having produced film festivals in college, I became associated with a wonderful fellow named John O'Keefe, then branch manager for MCA/Universal in NYC. On one occasion I mentioned to O'Keefe that a film should be produced and be shown to all waiting on line to take the Universal tour at Universal City, and Orlando, Florida. His positive response was, "Great idea. Go and make the film, and I will help you get it going."

That conversation caused me to find if Jr. Laemmle was still alive, as I wanted him to be the spokesperson for the retrospective. I was most fortunate in contacting Max Laemmle, who graciously proffered Jr.'s home address. That was the "seed" that germinated into a long period of letter exchanges between Jr. and myself, where I told him of my intentions to make a filmed short history of Universal Pictures, and having him (Jr.) as its host.

At the same time O'Keefe arranged a meeting between Henry "Hy" Martin who was president of Universal in NYC and myself to discuss Universal funding said film.

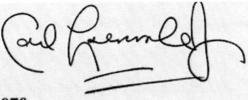

August 10, 1976

Mr. Neil R. Lipes
33 Southgate Road
Valley Stream, New York 11581

Dear Mr. Lipes:

I read your letter of July 30, with great interest.
If there is any way I could be of service to you
I would be glad to hear from you. You already have
my address. My home phone number is CRestview 6 7364
If you are ever in Beverly Hills, please call me.

Best regards.

Carl Laemmle, Jr.

P. S. I would be happy to see you and help in any
way I can.

Junior Laemmle's letter to Neil Lipes (courtesy Neil Lipes).

Sadly, Universal did not see the "merit" of such a project, and Martin declined active participation. More tragic was the fact that Jr. Laemmle already living with compromised health, took a turn for the worse, and died a short while later from MS. His tragic passing ended any hope to the production of a Universal Pictures retrospective.

Both Carl Laemmle, and his son Julius "Jr." Laemmle remain very much alive in my mind, and as such will never die, as long as they are spoken about and their films coveted.[6]

*   *   *

Universal City still exists in the same L.A. locale where Carl Laemmle, Sr., had festively opened it in 1915. However, it's now a giant conglomerate, as much a theme park as a studio, virtually unrecognizable from its original, pastoral chicken ranch site.

The view of the hills and the Pacific from the former Junior Laemmle home, atop Beverly Hills, 2010 (photograph by the author).

Landmarks from the Golden Age are few. Soundstage 28, the Phantom Stage, still stands, as does Soundstage 12, the *Broadway* Stage. A replica of the European village used in *Frankenstein* exists; the actual site burned many years ago.

Naturally, the same towering hills loom over the back lot, just as they did when Bela Lugosi played Dracula and Boris Karloff portrayed Frankenstein's Monster. These classics had a personality in common, of course ... a sad, rather tragic little man, whom many in Hollywood regarded as something of a hapless monster. However, in his daring, his showmanship instincts, and maybe even his personal hang-ups, he launched much of the mythology that is the worldwide corporate identity of Universal Studios.

Nevertheless, don't look for a statue, a postcard, or even a mention of Carl Laemmle, Jr., in Universal Studios in Hollywood, Orlando, Japan, or Singapore.

You won't find one.

Chapter Notes

Chapter 1

1. "Cinema," Time Magazine, 23 February 1931, p. 62.
2. Email to author from Kevin Chandler, 13 April 2003.
3. Warner Bros. Archives, Helen Chandler File, 24 June 1930.
4. A singer and actress on Broadway and in Hollywood, Lillian (like Helen) was a child actress and a victim of alcohol. Her 1954 memoir, *I'll Cry Tomorrow*, was an international best-seller and became a film with Susan Hayward receiving a Best Actress Oscar nomination for playing Lillian. Roth, who married at least five times, recovered from her alcoholism and later appeared on Broadway in the musicals *I Can Get It for You Wholesale* (1962) and *70, Girls, 70* (1971). She died May 12, 1980, at age 69.
5. Yale-educated Hume was a praised novelist of the Roaring '20s with such works as *Wife of the Centaur*. He was MGM's top Tarzan writer; in addition to *Tarzan the Ape Man* (1932), he provided the screenplays for *Tarzan Escapes* (1936) and *Tarzan Finds a Son!* (1939). His sister, actress Benita Hume (1906–1967), played in *Tarzan Escapes*. Also in Hume's credits are such films as *Flying Down to Rio* (RKO, 1933). Hume received an Emmy nomination for "The Fearful Decision," an episode of *The United States Steel Hour* (May 30, 1955); sharing the nomination with him was Richard Maibaum, later a key writer on the James Bond films, who claimed that Hume was the major influence on his career. Hume later wrote teleplays for such TV series as *The Rebel* and *The Rifleman*. He died in Palos Verdes, California, on March 26, 1966, ten days after his 66th birthday.
6. Born February 20, 1904, in England, Fletcher married four times: Helen Chandler (1935–1940), Diana Barrymore (1942–1946), Susan Robinson (1950–?) and Lael Tucker Wertenbaker (1970 until his death). Horror fans remember him well as Little Billee in *Svengali* (Warner Bros., 1931) and as Norton, the archaeologist who goes raving mad at the sight of Karloff's resurrected Imhotep in *The Mummy* (Universal, 1932). Other film credits include *Raffles* (Goldwyn, 1930), *The Monkey's Paw* (RKO, 1933), *Random Harvest* (MGM, 1942), and *The Undying Monster*

(20th Century–Fox, 1942). Among his many Broadway credits was the original *My Fair Lady*, in which he was star standby to Rex Harrison and later Edward Mulhare and Michael Allinson in the role of Prof. Henry Higgins (1956 to 1960). He later toured in a one-man show as George Bernard Shaw and was also an accomplished artist. Fletcher died in New Hampshire on June 22, 1988.

Chapter 2

1. Gene Fowler, *Good Night, Sweet Prince* (New York: Viking Press, 1944), pp. 326–328. Also: "Barrymore Has Private Menagerie," *The Hartford Courant*, 28 June 1931, p. D1.
2. Margo Peters, *The House of Barrymore* (New York: Knopf, 1990), p. 313.
3. Thanks to Dr. Karl Thiede, who provided these very hard-to-find financial figures for Barrymore's Warner Bros. films.
4. Thanks to the excellent staff of Warner Bros.' Archives, especially Sandra Joy Lee and Jonathon Auxier, for providing me with a copy of Barrymore's contract.
5. The other silent film versions are *Trilby and Svengali* (British, 1911) and *Three Tales of Terror* (Austria, 1912).
6. Carew later played "the Persian" in Lon Chaney's *The Phantom of the Opera* (1925) and had juicy featured roles in *Doctor X* (1932) and *Mystery of the Wax Museum* (1933). On April 22, 1937, ill and despondent, he checked into an auto court in Santa Monica and shot himself—leaving a note and money to pay for any damage the bullet might have done to his rented quarters.
7. Fowler, pp. 336–337.
8. A star in the London theater, she also emerged as the heroine in a real-life soap opera in which her husband, Sonnie Hale, left Evelyn for actress Jessie Matthews. The public embraced Evelyn, as did the divorce court judge—who publicly referred to Ms. Matthews as "odious."
9. *Svengali* production file, Warner Bros.' Archives.
10. "Film Fare for 1931 Considered," *The Baltimore Sun*, 4 January 1931, p. MR3.

11. The *L.A. Times* reported that she won the role because the play's director, Edgar MacGregor, felt she was "the ideal girl to play the somewhat sensational scenes in the comedy without creating offense." "Current Drama," *Los Angeles Times*, 19 October 1930, p. B11.

12. "Marian Marsh Selected for Star's Leading Lady," *The Baltimore Sun*, 25 January 1931, p. MR2.

13. Author's interviews with Marian Marsh, 14 May 1983, 18 July 1992, and 15 December 1992. The author visited Ms. Marsh at her home in Palm Desert, California, and found her a charming, generous hostess.

14. Faith Service, "Cinderella Comes to Life as Barrymore's Leading Lady," *Motion Picture*, November 1931, p. 59.

15. The source for this letter is Marian Marsh's correspondence offered in auction by Heritage Galleries, Dallas, Texas, in 2007. This writer was working as a cataloguer for Heritage at that time and examined and described most of the Marsh material. However, the Warner Bros. Archives report that Marian's *Svengali* salary was $300 per week, which would seem to indicate that her agent negotiated a raise for her before *Svengali* started shooting.

16. *Svengali* production file, Warner Bros. Archives.

17. "Carmel Myers Gets Film Job by Telegraph," *Los Angeles Times*, 24 May 1931, p. 23.

18. Anthony Slide, "Silent Stars Speak," *Films in Review*, March 1980, p. 141. Myers worked sporadically after *Svengali* and *The Mad Genius*, was a wealthy hostess in Hollywood, showed up as a silent movie star on the "Bird in a Gilded Cage" episode of *Chico and the Man* (November 21, 1975), and appeared with many other Golden Age stars in *Won Ton Ton: The Dog Who Saved Hollywood* (1976). She died November 9, 1980, age 81.

19. Crisp and Hare will both appear again in such films as Warners' *The Life of Emile Zola* (1937) and MGM's *Dr. Jekyll and Mr. Hyde* (1941).

20. *Svengali* production file, Warner Bros. Archives.

21. After being fired from *Svengali*, Douglas, according to the March 15, 1931, *Los Angeles Times*, signed a long-term contract as a Paramount featured player. However, his final film was Monogram's *West of Singapore* (1933). He died in Cuernavaca, Mexico, on May 4, 1978, at the age of 81.

22. "Marian Marsh to Play Role in *Svengali*," *Los Angeles Times*, 18 January 1931, p. 25.

23. Service.

24. Fowler, p. 338.

25. Warner Bros. pressbook for *The Mad Genius*.

26. On February 15, 1931, the same day that the *New York Times* announced John Barrymore would star in *The Idol*, *The Baltimore Sun* reported that Edward G. Robinson would star in the film opposite Marian Marsh ("Directors Slapping Actors to Make Them Angry Now," p. M1).

27. Carlisle Jones, "Barrymore Speaks His Mind," *Hollywood Magazine*, July 1931, p. 19.

28. "Barrymore Ends Fishing Cruise," *Los Angeles Times*, 4 March 1931, p. 22.

29. Jonah Maurice Ruddy, "The Dulwich Horror," reprinted in *Boris Karloff: The Frankenscience Monster*, Forrest J Ackerman, ed. (New York: Ace, 1969), p. 33.

30. Although his work found only a few fleeting moments in *The Mad Genius*, Bolm presented the complete ballet at the Hollywood Bowl in August of 1932. He died in 1951.

31. "Theatre receipts," *Motion Picture Herald*, 16 May 1931, p. 48.

32. "Theatre receipts," *Motion Picture Herald*, 23 May 1931, p. 46.

33. "Theatre receipts," *Motion Picture Herald*, 6 June 1931, p. 41.

34. Once again I am grateful to Dr. Karl Thiede for the rental information on both *Svengali* and *The Mad Genius*.

35. This information also comes from Marian Marsh's papers, which Marsh's daughter consigned to Heritage Galleries for auction in 2007.

36. *Variety*, 22 December 1959, p. 2.

Chapter 3

1. This autographed album page from Lionel Atwill to noted hairdresser Lily Dirigo was offered by R&R Auctions in October of 2008. Accompanying it was an album page autographed by Randolph Scott, also signed to Dirigo. Winning bid: $346.29.

2. Thanks to Kristine Krueger, National Film Information Service, Margaret Herrick Library, Academy of Motion Picture Arts and Sciences for providing this censorship information from Motion Picture Association of America, Production Code Administration Records (i.e., AAMP File).

3. *Motion Picture Herald*, 24 February 1934. Thanks to Gary Don Rhodes, who provided the exhibitor reports cited in this chapter.

4. Universal Studios had purchased Wylie's book *The Murderer Invisible* in blueprinting its *The Invisible Man* (1933), for which R.C. Sherriff provided the final screenplay and received sole on-screen credit.

5. Rumors perennially claimed Scott was one of the beast men in *Island of Lost Souls*, along with Alan Ladd and Buster Crabbe. Considering the very heavy makeup, it's virtually impossible to prove or disprove.

6. Randy Skretvedt, *Laurel and Hardy: The Magic Behind the Movies* (Beverly Hills: Past Times, 1994), p. 364.

7. A December 30, 1932, report from the Association of Motion Picture Producers, Inc., to the Hon. Will B. Hays in New York noted that there were several "animal pictures" in the works, including *The Big Cage* at Universal and *King of the Jungle* and *Murders in the Zoo* at Paramount. (The report missed a big one: *King Kong* at RKO.) Additionally, Universal had just completed *Nagana*, and the censor letter noted "we are now in receipt of a letter from the studio saying they are accepting our suggestions about trimming

down the animal scenes." Incidentally, *Nagana* included an episode in which crocodiles attack the bound heroine, played by Garbo look-alike Tala Birell.

8. John Andrew Gallagher, "Inside Zoo," *Video-Scope.*

9. Pressbook of *Murders in the Zoo,* provided by Kristine Krueger of the Academy's Margaret Herrick Library.

10. Film fans will remember Pawley as the sadistic cop who taunts James Cagney on the night of the latter's electric chair execution in Warners' *Angels with Dirty Faces* (1938). A passionate anti–Communist who found himself blackballed in Hollywood, Pawley took early retirement from show business, raised goats and wrote poetry, and died in Charlottesville, Virginia, on January 27, 1988, at the age of 86.

11. Jimmy Starr, *Los Angeles Evening Herald Express,* 7 February 1933.

12. "Savage Beasts Clash in Wild Film Melee," *Los Angeles Times,* 18 January 1933, pp. A1 and A3.

13. G. D. Hamann, *Lionel Atwill in the '30s* (Hollywood: Filming Today Press, 2004), pp. 20 and 21.

14. "Theatre receipts," *Motion Picture Herald,* 15 April 1933, p. 46.

15. "Theatre receipts," *Motion Picture Herald,* 22 April 1933, p. 44.

16. "Theatre receipts," *Motion Picture Herald,* 28 January 1933, p. 34.

17. "Theatre receipts," *Motion Picture Herald,* 21 January 1933, p. 36.

18. *Motion Picture Herald,* 24 February 1934.

19. *Motion Picture Herald,* 20 May 1933.

20. Joseph Breen rejected re-release of *No One Man, Sinners in the Sun, Lady and Gent,* and *Man from Yesterday* for "Illicit Sex." As for *Island of Lost Souls,* Breen allowed Paramount to release an extensively cut version in 1941.

21. Geraldine Baum, Ashley Powers, and Michael Muskal, "Monkey Escapes Ohio Carnage," *York Daily Record,* 20 October 2011, pp. 1A and 7A.

Chapter 4

1. Author's telephone interview, Dorset, VT, 9 October 2003; Author's interview, Dorset, VT, 16 July 2004.

2. G. D. Hamann, *Lionel Atwill in the 30s* (Hollywood: Filming Today Press, 2004), p. 5. Thanks to Mr. Hamann whose book contains many notices on the actor from Los Angeles newspapers of the 1930s and 1940s, a number of which appear in this chapter's timeline.

3. Gloria Stuart with Sylvia Thompson, *I Just Kept Hoping* (Boston: Little, Brown, 1999), pp. 57, 58.

4. Data on Atwill's 1938 contract comes from the Lionel Atwill Legal File, 20th Century–Fox Collection, UCLA Performing Arts Library.

5. The most factual and detailed published report on Atwill's "orgies" and legal troubles was Florabel

Muir's "They Wouldn't Believe Him," *New York Sunday News,* 13 September 1942.

6. Production data comes from the RKO Collection, UCLA Performing Arts Library.

7. Production information comes from the Universal Collection, USC Performing Arts Library.

Chapter 5

1. Mark Vieira, *Sin in Soft Focus: Pre-Code Hollywood* (New York: Harry N. Abrams, 1999), p. 172.

2. All censorship material in this chapter regarding *One More River* and *The Black Cat* comes from the *One More River* Motion Picture Association of America. Production Code Administration Records (AAMP File), Margaret Herrick Library, Academy of Motion Picture Arts & Sciences, Los Angeles, CA. Most sincere thanks to Kristine Krueger of the Academy's National Film Information Service for making it possible for me to view these extensive records.

3. Letter from Joseph Breen to Harry Zehner, 26 February 1934, *The Black Cat* AAMP File.

4. Letter from Breen to Zehner, 2 April 1934, *The Black Cat* AAMP File.

5. For the Universal date, budget and salary figures cited in this chapter, many thanks to Ned Comstock, who provided the information from the Universal Collection, USC Performing Arts Library, Los Angeles, CA.

6. Vieira, p. 153.

7. Scott Eyman, *Lion of Hollywood: The Life and Times of Louis B. Mayer* (New York: Simon & Schuster, 2005), pp. 342, 343. Breen was guilty, at least in the early 1930s, of being an anti–Semite. In his "scum of the earth" remark, Breen noted that "ninety-five percent of these folks are Jews of an Eastern European lineage."

8. Some of the other films condemned in 1933: *The Story of Temple Drake* (Paramount); *Convention City* (Warner Bros.), *The Worst Woman in Paris?* (Fox); France's *Grandeur and Decadence;* and Czechoslovakia's *Extase.*

9. Viera, p. 221.

10. Viera, p. 221.

11. On April 26, 1934, Elizabeth Yeaman of the *Hollywood Citizen News* reported that Universal was "quite confident, unofficially" that Charles Laughton would play Sir Gerald, and wrote, "the studio is not even looking at any other actors for the part of the sadistic husband." As this item came five days after *Variety* had reported Colin Clive's casting in the role, it was probably mere publicity. On May 1, Yeaman reported that Clive Brook, who'd played Diana Wynyard's husband in *Cavalcade,* was conferring with Junior Laemmle about playing Sir Gerald. This too was clearly just publicity. Thanks to G.D. Hamann for sending me these articles.

12. Before arriving in Hollywood, Ms. Wynyard made her Broadway debut in *The Devil Passes,* which opened at the Selwyn Theatre on January 4, 1932, and

ran 96 performances. The play would have interested
horror fans: Benn Levy (who scripted Whale's *The Old
Dark House,* 1932), wrote and directed, and the cast
included Basil Rathbone, Ernest Thesiger (who'd act
for Whale as Horace Femm in *The Old Dark House*
and as Dr. Pretorius in *Bride of Frankenstein*), Arthur
Byron (prominent in *The Mummy,* 1932) and Cecilia
Loftus (who'd play in Universal's 1941 version of *The
Black Cat*). A later credit of interest: "Hamlet" on
England's *ITV Play of the Week* (27 February 1956):
Paul Scofield played Hamlet, Wynyard was Queen
Gertrude, Mary Ure was Ophelia, and Ernest Thesiger
played Polonius. Wynyard died in London May 13,
1964, at age 58.

13. According to Elizabeth Yeaman in the *Hollywood Citizen News* (April 19, 1934), Universal had been
"dickering" with MGM for the loan of Robert Montgomery, who had just co-starred with Norma Shearer
in the notorious *Riptide.* Montgomery would have
brought star quality to the rather nebbishy role. Thanks
again to G.D. Hamann, who provided this clipping.

14. Unpublished and undated interview with Ms.
Darling by Richard Bojarski.

15. James Curtis, *James Whale: A New World of
Gods and Monsters* (Boston: Faber and Faber, 1998),
p. 230.

16. Gene Brown, *Movie Time* (New York: Macmillan, 1995), pp. 118, 119.

17. "Cardinal Declares War on 'Evil' Films," *New
York Times,* 13 July 1934, p. 1.

18. *Motion Picture Herald,* 25 August 1934.

19. Mae Tinee, "Splendid Cast, Director Offer a
Good Movie," *The Chicago Tribune,* 25 August 1934.

20. Breen died in Los Angeles on December 5,
1965, at age 75. In *The Aviator* (2004), directed by
Martin Scorsese and starring Leonardo DiCaprio as
Howard Hughes, Cate Blanchett as Katharine Hepburn (an Oscar-winning performance), Kate Beckin-
sale as Ava Gardner, and Gwen Stefani as Jean Harlow,
Edward Herrmann played Joseph Breen.

Chapter 6

1. "Screen Notes," *New York Times,* 20 June 1935,
p. 16.

2. Gerald G. Gross, "Something Old, Something
New as Warner Bros....," *The Washington Post,* 27 August 1935, p. 8.

3. Universal, in the woeful Depression years of
1931 through 1934, has lost approximately $1,800,000;
Warners, approximately $31,000,000.

4. The Edelman information appeared in the December 1937 issue. Author Rudy Behlmer quotes this
material in his excellent book *Inside Warner Bros.
(1935–1951)* (New York: Viking, 1985), pp. 61, 62.

5. "Penitent Mais, Defiant Legenza Executed for
Virginia Murder," *The Washington Post,* 3 February
1935, p. 1.

6. "Eva Coo: She and a Gangster Died," *The
Washington Post,* 30 June 1935, p. B2.

7. Many thanks to Ned Comstock for providing
me access to the Boris Karloff Script Collection at
USC. All script quotes in this chapter come from that
archive.

8. Thanks to Kristine Krueger, National Film Information Service, Margaret Herrick Library, Academy of Motion Picture Arts and Sciences, Los Angeles,
CA, who provided the AAMP censorship papers on
The Walking Dead.

9. Data on Karloff's salary and his correspondence and dealings with the studio regarding all five
films discussed in this chapter comes from the Boris
Karloff file, Warner Bros. Archives, Los Angeles, CA.

10. Joseph Fields (later Broadway playwright of *My
Sister Eileen*), Lillie Hayward (*My Friend Flicka* and
Disney's *The Shaggy Dog*), Peter Milne (collaborator
on such Warner product as *Gold Diggers of 1935*), and
Robert Andrews (who later penned Karloff's 1940 *Before I Hang* and scripts for Karloff's *Thriller* TV show,
including "God Grante That She Lye Still") all contributed to revamping the original Ewart Adamson
screenplay.

11. In a November 19, 1935, memo from producer
Hal Wallis to director Michael Curtiz and makeup
man Perc Westmore, Wallis objected to the test
makeup, including "white tucks of hair" (opining they
made Karloff look "like some kind of animal") and a
silvery makeup ("It looks like exactly what it is: a silver
metallic paint of some kind put on his face").

12. "Tri-State Killers Are Electrocuted," *The Washington Post,* 2 December 1935, p. 6.

13. Elza Schallert, "H.G. Wells—Outline of Hollywood," *Los Angeles Times,* 22 December 1935.

14. Pressbook, *The Walking Dead* file, Warner
Bros. Archives.

15. Mason Wiley and Damien Bova, *Inside Oscar*
(New York: Ballantine, 1986, 1987), pp. 64–66.

16. AMPP, 21 May 1936.

17. My thanks to Dr. Karl Thiede for providing
the final cost and domestic/foreign rentals and profit
figures for the five films covered in this chapter.

18. Cobbett Steinberg, *Reel Facts: The Movie Book
of Records* (New York: Random House, 1978), p. 394.

19. Data on his salary comes from the actor's file
at Warner Bros. Archives.

20. Behlmer, p. 62.

21. Parker went on to appear in several Warner
films of the late 1930s, including Karloff's *West of
Shanghai* (1937). He later played in such films as
MGM's *Kiss Me Kate* (1953), starred on TVs *Tales of
the Texas Rangers* (1955–1958), and married actress
Virginia Field (1951 until her death in 1992). Parker
died in Rancho Mirage, CA, on December 4, 1996, at
age 84.

22. He later became a successful TV producer of
such shows as *Peter Gunn* (1958–1961) and *It Takes a
Thief* (1968–1969). Oliver died in Los Angeles on January 26, 1995, at age 84.

23. In late 1938, Eason supervised the epic burning
of Atlanta sequence of *Gone with the Wind.*

24. Tom Weaver, "*West of Shanghai* (1937), *The Invisible Menace* (1938), *Devil's Island* (1939/40), *British Intelligence* (1940)," *Boris Karloff*, edited by Gary J. and Susan Svehla (Baltimore: Midnight Marquee Press, 1996), p. 202.

25. Weaver, p. 204.

26. The film won little splashes of publicity. This tidbit from the June 30, 1938, *Evening Herald Express*: When *Devil's Island* script girl Alma Dwight struck a match on her canvas chair, she set fire to her chair and her slacks. As the *Express* reported, "Karloff leaped to the rescue, soundly spanked out the fire."

27. At the Academy Awards that night, *The Adventures of Robin Hood* loses to Columbia's *You Can't Take It with You*, while Cagney lost to Spencer Tracy (MGM's *Boys Town*), Garfield to Walter Brennan (20th Century–Fox's *Kentucky*), and Curtiz to Frank Capra (for *You Can't Take It with You*).

Chapter 7

1. E.T.B, "*Arsenic and Old Lace*," *The Baltimore Sun*, 29 February 1944, p. 10. To be fair, some critics preferred Lugosi to Karloff. Also, Donald Kirkley, prior to the 1944 Baltimore opening, reported that *Arsenic's* business "didn't drop a stitch in consequence of the switch of stars" and had even "perked up in the last few weeks. There has been noticeable upsurge ticket buying by small boys and their willing parents" ("The Theatre Playbill," *The Baltimore Sun*, 27 February 1944, p. A6).

2. Donald Kirkley, "That Horror Man's in Town—But He's Really Quite Human," *The Baltimore Sun*, 23 December 1940, p. 20.

3. Donald Kirkley, "Screen: *Frankenstein*, with Boris Karloff, Colin Clive, Mae Clarke and John Boles, at Keith's," *The Baltimore Sun*, 27 November 1931, pg. 7.

4. The playwright's first Broadway comedy was *There's Wisdom in Women* (October 30, 1935, 46 performances).

5. "Josephine Hull, Actress, Dead; Stage Career Spanned Fifty Years," *New York Times*, 13 March 1957, p. 31.

6. "Karloff, Calm Menace," *New York Times*, 19 January 1941, p. X3.

7. "News of the Stage," *New York Times*, 6 March 1941, p. 24. Howard Lindsay reportedly tried to help Ms. Inglise secure other stage work in New York.

8. Gary Don Rhodes, "*Arsenic and Old Lace* (1941)," *Boris Karloff*, edited by Gary J. Svehla and Susan Svehla (Baltimore: Midnight Marquee Press, 1996), p. 246.

9. "News of the Stage," *New York Times*, 5 February 1941, p. 16.

10. "Elsa Lanchester Returns to Stage," *New York Times*, 6 February 1941, p. 24.

11. Frank Capra, *The Name Above the Title* (New York: Macmillan, 1971), pp. 309, 310.

12. Joseph McBride, *Frank Capra: The Catastrophe of Genius* (New York: Simon & Schuster, 1992), pp. 446, 447.

13. They remain, incidentally, the only Oscar-winning twins in Academy history.

14. Robert Cremer, *Lugosi: The Man Behind the Cape* (Chicago: Henry Regnery, 1976), p. 202. The Lugosi situation is interesting and puzzling. In *Lugosi: The Man Behind the Cape*, Lillian Lugosi Donlevy, Bela's fourth wife, claimed that Josephine Hull came to Los Angeles to visit the Lugosis in the summer of 1941, after *Arsenic and Old Lace* had closed in Chicago, and pleaded with Bela to take over the Jonathan role from Joseph Schildkraut, who "forgot his lines all the time and spoke to the audience." In fact, Josephine Hull was in the New York company that summer; the actress Lillian remembered visiting them was probably Laura Hope Crews, the Chicago Abby. Also, the Chicago Jonathan, of course, was Erich von Stroheim, not Joseph Schildkraut. Von Stroheim's performance, by most accounts, was impressive. At any rate, Lugosi originally accepted the offer but backed out.

15. In Hollywood, Joslyn played comic character roles in such films as *My Sister Eileen* (1942) and *Heaven Can Wait* (1943). After *Arsenic and Old Lace* he returned to Broadway only once—in *Collector's Item*, which opened February 8, 1952, and ran only three performances. Joslyn was memorable as the passenger who disguises himself as a woman in *Titanic* (1953), starred in the TV series *McKeever and the Colonel* (as the Colonel, 1962–1963), and paid three guest star visits to TV's *The Addams Family* (1964–1966). He died January 21, 1981, at the age of 79.

16. "Temporary Revised Shooting Script," *Arsenic and Old Lace*. Thanks to Ned Comstock of the USC Performing Arts Library for making it available to me. The script is part of the Boris Karloff Script Collection; apparently James Gleason, who appeared in the film as Lt. Rooney, gave Karloff his copy.

17. Bogart had enjoyed an impressive Broadway career, including *The Petrified Forest*, which led to his Warner contract when he recreated Duke Mantee in the 1936 film. He also made effective personal appearances at theaters: The screen showed him in various death scenes in his Warner gangster sagas, then the lights came up to reveal Bogart playing dead on the stage floor!

18. *Arsenic and Old Lace* production file, Warner Bros. Archives. Thanks to curators Jonathon Auxier and Laura LaPlaca. The file contains all the salary information and production material noted in this chapter.

19. Jack F. Hunter, "Ronald Reagan," *Films in Review*, April 1967, p. 211.

20. James Bawden, Interview with Raymond Massey, *Films of the Golden Age*, Summer 2010. The interview was published 27 years after Massey's death.

21. *Arsenic and Old Lace* production file, Warner Bros. Archives.

22. *Arsenic and Old Lace* production file, Warner

Bros. Archives. All shooting schedule information and memos cited in this chapter come from that file.

23. Capra, p. 311.

24. Bawden.

25. Stephen D. Youngkin, *The Lost One: A Life of Peter Lorre* (Lexington: University Press of Kentucky, 2005), p. 199.

26. For finding this fascinating information, I must thank again Jonathon Auxier and Laura LaPlaca of the Warner Bros. Archives.

27. Youngkin, p. 200.

28. This poem (apparently designed to be sung) was found among Karloff's papers during Heritage Galleries' 2008 Boris Karloff Archive Sale.

29. "*Arsenic* Menace Gets Ribbing at N.Y. Goodbye," *Variety,* 1 July 1942, p. 51.

30. M. William Phelps, *The Devil's Rooming House* (Guilford, CT: Lyons Press, 2010), p. 247.

Chapter 8

1. My thanks to Jacques Kelley, popular columnist for Baltimore's *The Sun* newspaper, for sharing this story—told to him by his parents—many years ago, when we were both students at Loyola High School in Baltimore.

2. Letter to author from DeWitt Bodeen, 15 July 1980. All of the quotes in this chapter from Bodeen on *Cat People* come from that letter.

3. All quotes in this chapter from the treatment and script come from the RKO Collection at UCLA (my thanks to Julie Graham) and the Val Lewton Collection, Library of Congress, Washington, D.C.

4. Richard Jewel, "RKO Film Grosses: 1931–1951," *Historical Journal of Film Radio and Television* 14, no. 1 (1994), p. 45.

5. Author's telephone interview with Ruth Lewton, San Jose, CA, 8 March 1993.

6. "Promises to Blow Lid Off Charges," *Los Angeles Examiner,* 25 April 1938.

7. "Simone Simon Admirer Held; Youth Who Climbed Pole to See Favorite Jailed for Inquiry," *Los Angeles Times,* 3 May 1938, p. A2.

8. She eventually went to jail on a deal: She'd serve nine months plus ten years' probation, but if she blabbed any more about Simone, the gold keys and/or the orgy record, she'd have to serve the full term ("Court Order Buries Secret of Golden Key," *Los Angeles Examiner,* 20 July 1938).

9. Accounts of this scandal include "Simone Simon Will Testify at Hearing," *Los Angeles Examiner,* 27 April 1938; "Golden Key to Her Home Given by Simone as Gift," *Los Angeles Examiner,* 3 May 1938; also various clippings—notably "Simone's Flame Had Golden Key to Star's Home" (unsourced, dated 2 May 1938), "Star vs. Secretary—Again" (by Lee Mortimer, unsourced and undated) in the Simone Simon file, Billy Rose Library for the Performing Arts, Lincoln Center, New York City.

10. "Simone Leaves Pouting Prettily," *Los Angeles Examiner,* 4 August 1938.

11. All studio archival information regarding salaries, budgets, and shooting schedules for *Cat People* and *The Curse of the Cat People* comes from the RKO Collection, UCLA Performing Arts Library. Many thanks to Julie Graham for making it available for my examination at the library in February and April 2010. Ms. Graham also provided access to early script drafts. Thanks as well to Richard May, Lauren Buisson, and Constantine Nasr.

12. Author's telephone interview with Simone Simon, Paris, 17 September 1994. All quotes from Ms. Simon in this chapter come from that interview.

13. Thanks to Kristine Krueger, of the National Film Information Service of the Academy of Motion Pictures Arts and Sciences' Margaret Herrick Library, for providing this censorship information.

14. Jewel.

15. Charles Higham and Joel Greenberg, "Mark Robson," *The Celluloid Muse* (New York: Signet, 1972), p. 236.

16. Author's telephone interview with Jane Randolph, Los Angeles, 28 June 1989.

17. "Tourneur Remembers: Recollections as Told to Joel E. Siegel," *Cinefantastique,* Summer 1973, p. 24.

18. *The Hollywood Reporter,* 13 July 1942.

19. Higham and Greenberg, p. 248.

20. "Hollywood Inside," *Variety,* 7 August 1942, p. 2.

21. Author's telephone interview with Elizabeth Russell, Beverly Hills, 3 February 1994. All quotes from Ms. Russell regarding *Cat People* and *The Curse of the Cat People* come from that interview and the author's other conversations and meetings with the actress in Baltimore and Los Angeles.

22. Who was the true auteur of this scene? In *The Celluloid Muse,* Jacques Tourneur claimed it was his idea, based on a real-life experience: He used to swim nude in a friend's pool in the San Fernando Valley, the friend kept two pet cheetahs, one escaped its cage, and it menaced Tourneur as he swam until a gardener shooed away the cat with a rake. (See Higham and Greenberg, p. 247.) Bodeen took great exception to Tourneur's story and told me, "The whole swimming pool sequence was my creation." In his liner notes for *Roy Webb: Music for the Films of Val Lewton* (Marco Polo, 2000), Scott MacQueen notes strong similarities of the scene to Chapter 16 of John Dickson Carr's 1941 mystery novel *Death Turns the Tables.* In that chapter a female named Jane visits the pool of the Esplanade Hotel, the lights go out, she fears a stalker and jumps into the pool without a bathing cap (as does Jane Randolph in *Cat People*), treads water, and finally swims to the edge of the pool where "a gloved hand descends on hers, fingers closing around her wrist." She screams, and her screams echo. The menace flees, help arrives, and Jane says, "Get me my robe, will you?" Clearly there are definite similarities, but *Cat People* has no "gloved hand," and *Death Turns the Tables* has no cat sounds, the robe isn't "torn to ribbons," and there's no Irena emerging from the shadows.

23. Thanks to Ned Comstock, curator of USC's Cinema and Television Library, for making a copy of the pressbook available.

24. "Picture Grosses," *Variety,* 9 December 1942, p. 9; "Picture Grosses," *Variety,* 16 December 1942, p. 9.

25. Author's interview with Marilyn Harris, San Gabriel, CA, 20 July 1997 and 26 July 1998.

26. *Daily Variety,* 29 October 1943, p. 48.

27. Thanks to Dr. Karl Thiede for worldwide rental and profit information on *Cat People, The Falcon's Brother, Hitler's Children, The Curse of the Cat People* and *The Body Snatcher.*

28. DeWitt Bodeen, "Writing the Movie, Recollections by its Author," *Focus on Film* 7 (1971), p. 56. Bodeen's quotes on *The Curse of the Cat People* in this chapter come from this article.

29. Author's telephone interview with Ann Carter, North Bend, WA, 27 March 2008. All quotes with Ms. Carter in this chapter come from that interview.

30. Author's telephone interview with Robert Wise, Los Angeles, CA, 13 May 1994. Also interview with author, Baltimore, 27 July 1996. All quotes from Mr. Wise in this chapter come from those interviews.

31. The Robert Wise Collection, USC Performing Arts Library. Thanks to Ned Comstock for providing me access to the script, hence making it possible to reconstruct the film's original ending.

32. "Headline News 1942–1943," *Variety,* 29 October 1943, p. 362.

33. "Picture Grosses," *Variety,* 15 March 1944, p. 33.

34. "Weekly B.O. Clicks of First Runs," *Variety,* 16 October 1944, p, 385.

35. Letter to author from DeWitt Bodeen.

36. A typed and signed copy of Napier's eulogy for Lewton is among the Lewton papers at the Library of Congress.

37. Thanks to Martin Grams, Jr., who found the proposal in an archive in Laramie, Wyoming while researching Greenway's TV show *The Green Hornet.*

Chapter 9

1. Alta Durant, "Gab," *Daily Variety,* 26 March 1942, p. 3. Supporting *The Ghost of Frankenstein* at both the Pantages and the RKO Hillstreet was Universal's *What's Cookin',* starring the Andrews Sisters.

2. Muriel Babcock, "Successor to Chaney Seen," *Los Angeles Times,* 12 February 1933, p. A1.

3. Author's telephone interview with Richard Denning, Hawaii, 6 June 1990.

4. Al Taylor, "The Forgotten Frankenstein," *Fangoria* 2, p. 40.

5. *Abbott and Costello in Hollywood* (New York: Perigee, 1991), which Furmanek co-authored with Ron Palumbo, remains the top book on the comedy team. Thanks to Bob for his sending me a copy of the October 7, 1942, shooting script and providing information on the early script drafts.

6. Author's telephone interviews with Curt Siodmak, Three Rivers, CA, 8 April and 1 July 1980.

7. For full coverage of Ms. Massey's life and career, see the author's *Women in Horror Films: 1940s* (Jefferson, NC: McFarland, 1999), pp. 163–181.

8. "Income Tax Liens Filed Against 21 in Screen Colony," *The Baltimore Sun,* 5 September 1942, pg. 2. Others hit included Busby Berkeley ($43,576), Basil Rathbone ($17,773) and Rathbone's wife Ouida ($18,008).

9. Thanks to Kristine Krueger, of the National Film Information Service, Margaret Herrick Library, Academy of Motion Pictures Arts and Sciences, Los Angeles, CA, for providing copies of these AAMP documents.

10. For the final cost of this production, thanks to Dr. Karl Thiede.

11. Thanks to Bob McElwee and his excellent online Greenbriar Picture Show for the budget figure on this film.

12. Author's telephone interview with Lillian Lugosi Donlevy, Culver City, CA, 13 December 1974.

13. A still of this scene survives, number 1279–8.

14. *The Hollywood Reporter,* 19 February 1943.

15. Thanks to G.D. Hamann, who sent me an email (October 13, 2012) with data on this game from *The Hollywood Citizen News,* 12 October 1942, and 19 October 1942, and the Los Angeles *Evening Herald Express,* 15 October 1942.

16. William Lynch Vallee, "Sentimental Monster," *Silver Screen,* July 1943. Thanks to the late Richard Bojarski, who provided me a photocopy of the article.

17. When Universal produced *House of Frankenstein* in April and May of 1944, the studio returned to the European village on the back lot.

18. Kuznetzoff is perhaps best-remembered as the fierce chef who chases Laurel and Hardy in *Swiss Miss* (Hal Roach–MGM, 1938), and as the convict who goes to the guillotine in Karloff's *Devil's Island* (Warner Bros., 1939). He worked with Ilona Massey again in *Lux Video Theatre's* "Purple and Fine Linen" (January 15, 1951). Also in the cast was Basil Rathbone. Kuznetzoff's character's name: Igor. He died in Port Washington, Long Island, New York, on August 10, 1954, age 65.

By the way, the shooting script contains two verses of the "Faro-La, Faro-Li" song not in the film. One sung to the drunken Franzec, and the other sung to newlyweds Rudi and his bride.

Were these verses originally shot and cut prior to release? In 1993, musician and film music historian Joseph Marcello sent me a copy of the "Faro-La, Faro-Li" recording that had been in Hans J. Salter's personal library. It's apparently the original pre-recorded track that Kuznetzoff sang to in the playback—the ending clear, without Chaney's shouts ("I don't *want* to live eternally!") overlapping. The Franzec–Rudi and Wife verses are *not* on this recording.

19. The actress's life poses colorful mysteries. She was the wife of Robert ("Believe It or Not") Ripley

from 1919 to 1926, during which time she won several beauty contests: "Miss Manhattan" in the 1924 Miss America pageant, "Miss Greater New York" in the 1925 Miss America pageant, and "Most Beautiful Girl in Evening Dress" in both the 1924 and 1925 Miss America pageants. She was also reputedly the longtime mistress of Louis B. Mayer, a relationship that might or might not have continued after her 1940 marriage to John Wesley Smith. Roberts died in Plymouth, Massachusetts, on July 24, 1970.

20. Telephone interview with author, New York City, 13 June 2012.

21. Marcia Daughtrey, "Ever See a Scream Walking?" *Movieland*, June 1946, p. 106. The article features an interesting story: Sara Swartz (also spelled as Sarah Swartz) had been an ingénue at Universal, and one day, circa 1917, saw that a cutting room was on fire. "Without hesitation," the story related, "she plunged into the holocaust and rescued a great deal of precious footage while suffering serious burns. She was hospitalized for many months, but when she was able to return to the studio, a grateful Mr. Laemmle gave Sara promise of a lifetime job with Universal." Swartz is seen and heard in *Bride of Frankenstein* as Marta, keeping vigil at the burned windmill with Una O'Connor's Minnie. She died March 30, 1949, in Los Angeles.

22. Bob Thomas, "Chaney Plays for Sympathy: Modern Monsters Not Motivated," *The Blade* (Toledo), 23 April 1963. In the same interview, Chaney claimed he doubled Glenn Strange in *Abbott and Costello Meet Frankenstein* after Strange "broke his ankle on the second day of the picture, and I did both roles." Production records reveal that Strange broke his ankle late in shooting and that Chaney did in fact double him, but for only one day.

23. On the Classic Horror Film Board, there's a popular thread, "Can You Hear Bela Speaking in *Frankenstein Meets the Wolf Man*?" Many claim they can hear Bela say, "It is here!" as he opens the bookcase and shows Larry where Frankenstein hid the diary. However, the dialogue "It is here!" is *not* in the shooting script. It's possible Bela ad-libbed it—I also think I hear the line—although what it might be is the "Hidden lock SNAPS, SQUEAKING" that Siodmak calls for in his script. If in fact that is Lugosi's voice, the editor likely missed it because (a) it's barely audible, and (b) the editor probably followed the script in preparing the cuts, and this line's not in the script.

24. *Profiles in History Catalog,* Addendum to Catalog 23, Fall 1994, p. 57. Suggested bid was $1,500.

25. Bob Furmanek has examined a cutting continuity of *Frankenstein Meets the Wolf Man* dated December 28, 1942, and reports it to be identical to the film as we know it.

26. Thanks to Dr. Karl Thiede.

27. "Picture Grosses," *Variety,* 17 March 1943, p. 9.

28. "Record First Run LA BO Totals," *Variety,* 29 October 1943, p. 45.

29. William G. Obaggy, "Bela Lugosi," *Horrors of the Screen* 3 (1964), p. 9.

Chapter 10

1. Jon Halliday, *Sirk on Sirk* (Boston: Faber and Faber, 1971), p. 71.

2. Thanks to Dr. Karl Thiede.

3. Mason Wiley and Damien Bova, *Inside Oscar* (New York: Ballantine, 1986, 1987), p. 123.

4. Rudy Behlmer, *Inside Warner Bros. (1935–1951)* (New York: Viking, 1985) p. 210.

5. Andrew Curry, "The Heydrich Equation," *World War II*, September–October 2011, p. 33.

6. Mario R. Dederichs, *Heydrich: The Face of Evil* (Drexel Hill, PA: Casemate, 2009).

7. Heinz Zollin Hohne and Richard Barry, *The Order of the Death's Head: The Story of Hitler's SS* (New York: Penguin, 2000), p. 495.

8. "Worst Act Since Dark Ages," *New York Times,* 12 June 1942, p. 6.

9. Summary Production Cost Sheet for *Prisoner of Japan,* originally titled *Isle of Forgotten Sins.* The report indicates the film was shot in one week, April 16 to April 23, 1942. Thanks to Arianne Ulmer Cipes, who provided me with a copy of the cost sheet.

10. Author's telephone interview, 24 November 2010.

11. Hedda Hopper, "Movieland Short Cut to Wealth or Ruin," *The Baltimore Sun,* 18 April 1943, p. SM4.

12. Ulmer told Peter Bogdanovich he'd replaced Ripley on *Prisoner of Japan* "because Ripley was not very normal ... he was a sick man ... mentally and physically." See Bogdanovich's interview with Ulmer in *Kings of the Bs,* edited by Todd McCarthy and Charles Flynn (New York: E.P. Dutton, 1975), p. 398. Ripley wrote and directed the acclaimed 1944 "B" *Voice in the Wind* (1944), directed the Robert Mitchum "moonshiner" smash hit *Thunder Road* (1958), directed some 1950s television, and became the first professor of Cinema Arts at UCLA—where he founded the UCLA Film Center. He died in 1961.

13. This very hard-to-find financial information comes from MGM records, dated 27 September 1943. Thanks to Buddy Barnett, who provided a copy of the studio's data on *Hitler's Madman.*

14. "Hollywood Tempests: RKO Seeks to Regain Investment in Two Disputed Films—Duel with Words," *The New York Times,* 11 October 1942, p. X3. Hollywood screen writers regarded Ludwig's remark as a major insult. In response, Bart Lytton claimed that Ludwig's story had "sprung unquestionably" from Lytton's own story, *Hangman's Village.* Arbitration followed in October of 1942 at the Screen Writers Guild Board. It was disastrous: Nebenzal's venture desperately needed the goodwill of the Hollywood community, and this bitter dispute rapidly earned the project a pack of enemies. In the end, Emil Ludwig and Albrecht F. Joseph received credit for original story. Screenplay credit went to Peretz Hirschbein (who'd worked with Ulmer on *Green Fields*), Melvin Levy, and Doris Malloy (who'd script Ulmer's *My Son, the*

Hero, 1943). Bart Lytton, who would receive credit for having written *Hangman's Village,* had scripted Ulmer's *Tomorrow We Live.* Edgar and Shirley Ulmer also contributed to the script, as did Douglas Sirk. Edna St. Vincent Millay received special billing for the use of her verses from "The Murder of Lidice." Howard Emmet Rogers, who would write the MGM retakes, received no credit.

15. Halliday.

16. The "Schufftan Process" (i.e., using a mirror mounted on the camera to create impressive effects) had contributed dynamically to Fritz Lang's *Metropolis,* and was perennially used in films until matte shots replaced it. Schufftan received royalties from the process and became a wealthy man.

17. Motion Pictures Producers and Distributors Association File, Margaret Herrick Library, Academy of Motion Picture Arts and Sciences, Los Angeles. Special thanks to Kristine Krueger of the National Film Information Service for this information, which includes all the censorship material cited in this chapter.

18. David Carradine, *Endless Highway* (Boston: Journey Editions, 1995), p. 41.

19. Joan Cohen, Notes, "The Art of Fritz Lang," *Hangmen Also Die!* screening, Margaret Herrick Library file on *Hangmen Also Die!*

20. It's odd that both *Hitler's Madman* and *Hangmen Also Die!* presented a fictional assassin, even though Germany had announced the names of Jan Kubis and Josef Gabcik as the real-life assassins. Walter Linden played Kubis and Albert Paulsen played Gabcik on two episodes of TV's *G.E. True* in 1963, "Heydrich: Part One" and "Heydrich: Part Two," in which Kurt Kreuger appeared as Heydrich. Fritz Wepper played Gabcik in German TV's *Heydrich in Prague* (1967).

21. Hedda Hopper, "Donlevy Dons Laurels," *The Washington Post,* 12 September 1942, p. B6.

22. Gene Tierney and Mickey Herskowitz, *Self-Portrait* (New York: Wyden, 1978).

23. "Frances Farmer Freed on Bail," *Los Angeles Times,* 21 October 1942, p. A2; "Frances Farmer Enters Guilty Plea," *Los Angeles Times,* 24 October 1942, p. A3. Both Farmer and Carradine had appeared in 20th Century–Fox's *Son of Fury* (1942), starring Tyrone Power, Gene Tierney and George Sanders.

24. James Robert Parish and Lennard DeCarl with William T. Leonard and Gregory W. Mank, *Hollywood Players: The Forties* (New Rochelle, NY: Arlington House, 1976), p. 397.

25. Hedda Hopper, "Movieland Short Cut to Wealth or Ruin."

26. Interview with author, Los Angeles, CA, 29 July 1998. This quote, and all succeeding ones from Ms. Morison in this chapter, come from that interview.

27. He received two "Best Music, Scoring of a Dramatic or Comedy Picture" Academy nominations: for Nebenzal's *Summer Storm* (UA, 1944) and *The Man Who Walked Alone* (PRC, 1945).

28. Halliday, pp.71, 72.

29. Predictably, *The Hollywood Reporter* (June 9, 1943) found Kennedy "miscast." However, *Boxoffice* (June 21, 1943) wrote that Carradine and Kennedy were the "standout characterizations," and the *New York World-Telegram* review (August 28, 1943) opined that Kennedy's was "the great performance" of the film. Other comic actors in *Hitler's Madman* were bespectacled stringbean Jimmy Conlin, a hanger-on in Preston Sturges comedies, who joined the show as Dvorak, the shopkeeper; and Victor Kilian, destined for fame on TV's *Mary Hartman, Mary Hartman,* as "the Fernwood Flasher," as Clara's father.

30. Watson played Hitler in nine films, beginning with the Hal Roach short *The Devil with Hitler* (1942), ending with MGM's *The Four Horsemen of the Apocalypse* (1962). Kosleck played Goebbels in *Confessions of a Nazi Spy* (1939), *The Hitler Gang* (1944) and *Hitler* (1962), as well as the *Motorola Television Hour* episode "The Last Days of Hitler" (1954).

31. The off-screen story is even stranger and possibly sadder. Acquanetta, claiming to be Native-American, was reportedly actually black—a fact Universal learned after starring her in several films. The studio promptly dumped her. Acquanetta steered far clear of this story and had her own take on her life and career when I interviewed her in July 1992.

32. Tom Weaver, *John Carradine: The Films,* introductions by Joe Dante and Fred Olen Ray, biography by Gregory William Mank) (Jefferson, NC: McFarland, 1999), p. 156.

33. The *Reporter* noted that the only other independent effort in recent Hollywood memory was Jon Hall's *The Captain of Koepenick,* which had cost $200,000 and had failed to find a distributor.

34. Telephone interview with author, Los Angeles, 18 February 1991; interview with author, Los Angeles, 19 July 1991. All quotes from Ms. Lee in this chapter come from those interviews.

35. Reportedly this film had its own share of off-screen drama. Original director Irving Reis quit; the *New York Times* claimed he couldn't tolerate stars Tim Holt and Bonita Granville. Edward Dmytryk, who replaced him, wrote in his memoir *It's a Hell of a Life But Not a Bad Living* that Reis quit after an argument with the film's producer, Edward "Doc" Golden.

36. Many thanks to Ned Comstock of the USC Performing Arts Library, who provided me access to the Dialogue Cutting Continuity script for the original version of *The Hangman* (dated March 3, 1943), the MGM Retakes Composite script (dated February 27, 1943), and the Dialogue Cutting Continuity for *Hitler's Hangman,* including the MGM retakes (May 22, 1943). This made comparison of the two versions possible.

37. An MGM retake scripted but not filmed: the scene in the University, which Rogers had rewritten to begin with close shots of Heydrich's approaching boots, and to climax with a rebellion by the male students—including the shooting of a student who says,

"You can force us into labor battalions and herd us into concentration camps—but you must keep your dirty hands off our women!" This action doesn't appear in the final film, nor do the MGM starlets show up in this scene, so it's assumed that MGM decided to retain the original scene from *The Hangman*.

38. Barnett.

39. Thanks to Gary Don Rhodes, who found the *Hitler's Madman* report in the Library of Congress and provided me a copy.

40. Barnett.

41. Thanks to Dr. Karl Thiede and Buddy Barnett for this information.

42. The TV print that ran for years was a poorly edited 89-minute version, with 46 minutes cut from the original 135-minute release. Among the cuts was the scene of Heydrich. It has recently been restored to its original form on DVD. *Hangmen Also Die!* received two Academy nominations: Best Sound and Best Musical Score.

Chapter 11

1. "*Voodoo Man* Rolls," *Variety,* 18 October 1943, p. 4.

2. Carradine perennially denied he ever recited Shakespeare on Hollywood Boulevard, or wore a cape when doing so. Nevertheless, many have recalled catching his act. Veteran actor Fritz Feld gave me a vivid eyewitness account during an interview at his home in Brentwood, CA, on July 11, 1987, remembering the Shakespeare, the cape, and that Carradine also entertained Hollywood cab drivers with classical recitals while they waited for late night passengers.

3. These lines, favorites of Carradine, are actually Richard's lines in *Henry VI, Part Three*. John Barrymore used them in his production of *Richard III* in New York in 1920. Carradine added them to his personal cutting of the play.

4. Carradine repeated this story whenever possible, twice on *The Dick Cavett Show* (1971 and 1980).

5. Many thanks to Ellen Bailey, a Pasadena Playhouse graduate, actress, and director, who has heroically organized the Playhouse Archives. She graciously welcomed me to the Playhouse February 17, 2011, and allowed me access to the archives, the source of most of the Playhouse information in this chapter.

6. As this was such a showcase for Carradine, it deserves mention that Playhouse founder Gilmor Brown and Morris Ankrum directed; Judith Evelyn played the Duchess of York. As noted, Michael Strange played Lady Anne. Ms. Strange, of course, had been the second Mrs. John Barrymore and was the mother of Diana Barrymore. Her casting is noted in Katherine von Blon's "Studio and Theater Comings and Goings," *Los Angeles Times,* 4 August 1935, p. A2.

7. *Los Angeles Daily Illustrated News,* 26 March 1936.

8. Information on Carradine's salary comes from his legal file in the Fox Archive, formerly housed in Special Collections at UCLA. The studio has recently reclaimed the material.

9. Larry C. Bradley, *Jesse James: The Making of a Legend* (Nevada, MO: Larren, 1980), p. 48.

10. Author's telephone interview, Keene, New Hampshire, 19 July 2000 and 23 January 2003.

11. Readers interested in these fascinating men can learn more about them in the author's book *Hollywood's Hellfire Club* (Los Angeles: Feral House Press, 2007), co-authored with Charles Heard and Bill Nelson.

12. Charles Hamblett, *The Hollywood Cage* (New York: Hart, 1969), pp. 217, 218.

13. "'The Profile' Names Actors Better Than He," *The Washington Post,* 27 June 1940, p. 11. Barrymore's List: Lionel Barrymore, Spencer Tracy, George Sanders, Paul Muni, Henry Fonda, Roland Young, C. Aubrey Smith, George Raft, John Carradine, and Maria Ouspenskaya.

14. Thanks to Martin Grams, Jr., prolific writer on radio history, for this information, which he learned from the show's writer, Norman Corwin.

15. Thanks to Bruce Forsberg, who provided me a copy of the annotated script for the May 31, 1942, broadcast.

16. Robert Lewis Taylor, *W.C. Fields, His Follies and Fortunes* (New York: Signet, 1968).

17. David Carradine, *Endless Highway* (Boston: Journey Editions, 1995), p. 3. All quotes from David Carradine in this chapter regarding his father, mother, and Sonia Sorel at the time of the Shakespeare company come from *Endless Highway,* pp. 48–52.

18. Since Carradine had acted there in the 1935 Shakespeare festival, several major stars had come through the Playhouse—including Victor Mature, Robert Preston, William Holden, and Dana Andrews. So had Laird Cregar, who'd acted with Carradine in *Blood and Sand* and, at this time, was starring as Jack the Ripper in 20th Century–Fox's *The Lodger.*

19. "A.M. Dailies," *Variety,* 9 August 1943, p. 8.

20. Author's telephone interview with Dean Goodman, San Francisco, CA, 9 July 1996. Unless otherwise noted, all quotes from Goodman in this chapter come from that interview.

21. Carradine's death scene has been cut from the currently available prints.

22. As noted, Allegro changed his professional name to David Bond and made his feature film debut in *Greenwich Village* (1944). His career had points of interest: in *A Double Life* (1947), Allegro/Bond appears in scenes from *Othello* (played by Ronald Colman in an Oscar-winning performance). He also acted on TV's *Ramar of the Jungle* in the "Urn of Destiny" episode (January 23, 1954) that also featured Sonia Sorel. The actor died in West Hills, California, on April 16, 1989.

23. Dean Goodman, *Maria, Marlene ... and Me,* (San Francisco: Shadbolt Press, 1993), p. 88.

24. The *Hollywood Reporter* gave "illness" as the cause for George Zucco's sudden departure from the

film. However, almost 50 years later, Stella Zucco, George's widow, reminded of the "illness" story, laughed, "Until his final illness, I don't remember George being sick a day in his life!" Interview with author, Santa Monica, CA, 19 July 1991.

25. *Los Angeles Times,* 6 October 1943.

26. "Second Front," *Time,* 8 November 1943, p. 32.

27. "Second Front."

28. "Second Front."

29. "Play Review," *Variety,* 26 October 1943, p. 3.

30. "Second Front."

31. Leonard Wolf, *A Dream of Dracula* (Boston: Little, Brown, 1972), pp. 289, 290.

32. "Carradine Troupe Will Tour to L.A.," *Variety,* 15 November 1943, p. 10.

33. *Variety,* 16 October 1944.

34. John Carradine Clipping File, Margaret Herrick Library, Los Angeles.

35. "Hollywood Inside," *Variety,* 27 January 1944, p. 2.

36. Sheilah Graham, *The Garden of Allah* (New York: Crown, 1970), p. 206.

37. *House of Frankenstein* Contract File, Universal Collection, USC Performing Arts Library, Los Angeles. Thanks to Ned Comstock for providing the material.

38. Author's telephone interview with Shirley Ulmer, Los Angeles, 24 March 1988.

39. Although the precise date isn't available, this event was later reported in several newspapers, including: "John Carradine in Plea for Sons' Custody," *Los Angeles Times,* 4 April 1945, p. A1; "Sheriff After John Carradine, Actor," *The Gastonia* (North Carolina) *Daily Gazette,* 16 August 1946, p. 6; and "John Carradine Flees to N.Y. to Avoid Alimony," *Chester* (Pennsylvania) *Times,* 17 August 1946, pp. 1–2.

40. On January 5, 1977, Onslow Stevens, so memorable a presence in the lives of both Carradine and Sonia, died at age 74 at the Hacienda Convalescent Center in Van Nuys under sad and mysterious circumstances. Suffering from depression and alcoholism, Stevens had been found in November by his wife Rose, "slumped in a wheelchair and in extreme pain," four hours after having suffered a broken hip at the center. He eventually died of pneumonia "due to or in consequence of a left hip fracture," and on February 10, 1977, the coroner ruled that Stevens had died "at the hands of another, other than by accident." A D.A. investigation followed to determine if there had been "gross negligence" and "involuntary manslaughter." As there appears to have been no further news, the death was presumably ruled as natural or accidental. Stevens is buried in an unmarked grave in "Restland" in Pierce Brothers' Valhalla Memorial Park, North Hollywood.

41. The Carradines starred in the play at Lake Hopatcong, New Jersey. The director was Dean Goodman, an alumnus of Carradine's Shakespeare company.

42. Carradine, 134.

43. Dotson Rader, "I Didn't Want to Fail," *Parade,* 29 September 1991.

44. "Notes on People ... Tiny Tim Still Finds Life Beautiful," *New York Times,* 1 July 1981, p. A21.

45. Tom Weaver, *John Carradine: The Films,* introductions by Joe Dante and Fred Olen Ray, biography by Gregory William Mank (Jefferson, NC: McFarland, 1999), p. 356.

46. Carradine, p. 574.

47. Carradine, p. 158.

48. The "love child" of artist Michael Bowen (who died in 2009 in Stockholm) and Sonia, Bowen is a prolific actor. Among his many credits: Danny Pickett on *Lost* (2006 to 2007) and Tracker in *Django Unchained* (2012). Bowen played "Buck" in *Kill Bill, Vol. 1 (2003)* reprising the role in *Kill Bill, Vol. 2* in 2004, the year his mother died. David Carradine, of course, scored as the evil Bill in both features—"channeling my father," as David put it. As this book goes to the publisher, Bowen has been appearing as "Uncle Jack," a murderous drug czar complete with a swastika tattoo on his neck, on AMC's mega-hit series *Breaking Bad.*

49. Carradine, p. 52.

Chapter 12

1. "

NARTB Would Bar All Horror Films on TV," *Variety,* 20 November 1957, pp. 30, 54.

2. For information, thanks to Bob Burns, Ned Comstock, Laura Wagner, and Tom Weaver.

3. At 8:00 p.m. *The Eddie Fisher Show* had its premiere on NBC, L.A.'s Channel 4, with guest stars George Gobel, Debbie Reynolds and Mike Todd. At 8:30, *The Red Skelton Show* returned for its first show of the new season on CBS, L.A.'s Channel 2, with Skelton as Freddie the Freeloader and guests Marie Wilson and Marilyn Maxwell. *Wyatt Earp* on ABC, L.A.'s Channel 7, went up against Skelton. So did *Doomed to Die* (1940), starring Boris Karloff, on L.A.'s Channel 13. The *Los Angeles Times* TV listing described *Doomed to Die* thusly:

> Story of the 3000-year-old Dr. Diablo whose hobby is poisoning and whose companion is a pet vulture.

In fact, *Doomed to Die* was the last of Karloff's Monogram *Mr. Wong* potboilers, without a mad doctor, poison or a vulture.

4. My thanks to Doug Norwine, who was a close friend of Mae Clarke during her final years. He provided me a copy of the script and the legal documentation that she had saved.

5. Mae Clarke's quotes in this chapter regarding James Whale, Colin Clive, Dwight Frye and Boris Karloff come from the author's interview with Ms. Clarke, Woodland Hills, CA, 11 May 1983.

6. "Mae Clarke Raps TV Portrayal," *Los Angeles Examiner,* 17 July 1958.

7. "Mae Clarke Raps TV Portrayal."

8. Terry Vernon, "Looking and Listening: With Diana as a Guest Can Como Still Relax?" *Long Beach Press-Telegram,* 19 October 1957, p. B12.

9. "'I Am Mae Clarke' Line Repeated for Trial Jury," *Los Angeles Times,* 16 July 1958.

10. "Shocked by TV Show, Mae Clarke Tells Jury," *Los Angeles Times,* 17 July 1958, p. B14.

11. "Has-Been Suit Decided Against Mae Clarke," *Los Angeles Herald,* 26 July 1958.

12. Arnaud d'Usseau, emerging from the blacklist, co-scripted (with Julian Zemet) *Horror Express* (1972), a British-Spanish feature starring Christopher Lee, Peter Cushing and Telly Savalas; the premise was a "Missing Link" creature (Juan Olaguivel) amok on the trans–Siberian express. He and Zemet also co-scripted *The Death Wheelers,* aka *Psychomania* (1973), in which a coven of bikers deal with the Devil and commit suicide in hope of eternal life. His final credit: the Norman Lloyd–produced TV movie *Ladies in the Corridor* (1975). Arnaud d'Usseau died in New York City January 29, 1990, age 73. Loring d'Usseau continued as program director at KTLA, later moving to KCET; he co-directed (with Rudy Behlmer) *Hollywood Without Makeup* (1963), a compilation of Ken Murray home movies with candid footage of many film stars. The climax of Loring's career was a 1981 Emmy win for producing *Meeting of the Minds,* the PBS series written by Steve Allen in which famous historical figures (e.g., Catherine the Great and Oliver Cromwell) met for colorful conversation. Loring d'Usseau died September 1, 2006, in Arcadia, California, age 75.

13. Author's interview with Richard and Nancy Lee Dix, Baltimore, MD, 6 March 1993. All quotes in this chapter from Richard and Nancy come from that interview.

14. One of the guests was George Lewis, who had been Baltimore's "Ghost Host" on Channel 45 in the 1970s and 1980s—and best man at the Dixes' wedding in 1951!

Chapter 13

1. Telephone interview with author, 27 April 1993. For arranging this interview, my thanks to Kirk Crivello.

2. Of great assistance was G.D. Hamann's, *Carl Laemmle, Jr. in the 1930s* (Hollywood: Filming Today Press, 2012), with many excerpts from Los Angeles newspapers of the 1920s, 1930s and 1940s.

3. Mark A. Vieira, *Sin in Soft Focus* (New York: Harry N. Abrams, 1999), p. 220.

4. Tom Weaver, John Brunas, and Michael Brunas, *Universal Horrors: The Studio's Classic Films, 1931–1946* 2d ed. (Jefferson, NC: McFarland, 2007), p. 121.

5. Mae Clarke used this adjective in regards to Junior Laemmle in a conversation with Doug Norwine, circa 1990.

6. Appreciation to Mr. Lipes, a great champion of Junior Laemmle, who generously provided a number of the illustrations and certain material for this chapter.

Bibliography

Interviews

Lionel Anthony Atwill, Dorset, VT, July 16, 2004.

DeWitt Bodeen, Woodland Hills, CA, December 8, 1981.

Ann Carter, North Bend, WA, March 27, 2008.

Geraldine Chandler, Los Angeles, CA, May 14, 2003.

Arianne Ulmer Cipes, Sherman Oaks, CA, April 6, 2010, and November 24, 2010.

Mae Clarke, Woodland Hills, CA, May 11, 1983.

Sonia Darrin, New York City, NY, June 13, 2012.

Richard Denning, Hawaii, June 6, 1990.

Nancy Lee Dix, Baltimore, MD, March 6, 1993.

Richard Dix, Baltimore, MD, March 6, 1993.

Lillian Lugosi Donlevy, Culver City, CA, July 31, 1976.

Dean Goodman, San Francisco, CA, July 9, 1996.

Verna Hillie, New York City, February 5, 1994.

Anna Lee, West Los Angeles, CA, July 19, 1991.

Ruth Lewton, San Jose, CA, March 8, 1993.

Kay Linaker, Keene, NH, July 19, 2000, and January 23, 2003.

Marian Marsh, Palm Desert, CA, May 14, 1983, July 18, 1992, and December 15, 1992.

Evelyn Moriarty, Los Angeles, CA, April 26 and 27, 1993.

Patricia Morison, Los Angeles, CA, July 29, 1998.

Jane Randolph, Los Angeles, CA, June 28, 1989.

Elizabeth Russell, Beverly Hills, CA, February 3, 1994.

Simone Simon, Paris, September 17, 1994.

Curt Siodmak, Three Rivers, CA, April 8, 1980, and July 1, 1980.

Robert Wise, Los Angeles, CA, May 13, 1994.

Marilyn Harris Wood, San Gabriel, CA, July 20, 1997, and July 26, 1998.

Stella Zucco, Santa Monica, CA, July 19, 1991.

Archives

Billy Rose Library for the Performing Arts, Lincoln Center, New York City, New York.

Manuscript Division, The Library of Congress, Washington, D.C.

Margaret Herrick Library, The Academy of Motion Picture Arts and Sciences, Los Angeles, CA.

Pasadena Playhouse Archives, Pasadena, CA.

University of California, Los Angeles, Performing Arts Collections, Los Angeles, CA.

University of Southern California, Warner Bros. Archives, Los Angeles, CA.

University of Southern California Film and Television Library, Los Angeles, CA.

Books

Ackerman, Forrest J. *The Frankenscience Monster*. New York: Ace, 1969.

Behlmer, Rudy. *Inside Warner Bros. (1935–1951)*. New York: Viking, 1985.

Birchard, Robert S. *Early Universal City*. Charleston SC: Arcadia, 2009.

Brown, Gene. *Movie Time*. New York: Macmillan, 1995.

Carradine, David. *Endless Highway*. Boston: Journey Editions, 1995.

Curtis, James. *A New World of Gods and Monsters*. London: Faber and Faber, 1998.

Dederichs, Mario R. *Heydrich: The Face of Evil*. Drexel Hill, PA: Casemate, 2009.

Eyman, Scott. *Lion of Hollywood: The Life and Times of Louis B. Mayer*. New York: Simon & Schuster, 2005.

Fowler, Gene. *Good Night, Sweet Prince*. New York: Viking, 1944.

Goodman, Dean. *Maria, Marlene, ... and Me*. San Francisco: Shadbolt Press, 1993.

Graham, Sheila. *The Garden of Allah*. New York: Crown, 1970.

Halliday, Jon. *Sirk on Sirk*. London: Faber and Faber, 1971.

Hamann, G.D. *Bela Lugosi in the '30s & '40s*. Hollywood: Filming Today Press, 2003.

Hamann, G.D. *Boris Karloff in the '30s*. Hollywood: Filming Today Press, 2004.

Hamann, G.D. *Carl Laemmle, Jr. in the 1930s*. Hollywood: Filming Today Press, 2012.

Hamann, G.D. *John Barrymore in the '30s*. Hollywood: Filming Today Press, 2012.

Hamann, G.D. *John Carradine in the '30s-n-'40s.* Hollywood: Filming Today Press, 2012.

Hamann, G.D. *Lionel Atwill in the 30s.* Hollywood: Filming Today Press, 2004.

Higham, Charles, and Joel Greenberg. *The Celluloid Muse: Hollywood Directors Speak.* New York: New America Library, 1972.

Ivanov, Miroslav. *Target: Heydrich.* New York: Macmillan, 1974.

Jacobs, Stephen. *Boris Karloff: More Than a Monster.* Sheffield: Tomahawk Press, 2011.

MacDonald, Callum. *The Killing of Reinhard Heyrich: The SS "Butcher of Prague."* New York: Da Capo Press, 1998.

McBride, Joseph. *Frank Capra: The Catastrophe of Success.* New York: Simon & Schuster, 1992.

McCarthy, Todd, and Charles Flynn, eds. *Kings of the B's.* New York: E. P. Dutton, 1975.

Peters, Margot. *The House of Barrymore.* New York: Alfred A. Knopf, 1990.

Rhodes, Gary Don. *Lugosi.* Jefferson, NC: McFarland, 1997.

Rhodes, Gary D., and Bill Kaffenberger. *No Traveler Returns: The Lost Years of Bela Lugosi.* Duncan, OK: BearManor Media, 2012.

Rhodes, Gary D., with R. Sheffield. *Bela Lugosi: Dreams and Nightmares.* Narbeth, PA: Collectables, 2007.

Schatz, Thomas. *The Genius of the System: Hollywood Filmmaking in the Studio Era.* New York: Pantheon Books, 1988.

Siegel, Joel E. *Val Lewton: The Reality of Terror.* New York: Viking, 1973.

Skretvedt, Randy. *Laurel and Hardy: The Magic Behind the Movies.* Beverly Hills, CA: Past Times, 1994.

Steinberg, Cobbett. *Reel Facts: The Movie Book of Records.* New York: Random House, 1978.

Stuart, Gloria, with Sylvia Thompson. *I Just Kept Hoping.* Boston: Little, Brown, 1999.

Svehla, Gary J., and Susan Svehla, eds. *Boris Karloff.* Baltimore: Midnight Marquee Press, 1996.

Vieira, Mark A. *Hollywood Dreams Made Real: Irving Thalberg and the Rise of MGM.* New York: Harry N. Abrams, 2008.

Vieira, Mark A. *Sin in Soft Focus.* New York: Harry N. Abrams, 1999.

Weaver, Tom. *John Carradine: The Films.* Jefferson, NC: McFarland, 1999.

Weaver, Tom. *Poverty Row Horrors!* Jefferson, NC: McFarland, 1993.

Weaver, Tom, John Brunas, and Michael Brunas. *Universal Horrors: The Studio's Classic Films, 1931–1946,* 2d ed. Jefferson, NC: McFarland, 2007.

Wiley, Mason, and Damien Bova. *Inside Oscar.* New York: Ballantine, 1986, 1987.

Wolf, Leonard. *A Dream of Dracula.* New York: Popular Library, 1972.

Youngkin, Stephen D. *The Lost One: A Life of Peter Lorre.* Lexington: University Press of Kentucky, 2005.

Magazines and Trade Journals

American Cinematographer, Baltimore Sun, Cinefantastique, Fangoria, Film Daily, Films in Review, Films of the Golden Age, Focus on Film, Hollywood Citizen-News, Hollywood Reporter, Los Angeles Evening Herald Express, Los Angeles Examiner, Los Angeles Times, Midnight Marquee, Monsters from the Vault, Motion Picture Herald, Newsweek, New York Times, Parade, San Francisco Chronicle, Silver Screen, Time, Variety, Video Watchdog, Washington Post, World War II Magazine.

Index